For Frances Wallace,
As part of our ongoing
exchange and cherished
friendship. love,
Jacqueline

Tense and Narrativity

Texas Linguistics Series

Tense and Narrativity

From Medieval Performance to Modern Fiction

By Suzanne Fleischman

 University of Texas Press   Austin

First edition, 1990

Requests for permission to reproduce material from this work should
be sent to Permissions, University of Texas Press, Box 7819, Austin,
TX 78713-7819.

∞ The paper used in this publication meets the minimum requirements of American National Standard for Information Sciences—Permanence of Paper for Printed Library Materials, ANSI Z39.48-1984.

Material from Suzanne Fleischman, "Discourse Functions of Tense-
Aspect Oppositions in Narrative: Toward a Theory of Grounding,"
Linguistics 23(1985) : 851–882, reprinted by permission of Mouton de
Gruyter. Material from Suzanne Fleischman, "Evaluation in Narrative:
The Present Tense in Medieval Performed Stories," *Yale French Studies*
70, reprinted by permission of *Yale French Studies.* Four lines from
"Shorts 1," from *W. H. Auden: Collected Poems,* edited by Edward
Mendelson, published in 1976 by Faber and Faber Limited and Ran-
dom House, Inc., reprinted by permission of the publishers.

LIBRARY OF CONGRESS CATALOGING-IN-PUBLICATION DATA

Fleischman, Suzanne.
    Tense and narrativity: from medieval performance to modern fic-
tion / by Suzanne Fleischman.—1st ed.
        p.   cm.—(Texas linguistics series)
    Bibliography: p.
    Includes index.
    ISBN 0-292-78090-7
    1. Discourse analysis, Narrative.   2. Grammar, Comparative and
general—Tense.   3. Discourse analysis, Literary.   4. Literature,
Medieval—History and criticism.   5. Fiction—History and
criticism.
    I. Title.   II. Series.
    P302.7.F54   1990
    808′.0014—dc20   89-35579
                                                              CIP
                                                              Rev.

Pour Y.M.
malgré lui

Contents

Tables

Figures

Abbreviations

COND	conditional	PFV	perfective
E	event (per Reichen-	PLP	pluperfect
	bach's tense model)	PR	present
FUT	future	PRET	preterit
FUT-OF-P	future-of-the-past	PROG	progressive
HP	historical present	PS	simple past
IMPER	imperative	PTC	participle
INDIC	indicative	R	reference point/period
IPFV	imperfective		(per Reichenbach's
NARR	narrative		model)
	(morphology)	S	moment of speech (per
NP	narrative present		Reichenbach's
P	past		model)
PA	past anterior (French)	SUBJ	subjunctive
PC	compound past	Subscripts:	
PERF	(present) perfect	[tense]$_a$	action
		[tense]$_v$	visualizing

Coding Markers:

\#   used in translations from Old French to mark the place of the
            particle *si*

(See appendix 1 for typographic conventions used in coding texts.)

Preface

The genesis of this book goes back some five years, when I first set out to "revisit" a long-standing conundrum of Romance philology: the seemingly idiosyncratic use of tenses found in much of the vernacular narrative literature of the Middle Ages. At that time I could not have foreseen how far beyond the boundaries of the original focus of inquiry my research would take me.

Interest in early vernacular tense usage has traditionally been confined to text editors, historical grammarians, literary scholars attentive to the linguistic questions raised by their texts, and of course students, wondering why medieval writers "couldn't get their tenses straight." Accordingly, the investigative tools and methodologies that have been brought to bear on this question have been for the most part those of traditional philology. One of my objectives in reexamining the question of medieval tense usage has been to expand the investigative framework, in hopes of arriving at a more satisfying interpretation of the phenomenon than those that have been proposed. In particular I have sought to introduce into my analysis some of the theory and methodology of contemporary text-linguistic and sociolinguistic research on the linguistic structure of "natural" narrative. The findings of this research can, I feel, enhance our understanding of apparent peculiarities of "narrative grammar" in other types of narrative as well. As Richard Bauman (1986) observes in a recent monograph on oral story performance, which in many ways complements this book, new perspectives do not necessarily demand the abandonment of old interests, but rather should lead to a reinvigoration of traditional concerns.

In the course of my research, the issues raised by the medieval texts have provided a springboard for exploring a number of broader theoretical questions that this book proposes to address: about differences between spoken and written textuality, about the linguistic correlates of orality and literacy, about the relationship of pragmatics to grammar, about narrative typology, and ultimately about the status of "narrative" as a category of linguistic performance whose protocols differ in certain respects from those of ordinary language.

As one of our most basic hermeneutic constructs, narrative marks a space of convergence for the concerns of a number of disciplines: literary criticism and literary theory; functional linguistics, with its emphasis on pragmatics and trans-sentential phenomena of discourse; sociolinguistics, specifically where it joins hands with cognitive psychology and artificial intelligence in an attempt to provide descriptive models of story structure and to offer insights into the linguistic strategies used by storytellers to perform narrative tasks; linguistic and literary anthropology (ethnomethodology), in their focus on "performance literature" as a text category with its own distinctive conventions; and historiography and philosophy of history, especially where they intersect with literary theory in probing the *differentia specifica* of "narrative" as a construct for organizing and making sense of the data of reality. This list could no doubt be expanded.

In the course of my research it has become apparent to me that investigators in these various fields grapple with many of the same fundamental issues, coming at them with the different (or not so different) concepts, terminologies, and sets of assumptions operative in their respective bailiwicks. Historians and literary theorists, for example, traverse much the same terrain in their discussions of "continuity" and "causality" as properties informing narrative, while linguists' controversies over "foregrounding" in discourse bear a striking resemblance to the debates among philosophers of history over "importance" in historical thinking. I have also observed that "narratologists" in these various fields—if I may use this term, coined by literary theorists, in a connotatively neutral sense—rarely exchange thoughts on these issues with one another, but tend rather to remain enclosed within locally established problematics.

Although I do not presume to have exhausted the critical literature on narrative in any one (let alone all) of these fields, one of my objectives in this book is to bring together insights from across disciplinary lines, insights that have contributed to shaping my own views about the linguistic structure of narrative and the strategies deployed by storytellers to accomplish certain uniquely narrative tasks. In one of the most penetrating studies I have consulted (*Time and Narrative*), the philosopher Paul Ricoeur calls upon historiography and literary criticism to join together in forming "a grand narratology" in which equal place would be given to historical and fictional discourse. The present investigation proposes to further that enterprise by soliciting the participation of a third major discipline in the grand narratology: linguistics. Through its explorations of the workings of narrative in the most primary of contexts—the conversational exchanges of daily life—linguistics lays an essential foundation on which all other disciplines concerned with narrative can build. "All the arts of narration," Ricoeur acknowledges, "and foremost among them those belonging to writing, are imitations of narrative as it is already practiced in the transactions of ordinary discourse." Whence the centrality of natural narrative and the principles governing its structure and organization to the global enterprise of narratology and to the conception of this book.

On the broadest level, it is my hope that this investigation will serve to reduce the sharp separation many investigators perceive between the literary and the conversational, between poetic and nonpoetic discourses, between linguistics and literature, and to demonstrate that natural-language data and certain analytical frameworks linguists use to describe them can be illuminating for the study of poetic texts. Most linguists who have ventured into the domain of literary/poetic discourse concur that insight into the workings of "artificial" narrative forms must be based on a thorough analysis of the natural narratives that punctuate our everyday verbal interactions. To these voices I hereby add my own.

Some of the ideas for this book have been rehearsed in article form (Fleischman 1985, 1986a, and forthcoming). Not surprisingly, my thinking on certain of the issues raised in these articles has evolved since their publication. I ask the reader's indulgence for any discrepancies that might be noted.

It is impossible to acknowledge individually the many people who contributed in one way or another to the genesis of this book. Special thanks, however, go to Susan Herring for sharing her narratological thoughts with me on various issues raised in the book; to Dina Sherzer and Linda Waugh for their insightful comments on an earlier version of the text and suggestions for its improvement; to Andrew Makuch of the University of Arizona Library for translation assistance; to Connie Dickey, Kathy Lewis, and especially Barbara De Marco for carefully proofreading the text in its various avatars and ferreting out infelicities of exposition; and to Jonathan Beck for listening to my grumblings and providing encouragement in moments of investigative doldrums.

Tense and Narrativity

Introduction

*Our ordinary language shows a tiresome bias in its treatment
of time. . . . The form it takes—that of requiring that every
verb form show a tense—is peculiarly productive of needless complications, since it demands lip service to time even where time
is farthest from our thoughts.* (QUINE, *WORD AND OBJECT*)

The reason *that throws light . . . consists in a narration. . . .
Alongside pure physico-mathematical reason there is . . . a
narrative reason. To comprehend anything human . . . one
must tell its history. . . . Life only takes on a measure of transparency in the light of [this]* historical reason.
(ORTEGA Y GASSET, *HISTORY AS A SYSTEM*)

0.1. A major project of text-oriented linguistics in recent years has been an inquiry into the linguistic foundations of narrative.
The goal of that project is to arrive at an understanding of the linguistic
strategies used by storytellers to construct verbal icons of experience, real
or invented. This book forms part of that project. Its focus is on the grammatical categories of tense and aspect as used in narrative, and specifically
on their NONREFERENTIAL or pragmatic functions. While these functions
are less obvious and less well understood than the basic REFERENTIAL or
grammatical functions, an understanding of the pragmatics of tense-aspect
usage is central to the broader objective that this book proposes: the development of a theory of tense in narrative.[1]

In his commentary on the radical departure from established novelistic
protocol marked by Camus's novel *The Stranger,* narrated almost entirely
in the PASSÉ COMPOSÉ, Jean-Paul Sartre (1947) suggests that it is in the
tense of a text that the secret of its special strangeness lies and that one task
of the critic should be the forging of a link between grammar and philosophy. A special strangeness indeed informs the excerpt given below from a
thirteenth-century French romance whose tense usage seems to defy grammatical logic, thereby presenting the critic prepared to take up Sartre's
challenge with a task all the more formidable:

Dedenz une garderobe ENTRE	I	She ENTERS [PR] a dressing room
ou une pucelete ESTOIT		where [there] WAS [IMP] a young damsel
qui aus piez du lit SE GISOIT		who WAS LYING [IMP] at the foot of the bed,
mes ele *ne la pot veoir.*		but she *could not see her* [PS].

El lit *s'EST lessie cheoir*   5   Onto the bed the lady of the castle
la chastelaine mout dolente;   *HAS fallen* [PC], grieving deeply;
iluec *SE PLAINT* et *SE DEMENTE*,   there she *SIGHS* [PR] and *LAMENTS*
et *dist:* "Ha! sire Dieus, merci!"   [PR],
                                                       and *said:* [PS] "Mercy, dear
                                                         Lord God!"
                                                       (*La Chastelaine de Vergi*, vv. 726–733)[2]

What strikes the reader immediately in this example is the seemingly idiosyncratic use of tenses. It is generally agreed that the basic function of tense in ordinary language is to establish the temporal location of situations predicated in a sentence or discourse. Yet the curious mixture of tenses in this example seemingly has little to do with temporal location: the five situations reported as punctual events (encoded by the predicates "enter a dressing room," "fall on the bed," "sigh," "lament," and "say") are all understood to occur in a fictional past and in the order in which they are reported ("sigh" and "lament" overlap). However, three of these situations are reported in the PRESENT (PR) tense, one in the COMPOUND PAST (PC), and one in the SIMPLE PAST (PS), as coded in the example. Inasmuch as time reference is usually established at the outset of a text and tends to be a property of fairly large stretches of discourse, it need not in principle be reiterated in each successive sentence; yet the grammars of many languages require that tense information be encoded (redundantly) on every finite verb—a state of affairs that might be viewed as a singularly uneconomical use of grammatical resources, as the opening quote from Quine suggests.

If these tense-aspect forms are not expressing temporality, neither do they seem to be expressing aspectual notions such as "completion" or "durativity": the predicates "was" (line 2) and "could not see her" (line 4) are both durative, though the first is reported by an IMPERFECTIVE PAST (IMP), the second by a PERFECTIVE PAST (PS). And of the three situations represented as completed, one is in the PR ("she enters a dressing room"), another in the PC ("she has fallen onto the bed"), and yet another in the PS (the introduction-to-speech verb "said").

Clearly, then, the contribution of the tense-aspect forms in this passage is something other than the basic grammatical functions normally associated with these categories. Fortunately, the *laissez-faire* economies of natural languages tend to make more efficient use of available resources than their artificially controlled counterparts in social and political institutions, one result being that in the narrative grammars of most languages tense-aspect morphology is often freed from its primary REFERENTIAL functions (discussed in chapter 1) and pressed into service for other, notably pragmatic purposes. One of the principal claims this book makes is that in narrative discourse the functions of tense and aspect are frequently pragmatic in nature; chapters 5, 6, and 7 accordingly are devoted to elaborating and illustrating these pragmatic functions.

Pragmatics is understood as referring to all types of meaning dependent on context. Of primary concern here are, on the one hand, *discourse context*—the portion of discourse or text that surrounds a given sentence or sequence of sentences—as well as the nature of the text as a whole (narration, conversation, oratory), and, on the other, *situation context*—the communicative context or setting in which the text as a speech-act occurs. The pragmatics of discourse is concerned in large part with the organization of texts as coherent wholes; this includes strategies for packaging the information in sentences as either topic or focus, signaling the relative saliency of different pieces of information, establishing intersentential cohesion, and other linguistically describable aspects of text structure. Situational pragmatics refers to aspects of the extratextual setting of the discourse, including its relationship to speech-act participants, the relationship of these participants—notably speaker and hearer(s)—to one another, and any other relevant features of the context of communication, linguistic or nonlinguistic.

Also relevant to this inquiry, and within the domain of pragmatics, are meanings and presuppositions that derive from our familiarity as members of a culture or subculture with certain culture-specific "frames"—a term coined by cognitive psychologists to refer to clusters of interrelated expectations associated with prototypical experiences or situation contexts. Though the frame concept was conceived with reference to real-world situations (e.g., a visit to the doctor, a Ph.D. exam), it is easily extended to *textual* worlds, which also fall into recognizable types—genres—to which similar sets of expectations attach. To the extent that all forms of discourse entail "horizons of expectations"—reader-response theorists' umbrella term for the shared knowledge, assumptions, and values that writers/ speakers tacitly draw on in constructing texts and that initiated readers/ listeners draw on in decoding them—these must also figure into any analysis of narrative language that claims a pragmatic orientation.

0.2. It has often been observed that tense usage in narrative is anomalous with respect to a language's normal use of tenses—that the relationships between time and tense in narrative are not the same as those obtaining in ordinary language. Attempts have been made, notably by Emile Benveniste (1959) and Harald Weinrich (1973), to explain the tenses of narrative not as anomalous but as regular within a special tense system that operates alongside that of nonnarrative language. Along similar lines, Dahl (1985) has observed that the possibilities for expressing temporal distance may not be the same in narrative and nonnarrative contexts; where the two differ, it is nonnarrative contexts that exhibit the greater number of tense-aspect distinctions (this observation supports Labov's more general claim [1972:377] that narrative shows a less complex linguistic structure than ordinary conversation). It is also the case that certain (non-Indo-European) languages have grammatical morphology, including tense-aspect, that is exclusive to narrative. While the languages here under survey show no uniquely NARRATIVE (NARR) morphology, we can identify particular sentence types (e.g., free indirect discourse), lexico-grammatical collocations (PAST-tense verb + nonpast adverb), and tense usages (HISTORICAL PRESENT and the so-called NARRATIVE IMPERFECT), whose acceptability depends on a narrative context. Finally, it has been observed across languages that the seemingly ungrammatical alternation of tenses illustrated in the Old French example above occurs only in sentences of narration and not in sentences of directly quoted speech, nor in commentary by the narrator.

These and other considerations have led a number of investigators to view narrative as a *marked* category of linguistic performance whose grammar differs in certain respects from that of everyday communicative language.

The markedness question has been debated largely by narratologists oriented toward literature, certain of whom take narrative to be synonymous with *written fiction* (e.g., Banfield 1982). By broadening the range of text types to which the label "narrative" applies so as to include both nonwritten and nonfictional texts, I propose to shed new light on this theoretical question of a special, marked grammar for narrative. The early Romance texts that make up the largest part of my data base were virtually all composed for oral recitation before a listening audience—for *performance*. The ramifications for a linguistic theory of narrative of this crucial pragmatic difference between interactive performance texts and texts involving absent-author communication will be discussed at various points in the book.

The claim that narrative constitutes a marked variety of language is not simply a theoretical question to be debated here for its own sake. It is central to the theory I put forth to account for tense usage in narrative, a theory based on the concept of markedness and specifically on the proposition that in a marked context the normal markedness values of an opposition may be reversed. In the unmarked context of ordinary (nonnarrative) language the PRESENT is generally regarded as the unmarked tense while the PAST is marked. And if we accept the claim that narrative constitutes a marked linguistic context, then according to the markedness-reversal hypothesis we should not be surprised to see an exchange of markedness values within the "special" tense system of narrative. A major thrust of my analysis is to demonstrate the operation of this hypothesis, in particular the proposition that *in a narrative context* the PRESENT—or any tense-aspect category other than the PAST[3]—is marked with respect to one or more of a set of properties that together define the unmarked tense of narration, the PAST. This proposition entails a particular view of PAST: as defined by the markedness framework, the category PAST is no longer a simple unanalyzable piece of grammatical information but a cluster concept involving multiple oppositional properties operative at different levels of the linguistic system—the REFERENTIAL, the TEXTUAL, the EXPRESSIVE, and the METALINGUISTIC.

0.3.   The model of language that provides a foundation for the markedness theory as well as for my categorization of tense-aspect functions is a multilevel functional model according to which elements of the linguistic system (lexical items, constructions, categories of grammar) can realize meanings in four interdependent components, here referred to as the REFERENTIAL, the TEXTUAL, the EXPRESSIVE, and the METALINGUISTIC. This model is an adaptation of a trilevel model proposed in Traugott (1982), itself a variation on a similar model put forth in Halliday and Hasan (1976), with the addition of a METALINGUISTIC component.

The REFERENTIAL component is concerned with the propositional content of utterances (referential meanings), with the function language has of being *about* something. At this level are located truth-conditional relations as well as other categories not interpretable solely in truth-conditional terms, including the so-called basic meanings of tense and aspect.

Located in the TEXTUAL component are a language's resources for creating and organizing discourse that is internally coherent ("text") and coheres with its situation context, and for signaling other information relevant to the structure of the discourse itself. Descriptions of this component typically emphasize the devices for creating textual cohesion. But the *textual* component is also the source of devices relating to other facets of the unfolding of a text. Particularly relevant in the present context are the strategies speakers use for controlling the rate of information flow in a discourse, for partitioning a discourse into smaller subunits and marking the boundaries between them, and for signaling levels of saliency or information relevance—for creating texture within text. This last operation is commonly referred to as foregrounding and backgrounding, or simply grounding.

Situated in the EXPRESSIVE component are meanings relating to the social, affective, and conative functions of language: its resources for expressing personal attitudes toward what is being talked about, toward the text itself, and toward the participants in the communicative transaction. Among the various linguistic resources located in the EXPRESSIVE component, the most important for our purpose are those serving to communicate evaluations and point of view.

The METALINGUISTIC component houses a language's resources for talking about itself. Language is often called upon to make statements that are essentially statements *about language.* Included under this rubric are the nomenclature of grammar and rhetoric, the vocabulary of stylistics, and, more generally, any meanings or functions that linguistic elements may have to signal a particular style, register, genre, or type of language. For example, the French PASSÉ SIMPLE has, in addition to temporal and aspectual meanings, a METALINGUISTIC function—which some now hold to be primary—of signaling a particular register of formal, normally written language. For languages that have an explicit narrative morphology, at least one function of this morphology is METALINGUISTIC: it identifies a discourse. Among the various resources located in the METALINGUISTIC component, the most important for our purpose is the "antinarrative" function of the PRESENT tense.[4]

In the metalanguage of literary narratology we find similar attempts to distinguish between elements of a text with strictly *narrative* functions— those that relate to the content of the story (paralleling my REFERENTIAL functions)—and those with *extranarrative* functions. The latter domain includes statements serving as "stage directions" (Barthes 1967) for the text (analogous to my TEXTUAL functions) as well as "explanatory, justificatory" statements whose function is "ideological" (Genette 1980; in my terms, EXPRESSIVE). Obviously this homology is only approximate; the EXPRESSIVE component encompasses considerably more than Genette's ideological discourse, for it is also the locus of elements whose functions are "conative" and "phatic," which define certain types of narrative as complex communicative events.

Both Traugott (1982) and Halliday and Hasan (1976) situate the contributions of tense and aspect to the linguistic message in the REFERENTIAL component. But this assignment accounts only for the primary or basic meanings of these categories—for tense as a grammaticalized marker of temporal deixis, and aspect as a nondeictic marker of the "internal constituency" (Comrie 1976) of a situation. One of the principal claims this book makes is that the functions of tense-aspect categories *in narrative* are not limited to these basic REFERENTIAL meanings; rather, tense and aspect do as much if not more of their work in the PRAGMATIC (TEXTUAL and EXPRESSIVE) and METALINGUISTIC components; moreover, the functions of tense-aspect that are exclusive to narrative are specifically pragmatic functions.

Given that in a narrative context tense-aspect can operate in all of the functional-semantic components, the question arises as to where it originates and what diachronic path it follows. Formulated in more general terms, the question is: Do grammatical forms start out in the REFERENTIAL component and subsequently go on to do TEXTUAL, EXPRESSIVE, and METALINGUISTIC work? Or, conversely, are the origins of grammatical categories to be sought in the pragmatics of discourse, as certain linguists (Givón, Hopper, Du Bois at various points in their writing) have proposed? It is significant that tense and aspect figure prominently among the grammatical categories around which this debate has centered. Hopper in particular has argued that aspect (notably PFV) markers are likely to originate at the TEXTUAL level as focus particles or markers of the textual foreground (Hopper 1979a, 1979b), while Traugott (1979) has argued for change in the opposite direction: REFERENTIAL → TEXTUAL/EXPRESSIVE. As she observes, "Over and over again in the history of languages, semantico-grammatical change seems to be . . . from non-deictic to deictic functions, from non-speaker-oriented functions to speaker-oriented functions, from non-pragmatic functions to pragmatic functions, from non-cohesive to cohesive functions." Among the theoretical issues on which this investigation purports to shed some light is that of the relationship between grammar and pragmatics.

0.4. The textual data base for this book consists of natural and artificial narratives from a range of genres,[5] primarily from Romance languages. A selection of these narratives (excerpts in the case of lengthy texts) is included in appendix 2.[6] One of the principal claims made here is that the specifically narrative functions of tense and aspect developed as motivated pragmatic responses to the conditions of narrative performance in interactive oral contexts. For this reason I have chosen to concentrate on texts from the later Middle Ages (eleventh–fifteenth cen-

turies), a period whose forms of thought and expression were still fundamentally *oral* and whose textual artifacts, which we now read—*après la
lettre*—as literature, still bear traces of their oral ontogenesis, certain of
which have survived chirographic transformation. Among the traces that
remain are conspicuous tense-aspect alternations whose logic seems to
defy conventional grammatical analysis.

Confusion des temps—as the tense-switching phenomenon has been referred to in French—turns out to be extremely widespread in the older Romance literatures, as well as in the narrative production of many other early
vernaculars. Over the years the tense-alternation question has spawned a
considerable body of critical literature—stylistic, literary, philological—
that by its sheer abundance would seem to point to the absence of satisfying interpretations of the phenomenon. In light of this volume of scholarship, one may wonder whether there is anything left to be said on the
matter that is not simply old wine in new, more fashionable bottles. I believe there is. However, the approach I take here involves a radical shift
in the premises and direction of inquiry, away from exclusive enclosure
within the problematics of medieval textuality—or literary textuality in
general—to an area of contemporary text linguistics that has of late drawn
considerable attention: the analysis of natural narrative.

Recently, the tense-switching phenomenon has begun to be explored in
a more rigorous and informed way by pragmatically oriented linguists
concerned with understanding how we construct and organize the natural
narrations that punctuate our everyday conversations and, concomitantly,
with identifying the linguistic strategies that make for effective storytelling. Much of this work has been carried out in the tradition of American
sociolinguistics associated with William Labov. In reading the relevant
literature I was struck by the similarity between the tense-switching patterns identified for natural narrative and those that occur in the early Romance texts; it was this similarity that motivated me to reexamine the medieval material in the light of findings of current text-linguistic research.
Admittedly, the inner-city Philadelphia *raconteurs* interviewed by Labov in
the 1960s have little in common with singers of medieval epic and reciters
of romances. But the cultural and time gap narrows progressively as we
learn more about the linguistic foundation of their shared expertise in *oral
story performance*.

Examination of a substantial corpus of early Romance texts reveals that
tense switching is virtually always a mark of orally performed narratives of
the type Nessa Wolfson (1978, 1979) has labeled performed stories, on the
basis of certain features that such texts share with theatrical presentations.

These features include direct speech, asides, repetition, expressive sounds and sound effects, and motions and gestures. Not all but at least some of them must be in evidence for a narrative to constitute a performed story and not merely an oral report of past events. The performed story should thus be understood as a prototype concept whose distinctive features are present to different degrees, and some not at all, in individual actualizations. The more fully a story is performed, Wolfson asserts, the more likely it is to exhibit tense switching.

Wolfson's research deals with natural narratives in contemporary American English. In her data, tense switching occurs only in those narrations in which the speaker "breaks through" into performance (cf. Hymes 1974). From what we know about conditions of text production and reception in the neo-Latin Middle Ages, we can be reasonably certain that the varieties of storytelling involved in medieval epics, romances, ballads, and so forth, qualified as performance (as defined by Wolfson), even when a written text was involved.[7]

In the extensive literature on tense usage in early Romance, insufficient account has been taken of the performance factor—not that medievalists have ignored the performative dimension of their texts, but their awareness of it often fails to carry forward into critical analysis. Medieval narratives are often read and analyzed as one would modern fiction, which is composed, transmitted, and received under quite different conditions. Current research into oral vs. written strategies in narrative suggests that in literate traditions "the meaning is in the text," while in oral situations "the meaning is in the context" and in the implications of communicative acts (Goody and Watt 1968; Olson 1977; Bauman 1986); listeners attend more to what is *meant* and readers to what is *written* (the actual words in the text). We are only now coming to recognize the linguistic implications of oral text performance and to articulate significant linguistic differences between narratives composed by literate writers for a literate readership and narratives composed for performance by professional storytellers in cultures still predominantly oral. Note, however, that orality is not being invoked here for its own sake. My purpose, like that articulated by Paul Zumthor in his provocative essay "The Text and the Voice" (1984b:68), is "not so much . . . to insist on the importance of orality in the transmission and indeed the creation of medieval poetry, but rather to appreciate and gauge what this orality implies; not so much to evaluate the size of the 'oral part' in the corpus of extant texts as to integrate into my perception and my reading the properties thus explained." What I wish to emphasize here is the crucial role I believe oral performance played in shaping the grammar and linguistic structure of vernacular narratives from the Middle Ages. Many of the disconcerting properties of medieval textuality, including its extraordinary parataxis, conspicuous anaphora and repetition, and striking alternations of tense, can, I submit, find more satisfying explanations through appeal to the incontrovertible orality of medieval culture.

0.5.   If the ontogenesis of tense switching is located in the pragmatic structure of oral story performance, as I believe it is, this does not mean that pragmatic uses of tense-aspect morphology are restricted to orally performed texts. Indeed, in planned written narratives produced by highly literate authors we find tense-aspect morphology similarly pressed into service for TEXTUAL and EXPRESSIVE purposes, as shown in the discussion of tense-aspect in modern and postmodern fiction that occupies much of chapters 7 and 8. How, if at all, are the medieval and modern uses related? What I would like to suggest is that certain stylistic phenomena now regarded as hallmarks of narrative *écriture*—for example, the HISTORICAL PRESENT (HP), the NARRATIVE IMPERFECT, and the tense usage characteristic of interior monologue—may have been adapted from popular narrative genres of earlier periods, and ultimately from the naturally occurring narratives of everyday speech at the time. Readers with a strong belletristic bias may find this claim disquieting; however, it appears to be well founded.

If written narrative of the postmedieval age has adopted—and adapted—the pragmatic uses of tense-aspect established by its orally performed precursors, it has not confined itself to these uses. The institution of writing and the different pragmatic structure of "absent-author communication" open up new possibilities for pragmatic exploitation of the apparatus of grammar, in particular of tense-aspect categories. For this reason I devote the last two chapters of the book to fiction, mainly French, of the nineteenth and twentieth centuries, showing how Flaubert and Proust exploit the possibilities of the IMPERFECT and Camus those of the PASSÉ COMPOSÉ, while Virginia Woolf pioneers in destabilizing narration through her uses of the PRESENT. As predicated by the markedness framework that underpins the theory of tense proposed here, these tenses are all *marked* in a narrative context. In choosing them as vehicles for the reporting of events, writers depart in various ways from the activity of narrating in favor of other modes of representing experience and/or the contents of constructed worlds. Among fiction writers surveyed here, those associated with the French *nouveau roman* (new novel) have conceivably gone the furthest in exploiting the options made available through the PRESENT tense. All genres that choose the PR as the basic tense for reporting information work in some way against the narrative norm; they are consciously or unconsciously antinarrative. As marked varieties of narrative, they accordingly privilege a tense that is itself marked in a narrative context. What we observe, in other words, is a second-order reversal of markedness values in a second-order marked context (the unmarking of PAST in narrative constitutes the first-order reversal).

The genres selected for discussion here that rely on the PR as the basic (unmarked) tense for reporting information might be viewed by some as strange bedfellows: medieval Romance epics, Hispanic ballads of the *romancero* tradition, modern fiction in the HP, and the postmodern *nouveaux romans*. Of these genres, two are products of orality (composition and performance), two of consummate literacy. The ideologies underlying them and the horizons of expectation they draw on could hardly be more diverse. Nonetheless, these genres all privilege a mode of representation that is not that of conventional narrators, whose PAST-tense reports of events are necessarily informed by a retrospective intelligibility, but that of eyewitness observers verbalizing in the PRESENT tense the (unconfigured) particulars of the visualized spectacles ostensibly passing before their eyes. While the historical and cultural distance separating vernacular epics and *nouveaux romans* could hardly be greater, striking similarities are observed in the linguistic strategies they deploy in the construction and articulation of a text (salient repetition, detemporalization of events, priority of the "descriptive" over the "eventive," a privileging of speech), similarities that might not suggest themselves were it not for their shared use of the PR tense. Verbal artifacts of postmodernism, the *nouveaux romans* pose conceivably the most powerful challenge to the tenets of realist fiction, and of normative narration in general, in their particular exploitation of a tense that, in its basic meaning, makes no commitment to temporality.[8]

0.6. One of the working hypotheses of this book that should by now be apparent is that certain linguistic protocols used in narration are, if not universal, at least widely attested across languages. This is not to ignore cross-language differences. It would be erroneous to assume that the pragmatic uses of tense-aspect in narrative are the same across genres and across languages. The grammars of different languages are obviously different, as are grammars of an individual language at different stages of its history. We might also wish to consider the proposition that no grammar is ever a stable system—rather, grammars are always in the process of being renegotiated by speakers in contexts of actual communication (Hopper's 1987 view of grammar as "emergent"). This is presumably how phenomena such as tense switching came into being in the first place. In any event, the tense-aspect oppositions available in a given grammar necessarily condition and constrain the pragmatic extensions this morphology can undergo. For example, in languages with PFV and IPFV aspects, this opposition commonly serves to mark the discourse contrast between events and description, whereas in languages in which perfectivity is not expressed morphologically this discourse contrast cannot be marked unambiguously, at least not in the same way. Similar options are conditioned by the PROG(RESSIVE) aspect.

It is also the case that for historical or stylistic reasons languages will either promote or avoid particular linguistic devices. Thus it has been observed that the HP has traditionally been less cultivated in fiction in English than in the narrative fiction of other languages, including French (Pascal 1962). Also different are the formal and stylistic conventions associated with storytelling practice in different cultures. These differences notwithstanding, there appear to be uses of tense-aspect in the linguistic structure of narrative that generalize across languages and across genres, and it is these I hope to capture, without, however, elevating them to the status of exceptionless universals. My goal is to strike a balance between the general and the particular, to posit cross-language tendencies where such can be reasonably supported by the data, while at the same time acknowledging differences within or departures from the broader patterns.

My conviction that certain pragmatic and metalinguistic uses of tense-aspect in narrative constitute potential universals motivates the spectrum of languages and diversity of genres included in this book. The major emphasis is on texts from French, notably from Old French. The medieval corpus also includes texts from Occitan, Spanish, and Italian. At appropriate points in the discussion data are also introduced from modern Romance languages and from English; in addition, reference is made to other languages in which "ungrammatical" tense usage has been observed but which, for reasons of space and lack of familiarity, I have chosen not to treat. It is my hope that readers with similar interests in the linguistic structure of narrative and with expertise in languages not included here might be inspired to test the claims put forth in this book against their own data. This would put us in an even stronger position empirically to assess the potential universality of certain pragmatic uses of tense and aspect—and of other components of the apparatus of grammar—in narrative language.

0.7. The organizational blueprint of this book is as follows. Chapter 1 surveys concepts and categories of grammar essential to the development of the theory of tense in narrative that is elaborated in chapter 2. Chapter 3 offers a critical overview of the literature on "ungrammatical" tense usage in narrative, focused on but not limited to the intrusion of PR tense into past narration. Chapter 4 then explores a number of typological questions about narrative as one of our primary hermeneutic constructs for converting the data of experience into language. Chapter 5 focuses on the linguistic structure of narrative—temporal structure and text structure, the latter based on the model proposed by Labov for natural narration. Because it figures so prominently in Labov's model, I also discuss in this chapter one of the principal EXPRESSIVE functions of tense-aspect in narrative: evaluation. Chapter 6 is devoted to TEXTUAL functions, while the remaining EXPRESSIVE functions are taken up in chapter 7. Finally, in its consideration of genres that challenge the conventions of normative narration by attempting to cast storytelling in the PR tense, chapter 8 explores a METALINGUISTIC function central to my theory of tense and narrativity.

Proceeding through the chapters of this book, the reader may perceive a curious resemblance between my own text-organizational strategy and a strategy of text structure characteristic of traditional oral storytelling. In oral cultures, the unfolding of narratives is not so much linear as circular: oral narrators frequently return to events previously narrated and re-present them such that new meanings emerge cumulatively through repetition. If the argumentation of this book is likewise less than strictly linear, returning periodically to questions raised earlier and reexamining them in different contexts, this should not be interpreted as the fallacy of imitative form, but simply as the structuring of the textual to accommodate the referential.

It will also be observed that the analytic terminology used in descriptions of narrative structure is often drawn metaphorically from grammar, in particular from grammatical categories associated with the *verb*. Among the more systematic descriptions offered by literary theorists, Todorov (1966, etc.) analyzes narrative structure in terms of "time," "aspect," and "mode," Genette (1980) in terms of "time," "mode," and "voice." It is not coincidental that the grammar of natural languages provides the conceptual and terminological metaphors for "grammars of narrative." The centrality of tense, aspect, and other verb-based categories to the accomplishment of certain specifically narrative tasks has no doubt motivated the choice of the verb as a prime metaphor for the description of narrative structure.

The cross-disciplinary nature of this book complicates the matter of an expository idiom. The two disciplines most prominently represented here, linguistics and literary theory, articulate their respective subject matter using different styles and different critical vocabularies. Preferring compromise over schizophrenia, I have endeavored to adopt a consistent, rigorous, but I hope not recondite usage, and to define all terminology invoked in a specialized sense by any of the disciplines represented here (italicized at first usage). I ask the indulgence of readers for whom this terminology is already household currency. I have also supplied translations for texts and examples and have translated citations into English. Given the tendency of translators to modify tense usage in the interest of smoothness or idiomaticity, I have chosen to use my own translations (unless otherwise indicated) even where published translations are available. Finally, to avoid ambiguity between tense-aspect categories and divisions of the time continuum, the names of which are often the same, I have adopted the convention of using lowercase for semantic/conceptual categories (e.g., past events, the speaker's present) and UPPERCASE for categories of grammar and their abbreviations (e.g., the PRESENT tense, the HP).

I Working Definitions and Operational Preliminaries

Dans ces "présents" nous semblons . . . capter le temps, qui à l'intérieur même des présents, des scènes, continue à s'écouler sous les formes d'un avenir qui devient passé.

(B. GROETHUYSEN, "DE QUELQUES ASPECTS DU TEMPS")

Behind the preterite there always lurks a demiurge, a God or a reciter. The world is not unexplained since it is told like a story; each one of its accidents is but a circumstance, and the preterite is precisely this operative sign whereby the narrator reduces this exploded reality to a slim and pure logos . . .

(BARTHES, WRITING DEGREE ZERO)

In this chapter I propose to outline the concepts and categories of grammar relevant to my analysis and to the theory of tense-aspect in narrative developed in chapter 2. The first three sections of the chapter are devoted to the grammatical macro-categories *tense, aspect,* and *situation type.* Section 1.4 discusses the locus of tense-aspect between "grammar" and "discourse." Sections 1.5–1.7 survey the tense-aspect categories of primary concern here, those of the past and present systems, with 1.7 focusing on the particularities of these categories in early Romance.

1.1. Tense

For the purposes of this investigation, "tense" is defined as *the grammaticalization of location in time.* More particularly, tense involves the location of situations predicated in a sentence or discourse relative to a reference time.[9] This reference time is normally the moment of speech but may be a surrogate temporal anchor indirectly linked to the moment of speech or conventionally established by the discourse. In contrast to other grammatical categories associated with the verb (aspect, voice, mood, evidentiality) tense is *relational* in that it involves at least two moments in time (which may coincide wholly or in part).

1.1.1. The definition of tense given above is based on a model proposed in Reichenbach (1947), in which tense relationships are described in terms of three orientation points along a hypothetical time line that moves from left to right. These are:

S: the *Speaker's* "now," or, more precisely, an arbitrarily fixed time point corresponding to the moment at which the speaker produces the utterance in question. This *deictic* "zero-point" may or may not coincide with:[10]

R: the temporal *Reference* point or period in relation to which a predicated situation is located. For so-called absolute tense relationships, R coincides with S, while for relative tense relationships R functions as a surrogate for S, which establishes itself as the anchor for the temporal location of predicated situations.

E: the predicated *Event* or Situation, whose location on the time line is reckoned in relation to R and/or S.

The sentences in (1.1) serve to illustrate the configuration of Reichenbach's three orientation points for situations reported by verbs in the SIMPLE PAST and PLUPERFECT (PLP), respectively. In addition to the surface tenses encoding E, and in (1.1b) also R, each sentence may be thought of as containing an underlying performative "I here and now state that . . ." which establishes S (bracketed in the examples below).

(1.1a)   [I here and now state:] Yesterday *I went to bed early.*

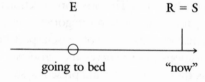

(1.1b)   [I here and now state:] Yesterday *Marcel claimed* he *had gone to bed early* the day before.

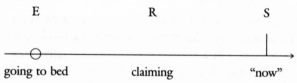

In (1.1a) the situation of "going to bed early" (E) is located in the past in relation to the moment S at which the speaker utters the sentence; S also serves as the reference point (R) for the deictic adverb "yesterday." In (1.1b) this same E is predicated as having occurred prior to a reference point established by the time of Marcel's "claim yesterday" (R), which is located in turn in relation to S.

The sentences in (1.1a) and (1.1b) illustrate what are referred to respectively as "absolute" and "relative" tenses. Absolute tenses assume the speaker's present as their reference point; in terms of Reichenbach's model, R = S. For relative tenses the reference point is established by the sentence itself (e.g., "yesterday" in the examples) or by context; it need not coincide with the speaker's present. Technically, the sentence in (1.b) is an "absolute-relative" tense (cf. Comrie 1985: chapter 3), for although E is located in relation to R, R is located in turn in relation to S—whence the representation E > R > S (i.e., E precedes R, which in turn precedes S). The deictic center, in other words, is still ultimately the speaker's present. For "pure relative" tenses, which are often nonfinite forms of the verb, R may be established entirely by the context, independent of S.

Though certain difficulties with Reichenbach's framework have been identified in the recent literature on tense (cf. Hornstein 1977; Comrie 1981, 1985; Dahl 1985), for our purpose it provides an adequate working model and has the advantage of being simpler and probably more familiar to readers than certain alternative models for representing tense relationships (e.g., Guillaume 1929; Bull 1960; or semantic approaches that draw on an intermediate formal language such as intensional logic). As in most descriptions of tense, however, in Reichenbach's model the linguistic domain over which tense applies is the sentence. Yet sentence-based grammatical models, even those that attempt to extend the notion of anaphora to temporal indexicality, often cannot account satisfactorily for temporal relationships that operate across linguistic units larger than the sentence, that is, for "tense in texts" (cf. Smith 1980; Kamp and Rohrer 1983). Moreover, many NONREFERENTIAL meanings of tense depend on contrasts that emerge only if we look at tense usage across stretches of connected discourse. The question then arises whether discourse, or context-dependent functions, should be incorporated as part of the meaning of tense-aspect categories. This question is deferred to §1.4.

Though Reichenbach's model is essentially sentence-based, it can be adapted without much difficulty to the structure of narrative discourse, even that of written fiction, which poses special problems with regard to the speaker and therefore to S. Extending Reichenbach's model involves, first of all, recognition of the fact that with each new sentence in the text S moves to the right along the time line; that is, the S of each successive sentence is later in the time of the telling than the S of the previous sentence. Although in principle, then, there is no single "now" that serves as the temporal deictic anchor for an entire text, in practice we often conceive of texts punctually, as if they were produced at a single moment in time that is the speaker's present.

Second, Reichenbach's model is predicated with respect to a communicative context involving face-to-face interaction between a *speaking* subject and an addressee, though the latter is not implicated formally in the model. In the deferred communication of *writing,* the analogue of S (i.e., the actual moment at which a sentence of the text is committed to paper—or now to disk) becomes less important as a temporal-deictic anchor for situations predicated *in* the text. This is especially true of much modern narrative fiction, which eschews all reference to its context of origin. If explicit linguistic traces of the real speaker—the author—are banished from narrative fiction, then S would seemingly become superfluous to a description of tense relationships in fiction; and if S is superfluous, then how can Reichenbach's model accommodate this type of narrative text?

There appear to be two possible ways in which the model can be adapted to the distinct pragmatic structure set up by fiction. One is optionally to detach R from S such that R is established independently by the discourse as the "current narrative plane" or "narrative present" of the story. In this case, tenses would be of the so-called pure relative variety, which need not be anchored to the present of the speaker-author at all, even indirectly. However, pure relative tenses tend to be expressed not by finite, tensed verbs but by participles or other nonfinite forms (cf. Comrie 1985:56–63), and it is impossible to construct a narrative on the basis of nonfinite verbs.

A preferable strategy for adapting Reichenbach's model to fictional narration is to assume that S refers not to the now of the author of the text but to the now of the author's surrogate inside the text—the fictional Speaker, or narrator, whether or not that Speaker refers to himself or herself as "I." This solution has the double advantage of being consonant with the pragmatic structure of fiction, described in chapter 4, and of retaining the essential link between R and S proposed by Reichenbach.

1.1.2.   The definition of tense offered above emphasizes the fact that tense is a *formal category of the grammar*. This is an important consideration inasmuch as the location of events in time can be handled in various ways other than through verb morphology. Compare the examples in (1.2), in which futurity is expressed respectively by a future tense (1.2a), by a future time adverb (1.2b), and by context (1.2c):

(1.2a) I think the Morrisons *will go* to Greece for their vacation.

(1.2b) The Morrisons leave for Greece *next Monday*.

(1.2c) A: Everybody seems to be spending the summers in Europe.
       B: Oh yeah? What about the Morrisons?
       A: They're going to Greece [implication: next summer].

For languages that have tense (not all languages do), this category provides a formal, grammatical means of expressing locations in time. But inasmuch as time reference can also be expressed lexically, contextually, or presuppositionally, tense morphology often becomes semantically redundant. Yet since this morphology is obligatory in tense languages, and since languages moreover seem to strive for functional economy in their use of available resources, there is a strong motivation for recycling tense morphology to do other types of (nontemporal) work in the discourse.

1.2. Aspect

Notwithstanding the controversies surrounding aspect in the linguistic literature, the working definition here is a simple one, oriented to the languages of primary concern. Both tense and aspect are categories associated with the verb, and in certain languages (e.g., the Romance group) tense information and aspect information are packaged together, synthetically, in the same morphology. Unlike tense, however, aspect is not a relational category, nor is it deictic; it is not concerned with relating the *time* of a situation to any other time point, but rather with how the speaker chooses to profile the situation.

Languages differ considerably with regard to the oppositions that are grammaticalized under aspect. The most prominent aspectual opposition cross-linguistically is the PERFECTIVE/IMPERFECTIVE (PFV/IPFV) contrast. A useful metaphor for describing this contrast is a camera lens that can adjust the focus on an object so that it may be viewed from different perspectives. Typically, PFV verbs denote single situations viewed *synthetically* "from the outside," that is, as unanalyzable wholes with well-defined results or endpoints, as in the example in (1.3) from French:

(1.3) L'année dernière Paul *a écrit* [PC] un roman. "Last year Paul *wrote* a novel."

Characteristically, PFV situations are punctual and their duration can be disregarded. They are also normally in the past and completed, though these features are not part of the meaning of PFV aspect, but *implicatures*[11] deriving from the fact that for most situations reported by PFV verbs the terminal boundary is in focus. By contrast, IPFV verbs view situations *analytically* "from the inside," making explicit reference to their internal development and leaving their endpoints out of focus entirely, as in the example in (1.4), again from French:

(1.4)   Quand il *rédigeait* [IMP] son deuxième chapitre, voilà son ordinateur qui est tombé en panne.   "While he *was writing* chapter two his computer broke down."

Although "writing chapter two" obviously has an initial and (we hope) a terminal boundary, these endpoints are disregarded, excluded from view, when the situation is reported by a verb with IPFV aspect. The emphasis is on the situation as process. The most common subdivisions of imperfectivity are "habitual" and "continuous" or "durative" action, the latter subdividing in certain languages into "progressive" and "nonprogressive" action.

The PFV/IPFV contrast is grammaticalized (i.e., expressed *morphologically*) throughout Romance, but only for the past; in English this contrast is expressed either *lexically* or for certain verbs via the PROGRESSIVE/NON-PROGRESSIVE (PROG/NONPROG) opposition, which is grammaticalized not only for the past but for the nonpast (present and future) as well. Not unexpectedly, use of the PROG/NONPROG contrast in English differs from its use in Spanish or Italian, which likewise have PROG aspect, while in French the meanings expressed by the PROG must be conveyed lexically (e.g., via the marked periphrasis *être en train de*).

Just as tense is understood to refer only to *grammatical* means of expressing locations in time, aspect refers only to grammatical means of expressing such notions as "completion," "durativity," and "iteration." This is not to say that these same notions cannot be expressed *lexically* via what is variously referred to as *Aktionsart, mode d'action*, or, according to a more recent typology, *situation type*. This latter category is frequently confused with aspect and is often in fact referred to as "lexical aspect."

1.3.   Situation types

In Vendler (1967:97–121) predicates are divided into four classes, or "situation types": *states, activities, accomplishments,* and *achievements*, distinguished according to a number of syntactic and semantic tests (summarized in Dowty 1979:60; Mourelatos 1981:191ff.; Foley and Van Valin 1984:36ff.). Briefly, the actions referred to by achievements ("recognize someone," "spot something," "find or lose something," "be born," "die") and accomplishments ("sing a song," "run a race," "smoke a cigarette," "build a house," "draw a circle," "recover from illness") are *telic*, that is, their meanings include natural endpoints. In the case of accomplishments these endpoints are resultant states: for example, "recovering from illness" ultimately produces the state of "wellness." The actions referred to by states ("know, believe, or own something," "desire or love someone") and activities ("sing," "run," "walk," "smoke," "swim," "push a cart," "drive a car") are *atelic*—they have no intrinsic endpoints. Though states and activities both refer to ongoing (atelic) situations, activities are more volitional, higher in transitivity (defined in *n*139), and can be described as "events." The two telic categories differ with respect to duration: insofar as accomplishments involve a process, they have inherent duration ("running a race" or "singing a song" over time), while achievements are inherently punctual and instantaneous: "finding something" obtains (= holds true) technically only at the precise moment the found object is discovered.

Though aspects and situation types are in principle independent, not all combinations of the two are permissible. For example, in languages with a PROG aspect, only activities, accomplishments, and to a lesser degree achievements are compatible with this aspect; thus "I am driving a car" (activity), "he was singing a song" (accomplishment), "we're losing money" (achievement), but questionably "I'm finding a job" (achievement). More acceptable in the PROG are activity counterparts of this last sentence, such as "I'm looking for a job" or "I'm trying to find a job" (the auxiliary *try to* "converts" the original achievement to an activity). States cannot normally occur in the PROG (*"I am knowing physics," *"Are you believing in Santa Claus?"), though PROG aspect does not itself alter a predicate's type. "Writing a novel" will always be an accomplishment irrespective of aspectual oppositions that may be superimposed on it by tense-aspect morphology, as shown in the sentences in (1.3) and (1.4) above.[12] Situation types can, however, be altered by quantification and by aspectual auxiliaries. The next sections consider these two factors in turn.

1.3.1. It is well known that definiteness and quantification may have an effect on the aspectual profile of a sentence (cf. Verkuyl 1972; Carlson 1981). Definiteness and quantification (of the grammatical object) are similarly factors in the determination of situation types. Taking as examples predicates occurring in the texts in appendix 2,[13] we observe that "to compose a song" (VI: 89), with a singular object, is an accomplishment; with a plural object ("to compose many beautiful songs," VI: 64) this predicate becomes an activity. The causative predicate "to stop some cars" (II: 25) is similarly an activity by virtue of its indefinite plural object; the singular version "to stop a car" (which does not occur in this text) would be an achievement. Yet the sentence that actually occurs in text II: "and then we try to stop some cars" (*et puis on essaie d'arrêter des voitures*) turns out to be an achievement; the plural factor is overridden by the ingressive, perfectivizing force of the auxiliary "try to" and the sequencing adverb "then," which together shift the focus onto the moment

when the situation begins. While an achievement situation refers by definition to a point, this point need not be the terminal boundary; it may instead be the initial boundary, the moment at which a situation begins to
obtain. As we shall see, reference to initial boundaries is often made
through use of perfectivizing auxiliaries.

Before leaving the matter of quantification, .I wish to point out its
heuristic value in revealing the superiority of the situation-type framework
over the alternative categories (*Aktionsarten, modes d'action*) that propose
to capture the notion of "lexical aspect." While the latter have scope over
the verb alone, situation types have scope over the entire predicate. As
noted above, while "to smoke" is an activity, "to smoke a cigarette" is an
accomplishment, "to smoke cigarettes" once again an activity, and "to start
to smoke (cigarettes)" an achievement. Situation-type differences of this
kind turn out to be highly relevant to the pragmatic use of tenses in narrative contexts. The findings of a number of studies that have sought to
correlate narrative tense usage in the Middle Ages to the semantics of verbs
(Gilman 1961; Szertics 1967; Schøsler 1986) are vitiated by the fact that they
operate with notions of lexical aspect that are limited to the verb alone and
therefore fail to reveal meaningful correlations with (NONREFERENTIAL)
use of tenses.

1.3.2.   In the course of my research I have observed
that a number of auxiliaries—including "stop," "finish," "begin to," "start
to," "go and" ("then he goes and tells her that . . .")—have the effect of
transforming non-achievement complements into complex achievement
predicates that focus on either the initial boundary ("begin to," "start to,"
"go and") or the terminal boundary ("stop," "finish") of a situation. While
these "perfectivizing" auxiliaries cannot themselves take achievement complements (*"he finished arriving home," ??"I started to recognize him"),
they are often pressed into service, like perfectivizing adverbs, to give an
achievement profile to state, activity, and accomplishment situations: *when
I began to think about it* (state → achievement) *I realized . . . ; so I finished
studying* (activity → achievement) *and went to the movies; at six o'clock I
started to cook dinner* (accomplishment → achievement). At various points
in the text I discuss the role of perfectivizing auxiliaries of this type, in
particular ingressive "begin to," in reconfiguring predicates so as to be
compatible with the NARRATIVE PRESENT (NP) tense.

1.4. Grammar, discourse, and the meaning of tense-aspect categories

Before proceeding to a discussion of individual tense-aspect categories, I would like to clarify my position on a theoretical question central to any discourse-pragmatic approach to tense and aspect, in particular one that focuses on the NONREFERENTIAL functions of these categories. The question is whether the *meaning* of a grammatical category should be seen as including the *functions* or *uses* of that category in particular discourse contexts. In his monograph on tense, Comrie (1985:26) argues that:

tenses have meanings definable independently of particular contexts; it is possible for a given tense to have more than one meaning, in which case some of the meanings may be more basic than others; it is also possible that a tense will receive particular interpretations in particular contexts, *but these are always explainable in terms of the interaction of context-independent meaning and context, and do not therefore form part of the meaning of the tense category in question.* This approach may be contrasted with an alternative, much in vogue with respect to tense and, even more so, aspect, according to which these categories should be defined primarily in terms of their contextual functions. (my emphasis)

In Comrie's view the failure to distinguish between "meaning," which is context-independent, and "implicatures," which are contextually determined, has been one of the main difficulties in working out an adequate characterization of tenses for language in general. While such is not the goal of this book, the distinction Comrie is insisting upon is nonetheless essential to showing the motivation for the TEXTUAL and EXPRESSIVE functions that tense-aspect categories assume in particular discourse contexts, notably narrative. The pragmatic *functions* of tense-aspect categories in narrative are not arbitrary; rather, I see them as motivated extensions of the *meanings* of those categories, extensions that, according to the view of grammar as "emergent" (Hopper 1987), may ultimately contribute to a reshaping of the basic meanings.

The next two sections of this chapter (1.5, 1.6) take up the basic meanings of a number of cross-language tense-aspect categories as well as the extended meanings (i.e., pragmatic functions) they can acquire in narrative contexts. Section 1.7 considers how these cross-language categories map onto individual-language tenses in early Romance. The emphasis on Old French reflects my own orientation as well as the fact that Old French has received considerably more attention from linguists and grammarians than any of its early Romance counterparts.

1.5. Tenses of the past system

Narration is a verbal icon of experience viewed from a *retrospective* vantage; the experience is by definition "past," whether it occurred in some real world or not. Hypothetical or future experiences are also commonly narrated as if they were past, for this, I submit, is the only way one can *narrate*. The tenses appropriate to the verbal activity of narrating are accordingly tenses that include past time reference as part of their basic meaning. Among these the PRETERIT and IMPERFECT (=PFV and IPFV PASTS, respectively) figure most prominently (§§1.5.1–3). The PERFECT (§1.5.4) is rare in narrative, for reasons connected to its basic meaning. It is common, however, for PERFECTS to evolve over time into PRETERITS, as has happened in several varieties of Romance, creating a state of nonisomorphism in which there are two PFV PASTS, with one doing double duty as a PERF. The ramifications of this state of affairs for narrative in French are discussed in §1.5.5. As a "before-past" or "past of the past," the PLUPERFECT has a temporal structure that may be represented as $E > R > S$; this tense typically serves to encode explanatory *background* situations that took place before the events of the current narrative plane. As the PLP is relatively straightforward, it is not elaborated on in this section. The "after-past" or "future of the past" tenses are discussed briefly in §1.5.6.

1.5.1. *The* PRETERIT. The prototypical tense of narration as a mode of reporting information is the PAST, specifically the PFV PAST, or PRET (for languages with a PFV/IPFV contrast), whose status as the unmarked tense of narration derives from its link to the notion of an event. The PFV aspect of the PRET is ideally suited to reporting experience that has been cognitively packaged into synthetic units amenable to representation as points along a time line. The affinity of the PRET for eventive situations explains its characteristic use to encode the sequence of happenings that constitutes the backbone of a narration.

It is the PRET's PFV aspect that endows a situation with a certain wholeness—a figure seen against a ground. Several investigators (Joos 1964; Weinrich 1973; Hopper 1979a, 1979b, 1982a) have therefore argued that the basic function of this PAST is to mark the *foreground* of a discourse, while the *background* is marked by its IPFV counterparts, the durative IMP or PAST PROG, whose analytic view of situations allows them to be perceived as unbounded stretches of individual moments. The controversy referred to in §1.4 is directly relevant to this claim that the basic meanings of PFV and IPFV aspect are TEXTUAL meanings related to grounding. As Comrie (1985), Martin (1971), and others have argued, neither the figural quality of the PRET nor its sequential quality is an intrinsic part of its meaning; rather, these properties emerge from the interaction of its basic meaning (PAST time reference + PFV aspect) with a specific discourse context—narration. In other words, the foregrounding ability of the PRET and the backgrounding ability of the IMP are contextual implicatures derivable from the synthetic and analytic visions of their respective aspects.

1.5.2. The IMPERFECT. As stated above, the two primary readings of the IMP are (a) habitual action and (b) durative or continuous action, illustrated by the Romance examples in (1.5) and (1.6), respectively:

(1.5) Quand j'*étais* petite j'*allais* souvent à la plage.   "When I *was* little I *would/used to go* to the beach a lot."

(1.6) Ayer papá *jugaba/estaba jugando al tenis* cuando se cayó y se le rompió la muñeca.   "Yesterday Daddy *was playing tennis* when he fell and broke his wrist."

Both readings are subsumed under the basic meaning of the IPFV aspect: The habitual IMP of (1.5) tells us that the situation of "going to the beach" occurred regularly *during a period of time in the past whose endpoints are not specified.* The durative IMP of (1.6) makes reference to "playing tennis" without regard to its endpoints; this situation is represented as ongoing and cotemporal with the punctual events of the father's falling and breaking his wrist, for which it provides a backdrop. Because IPFV PASTs represent situations analytically, from the inside, not synthetically in their totality like the PFV PAST, they tend to select those elements of an experience that, however interesting, are not essential to the narrative and do not serve to advance the plot. They are typically the tenses of commentary, explanation, and description.

As grammarians have pointed out, the IPFV aspect of the IMP (durative reading) and PROG P creates the illusion of "a past still alive," allowing the speaker to report situations that are entirely past as if they were in the process of unfolding. Guillaume (1929) locates this property of the IMP in its *vision sécante:* at the moment designated by R, one portion of the situation reported in the IMP (or PROG P) is already complete, has already become reality, while the other has yet to materialize; it leaves a "future" open. This *vision sécante* is represented in (1.7):

(1.7) A trois heures *J'ÉCOUTAIS* l'opera. "At three o'clock *I WAS LISTENING TO* the opera."

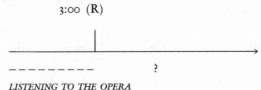

LISTENING TO THE OPERA

At the R established by the time adverb "at three o'clock" the speaker of this sentence was involved in listening to the opera, a process that began at some unspecified moment prior to R and continued up through R. This R is the past counterpart of what Groethuysen (1935–1936:165f.) calls the "dialectical now," the point of encounter between the past (as "known" and "completed") and the future (as "unknown" and "action") that expresses the dialectic of time itself. Ducrot (1979:10) notes that when a situation is reported in the IMP it is as if one does not see it come into being; it is seen, so to speak, as already there. The situation may also continue after R, though as Guillaume observes, the tense makes no statement about the continuation of the situation.

The IMP combines with different time adverbs and situation types to produce a variety of effects. The examples in (1.6) and (1.7), in which IMP verbs encode atelic activity situations ("playing tennis," "listening to the opera") co-occurring with either a *punctual time adverb* establishing R ("at 3 o'clock") or with another punctual situation ("fell down," "broke his wrist"), illustrate a classic IMP sentence type found in all varieties of discourse. It is this type of IMP sentence that founds Guillaume's *vision sécante*. But if we substitute a durational time adverb, as in the sentences in (1.8a)–(1.9a), the picture changes slightly:

(1.8a) L'année dernière à Paris IL FAISAIT CHAUD [IMP]. "Last year in Paris IT WAS HOT." [state]

(1.9a) L'année dernière JE DÉMÉNAGEAIS [IMP]. "Last year I WAS MOVING." [activity] (examples from Ducrot 1979)

Referring to examples such as these, Ducrot (1979:6) formulates the following global definition of the IMP: "When an utterance is in the IMP its *topic* is temporal and its *focus* is presented as a *characteristic property* of the topic which applies to it in its totality" (italics added). Transposed into Reichenbach's terminology, this definition states that a situation E reported in the IMP (the focus) is predicated to hold over the entire duration of its reference R (the topic), this R already having been established in the discourse by an earlier-mentioned past event, by a past time adverb (as in the examples above), or simply by context. The thrust of this definition becomes clearer if we consider the same sentences with PFV PASTs, as in (1.8b) and (1.9b) with the PC:

(1.8b) L'année dernière à Paris il a fait chaud [PC]. "Last year in Paris it was hot."

(1.9b) L'année dernière j'ai déménagé [PC]. "Last year I moved."

Here the eventive PFV P simply states that during the reference period established by the adverb (R = "last year"), E occurred on one or more occasions; (1.9b) asserts that the speaker changed residence—presumably once, though this is an implicature [14]—last year, while (1.8b) states that the temperature in Paris was at certain unspecified times last year above normal. By contrast, in the (a) sentences these predications hold for the entirety of "last year," providing a characterization of it. Given the stative predicate *faire chaud* (to be hot [weather]), the difference between (1.8a) and (1.8b) can only be expressed lexically in English. (1.8a) might be rendered as "last year was a hot year in Paris," (1.8b) as "last year in Paris there were times when it was hot." The relationships obtaining between E and R in these four sentences are represented in figure 1. Although the circles for the IMP Es are drawn congruent with those of their respective Rs, the IMP also allows for the possibility that E circles contain those of their respective Rs, that is, the unusual heat may have started before and/or continued beyond last year, or it may have taken the speaker of (1.9a) longer than just last year to complete his or her move. The IMP states only that for the entirety of R the situation E obtained.

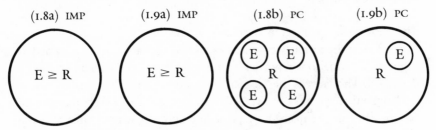

Figure 1. PERFECTIVE versus IMPERFECTIVE PASTS.

The sentences in (1.8) and (1.9) both involve atelic situations. Substituting telic situations (achievements and accomplishments) brings us to what has been referred to as the NARRATIVE IMPERFECT.

1.5.3. *The NARRATIVE IMPERFECT*.[15]   In the examples in (1.10)–(1.12) the IMPs (in uppercase) report unambiguously punctual eventive situations that would normally be reported in a PFV PAST:

(1.10) "Ce n'est rien," *dit il* [PS]. . . . Puis, au milieu du pansement [R] *IL S'INTERROMPAIT* [IMP/achievement] pour s'écrier: "Coup double! Tous les deux roides morts! . . . C'est le curé qui va rire. . . . Coup double! Ah! voici enfin cette petite tortue de Chalina." Orso *NE RÉPONDAIT PAS* [IMP/accomplishment]. Il *ÉTAIT* [IMP] pale comme un mort et *TREMBLAIT* [IMP] de tous ses membres.

"It's nothing," *he said* [PS]. . . . Then, in the middle of putting on the bandage [R] *HE INTERRUPTED HIMSELF* [IMP/achievement] to shout: "Double hit! Both of them still as corpses! . . . It's the vicar who's going to laugh. . . . Double hit! Ah! Here's that little turtle Chalina at last." Orso *DIDN'T RESPOND* [IMP/accomplishment]. He *WAS* [IMP] pale as death and *TREMBLED* [IMP] in every limb. (Mérimée, *Colomba*)

(1.11) Lorsque le notaire *arriva* [PS] . . . elle les *reçut* [PS] elle-même et les *invita* [PS] à tout visiter. . . . Un mois plus tard [R] elle *SIGNAIT* [IMP] *LE CONTRAT* et *ACHETAIT* [IMP] *UNE PETITE MAISON.*

When the notary *arrived* [PS] . . . she *received* [PS] them herself and *invited* [PS] them to look around at everything. . . . A month later [R] she *WAS SIGNING* [IMP] *THE CONTRACT* and *BUYING* [IMP] *A LITTLE HOUSE* [two accomplishments]. (Maupassant)

(1.12) In quello stesso anno [R] *NASCEVA* [IMP] a Firenze Dante Alighieri. "In that same year Dante Alighieri *WAS BORN* [IMP] in Florence" [achievement]. (cited in Ronconi 1943)

The static visual qualities invoked by grammarians to characterize the stylistic effect of the NARR IMP—picturesque, photographic—are intended to suggest that situations reported by this tense are not so much narrated as described. The PRET is the "action" PAST, the IMP the "visualizing" PAST. As Ronconi (1943:92) observes, the IMP can isolate a single moment of action, detaching it from those preceding and following it, just as a still photograph captures a single cut of a scene in motion and presents it frozen to the observer. This is diagramed in figure 2, using the example in (1.11).

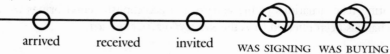

arrived　　　received　　　invited　　WAS SIGNING　WAS BUYING

Figure 2. The NARRATIVE IMPERFECT.

The two coordinated NARR IMP clauses in this example are like reduced relative clauses: "la voilà *qui signait . . . et achetait . . .*" As relatives, these clauses would normally be in the IMP in French, indicating that the subordinate verbs are cotemporal (simultaneous) with a past R. But encoding an event in a subordinate clause normally relegates it to background, which is precisely the opposite of what a narrator intends who chooses the NARR

IMP. By reporting these two situations as part of the sequence of narrative events *but with distinctive encoding* (the IMP rather than the unmarked PS), the narrator foregrounds and evaluates them, conveying, in addition to their propositional information, the information that they are unpredictable or contrary to expectation.

Along the lines of Ducrot, Ronconi (1943:93) observes that the sentence in (1.12) presents Dante's birth not as the instantaneous event it was but as a characteristic of the year 1265. The IPFV aspect of the NARR IMP cancels out, as it were, the inherent punctuality of this achievement situation, enabling it to "characterize the year 1265" as a whole, presumably in the sense that the year 1265 will go down in history because of the (retrospectively) momentous event of the birth of Dante. At several further points in our discussion we shall again observe the effects produced by the conflicting claims of aspect and situation type.

1.5.4. The PERFECT. The PERFECT is a category that combines aspect and temporality, though the temporal component is arguably an implicature deriving from the basic meaning of PERFECTS, which is to mark a situation as already *completed* in present time and/or to signal its present relevance (the latter meaning evolves from the former), as in examples (1.13a)–(1.15a):

(1.13a) I'm not hungry, thanks. I*'ve eaten.*

(1.14a) John *has been* to the Soviet Union three times.

(1.15a) *Jean de Florette* c'est un film que *j'ai* déjà *vu.* "*Jean de Florette* is a film I*'ve* already *seen.*"

Although I have included it in the section on PAST tenses, the PERF in narrative is more profitably viewed as a category of the PRESENT system. As Comrie observes (1976:52), the PERF says nothing directly about a past situation E (i.e., about when I ate, when John went to the Soviet Union, when I saw *Jean de Florette*), but relates a resulting present state (I'm not hungry, I know of John's travels to the Soviet Union, I'm familiar with the story of *Jean de Florette*) to the fact that E occurred at some moment in the past. The [+ past] implicature derives from the representation of E as [+ completed] at S, which serves also as its R. It is aspectually PFV and its temporal structure is E > R/S, in contrast to the R/E > S structure of its PFV counterpart the PRET, as in examples (1.13b)–(1.15b):

(1.13b) I'm not hungry, thanks. I *ate* a few hours ago.

(1.14b) John *went* to the Soviet Union three times last year.

(1.15b) *Jean de Florette* c'est un film que *j'ai vu* quand il venait de sortir. "*Jean de Florette* is a movie I *saw* when it just came out."

The PERF is in many languages unacceptable when combined with time adverbials that have definite past time reference, even when the reference is to a very recent past ("I'm not hungry, thanks. *I've eaten* a few hours ago"). This supports Comrie's observation that although the PERF expresses a relation between two time points, and is in this sense more like a tense than an aspect, it is not "about" the earlier situation (E).

The rarity of the PERF in natural narrative has been widely observed (Labov 1972; Givón 1983; Dahl 1985). Givón (1983:232) attributes its low text frequency to the fact that the PERF is typically used to report situations that are out-of-sequence, thereby infringing the narrative norm of sequential presentation. The low frequency of the PERF is also explained by the fact that this category establishes a connection to the speaker's now that cannot be neutralized. Yet narratives are not about the speaker's present, they are about the past. In narration, PERFs occur in two sharply profiled discourse contexts: first, in direct commentary by the narrator to the addressee outside the narrative proper, as in (1.16) from Old French:

(1.16) Aucassins fu armés sor son ceval, si con *vos avés oï* et *entendu*. "Aucassin was on his horse, fully armed, as now *you have heard*." (III:1–2)[16]

and second, within the narrative as a PERF linked to a *diegetic* PR,[17] as in (1.17):

(1.17) Tut sun aver qu'od sei *ad portét*, / Tut le depart [PR] par Alsis la citét. "All his wealth which he *has brought* [PC/PERF] with him, he distributes [PR] it all throughout the city." (*Alexis*, 91–92)

As mentioned above, over time the PERF in a number of languages has evolved into a PRET. This development is a logical semantic extension: from the meaning "state resulting from a past situation," to the "past situation itself, with present relevance," and ultimately to simply "past situation" (with no necessary present relevance). In Romance this has occurred in standard French, Northern Italian, and Daco-Romanian (see Harris 1982;

Fleischman 1983a), where the periphrastic PFV PAST now functions as a PRET side by side with a simple PFV PAST, while at the same time retaining its earlier PERF function. There has been a tendency in these languages for the two PFV PS to contrast according to discourse type: as an oversimplified generalization, the PC plays the PRET role in the spoken language and in informal writing, while the PS, now virtually excluded from the standard spoken languages, has been relegated to formal written genres.[18] It is to the relationship between these two PFV PS in French that we will now turn our attention.

1.5.5. *The PASSÉ SIMPLE and PASSÉ COMPOSÉ.*[19] The marginalization of the French PS has resulted in the privileging of a TEXTUAL function, the signaling of a particular type of discourse, at the expense of its REFERENTIAL function, the signaling of past time. As Roland Barthes observes, "obsolete in spoken French, the preterite, which is the cornerstone of Narration, always signifies the presence of Art; it is part of a ritual of letters. Its function is no longer that of a tense" (1967:30). Further on he adds, "when, within the narration, the preterite is replaced by less ornamental forms, fresher, more full-bodied, and nearer to speech (the present tense or the present perfect), Literature becomes the receptacle of existence in all its density and no longer just its meaning alone. The acts it recounts are still separated from History, but no longer from people" (1967:32). This observation points to the quintessential feature separating the PS from the PC: subjectivity. For native speakers of French, the PS is felt to be the vehicle of objective discourse from which all traces of speaker subjectivity have been eradicated. Even in fiction, the sole narrative form in which the PS co-occurs with a first person subject, situations reported in this tense constitute uninvolved narration, a past detached from the voice that narrates it.

By contrast, as Barthes suggests, the PC is inseparable from subjectivity; it marks the discourse of a speaker-observer whose psychological center permeates that discourse. Benveniste (1959) characterizes it as "the autobiographical form par excellence, the tense of an eyewitness narrator" (see below, this section) who recounts events from the perspective of a participant in them. When substituted for the PS in written narrative, the PC has the effect of removing the narration from the realm of the literary and bringing it to the level of everyday speech. This is presumably one reason why novelistic experiments in PC narration such as Camus's *The Stranger* (see §7.7.1) ultimately failed to produce a new narrative form.

The notion of eyewitness narration requires clarification, in that it appears to contain a contradiction. As one type of verbal representation of experience, narration is by definition a discourse informed by a retrospective intelligibility; it differs in this respect from eyewitness reports of experience, which seek to provide an unmediated commentary on simultaneously occurring action. As Schlicher writes (1931:48f.):

The experience of the mind in dealing with things which are in the process of happening is essentially different from its experience in dealing with events of the past. In the former case it is led along from one detail—act or occurrence—to the next, taking them in as well as it may, but with only a limited opportunity to judge them individually or grasp them in their relation to one another or their connection with other things outside of those just then taking place. . . . Whereas present experience is largely a mere suggestion of events, the past is a pattern in which . . . details have found their place according to their significance to [the speaker]. The individual act in the past may be seen as completed or continuing, as independent or as related to some other act. All this is possible because these acts can be passed in review at will, appraised and compared—a thing quite impossible or only partially possible at the time when they are taking place.

What Schlicher is getting at here is the fundamental cognitive difference that underlies a verbalization of events as one observes or experiences them and a post-hoc verbalization of events that have been retrieved from memory, having already become history. "The whole point of history," Arthur Danto observes (1965:183), "is not to know about actions as witnesses might, but as historians do, in connection with later events and as part of temporal wholes. History, in other words, only emerges once the game is over." To come back to Benveniste's reference to eyewitness narration, it must be understood that the activities of observation and narration, seeing and speaking, do not take place at the same time (cf. *n*21). What this term means is simply that a speaker is reporting on events in which she or he has personally participated.

As a PFV P necessarily linked to a speaking subject, the PC is the unmarked tense of conversational narratives in French, which are by-and-large recollections of personal experience (cf. text II in appendix 2). In nonconversational (i.e., literary, historical) narration,[20] the PC is a marked tense that insistently implicates a real narrator in a discourse, one of whose defining features is the elimination of all traces of a speaker; the PC seeks to blur the distinction between narration and memoirs as modes of representing one's experiences.

1.5.6. *The "After-Past."* Relatively infrequent in narrative are the FUTURE-OF-THE-PAST, with only two examples in the texts in appendix 2, given here as (1.18) and (1.19), and its functional analogue the "GO"-FUTURE-OF-THE-PAST, with three examples, given as (1.20)–(1.22):

(1.18) . . . on était en train de se demander si on *continuerait* ou non. ". . . we were beginning to wonder whether we *should go on* or not." (II : 35–36)

(1.19) . . . et aloient ja porparlant de quel mort il *feroient morir.* ". . . and along they went talking of how they *would have him killed.*" (III : 30–31)

(1.20) I really thought I *was gonna die.* (I : 50)

(1.21) Mi fermai otto giorni per dirigere gli attori che *dovevano rappresentarlo.* "I stayed there a week to direct the actors who *were to perform* it [*Don Giovanni*]." (V : 4–5)

(1.22) el aguililla . . . lo *iba a sacar.* "the eagle . . . *was going to pull him out.*" (VIII : 37–38)

Both tenses predicate a situation as having occurred after a past situation that serves as its R. The temporal structure of "after-pasts" can be represented as $R > S$; $R > E$. In the absence of precise temporal adverbs, the relationship between E and S is not specified: E may precede, follow, or overlap S. Both types of after-past are also aspectually IPFV: The FUT-OF-P in many languages combines FUT + IPFV PAST morphology. The so-called "GO"-FUT-OF-P combines an auxiliary in the IMP (PROG PAST in English) with an infinitive. This auxiliary is normally "go," though certain modals are also possible, as in the Italian example in (1.21) with obligative *dovere* (ought to).

In narrative these prospective tenses occur mainly in indirectly reported speech and thoughts, as in examples (1.18)–(1.20), including the style known as *free indirect discourse.* The FUT-OF-P should not be confused with the CONDITIONAL (COND), though in many languages, including English and the Romance languages, the same form expresses both functions.

1.6. Tenses of the present system

The present system includes, in addition to the PRESENT tense, the PERFECT and the FUTURE. The primary focus in this section is on the PR, in both SIMPLE and PROG forms, and on their use in narration with past time reference (§§1.6.1–3). Like the PERF, discussed in §1.5.4 above, the FUT is rare in narration and for the same reasons. It is discussed briefly in §1.6.4.

1.6.1. *The* PRESENT. The range of temporal references that the PR tense can have is greater than that of any other tense category. These include reference not just to the speaker's present but also to the future and the past, as well as reference to habitual, generic, gnomic, and timeless situations, illustrated respectively in the examples below:

(1.23) The Market *is down* 50 points today. (PR cotemporal with now)

(1.24) I *leave/am leaving* for Paris next week. (future)

(1.25) *I'm sitting* in my office when suddenly this student *walks in* and *says* to me . . . (past)

(1.26) The Deans' Conference *meets* on Thursdays. (habitual)

(1.27) Dogs *have* fleas. (generic)

(1.28) A good man *is* hard to find. (gnomic)

(1.29) Two plus two *equals* four. (timeless)

For convenience, the last four types are subsumed under the label "generic," subcategorized where appropriate as to whether the time reference is to all time moments in the story-world (local) or in all possible worlds (global).

It is often assumed that the primary or basic meaning of the PR is that illustrated in (1.23), cotemporality with the speaker's present. Yet if one takes this position, it is only through complex semantic circumlocutions that the range of other meanings can be explained, if at all. If, on the other hand, timelessness (in the sense of "temporal neutrality") is chosen as the basic meaning (that is, if the PR is viewed as *inherently unmarked for time*), then it is easy to see how the PR can assume, in particular discourse contexts, any of the possibilities for temporal reference listed above, thereby justifying its status as the unmarked tense category across languages (cf. Dahl 1985). Bolinger (1947:436) writes, "We might call the simple present tense the BASE TENSE, to which all other tenses are oriented but which is itself oriented to nothing, expressing merely the FACT OF PROCESS. The simple present . . . is 'timeless' not in the sense of 'eternal' but of 'non-committed about time.' Whenever, then, the speaker wishes to avoid the confinement of time implicit in other tenses, he uses the simple present."

1.6.2. "Visualizing" and "action" PRESENTS.

The PR in most languages is a static tense used to describe rather than to narrate, narration being a verbal activity for which the dynamic PAST is better suited. It was suggested above that for languages with a PFV-IPFV contrast, the IPFV PAST is the "visualizing" past, the PFV PAST the "action" past. I have adapted these terms from Buffin (1925), where they are invoked not with regard to the PAST but to distinguish between two virtually opposite uses of the diegetic PR (PR with past time reference), labeled respectively the *présent visuel* and the *présent moteur*. At the time Buffin was writing, certain connections now discovered to exist between tense, aspect, and *Aktionsart*/situation type had not yet been made. Thus he characterized the difference between these two varieties of PR simply in terms of whether the PAST equivalent in modern French would be the IMP (= visualizing) or the PS (= action).

Few languages have an IPFV-PFV contrast for present time; the PR in most languages is either IPFV or aspectually neutral (Comrie 1976:66). The difference between the visualizing and action PRs is most transparent in languages where it is expressed formally (e.g., by the contrast between SIMPLE and PROGRESSIVE aspect, as in English). However, form is not always a reliable indicator of the difference. For example, I have observed that the PR_a predictably co-occurs with telic situations, particularly achievements, while the PR_v co-occurs with accomplishments and with atelic situations (states and activities). In various languages states cannot normally occur in the PROG; they occur only in the SIMPLE (NONPROG) form ("I know/*am knowing calculus"). Yet the SIMPLE PR *form* of a stative verb does not change the fact of its being a visualizing PR. Irrespective of the availability of a formal opposition to provide distinctive encoding for these two varieties of PR, their difference at the TEXTUAL level reveals itself whenever the PR is used to represent past experience: as the labels suggest, visualizing tenses (PR or P) are used for *description*, action tenses for the *narration of events*. Henceforth, where appropriate I shall subscript tense labels as "v[isualizing]" or "a[ction]."

Consider the two passages given in (1.30), with clauses numbered for ease of reference:

(1.30a)   Rain *DRIFTS* about the windows (1), a pack of hounds *PADS BACK AND FORTH* in front of the house (2), someone *GOES UP* (3) and *KNOCKS* at the door (4).

(1.30b)   Rain IS DRIFTING about the windows (1), a pack of hounds IS PAD-DING BACK AND FORTH in front of the house (2), someone IS GOING UP to the door (3), now they'RE KNOCKING on it (4) . . . (cited in Traugott and Pratt 1980:299)

Traugott and Pratt observe correctly that speakers of English will identify the SIMPLE PR version in (1.30a) as a narrative in the HP, and the PROG PR version in (1.30b) as an eyewitness report produced, for example, by someone looking out the window. Parallel examples involving the SIMPLE/PROG contrast in English are discussed in Joos (1964:131), Comrie (1976: 77), Woisetschlaeger (1976:56), and Banfield (1982:165). Joos invokes this contrast specifically to refute the widespread view that the HP in English (always the SIMPLE PR form) represents events "as if they were occurring before our eyes." This is not quite the same, however, as saying that events are represented as if they were occurring before *the speaker's* eyes. As Groethuysen (1935–1936:166) remarks, the activity of observation is inseparable from the present, from now; correspondingly, speaking of what one *has seen* is to speak of past nows, of *presents* in the past.

Consider now the text in (1.31), immediately recognizable as a sportscast, in which SIMPLE and PROG forms of the PR alternate:

(1.31)   Aaron HITS A HIGH FLY BALL to center field (1). Donovan IS RUNNING BACK TOWARD THE FENCE (2), and the ball BOUNCES OFF THE CENTER FIELD WALL (3). The runner on second IS ROUNDING THIRD (4), and he CROSSES HOME PLATE (5). The crowd IS ON ITS FEET (6). (adapted from an example cited in Banfield 1982:165)

This text exemplifies a discourse form that will be referred to as *current report* (§4.3). Current reports are verbal representations of experience that purport to be simultaneous with the speaker's perception of the events being reported. Admittedly, it is only under rather specialized circumstances that the reporting of information is actually simultaneous with its perception (i.e., when the perception is of a more or less instantaneous event);[21] but when the event has significant duration the possibility arises of talking about it while it is going on (Chafe 1973:276). This difference points to a contrast involving situation types: on the one hand, achievements, which are instantaneous; on the other, states, activities, and accomplishments, which all involve duration. The passage in (1.31) contains three achievements, in sentences (1), (3), and (5), all reported in the SIMPLE PR. Sentences (2) and (4) contain accomplishments, and these are reported in the PR PROG. Sentence (6) can only be in the SIMPLE PR, given the constraint in English against the co-occurrence of states with PROG aspect.

As stated above, the SIMPLE-PROG opposition of English provides a formal (morphological) means of encoding the distinction between the action and visualizing PRs, the former typically used to report instantaneous event situations, the latter descriptions of ongoing process situations. This is not to say that activities and accomplishments, which have inherent duration, cannot be reported by the action PR. The mini-HP narrative in (1.30a) above contains three activities in sentences (1), (2), and (4) and one accomplishment in sentence (3), all in the SIMPLE (action) PR. The effect produced by using this PR is *to override the inherent duration of these situations, giving them the appearance of instantaneous achievements.* What we see here is a conflict between aspect and situation type; in this instance it is aspect that prevails.

I have deliberately chosen English examples to illustrate the difference between the PR_a and PR_v since this difference is more transparent in English, which can express it morphologically (and does so consistently in natural narratives) through the SIMPLE-PROG opposition. In languages that have no formal means to express the contrast (e.g., French, Latin), the two varieties of PR—which can be either diegetic or nondiegetic—have often been confused. Both the PR_a and the PR_v, however, signify that the data source for the experience is, or purports to be, direct perception. In contrast, experience resurrected from memory is reported through tenses of the PAST.

1.6.3. *Perception, memory, and tense.*   Chafe (1973) offers linguistic and psychological evidence for distinguishing four sources of input to consciousness: Data enter our minds first through *direct sensory perception.* They may then be held for a greater or lesser period of time in what he calls *surface memory,* having remained in consciousness from the time they were first perceived, or at least having remained so close to the surface of consciousness that they insistently return whenever deliberate attention to something else is released. Eventually, some of the data that have been in surface memory will enter *shallow memory,* whence they can be recalled into consciousness with a fair degree of accuracy and an effortless awareness of their temporal seriation. Finally, some of the data

that have been stored in shallow memory will enter *deep memory,* where they may remain for an indefinite period of time. For normal adults, recall from deep memory is significantly less accurate, and time relationships must be deliberately reconstructed (Chafe 1973:270). Chafe diagrams these inputs to consciousness as in figure 3.

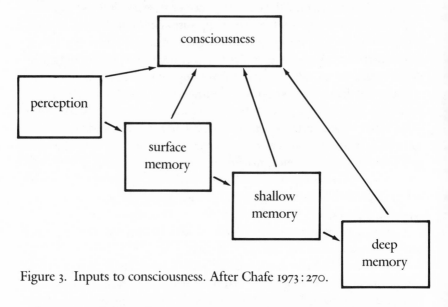

Figure 3. Inputs to consciousness. After Chafe 1973:270.

It was stated above that current reports ostensibly relate what a speaker perceives at the same time as the perception is taking place. With reference to the schema given in figure 3, Chafe observes (1973:276) that information of this type has progressed no further to the right than the box labeled "perception" and the arrow leading from that box into consciousness. Moreover, information of this type will be encoded in a PRESENT tense. By contrast, all information retrieved from one of the "memory" boxes will be encoded in a tense of the PAST. For now, suffice it to distinguish between the two broad categories of memory and perception as data sources for narration and current reports, respectively, with their corresponding P and PR tenses. In chapter 2 the category of memory will be broken down into its three subtypes, each of which will be shown to correlate with one of the tenses of the PAST system.

In a footnote to his discussion, Chafe (1973:276f.) reports on a cognition experiment carried out on individuals having *eidetic imagery* (so-called photographic memory). Apparently, when a scene is shown to such people and then taken away, the part of the scene that they are *still visualizing mentally* will be described in the PRESENT, while elements of the scene *re-membered* in the normal way will be reported in the PAST. Individuals with this capacity thus seem to make a clear distinction, documented linguistically, between what they are still seeing "in their mind's eye" and what they recall from memory. The literature on developmental psycholinguistics provides parallel evidence of this cognitive distinction and its association with tenses. Data from a number of experimental studies involving children's use of tenses in narrative suggest that certain tasks used in experimentation contain an inherent bias toward one tense or the other: tasks involving *recall* in the form of narrative have an intrinsic bias toward the PAST, while narrative elicitation based on looking at a picture book is biased toward the PR, given the *immediate visual* nature of the task (Herring 1986a). Herring notes, however, that even when confronted with the PR-based task of producing a story from a sequence of pictures, a significant number of school-aged children based their narrations in the *past*. These children, she observes, do not so much select a PAST-tense narrative mode as simply set out to narrate, and narration for them means PAST-tense.

1.6.4. *The* FUTURE.

The temporal structure of FUTURES is either S > R/E or S/R > E. The first formula corresponds to the English *will*-FUT or the SIMPLE FUTS in Romance (*je ferai, yo haré, io farò,* etc.), the second to "GO"-FUTS (*I'm going to do it, je vais le faire, voy a hacerlo*) or periphrastic FUTS with other auxiliaries, which mark a future event as having "present relevance" (see Fleischman 1982).

The FUT is rare in narrative for the same reason that the PERF is rare, and the discourse contexts in which the two occur tend to be the same. In natural narrations, FUTS occur either in commentary by the narrator, where time reference is not to the now of the story but to that of the speaker, as in (1.32), or, in *diegesis* proper, in relation to a NARRATIVE PRESENT (NP), as in (1.33).[22]

(1.32) Allí habló su camarera, bien *oiréis* [FUT] lo que *dira* [FUT] [quote follows]. "Then her chambermaid spoke up, now *you will hear* what *she will say.*" (VIII:41–42)

(1.33) Siete veces echan [NP] suertes: quién lo *volverá* [FUT] a buscar. "Seven times they draw lots [NP]: who *will go back* [FUT] to look for him?" (VII:5–6)

The first FUT in (1.32) refers to the time of the telling and to the context of the performance: "now you the audience will hear . . ." The second FUT ("she will say") is a metanarrative tense that refers neither to the time of the telling nor to that of the tale, but to what Genette (1980) calls "the space of the discourse"; this sentence might be paraphrased as "in the next sentence the chambermaid will say . . ." Narratives often contain temporal indications that are referential only to the linear disposition of the discourse: the adverb "now" often means only "at this point in the narration," while "next" and "then" function as textual sequencers. In a text like Robbe-Grillet's *Jealousy*, which seeks a negation of temporality and of conventional modes of representation (see chapter 8), *maintenant* (now) often means no more than "at this moment in writing, at this point in the text."

In modern historiographic narration one occasionally finds a tense referred to as the HISTORICAL FUTURE. This tense substitutes for a PFV P to represent a situation as having occurred after another situation reported either in the HP, as in (1.34)–(1.35), or the PAST, as in (1.36), which serves as its R. The H FUT has a temporal structure analogous to that of a FUT-OF-P ($R > E > S$), but differs from that tense, as we shall see, in attempting to camouflage its deictic pastness, that is, to delete the "$> S$" portion of the formula (examples from Imbs [1960]:46f.):

(1.34)   Cette fois, la république triomphe [HP$_a$]; et malgré son habileté, le duc de Broglie ne réussira [H FUT] qu'à retarder de quelques mois son avènement légal.

This time the Republic triumphs [HP$_a$]; and despite his ability, the Duke of Broglie will succeed [H FUT] only in delaying its legal implementation by several months.   (J. Lucas-Dubreton)

(1.35)   Il en est [PR] de l'expédition de Russie comme il en a été [PC] de l'affaire d'Espagne. On voit [PR] l'idée naître, grandir, s'emparer de l'esprit de l'empereur [Napoléon] jusqu'à ce que, selon un penchant qui s'aggrave [PR$_{gen}$] chez lui, il regarde [PR] comme fait ce qui peut [PR] et doit [PR] se faire, puisque sa raison l'a conçu [PC/PERF]. Et pourtant il n'en viendra pas [H FUT] à l'action sans avoir passé par de plus longues perplexités que pour l'Espagne. "Je n'étais pas d'aplomb," dira-t-il [H FUT] plus tard à Gourgaud en parlant de cette année 1811.

As for the expedition to Russia, it is [PR] the same as it was [PC] for the Spanish campaign. One sees [PR] the idea being born, grow, take hold in the Emperor's [Napoleon's] mind until, in line with a tendency that is exacerbated [PR$_{gen}$] in him, he sees [PR] as [already] done what can [PR] and ought to [PR] be done, because his mind has conceived it [PC/PERF]. And yet he will not convert it into action [H FUT] without having ruminated over it far longer than for Spain. "I was not at my best," he will say [H FUT] later to Gourgaud, speaking of the year 1811.   (H. Bainville)

(1.36) Le général Ott eut [PS] trois mille tués, et laissa [PS] cinq mille prisonniers entre les mains des Français. De cette bataille sortira [H FUT], pour le général Lannes, le titre de duc de Montebello.

General Ott had [PS] three thousand killed, and left [PS] five thousand prisoners in the hands of the French. From this battle will come [H FUT], for General Lannes, the title of Duke of Montebello.   (Bignon)

In all of these examples the FUT marks an event as having occurred after its R, which is established either by explicit reference to a preceding situation ("the triumph of the Republic" in [1.34]) or through context. The narrative historiographer uses the H FUT to report information not from his own retrospective vantage (i.e., not deictically from S) but "looking forward" from the now of the past R, even though the information could not have been known at that time: at the moment of the triumph of the Republic one could not know of the Duke of Broglie's subsequent attempts to delay its coming into being; likewise, what Napoleon would "later" say to Gourgaud could not have been reported at the time of the gestation of his idea for the Spanish campaign; nor could it have been known at the time of the battle referred to in (1.36) that General Lannes would eventually become the Duke of Montebello. The H FUT provides the historiographic narrator with an "internal" strategy for feigning a *prospective* temporal orientation (only now can one say *will*) while retaining the interpretive prerogative of what will always be a retrospective discourse. Moreover, in the example in (1.35), had the PS been used in place of the H FUT ("From this battle *came*, for General Lannes . . ."), this sentence would instantiate the prototypical *narrative statement* of historiographic discourse (see §5.5.3) in which the voice that speaks is that of a retrospective historical consciousness.

1.7. Tense-aspect in early Romance

A commonly held view among Romance philologists is that tenses in the medieval period were more aspectual than their modern counterparts. That is to say, given that tense information and aspect information are packaged synthetically in same morphology (inflections and/or auxiliaries), in older Romance it was more often the case that temporal distinctions would be neutralized in order for the morphology to express aspectual distinctions, whereas in modern Romance the situation is the reverse.[23] It has also been argued, with respect to French, that the early language tended to privilege what are here called situation types over aspect (Imbs 1956; Schøgt 1964; Martin 1971; Schøsler 1973). The latter claim is but one facet of a more widespread state of affairs whereby meanings that in the modern languages are expressed formally through grammar were in the earlier languages expressed lexically or simply as contextual implicatures. This claim provides a compelling explanation for at least one area in which the early Romance tense-aspect systems differ from their modern counterparts described above: the "durative" use of the PS in Old French, discussed below (§1.7.1). The functional overlap among tenses of the PAST system has posed problems for investigators of the early vernaculars. Not only did the PS overlap with the IMP in being able to report situations of extended duration, but the IMP could in turn be used to report "punctual" situations (§1.7.2), while the PS and PC divided up the functions of PRET and PERF (§1.7.3). This section also considers briefly the NP (§1.7.4), a major focus of attention in later chapters.

1.7.1. The "durative" PS.   Grammarians have often observed that the PS (PRET) of early Romance was "aspectually ambiguous" between punctual and durative readings.[24] Of the two functions of the modern IMP, habitual and continuous action, the latter was frequently expressed by the PS, as in example (1.37):

(1.37) Eufemien—si *out* [PS] a num li pedre.   "Euphemien—that *was* [PS] his father's name [lit., his father *had* [PS] Euphemien for a name]." (*Alexis*, 16)

Modern French would require the IMP in this sentence.[25] Among many examples of the durative PS occurring in the texts in appendix 2, consider:

(1.38) Aucassins *fu* [PS] armés sor son ceval,	Aucassin *was* [PS] on his horse, fully armed,
si con vos aves oï et entendu [PC].	as you have now heard [PC].
Dix! con li *sist* [PS] li escus au col	God! How [well] his shield *sat* [PS] on his neck
. . .	. . .
Et li vallés *fu* [PS] grans et fors . . .	And the lad *was* [PS] big and strong . . .
et li cevaus sor quoi il *sist* [PS] rades et corans	and the horse he *was sitting* [PS] on [*was*] swift and spirited. (III:1–9)

(1.39)   . . . li chevalier *furent* [PS] es uissiers tuit . . . et *furent* [PS] tuit armé . . . et les autres genz qui n'avoient [IMP] mie si grant mestier en bataille *furent* [PS] es granz nés tuit; et les galees *furent* [PS] armees et atornees totes. Et li matins *fu* [PS] biels, aprés le solei un poi levant.

. . . the knights *were* [PS] [assembled] in the transport ships . . . and *were* [PS] all armed . . . and the others, who had [IMP] less crucial functions in battle, *were* [PS] all in the large vessels; and the galleys *were* [PS] fully armed and decked out. And the morning *was* [PS] beautiful, just after sunrise.   (IV : 2–8)

Significant is the fact that the durative PS co-occurs only with *atelic* situations, most commonly with the verbs *être* (be), *avoir* (have), and modal auxiliaries, and often produces an inchoative reading. In the conflict between aspect and situation type illustrated by the above examples it is the intrinsic durativity of the stative situations that prevails over the PFV aspect of the PS and not, as Ménard (1973 : 140) has suggested, that people in the Middle Ages conceptualized as punctual events situations that to us involve duration, nor that medieval narrators differentiated less than we do between what is essential to the narrative (foreground) and what is accessory (background). As we shall see in chapter 6, medieval narrators were highly sensitive to the "texture" of their texts, but simply availed themselves of different linguistic strategies from those used by narrators writing in modern French to carry out TEXTUAL functions such as *grounding*.

Except for the verbs "be" and "have," which occur in the PS across genres, in dialogue as well as diegetic text, and well into the fifteenth century, the durative PS in Old French is confined to *narrative* texts, notably epics and twelfth-century verse romances (Faye 1933; Schøsler 1973). Like most of the important changes in tense-aspect usage in French, the decline of the durative PS, which went hand in hand with the increased use of the IMP, occurs around the beginning of the fourteenth century, during the passage from Old to Middle French. Martin (1971) sees the hesitations in tense usage of certain Middle French writers as an indication that the possibility of privileging the situation type of a verb over its aspect was being lost.[26]

1.7.2. The IMPERFECT. French grammarians are unanimous in pointing out the low frequency of the IMP throughout most of the Old French period. This tense begins to develop in the twelfth century, notably in the verse romances of Chrétien de Troyes, and continues in the prose romances of the thirteenth century. But at no point in the Old French period does it represent more than seventeen percent of total verb forms in a text (Martin 1971).

Lerch (1922) links the restricted use of the IMP in Old French to the language's preference for the PR (NP) to "represent action vividly"; with the decline of the NP, the IMP begins to come into its own. Yet the IMP replaces only the PR$_v$; insofar as action is represented vividly by the PR in Old French, it is by the PR$_a$, which substitutes for the PS not the IMP. It is in the thirteenth century that the textual frequency of the IMP begins to rise, as both the NP and the PS lose their ability to function as descriptive (visualizing) tenses (i.e., with the loss of the NP$_v$ and durative PS). It is at this stage in the development of French that the PS-IMP contrast begins to assume its modern TEXTUAL function of marking the discourse contrast between events and description. This contrast already begins to manifest itself in the tense usage of *Aucassin and Nicolette* (see Schøsler 1973).

A punctual use of the IMP that resembles the modern NARR IMP (§1.5.3) has been identified in Old French (Fotitch 1950), Old Italian (Bertinetto 1987), and most prominently Old Spanish (Menéndez Pidal 1908 : I,354; Gilman 1961; Szertics 1967). The passage in (1.40) is a paradigm epic combat scene from the *Cid:*

(1.40) Martin Antolinez et Diego Gonçalez firieron se [PS] de las lanças,
tales fueron [PS] los colpes que les quebraron [PS] amas.
Martin Antolinez mano metio [PS] al espada,
relumbra [NP$_v$] tod el campo tanto es [NP$_v$] linpia e clara;
diol [PS] un colpe, de traviessol *tomava* [IMP$_a$],
el casco de somo apart gelo *echava* [IMP$_a$],
las moncluras del yelmo todas gelas *cortava* [IMP$_a$],
alla levo [PS] el almofar, fata la cofia *legava* [IMP$_v$],
la cofia y el amofar todo gelo *levava* [IMP$_a$]
raxol [PS] los pelos de la cabeça bien a la carne *legava* [IMP$_v$] . . .

Martin Antolinez and Diego Gonzalez struck at each other [PS] with their lances,
the blows were [PS] such that both [lances] broke [PS].
Martin Antolinez placed [PS] his hand on his sword,
it gleams [NP$_v$] across the field so bright and shiny is [NP$_v$] it;
he [MA] dealt [PS] him a blow, he [DG] *caught* [IMP$_a$] it obliquely,
the upper part of his [DG's] headpiece he [MA] *threw* [IMP$_a$] it away,
the leather straps of his helmet he [MA] *cut* [IMP$_a$] them through,
the cowl of his mail stood up [PS], *reaching* [IMP$_v$] the protective cloth cap,
the cap and the cowl it all *stood up* [IMP$_a$] on him,
he [MA] scraped [PS] the hair off his [DG's] head, *getting* [IMP$_v$] down to
the very flesh . . . (*Cid,* 3646–3655)

Note that the IMPs in this passage do not report descriptive material but the major action of the encounter. Although they are concentrated at the assonance (in *a-a*) they are not determined by it; rather, they determine it (Gilman 1961:109). In the *romancero* passage in (1.41), reporting the content of a dream about King Roderick's revenge on Sancho II, the NARR IMPs (= IMP$_a$) do not occur at the assonance:

(1.41)　La reina con gran congoxa　dixo [PS] . . .
la noche passada　un mal sueño avia soñado [PLP]
y es que *venia* [IMP$_a$] el rey Rodrigo　con el gesto muy airado,
los ojos bueltos en sangre　que *iva* [IMP$_v$] muy apresurado
para ir a vengar la muerte　del desdichado don Sancho,
y que *bolvía* [IMP$_a$] sangriento,　y su cuerpo mal llagado,
y que *se llegava* [IMP$_a$] a mí　y me *tirava* del braço,
y *dezía* [IMP$_a$] estas palabras,　muy fuerte llorando . . .

The Queen with great anguish　said [PS] . . .
last night　a bad dream had I dreamed [PLP]
which is that King Rodrigo *came* [IMP$_a$]　in a very violent manner,
his eyes filled with blood,　*moving* [IMP$_v$] with great haste
to avenge the death　of the wretched Don Sancho,
he *came back* [IMP$_a$] all bloody,　with his body full of wounds,
and he *approached* [IMP$_a$] me　and *tugged* [IMP$_a$] on my arm,
and *said* [IMP$_a$] these words, loudly sobbing . . .

(from Menéndez Pidal 1957–1964:54)

1.7.3.　*The* PS *and* PC.　The relationship between simple and periphrastic PASTS in early Romance is a complex question that has received considerable attention, particularly in French. As a working generalization, to be nuanced in the following paragraphs, let us say that in the early vernaculars the PS is basically a PRET, the PC a PERF. Where tense usage differs between the diegetic (narrative) and mimetic (dialogic) sentences of a text, dialogue has generally been assumed to reflect contemporary usage more closely, while narrative may preserve an earlier usage (cf. §3.2).

　　It is generally acknowledged that PERF is the basic meaning of the early Romance PC.[27] At an initial stage, which I refer to as PERF$_1$ the PC functioned as a *PFV aspect of the* PR marking a situation as "completed in present time," as in example (1.42) from the Oxford *Roland*. I force this reading in the translation:

(1.42)   Roland *ad mis* [PC] l'olifan a sa buche,
Empeint [NP$_a$] le ben, par grant vertut le sunet [NP$_a$].

Roland *has* the olifant *placed* [PC] at his lips,
he positions [NP$_a$] it well, sounds [NP$_a$] it with all his might.

(vv. 1753–1754)

Yet by the time of the Oxford text (ca. 1100) the PC could already be used as a prototypical PERF to report *past situations with present relevance*. I call this stage PERF$_2$. In example (1.43) both types of PERF occur, marked accordingly:

(1.43)   Ço dist [PS] li reis: "Sunez en vostre corn" AOI
　　　　　[*laisse* break]
Gefreid d'Anjou *ad* sun greisle *sunét* [PC/PERF$_2$].[28]
Franceis descendent [NP$_a$], Carles l'*ad comandét* [PC/PERF$_2$];
Tuz lur amis qu'il *unt* morz *truvét* [PC/PERF$_2$]
Ad un carner sempres les *unt portét* [PC/PERF$_1$].
Asez i ad [NP$_v$] evesques e abez . . .

The King said [PS]: "Go sound your horn." AOI
　　　　　[*laisse* break]
The horn of Geoffroy of Anjou *has been sounded* [PC/PERF$_2$].
The French dismount [NP$_a$], Charles *has commanded* [PC/PERF$_2$] it.
All the comrades that they *have found* [PC/PERF$_2$] dead there
are borne off [PC/PERF$_1$] at once to a common grave.
There are [NP$_v$] bishops and abbots in great number.

(*Roland*, 2950–2955)

　　According to the figures reported in Blanc (1964), it is at the time of its functional shift to a prototypical PERF (i.e., to PERF$_2$) that the frequency of the French PC declines in narrative texts, becoming restricted to dialogue. In the earliest texts when it was still a PERF$_1$ (i.e., a PFV PR), the PC commonly substituted for the PS as a PRET (Vising 1888–1889:72ff.). As Schøsler (1973, 1985) points out, PERF$_2$ is the only meaning of the PC in the dialogue of *Roland*, but in diegesis the PC still appears with the PERF$_1$ function *with telic situations*. In this latter capacity it could substitute for the (punctual) PS, as in the PERF$_1$ in (1.43) above, which I have translated accordingly as a passive NP$_a$ ("the comrades are borne off"), the passive signaling completion of the action reported by the participle. Though examples of this PERF₁ usage are documented through the thirteenth century, it is already on the decline in the twelfth-century *chansons de geste*. Various investigators have interpreted this PFV use of the PC as an indication that as early as *Roland* (Stefenelli-Fürst 1966) or even the eleventh-century version of *Alexis* (Garey 1955), though more commonly in thirteenth-century texts, the PC in diegesis was already establishing itself in the PRET function it would ultimately develop, in a kind of "free variation" with the PS. The occasional equivalence of PS and PC has been also argued for Old Spanish. Consider the examples in (1.44) and (1.45) from the Old Spanish *Cid* and Marie de France's *Lanval* (late twelfth century):

(1.44) Mio Çid de lo que veye [IMP]   mucho era [IMP] pagado,
los ifantes de Carrion   bien *an cavalgado* [PC].
Tornan se [NP] con las dueñas,   a Valençia *an entrado*,
ricas fueron [PS] las bodas   en el alcaçar ondrado . . .

Mio Çid by what he saw [IMP]   was [IMP] most pleased,
the Counts of Carrión   *performed* well *on horseback* [PC].
They return [NP] with the girls,   they *arrived in* [PC] Valencia,
the wedding was [PS] opulent   in the noble citadel.

(*Cid*, 2245ff.)

(1.45) Quant del manger furent levé [PLP]
Sun cheval li *unt amené* [PC];
Bien li eurent la sele mise [PLP]
Mut *ad trové* [PC] riche servise!
Il prent congé [NPₐ], si *est muntez* [PC]
Vers la cité *s'en est alez* [PC].

When they had gotten up [PLP] from the table,
they *brought* [PC] him his horse;
The saddle had been put on [PLP] carefully.
He *found* [PC] the service most sumptuous!
He takes his leave [NPₐ], *mounted* [PC] his horse,
took off [PC] toward the city.

(*Lanval*, vv. 189–194)

Though I have translated these PCs as PRETs, following Menéndez Pidal (1908:355) and Beck (1988:138), respectively, other readings are possible. The last three verses of (1.44) might alternatively be read as a kind of inner speech reporting the Cid's thought, double-bracketed in (1.44′), about the men who have just married his daughters:

(1.44′) Mio Çid was most pleased by what he saw: [[The nobles of Carrión *have performed* well *on horseback*, they are returning now with the girls, they *have arrived* already in Valencia; the wedding was opulent in the noble citadel]].

The PCs in (1.45) might alternatively be read as PFV NPs (and the corresponding PLPs as markedly PFV PSs).[29] This PFV aspect is rendered by transposing the appropriate sentences into the passive, as I have done in (1.45′):

(1.45′) As soon as the meal *was over* [PLP], *there is* [PC] his horse already waiting for him (because it *has been brought to him*); the saddle *was put on* [PLP] carefully. The service *has been deemed* [PC] sumptuous. He takes his leave, *is up* [PC] on his horse (because he *has mounted it*) and *is off* [PC] to the city (because he *has left*).

Whether or not one accepts this reading, and notwithstanding examples such as those in (1.44) and (1.45) where we might be inclined to see a PRET function in early Romance PCs, there is little evidence to support a claim that in Old French or Old Spanish the PC was already evolving to a PRET; in French it is not until the fifteenth, even sixteenth, century that we have solid documentation of the PC being used to report past situations with no link to the speaker's present (cf. Wilmet 1970, 1976; Martin 1971; Martin and Wilmet 1980: §131; Schøsler 1985). The apparent counterexamples ("PRET PCs") found in French texts from ca. 1050–1300 are best regarded, as Schøsler (1973) suggests, as relics of the earlier usage, that is, as PERF₁ (a PFV aspect of the PR) substituting for the (PFV) PS. In Spanish the PC has never evolved to a PRET.

Leaving aside the durative uses of the PS (discussed in §1.7.1), there is consensus that the basic meaning of this tense in older Romance is PRET. However, in the early texts of both French and Spanish the PS can occasionally be found with the PERF₂ function, as in (1.46)–(1.48):

(1.46) Sachiez nos ne *venimes* [PS] mie por vos mal faire, ainz *venimes* por vos garder. "Know that *we have not come* [PS] at all to do you harm, rather *we have come* [PS] to protect you" [they are still there].   (Villehardouin, §146)

(1.47) Dixo [PS] el rey: "Non es [PR] aguisado oy;
vos agora *legastes* [PS]   e nos viniemos [PS] anoch."

"Said [PS] the King: 'It is [PR] not appropriate today;
you [have] just *arrived* [PS]   and we came [PS] last night.'"

(*Cid*, 2047f.)

(1.48)   Messire Gauvin, comment vos est?   —Sire, fet [NP] il, bien, la Deu
merci et la vostre qui delivré m'avez [PC] de mort. Onques mes ne fui [PS] je si
en aventure de morir comme j'estoie [IMP]. Mes, Deu Merci, vous m'en *deli-
vrastes* [PS].

My lord Gauvain, how are you?   —Sir, he goes [NP], very well, thanks to God
and to you who have saved me [PC] from death. Never was [PS] I in such danger
of death as I was [IMP] then. But, thank God, you *[have] saved* me [PS].

(*Prose Tristan*, §144 : 14–17)

In French this usage is rare after the thirteenth century (Schoch 1912 : 91),
though one still finds examples of it in Middle French, as in (1.49) from the
fifteenth-century farce of *Maistre Pathelin:*

(1.49)   Que *devint* [PS] vostre vielle cote hardie? "What *[has] become* [PS] of
your old heavy coat?"   (*Pathelin*, 352f.)

In all examples of this type the PS occurs in directly quoted speech.

In Middle French the PS can still be used to report a *recent* past situation, as long as the situation is considered in and of itself and not in relation to the speaker's here-and-now, as is also true of the PAST in American
English ("The screwdriver? I just *saw* it . . . a minute ago").

1.7.4. *The* PRESENT. In the early vernaculars the
SIMPLE PR can be used to express all the meanings discussed in §1.6 above.
Though this tense is in principle IPFV, the aspectual contrast is neutralized
in practice, inasmuch as the single PR form is used for both action and visualization. Both Old French and Old Spanish have in addition marked
IPFV forms of the PR, periphrastic constructions of limited use involving a
"go" or "be" auxiliary and a present participle, as in (1.50)–(1.52):

(1.50)   Del castiello que prisieron [PS]   todos ricos se parten [NP];
los moros e las moras   *bendiziendol estan* [PROG PR].
Vansse [NP] Fenares arriba   quanto pueden [NP] andar,
troçen [PR] las Alcarias   e ivan [IMP] adelant,
por las Cuevas d'Anquita   ellos *passando van* [GO-PROG].

From the castle which they took [PS]   the nobles all leave [NP];
The moors, men and women,   *are blessing him* [PROG PR].
They travel [NP] past Henares   as far as they can [NP] go,
cross [NP] the Alcarias   and headed [IMP] on,
by the Caves of Anquita   they *are going* [GO-PROG].   (*Cid,* 540–544)

(1.51) . . . dentro había [IMP]   . . . inside were [IMP] maidens
doncellas
vestidas a maravilla;   beautifully ·dressed;
las cincuenta *están tañendo* [PROG PR]   fifty of them *are playing* [PROG PR]
con muy extraña armonía,   a strange harmonic line,
las cincuenta *estan cantando*   fifty of them *are singing* [PROG PR]
[PROG PR]
con muy dulce melodía.   a sweet melody.
        (ballad of Roderick cycle: Menéndez y Pelayo 1945:8.88f.; *Prim.* # 5a)

(1.52) Al tens Nöé ed al tens Abraham
Ed al David, qui Deus par amat [PS] tant,
Bons fut [PS] li secles; ja mais n'ert [IMP] si vaillant.
Velz est [NP] e frailes, tut *s'en vat declinant* [GO-PROG]:
Si'st ampairét [PC], tut bien *vait remanant* [GO-PROG].

In the time of Noah and in the time of Abraham
And in that of David, whom God loved [PS] so well,
The world was [PS] good; never was [IMP] it so excellent.
[Now] it is [PR] old and frail, everything *is on the decline* [GO-PROG]:
It has gotten worse [PC], everything good *is coming to a halt* [GO-PROG].

                                                        (*Alexis,* 1–5)

Gougenheim (1929:2–35) cites Old French examples of the "go" construction in which *aler* ranges from a lexical verb of motion, to an auxiliary expressing durativity, to a semantically empty morph; in this last case the periphrasis is virtually equivalent to its simple counterpart and may have been used for prosodic reasons, as in (1.52) above. Gougenheim appeals to prosodics (assonance/rhyme) to explain the frequency of the construction in verse epics and verse chronicles.

In Old French the (diegetic) PR is rare in the earliest texts (De Felice 1957:34), but comes solidly into its own in the eleventh and twelfth centuries. In *Alexis,* the *chansons de geste,* and twelfth-century verse romances it is the predominant tense in narrative texts (Blanc 1964:100), expressing both action and visualization (as in texts X–XII). By the thirteenth century the visualizing function begins to be taken over by the IMP, leaving the diegetic PR as a substitute only for the PS and normally only with telic situations. The text frequency of the diegetic PR declines significantly during the Middle French period,[30] remaining in those genres with the strongest links to the oral tradition—the epic and what remained of verse romances—but no longer in historiography (Martin 1971:377). Buffin (1925:105) singles out the chronicle of the *Life of St. Louis* by the early fourteenth-century historiographer Joinville as a major turning point. By the end of the Middle French period the NP, which I see as having originated as a spontaneous pragmatic device of oral narration, begins to be cultivated as a stylistic phenomenon, though the so-called HP does not fully establish itself in French until the eighteenth century (see §§3.8, 8.3.2). In conversational narration, however, switching between P and NP apparently continued uninterrupted, as attested by Vaugelas's criticism of this linguistic habit in his *Remarques sur la langue françoise* (1663).

Having surveyed the grammatical categories relevant to an analysis of tense-aspect in narrative, I shall attempt in the next chapter to draw together the diverse observations set forth in this chapter into a coherent theory of tense-aspect in narrative language. This theory is based on the concept of *markedness*.

A Theory of Tense-Aspect in Narrative Based on Markedness

Voilà. Un robot rencontre une jeune dame . . .
Mon auditrice ne me laisse pas aller plus loin. Tu ne
sais pas raconter, dit-elle. Une vraie histoire, c'est
forcément au passé.
—Si tu veux. Un robot, donc, a recontré une . . .
—Mais non, pas ce passé-là. Une histoire, ça doit être
au passé historique. Ou bien personne ne sait que c'est
une histoire.   (ROBBE-GRILLET, *DJINN*)

2.1. The concept of markedness

Markedness was first introduced into linguistics in the 1930s by the Prague School phonologists Nicolai Trubetzkoy and Roman Jakobson. Since that time the concept has been extended to branches of linguistics other than phonology, notably syntax and semantics, as well as to other semiotic systems.[31] Markedness is founded on the idea that where there is an opposition involving two or more members (e.g., PFV/IPFV aspect, PAST/PR/FUT tense, narrative/nonnarrative language, fiction/nonfiction) one member of the opposition is often felt to be more normal, more common, or less specific (the *unmarked* member of the opposition) than the others, which are *marked* by the presence of some feature that the unmarked member lacks. It is commonly the case that the meaning of the unmarked category encompasses that of the marked category. The clearest example of this is where explicit expression of the meaning of the marked category is optional—where the unmarked category can always be used, even in situations where the marked category is appropriate (e.g., the HP or NP vis-à-vis the unmarked PAST tense). The criteria for assigning markedness values may be semantic, morphological, statistical (frequency), and/or contextual, and are logically independent of one another. They may even conflict—hence the controversies over markedness with respect to language-particular oppositions. At issue here are *semantic* criteria, though frequency comes into play in "local" or "contextual" markedness, discussed below (§2.1.2).

While the marked member of an opposition necessarily signals "the presence of a unit of information *x*," the unmarked member (if we take into consideration all its uses) signals "the presence or absence or nonpertinence of x." Since the feature x constitutes the "mark" of the opposition, we may characterize the opposition as an asymmetrical relationship between the presence of x and the nonnecessary presence (presence, absence, or even nonpertinence) of x (Waugh 1982:310). The fact that the marked category is more narrowly specified than the unmarked category leads to various effects or implicatures of markedness, which should not be confused with its *definition*—for example, the tendency for the unmarked category to occur with greater frequency than the marked category, the tendency for the marked category to occur in fewer different contexts and to be less universal than or nonuniversal vis-à-vis the unmarked category, the tendency for the marked category to be acquired later by children, and so forth. If it should happen that the marked category is statistically *more* frequent in particular texts or a particular type of discourse, this should not be interpreted to mean that the markedness values are wrong or uncertain, but rather that the text frequency of a category is due to the interaction of various factors including, as we shall see, occurrence in a context that is itself marked.

2.1.1. Markedness and tense-aspect opposi-
tions.   In most languages that grammaticalize a tense opposition between P and PR (or PR and NON-P; cf. *n*32), P is the marked category and PR/NON-P the unmarked category in normal language use. Whereas P carries a specific "mark" for time reference (it reports situations as past with respect to S), the basic meaning of PR, as argued in chapter 1, specifies neither past time nor present time—though it can be used to refer to situations both past and present—nor does it deny past time. Situations reported in the unmarked PR tense can have past time reference (the HP or NP), or specifically nonpast time reference (the "PR cotemporal with now" and the *praesens pro futurum*), though in many contexts the PR expresses neither the presence nor the absence of past—time reference is irrelevant. Each of these possibilities correlates with a particular interpretation of the unmarked category.

In the so-called *zero-interpretation,* which is the broadest and most general, the presence or absence of the "mark" x is irrelevant—what Jakobson calls "nonsignalization of x." For the PR tense this zero-interpretation is the basic meaning of "timelessness" or "atemporality" illustrated in examples (1.26)–(1.29) of chapter 1. In these examples the PR is used not so much because it refers to a given time but because it is the only tense that can be used with minimal reference to time (cf. Dahl 1985). The unmarked category in its zero-interpretation is often used when the objective is to make no active reference to the mark.

The *minus-interpretation* signals the absence of the feature associated with the marked category—what Jakobson refers to as "signalization of non-*x*." For the PR tense the minus-interpretation is the "PR cotemporal with now" illustrated in example (1.23). The fact that the unmarked term of an opposition can have a minus-interpretation (signalization of non-*x*) or a zero-interpretation (nonsignalization of *x*) has led to some confusion about the status of the opposition between marked and unmarked categories (see Waugh 1982:305f.).[32] For the P and PR tenses the opposition in general meanings is between "marking of (past) time" and "nonmarking of past time," while on the level of more narrowly specified meanings the opposition is between "marking of past time" and "marking of nonpast time." In the zero-interpretation of the PR, time is largely unspecified; only the minus-interpretation involves a positive reference to present time.

The unmarked term of an opposition may also have a *plus-interpretation* fostered by a specific context. The plus-interpretation is that which could also be signaled by the marked term. For the PR tense this is the meaning of "past time" that surfaces specifically in narrative contexts. But although both the P and the PR (HP or NP) can be used to refer to past events, the two are not therefore equivalent. Given the availability of forms specifically marked for pastness (PRET, IMP) that could report a past situation more directly, the choice of a PR involves special connotations. Use of the PR in narrative enables particular TEXTUAL or EXPRESSIVE effects because the meaning "simultaneity with S" (the minus-interpretation) is always open; in other words, because of the play between the reading "simultaneity with S" offered by the *tense* itself and the explicit rejection of this reading in the rest of the *discourse* (the temporality of *narrative* is past), the diegetic PR is able to suggest, for example, a sense of action occurring before the speaker's eyes.

2.1.2. *Markedness relationships in marked contexts.*

Andersen (1972) has suggested that the marked form may be an icon of the marked context in which a sign occurs: that is, in contexts that are themselves marked, the normally marked member of an opposition is the one commonly encountered. This is an instantiation of the general phenomenon of "pragmatic unmarking," whereby a marked item loses its distinctiveness (its mark) in a particular context through frequency of use. Albeit formulated with regard to phonological oppositions, Andersen's dictum can easily be extended to other semiotic oppositions, including tense-aspect. As has been observed (Comrie 1976; Chvany 1984; Bache 1986), in many languages the markedness values of the PFV-IPFV opposition differ for present and past contexts: combined with the unmarked PR tense, IPFV aspect is unmarked, PFV aspect marked; but in combination with the marked P, PFV aspect (i.e., the PRET/AORIST) is unmarked, IPFV aspect (the IMP) marked. The idea that markedness values often reverse in oppositions dominated by marked contexts provides a strong linguistic foundation for the view that the unmarked tense of narrative is the (PFV) P. For if the PR is the most neutral or unmarked tense of ordinary language (the unmarked context), then according to Andersen's hypothesis it is not unpredictable that the unmarked tense in the marked context of narrative is the P.

The theory of tense in narrative elaborated in §2.2 is founded on the proposition that the PFV P (= PRET) is the (pragmatically) unmarked tense of narrative language and that this tense, interpreted here as a cluster concept, carries a positive mark for each of a set of constituent properties operative at different levels of the linguistic system. This cluster concept approach to tenses takes as its point of departure Herring's analysis of the HP in terms of the markedness oppositions that distinguish it from the P (Herring 1985b, 1986a, 1986b). One of the principal claims of this book is that when in a narrative the PR—or any tense other than the PRET—is chosen, the narrator's objective (often unconscious) is to neutralize one or more of the properties that collectively define PRET as the unmarked tense of narration and in turn define the norms for narrative discourse. If we take the narrative prototype to be a distanced, objective, factual chronicling of a specific sequence of ordered, causally linked past events (see §4.2.2),[33] its constituent properties reveal themselves: *past* time reference, *perfective* aspect, and a *distanced, objective* perspective on events that are *realis*,[34] *semelfactive* (unique occurrence), and *sequentially ordered*.[35] An important entailment of this approach is that P[RET] is no longer viewed as a simple unanalyzable piece of grammatical information but as a cluster concept involving a number of markedness oppositions operative at different levels of the linguistic system—the REFERENTIAL, the TEXTUAL, the EXPRESSIVE, and the METALINGUISTIC (see table 1).[36]

One advantage of basing a theory of tense in narrative on markedness is that the theory is thereby able to account for the fact that *tenses in narrative are not restricted to a single pragmatic (TEXTUAL or EXPRESSIVE) function* in a particular language or genre, or even in an individual text. The fact that markedness values commonly reverse in oppositions dominated by a marked context allows for the possibility that "global" markedness values (of a language, genre, text, or individual speaker/writer) may reverse at the "local" level. In other words, any context or subcontext may set up its own norms in contrast to those of the larger context: a figure in relation to the ground. Thus we encounter narrative subtypes such as the French *chansons de geste* or the *nouveau roman* (both taken up in chapter 8) in which the unmarked and statistically most frequent reporting tense is not P but PR. The recursive nature of markedness reversals within successively embedded contexts is represented graphically in figure 4, using the example of the Old French *chansons de geste*.

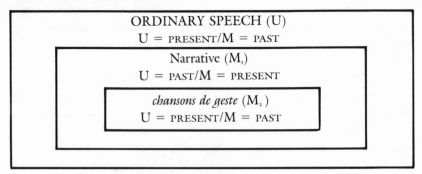

Figure 4. Markedness reversals in embedded marked contexts.
U = unmarked; M = marked. Numerical subscripts refer to successively narrower discourse contexts, represented graphically by the nested boxes; each context is
unmarked vis-à-vis the one it contains and marked vis-à-
vis the one that contains it.

As noted above, statistical frequency is in principle independent of global (inherent) markedness, but it is relevant to local markedness in creating the expectations that determine the relative informativeness of a sign in context. As Bronzwaer (1970:174) observes, "linguistic signals are not so much a matter of features selected according to rules as deviations from norms, marked by clearly visible contrasts with contextual features."

2.2. Markedness and tense-aspect categories in narrative

2.2.1. *The* PAST *and* PRESENT *as cluster concepts.*

As stated above, an alternative to the traditional view of tenses as simple, unanalyzable pieces of grammatical information is to view them as clusters of oppositional properties to which markedness values apply. The relation-ship between the PR (specifically the PR_a) and the PRET, formulated in terms of these properties, is given in table 1, which proposes certain refine-ments to a similar conceptualization put forth in Herring (1985b). The properties listed in the horizontal row labeled PRETERIT are the marks of this tense, grouped according to the functional-semantic component (RE-FERENTIAL, TEXTUAL, EXPRESSIVE, or METALINGUISTIC) in which they operate. The feature values indicated in table 1 are those that hold for ordi-

Table 1. Markedness Oppositions for the PAST and PRESENT Tenses in Ordinary (Nonnarrative) Language

LEVEL OF THE LINGUISTIC SYSTEM	REFERENTIAL			TEXTUAL		EXPRESSIVE			META-LINGUISTIC
Properties	Time	Aspect	Semelfactivity	Sequentiality[a]	Grounding	Reality Status	Perceived Distance	Objectivity	Discourse Mode
PRETERIT (M)	+ past	+ PFV	+ semelfactive	+ linked events	+ foreground[b]	− realis[c]	+ distant	+ objective	+ diegesis
PRESENT (U) Plus-interp.	+ past	+ PFV[d]	+ semelfactive	± linked events[e]	+ foreground	− realis	− distant	− objective	+ diegesis
Zero-interp.	0 past (atemporal)	0 PFV	− semelfactive	0 linked events	0 foreground	0 realis	0 distant	0 objective	0 diegesis
Minus-interp.	− past	− PFV	± semelfactive[f]	− linked events	− foreground	+ realis	− distant	− objective	− diegesis

Note: A plus sign indicates the presence of the "mark" in question, a minus sign its absence, and "0" the nonpertinence of the mark.

a See n35.

b Though in ordinary language the PRET (PFV P) is a foregrounding tense (vis-à-vis the PR), in a narrative context it is [− foreground] since it is the expected (unmarked) tense for reporting events. This criterion for determining foreground departs from the conventional view in discourse studies (reexamined in chapter 6) that holds "events," and therefore the PFV P, to be the foreground of a narrative.

c The [− realis] value of the PRET holds only for the context of nonnarrative language (cf. n34); in narrative the values are reversed and the PRET is [+ realis].

d The aspectual feature [+ PFV] and the feature [+ semelfactive] distinguish the PR_a from the PR_v; the latter is [− PFV] and [+ semelfactive].

e "Sequentiality" is variable for the reason that a series of events reported in the diegetic PR_v is not universally felt to convey the same sense of sequential cohesion as if the events had been reported in the PRET (but see n34); for French in particular it has been argued that sequentiality is conveyed only by the PASSÉ SIMPLE. I shall return to this question in chapter 4.

f The minus-interpretation of the English SIMPLE PR is habitual action (i.e., [− semelfactive]).

nary (nonnarrative) language, where the PRET is marked relative to the PR. As pointed out in the notes to the table, for certain of these properties the values are reversed in a narrative context where the PRET is unmarked and the PR marked.

The REFERENTIAL, TEXTUAL, and METALINGUISTIC properties that the PR in its plus-interpretation shares with the PRET collectively define what is here referred to as the diegetic PR₂. These properties include, in addition to occurrence in diegesis proper: past time reference, perfective aspect, reference to a unique situation, foregrounding, and, optionally, sequentiality. Qualifications regarding foregrounding and sequentiality are noted in table 1. Where the diegetic PR differs from the PRET is primarily with regard to the properties located in the EXPRESSIVE component. As pointed out in chapter 1 (§1.5.5), "lack of distance" and "lack of objectivity" are features intrinsic to an account of events rendered in the PR tense, features that derive from the cognitive limitations imposed by eyewitness reporting. These features of the PR are not overridden in a narrative context, and it is in part because they are nonnegotiable that this marked tense (for narrative) is chosen over the unmarked PRET. The PR is also chosen because of the latent meanings available through the minus-interpretation, meanings that are not explicitly actualized in a narrative context but remain "under erasure" in the form of "traces," to use a terminology popularized by Derrida.

The features listed in the row labeled "minus-interpretation" in table 1 collectively define the "PR cotemporal with now." As Herring (1986b) has suggested, many of these minus features can be redefined as "positive" terms that express more transparently the nuances that emerge in the interplay between plus- and minus-interpretations (the "structure of difference") that is always a possibility whenever the PR is used in narration. These positive readings are given in table 2.

As shown in table 1, the diegetic PR, which occurs specifically in a narrative context, privileges a number of "marks" that the PR shares with the PRET. However, the stylistic effects listeners or readers commonly perceive in narratives that make use of the diegetic PR derive not from the plus-interpretation but from meanings contributed by the tense in its minus-interpretation, as Herring (1985b, 1986b) has suggested, or in its zero-interpretation, but in either case from meanings that the PR *does not* share with the PRET. The logic of this should be apparent; narrators will choose the PR—or any marked tense—to obtain meanings that the PRET cannot offer. For example, the "atemporality" of the PR in its zero-interpretation makes it possible to detach events from a particular historical moment and endow them with a sense of timelessness; this lack of active reference to

Table 2. Markedness Values for the "PRESENT Cotemporal with Now"

Properties	REFERENTIAL			TEXTUAL		EXPRESSIVE			META-LINGUISTIC
	Time	Aspect	Semelfactivity	Sequentiality	Grounding	Reality	Perceived Distance	Objectivity	Discourse Mode
Minus interp.	– past	– PFV	± semelfactive	– linked events	– foreground	+ realis	– distant	– objective	– diegesis
Positively defined	now	IPFV durative	repeatable, habitual events	detached events; suspended event line	foreground	here-and-now	immediate	subjective; evaluated	description; mimesis (i.e., speech)

time, together with the "nonsemelfactive" feature of the PR, motivates use of this tense for genres in which events are for one reason or another regarded as nonunique. Among these genres are jokes, tall tales, and myths, which in addition privilege the "irrealis" feature that the PR acquires in narrative through a markedness reversal (cf. §4.7).

As for meanings contributed by the minus-interpretation (see table 2), it should now be apparent that the eyewitness perspective of current reports derives from a combination of tense and aspect features expressing simultaneity with now. The descriptive capacity of the PR (an implicature of its IPFV aspect), together with its optional nonsequential feature, motivates use of this tense to isolate or detach situations from the routine queue for a close-up view (the same for the NARR IMP, likewise IPFV). The ability of the PR to interrupt or suspend the narrative event line also makes possible the suspense that typically accompanies peaks of narrative tension, which are often reported in the PR. The fact that the PR is the unmarked tense of the mimetic rather than the diegetic mode, the tense of actual *speech*, motivates its use to transform narration into *performance*, thereby emphasizing, above and beyond the information value of a story, its value as a piece of verbal craftsmanship. Finally, the immediacy and subjectivity of the PR motivate its use for internal evaluation, as well as for the representation of the contents of other minds through the discourse form known as interior monologue. These functions are elaborated in subsequent chapters.

Tables similar to table 1 could be drawn up to contrast the PRET with the other marked tenses of narrative, the PERF/PC, the IMP, and the PR$_v$. In the interest of space I simply list the constituent features of these tenses (for minus-interpretations in ordinary language) in the vertical matrices given in (2.1)–(2.3):

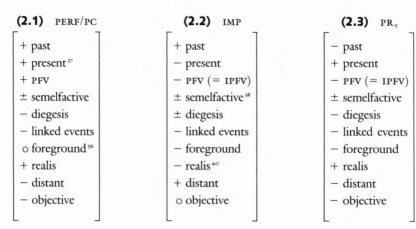

(2.1) PERF/PC	**(2.2)** IMP	**(2.3)** PR$_v$
+ past	+ past	− past
+ present[37]	− present	+ present
+ PFV	− PFV (= IPFV)	− PFV (= IPFV)
± semelfactive	± semelfactive[38]	± semelfactive
− diegesis	± diegesis	− diegesis
− linked events	− linked events	− linked events
o foreground[39]	− foreground	− foreground
+ realis	− realis[40]	+ realis
− distant	+ distant	− distant
− objective	o objective	− objective

Note that the feature matrix for the PR$_v$ is identical to that of its action counterpart given in table 1 save for the aspect feature: the PR$_v$ is explicitly [− PFV] (= IPFV), while the PR$_a$ is [0 PFV], thereby allowing a [+ PFV] reading in the plus-interpretation. As a tense of pure description analogous to the "continuous" IMP, the PR$_v$ reports nonsequential situations viewed as ongoing ([− linked], [− PFV]). The PR$_v$ differs from its past counterpart, the IMP, in its immediacy and explicit subjectivity ([− distant], [− objective]); for texts in which both tenses occur in sentences of description, the opposition may be used to set off the descriptive foreground (PR$_v$) from the descriptive background (IMP). The [+ present] feature of the PERF/PC combines with [− distant] and [− objective] to create a link to the here-and-now of the speaker—the so-called present relevance that sets the PERF apart from the PRET and accounts for its low text frequency in narrative.

2.2.2. Tenses as indices of "narrating personae."

In chapter 1 (§1.6.3) a basic cognitive difference was shown to underlie the linguistic difference between a report of what one sees simultaneous with its perception and a report of information that has been filtered through and retrieved from memory. In the preceding section of this chapter (§2.2.1) the principal tense-aspect categories used in narration— PRET, PERF/PC, IMP, and PR—were redefined as clusters of oppositional properties; these properties, to which markedness values may be assigned, collectively define the prototypical narrative sentence and its unmarked tense, the PRET. We are now in a position to relate these tense-aspect categories to the four sources of input to consciousness given in figure 3. The connections are represented schematically in table 3, which correlates Groethuysen's phenomenological reflections on narrative (1935−1936) with Chafe's observations (1973) on grammar in relation to memory. As shown in table 3, each of the four tenses at issue can be correlated with a particular *mode of representation*, with a particular *activity* carried out by the narrator, and with what I refer to as a *narrating persona*.

In verbal reports whose data source is perception, the activities of seeing and speaking are carried out simultaneously, as it were, via the PR tense, whose set of defining properties uniquely qualifies it for this task. In verbal reports whose source is memory, the narrative vehicle is appropriately a tense of the PAST (observation/experience occurs prior to speaking). The discourses of memory may be subcategorized as follows, each with its associated reporting tense:

(a) that which emanates from the memory of a speaking subject reporting on experiences that are still very much present—in experiential time if

Table 3. Tense, Memory, and Narrative Perspective

DATA SOURCE	NARRATING PERSONA	TENSE	MODE OF REPORTING	ACTIVITY
Perception	Performer	PR	Mimetic	OBSERVATION/RE-PRESENTATION: I speak what *I see*.
Surface Memory	Memorialist	PERF/PC[a]	Autobiographical[a]	EVOCATION: I speak what *I have seen* as it relates to me now, an erstwhile participant in the events I have retrieved from my personal memory.
Shallow Memory	Historian	PRET	Diegetic	NARRATION: I speak what has become an objective knowledge. Through an effort of retrospection I can recall what *I once saw*, its original temporal structure still intact, though it is now distanced and detached from me as an erstwhile observer.
Deep Memory	Painter	IMP	Pictorial	DESCRIPTION: The original structure of what I saw/experienced has become blurred. Elements of it return to consciousness not through a voluntary effort of recall but by chance, and with a vitality lacking in experiences retrieved from shallow memory via the PRET. *I speak what I saw as if I were reliving it*; what happened has become a part of my "self," defined as the sum of my experiences. The "existential" ego has replaced the "observing" ego.[b]

[a] In the sense that the PERF/PC rests on the Augustinian notion of the past being a "present in memory," a past whose traces traverse the present (*Confessions*, book XI). Recall Benveniste's assertion (1959) that the French PASSÉ COMPOSÉ is the "autobiographical tense" par excellence.

[b] In Groethuysen's words: "dans le souvenir le spectateur disparaît de même que le spectacle, spectateur et spectacle se confondent. Je ne suis plus en face de ce qui arrive. Je ne *vis* pas en face de ce qui se passe. Je retrouve dans mon souvenir ce qui se passait comme ma vie, comme vécu. Je ne le vois pas, et c'est parce que je ne le vois pas que je le vis" (1935–1936:189).

not in real time; what we are dealing with is not the story but its image, its trace in memory. The tense of this discourse is the PERF/PC;

(b) that of events that retain no connection to a speaking subject and, as it were, speak themselves, an objective report of experiences that memory has converted into knowledge but that can be accessed in their original temporal order through an effort of recall (*le rappel*). The tense of this discourse is the PRET/PS;

(c) that which reports experiences that cannot be evoked at will but surface involuntarily, and without regard to their original sequence, from the depths of what has been assimilated not as an objective knowledge distinct from the self but as an integral part of the self. This is the discourse of remembrance (*le souvenir*); its tense is the IMP.

Narrators are not obliged to choose one of these modes of representation and stick to it; they can move from one to another by an appropriate shift in tense, and in so doing adopt the "narrating persona" of the mode in question. The narrator who speaks in the unmarked PRET adopts the perspective of the historian. With a shift to the IMP, we see events no longer from the perspective of the historian but from that of the painter, who depicts rather than narrates.[41] As tenses of narration, the PR and the PC contrive in different ways to link the speaker's world to that of the story: the PC views events from the perspective of a memorialist whose report, unlike that of a historian, makes explicit reference to personal experience and carries a *supplément énonciative* (Boulle 1981), while the PR, the tense conventionally used for mimetic discourse (actual speech and its direct representation), enables narrators to remain within the diegetic mode but at the same time to "represent" (rather than "narrate") what they purport to observe, and to "perform" the report of it.

3 "Ungrammatical" Tenses: Background of the Question

Experience which is passed on from mouth to mouth is the source from which all storytellers have drawn. And among those who have written down the tales, it is the great ones whose written version differs least from the many nameless storytellers.
(BENJAMIN, "THE STORYTELLER")

Au commencement était l'oral.
(ZUMTHOR, LA POÉSIE ET LA VOIX DANS LA CIVILISATION MÉDIÉVALE)

3.1. Scope of the phenomenon

Over the years, investigators have remarked on what appears to be ungrammatical tense usage—in particular, but not limited to, the intrusion of PR tense into past narration—in texts from a diverse spectrum of languages, ancient to modern, and in a range of narrative genres: historical and fictional, documentary and poetic.[42] For the early Romance languages, idiosyncratic tense switching has been discussed most extensively with respect to medieval epic,[43] but the phenomenon has been documented in other narrative genres as well: hagiographic/religious texts, notably saints' lives and passion narratives;[44] texts of historiographic purport, including the Old and Middle French chronicles of Joinville, Robert of Clari, Villehardouin, Wace, and Froissart;[45] shorter narrative genres such as the *fabliaux,* the Celtic inspired *lais,*[46] and the *Three Hundred Tales (Trecentonovelle)* of the fourteenth-century Italian writer Franco Sacchetti; a wide variety of Old French romances—verse as well as prose;[47] the thirteenth-century French prosimetric tale of *Aucassin and Nicolette;*[48] the fifteenth- and sixteenth-century Spanish ballad tradition known as the *romancero;*[49] the Old Occitan *vidas* and *razos,* short narrative pieces composed to accompany the songs of the troubadours once these came to be collected in songbooks (thirteenth–fourteenth centuries);[50] and marginally in the fourteenth-century Spanish *Book of Good Love (Libro de buen amor)* attributed to a Juan Ruiz.[51]

This survey is not exhaustive. Further scrutiny of early narrative texts, particularly those assumed to have been performed orally, would no doubt reveal tense switching to be even more widespread than indicated here. However, my objective in this study is not an exhaustive presentation of data, counted and classified according to the parameters scholars have heretofore deemed pertinent to the analysis of medieval tense usage. To a large extent this work has already been done, and I draw on it frequently in recognition of the philological acumen that has gone into combing the texts and identifying, sorting, and interpreting the vast array of data. For my part, I have reexamined many of the Romance texts cited above and looked independently at a number of others in order to constitute a corpus of sufficient breadth, in terms of genres and language representation, to justify the broader claims this book proposes.

It is not my intention in this chapter to retrace the peripatetics of the extensive critical discussion that has focused on tense idiosyncrasies in early Romance. In the sections that follow, I propose merely to indicate and comment on major directions of inquiry, introducing where appropriate the findings of investigators into narrative traditions outside Romance.

3.2. Diegetic and mimetic discourse

As early as Schoch (1912) and Foulet (1920) it was noted that the diegetic portions of Old French texts showed a greater "freedom" in the use of tenses than did passages of direct speech (dialogue). This avenue of inquiry was pursued by Manfred Sandmann, who is credited with having established for the Romance tradition that "ungrammatical" tense usage occurs exclusively in diegetic and never in mimetic discourse. Any linguistic analysis of early Romance tense usage, Sandmann argued, should therefore be based on dialogue, which he took to be a faithful representation of the spoken language at the time (Sandmann 1957 [1973]:171f.). Foulet, somewhat earlier (1920:283), expressed a similar view, if less categorically: "It is in dialogue represented in its original form, whether real or constructed, that we are most likely to encounter the popular usage of the time." Sandmann's observation that tense switching is confined to diegesis has been confirmed by all subsequent studies on early Romance and appears to hold for other linguistic traditions as well.[52] However, it is quite another matter to equate textual dialogue with living speech, as Foulet, Sandmann, and most recently Wigger (1978) have proposed.

Various linguists have looked into the relationship between naturally occurring speech and constructed dialogue (in artistic and conversational texts).[53] One thing that has been pointed out is that dialogue often strikes us as more "real" than transcripts of actual conversations, which are filled with disconcerting disjunctions, false starts, repair mechanisms, and so forth. Textual dialogue filters out the performance errors ("performance" in the Chomskyan sense), conferring on speech an illusion of grammatical perfection that spontaneous utterances typically lack. As Banfield (1982:248) observes, direct quotation in constructed texts is not a recording of speech; it is an imitation (mimesis) that can be said to represent speech inasmuch as it represents, along with the propositional content of the original speech act, the act of speaking itself. Dialogue furthermore fulfills an important EXPRESSIVE function in narrative: as a feature serving to create "involvement" (Chafe 1982) in a text, constructed dialogue is "a means by which experience surpasses story to become drama" (Tannen 1986:312). It is for this reason that dialogue figures prominently among Wolfson's defining features of performed stories (cf. also Wierzbicka 1974; Labov 1982; Bauman 1986).[54] With regard to tense usage, Wolfson (1982:8) notes that while novelists and playwrights often use the PR to "lend realism" to their dialogue, we cannot assume that their use of this technique *as authors* is the same as if they were spontaneously recounting a narrative in an informal setting.

In light of these considerations, we are obliged to reject the strong version of the philologists' claim, namely that mimetic discourse (from which tense switching is absent) provides a reliable picture of tense usage in the medieval vernaculars *as they were spoken* (ultimately a moot question, since one term of the equation is no longer amenable to scrutiny), as well as the corollary piece of this argument, taken up in §3.4 below, that the tense alternations occurring in diegetic text must therefore be attributed to a literary *écriture*. The regularity of tenses in dialogue and the consistency of usage across texts does, however, support a more moderate version of the claim—that the tense patterns of dialogue are probably closer to what was actually spoken than those of diegesis (cf. Schøsler 1973, 1985).

3.3. Grammatical "freedom" of the early vernaculars

Attempts to explain tense switching—and other grammatical "anomalies" of early Romance—have often involved an appeal to the supposedly greater freedom and flexibility of the older languages (cf. Foulet 1919; Sutherland 1939; De Felice 1957), particularly with respect to verbal syntax. While it is true, as Beck (1988) demonstrates, that tense-aspect categories in Old French are more elusive with regard to function than what is implied in certain statistically based studies, the "functional multiplicity" of grammatical categories in the older language has often been interpreted to mean lack of grammar. What many investigators have failed to consider is that the language that constitutes their object of study was not yet a codified, written idiom, nor one in which linguistic functions were heavily grammaticalized. Cerquiglini et al. (1976) make a compelling case for viewing the language of the extant Old French texts as in essence a *spoken language*, the communicative instrument of a fundamentally oral culture, adapted—sometimes better, sometimes less well—to writing. This claim is of major import for the present inquiry. What the early texts confront us with is the "literary elaboration" of a language that, while it served as the vehicle for a vernacular poetic tradition already in place by the twelfth century, "had not yet become the object of a grammatical discourse" (Cerquiglini et al. 1976:191). Many of the grammatical and paleographic idiosyncrasies analyzed by Cerquiglini et al. bear striking resemblance to phenomena confronting contemporary descriptive linguists whose object is likewise a spoken idiom. When set down on paper, spontaneous spoken discourse typically strikes the literate observer as grammatically quite flexible, not to say ungrammatical. As I propose to demonstrate in the chapters that follow, the disturbing freedom of tenses that investigators have perceived in the early vernaculars must be understood, on the one hand, as a function of the *oral* nature of the discourse and, on the other, as an instance of languages putting their available morphology to use for purposes not strictly grammatical but *pragmatic*.

3.4. Tense alternation as a mark of "literary" *écritures*

Romanists have long sought to interpret the peculiar tense alternations of the early texts as a poetic technique linked to literary, in particular archaizing literary, styles. Foulet (1920) ascribes tense switching to a consciously *poetic* discourse whose syntax he found to differ from that of narrative prose.[55] For Sutherland (1939:330f.), "it is [similarly] clear that . . . the alternation between past and present is part of a definite literary technique." Like others before and after her, Sutherland sees poetic tense usage as "a matter of style rather than syntax" (1939:333), with style understood as being "limited to a specialized literary technique" while syntax is "a genuine reflection of a development in the colloquial language" (Worthington 1966:398f.). Gilman (1961:16) echoes this view when he states that in talking about tense usage in the *Cid* "I am talking about *style* and not about language."

Most linguists, I suspect, would be uncomfortable with this dichotomy between *style,* construed as the private property of literary or poetic language, and *syntax,* viewed as belonging to everyday linguistic performance. As Jakobson observes, "the facts of style cannot be opposed to the

facts of language; the inventory of 'options' and the meaning of their oppositions are given in language" (Jakobson 1938:106; cf. also Traugott and
Romaine 1985). If tense switching is to be regarded as a matter of style—
quite a reasonable view—then we ought at least to broaden the linguistic
domain over which style is understood to operate, regarding as "stylistic"
anything in language that reflects a *choice* on the part of a speaker or writer.
Equally important, we must recognize that rhetorical-expressive choices of
this sort are often made unconsciously. Certain speakers who switch tenses
in storytelling are unaware that they do so until it is pointed out to them,
and even speakers who are aware of it do not necessarily understand why
they do it—nor can they state the conditions under which switching occurs. The ontogenesis of the tense-switching phenomenon is, I submit,
linked to a particular "style" of narration, which Wolfson has labeled the
"performed story."

Romanists who have sought to explain the tense anomalies of the older
languages as a feature of literary style have in general interpreted switching
between P and PR—the most conspicuous of the alternations—as variation that is essentially *ungrammatical* but tolerated for its esthetic value:
"the vicarious present must have produced an effect of stylistic elegance
signalling the ritual dignity of art" (Paden 1977:557); or to comply with the
rhetorical desideratum of *variatio:* "one often has the impression that in
Old French the historical present is freely used . . . simply for stylistic
variation" (Ménard 1973:§145); "the monotony of a single temporal to-
nality can thereby be avoided" (Ollier 1978:102).[56] In one of the most
nuanced of the stylistic analyses—which anticipates a direction to be taken
here—Hatcher (1942) likens the narrator's movements within the verbal
system in *Roland* to the movements of a movie camera: shifting into the PR
to cover action in the foreground, then back to the PS as actors and events
emerge from or recede into the background. She observes that the basic
narrative tense of *Roland* is the PR,[57] with the PS and PC used to refer to
"prenarrative events," that is, situations chronologically prior to those of
the current narrative plane. Switching between PR and PS functions to
shift the narrator's role from "eyewitness of events" to "historian." If we
reformulate the above observations (distilled from a lengthy and nuanced
analysis of the text) in the terms of our trilevel model, what Hatcher appears to be suggesting is that tense switching operates in three of the
functional-semantic components: she identifies a REFERENTIAL (temporal)
function in the switch between PR and P, which mark, respectively, the
current narrative plane (PR) and situations chronologically prior to it

(PR/PC);[58] but she also hints at TEXTUAL and EXPRESSIVE functions: on the one hand, the marking of narrative foreground and background and, on the other, shifts in point of view on the part of the narrator. These functions are elaborated in chapters 6 and 7, respectively.

3.5. Prosodic considerations

Among the hypotheses most frequently invoked to account for idiosyncratic tense usage in medieval verse narratives is the supposed need to accommodate demands of prosody. Thus Visser (1964, 1966) argues that rhyme and especially meter govern the use of HP in place of P in Middle English, insisting that this substitution occurs exclusively in verse texts.[59] Emery (1897) makes the same argument for popular Latin (Plautus and Terence), though she admits that poets must be credited with the ability to adapt their verses to normal language usages. Romanists have likewise leaned heavily on meter, and even more on rhyme or assonance, to explain the appearance of certain tense-aspect categories, notably in verse-final position (cf. Yvon 1960; Myers 1966; Montgomery 1968; Sandmann 1974). The examples in (3.1) below are taken from five Spanish *romances* in which an introduction-to-discourse formula in the second hemistich is syntactically manipulated to fit rhymes in -*aba*, -*ía*, -*an*, -*ar*, and -*ó*, respectively (the first-hemistich verb is consistently in the PS). For clarity all tenses are labeled and coded (see appendix 1).

(3.1a) Allí *habló* [PS] un moro viejo, / de esta manera *HABLABA* [IMP].
"Thus *spoke* [PS] an old Moor, / in this way DID HE SPEAK [IMP]."

(3.1b) La niña le *respondiera* [PLP] / y estas palabras *DECÍA* [IMP].
"The girl *answered* [PLP] him / and these words DID SHE SAY [IMP]."

(3.1c) Allí *hablaron* [PS] sus doncellas, / bien OIRÉIS [FUT] lo que DIRAN [FUT]. "There *did* her ladies *speak* [PS], / now you WILL HEAR [FUT] what they WILL SAY [FUT]."

(3.1d) *Respondióle* [PS] el marinero, / tal respuesta le *fue* [PS] a dar. "The sailor *answered* him [PS], / such a response he *proceeded* [PS; lit., *went*] to give him."

(3.1e) Allí le *habló* [PS] el rey, / bien OYREIS [FUT] lo que *habló* [PS]. "There the King *spoke* to him, / now you WILL HEAR [FUT] what he *said* [PS]."

Sandmann (1974:283) cites these verses from the *romancero* in support of his position that tense choice was frequently determined by rhyme. But as I see it, these data can be interpreted as showing just the opposite—that the sixteen-syllable, two-hemistich line of the *romancero* offered sufficient syntactic flexibility that a skilled poet-singer did not have to violate grammar in order to accommodate a rhyme or maintain the prescribed syllable count. In (3.1d), for example, the use of a verbal periphrasis (*fue a dar*, "he proceeded to give") in place of the same verb in the PS (*dió*, "he gave") yields the correct number of syllables and preserves the assonance in *-á*, with no need to "substitute" another tense for the PS.

A more formidable obstacle to the prosodic hypothesis as a universal explanation for tense switching is the fact that tense alternations occur in the anisosyllabic verse of the *Cid*, where meter is not a consideration, as well as in narrative prose, where neither rhyme nor meter is a factor. If the incidence of tense switching is generally lower in prose than in verse, as studies have indicated (cf. Blanc 1964), this probably has less to do with prosodic considerations per se than with the relative chronology of verse and prose as vehicles for narration. By the thirteenth century a shift was well under way from orally performed (and for certain genres also orally composed) texts *in verse* to *prose* texts composed in writing and to an increasing degree for private reading. The impact on syntax of this shift, which went hand in hand with the development of literacy, is explored more fully in §3.10.

3.6. Aspectual hypotheses and "situation types"

It was suggested in chapter 1 (§1.7) that "tenses" in early Romance often functioned aspectually: various investigators have appealed to this hypothesis in order to account for the "anomalous" tense usage of the early texts.

For Antoine (1959), the privileging of the aspectual component of tense-aspect categories was a strategy of syntactic compensation linked to the parataxis of Old French syntax. In the early language, he observes, unexpected tense variation tended to occur where successive clauses were merely juxtaposed with no formal connective tissue (asyndeton). Conversely, where there was clausal conjunction, tense continuity was maintained. From this pattern he infers that tense alternations are essentially a phenomenon of aspect and goes on to postulate as a general principle an inverse relationship between the prominence of aspect in a language and the presence of explicit markers of clausal conjunction (1959:585–589).

Antoine is clearly on the right track in proposing a connection among tense switching, aspect, and parataxis: a major function of the aspectual PFV/IPFV contrast has now been shown to be the marking of "textual subordination" or grounding. Regrettably, though, he discusses these connections only briefly, almost in passing, and his ideas seem not to have caught the attention of other Romanists with similar concerns. Hypotheses involving tense switching and aspect have been proposed, seemingly independently, for Old Spanish.

Gilman (1961:50) observes a tendency in the *Cid* for "imperfective" verbs to occur in the PR while "perfective" verbs select one of the PAST tenses (PS or PC), in all cases with past time reference. Thus what is actualized through use of the PR, he argues, is not a temporal meaning of presentness but "indeterminate duration,"[60] while the PS functions not so much to express pastness as perfectivity. Szertics (1967) advances a parallel interpretation for the contrast between the IMP and the PS/PC in the *romancero*, which he sees as signaling above all "ongoing" vs. "completed" action, respectively; the diegetic PR also expresses ongoing action, albeit more so with "perfective" than with "imperfective" verbs.

A correlation between the diegetic PR and perfectivity has been observed in a number of languages, as discussed further in chapters 4 and 5. It is not clear, however, whether Szertics (or Gilman) is using the terms "perfective" and "imperfective" to refer to grammatical aspect or to situation type. As stated in chapter 1, meanings like "durativity" or "punctuality" (which Romanists frequently refer to as "imperfectivity" and "perfectivity," respectively) can be expressed either grammatically via aspect or lexically via the situation type of the predicate. The latter is fixed, the former subject to modification. In most instances aspect and situation type go hand in hand—hence the frequent statements of pedagogical grammars to the effect that the IMP is used for description (which generally involves states and activities), the PRET for actions and events (achievements and accomplishments). But where there is a contradiction between aspect and situation type, the contribution of one or the other is neutralized. Just as the older Romance vernaculars tend to privilege aspect over tense, they also appear to privilege situation type over aspect in cases where the two are in conflict, as in the case of the "durative PS" (§1.7.1) or the "punctual IMP" (§§1.5.3, 1.7.2).

The potential "reciprocity" between aspect and situation type can also be invoked to explain the predilection of the diegetic PR—specifically the PR$_a$—for achievement predicates, either intrinsic achievements or situations that convert to achievements through the agency of punctual time

adverbs ("suddenly," "all of a sudden," "just then," "thereupon," etc.) and/
or ingressive auxiliaries ("begin to," "go and") that focus on the *initial*
boundary of the situation, which is an instantaneous point. By way of example, consider the predicates of the "Car Breakdown" narrative given as
text I in appendix 2.

Text I contains ten instances of the simple PR in diegesis. Of these, eight
are inherently achievements: "these guys come out" (26), "he opens the
car" (30), "everyone gets out" (31), "the girl says" (35), "he says" (40), "he
gets in the car, sits down, and turns on the motor" (42–44). The two remaining situations, "the buzzer sounds" (25) and "sparks fly" (34), are inherently activities; however, they become achievements in conjunction
with the adverb "all of a sudden," reinforced in the second instance by the
ingressive auxiliary "start to." The set of narrative clauses in lines 42–44 is
likewise introduced by "all of a sudden."

Investigators who have studied the diegetic PR have repeatedly noted
the tendency for this use of the PR to co-occur with adverbs like "suddenly." Reporting on the PR of conversational narration in Honduran
Spanish, Ess-Dykema (1984) observes that this tense co-occurs specifically
with achievement predicates, and moreover a PR-tense auxiliary imposes
an achievement profile on verbs that are not inherently achievements. The
connection she perceives between achievement situations and the diegetic
PR$_a$ seems to hold for a number of languages; however, her interpretation
of the conversion process through which nonachievements become achievements puts the cart before the horse. It is the *lexical* information provided
by the auxiliary, which expresses ingressivity or explicitly marks the point
of entry into a new situation (e.g., "start," "go"), that serves to convert
these periphrastic predicates into achievements (cf. §1.3.2); once they have
become achievements, the conditions are then favorable to attract the
diegetic PR$_a$. For predicates not requiring an adjunct of this type to shift
the focus explicitly onto the initial moment of the situation, the PR$_a$ is used
for the main verb. New or unexpected developments on the narrative line
are predictably encoded as achievements, specifically with a focus on the
initial (rather than the terminal) endpoint. As shown by the data above
from text I, it is precisely this type of situation that carries the distinctive
encoding provided by the diegetic PR$_a$.

The fact that certain verbs, when used as auxiliaries, can convert other
situation types into achievements also suggests why the diegetic PR occurs
most commonly—across languages and across narrative genres—with particular types of verbs: (1) inchoative auxiliaries like "begin" or "try":

(3.2) Adonc CONMENCENT li marinier a ovrir les portes des uissiers et a giter les pons fors; et on COMENCE les chevax a traire; et li chevalier CONMENCENT a monter sor lor chevaus, et les batailles se CONMENCENT a rengier si com il devoient. "Then the sailors BEGIN TO open the doors of the transport ships and to throw down the ramps; and they BEGIN TO bring out the horses; and the knights BEGIN TO mount their horses, and the battalions BEGIN TO form as they were instructed." (IV : 28–32)

(3.3) Alors on a décidé de faire du stop . . . et puis on ESSAIE D'arrêter des voitures. "So we decided to hitchhike . . . and then we TRY TO stop some cars." (II : 22, 25)

(2) verbs of motion, including combinations of a motion verb and a *verbum dicendi:*

(3.4) Et li chevalier issirent des uissiers, et SAILLENT EN LA MER trosque a la çainture. "And the knights disembarked from the transport ships, and JUMP INTO THE SEA up to their waists." (IV : 16–17; cf. also IV : 15, 23–25, 34, 59, 70)

(3.5) . . . so then he GOES AND SAYS he won't have anything to do with it! (personal data)

(3) *verba dicendi* themselves:

(3.6) DIENT [PR] paien: "De ço avun nus asez." . . . DIENT [PR] Franceis "Il nus i cuvent guarde." "The pagans SAY [PR]: 'We have enough of this.' . . . The French SAY [PR]: 'We must be on our guard.'" (*Roland,* 77, 192; cf. also §3.9.1 below)

and (4) verbs of perception—notably "see" and "hear"—in the abstract, cognitive sense of "learn, realize, come to understand (something one did not know previously)":

(3.7) Quant VEIT Tierri qu'or en ert la bataille, sun destre guant en ad presentét Carle. "When Thierry SEES that the battle is about to take place, he has his right glove given to Charles." (*Roland,* 3850f.)

(3.8) Quant l'OT li reis, fierement le reguardet. "When the King HEARS this, he stares at him in fury." (*Roland,* 745)

The verbs of perception are typically presented as the cause of the ensuing action (when = because).

The connection posited by various scholars between tense switching and aspect is linguistically well founded. Yet none of the discussions I have referred to provides a compelling explanation for why IPFV aspect is the meaning privileged by certain uses of the IMP and above all by the PR in narrative nor indicates what particularly narrative purposes are served by choosing IPFV forms.

Given that IPFV tenses view a situation as process and without regard to its endpoints, they remove the possibility of its being apprehended as a completed whole. They are in this sense ideally suited for reporting experiences represented as the perception of an eyewitness (cf. §1.6.2) and are at the same time antithetical to narration. For intrinsic to narration—understood as a retrospective verbalization of experience that is packaged *post hoc* into "events," chunks of *completed action*—is perfectivity; hence the universal tendency of languages to select the PFV PAST as the unmarked narrative tense. Yet narrators often choose to depart from the normal retrospective perfectivity of narration so that their reports may instead give the appearance of being verbal replicas of an experience as it was occurring and at the same time registering itself on the consciousness of the observer. If this is their objective, narrators will accordingly choose a tense—IMP or PR— whose IPFV aspect enables situations to be viewed not as completed wholes whose endpoints are in focus, but as ongoing processes whose endpoints are left out of consideration. Among the IPFV tenses, it is the PR that, by the virtue of meanings "under erasure" from its minus-interpretation, is ideally suited to the task of representing experience prospectively and as process, as if it were happening now.

Even in languages whose verb morphology is primarily tense oriented (e.g., modern Romance), the meanings of most tense-aspect categories include both temporal and aspectual information. In narrative, past time reference is a given and need not be reiterated in each sentence. Where it is redundant, the primary temporal voice of a tense-aspect form may be muted, allowing the secondary aspectual voice to be heard. What is privileged, then, in narrators' use of the diegetic PR, or of the IMP to report punctual situations, is the IPFV aspect that enables situations to be presented as not yet concluded, as still in progress. This also suggests why the diegetic PR substitutes in certain languages only for the PFV and not (redundantly) for IPFV P,[61] and similarly, why it selects *achievement* predicates.

Of the four situation types described in §1.3, states are by definition durative (they continue until terminated, having no natural endpoints); of the three eventive types, only achievements do not occur naturally over a certain duration—hence the motivation for using an IPFV tense to "draw them out" and mask, as it were, their intrinsic punctuality. Various investigators have erroneously inferred from the fact that the diegetic PR *substitutes for* PFV forms that it is therefore itself aspectually PFV (for references and discussion, see Sorella 1983: 312ff.). But this would be a redundant use of grammatical resources and one that defeats the argument that tense is functioning aspectually. Why replace one PFV tense with another if the goal is to modify the aspectual profile of a situation?

3.7. The HISTORICAL PRESENT: The "past-more-vivid"

The explanation most frequently encountered for the seemingly idiosyncratic use of PR tense in early Romance is also the one traditionally put forth to account for the so-called HISTORICAL PRESENT. According to this explanation, use of the PR is a technique for reporting events that are vivid and exciting, or for enhancing the dramatic effect of a story by making addressees feel as if they were present at the time of the experience, witnessing events as they occurred. Various grammarians have suggested that HP narrators become so involved in their stories that they recount the action as if they were reliving it simultaneously with its telling, or, alternatively, that they experience the events subjectively rather than viewing them objectively distanced in the past.

Such descriptions assume, moreover, that the HP renders the past more vivid by shifting events out of their original (past) time frame and into that of the act of narration (present). Past events "come alive" with the HP because it is formally identical to the tense used to mark situations as cotemporal with the speaker's now. In virtually all interpretations of the HP (across languages) as a "dramatic present" or "past-more-vivid," the perceived effects of vividness or immediacy are traced to the minus-interpretation of the PR tense, that is, a variable span of time that includes the speaker's now. Yet there is nothing in HP usage to justify a positive reference to present time. The IPFV aspect of the PR, plus the fact that in the absence of explicit time reference present time is assumed,[62] licenses the meaning "PRESENT cotemporal with now"; but it is the basic neutrality of the PR with respect to time that allows this tense to be used in past contexts.

Among investigators who have examined the diegetic PR in various linguistic traditions, some reject the past-more-vivid interpretation on grounds that the most vivid or dramatic events of a story are often reported not in the PR but in a P tense and, conversely, that the PR is at times used for events that cannot be construed as salient. Kiparsky (1968) comes out strongly against the idea that this particular use of the PR conveys some special vividness; he sees the diegetic PR (in early Indo-European languages) as a kind of neutral tense into which the narrator moves, having established through the form of a previous verb that what is being talked about is the past.[63] In such contexts, Kiparsky argues, it is superfluous to repeat a morpheme expressive of past time—hence comes an intermingled sequence of verbs, some explicitly P, some not. The latter are called PR by grammarians; but we must not infer from their appearance in a narrative that the story at that point bears some positive resemblance to present time, i.e., that it is more vivid or dramatic than portions of the story recounted in the past, or that it arouses the narrator's empathy (Kiparsky 1968:30–33).[64]

The point made by Kiparsky and those who support his position is clearly accurate: there is no strict isomorphism between the diegetic PR and salient events in a narrative (I defer to chapter 6 the question of whether it is even legitimate to talk about *a priori* importance with regard to the contents of a narrative). Whether this poses a valid obstacle to the "past-more-vivid" hypothesis is another matter.

As Wolfson points out, in conversational performed stories the P/PR alternation is an *optional* feature that is never actualized in all possible instances. She attributes to the switching phenomenon an *interactive* function that causes it to surface in some settings and not in others (cf. Wolfson 1982: chapter 4). This consideration alone, which applies equally to poetic performed stories, seriously weakens the objection that some important events are encoded in the P rather than the PR. Moreover, a speaker's use of tenses will not be consistent across multiple retellings of the same story.[65] Comparison of the manuscripts of medieval texts existing in more than one version reveals a similar state of affairs: often verbs in the diegetic PR in earlier manuscripts appear in the PS in later manuscripts (cf. texts IV and VI, where these PRs are marked with an asterisk). Comparison of the multiple versions of an Old French *chanson de geste* or a Spanish *romance* likewise reveals the PR to be an optional strategy, although for these genres the different manuscript or print "versions" often reflect entirely different performances, a fact that invalidates strict comparison. A more legitimate comparison can be made among copies reflecting a single version, that is, a single manuscript tradition. Schøsler (1986) analyzes tense variation among the nine extant manuscripts of the Old French *Charroi de Nîmes,* ranging in date from the mid-twelfth to the early fourteenth centuries. The fact that she compares individual verses across the nine texts suggests that the texts descend from a single common original, which is not the case (four distinct manuscript traditions are represented). Nonetheless, of approximately 150 instances in which the manuscripts offer different tenses in identical or nearly identical syntactic contexts, nearly a third involve the PR and the PS.

Another response to the objection that certain of the "crucial events" in a story are reported in the P rather than the PR emerges from Longacre's analysis of "narrative profile," with particular reference to his notion of "discourse peaks" (Longacre 1976:217–228, 1981). Most discourse, narrative or other, is not spoken or written on a uniform level of excitement or tension. There is mounting and declining tension, generally within a global cumulative development. As Longacre (1981:347ff.) argues, it is the peaks of discourse intensity that mark out the "profile" of a whole text that includes one or more such units. Narrative peaks are marked in surface syntax in various ways: repetition and paraphrase (slowing down the camera, as it were, so that the peaks do not go by too fast),[66] inclusion of a mass of detail beyond what is called for in routine narration, and, most important for our purpose, reversal of certain established correlations between grammatical forms and discourse functions. Peaks, Longacre notes, typically emerge as zones of analytical difficulty in the linguistic analysis of texts precisely because *it is at these points that the "spectral lines" can shift:* for example, verb forms that regularly signal a particular kind of information (more salient vs. less salient, events vs. description, etc.) may occur in a distribution other than that predicted from previous sections of the narrative (Longacre 1981:351). Thus, for example, if in a text the PR is normally associated with foreground and with evaluated events, the P with background and unevaluated material, we should not be surprised to see these correlations (simplified here for convenience) reversed at certain of the "most important" points in the story (peaks), which tend, as Longacre notes, to be zones of linguistic turbulence. We might interpret in this perspective Schøsler's finding (1985, 1986) that tense variation across the different manuscripts of certain Old French texts is at its highest at the "most dramatic moments" of the story. Peaks, in other words, constitute a marked discourse context in which the markedness relationships normally operative in a text predictably reverse.

The above considerations should suffice to defuse the objection various investigators have raised to the "vividness" interpretation of the diegetic PR—namely, that highlighted events are not consistently reported in the PR; this consideration neither cancels the effect of vividness perceived in certain instances of the PR tense in narrative nor invalidates the vividness hypothesis. My own position on the matter, though, is that vividness, or dramatization, is not the essential *function* of the diegetic PR, but merely an *effect* deriving from the IPFV aspect of the PR and from various meanings realized in the EXPRESSIVE component (cf. table 1).

3.8. The NARRATIVE PRESENT, HISTORICAL PRESENT, and PRESENT tense

Much of the philological work on tense usage in early Romance carries an assumption, implicit or explicit, that the PR-tense phenomenon of medieval epics, romances, saints' lives, and chronistic narrations, referred to here as the NARRATIVE PRESENT (NP), is essentially the same grammatical animal as the HISTORICAL PRESENT (HP) of later written genres, notably historiography, novels, and short fiction (cf. Foulet 1920; Hatcher 1942; Worthington 1966). Some investigators discriminate in principle between these two varieties of diegetic PR (Sandmann, at various points in his writings; Gilman 1961; Blanc 1964; Ollier 1978), though the basis for their distinctions is not always transparent. There is some validity to Paden's claim (1977) that the modern HP represents a blend of the earlier diegetic PR (what he calls the "vicarious present") and the "PR-cotemporal with now," though this claim requires some refinement.

A related question debated among Romanists is whether the medieval diegetic PR (under whatever label) should be regarded as a form of PR tense, given that its reference is to past events. Most subscribers to the "dramatic present" interpretation (e.g., Sutherland 1939; Sandmann 1953) treat the NP as a bona fide PR tense; Paden (1977), following Kiparsky (1968), calls it "a neutral tense which behaves like a P," while Ollier (1978) sees it as a device for introducing the "present of the living speaker" into the past story-world (and thereby ostensibly collapsing the distance between the two). This question has been the object of some discussion; however, in a pragmatically based, functional model of language, it becomes a non-issue. As argued in chapter 1 (§1.4), by distinguishing between the basic meaning of tense-aspect categories and their extended meanings, functions, or implications in particular contexts, we obviate the need to debate whether the medieval NP is or is not a variety of PR tense. The more appropriate question is why the PR tense has been mobilized across so many languages to carry out a number of pragmatic functions in the normally past-tense discourse of narrative.

To answer this question, let us begin by returning briefly to the question posed earlier of the relation between the HP and the NP (the latter understood as the variety of diegetic PR that occurs specifically in performed stories), in order to consider this relationship in diachronic terms. It should be kept in mind that the HP in most languages is regarded as a cultivated rhetorical device that typically involves some continuity of the PR tense rather than switching between P and PR;[67] its medieval counterpart was by all indications a spontaneous phenomenon,[68] in which the PR alternated with the P according to patterns that, if research on natural narrative may serve as a guide, can now be described on the basis of relevant linguistic criteria rather than impressions and intuitions.

A number of investigators have situated the origins of the HP in the *popular speech* of an earlier period. Thus Foulet (1920:280) hypothesizes: "if from its beginnings spoken French had not used the present to designate the past, the HP would not appear in our written language" (similarly Buffin 1925; Wartburg 1937). Parallel views on the colloquial origin of the HP have been expressed with respect to Italian (Ronconi 1942; Ageno 1964), Latin (Emery 1897; Wackernagel 1920; Hoffman and Szantyr 1963; Grassi 1966), Old Icelandic (Sprenger 1951), English (Jespersen 1935; Visser 1966:§779), and no doubt other languages. Visser, however, denies any connection between the popular speech phenomenon and the diegetic PR documented in Middle English poetic texts. His view of the relationship between the Middle English "substitutive PR" (roughly = NP), the "vividly reporting PR" (= HP), and the diegetic PR of colloquial conversational narration is diagramed in figure 5a. The distinctive features Visser operates with are "vividness" and "tense switching."

This picture contrasts with the consensus view on the relation between these varieties of diegetic PR in Romance, given in figure 5b, which implies that the influence of conversational usage on poetic usage occurred early on (a notable dissenter is Sandmann). In line with my claim that tense switching is—or at least originates as—a pragmatic device of spontaneous oral narration, figure 5b illustrates graphically the popular origin of the diegetic PR in the natural narrative language of what was still essentially an oral culture, whence it migrated into artificial narrative forms and ultimately, as we shall see (§8.3), into narrative *écriture*.

The connection between tense switching and techniques of oral narration that forms a cornerstone of this analysis has not passed unnoticed; neither has it been given the prominence it deserves. A half-century ago Kuen (1934:493) observed that tense switching in Old French was characteristic of the older poems that were still *sung*, but tended to disappear both in poems intended for a reader and in prose. As a generalization this statement is not inaccurate. Several investigators (Sutherland 1939; Sand-

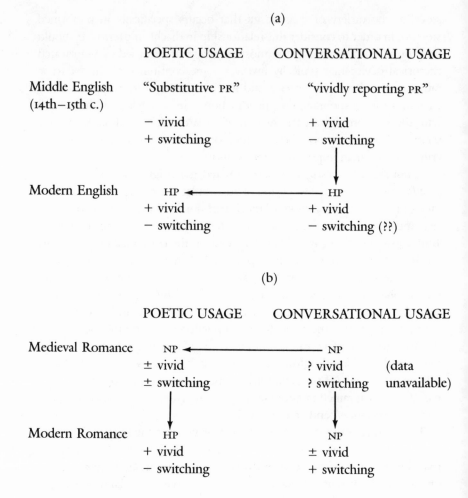

Figure 5. NARRATIVE PRESENT and HISTORICAL PRESENT: (a) in English (after Visser 1966); (b) in Romance.

mann 1953; Ruelle 1976) have also pursued the possibility of a connection to musical recitation, given that most genres in which tense switching occurs are known to have been recited or chanted, presumably with some musical accompaniment.[69] Regrettably, the musical hypothesis, like the prosodic hypothesis discussed in §3.5, is too limited in applicability to account for the range of narrative genres in which similar patterns of tense switching occur. More promising was Wartburg's observation that "Old

French narrative frequently mixes the PR, the simple tenses, and the compound tenses in a way similar to modern conversation, which often alternates, audaciously, the PR and the PC" (Wartburg 1937 [1971]:94). Uitti (1973:50f.) pursues this line of argument, adding that the direction of the shift (i.e., P → PR or PR → P) is usually immaterial; what matters is the alternation.[70] Uitti includes tense switching within a repertoire of "highly sophisticated oral techniques" (1973:51); it is unclear from his statement whether "sophisticated" is meant to suggest that the phenomenon was conscious and deliberate. Studies on naturally occurring narration—or simply listening to oneself tell stories—suggest that it is not.

3.9. Participant tracking

Several investigators have proposed that tense switching in early Romance serves to distinguish or individuate participants in the story world—what I refer to as the "participant tracking" function. Gilman (1961) claims that in the *Cid* clauses with the hero as subject show a preference for PFV verbs,[71] while clauses with collective subjects attract IPFV, notably PR verbs; Schøsler (1985) observes a similar distribution of P and PR verbs in the Old French *Prose Tristan*. There is a motivation for the affinity between individuation and perfectivity in the quantifying nature of aspects; PFV aspect on the verb corresponds roughly to the categories count and singular on the noun, while IPFV aspect corresponds to the categories mass and plural (cf. Jakobson 1957). Unfortunately, these correlations do not hold across texts with any meaningful frequency. In the passage given in (3.9) from the *Prose Tristan*, tenses of the PAST (PS and IMP) mark the collective or at least unindividuated actions of King Marc's court, while the actions of individuated participants (Tristan and Lancelot) are encoded in the PR:

(3.9)   Mes il [= Marc's court] *DOUTOIENT* [IMP] tant le roi Marc que *il n'i ot* [PS] nul qui s'en osast [IMP SUBJ] entremetre. Quant il [= Tristan and Lancelot] *SONT* [PR] hors de la cité, Tristanz, qui moult *EST* [PR] desirant de savoir et de conoistre celi qui *l'ENMAINE* [PR], *PARLE* [PR] et *DIT* [PR].

But they *WERE* SO *AFRAID* [IMP] of King Marc that *there was* [PS] *no one* who dared intervene. When they [= Tristan and Lancelot] *ARE* [PR] outside the city, Tristan, who *IS* [PR] desirous to learn of and to know the one who *IS LEADING* [PR] him, *SPEAKS* [PR] and *SAYS*.

(*Prose Tristan*, §43:23ff., from Schøsler 1985:112)

Though various investigators have looked for stable correlations between tense-aspect categories and story-world participants,[72] there appears to be no consistency across texts, or even within a single text. This lack of stable correlations should not, however, be seen as undermining the hypothesis that tenses can function pragmatically to track story-world participants. The inconsistencies merely reflect the different contextual norms against which the switches operate.

3.9.1. *Participant tracking with* verba dicendi.

Investigators have observed that speech-introducing verbs (referred to as *inquit formulas*) in Old French are almost without exception in IPFV tenses (PR or IMP) when the quoted speech that follows is that of collectivities, while the speech of individuals is introduced by PFV tenses of the PAST (PS or PC). Compare in this regard some inquit formulas from *Roland*, given in (3.10), which are typical of the *chansons de geste:*

(3.10a)   *DIENT* [PR] paien: "De ço avun nus asez." . . . *DIENT* [PR] Franceis "Il nus i cuvent guarde." "The pagans *SAY* [PR]: 'We have enough of this.' . . . The French *SAY* [PR]: 'We must be on our guard.'"   (*Roland*, 77, 192)

(3.10b)   *Dist* [PS] li paiens: "Mult me puis merveiller de Carlemagne . . ." "The pagan *said* [PS]: 'I am very surprised at Charlemagne . . .'"   (*Roland*, 537)

(3.10c)   Li quens Rollant . . . Dunc *AD* **parléd** [PC] a lei de chevaler: "Sire parastre . . ." "Then Count Roland *HAS* **spoken** [PC] in a manner befitting a knight: 'My noble stepfather . . .'"   (*Roland*, 751ff.)[73]

Fotitch (1950 : 51) seeks to explain the IPFV bias of inquit formulas introducing the speech of collectivities by arguing that such choric speech can hardly be considered an objective recording of words actually uttered; rather, it represents a synthesis of general opinion or a general reaction to some important event. Hence the shift from the objective reporting mode (associated with the PS) to a subjective expression of "empathy with the substance of speech, i.e., with the discourse itself" (but see *n*134). Lerch (1922) had earlier argued that these IPFV *verba dicendi* created a "vivid visualization" of the act of speaking.

As for Lerch's argument, recall that direct speech is itself a device for dramatizing narration and creating involvement; it should therefore have little need for reinforcement via a "vivifying" *verbum dicendi*. Fotitch's claim, however, is also difficult to sustain as a cross-language generalization, since IPFV *verba dicendi* are found not only in cases where a narrator empathizes with the content of quoted speech but also where direct quotation is used to underscore a *lack of empathy* with the quoted story participant, as in the passage from text II reproduced in (3.11) below. Here the narrator, a young female hitchhiker, quotes the annoyed wife of the driver who has finally offered her and her friend a ride:

(3.11) Alors IL Y EN A une qui me DIT: "Je ne vois vraiment pas pourquoi mon mari s'est arrêté. Eh bien oui. D'habitude, vous savez . . . Vous avez eu beaucoup de chance qu'il vous prenne."

Then THERE'S this one of them SAYS to me: "I really don't see why my husband stopped [for you]. I mean, really. Usually, you know . . . You were really pretty lucky he picked you up."   (II : 97–101)

Perhaps the most we can say about direct quotation introduced by an IPFV *verbum dicendi* is that it is evaluative. Along this line, Ess-Dykema (1984 : 287) points out that in natural narrative data from contemporary Honduran Spanish a PR-tense inquit formula tends to accompany quoted speech that itself contains *internal evaluation* devices, such as intensifiers, comparators, expressive phonology, gestures, and repetition. This EXPRESSIVE interpretation of inquit formulas seems overall more compelling than a TEXTUAL interpretation (proposed independently in Cerquiglini 1981 and Ess-Dykema 1984, and not incompatible with the EXPRESSIVE interpretation), according to which the PR-tense *verbum dicendi* anticipates the shift that is about to take place from the narrative mode, associated with the P tense, to the speech mode, associated with the PR.

The tense usage of *verba dicendi*—the highest-frequency verbs to appear in the diegetic PR across languages and across genres—remains a point of analytical difficulty. One question linguists have debated is whether the quoted material is syntactically and semantically part of the sentence that contains it. Munro (1982 : 316) makes a convincing case for interpreting *verba dicendi* together with their direct-speech complements as single complex predicates that can be used to *characterize* a speaker as well as report an event.[74] This characterizing function provides an *a fortiori* motivation for the IPFV aspect of inquit formulas. Finally, it will be observed that in narratives of personal experience PR-tense *verba dicendi* co-occur overwhelmingly with persons other than ego, and commonly with third-person subjects. In certain styles of (nonstandard) English, "say" can occur with the first person, but interestingly it is always "I says," or more commonly "says I" (with pragmatically marked word order), never "I say" (Casparis 1975 : 116; Bellos 1978).

3.9.2. Evaluation via participant tracking.

Though no consistent correlations have been noted between specific tense-aspect categories and participant types (e.g., individuated vs. collective, major vs. minor character), the TEXTUAL function of tracking story participants (including narrators when they also figure as story characters) appears to be well documented both in our medieval corpus of artificial narratives and in natural narratives of personal experience. In the short text given in (3.12), the P/PR alternation serves to contrast situations associated with the narrator, rendered almost consistently in the P, with those of his third-person interlocutors, in the PR:

(3.12)   And so, *I walked* . . . uh *WALK* up through customs,
and there's a . . . there's a middle-aged woman there,
and she *LOOKS* at me and she *GOES*— [75]
I *handed* her my passport and she *GOES*—"How long have you been out of the country?"
and *I said,* "Oh, a couple years"
and she *GOES,* "Really? Where've you been, Mexico?"
and then *I said,* "No, I've been in India."
She *GOES,* "India!"
And so then this . . . then this . . . uh young guy,
who I S the guy who's supposed to go through your suitcases, you know,
he *LOOKS* at me and he *GOES* uh—, "Why don't you open up this suitcase?"
(from Herring 1986a, 1986b)

I have observed that narrators across languages tend, like the speaker of this text, to avoid reporting their own actions—and even more so introducing their own speech—in the PR tense. It is not entirely clear why this is the case. Avoidance of the PR may simply be a politeness strategy (do not foreground ego!). If so, this hypothesis would also account for "says I," which casts ego in the grammatical person of the other (it is acceptable to foreground the speech and actions of others). Alternatively, it might be argued from a cognitive standpoint that we have less need to foreground our own words and deeds, which being our own are intrinsically salient in our horizon of concerns and therefore have less reason to be TEXTUALLY marked for saliency. However, such TEXTUAL marking is generally not for our own benefit (though we are always to a degree our own interlocutors), but for that of our listeners. In line with Munro's suggestion that complex speech-act predicates "characterize" an individual, we might relate the apparent constraint on co-occurrence of PR-tense *verba dicendi* with ego to the awkwardness we experience in trying to characterize ourselves. This is not to say that first-person narrators do not construct a "character" for ego just as they do for other story participants; however, effective narrators do this largely through internal strategies other than self-quotation, which, especially when overused, can undermine the desired effect. When narrators resort to self-quotation, the tendency is to "soft-pedal" the technique through a *verbum dicendi* in the PAST, or, in styles of English that allow "says I," to attribute the words of ego to a grammatical third person.

The participant-tracking function is discussed further in chapters 6 and 7, where it is shown how narrators use tense switching both at the TEXTUAL level, to segment a narrative into chunks or *spans* of text focused on different story participants,[76] and at the level of EXPRESSIVITY to evaluate internally a narrator's relationship to story participants, including his or her own character-I.

3.10. From oral performance to *écriture:* Oral residue in written texts

Of the Old French texts that exhibit tense switching to any meaningful degree, all—or virtually all—conform to the working definition of performed stories proposed by Wolfson. Virtually all, since vestiges of the oral switching phenomenon appear in later texts assumed to have been composed in writing and for private reading; however, well into the medieval period "reading" entailed an oral articulation of the sounds being decoded.[77] The French verb *lire* (to read), where it occurs, normally indicates that a text will be read aloud to others. Gallais (1964:486) claims that no French romance up to the mid-thirteenth century shows signs of having been composed exclusively for private reading; all have marks of oral delivery.

The thirteenth century stands as a turning point at which some written texts still look back to earlier techniques of oral composition, including the mixing of tenses, while others look forward to "modern" tense relationships. It is likewise this century that first sees the use of prose for genres that were previously composed in verse, notably romances and historiography. Sutherland (1939:333) writes:

Works that continue in prose the oral narrative of the [verse] romances retain the traditional technique of the twelfth-century poems, and keep in the early thirteenth century an extensive use of the present indicative; the prose *Lancelot* shows a high proportion of present to past tense of the verbs.[78] Villehardouin seems to be moving toward the modern system, though he still has a fair proportion of present tenses, a usage which may be attributed again to his *oral style of narration*. Narrative literature in the fourteenth century is already very consistent in its use of the past tense; the short story, as well as history, is conceived as continuous narrative, rather than a succession of episodes, and displays a logical and careful notation of sequence in real time. Froissart, who appears to be an exception, with his trick of using the present indicative where we should expect the imperfect, is obviously narrating in a personal and intimate style, of necessity *more akin to the contemporary spoken language*. (my emphasis)

Blanc (1964) graphs the relative frequencies of tenses in Old French texts from ca. 1100 (*Roland*) through the fourteenth century. During this period the speaker-oriented PR and PC follow a downward development in roughly inverse proportion to the upward trend for the storytelling tenses, PS and IMP. The gradual decline in the use of speaker-oriented tenses and concomitant rise in the use of narrative tenses produces an X-pattern on Blanc's graph (1964:100), particularly salient with respect to the PR and PS. Notable is the fact that this change in tense usage parallels an evolution from the orally performed verse texts of the earlier period to the later prose texts composed in writing and, to an increasing degree, for a reader. This change in techniques of text composition and transmission that accompanied the development of literacy must not, however, be viewed as "progress" from more primitive to more "sophisticated" narrative techniques (Sutherland 1939), nor as evidence that writers were simply becoming more "logical" and more "precise" in their choice of tense forms, making distinctions wherever possible (Garey 1955). Neither sophistication nor logic is at issue here. Nor are we dealing simply with "a change in literary taste" (Worthington 1966:408). The considerations that seem to account for the changing use of tense-aspect categories as narrative textuality evolves are of a linguistic/pragmatic nature: on the one hand, the difference in pragmatic structure between texts composed for oral performance in an interactive setting and texts composed for private reading, and, on the other, the gradual transfer of certain narrative functions from purely contextual or paralinguistic expression to expression via the grammar that was emerging as the language gradually adapted itself to writing. Blanc's analysis provides valuable statistical support for my view that the ontogenesis of the diegetic PR, or more accurately of the P/PR alternation, is to be sought in the pragmatic structure of oral narration.

Given my insistence on linking tense switching to oral performance, one might wonder at its appearance in later, nonimprovisational genres presumably composed in writing and for private consumption, such as historical chronicles and prose romances. Notwithstanding their composition in writing, certain prose chronicles were destined for oral performance. A case in point is the *Conquest of Constantinople* by Villehardouin, whose distinctively oral style has been remarked on (Sutherland 1939; Beer 1968, 1981). His account of the Fourth Crusade, "composed in the vernacular by an illiterate" (Beer 1981:55), announces itself as an orally dictated text: "Jouffrois li mareschaus de Champaigne . . . ceste ouvre *dita* . . ." (Geoffrey, Marshal of Champagne . . . *dictated* this work, §120). Also dictated was the crusade narrative of Villehardouin's contemporary Robert of Clari, "qui i fu et qui le vit et qui l'oi le tesmoingne . . . et *a fait metre en escrit* le verité" (who was there and who saw it and heard the testimony . . . and *had the true account of it committed to writing*, §120:4–6). Nor are these isolated cases: as we shall see, the dictation mentality did not disappear even when literate individuals began committing their own texts to writing. While chronistic narration may legitimately be regarded as a written literate genre, "literate" need not preclude oral composition or recitation. This is not to deny differences between dictated and fully oral (improvisationally composed) texts, a contrast brought home by Ong's (1982b) reflection on the distances separating traditional oral poets from the blind Milton sitting down to dictate *Paradise Lost*.

Texts can represent all kinds of adjustments to orality-literacy polarities, and manuscript culture in the West was always to a degree oral. As Ong observes (1982b:153), certain institutions surviving from oral-aural culture favored the oral cast of mind and the survival of oral elements. Crucial among these was the orientation of all academic instruction toward oral performance; outside the academy, too, the oral mindset was sustained by certain special vernacular practices, such as the singing of ballads (cf. §8.2). Even after print, textuality only gradually achieved the place it has today in cultures where most reading is silent. Hence it is not surprising to find "oral residue" in texts known to have been composed under increasingly literate circumstances.[79]

Bäuml (1984:41f.) sees as incontrovertible the process whereby certain marks of orality are "by their writtenness" converted into stylistic attributes of written texts. Though tense is not among the orality features he discusses, the passage from the NP to the HP would be a prime example of this process. In written texts orality features often have a referential function quite different from the mechanical one they had in their oral antecedents. Bäuml illustrates this point with respect to epic formulas.

Formulas are a mechanism essential to the process of composition-in-performance as well as to the reception and retention of primary oral epics.

Formulas are also culturally essential references to the tradition they formulate and transmit. In the process of formulaic *written* composition, formulas no longer fulfill a crucial mechanical function, but take on a referential function: they refer to a specific (oral) type of text, and thus represent the convention which determines the composition of the written text (Bäuml 1984 : 42f.).

A parallel argument can be made for tense switching. The mechanical functions of the medieval NP are its pragmatic functions in oral storytelling, functions related in part, as we shall see in chapter 6, to the paratactic structure of the texts. In written texts that were still read aloud (e.g., chronicles and prose romances), the mechanical features relating to *performance* were still functionally motivated, whereas those relating to oral *composition* had lost their mechanical raison d'être.[80] Tense switching nonetheless retained a referential function (in Bäuml's sense) in written texts by invoking a textual convention of the earlier literature composed in performance. Tristram (1983) makes precisely this argument for a group of Middle Irish texts that preserve features of oral transmission—among them tense switching—despite conspicuous evidence of written composition. She proposes, in fact, that NP usage be taken as an index of the degree to which the manuscript form of a tale still reflects its oral origins.

Commenting on the persistence of oral mental habits of thinking as manifested in the physical act of writing during the European Middle Ages, Ong observes that "composition in writing, working out one's thoughts pen-in-hand, . . . became widespread for literary or other prolonged compositions at different times in different cultures. It was still rare in 11th-century England, and, when it occurred, even this late, could be done in a psychological setting so oral that we find it hard to imagine. The 11th-century Eadmer of St. Albans says that, when he composed in writing, he felt he was dictating to himself" (Ong 1982b : 95, following Clanchy 1979 : 218; cf. also Crosby 1936; Riquer 1959). Most oral theorists acknowledge the existence of transitional texts exhibiting features of both orality and literacy.[81] Given that the medieval performed stories in our corpus are now available only as written texts, it is useful to draw up at least a provisional typology of oral text types.

In his *Introduction à la poésie orale*, Zumthor (1983) proposes a four-part typology of oral situations. The purest form, "primary" orality, assumes no intervention of a writing system. The two subsequent stages, "mixed" and "secondary" orality, both involve the coexistence of orality with writing: the secondary variety presupposes a fully literate culture (one in which all experience is marked by the presence of writing); hence the oral text is (re)composed from a written base in a culture in which writing predominates over the voice. In the mixed variety, although the culture is in possession of a writing system, the influence of writing remains external, partial, or for some reason deferred. Finally, Zumthor speaks of orality "diffused by the media"—mediated by technology, hence subject to displacement in time and space (what Ong 1982b labels "secondary orality").[82] The oral literature of the European Middle Ages (which is not considered in Zumthor's 1983 book) would seem to come closest to his mixed variety, though some would argue for primary orality in the case of the epic songs, or *chansons de geste*. According to the now prevailing theory, these epic songs were continually recomposed in performance via a poetic analogue of Chomsky's "rule-governed creativity," through memorization of a skeletal plot and recipient-designed recomposition of the text in performance, using conventionalized building blocks on the levels of theme, motif, and formula (for details, see Duggan 1973). In a later essay Zumthor (1984a) assigns medieval Romance poetic texts to either the mixed or secondary categories. By the eleventh and twelfth centuries oral discourse was beginning to function in a universe of communications that had evolved the notion of "texts." The importance of secondary orality increases in particular from the thirteenth century on, a turning point that, as noted above, is likewise crucial in terms of the development of grammar.

The point of the preceding discussion is to argue for the *cognitive orality* of the medieval narratives here under consideration, which necessarily leaves its mark on linguistic structure. Ong and others who have addressed themselves to the issue of orality and literacy in medieval Europe have shown convincingly that a fundamentally oral mindset underlies all vernacular texts from this period, irrespective of the intervention of writing in their textual genesis. "Ungrammatical" tense usage is but one example of the "oral residue" (Ong 1965) that persists in written texts and takes on new functions as textuality evolves from more oral to more literate.

3.11. Performed stories: Medieval and modern, natural and artificial

Medievalists might question the legitimacy of applying to so-called literary texts from the Middle Ages a methodology designed for the analysis of quotidian narrations produced spontaneously in conversation.[83] In the same spirit Wolfson (1979) criticizes certain earlier work on the diegetic PR for ignoring distinctions of genre. Apropos of Kiparsky's (1968) comparison of the diegetic PR in different languages and text types, she insists that, "whatever the validity of [his] syntactic hypothesis, it must be remembered that he is dealing with HP in the literature of ancient languages; there is no reason to expect . . . that this feature should have the same function in modern languages." To this she adds that investigators have on the whole failed to distinguish between use of the device in "literary" and in "spoken" language (Wolfson 1979 : 168).

In principle I concur with Wolfson's position that the function of a linguistic phenomenon widely documented across languages and across textual genres need not be the same wherever it occurs. For this reason I have insisted on distinguishing the diegetic PR that occurs in the early performance genres, which I have labeled the NP, from the HP of later written genres. Nor do I assume, even for a given *état de langue*, that the functions of a tense-aspect category are identical in all text types. This is true *a fortiori* for Old French—a label that subsumes a number of dialects over a period of several centuries during which major linguistic changes occurred. On the other hand, a refusal to consider potentially similar data from different periods or text types seriously limits the scope of one's findings and undermines the possibility of arriving at revealing generalizations of the kind obtainable through carefully controlled comparison of languages, discourse types, genres, or texts.

To come back to Wolfson's objection, my own probings into this matter suggest that with regard to performed stories the crucial opposition is not the one she invokes between "spoken" and "literary" language—where does "oral literature" fit in?—but between narrative designed as absent-author communication (most varieties of written narrative) and narrative designed for interactive oral performance. A major thrust of my analysis is thus to demonstrate the functional parallelism of tense switching in the performed stories of the Middle Ages and in those of everyday conversation. Clearly there are significant differences between these two varieties of narrative—the one being what Zumthor has referred to as a "monument," the other a "document." Let us consider some of these differences, in an effort to dispel doubts about the legitimacy of applying to artificial texts a methodology developed for natural-language data.

To begin with, medieval narratives, even the shorter genres, are significantly longer than most conversational narrations, which typically have only one point to make. Yet medieval performed stories are typically *episodic* in structure, a consequence of being performed in multiple internally cohesive segments, much like television serials. Epics and romances, as well as chronistic and hagiographic narratives, tend to consist of a series of semi-independent shorter narrations (episodes), each of which has a coherent macro-structure not dissimilar to that of conversational texts (a model for this structure is outlined in chapter 5). Thus texts III, X, XI, and XII of the appendix present us with structurally complete narratives, although they have been excerpted from longer stories. Their plots may be summed up as follows: Aucassin engages in combat with and defeats Count Bougar of Valence (III); the Cid battles and defeats an escaped lion, shaming his cowardly sons-in-law (IX); two vassals of Count Euphemien of Rome go out in search of his lost son Alexis, but when they come upon Alexis they fail to recognize him, dressed as a beggar, and so return home (XI); Yvain engages in combat with and defeats Esclados the Red (XII). The excerpt from Villehardouin given as text IV subdivides into three mini-narratives: vv. 1–27, 28–41, and 42–end, all subsumed within the larger episode of "the taking of the tower of Galatha" (§§155–161 in Faral's edition),[84] in its turn part of a larger narration of the events of the Fourth Crusade. As Ong (1982b:148) has observed, a narrator in an oral culture normally and naturally operated in episodic patterning—"the natural way to talk out a lengthy story line, if only because the experience of real life is more like a string of episodes than it is like a Freytag pyramid."

In his typology of narrative forms, Longacre (1983) distinguishes between "climactic" and "episodic" narrative, marked respectively by a plus and a minus value for the feature "tension." But much "episodic" narrative can be shown to consist of a series of "climactic" mini-narratives, each having its own buildup, peak, and resolution. Such is generally the case with narratives designed for performance in multiple units (sittings, chapters, etc.), such as verse romances and especially the *chansons de geste*. Rychner (1955:44f.) comments apropos of several *chansons de geste* that the number and order of the episodes is more a fact of being committed to manuscript than of actual composition. Epic jongleurs, he conjectures, were no more concerned than their listeners about the narrative coherence of a story that could not, in any case, be assimilated in its entirety. Differences involving text length and episodic vs. climactic structure should not, then, concern us unduly.

A point stressed by Wolfson in her discussion of conversational storytelling is that tense switching is a variable that occurs exclusively in performance narration, and conversational performance is virtually always spontaneous and *improvisational*—what Ochs (1979) refers to as "unplanned discourse." To be sure, performance literature is less improvisational than conversational performance, being generally subject to formal and compositional constraints (a fixed meter, rhyme or assonance, formulaic language, subdivisions of a fixed length, etc.). However, we know from living oral traditions that skilled professional storytellers can work comfortably within such formal limitations to construct a poetic syntax that does not strike listeners as deviant within the horizon of linguistic expectations that performance literature sets up. In fact, Scholes and Kellogg (1966:50) maintain that oral composition of prose sentences is universally more difficult than oral composition of metrically perfect verse. Be that as it may, the crucial factor for tense switching, as I see it, is not that narratives must be unplanned, but that they must be *acts of performance,* as defined by the presence of such features as dialogue, asides, repetition, expressive sounds and sound effects, and motions and gestures.[85]

Accepting that medieval narratives satisfy the criteria for performed stories, there is also the fact that the relationship of the extant text to living speech is different in natural narrative performance from what it is in the performance of artificial narratives from the Middle Ages, given that the medieval texts we possess do not represent faithful transcriptions of independent, self-sufficient performances that always occurred, initially, without writing (Bill Paden, personal communication). Two issues are involved here: first, the fidelity of the extant text to an original oral performance and, second, the question of oral vs. written composition.

The first of these poses an unresolvable difficulty. As Zumthor (1984a) notes, the fact that these texts have come down to us mediated by writing means that our efforts to approach their orality will be at best approximative; however the texts may have originally been composed and received, we confront them as fixed written documents from which much of the paralinguistic and pragmatic information they contained as "storytelling events" has been lost. And in light of the numerous alterations introduced in the process of scribal transmission and in modern editing, it is obvious that these texts that *we now read* cannot be regarded as faithful renderings of erstwhile oral performances. But must we therefore abandon all efforts to determine what features of these texts can be explained by orality? I think not.

The second issue is still debated among Romance philologists and medievalists: whether certain genres, notably the epics, were orally composed. The term "oral composition" refers to composition-in-performance, and certain oralists restrict "oral poetry" to texts composed in this fashion. Here, however, the focus of the term "oral texts" is on the process of communication—via oral performance—rather than on the method of composition, which might have been either oral or written. The question of oral composition is not central to the present inquiry; the crucial issue is once again *performance*—the fact that these texts were produced in a culture whose forms of thought and expression were still fundamentally oral, and were composed—whether orally or in writing—for presentation to a live audience by professional storytellers/singers for whom effective techniques of oral delivery came much more naturally than they do for those of us whose cognitive and linguistic structures are permeated by writing.

In short, there appear to be linguistic strategies particular to performed stories that cut across language, genre, or literacy lines. It is by appeal to these that I justify using a methodology designed for natural narration to shed light on the functions of tense-aspect in artificial narratives—in the first instance in performance narratives from the Middle Ages, but ultimately also in planned, written genres that draw certain of their stylistic devices from their oral predecessors.

The issue of narrative genres is one of a number of typological questions about narrative to which we shall now turn our attention.

4 Narrative Discourse: Typological Considerations

What makes a writer is this: until she —or he, of course— writes down whatever happens, turns it into a story, it hasn't really happened, it hasn't shape, form, reality.

(AMANDA CROSS, NO WORD FROM WINIFRED)

Between those happenings that prefigure it
And those that happen in its anamnesis
Occurs the Event, but that no human wit
Can recognize until all happening ceases.

(W. H. AUDEN, FROM "SHORTS I")

4.1. Verbal representations of experience: Story structure and reality structure

The translation of experience—real or imagined—into language can take a variety of forms, one of which is the story. Notwithstanding cultural differences concerning their well-formedness (see *n*88), stories are one of the most basic of our acquired constructs for organizing and making sense of the data of experience. As a hermeneutic device, the story form functions as an organizational matrix, not only for recalling our experiences in order to communicate them to others, but also for shaping those experiences for ourselves into structures conforming to culturally determined expectations of newsworthiness and/or how we would like the world to be. Psycholinguistic literature on narrative has shown that people often use story *schemata* (see §4.1.3) to *recreate* versions of their past experiences, and in so doing elaborate or revise altogether the organizational structure of the actual experiences (Stein 1982). This raises an important pretheoretical question that has been debated by narratologists of various stripes: the relationship between reality structure and narrative structure and the tacitly assumed priority of the former over the latter.

4.1.1. Narrative theory generally starts out by drawing a distinction between the organizational structure of real experience or a possible world and that of its representation in a narrative. As Richard Bauman writes (1986:5), "Events are action structures, organized by relationships of causality, temporality, and other such linkages; narratives are verbal structures, organized by rules of discourse. Most commonly narratives are seen as verbal icons of the events they represent, and the problem is one of determining the nature and extent of the isomorphism between them and the means by which this formal relationship is narratively achieved." The priority of event structure over narrative structure is a presupposition underlying much of the linguistic work on conversational narrative. Consider in this regard Labov's (1972:359f.) definition of narrative as "one method of recapitulating past experience by matching a verbal sequence of clauses to the sequence of events which (it is inferred) actually occurred." What is presupposed is the givenness of reality structure—that experience offers itself up to us already packaged in the form of "events," which a narrator then arranges in a text to conform to particular communicative and esthetic objectives.

But can we simply assume that events are prior to and independent of the narratives that recount them, or might it not be the case that narrative is itself the "cognitive instrument" (Mink 1968) for imposing a structural coherence on the otherwise inchoate substance of experience? Implicit in the *fabula-sjuzhet* opposition introduced by the Russian formalists is the idea that event structure is retroactively constituted from the discourse that narrates it. *Fabula* refers to the events of a story abstracted from their disposition in a text and reconstructed in their chronological order, together with the participants; *sjuzhet* refers to the representational discourse (spoken, written, pictorial, theatrical, cinematic) that undertakes the telling of these events, not necessarily in the order in which they occurred.[86] The implied priority of narrative structure over reality structure in the *fabula-sjuzhet* opposition relates presumably to the fact that this opposition was formulated with reference to fiction, the events of which obviously have no existence prior to and independent of the text. However, the "bias of objectivity" has been called into question, most insistently by philosophers of history and narrativist historians (Gallie 1968; Mink 1968; White 1980). Ong (1982a:12) offers the following straightforward and compelling articulation of this position: "Reality never occurs in narrative form. The totality of what happened to and in and around me since I got up this morning is not organized as narrative, and as a totality cannot be expressed as narrative. To make a narrative, I have to isolate certain elements out of the unbroken seamless web of history with a view to fitting them into a particular construct which I have more or less consciously in mind." This carving up of reality into constructs of experience, and the organization of these constructs into a verbal representation through which they acquire meaning, is the *configurational* operation of narrativization (for a penetrating discussion of this process, see Ricoeur 1984, esp. 155–161).

4.1.2.   Narrativization appears to be a two-step process consisting of cognitive and linguistic operations. The first operation involves an unconscious segmentation of the seamless experiential continuum into cognitive units that we call "events" (the vexed question of defining an event is addressed in §4.1.4). The second operation—the linguistic encoding of these events as a sequence of predicates, and eventually of clauses, of various types—is one of linearization and perspectivization, the goal of which is to impose a particular order and coherence on the events and to render their configuration meaningful. The process of narrativization is necessarily an individual, subjective act whereby experience is passed through the filter of a focalizing consciousness whose point of view the story will reflect.[87] No two narrators will configure an experience, or evaluate its component elements, in precisely the same way.

As suggested above, there are stronger limitations on story form than on the form of events in real life: for one thing, there are often no obvious beginnings and more often no clear-cut endings to event sequences in daily life; these boundaries are superimposed on experience by *story schemata* (see §4.1.3) in accord with our expectations of narrative well-formedness. But in addition to the problem of segmentation there is the matter of linearizing what is inherently nonlinear (for a probing discussion of this problem, see Toliver 1974 : part 1). The internal states that accompany sequences of actions as ongoing states supporting them must be verbalized in a narrative at a single point in the linear sequence. As we shall see in chapter 6, one way in which narrative handles this problem of sequencing the simultaneous is through the contrastive use of tense-aspect categories: typically IPFV tenses are used to report the ongoing states and activities that serve as background to the set of ordered events that are reported by PFV forms.

4.1.3.   "Schemata" and "frames."   In converting the data of experience into narrative language, speakers rely heavily on what cognitive narratologists refer to as story schemata. These are sets of expectations about the internal structure of stories that serve to facilitate both encoding and retrieval of information—mental representations of the parts of a typical story and the interrelationships among those parts (Mandler and Johnson 1977 : 111f.). Chapter 5 examines in detail the schema proposed by Labov (1972) and Labov and Waletzky (1967) for the structure of natural narrative.[88] As structures for organizing experience into narrative, schemata are conceptually analogous to the plot structures of literature. In his statement that "the narrative work is an invitation to see our praxis as it is ordered by this or that plot structure articulated in our litera-ture," Ricoeur (1984:83) is not suggesting that life copies art (not an alto-gether outlandish idea); he is simply alluding to our reliance on certain cognitive constructs (schemata, plots) as hermeneutic devices for organiz-ing and making sense of the data of experience.

Cognitive psycholinguistics has also developed the concept of *frames* to refer to the sets of expectations we associate with conventionalized situa-tions (e.g., a visit to the doctor, a trip to the supermarket, a university semi-nar, running in a race, etc.; see Tannen 1979; Chafe 1987). Though the frame concept was developed to account for how we anchor different types of real-world experience (cf. Goffman 1974), the concept can be extended to the conventionalized situations of textual (including fictional) worlds. Frames appropriate to medieval narratives would include physical com-bat—between large collectivities in the epics, between individual knights in the romances; the *coup de foudre* of courtly heroes' first encounters with their ladies; and the exchange of embassies and messengers—a device for conveying (and reiterating) information via direct speech. In later chapters we shall examine variants of the combat frame. The participants in a nar-rative speech act (speaker/author and hearer/reader) rely heavily on frames in the encoding and decoding of meanings in texts.

4.1.4. Events.   Among the cognitive structures we use to map experience onto language, the most basic—and the one most closely involved with the categories of tense and aspect—is the *event*. We talk constantly about events, which would seem to imply that we know what they are. Yet when pressed to define events, we immediately become aware of the complexity of the issue.

The *OED* defines an event as "anything that happens or is contemplated as happening." For narratological purposes, this definition won't get us very far. Definitions offered by literary investigators are scarcely more il-luminating: Dorfman (1969:5) defines an event as "anything that happens, an incident of some kind, particularly if some importance is attached to its occurrence." Chatman (1978:32), who devotes an entire chapter to "events," defines them as simply "actions" or "happenings" (depending on whether the affected participant is an agent or patient). Rimmon-Kenan (1983:15) adds that when something "happens," the situation usu-ally changes: "an event . . . may be said to be a change from one state of affairs to another." This statement hints at a connection between events and perfectivity or telicity that Polanyi's definition makes explicit; for Polanyi (1985:10), an event is "an occurrence in some world which is described as having an instantaneous rather than a durative or iterative character."[89] Rimmon-Kenan recognizes, however, that simply positing a "change" does little to solve the segmentation problem.

Most events can be broken down into a set of micro-actions and intermediary states; conversely, numerous individual events are often subsumed under global event labels, such as the Fall of the Roman Empire or World War II—what Ricoeur (1984:46) refers to as "project events."[90] The segmentation problem carries over to the linguistic level: corresponding to "project events" are "project verbs" ("make war," "take a trip," "write a book") that organize numerous micro-actions into a single, undifferentiated activity predicate. Clearly we have not gotten very far in circumscribing the notion of "events."

Banfield (1982:265) emphasizes the *countability* and *sequentiality* of events: "an event is a discrete unit occurring in time which may be counted and, hence, which is defined by the sequential relationship with the unit(s) which precede or follow it in the series." She adds, however, that her concern is not to decide which units qualify as events, nor to analyze them into their constituent subunits—the segmentation problem. Her definition, like Polanyi's, points to the punctual, perfective nature of what we think of as events. This definition does not, however, make clear what kind of "discrete units" are involved: units of experience? units of language?

Linguists concerned with natural narrative have made little if any progress over their literary counterparts in their attempts to define the event; the main differences seem to be an unquestioned assumption of the priority of event structure over narrative structure and a greater concern with the problem of segmentation. The latter is at the crux of the discrepant interpretations of the diegetic PR in conversational narration.

While investigators seem to agree that a narrative is composed of a series of temporally ordered acts, Wolfson (1982:115), responding to criticisms from Schiffrin (1981), argues that these minimal units of action do not in themselves constitute events; rather, through the operation of tense switching this indistinct series of acts is divided up "and each span or cluster *which is thus created*" (my emphasis) she calls an event. Unfortunately, this definition provides no means to identify events in texts in which tense switching does not occur. The advantages it offers over certain other definitions are, first, acknowledgment of the *speaker's role* in organizing experience into narrative units (they are not given *a priori*), and, second, recognition of the fact that events only come into being as a result of linguistic operations. However, these operations are not limited to switching between P and PR tense.

The sentences given in (4.1) illustrate the dependence of events on language:

(4.1)   First he was unable to stand upright. Next he was incapable of inserting the key into the door. (from Halliday and Hasan 1976)

Halliday and Hasan observe that here there are clearly no "events": there are only "linguistic events," and the time sequence is located in the speaker's organization of his own discourse (1976:238f.). Gleason (1968), who pioneered in exploiting the difference between events and nonevents, also observes that different languages approach the time sequences between neighboring events in quite different ways. If this is so, is it pointless to try to formulate a cross-linguistically valid definition of the event? Should we content ourselves with the fact that speakers have an intuitive sense of what events are and leave it at that? I believe some headway can be made if we approach the event as a cognitive construct that mediates between experience and language, yet belongs strictly to neither domain.

We have observed that narratologists often treat events as if they were ontologically given and capable of being mapped onto grammar in a fairly straightforward way. Thus Robert Scholes (1981:205) ponders, "What is an event? A real event is something that happens: a happening, an occurrence, an event. A narrated event is the symbolization of that event: a temporal icon." As pointed out above, it is difficult to sustain the notion of "real events" altogether prior to and independent of the discourse that articulates them. We are on firmer ground ontologically if we acknowledge that *the event is but a hermeneutic construct for converting an undifferentiated continuum of the raw data of experience, or of the imagination, into the verbal structures we use to talk about experience: narratives, stories.* The relationship of experience, events, and stories emerges from the following statement from Shuman (1986:20):

Stories, experiences, and events are different entities. Roughly, experiences are the stream of overlapping activities that make up everyday life. Events, unlike experiences, have potentially identifiable beginnings and endings. . . . Stories frame experiences as events. Stories are one of the forms that transform experiences into bounded units with beginnings, endings, and foci, and events are one kind of bounded unit. A story is the representation of an event segmented into sequentially arranged units.

There has been a tendency in narrative scholarship to assign experience a sense of objectivity so that experiences become invested with reality, in contrast to stories, which are supposedly understood subjectively. This unfortunate tendency has led scholars to confuse events with experiences, *as though one could experience an event. Events are ways of categorizing experience;* in a sense the category "event" makes experiences accessible to understanding by providing a language for talk-ing about experience. (my emphasis)

Having posed the question of the relationship between reality structure and narrative structure, and having examined certain of the cognitive con-structs we use to move from one to the other (events, schemata, frames), let us turn our attention now to the *differentia specifica* of "narrative" as a category of linguistic performance, and to certain of the oppositions that subtend this category and are relevant to a study of tense and aspect.

4.2. *Differentia specifica* of narrative textuality

The definitions of narrative that have been proposed are as numerous and varied as the disciplines it encompasses. In choosing to review certain of these proposals here, I proceed not out of any intrinsic fascination with definition, but in order to arrive eventually at a set of criteria that set nar-rative language apart from other types of utterance, in particular criteria that relate to tense-aspect.

Barbara Herrnstein Smith defines narrative as "someone telling some-one else that something happened" (1981:228). The advantage of this "most minimal and most universal" characterization, she observes, is to emphasize narrative's function "as part of a social transaction," the prod-ucts of which (i.e., novels and other written fiction) should not be re-garded as "detached and decontextualized entities." The significance of this statement—unusual from the pen of a literary theorist—with respect to the pragmatics of fiction will become apparent later on.

4.2.1. Whereas literary theorists generally define nar-rative in terms of global properties, linguists concentrate on its internal structure: macro-structure (the major parts of a typical story) as well as micro-structure (organization at the sentence and clause levels). Labov and Waletzky (1967) define a minimal narrative as any sequence of clauses that contains at least one *temporal juncture* (two clauses temporally ordered with respect to one another). Prince (1982) adds that the two or more ordered situations referred to in these clauses must not presuppose or en-tail one another. For other definitions of a "minimal story," see Stein (1982:496ff.), Beaugrande (1982:406ff.), and various articles in the special issue on stories of *Journal of Pragmatics* (6.5 [1982]).

Most investigators emphasize that narrative involves *a sequential order of presentation,* specifically one in which the order of narrative units (clauses) parallels the order in which events are presumed to have occurred in the world modeled by the text. This match between the order of events in the *fabula* and the order of linguistic units in the *sjuzhet* is referred to here as *iconic sequence.* For Banfield (1982), it is the specific property of sequentiality that sets "narration" apart from "representation," the latter falling under the rubric of what is often (infelicitously) referred to as "communicative" discourse (i.e., the nonnarrative mode in the frameworks of Benveniste or Weinrich, discussed in §4.5 below). Narrative, Banfield argues (1982:268), does not "re-present" the passage of time, it "re-counts" it, segmenting it into countable and orderable narrative units. The units she has in mind—prototypical *narrative events*—have, as we shall see, a particular tense-aspect profile.

4.2.2. Though it is not intended as a definition but simply as a characterization of the narrative norm or prototype, the passage quoted below from Herring (1986b) yields a definition especially suited to our purpose. She describes narrative discourse in terms of the unmarked values for a set of oppositional properties (italicized below) that collectively define its unmarked *tense:* the (PFV) PAST (1986b):

The prototypical past-tense narrative is concerned with *events,* rather than static description, and the events are not narrated in random order but rather in a *sequence* which is iconic with the temporal order in which they actually occurred (cf. Labov's definition of narrative). Further, the completion of one event is implied by the inception of that which follows, a fact which may give rise to an interpretation of aspectual *perfectivity* for the (simple) past tense, where no other aspectual value is specifically indicated (Hopper 1979a, 1979b). The prototypical narrative is *factual* and *time-bound,* in that it chronicles a *unique sequence of events* which took place at a specific point (or over a specific bounded interval) in time. There is also a sense in which the ideal narrator is *objective,* maintaining a *distance* between him or herself and the events narrated in order to relate them as they actually occurred, in linear order, and with a minimum of personal evaluation or digression. It is this complex of features which, in the absence of indications to the contrary, the "narrative past" typically evokes.

I stress that this is not, in principle, a definition of narrative. If it were, then we would be hard pressed to explain the fact that many narratives show marked values for certain of the properties at issue (e.g., narratives that are fictional, or narrated subjectively or by an "unreliable narrator";

narratives that rely heavily on the PR, or in which the ordering of the *sjuzhet* is deliberately noniconic). But the existence of narratives with marked features does not invalidate the notion of a narrative norm. To the contrary: without a norm, defined as a set of unmarked values, the marked values could not produce the effects they do. Notwithstanding my caveat above, the net result of identifying this set of properties and determining their unmarked values is a linguistically based definition of narrative.

In a note to the passage quoted above, Herring remarks that in the idealized act of narration, pragmatic considerations (e.g., making one's narrative relevant and interesting in order to maintain the listener's attention, forestall interruptions, and get across a point of view) are presumably secondary to the primary goal, which is informative. However, the role of pragmatic considerations in a speaker's selection of the storytelling mode over other modes of reporting information should not be underestimated. As Traugott and Pratt (1980:250) observe, "The story is distinguished by the fact that it is an utterance type used when one is recapitulating experience *for display purposes* rather than for information giving purposes or for some other purpose" (my emphasis). This allusion to performance is echoed by Ducrot (1979:10), who suggests that "to narrate is not only to inform listeners that such and such events took place, but to make them relive the experience, to give them the feeling of being there"—phrases one sees repeatedly associated with the diegetic PR. An important pragmatic function of the diegetic PR that conversational narratologists have identified is *evaluation*. What purpose does evaluation serve if not, at least in part, that of telling a good story (cf. van Dijk 1975; Tannen 1984b)? To conclude this section, then, we might consider the proposition that one of the (presumably unconscious) agendas speakers have in choosing narrative over other modes of reporting information is to "display" and win approval for their own skill as storytellers.

4.3. Stories, narratives, and other verbalizations of experience

The terms "narrative" and "story" have been—and will continue to be—used here interchangeably, inasmuch as the texts under consideration fit both categories. Technically the relationship is a hyponymous one: all stories are narrative, but not all narrative accounts are stories. Polanyi (1986) defines story as a *specific* (vs. generic) *past-time* narrative that has a *plot* and makes a *point*. Likewise, all narratives are verbal reports of experience, but not all verbalizations of experience are narrative. It is appropriate, therefore, to examine briefly the various discourse forms used to convert experience into language.

4.3.1. Reports. *Reports* (e.g., police reports) share with stories the features of referential uniqueness (they refer to specific events that happened once) and past temporality. They differ from stories in that they do not make a point: the question of why someone did something at a particular moment in a particular world then something else at a subsequent moment in that world is external to the text. Nor do reports illustrate some general truth—a "message"—with implications for the world of the telling as well as for the world of the tale (Polanyi 1981, 1986). Reports, then, may be seen as narratives lacking in evaluation.

One important pragmatic difference between stories and reports is that storytellers are responsible for demonstrating the relevance of their texts to the discourse and situation context—listeners should not be left wondering "what's the point?"—whereas with reports it is often the responsibility of the listener to determine the relevance of the information presented (Polanyi 1982:514). Obviously, the teller of a *fictional* story (the real teller, the author) is not confronted with quite the same "burden of relevance" as the speaker who inserts a narrative into a conversation. It is not incumbent upon a novelist to convince a reader that the novel is appropriate reading matter at a particular moment in the reader's life. It is the reader who chooses the text and also chooses when to pick it up and put it down. The position of professional story performers is closer in this regard to that of natural narrators; story performers generally "make a pitch" for their texts—hence the *captatio benevolentiae* with which many medieval tales begin. In earlier fictional genres, before fiction became inexorably detached from its origin (producer), the burden of demonstrating the appropriateness of a text would often devolve on the fictional Speaker (implied author or narrator), who provided an "apology," a justificatory preface for the story contained in the book (see Watts 1984).

4.3.2. Current reports. Experience can also be verbalized in the form of *current reports:* eyewitness descriptions of events (e.g., sportscasts, action news coverage) in which the activities of seeing and speaking are ostensibly carried out at the same time. The now of the events being reported coincides with the now of the reporting, which is the speaker's present. The sentences of current reports carry the features [+ simultaneous] and [+ present] or [− past], signifying the simultaneity of each event (E) with the moment at which it is perceived and reported (S). Appropriately, the verbal vehicle of current reports is the PR tense. Insofar as "narration" is understood to mean narration *of past experience,* the two distinctive features of the current report form noted above would appear to disqualify it from being a form of narrative; hence the contradiction in Casparis's (1975:10) characterization of the current report as a discourse in which "an unpredictable sequence of sense impressions is *narrated simultaneously*" (my emphasis). Comrie (1976:77), however, points out that although the time reference is to the present, the discourse structure of current reports is that of a narrative (dynamic) rather than that of a description (static)—the mode normally associated with the PR in its unmarked uses.

4.3.3. Generic narratives. *Generic narratives* relate what used to be the case in the past or what normally occurs in the present and are marked for the feature [+ habitual]. Polanyi (1986) refers to these as "procedures." Developmental psycholinguists have observed that the stories elicited from young children in response to requests such as "Tell me what happened at the supermarket yesterday" are frequently generic in nature—generalized descriptions of the supermarket frame rather than specific accounts of what happened yesterday.

4.3.4. Irrealis narration. "Irrealis" is used here as a cover term to refer to verbalizations of experience that is unrealized, either because it is predicated as taking place in the future or because it is in some sense hypothetical.

The "future" category includes science fiction as well as prophetic, utopian, apocalyptic, oracular, or oneiromantic tales, all of which Todorov (1969) subsumes under the rubric of "predictive" narratives, Polanyi (1986) under "plans." There is, however, an important difference between these two types of verbalization of projected experience: in plans, which are not narratives, events are recounted in the FUT tense (at t_n in the future I will do x and at t_{n+1} I will do y, etc.); in predictive genres, although events are assumed to have future time reference, they are nonetheless reported in the PAST. In other words, they are *narrated*. All narratives, even those that refer to the future, speak of the unreal as if it were past, as if the events had actually occurred. Many modern novelists have sought to break with this convention and to cast their fiction in the PR or even FUT tense.[91] As I shall argue in chapter 8, which surveys PR-tense genres, the verbal activity involved in these genres is no longer strictly "narration." For now, suffice it to point out that the time reference of a fictional narrative is independent of the tense used to narrate it. Once a tense is mobilized as the vehicle for fictional narration, whatever temporal value it has in everyday language (its REFERENTIAL meaning) is neutralized.

Of the two irrealis categories referred to above, the larger by far is the hypothetical, for the simple reason that it includes fiction, which is considered separately below (§4.4). This category also encompasses narrations of the contents of dreams, visions, or hallucinations, which in the languages I know best typically select the IPFV PAST. Other irrealis genres select the PR. Thus a story that begins "There's this guy *WALKS* into a bar and he *SAYS* to the bartender . . ." will normally be identified as a joke [− realis], while this same sequence of events rendered in the P ("A funny thing *happened* to this guy I know the other day; he *walked* into a bar and *said* to the bartender . . .") will signify for most speakers of English that what they are about to hear is a narration of real events. Herring (1986b) points out apropos of this example that even if a joke is based on a true story, its actual occurrence in past time is subordinated to the timeless entertainment value derived from its telling and retelling. The same claim can be made for traditional oral storytelling where the tales are generally familiar; the purpose of performing them is not a REFERENTIAL one of informing an audience about events that happened, but a social and cultural one combining entertainment with an important ritual of group solidarity. The conspicuous use of the PR in these genres—as in traditional children's stories, which seem to delight their listeners all the more with each retelling—is linked to the timelessness of the stories *as entertainment*.

4.3.5. Plot summaries. The *retelling of plots* (e.g., of novels, films, operas, plays) is also predictably carried out in the PR, the typical eliciting question being similarly in the PR ("What IS *Crime and Punishment* about?"). Interestingly, the plots of television serials tend to be recounted in the P, in response to questions posed similarly in the P (e.g., "What *happened* on *Masterpiece Theatre* last week?").[92] Though verbal-visual narratives actualized via the medium of television and those actualized via film or drama are equally irrealis (fictional), the former—at least until the advent of the video-recorder—would presumably be filed in a cognitive directory labeled "over, not retrievable," which might explain their being retold in the P; films or plays, on the other hand, are thought of as available for repeated viewing and are thus filed—along with written fiction, whose inscription ensures permanence—in a directory labeled "atemporal" or "timeless," whence their retelling in the PR.

Hamburger (1973) sees the characteristic PR of plot summaries as reinforcing the essential atemporality of fiction (cf. §4.4.5). Yet this same PR is used to summarize the events of a historical person's life. An example is text XIII, a written synopsis of the major events in the life of the narrator's grandfather. This summary functions like a verbal photograph or canvas that "freezes" the (past) events of the protagonist's life, making them available for scrutiny at any moment. In other words, it renders them timeless. It is presumably in this sense that Hamburger (1973: 109) refers to the synoptic PR as "an a-temporal present tense *about ideal objects* (not reality statements)" (my emphasis). The same reasoning may be extended to the use of the PR for the chapter headings used in earlier fictional genres (e.g., "Chapter 5: Gil Blas BECOMES a man of good fortune. He MEETS an attractive person.").

4.4. Narrative fiction

With the exception of Propp (1958), whose morphology of narrative structure was conceived with reference to the folktale, narratologists concerned with the structure of artificial narrative forms have directed their attention largely to modern fiction, which some see as the paradigm form of narration.[93] The question of defining "fiction" has been the subject of a considerable debate that lies outside the scope of the present inquiry.[94] My concern is less with determining where the fictionality of a text is located (discussed briefly in §4.4.1) than with the behavior of tenses in fictional vs. nonfictional narration.

4.4.1.   The fictionality of a text has traditionally been located either in an author/composer's *intent* to create a fiction (Searle 1975, 1979), or in a contractual agreement between the text producer and its consumers to treat the discourse as fiction (Schmidt 1976). While for most modern texts this involves fairly straightforward determinations, for texts of earlier periods and/or traditional oral cultures the matter is less simple. From a typological survey of oral poetic forms, Kiparsky (1974: 19) concludes that for oral cultures, whether the content of a story is true or false and whether it is believed or not believed "are irrelevant and often unanswerable questions"; the fact-fiction opposition, insofar as it is relevant at all as a parameter for classifying narratives, is better viewed as a difference between "things told as knowledge" and "things told primarily for entertainment." While Kiparsky is correct in pointing out the questionable diacritical value of "truth" or "credibility" in the discrimination of fact from fiction, the same holds for "knowledge" and "entertainment," which, *a fortiori* in oral cultures, do not surface as discrete categories. The epic songs performed by professional singer-storytellers provided a "popular historiography" for much of medieval Europe (see Duggan 1987).

The difficulty with the proposals mentioned above is that they locate the fictionality of a text in mental attitudes of the text composer and/

or recipients, without indicating *how* those attitudes are communicated. Searle's claim that a text cannot be fictional unless its composer intends it to be so is certainly valid, but how does this intent manifest itself? Adams (1985) points out that once a writer decides that a text is to be fiction, he or she creates *a distinct pragmatic structure.* Fiction, in other words, can be identified by the text's pragmatic context (i.e., the participants in the narrative contract and their relationship to the utterances of the text), rather than by the use to which readers put the text. This will become clearer in the following section.

4.4.2.   Let us adopt the following pragmatic definition of fiction proposed by Adams (1985:10), which is based on an act that a writer performs but which is not a speech act: "The writer creates a fiction when he attributes what he writes to another speaker; . . . he attributes the performance of his speech acts to a speaker he creates." This act of transferring "origin," of attributing the text to someone else, results in the formation of an *embedded communicative context* with a fictional Speaker and Hearer (the narrator and narratee, respectively). The pragmatic structure of fiction consists in the relationship among all the language users of the text: particularly, between the writer and the fictional Speaker and Hearer, on the one hand, and the reader and the fictional Speaker and Hearer, on the other, as well as their relation to the text itself. Adams diagrams this relationship as in figure 6.

WRITER   [Speaker   (text)   Hearer]   READER

Figure 6. The pragmatic structure of fiction. After Adams 1985:12.

Everything enclosed within square brackets belongs to the embedded communicative context, which is fictional. Only the participants in uppercase belong to the real communicative context, such as it is in situations of deferred written communication.

In nonfictional narration, WRITER = Speaker and READER = Hearer within a single communicative context in which all participants are historical agents (who need not, however, be present together). In fictional narration, according to this model, there is a second-level fictional communicative context embedded into the real one; all speech acts carried out in the text refer to the embedded communicative context, that is, to the Speaker and Hearer, both of whom are fictional personae (cf. also Cohn, forthcoming).[95]

4.4.3.   An ongoing controversy among literary narratologists concerns whether narrative—in the narrow sense of written narrative fiction—conforms to the so-called communication model of language, according to which every utterance presupposes both a speaker and an addressee (= hearer). Wolfgang Kayser, Tzvetan Todorov, and Barbara Herrnstein Smith are representative of a number of literary theorists who believe that all narrative works of art by definition include a Speaker, who is the narrator. The opposite viewpoint, implicit in the theories of Emile Benveniste and Harald Weinrich (see §4.5), holds that certain features of the pragmatic context, notably the person and time of the speaker, are *not* recoverable from the linguistic features of *narrative* utterances as they are from nonnarrative utterances. This position has been argued explicitly by Käte Hamburger, S.-Y. Kuroda, and Ann Banfield, and has been used as evidence to support the position that narrative constitutes a marked use of language.

According to the extreme formulation of this position (Hamburger 1973), a text with no overt linguistic signs of a narrator (i.e., what is traditionally called third-person narration) has no speaker and thereby fails to meet one of the pragmatic conditions of communicative language. An unfortunate consequence of Hamburger's view is that first-person narration and third-person narration are assigned to different domains of language, the former to the "communication mode," the latter to the "historical mode" (Benveniste's *discours* and *histoire*, respectively), notwithstanding their being equally fictional and equally narrative.

A more moderate version of this position has been argued by Banfield (1982), on the basis of two sentence types that she sees as confined to literature (i.e., they cannot occur in interactive speech): optionally narratorless sentences and sentences of free indirect discourse. These express pure objectivity and pure subjectivity, respectively, and both, she claims, are speakerless. While, for Hamburger, fiction in a first-person voice is not narrative but a "feigned reality-statement," for Banfield narrative can include "first-person narration that addresses no one." She excludes only the second person from the narrative context.

The pragmatic definition of fiction proposed by Adams (diagramed in figure 6) obviates the difficulties encountered by both Hamburger and Banfield. According to this view, the pragmatic structure of fiction includes both a Speaker and an Addressee, not necessarily as part of the text but as part of the context. For every discourse there is a speaker, but in fiction that Speaker is fictional. In speaking the text the Speaker may refer to himself or herself (as in first-person narration) and/or to the Addressee, but need not and often does not do so (as in third-person fiction). Yet both participants are integral and necessary components of the pragmatic structure (Adams 1985: 13). Once fiction is understood in this way, Hamburger's separation of first- and third-person narration and her exclusion of the former from the category of narrative are seen as unnecessary moves. More importantly, however, the pragmatic structure of fiction obliges us to reject the claim that narrative—that is, narrative fiction—falls outside the domain of "communicative language,"[96] though there is ample linguistic evidence, nonetheless, to support the view of narrative as a grammatically and pragmatically marked category of utterance.

4.4.4. We have established that every text has a Speaker. The grammatical category of "person" comes into play in the determination of who that Speaker is—what is referred to as "narrative voice." Narration is traditionally said to be in either a first-person or a third-person voice, though the term "third-person narration" has been criticized because of its implication that the Speaker is speaking not as a first person but as a third person, which is impossible; a speaker is by definition an ego who can speak only "in the first person" (see Tamir 1976). What is conventionally understood by "third-person narration" is that the voice that speaks the text is not associated with a story participant; it may even correspond to an unpersonified textual stance. As alternatives to the traditional labels I at times use the terms "experiential" and "vicarious" narration. "Experiential" should be understood as referring to the experiences *of the narrator,* in contrast to the experiences of others, which are vicarious.[97] Moreover, experiential normally implies that the point of view from which events are recounted is that of the narrator by virtue of his or her participation in them. As we shall see in chapter 7, departures from this unmarked point of view are frequently signaled by tense-aspect shifts.

The distinction between experiential and vicarious narration cuts across the historical-fictional continuum in an interesting way (cf. Cohn, forthcoming). "Historical" is understood here in the layman's sense of referring to real events, and as such overlaps but is not synonymous with "experiential," which is limited to events in the speaker's personal history. Historical narration may be either experiential or vicarious. It is experiential if the historian was—and, more important, is shown linguistically to have been—a participant in events (e.g., the thirteenth-century French chroniclers Villehardouin and Robert of Clari, whose subjectivity so permeates their texts as to undermine their value as historical documents). This judgment obviously reflects the modern historiographic bias summed up in

Benveniste's statement that "the historian cannot historicize himself without fundamentally undermining his purport" (1959 [1966]:245). Yet for thirteenth-century France, eyewitness participation in events was virtually a requirement for historiography (Zink 1985).

With regard to discourse that is fictional, our initial impulse would be to include it under the heading of "vicarious narration," since the events reported are not being marketed as real-world experiences of the author. However, the pragmatic definition of fiction proposed above essentially frees fiction from considerations of reality or truth value, which are often impossible to determine anyway, and transfers the question of experiential vs. vicarious narration to the embedded communicative context. Insofar as events are presented *as if* they were the experience of the narrator as an historical personage, the narration is experiential—hence Hamburger's term "feigned reality statement" to characterize first-person fiction. Third-person fiction is *a priori* vicarious. The move from first- to third-person fiction that took place during the nineteenth century can be seen in part as a move to substitute the distanced and dispassionate historian for the memorialist who retraces the earlier trajectory of life from his or her present vantage. For languages with a PC/PS contrast this did not, however, entail a corresponding change in narrative tense; the memorialist's PC was never a generalized tense of written literary narration.

While in general experiential narratives show greater "involvement" than their vicarious counterparts (Eisner 1975) and are therefore more likely to be performed, skilled storytellers are capable of producing highly "involved" narrations even when the events they evoke are quite distant from their own now, so distant even as to qualify as legend; for involvement is conditioned by experiential time, which has little to do with the actual distance of events in physical time. Salient events in a narrative may be remote in real time yet proximate in the subjective experiential time of the narrator. The linguistic coding of such events, which often takes the form of a grammatically illogical but pragmatically motivated use of tenses, is discussed elsewhere (Fleischman 1989b).

4.4.5. Fiction shares with nonfictional forms of narrative the use of the P (PRET) as the basic, or unmarked, tense. Yet in the fictional mode, it has been observed, this tense loses its REFERENTIAL meaning of signaling past time. Consider the passages in (4.2a) and (4.2b), identical save for tense:

(4.2a) Howard *TURNS* with his bottle and *GOES* back through the house, to the gaunt, flowerless Victorian conservatory at the back of it. The pink sodium lights *SHINE* in through the glass roof; this *IS* now the only illumination. The place *BOOMS* with violent sound. Dancers *SWAY* their bodies. . . . The German girl in the see-through blouse *HAS started,* in a corner, with a group of men around her, to take it off. She *LIFTS* it upward, over her head, and it *WHIRLS* in the air above them for a moment . . . (Malcolm Bradbury, *The History Man,* p. 86; cited in Bache 1986:87)

(4.2b)   Howard *turned* with his bottle, and *went* back through the house, to the gaunt, flowerless Victorian conservatory at the back of it. The pink sodium lights *shone* in through the glass roof; this *was* now the only illumination. The place *boomed* with violent sound. Dancers *swayed* their bodies. . . . The German girl in the see-through blouse *had started* in a corner, with a group of men around her, to take it off. She *lifted* it upward, over her head, and it *whirled* in the air above them for a moment . . .

Bache observes that the deictic time values associated with the PRESENT and PAST tenses in the normal speech mode do not hold in these passages. The PAST does not assign narrated events to a past time sphere. Both PAST and PRESENT are nontemporal in that they do not relate situations to the moment of utterance (S), and the PAST-PRESENT contrast is effectively neutralized (1986:87). This loss of referentiality for tenses, along with other related criteria, has led a number of theoreticians to the position that fiction—and its PAST tense—are atemporal (Hamburger 1973; Weinrich 1973; Sternberg 1978). If the PAST in fiction is not temporal, then what is its function?

Reflecting on the PASSÉ SIMPLE of French, Roland Barthes writes (1967:30): "allowing as it does an ambiguity between temporality and causality, [this tense] calls for a sequence of events, that is, for an intelligible narrative." For Barthes, the PASSÉ SIMPLE embodies the two defining primes of narrative textuality: temporal sequence and logical cohesion (causality). A similar view may be inferred from Weinrich's insistence that the PASSÉ COMPOSÉ, which he finds lacking in sequentiality, can never fully replace the PS.

For Weinrich, as for Hamburger, the function of the P tense in fiction is what I would classify as an EXPRESSIVE function: marking events as "fictional"—hence outside of time. (Alternatively we might view this function as TEXTUAL: P marks the *discourse* in which the events are narrated as "fiction.") Weinrich concedes, however, the "narrative tenses" (as he defines them, cf. §4.5.2) cannot by themselves distinguish between a historical (past) and a fictional (timeless) world. The fact that P is the unmarked tense of both types of narration would seem to undermine any claim that its pragmatic function is to mark a discourse as expressly fictional. It seems more reasonable to suggest that the function of the P in fiction is rather to suggest verisimilitude. The P endows a fictional discourse with an historical "as if": "let us pretend for the duration of this textual transaction that such and such events occurred in some past world." What licenses the "as if" is the fact that the P is the prototypical tense of *realis, historical* narration. Recounting the dilemma of eighteenth-century novelists responding to the new challenge of writing in prose, Bronzwaer (1970:42) comments, "in a nutshell, the question was how to reconcile the preterite, traditionally the vehicle of historical narration, with a fictive story that had, when all was said and done, not really happened."

In connection with the claim that fiction and the P tense in fiction are nontemporal, Ricoeur (1985:98) ponders the question of why the grammatical form of the P is retained if its referential meaning is abolished. His answer is entirely consonant with, indeed predictable from, the pragmatic structure of fiction.

As stated above, all speech acts in a fictional text relate to the embedded communication context; the here-and-now of the speaker (S), which provides the deictic anchor for all utterances, is that of the fictional Speaker. As Ricoeur puts it (1985:98), "Every story is told *in the past* for the voice that tells it" (my emphasis). From the standpoint of the reader (or listener) participation in a contract of narrative fiction entails an acceptance, for the duration of that contract, that the events reported by the narrating voice belong to the past of that voice—what Ricoeur calls the "as if past." Once it is understood that all deictic operations in a fictional narration refer to the embedded communicative context, we have a compelling motivation for use of the P tense. If fiction were really a nontemporal discourse, as some have claimed, its logical grammatical vehicle would be the PR, whose basic meaning is atemporality, or timelessness. An important presupposition of the preceding statement is that *the pragmatic functions of tense-aspect categories (often referred to as "extended" or "secondary" meanings) are inherently motivated.* Just as the P is not randomly chosen as the unmarked narrating tense of fiction, neither is use of the PR in the passage in (4.2a) arbitrary. The HP of modern fiction is taken up in chapter 8. For now, suffice it to say that the effect Bradbury seeks to convey in the passage in (4.2a)—that the narrator (= Speaker) is reporting on the activities of the conservatory as he perceives them at that moment—is directly a function of temporal and aspectual properties of the PR in ordinary (nonnarrative) language.

4.5. Modes of discourse: "Storytelling" and "communication"

Among theoreticians who have claimed a special linguistic status for narrative, the most influential have been Emile Benveniste and Harald Weinrich, whose typological models frequently serve as a point of departure for discussion. As these typologies are by now familiar, I shall limit myself to points specifically relevant to the present inquiry.

Benveniste (1959) and Weinrich (1973) have each identified a special domain of linguistic performance, which I will refer to generically as the "storytelling mode," that differs in certain respects from the mode of ordinary verbal exchange, which for lack of a better term I call the "communication mode." Benveniste labels these modes respectively *histoire* and *discours*, Weinrich *erzählte Welt* and *besprochene Welt* (conventionally translated as "narrative" and "commentative"). The opposition between the two modes of discourse is founded on grammatical considerations involving the categories of tense and person and was formulated in both cases with reference to the grammar of modern French, whose two PFV PAST tenses, the PASSÉ SIMPLE (PS) and PASSÉ COMPOSÉ (PC), stand in a unique and not uncontroversial relationship to one another. One cannot apply these models, *as formulated*, to other languages or even to earlier stages of French; adjustments must be made in accord with the oppositions available in the verbal system of the language in question.[98]

4.5.1. Histoire *and* discours.
For Benveniste (1959 [1966]:239), *histoire* has now become restricted to the written language and is invoked for "the *narration* of *past events*" (his emphasis) in which no linguistic traces of a speaker appear. This definition calls for clarification in light of certain misinterpretations to which it has given rise. First, the distinction between *discours* and *histoire* is not synonymous with that between spoken and written language; while the historical mode is actualized only in writing, the communication mode can occur in either spoken or written form. Thus a text such as the theft narrative recounted by Lorenzo da Ponte (appendix 2, text V), notwithstanding its written composition, would be assigned to *discours*, for reasons that will become apparent. Benveniste insists that in *histoire* all marks of speaker subjectivity are expunged. Excluded therefore are all "autobiographical" linguistic forms, in particular first- and second-person deictics. But he acknowledges—a point that has often been glossed over—that in *fictional* narration first-person forms can and often do occur (1959 [1966]:244n). Only in

the discourse of history *sensu strictu* is there no linguistically identifiable narrator mediating between the story-world and the reader; only there do events appear to speak themselves. Sentences of *discours,* on the other hand, presuppose both a speaker and an addressee and are ostensibly uttered with an intention on the part of the speaker to influence the addressee in some way or at least to add to his or her knowledge.

The prototypical tense of *histoire,* according to Benveniste, is the PS, which is also the only tense excluded from *discours*—hence its META-LINGUISTIC function as a marker of this mode of discourse. Alongside the PS in *histoire* are the IMP, PLP, FUT-OF-P,[99] and marginally the past counterparts of the "prospective" forms (*il allait/devait faire*). By contrast, *discours* permits all tense-aspect categories except the PS, though it operates principally via the PR, FUT, and PERF, all of which are excluded from *histoire.* The IMP straddles the two modes. By the PR Benveniste refers primarily to the "PR cotemporal with the now" (the minus-interpretation) and excludes the HP, an *"artifice de style"* (1959 [1966] : 245*n*) confined to *histoire.* By PERF he intends principally the PC, in both its PRET and PERF functions, but also the FUT PERF—in other words, the perfective/anterior counterparts of PR and FUT (expressing both aspectual completion and temporal anteriority).

Benveniste points out that within a text that qualifies as *histoire,* the narrator can move in and out of storytelling mode by simply shifting from one set of tenses to the other; that is, the labels *discours* and *histoire* do not apply to texts in blanket fashion, but to individual sentences. Each time directly reported speech or evaluative commentary is introduced into narration, the text shifts at that moment from the storytelling mode to the communication mode. The type of commentary Benveniste has in mind that moves a text from *histoire* to *discours* is what Labov (1972) has referred to as *external evaluation*—the narrator steps out of the diegetic world and comments as an "I-speaking-now" on some element of it. With *internal evaluation,* as we shall see in chapter 5, the text can remain in the storytelling mode and events continue to "speak for themselves."

Benveniste acknowledges that the activity of narration can be carried out in either *histoire* or *discours.* Precisely because narration is possible in either mode, he is careful to point out (1959 [1966] : 242*n*) that what he is referring to in his discussion of tenses are "tenses of historical narration" (*temps du récit historique*) and not "narrative tenses" (*temps narratifs*). He clearly recognized the ambiguity of the latter term, though his caveat has not prevented the anticipated misunderstandings. In modern French both the PS and PC are "narrative tenses," albeit operative in different modes:

the PS is the unmarked tense for narration in *histoire*, the PC for narration in *discours*. In this regard each has a METALINGUISTIC function of signaling that particular mode of discourse. Natural narratives (e.g., texts I and II in appendix 2) would be assigned by Benveniste not to *histoire* but to *discours*. On this point he is in agreement with Weinrich, who likewise excludes naturally occurring narrations from the storytelling mode.

4.5.2. Erzählte Welt *and* besprochene Welt.

Weinrich (1973:304) states that the story given in appendix 2 as text II gives the impression of being "badly narrated," an impression that derives from its "chaotic temporal sequencing." By this he is referring to the relatively high ratio of "heterogeneous" transitions (shifts from a "narrative" to a "commentative" tense or vice versa) to "homogeneous" transitions (continuity of tenses in the same mode). For Weinrich "narrative" tenses in French include the PS, IMP, PLP, and FUT-OF-P, "commentative" tenses the PR, PC, and FUT. He calculates that text II contains sixty-six heterogeneous to forty-eight homogeneous transitions, thereby violating what he considers to be a prime condition of "textuality": a relative predominance of homogeneous transitions. Weinrich's more rigid distribution of tense-aspect categories between the two modes (no overlap, at least for event tenses) and his insistence on homogeneous transitions as a condition for cohesive textuality suggest that grammars have a built-in semiotic feature whose function is to signal "this discourse is speech" or "this discourse is narration." Hence the supposed infelicity he perceives in tense shifts from one "speech attitude" (his term) to the other.

Weinrich acknowledges, however, that the insertion of commentative tenses into narrative text (what he calls "tense metaphors") can fulfill an EXPRESSIVE function, which derives from the [± tension] feature (*Spannheit*) that founds his contrast between the two modes. Commentary is characterized by a tension or involvement (*gespannte Haltung*) of the participants in the speech act, narrative by a relaxation of tension, or detachment (*entspannte Haltung*), resulting from the fact that the speech-act participants are not explicitly implicated in the discourse. If novelists choose to make their novels exciting or thrilling (*spannend*) through "tense metaphors," this is a mechanism of compensation: that is, the use of commentative tenses, which are marked for the involvement and immediacy of the [+ tense] mode, to a degree counterbalances the lack of tension inherent to the narrative mode. In choosing these tenses a narrator narrates *as if* commenting (1973:35).

An important point Weinrich raises, which explains his feeling that spontaneous oral narratives lack cohesion (textuality), is that the French PS carries a feature of [+ sequential] that the PC, its counterpart in the spoken language, does not. Like many commentators on the French tense system, Weinrich insists that the disappearance of the PS from the spoken language has not been entirely compensated for by the PC, given that the latter necessarily carries a link to the speaker's here-and-now that the PS does not. The temporal anchor point (R) for the PC is always the speaker's now (R = S), while that of each PS verb in narration is the past now of the event previously narrated in the sequence (see figure 8 below), none of which is predicated in relation to S (but see *n*100). To paraphrase Weinrich's argument (1973 : 306ff.) in the terminology used here, a series of PSs creates in and of itself a coherent text, whose defining features are sequentiality and logical causality. In oral narration or in a text like Camus's *The Stranger* (see §7.7.1), from which the PS is excluded, the substitute event tenses, PR and PC, cannot by themselves provide sequential cohesion; hence there occurs a proliferation of adverbial sequencers such as *puis* (then) and *alors* (so). Adverbs of this kind, Weinrich claims, can superimpose the property of sequentiality on a string of utterances, thereby bridging the gaps between the isolated, nonsequential clauses in which events are reported by the PC. Grafted onto a sequence of PCs, these adverbs provide the textual cohesion that the PC cannot convey by itself (1973 : 310f.).[100]

Though Weinrich does not recognize the PC as a canonical tense of narration, he acknowledges that in certain genres (natural narrative) or certain texts (*The Stranger*) it may be pressed into service as a narrative tense. Where it occurs in conjunction with other commentative tenses (i.e., in "homogeneous" sequences), the PC carries out its normal functions in nonnarrative language. Where it alternates with narrative tenses such as the IMP and PLP ("heterogeneous" sequences), it functions narratively— which is not, however, to place it on an equal footing with the PS, given the need for adjunct markers in the form of temporal adverbs to provide the sequentiality necessary to produce cohesive text.

For Weinrich, natural narratives or a text like *The Stranger* preserve a sense of telling a story "as if in commentative mode" (1973 : 311), by virtue of the fact that their event tenses are PC and PR. Moreover, the difference between storytelling in the narrative and in the commentative mode concerns only the tenses used to report *events:* PS in the narrative mode, PC/PR in the commentative mode. Tenses of description and of other *noneventive* collateral material remain the same: IMP and PLP. What is essential to Weinrich's analysis of tense usage in narrative is the marking of this discourse contrast, which in many recent discussions of information saliency is referred to as *foreground* vs. *background* (a different approach to *grounding* is put forth in chapter 6). Weinrich is explicit in his insistence that the primary function of the PS/IMP contrast (or PR-PC/IMP contrast in spoken narration) is a TEXTUAL one: *la mise en relief* (1973:115). The PS (or its commentative analogues) reports the essential events of the story, while the IMP reports supporting descriptive material. For Weinrich, then, the TEXTUAL function of the PS/IMP is basic, the REFERENTIAL function (contrasting PFV and IPFV aspect) secondary. Among linguists who have explored this opposition in natural narrative, Hopper (1979a, 1979b, 1982a) has sought similarly to locate the ontogenesis of the PFV/IPFV contrast at the TEXTUAL level.

As stated above, for Weinrich texts produced in conversational storytelling do not constitute legitimate "narration": they are but "impoverished narrative fragments of minimal substance, scarcely distinguishable from the commentative continuum" (1973:301). Like Walter Benjamin (1969), Weinrich is skeptical that bona fide storytelling exists today anywhere outside the domain of fiction and nostalgically laments the decline of an *oral* narrative literature of the kind that existed in the Middle Ages. Regrettably, Weinrich has failed to recognize certain striking linguistic similarities between the oral narratives of the Middle Ages and the "depreciated narrative fragments" that constitute, for him, natural narration. Crucial among these similarities—and what distinguishes these narrative situations from that of the modern novel—is the fact that in both natural narrative and medieval story performance the speaker and hearer(s) are linguistically implicated *in the text,* and not just present in the pragmatic context (see §4.6).

4.5.3. Despite apparent similarities, the discourse typologies of Benveniste and Weinrich differ in important respects. The differential assignment of tenses to the storytelling and communication modes has already been noted. A further difference concerns the role of the narrating ego. For Weinrich, the status of the speaker in narrative and commentative discourse remains the same; what changes is the "speech attitude," i.e., the subjective relationship that the narrator establishes with the content of the text and seeks in turn to communicate to the addressee(s). We might characterize this relationship in terms of the feature "involvement." For Benveniste, on the other hand, it is not a question of the speaker's subjective relationship to the content of the text, but of the presence or absence in the text of formal marks of a speaking subject. Whereas, for Weinrich, the speaker in the storytelling mode is [− involved], for Benveniste, "no one speaks." Banfield (1982 : 271) connects this speakerless discourse directly to writing: "writing makes possible the development of a narrative style where the act of production, of performance, leaves no trace in linguistic structure."

Reacting to claims such as these for a speakerless discourse, Ricoeur (1985) ponders whether it is possible for past events (real or imagined) to appear on the horizon of a story without anyone speaking in any way, or whether instead the perceived absence of a narrator from the historical mode is not simply the result of a strategy whereby the narrator "makes himself absent" from the narrative (1985 : 64)—a view closer to Weinrich's. For narrative historiography, where presumably speaker/narrator = historian, this should suffice. Narrative fiction, as we have seen, operates a division between a real speaker (the author) and a fictional surrogate inside the text (the narrator). The former, like the historian, always "makes himself absent," while the latter frequently injects subjectivity into linguistic structure.

4.5.4. Neither the model of Benveniste nor that of Weinrich is ideally suited to medieval vernacular storytelling. In the first place, the language of these texts, which are functionally "narrative," is nonetheless a "communicative" language (cf. §3.3); all tenses belong to the mode of interactive speech. Second, the texts are all directly or indirectly products of oral-aural communication, with overt linguistic traces of their origin in performance (real or purported). Yet they are undeniably narrative, like their counterparts in everyday conversation, which similarly pose problems for theorists like Benveniste and Weinrich. As noted above, both concede that narration can take place in the communication mode, a fact that would appear to weaken the basis for the opposition.

Despite these difficulties in generalizing the two models, the basic idea that languages do not treat narrating and asserting, or narrating and referring, in the same way is linguistically well founded and is supported by cross-language data. It is also true across languages that narration selects certain tenses to perform certain expressly narrative tasks. Some or all of these tenses may also be used in the communication mode, but their functions will not always be the same. In other words, *it is the ways in which tense and person function in narrative, and not the presence or absence of certain tenses or grammatical persons, that justifies the claim here that narrative is a distinctive category of linguistic performance.* Only in narration, for example, can the PR tense acquire a temporal value of "past"; only in narration can the English simple PR or the French IMP receive a punctual interpretation. Furthermore, many narrative functions override considerations of speech vs. writing, literature vs. conversation, history vs. fiction, or first-person (experiential) vs. third-person (vicarious) voice. All of this suggests the desirability of retaining a basic distinction between "storytelling" and "communication," while broadening the scope of the storytelling mode to encompass, in addition to written fiction, also spoken and experiential narratives with explicit linguistic traces of their origin as speech-acts.

4.6. Linguistic marks of storytelling

The narrative stance of the modern novel, which has been defined by such theoreticians as Barthes and Blanchot in terms of the (METALINGUISTIC) use of the PS, nonpersonal narration (what Barthes, following Benveniste, refers to as the "third person of the novel"), and represented thought, is quite different from the narrative stance of medieval story performance, even of genres such as the epic, which often give the impression of "singing themselves," without a narrative consciousness or a composer's guiding hand (Jauss 1963).

4.6.1. *Signs of the Speaker.*

In performance texts from the Middle Ages, as in the narrative forms of any oral culture, the voice of the Speaker is necessarily expressed through the voice of a real person—the performer, who generally makes a virtue of the fact that his presence cannot be concealed. Linguistic marks of this Speaker (first-person deictics and tenses of the communicative mode) are frequent, as shown in the following examples, chosen randomly from the Old French/ Old Occitan corpus:

(4.3) Mes or *parlons* de cez qui furent, / si *leissons* cez qui ancor durent. "But *let us now speak* of those from bygone days and *let us leave off* talking of those still alive." (*Yvain*, 29–30)

(4.4) Es *eu* per s'amor *tornarai* / A Jaufre, e-l *desliurarai* / De la presun un es entratz. "And out of love for him [the King of Aragon] *I shall return* to [my tale of] Jaufre and *I shall deliver him* from the prison into which he has gotten himself." (*Jaufre*, 2631ff.)

(4.5) Mil Sarrazins i descendent a piet / E a cheval sunt .xl. millers. *Men escïentre* ne.s osent aproismar . . . "A thousand Saracens go down there on foot, and 40,000 more are on their mounts: *as I perceive it,* they don't dare approach . . . ." (*Roland*, 2071–2073) [101]

(4.6) Mas *no-m qual dir, a mon semblan* / los gais envits que chascus fai, / Mais aitan sivals ne *dirai* . . . "But *it doesn't behoove me, I don't think,* to tell about the pleasurable moves each lover makes; but this much *I will tell* . . ." (*Flamenca,* 6496ff.)

Linguistic traces of a Speaker/narrator also occur in the form of statements like those in (4.7) and (4.8), where the deictic adverb "like this" marks out a space in the text presumably filled in performance by a gesture:

(4.7) . . . el leon quando lo vio *assí* envergonço ante mio Çid la cabeça premio y el rostro finco. "The lion, when he saw him, humbled himself just *like this:* he bowed his head before the Cid and lowered his face." (*Cid,* 2298f. [IX:41–44], noted in Walsh, forthcoming; cf. also IX:58)

(4.8) . . . el coraçon le salta, *assí,* a menudillo. ". . . her heart leaps, *like this,* over and over." (*Libro de buen amor,* 810c)

In performance narration the silencing of the Speaker is a pragmatic impossibility. Though medieval genres exhibit differing degrees of distance between narrators and their material (see Pickens 1979; Fleischman 1983b), even the most objective and distanced stance—that of the historian—cannot be equated with that of the modern novel, in which the narrator can effectively disappear (i.e., delete all self-reference).

One might be tempted to see a precursor of the impersonal novelistic stance in the conspicuous *anonymity* of so many medieval texts, produced in a culture in which the notion of literary property had not yet emerged. But anonymity refers to an author, and even in texts where no author claims to be speaking, the physical person, voice, and gestures of the Speaker-performer cancel out any possibility of a disembodied narrative voice. Even where a Speaker claims to be the composer (e.g., "Juan Ruiz," the Spanish equivalent of John Smith, who claims authorship of the *Book of Good Love*), such statements are often of dubious reliability (on the complex question of autobiography in the Middle Ages, see Zumthor 1975; Zink 1985).

4.6.2. *Signs of the addressee.* With the exception of the epistolary novel and the storytelling mode known as *skaz* (see §4.6.3 below), modern fiction generally excludes explicit reference to the Hearer; this does not mean that fictional texts are not *recipient-designed* with both Hearer and Reader in mind, and one can often reconstruct the

"implied reader" on the basis of assertions and presuppositions in the text. There have also been narrative experiments which purport to reflect the Hearer's point of view. Michel Butor's *Second Thoughts* (*La Modification*) begins:

(4.9) Vous avez mis le pied gauche sur la rainure de cuivre, et de votre épaule droite vous essayez en vain de pousser un peu plus le panneau coullissant.

Vous vous introduisez par l'étroite ouverture en vous frottant contre ses bords, puis, votre valise. . . . Vous la soulevez et vous sentez vos muscles et vos tendons . . .

You have placed your left foot on the grooved brass sill, and with your right shoulder you are trying in vain to push the sliding panel a little wider open.

You are edging your way in through the narrow opening, brushing against sides, then your suitcase. . . . You are lifting it up and you feel your muscles and tendons . . . (*La Modification*, translation adapted)

Butor attempts to sustain this perspective—a virtual mirror image of the current report—throughout. But such texts are a rarity in written literature.[102]

For oral literature, the pragmatic situation is radically altered by the physical presence of a second person who typically combines the functions assigned in fiction to Hearer and Reader. We are no longer dealing simply with stories but with storytelling events. Oral cultures are in general empathetic and participatory rather than objectively distanced (cf. Ong 1982b); oral modes of expression, whether spoken or written, focus on contextualized participant interaction in contrast to the decontextualized, nonparticipant-oriented presentation of material in literate modes (Traugott and Romaine 1985). More crucial in oral storytelling are *recipient design* and *local occasioning*. "Recipient design" refers to the adaptation of a story to one's beliefs about listeners' beliefs about and knowledge of the story-world (this accounts for the fact that in traditional tales fragmented chronology, ellipses in the plot, cataphoric references, and leaps in time are not problematic).[103] "Local occasioning" refers to a demonstration of how the story relates—is locally occasioned—to the point in the discourse at which it is inserted (cf. van Dijk 1975; Polanyi 1981).

Local occasioning may be less of a concern in poetic or folkloristic oral texts than it is in natural narratives, inasmuch as the communicative context is given, so to speak: listeners have voluntarily come together in conventionalized settings to hear stories performed—a state of affairs that virtually eliminates the "burden of relevance" incumbent upon natural narrators, who must demonstrate the pertinence of their stories to the current topic of conversation. Performance narratives in oral cultures are part of a communication mechanism whereby coded messages are relayed to a receptive audience well acquainted with the images evoked by the artist (Scheub 1977:363). The conspicuous repetitions (see Fleischman 1986b, 1989a), cataphoric references (see §§5.3, 8.4.1), and belabored stanzaic transitions of the *chansons de geste* (§6.5) may thus be seen as poetic devices for creating solidarity and establishing a rapport between poet-singers and their audiences.

The most conspicuous linguistic marks of the addressee in medieval narratives are the frequent minstrel formulas of direct address such as Old Spanish *sabet* (you know),[104] Old French *sachiez* (know!), *podeiz saveir* (you may know), *es vus, afévos* (look! before you is . . .), and *or oez/or entendez* (hear now)—subliminal punctuation whose METALINGUISTIC function is to remind listeners of their active engagement in a storytelling event. Analogous examples of sociocentric elements could easily be cited; there is scarcely a text in the medieval Romance repertoire in which they do not occur.[105]

4.6.3. *Skaz.*

4.6.3. *Skaz.*   The linguistic traces of the second person discussed thus far have all been extradiegetic: direct addresses by the storyteller to the audience, with time reference to the now of the telling. By contrast, literary theorists have identified a particular type of first-person narration that imitates the form of direct speech to the extent that *within diegesis* a fictional storyteller addresses a tale to an audience whose presence is linguistically inscribed in the tale along with the voice of its teller. The Russian formalists have labeled this style of storytelling *skaz,* the Russian word for "speech" (cf. Bakhtin 1971). As the formalists have defined it, a story told in *skaz* is not itself speech, but gives the illusion, in writing, of storytelling occurring in an interactive context.

Adapting the model for the pragmatic structure fiction given in figure 6, we can represent the structure of *skaz* by embedding an additional communicative context between the Speaker-Hearer and the "text" (*sjuzhet*) itself, as in figure 7. In theory, the embedding of communicative contexts could be carried out in infinite regress—the *mise en abîme,* though not without posing serious obstacles to the reader or listener's ability to follow the story.

A number of medieval narratives fit the *skaz* model. In so-called frame-narratives such as Boccaccio's *Decameron* or Chaucer's *Canterbury Tales* the

WRITER or
COMPOSER
[Speaker₁ {speaker₂ (text) hearer₂} Hearer₁]
READER or
LISTENERS

Figure 7. The pragmatic structure of *skaz.*

communication frame is often little more than a unifying device for a heterogeneous collection of tales. More interesting is the thirteenth-century bawdy tale of "Castia-gilos" ("The Jealous Husband Punished") attributed to the Catalan troubadour Ramon Vidal de Besalù. The "text" of "Castia-gilos" is set into a multilevel frame that includes its performance context. It is impossible to know whether Ramon Vidal actually designed the story as *skaz,* or whether the text that has come down might not represent a transcription, by a scribe in attendance at Vidal's performance, of what was originally speech—the storytelling event—in which Vidal's introduction (as Speaker₁ [= COMPOSER]) as well as the interactive discourse between speaker₂ (an anonymous *performer*) and hearer₂ (listeners at the court of King Alfonso of Castile) have been retained. In either case, "Castia-gilos" offers precious documentation of medieval story performance as it was actually carried out.[106]

4.7. Tense and aspect as metalinguistic signals of narrative genres

From the issues raised in this chapter together with the information on tense-aspect categories provided in chapter 1, certain inferences may be drawn concerning tense, aspect, and narrative genre.

First, it appears that as part of their linguistic competence adult speakers possess a typology of narrative forms. The most basic divisions of this typology might be along the lines *realis* vs. *irrealis* (real vs. hypothetical, fiction vs. nonfictional), and *time bound* vs. *timeless,* or *accessible* vs. *ephemeral* (whether or not a story is still available—through writing, audio or video recording, or a society's collective memory), though these oppositions are not always clear-cut. Second, there appear to be grammatical features, including tense-aspect categories, that correlate predictably with these narrative primes. Relying on our (unconscious) knowledge of these correlations, which are culture-bound, skillful narrators can use them for particular purposes—for example, the joketeller alluded to above who adopts the PAST tense so that listeners will be inclined to interpret his tale as a true story. Narration in the PRET, the unmarked tense of the narrative mode, correlates with stories that are or purport to be *realis* (including conventional fiction, which purports to be someone's experience) and *time-bound.* Genres that choose a basic reporting tense other than the PRET tend to be *irrealis, accessible,* and/or *timeless.*[107]

The IPFV aspect of the PR and IMP enables these tenses to represent past experience as if it were occurring, unmediated by the reflective consciousness of the experiencer. In many languages the IMP is used for irrealis forms such as children's make-believe games or dream narrations. The few IMPs that occur in *Roland* are appropriately concentrated in the dream visions (vv. 719–720, 726, 2556–2560). Both the IMP and the PR are used for genres that refer to a legendary or mythical past (e.g., the Sanskrit *Ṛgvedas,* the Tamil Puranic stories), and the epic universally. As Gonda (1956 : 25) observes, "In mythical thought chronology is unessential. Mythical reality is timeless; it is, or was, before all times, 'in the beginning,' as well as actual, and present. Though timeless, it can always be repeated and represented here and now." Compare in this regard Goldin's description of the *laisse* unit in *Roland* (1978 : 42): "The formulaic laisse immobilized time, transformed it into an edifice . . . in which all the heirs of Charlemagne were assembled. Through . . . the singing of the song, their forebears became their companions, the empire of their descendants was restored. Charlemagne was *nostre emperere.*" In mythical or legendary genres there is often no sense of the past being differentiated from the present. The PR tense in its zero-interpretation is thus ideally suited to representing the timeless quality of epic. This connection is developed in chapter 8.

Legendary material, particularly when it is local legend, may also be related in the PC. Boyer (1985a : 79f.) reports on a French radio interview in which a speaker-narrator recounts the origins of a locally popular legend about "the-man-who-killed-a-horse-with-one-punch." The basic tense of the narration is the PS, albeit with frequent shifts into the PC. Boyer interprets these shifts as a METALINGUISTIC signal by the speaker that he is no longer telling a *story* (PS) but marking the fact that this is a *legend* (PC), which has come out of the past (where it might have remained buried) and continues to live in the present in the *memory* of a particular group.[108] In light of what has been said above about the PS and PC in French, this speaker's (no doubt unconscious) tense alternations are entirely motivated.

In this chapter I have sought to establish the profile of narrative as a category of linguistic performance, to situate it within a typology of discourse forms for translating experience into language, and to identify parameters and oppositions relevant to a typology of narrative forms. In the next chapter we shall see how certain of these parameters and oppositions come into play in the linguistic structure of narratives.

5 The Linguistic Structure of Narrative

The storyteller takes what he tells from experience—his own and that reported by others. And he in turn makes it the experience of those who are listening to his tale.

(BENJAMIN, "THE STORYTELLER")

Part I. Temporal Structure

5.1. Speaker-now and story-now

Narratives are intrinsically structured with two time frames: the time of the telling of the story and the time during which the events of the story are assumed to have taken place. I refer to these respectively as *speaker-now* and *story-now*.[109] Each of these time frames has a set of tense-aspect categories normally associated with it—the tenses of communication and narration, respectively, actualized via different forms in different languages. All tense-aspect categories are normally associated with speaker-now, save for any explicitly marked as NARR; however, the primary speaker-based tenses are PR, FUT, PAST (PFV and IPFV), PERF, and their perfective/anterior counterparts. Story-now is normally restricted to categories of the past (P—PFV and IPFV, PLP, FUT-OF-P), an entailment of the definition of narration. This is not to say that speaker-based tenses are excluded from narration. The point is rather that when they occur in narration they can refer either to speaker-now or story-now, and the difference is important. When their time reference is to speaker-now, they retain the temporal (REFERENTIAL) meanings they normally have in ordinary language, though, as we shall see in the following paragraphs, their contribution to the text can also be pragmatic. When their time reference is to story-now, their contribution to the discourse is always something other than temporal location. It is the nontemporal meanings that are of primary concern in this book.

5.1.1.   *The generic* PR.   The PR may refer to speaker-
now or to story-now, or to neither specifically, in the case of the generic or
temporally neutral PR (zero-interpretation). In examples (5.1)–(5.4), taken
from the texts in appendix 2, the italicized clauses contain generic PRs that
extend the temporal scope of the respective predicates to include all relevant time moments, both within the story world (local) and beyond it
(global):

(5.1)   . . . so we were in this car, in this—an' we were in Allentown, *it's real
dinky an' it's like real hick town off o' Allentown.*   (I : 18–21)

(5.2)   . . . c'était un petit chemin, c'était vraiment un petit chemin. La *route est
à peine . . . elle est . . . mais elle est pas très fréquentée . . .* ". . . it was a pretty
small road, [I mean,] it was really a small road. *The road is hardly . . . it's . . . but
hardly anybody uses it.*"   (II : 64–68)

(5.3)   . . . hablóle en algarabía, *como aquel que bien la sabe.*   "He spoke to him
in Arabic *like one who knows it well.*"   (VII : 47–48)

(5.4)   . . . pues que el cuerpo sin el alma *solo un dinero no vale.*   ". . . for a body
without a soul *is worth not a penny.*"   (VII : 57–58)

Generic PRs, whether global or local, provide a means for injecting evaluation into a narration, generally of the external variety (see §5.5.2).

5.1.2.   *The speaker's* PR.   As stated above, tenses in
a narrative that refer to speaker-now do not have a REFERENTIAL function
of establishing time reference within the story-world; their functions relate
generally to the pragmatic context of the narration. They often fulfill a *phatic*
function of calling attention to the channel of communication (Jakobson
1960)—in the case of medieval narratives, reminding the audience that a
tale is being performed, as in (5.5) and (5.6):

(5.5)   Unas novas *vos vuelh contar* que auzi dezir a un joglar . . .   "A new tale *I
want to tell you* which I heard a minstrel recite."   ("Castia-gilos," 1–2)

(5.6)   Mas *no-m qual dir,* a mon semblan, los gais envits que chascus fai, mais
aitan sivals ne *dirai . . .*   "*But it isn't appropriate for me to tell,* I don't think, of
the pleasurable moves each one makes. But this much *I will tell.*"

(Flamenca, 6496ff.)

Tenses anchored to speaker-now, particularly when coupled with second-person pronouns, may also have a *conative* function of underscoring the interactive dimension of narrative performance by appearing to draw listeners into the diegetic universe. Consider the examples in (5.7) and (5.8):

(5.7) Aucassins ala par le forest . . . *ne cuidies mie* que les ronces et les espines l'esparnaiscent. "Aucassin wandered through the forest . . . *don't think for a moment* that he was spared the brambles and the thorns."

(*AN*, 24:1–3; cf. also III:12ff.)

(5.8) Allí hablaron sus doncellas, *bien oiréis lo que diran.* "Then her ladies in waiting spoke up, *listen well now to what they will say.*"   (VIII:23–24)[110]

In each case the narrator momentarily steps out of story time to address listeners directly. Not infrequently the phatic and conative functions go together, as in the minstrel formulas discussed in §4.6.2.

5.1.3. The diegetic PR. The fact that speaker-based tenses are NON-REFERENTIAL when used in narration (they do not refer to the events of the story) has particular consequences for the PR, the most prominent of all speaker-based tenses found in narrative texts. The "PR cotemporal with now" (minus-interpretation), as in (5.5) and (5.6), does not occur in narrative diegesis; it occurs exclusively in commentative sentences outside the story proper and its functions are pragmatic. While the functions of the PR anchored to story-now (plus-interpretation) are also pragmatic, this PR occurs only in diegetic sentences, and its functions are pragmatic with regard to the story itself rather than to the speech-act participants and context. If we substitute a P for an HP or NP, the semantic interpretation remains unchanged; however, substituting a P for a PR cotemporal with now (e.g., those in [5.5] or [5.6] above) does change the semantic interpretation.

5.2. Retrospective discourse and prospective time

The "retrospective vision" of narration as a mode of utterance follows logically from two propositions that have now been established: (a) every text has a speaker, and (b) every act of narration involves two temporal planes, the present of the speaker (and hearer) and the past of narrated events.[111] In terms of Reichenbach's tense model this means that a speaker looks *back* on an experience and configures it into a sequence of events (Es) viewed from the vantage of his or her present (S), which serves (directly or indirectly) as the temporal reference point (R) for those events. With this formula in mind, consider the following definition of the linguistic (temporal) structure of narrative: "A sentence occurs in a narrative context if the temporal point of reference (in Reichenbach's sense) is determined by the point in time at which the last event related in the preceding context took place" (Dahl 1985:112). If we imagine a time line that moves from left to right, with the past on the left and the future on the right, what Dahl is saying is that the temporal structure of narrative involves a prospective movement along that time line, starting from the left and moving *forward* in time, as each E in the sequence serves to establish the R for the next. This is diagramed in figure 8. The diagram models the minimal narrative given in (5.9), consisting of three clauses each containing a prototypical narrative event.

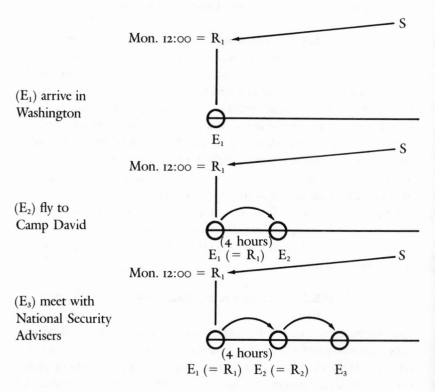

Figure 8. The temporal structure of narrative.

(5.9)   President Reagan *arrived back in Washington* (E_1) at noon on Monday. Four hours later he *flew to Camp David* (E_2) where he *met with National Security advisers* (E_3).

The R for E_1, Reagan's arrival in Washington, is established by the adverb "at noon on Monday," which is in turn located in relation to S. Only at this point does Dahl's definition become relevant, since a minimum of two clauses are required for a narrative. The R for E_2, Reagan's flight to Camp David, is provided by E_1 (E_2 is said to occur four hours after E_1). E_2 then provides the R for E_3, Reagan's meeting with National Security advisers, though there is no temporal adverb corresponding to this R; its occurrence after E_2 is inferred from *iconic sequence* (see §5.3) together with our knowledge of the story-world (in this particular world presidential conferences are often held at Camp David).

Although the temporal orientation of this discourse is *prospective* (i.e., the linear movement of the text follows the order of the events), the perspective on these events nonetheless remains *retrospective;* that is, all Es are viewed in retrospect from the vantage point of S. Before attempting to resolve this seeming paradox, however, I offer a demonstration that the perspective of figure 8 and the mini-narrative it models are in fact retrospective.

If we substitute for the adverb "four hours later" in (5.9) its "prospective" synonym "in four hours," the result is problematic:

(5.10)   President Reagan arrived back in Washington at noon on Monday (E_1). *In four hours* he flew to Camp David (E_2), where he met with National Security advisers (E_3).

The problem with (5.10) arises from a difference between the two time adverbs, notwithstanding their (partial) synonymy. "Four hours later" is a retrospective nondeictic adverb whose R is determined by context; in this example, the R of this adverb is established by the event of Reagan's arrival in Washington (E_1). But any contextually salient time or event will do, and there are no restrictions on tenses with which this adverb can co-occur. By contrast, "in four hours" (in its punctual reading) can only refer to a point in time four hours later than either S or R, and it always marks a prospective view of time relative to that reference point (S or R). Thus it is compatible only with tenses that likewise involve a "prospective" orientation, as in (5.11):

(5.11)   President Reagan arrived back in Washington at noon on Monday. (E₁)

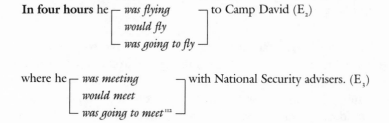

In four hours he ⎡ *was flying* ⎤ to Camp David (E₂)
            ⎢ *would fly* ⎥
            ⎣ *was going to fly* ⎦

where he ⎡ *was meeting* ⎤ with National Security advisers. (E₃)
        ⎢ *would meet* ⎥
        ⎣ *was going to meet*¹¹² ⎦

The difficulty with (5.10), then, results from an incompatibility between the *prospective* orientation of the temporal deictic adverb (*"in four hours"*) and the *retrospective* orientation of the SIMPLE PAST verb.

Observe also that the sequence of sentences in (5.11) offers a different point of view on events from that in (5.9). All Es in (5.9) are reported from the point of view of the speaker at S, whence they are seen as completed (PFV). By contrast, the prospective E₂ and E₃ sentences of (5.11) are reported from the point of view of Reagan at the time of E₁; it is from his point of view at the time of his arrival in Washington that these events are still unrealized and therefore reported by tenses with IPFV aspect. Sentences of this type are explored further in chapter 7.

Let us return now to the matter of reconciling the *prospectivity* of time movement in narrative with its fundamentally *retrospective* point of view. Mendilow (1952:106f.) sees a correlation between retrospection and first-person narration, and prospection and third-person narration, though both are written in the PAST (his concern is with narrative fiction). It is not difficult to see how he arrives at this homology: the unpersonified narrative stance of third-person fiction gives the impression of a story being written forward from the past, inasmuch as no real speaker is there to stake a claim at S, as is the case in first-person fiction. In first-person novels the action is perceived as having taken place; third-person novels create the illusion that the action is taking place.

As it turns out, the prospective temporal orientation that Mendilow associates with third-person narration is appropriate to first-person narration as well. As indicated in Dahl's (1985) definition cited above, this forward look is a defining feature of all narrative language. But where does it come from? As I see it, prospectivity surfaces in the cognitive space in which experience is mapped onto language. As Mink (1968:687) puts it, it is only when we *tell the story* that we "retrace forward" what we have already "traced backward." Nor is this a mechanical operation, as Mink's statement might imply. The process of creating a verbal icon of an experience in language "reopens the space of contingency that once belonged to the past when it was present. It may reinstate a feeling of wonder, of suspense, thanks to which 'contingencies' recover a part of their initial surprising force" (Ricoeur 1984 : 157ff).

Chapter 1 established that narration has its source in memory, and as such is epistemologically retrospective; but as has been suggested at various points in this discussion and will become clearer when we consider the matter of *evaluation* (§5.5), a primary distinctive feature of narrative that sets it apart from chronicles or other reports of past experience is its ability to recreate the experience of the events, in other words, to replicate *post hoc* the contingent prospection of the current report form—whose data source is not memory but direct perception, whose aspect is the IPFV, and whose tense par excellence is the PR. A major goal of effective storytelling, I submit, is to mask the inherent retrospectivity of narration; and among the principal linguistic tools for accomplishing this task are tense and aspect.

5.3. Iconic sequence and the narrative norm

At several points in this discussion reference has been made to *iconic sequence* as the unmarked ordering principle of narrative. This term refers to the *diagrammatically iconic* relationship that obtains in normative narration between the sequence of events of the *fabula* and sequence of clauses in the *sjuzhet* in which those events are reported.

Pierce (1932) distinguishes three types of iconicity: imagic, diagrammatic, and metaphoric. It is the second of these types that is at issue here. An iconic *diagram* is a systematic arrangement of signs, none of which necessarily resembles its referent in respect to any prominent characteristic, as is the case with an iconic *image;* rather, it is the relationship of the signs to one another that mirrors the relationships of their referents. The paratactic, noncoordinated structure "sentence$_1$, sentence$_2$," without additional diacritics (such as intonation), may have only those meanings of which the linear order is an iconic diagram: such structures may be causal or conditional, as in (5.12a), where the unmarked readings are "if *x*, then *y*" or "*y* because of *x*":

(5.12a)   You go out without your jacket, you're going to be cold.
            [*x*]   [*y*]

or temporally sequential, as in speaker B's response in (5.13a), which imposes the reading "first *x*, then *y*":

(5.13a)   A: Why didn't you come to the party last night?
          B: I finished writing my paper, I went to bed.
               $[x]$ $[y]$

These same readings, and only these, appear to hold even if the clauses are conjoined by a minimal connective such as "and." But if we reverse the order of clauses in these sentences, additional diacritics must be supplied in order to preserve the intended relationships between the events, as in the corresponding (b) sentences:

(5.12b)   You're going to be cold *if* you go out without a jacket.
            $[y]$ $[x]$

(5.13b)   I went to bed *after* I *had* finished writing my paper.
         $[y]$ $[x]$

There is often a trade-off between linear order and other means—including morphological, lexical, or prosodic diacritics—for expressing the semantic relationship between two clauses. Thus in (5.13a) a minimal narrative is produced by simply juxtaposing two clauses whose order is iconic to the assumed real-world chronology of the events they report. By contrast, (5.13b) configures the same scenario in terms of a foregrounded action in the main clause ("finishing the paper") to which the action of "going to bed" is backgrounded by means of a subordinating conjunction ("after") and a tense of anteriority—the PLP.

Halliday and Hasan (1976:228f.) argue that in sentences like those in (5.13) the cohesive power lies in the underlying semantic relation of *succession in time,*[113] not in temporal adverbs or other conjunctive elements that function simply as adjuncts. We are willing to fill in the temporal—and causal—gaps on the assumption that there is cohesion, even when it has not been explicitly (formally) demonstrated. In Gestalt perceptual studies this diegetic imperative is referred to as the principle of *good continuity.*[114] Though the examples in (5.12) and (5.13) are elementary, they typify the clausal linkages found in much oral narration. The relative absence of formal cohesion markers, which addressees must reconstruct as part of the process of decoding the text, is one of the conspicuous features distinguishing oral from written discourse.

Linguistic definitions of narrative are generally founded on the assumption that iconic sequence is the default clause order, or narrative norm. Thus Labov (1972:359f.) defines narrative as "a method of recapitulating past experience by matching a verbal sequence of clauses to the sequence of events (it is inferred) actually took place." Similarly, Comrie (1985:28) writes, "A narrative is by definition an account of a sequence of chronologically ordered events (real or imaginary), and for a narrative to be well formed it must be possible to work out the chronological order of events from the structure of the narrative with minimal difficulty; this constraint of minimal difficulty means the easiest way to present these events is with their chronological order directly reflected in the order of presentation" (cf. also Dahl's definition cited in §5.2 above). In view of these definitions, one might wonder what the basis is for assigning default status to iconic sequence and to what extent iconic sequence holds across genres.

For one thing, there is considerable psycholinguistic evidence in support of iconic sequence (see Mandler and Goodman 1982). Also, in certain languages with explicit NARR morphology, iconic sequence is a requirement (cf. Grimes 1978:34, 42; Enkvist 1981). Ong (1982b:147) writes, "We find ourselves today delighted by exact correspondence between the linear order of elements in discourse and the referential order, the chronological order in the world to which the discourse refers. We like sequence in verbal reports to parallel exactly what we experience or can arrange to experience. When today narrative abandons or distorts this parallelism . . . the effect is clearly self-conscious: one is aware of the absence of the normally expected parallelism." Playing with sequential ordering is obviously an important convention of literary fiction; it is a means of drawing attention to certain things, bringing about esthetic and psychological effects, showing different interpretations of an event, and indicating subtle differences between expectation and realization (Bal 1985). But even for complex artistic genres such as novelistic fiction, where a strict linear chronology is more the exception than the rule, the assumption that iconic sequence is the default order nonetheless appears to be valid. Deviations from this arrangement must be seen as indications of artistic purpose, since all rearrangements of chronology depend upon chronology for their effects.[115]

Oral literature, on the other hand, does not rely on iconic sequence to the same degree. Ong (1982b:147) claims that iconic sequence becomes a major objective only when the mind interiorizes literacy. In societies that maintain the practice of traditional oral storytelling, the tales are generally familiar, being part of a shared cultural heritage. In storytelling of this type, an accurate or logical chronology is not essential. Narrators will often begin *in medias res* and relate events not in any strict linear sequence. The chronology of the *Cid* has been shown to be of this type (Chasca 1967), also that of many Old French epics,[116] which abound in cataphoric references (references to events as *realized* that are chronologically *later* than the present of the current narrative plane). To cite but one well-known example from *Roland,* Ganelon's betrayal of Roland is cataphorically referred to early in the text in the PS:

(5.14)   Guenes i vint qui *la traïson fist* [PS].   "Ganelon arrived there, [the one] who *committed the treason* [PS]."   (v. 178)

even though the events constituting the betrayal are at that point in the story still in the future, and the recognition of those events as treasonous even further in the future. In traditional poetry, cataphoric references of this type operate to divide temporality for a moment between the two nows of storytelling: underlying v. 178 is something like "Ganelon came, who—as you know, having heard this story many times before—committed treason." Ong (1982b: 144) comments apropos, "What made a good epic poet was not mastery of a climactic linear plot . . . [but] among other things . . . possession of supreme skill in managing flashbacks and other episodic techniques. Starting in 'the middle of things' is not a consciously contrived plot but the original, natural, inevitable way to proceed for an oral poet approaching a lengthy narrative."[117]

Peabody (1975) offers a compelling demonstration of the incompatibility between linear plot and oral memory that dovetails with anthropological evidence linking concepts of time to literacy: cyclic time is found to be characteristic of nonliterate societies, linear time of literate groups. If we accept this idea, we must then acknowledge the seriousness of its implications for medieval vernacular epic, for it calls into question critics' attempts to discern in the epic poems temporal blueprints that satisfy our modern sense of narrative architecture but are conditioned by writing and literacy. Time in *Roland*—a paradigm text in this regard—is discontinuous and cyclical rather than linear. Life is conceived of as stasis rather than flow—a negation of linear time (see §8.1).

These observations suggest that as a norm for the temporal ordering of narratives iconic sequence may not be appropriate to the overall structure of traditional oral genres. For lengthy narratives, a linear plot comes only with writing. But within lower-level narrative units such as episodes or scenes, which often correspond to prosodic or performance units, there is distinctly greater iconicity, even in the case of epics. The temporal ordering of text IX, the episode of the lion from the *Cid,* is rigorously iconic; likewise text VIII, a *romance* dramatizing the moment of the Roland legend in which Roland's fiancée Alda learns of the death of her husband-to-be.

However, the *romances*—episodic in the sense that they typically relate fragments of larger stories—are on the whole noniconic (see §8.2.2). The atypical iconicity of this text may relate to the fact that it reports very few "events."

As in our discussion of the event (§4.1.4), in talking about iconic sequence we must keep in mind that temporal ordering in narrative is a cognitive and ultimately linguistic process that does not directly map a real or imagined world. Insofar as an event is but a hermeneutic construct, albeit a necessary one for talking about experience, the idea that a complex experience can be reduced to a sequence of events laid out in linear order and translated into a sequence of *narrative clauses* is likewise a hermeneutic idealization, even for the simplest of narratives. Events can obviously be of shorter or longer duration; they can overlap or be coterminous; they may repeat; one may be included within another (see Genette 1980). All these relationships, which are frequently expressed by tense and aspect, can be accounted for in a linguistic model of narrative structure, to which we shall now turn our attention.

Part II.   Text Structure

5.4.   The global structure of narrative

A number of models have been proposed to describe the macro-organization of natural narratives. Conceivably the most familiar is that elaborated in Labov (1972) and Labov and Waletzky (1967), which I adopt here in its later formulation, incorporating some refinements of my own.

A fully developed narrative exhibits all or most of the following components: *Abstract, Orientation, Complicating Action*—in which the major events of the story are set forth, *Peak, Evaluation, Result* or *Resolution,* and *Coda.* Each of these components responds to a particular question:

a. Abstract: what was this about?
b. Orientation: who, what, when, where?
c. Complicating Action: *then* what happened?
d. Peak: what was the highpoint?
e. Evaluation: so what?
f. Resolution: what finally happened?
[g. Coda: what is the relation to the present context?]

Labov observes that in principle only Complicating Action is essential to a narrative. The Abstract, Orientation, Resolution, and Evaluation answer questions that bear on the functions of *effective* narration: the first three to clarify referential functions, Evaluation to make explicit why the story is told—its *raison d'être*. The Coda, found less frequently than any other narrative element (whence the bracketing above), does not answer but puts off a question: it signals that questions c, d, and f are no longer relevant, providing definitive closure.

The following paragraphs describe each of these components in turn, beginning with the optional Abstract and Coda, which together provide a frame for the narrative proper (the "story") linking it to the context of its telling. The relationship of the story and its subcomponents to the context of its telling is diagramed in figure 9.

In terms of temporal reference, the two outermost boxes (Abstract and Coda) refer to speaker-now and thus rely on tenses associated with the communication mode; the two inner boxes (Orientation, Complication/ Peak/Resolution) refer to story-now and rely on the tenses of the narrative mode.

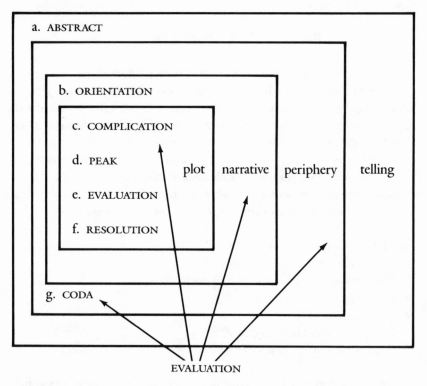

Figure 9. The global structure of narrative. After Polanyi 1986.

5.4.1. Abstract. Narrators often begin by establishing the point of a story or by giving the most salient events in a nutshell, as in (5.15):

(5.15) Let me tell you about the time the roof started leaking right in the middle of our dinner party!   (personal data)

In medieval storytelling Abstracts often take the form of narrator prologues that occur in absolute text-initial position (hence the absence of this component from certain texts in the appendix that constitute internal segments of longer narrations). In episodic texts, particularly those performed in multiple segments, individual episodes may contain an Abstract, as in IX:7–8: . . . *mala sobrevienta sabed que les cuntio.* ". . . a frightening escapade befell them, know this!" The *razo* of the troubadour Peire Vidal (text VI) opens with an Abstract in the form of a concise reference to the particular feature of Peire's persona that is developed in, and constitutes the point of, the *razo:* his expertise as a would-be lover. The Abstract from "Castia-gilos" given in (5.16):

(5.16) Ar auiatz, senher, cals desastre li avenc per sa gilozia.   "Now listen, my Lords, to the disaster that befell him because of his jealousy."
                                                    ("Castia-gilos," 44f.)

similarly encapsulates the point or message of the story, a moral fable warning husbands about the dangers of jealousy, while the Abstract in (5.17) from the Old French *Song of William* is more a straightforwardly referential summary of events:

(5.17) Plaist vus oir de granz batailles e de forz esturs,
de Deramed, uns reis Sarazinurs,
cum il prist guere uers Lowis nostre empereur?
Mais dan Willame la prist uers lui forcur,
tant quil ocist el larchamp par grant onur.
Mais sovent se combati a la gent paienur,
si perdi_de ses humes les meillurs,
e sun nevou dan Vivien le preuz,
pur qui il out tut tens al quor grant dolur.
    Lunesdi al uespre
Oimas comence la chancun d'Willame . . .

Does it please you to hear about great battles and fierce combat, about Deramed, a Saracen King, [and] how he waged war against our Emperor Louis? But Sir William carried out an even stronger offensive against him [Deramed], until he killed him at Larchamp to his great glory. But often he had occasion to do battle with the pagans, [where] he lost some of his best men and his nephew Vivien the valliant, for whom his heart was always sorely grieved.

    Monday at vespers

Here now begins the Song of William . . .   (*Song of William*, 1–11)

Observe that this summary of events *about to be sung* is rendered in the PAST. According to the time of the telling these events are future, but for the audience, to whom they are familiar, they are past. The epic genre reverses in an interesting but not unpredictable way one of the tense correlates of narrative typology proposed in chapter 4. There it was pointed out that narration is normally carried out in the P and plot summary in the PR (§4.7). But in this marked genre of storytelling the summative Abstract is in the P, and the unmarked tense of narration is the PR—a reversal of markedness values in a marked context.

Abstracts can fulfill an important hermeneutic function of signaling to the listener at the outset how the narrator reads the events of the story. Abstracts of this type, such as that of text I given in (5.18) below, are *externally evaluative:*

(5.18) Oh it was so crazy. I remember this. Maybe I shouldn't say it now. It was really a weird thing.   (I:1–4)

This reading of the experience is reconfirmed in the final Evaluation section of the text (see lines 50–54).

It will be noted that the referential scope of Abstracts often encompasses that of Orientation, Complicating Action, and Evaluation: Abstracts not only state what the narrative is about, but also why it is being told.

        5.4.2. Coda. The Coda is a device for returning the verbal perspective to the time frame of speaker-now. As a rule, the sequence of events reported in a narrative does not extend up to actual present time. By means of a Coda the narrator can bridge the gap between the end of the story and the present. The sentences in (5.19) and (5.20) are typical of conversational narrative Codas:

(5.19) . . . and, you know, *I've been looking for one like it ever since.*

(5.20) . . . although *I've never seen the guy since,* I'll never forget that look on his face.   (personal data)

The Coda's function of connecting past events to the speaker-now explains the high frequency in Codas of the PERF—traditionally defined as a PAST with "present relevance"—and of other tenses associated with the communication mode. Consider the Coda given in (5.21), which closes Lesage's *Gil Blas:*

(5.21) *Il y a déjà trois ans,* ami lecteur, que *je mène une vie délicieuse* avec des personnes si chères. Pour comble de satisfaction, le ciel *a daigné* m'accorder deux enfants, dont l'éducation *va devenir* l'amusement de mes vieux jours, et dont *je crois* pieusement être le père.

It is now three years, dear reader, that *I have been leading a delightful life* with such dear people. As a crowning satisfaction, heaven *has seen fit* to bestow upon me two children, whose upbringing *will become* the pastime of my old age and whose father *I* dutifully *believe* myself to be.   (*Gil Blas,* 2:512)

5.4.3. *Orientation.* At the outset of a narrative it is necessary to identify the time, place, story participants and their activity, and the setting or context in which the events of the story will take place. While this can be accomplished in the first few *narrative clauses* (see §5.7.1), most stories begin with an Orientation section composed of *restricted* (§5.7.2) and *free* (§5.7.4) clauses that provide this background information. I give in (5.22) the Orientation that opens text IX:

(5.22) En Valençia seye [IMP] mio Çid con todos sus vassallos, con el amos sus yernos los ifantes de Carrion. Yazies [IMP] en un escaño, durmie [IMP] el Campeador. "The Cid was [IMP] in Valencia along with all of his vassals, with him also his two sons-in-law, the infantes of Carrión. He was lying [IMP] on a bench, the Cid was asleep [IMP]."   (IX:1–6)

(Cf. also I:1–10; II:1–15; III:1–22; IV:1–10; V:1–11; VI:5–25; VII: 1–4; VIII:1–18.)

The most frequent tenses in Orientation are IPFV Ps expressing continuous or habitual action. Thus in English (see text I) we find a heavy concentration of stative ("it was our birthdays") or PROG ("we were all going out for lunch") PASTs; Spanish (example [5.22]) and Modern French (text II) similarly select verbs in the IMP for Orientation clauses, which sketch the kind of thing that *was going on* before the first narrative event of the story or during the entire episode, or for events *collateral* to the main narrative events. Also common in Orientation are before-pasts (PLP or PA) for explanatory circumstantial material—what *had already happened* to produce the situation in which the events of the story will take place, as in XI : 3: *Quant il ço sourent qued il* **fud** *si* **alét** [PA] "When they learned that he [Alexis] *had gone*" (cf. also II : 3–15).

The tense-aspect categories most commonly found in Orientation in our texts—IMP, PROG P, PROG PR, PLP/PA—support the correlation that has been posited between backgrounded clauses and IPFV aspect. However, in the early Old French texts (e.g., *Alexis, Roland, Yvain*), certain descriptive functions now expressed by the IMP were handled by the durative PS (cf. §1.7.1). The PS is still the predominant tense for Orientation in *Aucassin and Nicolette* (text III), though the roughly contemporaneous text by Villehardouin (text IV) shows heavier use of the IMP. Villehardouin's text also shows PRs in Orientation clauses, but significantly they are not diegetic: *sachiez* (l.45) refers to speaker-now ("And *know* in truth that . . ."), while *appelle* (l.52) is locally generic ("the Jewish quarter, which *is called* Estanor"). The PR, when it occurs in Orientation", is not diegetic (but see *n*118); it is functionally different from PRs appearing in narrative clauses of the Complicating Action, whose temporal reference is always to story-now. The commutation test (substituting a P for a PR) confirms the contrast.[118]

In principle, all *free* Orientation clauses could be placed at the head of a narrative, as in text VII (lines 1–4); in practice, though, orientation tends to be embedded throughout a text, in the Complicating Action (as marked in the texts), in Evaluation (I : 47; II : 111–115; XI : 24; XII : 21–27, 31–33, 41–42), even in Resolutions (II : 107–108). Free Orientation clauses (§5.7.4) are by definition displaceable to any point in the text: for example, the Cid's formulaic epithet *el que en buen ora nació*, "the one born at a propitious hour" (cf. also II : 114–115; III : 3–9, 35–36; VI : 5–25, 78; IX : 30). *Restricted* Orientation clauses are not freely displaceable; their reference is limited to a particular scene or set of events. Examples occur in all the texts (I : 14–22; II : 18–21, 24, 27–32, 35–37, 41, 45, 52–53, 56–60, 63–69, 75, 78–87, 89–92, 94–95, 103–104; III : 51–53; IV : 18–21, 35, 39–49, 51–53, 55, 61–65, 68, 72, 75–76, 80, 83; V : 8–11, 27–30, 38–40; VI : 49–50, 57, 65–66; IX : 55–56; X : 8, 11; XI : 16; XII : 4, 15–20, 41–46) and should be looked at in context.

5.4.4. *Complicating Action.* The Complicating

Action consists of the set of *narrative events* that together make up a story. This is as a rule the longest section of a narrative (I : 11–49; II : 16–109;

III : 23 – end; IV : 11 – 83; V : 12 – end; VI : 26 – 88; VII : 5 – end; VIII : 15 – end; IX : 9 – 62; XI : 3 – end; XII : entire passage), in which both Orientation and Evaluation may be embedded. In addition to the events that constitute the *primary sequence* (the ordered set of singulative events separated from one another by temporal juncture that form the backbone of the story), which are reported in *narrative clauses* (clauses preceded by a letter in the appendix texts), the Complicating Action contains several other clause types, discussed in §5.7.

5.4.5. *Peak.* The Peak marks a point in the Complicating Action at which discourse tension reaches a climax, after which it decreases, either to rise again or to decline definitively toward a Resolution. Peaks are frequently marked in surface syntax by various devices for "rhetorical underlining," including repetition and paraphrase, insertion of a mass of detail beyond what is called for in routine narration, and, notably, direct speech—all devices to "slow down the camera" so that the Peak does not go by too quickly (Longacre 1981 : 374ff.).[119]

Peaks occur as follows in the texts in appendix 2: in the "Car Breakdown" narrative (text I) at clause o as the stranger starts the motor of the girls' car. In the "Hitchhiking Adventure" (text II) the first Peak occurs at clause l as the girls are deposited in the middle of nowhere by their first ride. This Peak is marked by direct speech. The second Peak occurs at clause v with the driver's wife's amazement (again reported in direct speech) at her husband's decision to pick up the hitchhikers. In *Aucassin and Nicolette* (text III) the Peak occurs at clauses s/t as Aucassin deals the decisive blow to Count Bougar. In Villehardouin's chronicle (text IV) the battle for the tower of Galatha is punctuated by a series of Peaks at clauses d, q, and u, all highpoints of the action. In Da Ponte's "Theft Narrative" (text V) one Peak occurs at clause l as the narrator discovers the loss of his money, a second at t, a clause of direct speech in which the servant Caterina is implicated in the crime. In Peire Vidal's *razo* (text VI) the Peaks occur at clauses f and j as Peire steals a kiss from Lady Adelaide and she subsequently realizes who it is that has kissed her. In the ballad of Beltrán (text VII) the Peak occurs in dialogue (line 68) as the Arab confirms Beltrán's death and points out the location of his body. In the ballad of Alda (text VIII) the Peak comes in the last narrative clause (h), the arrival of the letter containing news of Roland's death. In the epic texts (IX and X) there are no clearly marked Peaks, though the tension seems to rise in passages of direct speech: in text IX as the Cid's vassals awaken their lord with news that the lion has escaped (lines 35–36), in text X in the laments of the pagans collectively and of Bramimonde. In the episode from *Alexis* (text XI), the Peak occurs at clause i, as Euphemien's men find Alexis but fail to recognize him in beggar's attire. This event is repeated four times in a space of seven verses. The entire episode that constitutes text XII is reported at a high level of dramatic intensity, which peaks at clause o, the definitive blow dealt by Yvain to his opponent. As Peaks are only apparent in context, interested readers should examine the texts in their entirety in appendix 2.

An alternative model for the macro-structure of narrative and one not incompatible with Labov's is Longacre's "profile" model (1981), according to which the flow of a narrative—and of other types of discourse—is analyzed in terms of the buildup and relaxation of tension around a series of Peaks that collectively define the profile of the text. It should be apparent that the profile model can be superimposed onto the Complicating Action, thereby building into Labov's model the recursivity needed to describe the organization of more complex narrative forms.

Observing that Peaks are typically zones of linguistic turbulence (marked discourse micro-contexts) where predictable correlations between grammatical features and levels of information relevance operative elsewhere in the text are often canceled or even reversed, Longacre (1976:219f.) notes that a frequent strategy for achieving the highlighted vividness of narrative Peaks is through tense switching, in particular through a shift into the PR. In eight (possibly nine) of the twelve narrative texts in the appendix, Peaks are marked by a verb in the PR: texts I, II, III, IV (all three Peaks), VI(?),[120] VII, VIII, X, and XII. In three of these cases the Peak occurs in quoted speech (II, VII, X), though in II and X there is also an inquit formula in the PR.

5.4.6. Resolution. The Resolution of a story is normally reported in the final clause(s) of the Complicating Action. Complication builds to a final Peak, after which comes a clause answering the question "What *finally* happened?" In text I, this is given in clause p, the tattooed stranger's exit from the car; in text II in clauses w/x, the girls' arrival back at camp in time to meet the bus; in text V in clause v with the recovery of the money; in text VI at z (reiterated as z') with Lady Adelaide's granting of the long-desired kiss to Peire Vidal. In text VII the Resolution coincides with the Peak (line 68). The Resolution in text VIII—the news of Roland's death—is encoded uncharacteristically in what appears to be a subordinate clause.[121] Texts III, IV, IX, and XI offer only an interim kind of closure (i.e., of individual episodes, which are then followed by new episodes with their own internal structuration). In text

III this interim Resolution comes in clauses aa/bb as Count Bougar gives his promise to stop fomenting trouble; narrative clauses follow in which he is led away to safety. In text IV the Resolution of the tower of Galatha episode occurs in the final clauses v/y/z, in which the tower is captured with the Greeks sequestered inside. This is followed by a restrictive clause containing a report on prisoners and casualties. The outcome of the entire episode is summed up in lines 84–85, a recapitulative Abstract, which functions as a bridge between the tower of Galatha episode and the one that follows. The episode given as text IX is resolved in clause u, as the lion is returned to his cage, after which the focus shifts to the cowardly behavior of the Counts of Carrión. In text XI the poet validates the grief of Alexis's family in an evaluative Resolution (lines 36–37) following five stanzas of verbal breast beating reported largely in direct speech (omitted from the excerpt). In text XII the Resolution of the combat comes with Esclados's departure from the battlefield (clause r). This information is not actually narrated, but reported in a conditional sentence (*"If he fled*, he is not to be blamed"), whence the fact of the event is inferred. In the two *laisses* from *Roland* given as text X there is no explicit Resolution.

5.5. Evaluation

Evaluation refers to the various EXPRESSIVE strategies through which narrators comment on the propositional content of their stories and communicate their significance. A strategic component of effective narration, evaluation operates both at the global level of the text as a whole and at the local level of individual elements.

At the global level, evaluation functions to put off the question "so what?"; it conveys the information: this experience I am telling you about was terrifying, dangerous, wonderful, amusing, weird, crazy—in short, that it was out of the ordinary and therefore worthy of being recounted (Labov 1972:370f.). Evaluation thus serves to communicate the message or point of a story. Labov insists that a narrative containing Orientation, Complication, and a Resolution is not a complete narrative; while such a text may carry out the REFERENTIAL function adequately, it lacks significance—it has no point. The point of a story, however, often transcends the events themselves: the narrative may be merely a vehicle for communicating the speaker's feelings about a given state of affairs—a parable or *exemplum* of sorts, from which the hearer is to draw certain conclusions. Evaluation also has a conative function of involving the hearer in the story.

At the local level, narrators will use evaluation to "modalize" particular elements of a text—events, agents, settings—in order to ensure that those elements considered noteworthy will come across as such, and to forestall differences in interpretation that might result from impartial "phenomenological" reporting. What transforms a straight chronicle of events into a narrative is in large part *evaluation*.

5.5.1. The locus of evaluation.   As stated above, narrators often seek to underscore points at which the discourse tension reaches its Peak and/or is about to resolve itself. This is frequently accomplished by introducing a formal Evaluation section just before or after the Peak or just before the Resolution. In text I an evaluation block of this type occurs at lines 45–48, as the narrator articulates the girls' fear that the stranger might drive off with them. In text II the narrator repeats the phrase "it was really luck" (lines 102, 111) to highlight the fortuitousness of their encounter on the road. In text V Da Ponte evaluates, with a certain retrospective irony, the discovery that his money was missing (line 26) by prefacing that clause with "and what was my surprise" (25). In text IX the Resolution (the Cid's return of the lion to its cage) is followed by the evaluative statement "they think it a miracle, those who are gathered there." In text XII the Peak (clause o) is surrounded by evaluation, while the Resolution of the episode is a single narrative clause (line 60) embedded in a block of evaluation (52–62).

Inserting an explicit evaluation section just before the Resolution serves to underscore the dramatic nature of the Resolution, which is often a happening that could not have been predicted. The clearest illustration of this in our corpus occurs in text VIII in the two evaluative verses describing the letters from which Alda will learn of Roland's death (the passage is given in [5.27] below). This "suspension point" at which Western narrators typically inject evaluative comments or questions between the Complication and the Resolution is *not*, however, a universal feature of narrative structure (Grimes 1975:42).

5.5.2. External evaluation.   The type of evaluation found in most of the passages referred to above is what Labov calls *external evaluation:* the narrator exits the diegetic world—and story-now— to address a comment directly to the addressee(s). Medieval story performers are on the whole highly interventional.[122] In text IX, after describing the clumsy attempt of the Counts of Carrión to sneak out of the court, the *Cid* poet says, "Never did you see such a comedy as passed through that court!" In XI:28, after Euphemien's men return to Rome having failed in their attempt to locate Alexis, the narrator comments apropos of Euphemien, "As if you need ask whether he was sad!" And at the close of *Alexis,* when the saint and his family are at last reunited in heaven, the narrator steps out of the story-world and says to us:

(5.23) Ne vus sai dirre cum lur ledece est grande.   "I cannot tell you how great is their joy."   (*Alexis,* 610)

Apropos of a particularly upsetting military setback Villehardouin comments:

(5.24) Et sachiez que ce fu *la plus granz dolors* qui onques avenist en ost. "Know that it was *the greatest misfortune* that ever befell an army." (Villehardouin, §85)[123]

In the verses cited in (5.25) below, the narrator of the Old Spanish *Life of St. Mary the Egyptian* similarly exits the narrative to "explain"—in the PR of his own now—the saintly woman's disheveled appearance:

(5.25) No es maravilla si es   It is no surprise if she is bedraggled,
            denegrida
fembra que mantiene tal vida.   a woman who leads such a life.
Ni es maravilla si color muda   Nor is it a surprise if her skin darkens
qui cuarenta annyos anda desnuda.   walking barefoot for forty years.
                                (*Vida de Santa María Egipciaca,* 776–779)

Text XII is heavily evaluated throughout; the most salient examples of external commentary are the narrator's observation, "It's a wonder such a fierce and bitter battle could last so long" (35–36), and the clause (italicized) that evaluates the Resolution, "If he fled, *he is not to be blamed*" (59).

5.5.3. *Internal evaluation.* Not all evaluation has the structural property of suspending the Complicating Action. Evaluation is often *internal,* embedded directly into the complication through a variety of strategies, only some of which are discussed here (see Labov 1972:372ff.; Eisner 1975:23–44; Polanyi 1986).

Internal evaluation may be carried out *lexically* through intensifiers, comparators, or otherwise value-marked vocabulary. Consider the examples in (5.26) and (5.27), selected from among many available in the texts in the appendix (evaluative items italicized):

(5.26)   he was like *real*—with *all tattoos* and *smelled*—   (I:47)

(5.27)   . . . *tintas* venian de dentro, de fuera *escritas con sangre.*   ". . . they [the letters] came *stained* on the inside, on the outside *written in blood.*"   (VIII:55–56)

The example in (5.28) below is typical of Villehardouin's reporting technique, in which evaluation is carried out internally via the lexicon rather than externally as in (5.24) above:

(5.28)   Einsi partirent *par mal* l'empereres Baudoins de Costantinople et Bonifaces li marchis de Montferrat, et *par malvais conseil.* "Thus *alas!* did Baldwin of Constantinople and Boniface, Marquis of Montferrat, depart, *victims of unwise counsel.*"   (Villehardouin, §278)

Philosophers of history have identified a particular class of sentences— *narrative statements*—whose most general characteristic is that they refer to at least two time-separated events, both in the past, though they only predicate (are only *about*) the earliest event to which they refer. By way of example, Danto (1965) cites the sentences given in (5.29)–(5.31):

(5.29)   And so, at Sarajevo, the first shot of the First World War was fired.

(5.30)   Aristarchus anticipated in 270 B.C. the theory which Copernicus published in A.D. 1545.

(5.31)   Piero da Vinci begat a universal genius.

These statements are pragmatically felicitous only when uttered at a point in time corresponding to the moment of historical consciousness, from which vantage the historian can view the focal event retrospectively in order to determine its significance for the narrative. They are also without exception reported in the (PFV) P. The sentence in (5.29) would be pragmatically deviant had it been uttered at Sarajevo at a moment cotemporal with the firing of the shot, that is, in the discourse mode of eyewitness report. Similarly, the sentence in (5.31) is infelicitous if uttered during Leonardo's lifetime, before history would judge him to be a "universal genius." [124]

Sentences of this type can only occur in narration. They constitute a hallmark of the "evaluative prerogative" of the narrative historian, a stance not available to the chronicler or annalist. The point of such sentences,

Dray (1971:160) argues, is not to show why something came about, *but to demonstrate its significance to the point the narrator is seeking to make*. Conspicuous in narrative statements are lexical evaluators like "fatal," "detained," "doomed," "victim" (cf. Villehardouin's "it was a fatal moment when . . . ," "that ill-fated expedition," "victims of unwise counsel"), which dramatize what some see as an essential feature of historical organization: the narrative restructuring of reality in light of some subsequent event, ideology, or principle. What Danto (1965) refers to in this context as the "retroactive re-alignment of the past" is an inalienable property of narration as a retrospective hermeneutic activity. In *Remembrance of Things Past* Proust is obsessed by this seemingly inevitable restructuring that the past undergoes in the act of passing through the crucible of the mind; his search to recapture it in its experiential purity (the linguistic consequences of this *recherche* are considered in chapter 7) is in essence an attempt to strip experience of the evaluative accretions it acquires as it passes through the filter of a narrating consciousness.

Internal evaluation is also carried out by presenting commentary in the form of direct quotation—of the narrator's words or, better, those of another story participant. In the *Cid* it is the people of Burgos, not the narrator, who utter the celebrated line:

(5.32) ¡Dios que buen vasallo! ¡Si oviesse buen señor!   "God, what an exemplary vassal! If only his lord were on a par!"   (*Cid*, 20)

The example in (5.33) below from *Roland* contains a lexical item central to evaluation in Old French: the adverb *mar*, which Cerquiglini (1981:173) characterizes as a "thetic modalizer" through which the speaker of a sentence communicates an unfavorable judgment about its propositional content:

(5.33) Il [Roland] dist al rei: "Ja *mar* crerez Marsilie."   "Roland said to the King [Charlemagne]: '*Woe will be unto you* who believes Marsile.'"   (v. 196)

By reporting the quoted statement as Roland's utterance the composer-narrator underscores Charlemagne's folly in believing the promises of the pagan King Marsile and hints at the disaster to come. Parallel examples from the texts in the appendix include Diego González's exclamation "Never again will I see [my homeland] Carrión" (IX:24), a subtle commentary on his cowardliness; the warning to the stranger who enters the girls' car in the "Car Breakdown" narrative (I: clause k)—clearly more dramatic and less overtly interventional than had the narrator simply continued: "And I was real scared because I didn't think the guy knew what he was doing." Aucassin's histrionic "Oh God! . . . are these my mortal enemies?" (III : 33–34) effectively conveys the idea that his adversaries are out for blood. Examples could easily be multiplied; performed stories abound in directly quoted speech, which both characterizes and evaluates.

An internal evaluation strategy frequent in epic narration is *evaluative action:* telling what people did rather than what they said. This allows events to "speak for themselves" and, inasmuch as it involves no departure from the diegetic world or from story-now, provides a more subtle, less obtrusive form of commentary than judgments addressed directly to the addressee. A precondition for this type of evaluation, however, is a social context in which values are shared. Otherwise, the evaluations pass unrecognized or may even be misconstrued. To the extent that they are interpreted correctly, evaluations of this type provide a window onto the world view and cultural presuppositions of the narrator (or, in fiction, the author), which constitute the ideology of the text. In fiction, evaluative action offers one of the few avenues through which the point of view of the author reveals itself, *a fortiori* in situations involving an "unreliable narrator."

Evaluative action, as Labov points out, typically has the effect of dramatizing a narrative. The prominence of this technique in the *chansons de geste* has been widely observed. The Oxford *Roland* closes with the following description of Charlemagne, who has just returned from a pyrrhic victory over the pagans and is immediately called off again to battle:

(5.34) *PLURET* des oilz, sa barbe blanche *TIRET*.   "His eyes *WEEP*, he *STROKES* his white beard."   (*Roland,* 4002)

Two minimal narrative clauses in the PR tense communicate *in nuce* a major ideological crisis confronting the military-feudal world. The passage given in (5.35) below is from text IV: the Latin army has arrived at Constantinople and begins preparations for the assault on the Greeks holding the tower of Galatha:

(5.35) Adonc *CONMENCENT* li marinier *A OVRIR LES PORTES* des uissiers et *A GITER LES PONS FORS;* et on *COMENCE LES CHEVAX A TRAIRE;* et li chevalier *CONMENCENT A MONTER SOR LOR CHEVAUS,* et les batailles *SE CONMENCENT A RENGIER* si com il *DEVOIENT.* Li cuens Baudoins de Flandres et de Hennaut *CHEVAUCHE,* qui *L'AVAN GARDE FAISOIT,* et les autres batailles aprés chascune, si cum eles *CHEVAUCHIER DEVOIENT.* Et *alerent* trosque la ou l'emperere Alexis *avoit esté logiez.*

Then the sailors *BEGIN TO OPEN THE DOORS* of the transport ships and *TO THROW DOWN THE RAMPS*; and they *BEGIN TO BRING OUT THE HORSES*; and the knights *BEGIN TO MOUNT THEIR HORSES*, and the battalions *BEGIN TO FORM* as they *WERE INSTRUCTED*. Count Baldwin of Flanders and Hainaut *RIDES FORTH*, [the one] who *WAS LEADING THE VANGUARD*, and the other battalions each in turn, as they *WERE INSTRUCTED TO RIDE*. And they *proceeded* to where the Emperor Alexis *had been camped*.   (IV : 28–38)

With this series of short narrative clauses in the PR the tempo accelerates and we begin to feel the drama and excitement that for Villehardouin and his companions accompanied the entry into action.

From these two examples it should be apparent that narrative events may themselves be evaluative, which is where tense switching comes into play.

Conversational narratologists have convincingly demonstrated that a switch to the PR tense within diegesis functions as an EXPRESSIVE device for carrying out *internal evaluation* (Schiffrin 1981; Silva-Corvalán 1983). It allows the narrator to report events as if they were taking place simultaneously with their telling, in the fashion of a current report, so that members of the audience can see and hear for themselves what happened and interpret for themselves the significance of those events. Rather than interpret events for the listeners, the narrator allows events to speak for themselves, relying on more subtle linguistic devices including tense switching to do the work of evaluation.

5.5.4.   In Fleischman (1986a) I argue for the appropriateness of this hypothesis, which was developed for natural narration, to artificial narratives in Old French, in particular to performed stories from the thirteenth century (*Aucassin and Nicolette*, Villehardouin's chronicle). By this time the use of tenses for pragmatic purposes is already coming to resemble that of modern French, *mutatis mutandis*, and of other modern languages (English, Spanish) that conversational narratologists have studied from this perspective. But in texts from an earlier stage of French, as in certain Old Spanish texts, the internal evaluation function of the NP is not confined to narrative clauses of the Complicating Action, nor is evaluation limited to the NP.

Consider the passage from text VII given in (5.36), a segment of the lyric meditation on Beltrán's father, who returns to the battlefield to search for his dead son's body:

(5.36)   *VUELVE RIENDAS AL*   1   He *GIVES REIN TO HIS HORSE*
CABALLO,

y *VUÉLVESELO A BUSCAR*
de noche por el camino
de dia por el jaral.
Por la matanza *VA* el viejo,

por la matanza adelante;
los brazos *LLEVA CANSADOS*
de los muertos rodear;
no *HALLABA* al que *BUSCA*,
ni ménos la su señal . . .

and *GOES OUT IN SEARCH OF HIM*,
by night on the pathways,
by day through the brush.
5 The old man *GOES OUT* in search of
carnage,
of the carnage [that lies] ahead;
his arms *ARE WEARY*
from turning over corpses;
he *COULDN'T FIND* the one he *SEEKS*,
10 nor even any trace of him . . .

(VII : 11–20)

In this passage only the clauses in lines 1–2 are sequential narrative clauses reporting new information (Beltrán's father spurs his horse, then sets out on his quest). The NP in line 5 refers anaphorically to the event narrated in line 2 (the repetition is itself evaluative), but this time added to the verb is a highly evaluated complement—*por la matanza*—repeated in line 6 in a parallel construction. The situation reported in the NP of line 7 is not an event at all but a description ("his arms are weary"). In languages that make use of a *visualizing* NP as well as the more common action variety, this tense can be used EXPRESSIVELY to evaluate noneventive material (participants, settings, objects). The poignancy of the information reported in this sentence (lines 7–8) is brought out at least in part by the evaluative NP, which prompts us to visualize (a metaphor for empathy) the physical and emotional fatigue of Beltrán's father turning over body after body hoping—but at the same time hoping not—to find his son among the casualties. The final NP in line 9 refers once again to an activity ("seeking") but not to a narrative event. The entire ballad is a lyrical circumspection on this search; thus the narrator returns to this verb (*buscar*), evaluating it through a variety of linguistic means (tense, lexical adjuncts, repetition).

The episode from Chrétien's *Yvain* given as text XII is also highly evaluated, though there are relatively few narrative clauses. In striking contrast to the contemporaneous *chansons de geste* in which the EXPRESSIVITY of a narrator is minimal, Chrétien's romances are distinguished by the presence of an evaluating Speaker. The encounter between Yvain and Esclados contains both external evaluation (if he fled, "he is not to be blamed," 59, also 35–40) and internal evaluation, the latter carried out lexically ("mortal hatred," 3, "test each other cruelly," 21, proceeded "honorably," 41, armor "stained with brains and with blood," 55f., etc.), through comparators ("never do they move further from their positions than . . . ," 22–23, "never were two knights more eager to hasten each other's death," 24–25, also 32–33, 52), and notably through negative predications ("defending himself was to no avail now," 61, also 16, 22–27, 32–33, 38–40, 42–44, 59; cf. §5.7.1 below). At times these strategies are combined with evaluation carried out via the PR tense. For example, in the first passage of evaluative Orientation describing the state of the shields after a number of blows have been exchanged (15–20), we see the pieces of the shields "left hanging" (15: NP$_v$), with "so many holes" (17: lexical evaluation together with "resultant state" PC/PERF) that they can "no longer cover nor defend" their bearers (16: negation, NP$_v$s), hence the blows "land" (20: "mass" NP) on their unprotected flesh (18–19: evaluated vocabulary). The other evaluative Orientation passages in this text similarly combine the NP$_v$ with lexical intensifiers (31: their hauberks "are now so hot") and with negators and comparators (32–33: "neither is worth much more than a frock").

The evaluative function of the PR in this text extends to the PC (11–13, 17), which at this stage in the development of French still functioned primarily as a PFV aspect of the PR tense (cf. §1.7.3). Whereas the NP$_a$ packages information in the form of events, specifically achievements, the PC packages it in the form of resultant states. Thus in narrative clauses a–i we *see* the two combatants acknowledge (a) and approach (b) one another, exchange blows (c: multiple iterations of the same act condensed into a mass verb), pierce through each other's shields (d), smash each other's hauberks (e), shatter and splinter each other's lances (f–g), the pieces flying into the air (h), and begin to attack with swords (i: another mass verb). All of these actions are narrated by the NP$_a$, as if the narrator were seeing them *happen*. By contrast, the actions reported by the PC in lines 11–13, 17 are not narrated; they *have happened*, and what we see are the results: the shield straps "have been cut" (11/12), the shields themselves are now "split" (11/13) and have "many holes" (17).

This combat episode consists entirely of Complicating Action, into which are embedded, at times together, Orientation and Evaluation. The episode begins in the P (1–4) with a relatively low level of narrative tension as the combatants take their positions. The tension rises in line 5 as the major action of the episode begins and the PR tense takes over from P: "performance" takes over from "narration." From this point the tension builds steadily toward the Peak in line 48. Throughout the pre-Peak section avatars of the PR predominate (NP$_a$, NP$_v$, PC): narrative events are consistently reported in the PR (NP$_a$), as are their results (PC); where the narrative line is interrupted by *internally evaluated* description and commentary, such material is reported in the NP$_v$. The narrator shifts into the P only for sentences of *external evaluation*, which includes, on the one hand, hypothetical alternative scenarios—what the combatants did not do or might have done (42–44)—and, on the other, sentences of evaluation externally focalized from within (see §§7.1, 7.7.3)—judgments by the narrator that presume access to information (thoughts, feelings) that only the characters can possess (24–25, 38–40, 44). Once the Peak is over, narration resumes in the P as the tension declines rapidly toward the Resolution. The P continues to be used for evaluative Orientation externally focalized from within (52, 57–58, 59–61) and takes over from the NP$_a$ for the few remaining narrative events (p–r). The PA in 53–54 (he [Yvain] "had . . . his [Esclados's] head split apart") has the same "perfective" relation to the PS as the PC does to the NP$_a$: just as in the previous excerpt we are not shown the actions that render the knights' shields useless but only the results, neither are we shown Yvain's sword penetrating the head of Esclados. We see the blow to his helmet, reported in the PR$_a$ (48); some five lines later we are told that the sword "had cleaved through" his head.

The helmet blow that penetrates the opponent's head is a stock element of combat scenes in both epic and romance. Compare the presentations of this conventional motif from texts III and XII, given in (5.37a) and (5.37b), respectively. The numbers in parentheses indicate the natural order in which the events occur:

(5.37a)   . . . se le *FIERT* [NP$_a$] par mi le hiaume (1) si qu'i li *ENBARE EL CIEF* [NP$_a$] (2). Il *fu si estonés* [PS] (3) qu'il *caï a terre* [PS] 4. "[Aucassin] *STRIKES* [NP$_a$] through the helmet (1), such that he *BASHES HIM IN THE HEAD* [NP$_a$] (2). He [Bougar] *was so stunned* [PS] (3) that he *fell to the ground* [PS] (4)."

(III : 56–59)

(5.37b)   Son hiaume *ESCARTELE* [NP$_a$] au chevalier mes sire Yvains (1); del cop *fu si estonez* et *vains* [PS] li chevaliers (3); molt *s'esmaia* [PS] (4) . . . qu'il li *ot* desoz le chapel *le chief fandu* [PA] jusqu'au cervel (2). "He *SMASHES* [NP$_a$] the knight's helmet, my Lord Yvain [does] (1); the knight *was stunned* and *weakened* [PS] by the blow (3); he *was confounded* [PS] (4) . . . for he [Yvain] *had*, beneath his [Esclados's] hood, *his head split apart* [PA] down to the brain (2)."

(XII : 48–51/53–54)

There are several pertinent differences between these two renderings of the "definitive blow," which in both cases marks the Peak of the episode. Most obvious is the differential packaging and ordering of the information: the narrator of *Aucassin and Nicolette* presents this material as a straightforward sequence of four narrative events whose clause ordering is iconic to the order of events in the *fabula*. In the first two of these clauses the situation is presented from the perspective of the hero: Aucassin is the discourse topic and also the grammatical subject of the sentences (the two frequently travel together) that are reported in the PR. At clause (3) the topic/subject switches to the defeated opponent, and this shift is marked by a shift to the PS.

Chrétien's narrator configures this information somewhat differently: iconic sequence is not maintained in that the clauses are ordered 1–3–4–2. Also, only three of these clauses are "narrative clauses" that report events; the last one (2) reports its information (the cleaving of the opponent's head) as a resultant state in the PA. It is the departure from iconic sequence that accounts for the PA of clause (2). The temporal reference point for this clause is established by the events of the two preceding clauses (3) and (4), which are reported in the PS—Esclados "was stunned and weakened" (3) and "was confounded" (4) because his head "*had been* split apart" (2; compare the PLP sentence in [5.13b]).

In the configuring of information in this conventional combat motif, both narrators foreground and evaluate (the two functions often travel together—the one emanating from the TEXTUAL, the other from the EXPRESSIVE component; cf. §6.2) the information reported in sentences of which the hero is the discourse topic, while sentences with the opponent as topic remain backgrounded and unevaluated. There is, of course, no requirement that evaluation be reserved for the participant(s) for whom the narrator shows greater empathy (cf. text I, in which the narrator uses the NP to evaluate actions of the seemingly shady character who enters the girls' car). It is simply the case in this example that both narrators link evaluation to empathy. Thus in both versions clause (1) is "about" the hero (he is the topic), who is also the grammatical subject; the action reported in this clause is encoded accordingly in the evaluating PR. Also, for both narrators the opponent is both topic and subject of clauses (3) and (4), the actions of which are reported in the unmarked PS. Once again, the crucial clause distinguishing the two passages is clause (2).

The situation reported in this clause is a highly transitive one involving two participants, an *agent* (the hero) and an *experiencer* (the opponent). In principle, it could be mapped onto syntax from the perspective of either participant, although the unmarked manner of presentation would be via an active transitive sentence with the agent as grammatical subject (the hero bashes in the head of the opponent). This is in fact what both versions offer. The difference is one of topicalization. In (5.37a) the hero (Aucassin) is both subject and topic of the sentence in clause (2), which is accordingly reported in the evaluating PR. In (5.37b), however, although the hero is the grammatical subject (*il* = Yvain), the sentence is "about" the opponent Esclados (there is topic continuity across clauses 3–4–2). As mentioned above, Chrétien's narrator does not evaluate or foreground sentences of which Esclados is the topic (at least when paired with Yvain), which might explain why a P rather than PR tense was chosen for this clause; the choice of a "before-past" tense (PA) has to do with the fact that the information it contains is reported out of sequence.

There are two final points concerning evaluation.

5.5.5.   Internal evaluation has been recognized as an essentially oral strategy, external evaluation as a literate strategy (Tannen 1982a). These correlations refer to basic "casts of mind," not to whether a text is spoken or written, and dovetail with Labov's observation (1972:373) that external evaluation is common in the natural narrations of educated, middle-class speakers, while internal evaluation tends to be preferred by older, highly skilled narrators from traditional working-class backgrounds. *Mutatis mutandis,* Labov's observation may shed light on the prominence of internal evaluation among medieval story performers, notably the illiterate composer-singers of epic.

5.5.6.   There are no "absolute" evaluation devices; the mechanism operates contextually according to a basic "figure-ground" relationship. Given that evaluation is carried out by encoding in a distinctive or marked way the propositional information to be accorded attention, the more distinctive the encoding, the more the evaluated information stands out against the ground of the rest of the text. However, evaluation devices can also be used for normal encoding or overused to the point of losing their distinctiveness—what is referred to as "pragmatic unmarking"—and their evaluative force (cf. Polanyi 1982, 1986). Thus in fiction written entirely or almost entirely in the PR (e.g., the Old French *chansons de geste*), the PR tense cannot be seen as strictly evaluative. The motivations for choosing the PR as the unmarked tense of narration are explored in chapter 8.

5.6. Adapting the natural narrative model to complex narrations

Although Labov's model was designed to represent the structure of simple natural narratives with, usually, but a single point to make, the framework can be adapted to structurally more complex texts. For one thing, narrative structure involves considerable recursivity, whether or not this is formalized as "episodes." After an apparent resolution, new complications arise, reach their respective peaks, and lead to new (positive or negative) resolutions. Markedly episodic movement often represents an adaptation of text structure to the pragmatic conditions of seriated oral narration, whether performed by professional storytellers or on weekly television. As pointed out in §3.ii, lengthy medieval narratives are known to have been performed in multiple sittings, each of which had to be of sufficient structural integrity to constitute an independent performance. Shorter narratives (e.g., the 625-line Old French *Life of St. Alexis*) fit Labov's model as whole texts, showing all the major structural components.

The Hildesheim *Alexis* (eleventh century) begins with a moralizing Abstract-prologue (verses 1–12) announcing the coming of an event that will once again set the world right. Next comes a brief section of Orientation (13–20) describing Alexis's family and background. The Complication builds (23–601), punctuated by a series of Peaks—Alexis's flight from bride and country (74f.); the Romans' discovery of the long-sought-after holy man, now dead, under Alexis's father's stairs (346–348); Alexis's parents' discovery that this holy man is their own son (387f.)—then declines toward the Resolution, Alexis's burial as a saint (596–601). In an evaluative Coda-epilogue (605–625) the narrator brings the story up to present time, where Alexis is reunited with his earthly bride in heaven and has a beatific vision of God. The epilogue concludes with a reminder of the morally debased state of the (Speaker's) present world and an exhortation to the audience to appeal to Alexis to intercede with God on their behalf (the "point"). Evaluation, both internal and external, occurs throughout the text.

Labov's model is further adaptable to more complex artificial narratives in that a secondary narrative or by-story may be embedded into the main story. According to one variant of this pattern, the secondary Resolution is made a necessary condition for Resolution of the main story. Alternatively, two independent story lines may be interwoven, often with only minimal connection to one another.[125] Classic examples of this "interlace" structure, common in Old French courtly romances (cf. *n*78), are Chrétien's *Yvain*, in which the hero's saga is intertwined in episodic counterpoint with that of his fellow knight Gauvain, and the anonymous *Death of King Arthur*, which shifts from Lancelot's story to that of Arthur (5.38a), then back again to Lancelot (5.38b):

(5.38a)   . . . et por ce qu'il estoit tant amez de toutes parz, en vint tant que, se Lancelos fust rois tenanz terre, ne cuidassent mie moult de genz qu'il assemblast si grant chevalerie comme il assembla adonc. *Mes atant* **lesse** *ore li contes a parler de lui et* **retorne** *au roi Artu.*

Or *dit li contes que* a celi jor que li rois Artus atermina a ses homes qu'il venissent a Kamaalot . . .[126]

. . . and because he was so widely loved, it came to pass that even if Lancelot had been a land-holding monarch, many people would not have thought he could gather together so many knights as he did then. *But thereupon the story leaves off talking about him and returns to King Arthur.*

Now the story relates that on that day King Arthur set a date for his knights to return to Camelot . . .   (*Death of King Arthur,* §§106–107)

(5.38b)   *Mes atant s'en test ore li contes a parler d'eus et retorne a Lancelot et a sa compagnie.*

En ceste partie dit li contes que, après ce que la reïne fu rendue au roi, se parti Lancelos de la Joieuse Garde . . .

But thereupon the story ceases [lit., is silent] to speak about them and returns to Lancelot and his company.

In this part the story tells that after the Queen had been returned to the King, Lancelot departed from Joyeuse Garde . . .   (*Death of King Arthur,* §§121–122)

Narratologists have shown that the schemata used to describe the structure of natural narratives can, through such text-syntactic strategies as subordination, recursiveness, and embedding, be adapted to the more complex structures of literary and other artificial narrative forms (cf. van Dijk 1975; Longacre 1976; Pratt 1977; Prince 1982; Watts 1984). A strong formulation of this position is that of Labov and Waletzky (1967:12), who insist: "It will not be possible to make very much progress in the analysis and understanding of . . . complex narratives until the simplest and most fundamental narrative structures are analyzed in direct connection with their originary functions. We suggest that such fundamental structures are to be found in the oral versions of personal experiences." The data of the present study bear out this claim: in significant ways personal experience narratives constitute structural microcosms of the more elaborate oral narratives performed for audiences in the Middle Ages and even today in societies in which traditional oral storytelling still fulfills an important sociocultural function. Ultimately, many of the linguistic strategies for organizing and evaluating narrative that developed in performance contexts have been adapted to more complex forms of written and literate narrative.

5.7. The clausal structure of narrative

Labov (1972) has identified several different clause types occurring in nar-

rative, distinguished according to function and constraints on their movement to different points in the text ("displaceability").

5.7.1. Narrative clauses. At several points in this
discussion reference has been made to *narrative clauses*. The moment has
come to define them. A narrative clause is one that contains a unique event
that, according to the narrative norm, is understood to follow the event
immediately preceding it and to precede the event immediately following
it. Narrative events are separated from one another by *temporal juncture,*
which is semantically equivalent to the temporal conjunction "then": a
happened, then b, then c, and so forth. Inasmuch as narrative clauses are
temporally ordered, any change in their ordering (displacement across a
temporal juncture) alters the inferred sequence of events in the original
semantic interpretation (the *fabula*). This becomes apparent if one attempts to juggle the lettered clauses in any of the texts in appendix 2. The
prevailing view has been that only *main* clauses are relevant to temporal
sequence, since subordinate clauses can often be "displaced" to varying degrees without disturbing the chronology of the *fabula*.[127] Following this
line of argument, narrative clauses have also been defined as those that advance the story line or "move narrative time" (cf. Dry 1981, 1983). By reading down the sequence of lettered narrative clauses in any of the texts in
appendix 2 (the reader is encouraged to do this) the backbone of a story or
primary sequence emerges (Labov and Waletzky 1967).

It will be observed that the events reported in the lettered narrative
clauses are all punctual and completed; their time reference is conventionally assumed to be that of the "current narrative plane" of the story
(i.e., past). The expected tense-aspect category is therefore the PRET, in
whatever form this category takes in individual languages. In this particular textual environment—narrative clauses of the Complicating Action—
we also find the PR (the action PR) substituting for and referentially
equivalent to the P. The (nonstative) PRs of texts I–VI and XI are all aspectually PFV, encoding singulative punctual events separated by temporal
juncture.[128] Exceptions to the "rule" of separation by temporal juncture are
PR verbs in *coordinated clauses* (§5.7.3), while mass or project verbs constitute an exception to the singulative rule.[129] A significant portion of the action in text XII is reported in the form of mass (lines 5, 10, 20, 27) or
project (line 21) situations. Reciprocal pronominal verbs (e.g., "they strike
one another's faces with their blades," line 34), which abound in text XII,
are often used to encode mass situations. An important property of mass
situations pertinent to this analysis is that when they are reported in the
diegetic PR they take on the appearance of singulative achievements. Here

again the commutation test proves illuminating: these PRs could in all instances be replaced by PFV Ps without changing the semantic interpretation, but not by IPFV Ps. If IMPs are substituted, the situations referred to by these verbs cease to be interpreted as narrative events and become the kind of nonsequential descriptive information normally found in free or restricted clauses but not in narrative clauses.

The question arises whether negative predications can constitute narrative events inasmuch as they refer to unrealized happenings. Most investigators who have considered the question feel that negated clauses are not narrative clauses but form part of the background or "collateral" material against which the meaning of realized events is to be interpreted (cf. Labov 1972; Grimes 1975; Halliday and Hasan 1976; Talmy 1978; Costello 1979; Hopper and Thompson 1980). The reasoning runs as follows: narrated events are asserted; negation normally constitutes a digression into a possible but nonreal world. In other words, the statement "*x* did not happen" carries an entailment "but it could have," and this unrealized alternative scenario serves to *evaluate* what did happen. In the "Car Breakdown" narrative, after the stranger gets in the car the narrator says:

(5.39)   . . . and everyone gets out *except me and my girlfriend* . . . *we just didn't feel like getting out.* And all of a sudden all these sparks start t' fly . . .   (I : 31–34)

This negated information (italicized) serves to evaluate the information reported in the last narrative clause ("all of a sudden all these sparks start t' fly"); it dramatizes this event by reminding us that the girls are still in the car (actual scenario) and potentially in danger, although they could have gotten out (unrealized alternative scenario). Example (5.40) from *Yvain* is even more explicit (Chrétien generally leaves little room for question):

(5.40)   . . . toz jorz a cheval se tienent / que *nule foiz a pié ne vienent.* "[Yvain and Esclados] remain always on horseback, *never resort to combat on the ground.*" (XII : 45–46)

In this example the negated proposition serves to evaluate the information in the preceding clause. Even if we are ignorant of the code of chivalric combat (most readers of this book presumably fall into this category), the negative clause clues us to the relative status of combat on horseback vs. combat on foot.

In short, although negative predications appear not to constitute narrative events, they are nonetheless evaluative (cf. also XII : 16, 22–23, 25, 26, 32–33, 38–40, 42–45, 59).

Van Dijk (1975:280) points out that there are certain "not-doings" that must be considered events in their own right, notably in instances where doing something would be expected or required under given circumstances. Thus he claims that "not saving a child from drowning" would qualify as an event, whereas "not shooting oneself through the head" would not. But even the latter can reasonably be viewed as an event *if it is essential to plot development*—for example, because our hero *did not shoot himself in the head* after all in that moment of despair, he was able to continue his work and ultimately win a Nobel prize (had he shot himself in the head, the story would presumably be over). The criterion of plot advancement seems to be essential in distinguishing between negated clauses that do and do not qualify as narrative events. The most salient examples in our texts of negative events are two clauses from the "Theft narrative" (text V) in which Da Ponte discovers that his money is *not* in his pocket (clause l) *nor* in his room at the inn (clause n). Without these negated clauses the logic of the plot collapses.

Semantically double-negative predications—"not not-doing *x*"—also constitute "events" inasmuch as they are paraphrasable in the affirmative as "managing to do *x*." Cf. III: clause q: "Aucassin *did not fail to* spot him" (= A. spotted him); VI: clause t: "he *couldn't keep her from* making a fuss" (= she made a fuss).

5.7.2. *Restricted clauses.*   In contrast to narrative clauses, *restricted clauses* are not rigidly ordered. They report situations that often subsume others reported in the temporally ordered clauses (e.g., "*I was cooking dinner* when the doorbell rang"). Restricted clauses generally report extended situations and have temporal reference covering a specific scene or episode. The restricted clause of Peire Vidal's *razo* "and there [he] *composed* many beautiful songs, recalling the kiss that he had stolen" (VI: 65–66) has temporal reference over the entire period of Peire's overseas exile and includes all the individual song-events reported in the next ten lines. The verbs in lines 62, 69, 71–73 of the "Hitchhiking" narrative (text II) all refer to durative (waiting, starting to give up) or iterative (cars stopping and/or turning) situations reported as ongoing during the time the girls were standing at the crossroads waiting for a ride. The Cid's activities described in (5.41) are similarly reported as events of extended duration:

(5.41) *Yazies* [IMP] en un escaño, *durmie* [IMP] el Campeador.   "He *was lying* on a bench, the Cid *was asleep*."   (IX:5–6)

Because they are not rigidly ordered, restricted clauses may be reshuffled or displaced over limited sections of a narrative without changing the inferred chronology of events in the story-world. The passage given in (5.41) above could be relocated to any point in the first twenty-eight lines of text IX (with necessary adjustments for anaphoric reference) without altering the chronology of the *fabula*. In text XII the entire section from lines 21 to 27 is displaceable virtually anywhere between lines 3 and 47.

A number of the texts surveyed contain a particular type of restricted clause that I call the *summative result clause*. Unlike narrative clauses, which report unique countable events, clauses of this type function as retrospective summaries of a series of previously reported situations. Like the narrative statements discussed above (§5.5.3), summative statements involve a configurational judgment on the part of the narrator, and as such are evaluative. Also, like narrative statements, they are consistently in the PRET. Given these similarities between summative result clauses and the narrative statements that constitute a distinctive feature of narrative historiography, it is perhaps not coincidental that among the narratives included in this sample summative result clauses occur most prominently in the two texts with historiographic purport: *Roland* and Villehardouin's crusade chronicle. In the statement "and the Greeks *put up a great show of resistance*" (IV:21), Villehardouin telescopes into a single event—and at the same time evaluates—the individual defense maneuvers subsumed under the deverbal abstract "resistance." Similarly, in the sentences given in (5.42a–d) below, also from Villehardouin, the summative result clauses seem to institute mid-level boundaries, chunking the episode (or the text as a whole for structurally very simple narratives) into smaller subunits:

(5.42a)   And there our men collected a great deal of booty.   (IV:41)

(5.42b)   . . . and he performed so well that he received great praise for his
service.   (IV:67–68)

(5.42c)   . . . and there were a great number captured and killed.   (IV:72)

(5.42d)   . . . there were many prisoners and casualties.   (IV:83)

Likewise in *Roland*, where the basic reporting tense is the PR, summative result clauses in the P (italicized in the examples below) often establish an event or episode boundary, which may or may not correspond to the final verse of a *laisse*, as in (5.43) and (5.44), respectively. Like the examples from Villehardouin, the *laisse* given in (5.43) is a description of battle, which concludes by stating the outcome—"few escaped":

(5.43)   Paien s'en fuient cum Dam-
nesdeus le volt;
encalcent Franc e l'emperere avoec.

The pagans flee as God wills it;

the French pursue, the Emperor with
them.

Ço dist li reis: "Seigneurs, vengez vos
doels . . ."

The King said: "Seigneurs, avenge
your griefs . . ."

Respondent Franc: "Sire, ço nus
estoet."

The Franks reply: "That is our duty,
Lord."

Cascuns i fiert tanz granz colps cum il
poet.

Each one strikes blows as hard as he
can.

Poi s'en estoerstrent d'icels ki sunt iloec.

Few escaped of those [pagans] who are
there.

(*Roland*, 3625–3632)

The passage given in (5.44) is from Charlemagne's poignant lament as he
surveys the casualties at Rencesvals:

(5.44)   Carles escriet: "U estes vos,
bels nies?

Charles cries out: "Dear nephew,
where are you?

U est l'arcevesque e li quens Oliver?

Where is the Archbishop and Count
Oliver?

U est Gerins e sis cumpainz Gerers?

Where is Gerin and his companion
Gerer?

U est Otes e li quens Berengers,
Ive e Ivorie que jo aveie tant chers?

Where is Otun and Conte Berenger?
Yves and Yvoire, men I have loved so
dearly?

Que est devenuz li Guascuinz Engeler,

What has become of Engeler the
Gascon?

Sansun li dux e Anseïs li bers?

Sansun the Duke and Anseïs, that
fighter?

U est Gerard de Russillun li veilz,
Li .xii. per que jo aveie laisét?"

Where is Gerard the Old of Rousillon,
the 12 Peers, whom I left in these
passes?"

De ço qui chelt, quant *nul n'en
respundiét.*

But what does it matter, when *no one
answered?*

"Deus!" dist li reis, "tant me pois
esma[i]er
Que jo ne fui al estur comencer!" . . .

"God!" said the King, "how much I
must regret
I was not here when the battle began!" . . .

(*Roland*, 2402–2413, translation adapted from Goldin)

In the last verse of this passage, the summative result clause in the PS coupled with the preceding clause of external evaluation ("But what does it matter?") provides a stark interruption (boundary) in Charlemagne's anguished *planctus,* underscoring the finality and senselessness of the massacre of his men.

It was pointed out above that the two tense-aspect categories occurring in narrative clauses are PFV PAST and PR (PR$_a$), both used to report punctual situations with temporal juncture. Inasmuch as restricted clauses can be displaced across temporal junctures, and often report durative situations ongoing at the time of the narrative events, they predictably favor IPFV categories expressing continuous, habitual, or iterated action, notably the IMP and, where available, PROG forms.

In English the SIMPLE PR does not occur in restricted clauses (with other than stative verbs), but the PROG PR does. As the formal exponent of the PR$_v$, the PROG PR is used to report situations ongoing at the time of narrative events referred to by the SIMPLE PR$_a$, as in example (5.45):

(5.45) I'M *WALKING* into the house when all of a sudden I *SEE* this squirrel hanging on a chain from the ceiling! (personal data)

In this example both PR forms could be replaced by P equivalents, the first IPFV/PROG, the second PFV/SIMPLE, with no change in REFERENTIAL meaning:

(5.45') I *WAS WALKING* into the house when all of a sudden I *saw* this squirrel hanging on a chain from the ceiling!

As an IPFV backgrounding tense the English PROG PR has no formal PR counterpart in modern French; this function can only be carried out by the IMP. Diegetic PRs do not occur in restricted clauses in French, at least not in natural narration (compare text II).[130] But such was not always the case. The narrative grammar of the earliest performance texts in French is closer to that of Modern English in its use of the PR in both narrative and restricted clauses, albeit without distinctive forms for the action and visualizing functions expressed respectively by the English SIMPLE and PROG forms. The SIMPLE PR of the *chansons de geste* expresses both functions, as will once again be the case in HP narration.

5.7.3. *Coordinate clauses.* Following Labov, *coordinate clauses* are narrative clauses that may be *interchanged with one an-*

other without altering the original sequence of events, as in the boldfaced clauses in the examples in (5.46)−(5.48):

(5.46) o. L'oste e la moglie . . . chiamano tutti i servi, p. cercano, q. esaminano, r. minacciano; s. ma nessuno confessa di aver guardato in quel letto	The innkeeper and his wife . . . summon all the servants, **they search,** **inspect,** **threaten;** **but no one confesses to having looked in that bed**

(V : 33−37)

(5.47) i. et il mist le main a l'espee, j. si comence a ferir a destre et a senestre **k. et caupe hiaumes et naseus et puins et bras** **l. et fait un caple entor lui,** [. . .] **m. et qu'il lor abat dis cevaliers** **n. et navre set** **o. et qu'il se jete tot estroseement de le prese**	And he placed his hand on his sword, starts to attack left and right, **and slashes helmets and nose guards,** **and wrists and arms,** **and wreaks slaughter all around him,** [. . .] **And he slays ten of their knights,** **and wounds seven,** **and throws himself headlong** into the fray[131]

(III : 37−48)

(5.48) Cleimet sa culpe, si reguar- det amunt, Cuntre le ciel **amsdous ses mains ad joinz,** Si **priet Deu** que pareïs li duinst.	He confesses his sins, # **lifts up his eyes,**[132] **Both his hands has lifted up** to heaven, # **prays God** to grant him Paradise.

(*Roland,* 2239−2241)

(Cf. also VI:c/d, m/n, aa/bb; VIII:d'/e'; IX:a/b, e/f; X:h/i/j/k; XII: e/f/g; l/m/n/o.) Coordinate clauses are generally used for event situations reported as going on simultaneously, where no relationship of logical sub-ordination obtains.

There has been debate among conversational narratologists about whether coordination inhibits tense switching. Wolfson observes a tendency in her data for switching *not* to occur across coordinated clauses, in particular those involving a verb of motion and a verb of speech (discussed below). In line with her hypothesis that switching between P and PR functions to establish event boundaries, she seeks to explain the apparent continuity of tenses across coordinated clauses by claiming that these clauses constitute "single events." Though my data as well as those of other investigators (Schiffrin 1981; Silva-Corvalán 1983) tend to support the hypothesis of tense continuity across coordinated clauses, as shown in the examples in (5.46)–(5.48) above, Silva-Corvalán (1983) convincingly demonstrates that conjunction is not a necessary condition for uniting acts into one "event." Furthermore, Silva-Corvalán's data (for Mexican Spanish) show that while tense switching does not seem to occur across *conjoined verbs of a single clause or sentence* (i.e., where there is necessarily subject continuity), it can occur across *coordinated full clauses,* even with subject continuity. Expression of the subject in a pro-drop language like Spanish—or Old French—generally indicates some kind of topic discontinuity; like clausal conjunction in English, an expressed subject in a pro-drop language allows tense switching because of a correlation with subject/topic discontinuity (Silva-Corvalán 1983:772). The early Romance data provide occasional examples of switching even across *conjoined verbs* with subject continuity, as in the starred clauses in the passage from text VI given in (5.49):

(5.49) b. Peire Vidal *INTRA* [PR] en la cambra
　*c. e *venc s'en* [PS] al leit de ma dona N'Azalais
　*d. e *TROBA* [PR] la dormen.
　e. Et *AGENDILLA SE* [PR] davan ella
　f. e *BAIZA* [PR] li la boca.
　g. Et ella *sentit* [PS] lo baizar
　h. e *crezet* [PS] qu'el fos En Barrals, sos maritz,
　i. e rizen ela *se levet* [PS].
　*j. E *GARDA* [PR]
　*k. e *vit* [PS] qu'el *ERA·*l fol de Peire Vidal;
　l. e *comenset* [PS] a cridar e a far gran rumor.

　b. Peire Vidal *GOES INTO* [PR] the room
　*c. and *came up* [PS] to Lady Adelaide's bed
　*d. and *FINDS* [PR] her sleeping.
　e. And *KNEELS DOWN* [PR] beside her
　f. and *KISSES* [PR] her on the mouth.
　g. And she *felt* [PS] the kiss
　h. and *thought* [PS] it was Sir Barral her husband.
　i. And smiling, she *got up* [PS].

*j. And *LOOKS* [PR],

*k. and *saw* [PS] that it *WAS* the prankster Peire Vidal.

l. And *began* [PS] to scream and make a ruckus.   (VI:30–40)

Except for these two switches (c/d, j/k), tense continuity in this passage does correlate with subject/topic continuity: the actions of Peire Vidal in clauses b–f are reported in the PR; when the topic switches at clause g to Lady Adelaide, the tense switches to the P. In §3.9 I referred to this TEXTUAL function of tense switching as "participant tracking," a function all the more important in pro-drop languages (like Old Occitan) that normally omit anaphoric pronouns. The relation between tense continuity and subject/topic continuity is explored further in chapter 6.

A special case of conjoined clauses relevant to tense switching involves *action-speech sequences,* i.e., the conjunction of a verb of motion with a *verbum dicendi.* Wolfson (1982) and Silva-Corvalán (1983) have advanced parallel arguments to explain the observed tendency for tense continuity to be maintained across structures of this type.[133] The early Romance data similarly show tense continuity across coordinated action-speech sequences, as in (5.50):

(5.50) Si la *VONT QUERRE* en une chambre ou ele estoit, et li DIENT: "Dame, li haut home de vostre terre vos atendent . . ." " # [they] *GO LOOK FOR* her in a room where she was and *SAY* to her: 'My lady, the noblemen of your land await you.'"   (*Death of King Arthur,* §137:7–9)

However, examples of switching also occur. Of six instances of the action-speech sequence in "Castia-gilos," tense is maintained in three; in the remaining instances, given in (5.51)–(5.53), the tense switches:

(5.51) . . . vas l'alberc d'En Bascol *S'EN COR* [PR] et *dis* [PS] li . . . ". . . he *RUNS* toward the lodging of Sir Bascol and *said* to him."   (105–106)

(5.52) . . . et *AGENOHLA S'EN* [PR] mantenen e *dis* [PS] . . . ". . . and he immediately *FALLS TO HIS KNEES* and *said.*"   (230–231)

(5.53) Lo caval *LAISSA* [PR] al trotier e *dis* [PS] . . . "He *LEAVES* his horse with the groom and *said.*"   (204–205)

Though these switches are all from action verbs in the PR to speech verbs in the PS,[134] the data also yield examples, albeit less frequent, of switches in the opposite direction (P action verb → PR speech verb), as in (5.54):

(5.54) Parmi le piz sun espiét li *mist fors* [PS], e *DIT* [PR] aprés: "Un col[p] avez pris fort . . ." "He *drove* his spear through the middle of his chest, and then he *SAYS*: 'A heavy blow you have taken.'"   (*Roland*, 1947f.)

This example would seem to support Wolfson's hypothesis that a tense switch establishes an event boundary: the adverb *aprés* (after, then) that accompanies the *verbum dicendi* reinforces the notion that the two clauses represent separate events.

The action-speech sequence also occurs in subordinating constructions, typically of the form "when *x did y*, he *SAYS z*," as in the following examples from Old French chronicles:

(5.55) Et quant il *furent assemblé* [PS] al paveillon le fil l'empereor Sursac, si lor *CONTE* [PR] ceste novelle.   "And when they *were assembled* [PS] in the tent of the son of the Emperor Sursac, # [he] *RECOUNTS* [PR] to them this piece of news."   (Villehardouin, §183)

(5.56) Quant li message *vinrrent* [PS] a le court l'empereeur d'Alemaingne . . . si li *DISENT* [PR] le message que on leur avoit carquié a dire.   "When the messengers *arrived* [PS] at the court of the German Emperor . . . # [they] *TELL* [PR] him the message they were entrusted to tell."   (Clari, §30 : 8 – 11)

In constructions of this type, discussed further in chapter 6 (§6.1.4) in conjunction with other "when"-clauses, tense is both maintained and switched.

5.7.4. Free clauses. *Free clauses* are those that have no fixed relationship to temporal sequence and can range freely throughout a narrative, as in the following example from *Aucassin and Nicolette:*

(5.57) Li vallés fu grans et fors, et li cevax so quoi il sist fu remuans.   "The lad was big and strong, and the horse he sat on was spirited."   (III : 35 – 36)

These clauses could be moved to any point in the text, their displacement having no effect on the temporal or causal logic of the story. They in fact appear with almost identical wording (conceivably a formula) in the preceding Orientation section, lines 6–9. The formulaic epithet from the *Cid: que en buen ora nació* (the one born at a propitious moment, IX : 30) can likewise be displaced to a position following any clause in the text in which the hero's name appears. This formula, including syntactic variants, occurs forty-five times in the text, with the verb *naçer* (to be born) in the PS (active and passive) and the PR.

5.8.   Conclusion

In this chapter I have sought to outline the concepts and parameters essential to an analysis of the linguistic structure of narrative—temporal structure as well as text structure.

In considering temporal structure I have emphasized that all acts of narration involve two different time frames, that of the narrating (speaker-now) and that of narrated events (story-now). Inasmuch as tenses in a narrative can refer to both of these time frames, it is crucial to discriminate between them, since the functions of tenses (notably the PR) often differ depending on which world they refer to. I have also attempted to resolve here an apparent paradox of narrative temporality, namely that within an inherently retrospective discourse the movement of narrative time is prospective. As I see it, the resolution of this paradox is to be sought in the process of "narrativization"—a configurational operation whereby the unordered data of an experience are converted into structures of language, for it is only in telling the tale that we retrace forward what we have already traced backward.

The question of iconic sequence provides a bridge from temporal structure to textual structure by positing as a norm for the linear arrangement of narrative texts a match between the order of the *fabula* and that of the *sjuzhet*. And although artificial narratives more often than not depart from iconic sequence, I have argued that the artistic effects produced by these departures depend on an assumption that sequential presentation constitutes a norm for the ordering of material in a narrative.

The textual structure of narrative has been analyzed here according to a modified version of the model proposed by Labov and Waletzky (1967) for natural narration, a model that I believe can be profitably adapted to the more complex structures of artificial narrative genres. In outlining the various macro-structural components and clause types found in narrative, I have concentrated on how these correlate with tense-aspect categories. In the next two chapters I shall draw on this organizational infrastructure in explicating the pragmatic functions that tense-aspect is called upon to perform in narrative.

6   Textual Functions

Order, rules, and boundaries constitute much of the differ-
ence between the controlled games of art and the com-
parative chaos of open historical situations.

(HAROLD TOLIVER, *ANIMATE ILLUSIONS:*
EXPLORATIONS OF NARRATIVE STRUCTURE)

A minimal unit of narrative rhythm is one that clarifies
a portion of its own muddle and fulfills itself sufficiently to
relax our vigilance and give pause to the forward urge of
the work.   (IBID.)

This chapter is concerned with how narrators use tense-
aspect morphology for discourse-pragmatic purposes relating to the structure and design of a text. Part I focuses on the use of tense-aspect contrasts
to create *texture* within text, that is, to mark levels of information saliency—what is referred to in discourse literature as *grounding*.[135] Part II is
concerned with the role of tense-aspect in the *spatial* organization of texts,
specifically as a device for marking narrative "boundaries." Part III examines *temporal* uses of tense-aspect categories, not in the REFERENTIAL
sense of indicating time relationships between predicated situations, but as
a TEXTUAL device to regulate the pace or *tempo* of the discourse, which is a
function of clause structure, especially clause length, and of the rate at
which new information is introduced.

Part I.   Grounding: The "Texture" of the Text

6.1.   The foreground-background contrast

In any discourse some parts of the message are more important to the
speaker's communicative goals than others. In recent linguistic literature
on narrative this contrast is often referred to as *foreground-background*—an
extension into the domain of text structure of the Gestalt figure-ground
opposition for the perception of spatial relations.[136] As formulated by
Hopper and Thompson (1980:28of.), "In any communicative situation,
narrative or non-narrative, some parts of what is stated are more rele-

vant or central than others. That part of a discourse that does not immediately contribute to a speaker's goal, but which merely assists, amplifies,
or comments on it, is referred to as BACKGROUND. By contrast, that
material which supplies the main points of the discourse is known as
FOREGROUND. . . . The foregrounded portions together comprise the
backbone or skeleton of the text, forming its basic structure; the backgrounded clauses put flesh on the skeleton, but are extraneous to its structural coherence." [137]

In most studies grounding is construed as a binary opposition: an undifferentiated textual foreground is set off from a similarly undifferentiated
background. However, my own explorations into the grounding mechanisms used in early Romance, as well as work by other investigators on
different languages, suggest that a *continuum* approach to information saliency is more consonant with the linguistic data than a simple binary distinction of foreground vs. background.

Insofar as grounding in discourse is a universal, having its origins in
essential cognitive, communicative, and perhaps psycholinguistic functions, we should expect this distinction to manifest itself somehow in the
linguistic structure of narrative discourse in all languages. [138] We should
not, however, expect to find a universally consistent mapping of foreground and background onto grammatical categories or constructions
across languages. Some languages use primary vs. secondary verb inflections to contrast the crucial material of a story from that included for detail
or color; other languages use focal vs. nonfocal pronouns to distinguish
between more prominent and less prominent story participants (Grimes
1975:99). In still other languages these same functions can be carried out
via tense-aspect contrasts. These strategies all involve morphology; yet
grounding can also be signaled by contrastive word-order patterns (Hopper
1986) or clause types (main vs. subordinate). The need to indicate relative
saliency (of events, participants, settings, etc.) appears to be a universal linguistic agenda in connected discourse. To carry out this agenda languages
mobilize a variety of grammatical oppositions whose basic (REFERENTIAL)
functions are often something quite different. Nor will a language rely on
just one strategy to mark saliency. Typically, grounding will be carried out
by a number of different markers (which need not all coincide), yielding a
saliency hierarchy in which foreground and background are simply the
most basic divisions.

6.1.1. A prevailing view in discourse literature is that
the foreground of a narrative consists of the ordered set of events, reported

by PFV action verbs (accomplishments and achievements), that constitute the main plot line, while background consists of descriptive, collateral material, typically packaged as IPFV stative and activity predicates. With respect to clause type, the conventional view is that foreground information tends to be carried by main clauses, while background information appears in various types of subordinate clauses. But we shall see that these formulas are not appropriate to all languages or to all types of narrative, nor is the foreground-background contrast necessarily synonymous with the distinction between events and description. In order to demonstrate this claim it is useful to examine more closely the criteria that have been invoked to identify foreground and background with respect to narrative, since the contrast has been understood in different ways. These criteria are not mutually exclusive; on the contrary, they often entail one another.

6.1.2. Following Labov and Waletzky (1967), various investigators have equated the foreground of a narrative with *the sequence of temporally ordered main clauses* in which the narrative events of the story are set forth; any change in the ordering of these clauses alters the temporal order of the *fabula*. Backgrounded clauses (restricted clauses, free clauses, and various types of subordinate clauses) are not "on the time line" because they are not ordered with respect to one another and allow for degrees of displacement without disturbing the temporal order of the *fabula*. This sequential interpretation of foregrounding underlies the analyses in Hopper and Thompson (1980), Dry (1983), and Reinhart (1984), the last of which at least acknowledges that sequentiality is solely a property of texts and not of the worlds they model.

One difficulty with equating foreground with the narrative event line—which also points up the weakness of a binary view of grounding—is that in any narrative not all temporally ordered events are of equal importance. Looking down the sequence of lettered narrative clauses in text II, for example, we observe that those reported in the PC seem to be less crucial than those reported in the PR, similarly in texts V and VI with respect to the PS and the PR. Wehr (1984:106) arrives at the same conclusion from her analysis of grounding in the Old French *Quest for the Holy Grail;* she associates the PS with "the main narrative plane" (i.e., the event line), the PR with "foreground" (i.e., high-focus events on that line).

Another difficulty with the sequential interpretation of foregrounding, at least in its classic formulation, concerns the correlation between foreground/background and main/subordinate clauses. The assumption that founds this correlation is that syntactic subordination is a grammatical icon of narrative subordination, i.e., that the material the narrator considers less salient will be relegated to subordinate clauses. However, it has been shown that subordinate clauses can be temporally ordered and thereby constitute part of the main narrative line (Dry 1983; Reinhart 1984; Thompson 1987).

Thompson (1987) goes to some length to demonstrate that in addition to reporting temporally sequenced events "time-line subordinate clauses" do TEXTUAL work: in particular, they operate to create cohesion and maintain the continuity of the narrative line. Scrutinizing her examples as well as examples of time-line subordinates in my own data, I have observed that sequential subordinates—virtually all temporal adverbial clauses with PFV aspect—occur predictably *after an interruption in the narrative line* (e.g., after an insertion of commentary or otherwise nonsequential material). Consider any of the following clauses from our sample texts: III:32, IV:22, VI:41f., IX:57f., and XI:3f., which should be looked at in context in appendix 2. As Thompson suggests, these time-line "when"-clauses (or analogous clauses with "before," "after," "until," or a gerundive) do function to signal a continuation of the narrative (plot) line that has been broken.

Given that the most natural ordering procedure in narrative is to report events in iconic sequence (even though strict adherence to this procedure would probably make for a flat and rather boring story), departures from iconic sequence—such as back reference, forward reference, simultaneity, overlap, repetition—must be signaled. As suggested in chapter 5, departures from sequential ordering may be used for foregrounding. In written (and to a more limited degree oral) narrative, deviations from iconic sequence are often signaled by means of subordinate clauses introduced by temporal conjunctions. However, only PFV temporal subordinates (e.g., the "when"-clauses referred to in the preceding paragraph, but not the one in VI:23) are on the time line; the reasons for this will become apparent.

One of the strengths of the demonstration in Thompson (1987) is that it reveals the extent to which the status of the homology between clause type and grounding has been exaggerated (the objective of her paper is to explain certain exceptions to this homology) and why it should be regarded as no more than a strong tendency realized maximally in the unmarked (if not very common) situation of rigorously chronological narration. Clearly, it is a strong tendency, and as such it establishes one of the grammatical correlates of the narrative norm. I shall consider below certain literary counterexamples involving foregrounded subordinates whose effects depend on the expectation of iconicity between grammatical subordination and background.

6.1.3. Foreground has also been taken to be synonymous with *what is humanly important*—for human beings certain kinds of situations are intrinsically more important than others and it is these that speakers are most likely to foreground. The question thus becomes one of determining the kinds of situations speakers tend to find important and center their narrations around. Hopper and Thompson (1980) suggest that foregrounded situations are typically situations of high transitivity.[139] Testing Hopper and Thompson's claim, however, Kalmár (1982) finds that the relationship between transitivity and foregrounding needs further refinement; specifically, the complex of features constituting transitivity relates more to *sequentiality* (one of several indices of discourse saliency) than to foregrounding per se. The "saliency hierarchy" proposed in Chvany (1984, 1985) suggests improvements to Hopper and Thompson's schema, with transitivity being only one of a set of indices of saliency, and therefore of foreground.

While the criterion of intrinsic importance is psycholinguistically motivated—people do tend to construct stories around situations they consider interesting or important—we cannot assume cross-cultural unanimity about what is interesting or important and therefore intrinsically foregroundable; nor is it always the case, as also observed with regard to evaluation, that the actual events of the story are what the speaker considers most important. Relevant here is an example from a conversational narrative discussed by Polanyi (1981 : 324n) in which a teenage girl who is not allowed to date boys with cars might alter the location of a story she is telling her parents about the funny thing her date said last night in the front seat of his car. Such a detail of orientation, however, might well be foregrounded in recounting the same episode to her girlfriends. In other words, what is conventionally thought of as an item of lesser importance—the setting of an event—can be foregrounded to communicate certain (often not explicitly stated) information. The setting formula from *Roland, halt sunt li pui* (the hills are high), foregrounded both through repetition (five occurrences in the Oxford text) and a PR-tense verb, functions more as a lyrical element than as orientation per se; its symbolic significance transcends its referential meaning as the locus of a particular set of events (see Crist 1981).

It should be apparent that the criteria of "importance" and "sequentiality" do not always coincide. Reinhart (1984 : 787) claims that there is no reason to expect that the narrative temporal sequence should be more important than the nonnarrative units, though in the narrative norm the two often go together. Reinhart's argument for the independence of foreground from the sequential event line is founded on the perceptual neutrality of the Gestalt distinction, in which figure need not be intrinsically more important than ground. While this is true, it is also the case that whatever functions as figure will acquire importance by virtue of being figure (the chicken and the egg). This is what is implied in the French term *mise en relief*. But here we are already moving away from "importance" as an intrinsic quality of situations toward a contextually determined, hence relative, saliency, discussed in §6.1.5.

In the storytelling of traditional oral cultures the most important or salient information is often *not* the sequence of narrative events that constitute the plot line, to the extent that there is a plot line at all. The entertainment value of a storytelling event often derives from the skill of the storyteller in expanding and elaborating the *descriptive* details that the audience relishes (Herring 1986b), details that can be foregrounded against the background of routine description. Consider the passage in (6.1) from *Roland*, in which the nobility of Charlemagne is brought out through foregrounded descriptive clauses in the PR$_V$ (italicized):

(6.1) *Li empereres se fait [NP$_V$] e balz e liez* . . .
Li empereres *est* [NP$_V$] en un grant verger,
Ensembl'od lui Rollant e Oliver . . .
E si i furent [PS] e Gerin e Gerers:
La u cist furent [PS] des altres i out [PS] bien . . .
La siet [NP$_V$] li reis ki dulce France tient [NP].
Blance ad [NP$_V$] la barbe e tut flurit le chef,
Gent ad [NP$_V$] le cors e le cuntenant fier;
S'est [PR] k·il demandet [PR], ne l'estoet [PR] enseigner . . .

The Emperor is [NP$_V$] secure and jubilant . . .
The Emperor *is* [NP$_V$] in an ample grove,
With him there [are] Roland and Oliver . . .
And Gerin and Gerer were [PS] there also:
Where those men were [PS] there were [PS] many others too . . .
There sits [NP$_V$] the King who holds [NP] sweet France.
His beard is [NP$_V$] white, his head flowering white,
Lordly is [NP$_V$] his body, his countenance fierce;
Should someone come asking [PR] for him, there would be no need [PR] to
point him out . . .   (*Roland*, 96–119)

In Chrétien's romances descriptive elements can be foregrounded by either the PR or the IMP, against the background of the PS, which in the late twelfth century was still the unmarked tense of description, particularly for stative verbs. Fotitch (1950:54ff.) points out that Chrétien tends to use the IMP for descriptions of story elements that are unusual or out-of-the-ordinary (persons, places, clothing), as in the example of the sword bridge from *Lancelot* given in (6.2):

(6.2) *Et li ponz* qui est [PR] en travers	*And the bridge* which goes [PR] across it
estoit [IMP] de toz autres divers;	*was [IMP] different from any other;*
qu'ainz tex ne fu [PS] ne ja mes n'iert [FUT]	never was [PS] there one like it before nor will there ever be [FUT],
Einz ne fu [PS], qui voir m'an requiert [PR],	Never was [PS] there, whoever desires [PR] to know the truth,
si max ponz ni si male planche:	so evil a bridge nor so difficult a board;
d'une espee forbie et blanche	*Of a gleaming white sword*
estoit [IMP] li ponz sor l'eve froide;	*was [IMP] the bridge over the cold water;*
mes l'espee estoit [IMP] forz et roide,	*but the sword was [IMP] strong and stiff,*
et avoit [IMP] deus lances de lonc,	*and was [IMP] the length of two lances.*
De chasque part ot [PS] un grant tronc,	On each side there was [PS] a large tree trunk,
ou l'espee estoit [IMP] closfichiee.	*to which the sword was [IMP] nailed.*

(*Lancelot*, 3015–3027)

All the information in this passage is "off the event line"; however, the narrator (Calogrenant) divides this information into two categories: on the one hand, his own commentary and more realistic descriptive details, reported in the PS, on the other, the extraordinary features of the fantastic bridge, foregrounded by the IMP. (Note that all six situations reported in the IMP are states, for which in twelfth-century texts we would *a fortiori* expect the PS.)

The elaborate descriptions of pageants, tournaments, clothing, and courtly festivities that modern readers may find tedious in medieval courtly romances are a requisite component of the genre, without which the stories would not have been successful, just as contemporary intergalactic adventure narratives would be incomplete without detailed descriptions of extraterrestrial creatures and their eccentric accoutrements and habitats.

Such passages of narrative stasis, during which the plot line advances minimally if at all, are nonetheless crucial to these stories as cultural artifacts, and as such not unexpectedly bear linguistic marks of foregrounding. The distinction between events and description is not obliterated; my point is simply that this distinction does not translate straightforwardly into foreground and background, respectively.

6.1.4. A third criterion for identifying foregrounded material in a narrative is whether or not a clause serves to *advance the plot* (Kalmár 1982) or *move narrative time forward* (Dry 1981, 1983). I include plot movement ("causality" in Aristotle's sense; *Poetics*, 8) and time movement under the same rubric since in narrative they represent two sides of the same coin: *post hoc, propter hoc*. This criterion is essentially an entailment of sequentiality and of the association of foreground with a particular event profile: PFV achievement or accomplishment situations.

Dry (1983) has observed that sentences that foster the impression that narrative time is moving are those that make reference to temporal *points* rather than spans of time, usually the endpoints of situations; if such sentences refer to a time line, then their sequence constitutes the narrative foreground. Sentences that make reference to endpoints usually involve PFV aspect and telic situations (achievements and accomplishments),[140] though atelic situations can also propel time if a prior change of state can be inferred, either by implicature from the preceding sentences or through the agency of modifying elements such as time adverbs and/or perfectivizing (notably ingressive/inchoative) auxiliaries, as in the examples in (6.3) and (6.4):

(6.3) We were in the front; we just didn't feel like getting out. *And all of a sudden* all these sparks *start t'* fly [activity]. (I:32–34)

(6.4) This was more than silence . . . Here there was nothing to feel. *Suddenly* she was aware [state] of her heart beating rapidly. (cited in Dry 1981:239)

In both examples intrinsically atelic situations ("sparks flying," "being aware of something") are converted into achievements through the agency of punctual time adverbs, plus in (6.4) an ingressive auxiliary that shifts the focus onto the initial endpoint or boundary of the situation, the moment at which the sparks began to fly.[141] Only time adverbs that refer to points ("suddenly," "just then," "at that moment"), not those that refer to spans ("for a while," "then" in the sense of "at that time"), can be used to move narrative time. Similarly, only temporal conjunctions that refer to points, not to spans, can produce the time-line subordinate clauses discussed above.

As Dry (1983) points out, only PFV "when"-clauses are on the time line and generate a sense of temporal progression, as in the examples from appendix 2 referred to in §6.1.2 above and those in (6.5)–(6.7):

(6.5) *Quant l'ot [PS] Marsilie,* vers sa pareit se turnet [NP$_a$]. "[At that moment] when Marsile heard [PS] it, he turns [NP$_a$] his face to the wall."

(*Roland*, 3644)

(6.6) *Quando vio [PS] mio Çid asomar a Minaya* . . . valo abraçar [NP$_a$] sin falla. *"When Mio Cid saw [PS] Minaya come into view . . .* he goes to embrace him [NP$_a$]."

(*Cid*, 919f.)

(6.7) E *cant el trencar las auzi [PS],* tost en ·l· escala salhi [PS]. "And *when he heard [PS] them hacking* [away at the door], quickly he climbed [PS] onto a ladder." ("Castia-gilos," 311f.)

In these sentences "when" means "after, as soon as" and sequences the endpoints of the situations referred to in the main and subordinate clauses. "When"-clauses with before-past tenses can also move time (they signal endpoints by definition) provided they introduce *new information* and do not simply refer to situations already mentioned in the discourse in order to pick up the narrative line following a break. In the example in (6.8) from Chrétien's *Erec,* the *italicized* PA clauses are of the latter, anaphoric type that do not move time and are by far the more common in medieval narrative; only the starred clause in v. 502 introduces a new event, and as such advances the narrative:

(6.8) Cil atornoit [IMP] an la cuisine
por le soper char et oisiax.
De l'atorner fu [PS] molt isniax;

bien sot [PS] aparellier et tost
char cuire et en eve et an rost.

Quant ot le mangier atorné [PA]
tel con l'an li ot comandé [PA]

In the kitchen [the servant] was preparing [IMP]
meat and fowl for their supper.
490 He was [PS] very prompt in his preparations;
he knew [PS] well how to prepare
and quickly cook meat, both boiled and roasted.

As soon as he had prepared [PA] the meal
as he had been ordered [PA],

l'eve lor done [NP$_a$] en deus bacins,   495 he gives [NP$_a$] them water in two
basins,

tables et napes, pains et vins;   tables and tablecloths, bread and
wine;

fu [PS] tost aparellié et mis,   [it] was [PS] quickly prepared and set
forth,

et cil sont au mangier asis [PC].   and they are seated [PC] at dinner.[142]

Trestot quanque mestiers lor fu [PS]   Everything that they needed [PS]

ont a lor volanté eü [PC].   500 they had [PC] in abundance.

Quant a lor aise orent sopé [PA]   *When they had eaten [PA] at their
leisure*

**et des tables furent levé [PA]*   502 **and had gotten up [PA] from the
table,*

Erec mist [PS] son oste a reison . . . Erec questioned [PS] his host . . .

(*Erec*, 488–503)

Though the clause in v. 502 could be rewritten as a time-line narrative
clause ("when they had eaten at their leisure, *they got up from the table,*
then Erec questioned his host"), it would be hard to argue for its being
foregrounded.

The IPFV "when"-clauses in which "when" = "whenever" (iterative/
habitual), as in (6.9), or "while" (continuous), as in (6.10), do not refer to
endpoints and therefore cannot report sequential situations; consequently,
they do not move narrative time.

(6.9)   E *quan Peire Vidal se corrosava [IMP] ab ela,* En Barrals fazia [IMP] ades la
patz.   "And *whenever Peire Vidal would get upset [IMP] with her,* Sir Barral would
make peace [IMP] straightaway."   (VI:23f.)

(6.10)   Car *quant le chevalier y pensoit [IMP] le mains, environ .III. mois après,* ilz
vinrent [PS] en son hostel de Corasse . . . messagiers invisibles.   "For *when the
knight thought about it [IMP], some three months later,* there came to his lodging in
Corasse some unseen messengers."   (Froissart §12:174, l. 13)

Durative examples like (6.10) are rare in Old and Middle French, given the
inherent punctuality of *quant*. The few examples in which *quant* cooccurs
with a verb in the IMP are iterative/habitual (Martin 1971:316).

"When"-clauses have been a topic of debate among conversational narratologists concerned with tense switching. While there is agreement that
the sequence "when *x, y*" favors tense continuity and that the diegetic PR

tends not to occur in the "when"-clause, there is disagreement as to why this is so. Wolfson (1982) argues that the "when"-clause provides non-sequential background information, setting the scene or providing a temporal reference for the main clause that follows; the two clauses together constitute a single event—whence tense is maintained (this is in line with her claim that tense switching serves to mark boundaries between events). For IPFV "when"-clauses in which "when" = "while" ("when the baby was having a bath, the telephone rang") the backgrounding argument is reasonable, though it is difficult semantically to see how the baby's bath and the telephone ringing constitute a single event. For PFV time-line "when"-clauses of the type discussed above ("when the telephone rang, the baby started to cry"; "when/once the baby had eaten, she stopped crying and went to sleep") the argument is altogether untenable. Schiffrin (1981) and Silva-Corvalán (1983) both reject Wolfson's claim that the two clauses constitute a single event, though Schiffrin's explanation for tense continuity in this environment is not all that dissimilar from Wolfson's: she sees the tendency for tense to be maintained as reflecting the fact that the nonsequential material contributed by the "when"-clause adds background information "within the same temporal slot" as the event reported in the main clause.

The medieval Romance data are less consistent with respect to "when"-clauses than the conversational data. To the extent that temporal subordinates are used at all, tense continuity is more common than tense switching. Where switching occurs, in roughly twenty-five percent of cases overall, it is generally from a P "when"-clause to a PR main clause, as in (6.5)–(6.7), though the reverse pattern occurs too, as in (6.11) and (6.12):

(6.11)   Quant l'*OT* [NP$_a$] Rollant, si *cumençat* [PS] a rire.   "When Roland *HEARS* [NP$_a$] this, he *started* [PS] to laugh."   (*Roland,* 302)

(6.12)   Quando gelo *DIZEN* [NP$_a$] a mio Çid el Campeador/una grand ora *pensso* [PS] e *comidio* [PS].   "When they *TELL* [NP$_a$] it to Mio Cid the Warrior Hero, he *thought* [PS] and *reflected* [PS] for a long time."   (*Cid,* 2827f.)

Where switching occurs, it does so most commonly in sequences where the "when"-clause verb is of perception—"hear" or "see" in the perfective cognitive sense of "learn, realize, come to understand, acquire information"—which provides a causal impetus for the action that follows in the main clause.

Commenting on the development of the expression of temporal relationships ("before" and "after") in Old French, Blanc (1964:123) notes that in the early, orally composed genres these temporal relationships were often not expressed at all, at least not grammatically. In the epics it is often sufficient to juxtapose two events, a difference in tense or aspect indicating the chronological relationship between them, as in (6.13):

(6.13)   Seisante milie en i cornent [NP$_a$] si halt . . .
Paien l'entendent [NP$_a$], ne·l tindrent [PS] mie en gab;
Dit [NP$_a$] l'un a l'altre: "Karlun avrum nus ja."

Sixty thousand of them sound their horns [NP$_a$] so loud . . .
The pagans hear [NP$_a$], they did not take it [PS] as a joke;
One says [NP$_a$] to the other: "Charles will be upon us soon."

(*Roland*, 2111–2114)

We can recast this example as in (6.13') making the temporal relationships explicit:

(6.13')   Sixty thousand of them sound their horns so loud. *When the pagans heard this*—they did not take it as a joke—*they say/said to one another* . . .

In the actual example, the clause of narrator commentary in the PS provides the transition between the two sequential clauses in the PR that have no grammatical connective to indicate the temporal relationship made explicit in the paraphrase. Paratactic expression of temporal sequence continues in the prose sections of *Aucassin and Nicolette* and even in the *Prose Lancelot*. In these texts there is some use of *quant* (if a temporal subordinator is used at all), accompanied not infrequently by a tense switch between the two clauses, as in the examples in (6.5)–(6.7) above. In general the romances express anteriority and posteriority more explicitly, via either a telic verb in the PS or a "when"-clause together with a tense of anteriority (PLP/PA), as in the example in (6.8). By the thirteenth century, in addition to explicit tenses of anteriority, a wider range of temporal conjunctions (*puis que, apres que* [after], *einz que, ançois que* [before], *des que, endementiers que, entreusque* [when, while]) is introduced (cf. Foulet 1919: §426).

Many of the connectives relevant to time movement—"before," "after," "when"—normally introduce presuppositional or old information (e.g., the two anaphoric "when"-clauses in [6.8]). It is also the case in narrative discourse that *new* information is introduced in presuppositional (i.e., subordinate) structures, as in the nonanaphoric "when"-clause of the same example (v. 502). Consider now example (6.14a), in which a *new situation* is reported in a subordinate clause introduced by "after":

(6.14a)   Harry went down to the delicatessen. *After buying his bagels,* he discovered his car had been stolen from the parking lot.

In the revised scenario given in (6.14b) the same presupposed information no longer moves narrative time because it is no longer new:

(6.14b)   Harry went down to the delicatessen and bought some bagels. *After buying his bagels,* he discovered his car had been stolen from the parking lot.

If we equate foreground with the set of clauses that propel narrative time, as has been suggested, then the italicized clause in (6.14a) is foregrounded, while the same clause in (6.14b) is backgrounded.

Dry (1983) manipulates similar examples to show how the same information can be packaged alternatively as foreground or background and in so doing points up, indirectly, the fragility of intrinsic importance as a criterion for identifying the foreground of a text. She concludes, however, that the set of sentences that literary critics have intuitively identified as "important," "essential," and "propelling" turn out *grosso modo* to match the set of sentences that trigger the illusion of temporal movement (i.e., the set of sequential "events"), though "importance" is not determined by any inherent prominence of the content of sentences but by linguistic features such as aspect, situation type, and the semantics of temporal connectives (Dry 1983 : 49). Just as I have insisted that temporal structure does not exist in the world independently of language, independently of the transformation of experience into narrative, neither does narrative language mirror *a priori* determinations of saliency; rather, it creates them.

The example in (6.14b) was not introduced simply to make a point about subordinate clauses and grounding. If we substitute tense alternations for the subordinating syntax, the anaphoric structure of this passage strongly resembles that of many medieval performance narratives, in particular the orally composed epics. In part III of this chapter I shall look into the pragmatic factors underlying an anaphoric text structure of this type.

6.1.5.   A fourth criterion for deciding foreground in a narrative is the degree to which an element is *unpredictable* or *unexpected* in

"Mitchell—herd of four."

(6.15) "Mitchell—herd of four." Drawing by Maslin; © 1985.
The New Yorker Magazine, Inc.

a particular context—what Weinrich refers to as *l'événement inouï* (1973:
115). Any element in a discourse, irrespective of its intrinsic human interest,
can be foregrounded through what the Russian formalists have referred
to as "defamiliarization": placement of an item in a context that renders it salient by virtue of contextual unexpectedness. This interpretation
of foreground is pointedly illustrated in the *New Yorker* cartoon in (6.15).
Clearly, there is nothing intrinsically important about hippos; in fact most
grounding-related hierarchies would predict nonhuman, nonindividuated
participants to be less newsworthy and therefore less foregroundable than
individuated human participants. The verbal—and visual—foregrounding
effect derives solely from the unexpectedness of the herbivorous mammals,
standing erect, in a restaurant frame.

It is the criterion of unpredictability more than any other that reflects
the perceptual neutrality of the Gestalt figure-ground opposition. Grammatical correlates of grounding are still posited; but, like markedness values, they are relative and potentially reversible without undermining the
foundation on which they are predicated. What unites diverse examples
of markedness and diverse examples of foregrounding is *informativeness*.
From the point of view of information theory, an element unexpected in a

particular context is more informative than an expected one, and this contextual informativeness (or markedness) interacts with the information inherent in lexical and grammatical signs.

By adopting a *contextual* approach to foregrounding we also obviate the temptation to postulate as quasi-universals grammatical correlates of grounding that are really only strong cross-language tendencies involving, for example, transitivity, aspect (PFV vs. IPFV),[143] case marking, situation type (telic vs. atelic), clause type (main vs. subordinate), and, what is primarily at issue here, tense. While the correlation PS = foreground, IMP = background provides a *norm* for distinguishing sequential material from nonsequential material in certain languages and certain narrative genres, it is not a universal. I would go further and say that it is inaccurate to call the PS/PRET a foregrounding tense, if we understand foregrounding to mean the unpredictability or markedness of an item in context; in the context of the event line of a narrative the PS/PRET is the *predictable* tense choice (hence the unmarked narrative tense) and is therefore not used to foreground (cf. also Wehr 1984: part II).

If the contrast between foreground and background is not universally synonymous with the contrast between sequential "events" and "nonevents" (description, commentary), then a preferable approach to grounding in narrative would seem to be to treat events and nonevents (sequential and nonsequential material) as separate discourse categories, each with its own linguistic devices for foregrounding. Inasmuch as foregrounding, like evaluation, implies distinctive linguistic encoding, foregrounding tenses will always be tenses other than the unmarked tense for the category in question. In the example from Chrétien's *Lancelot* cited in (6.2), it is only against the background of the durative PS, the unmarked tense for description, that the IMP can be used to highlight particular descriptive information. In *Roland,* on the other hand, where the IMP has a very low text frequency,[144] it is the NP_V that foregrounds noneventive material. In both cases grounding "on the event line" is carried out by the NP_a-PS contrast. By the thirteenth century, the grounding "norm" is already coming to resemble that of modern French and a number of other languages that use the PR_a and PRET to mark foreground and background, respectively, on the event line, while description is uniformly in the IMP (see text II).

Interpreted in a context-sensitive way, the foreground-background concept allows for the kinds of reversals of expectations that produce many of the most striking effects in artistic narration. As Chvany (1984:245) observes, once the normative grammatical correlates of grounding are established on the basis of simple, sequential texts, the same grammatical properties can then be used as independent indices of grounding in non-sequential (or otherwise more subtle) literary texts whose authors play with our expectations. Among the correlates of grounding discussed above is the iconic relationship between syntactic subordination and background-ing. Consider the examples in (6.16) and (6.17):

(6.16)   Mr. Ramsey, stumbling along a passage one dark morning, stretched his arm out, *but Mrs. Ramsey having died rather suddenly the night before,* his arms, though stretched out, remained empty. (Virginia Woolf, *To the Lighthouse,* p. 194)

(6.17)   *Zadušiv ego,* ona bystro ložitsja [HP$_a$] na pol.   "*After smothering him* [the baby] she [the nanny] quickly lies down [HP$_a$] on the floor."
(Chekhov, "Sleepy," cited in Chvany 1984 : 249)

In the first example the news of Mrs. Ramsey's death is announced in pass-ing, as it were, in a subordinate clause embedded into a sentence in which not she but her husband is the topic. Similarly, in the second example, as Chvany observes, Chekhov backgrounds the humanly more remarkable ac-tion of "smothering the baby" in a subordinate clause; the effect of this manipulation is a subtle but dramatic shift to the point of view of the ex-hausted nanny, for whom sleep has become the most important activity, reported accordingly in a main clause and foregrounded by a PR-tense verb.

In examples such as these, unless the normative grammatical correlates of grounding are in place, the stylistic or artistic effects produced by re-versing them are impossible. A contextual approach to grounding, like a contextual approach to markedness, is moreover consonant with my posi-tion that the organization of material in a narrative reflects not an *a priori* configuration of experience, but an experience configured by an individual subject.[145] The subjectivity involved in determining what is to be high-lighted in a report of events manifests itself through reliance on—or delib-erate skewing of—the linguistic strategies conventionalized by the lan-guage for grounding and evaluation.

6.2. Toward a theory of grounding

The connection between foregrounding on the TEXTUAL level and evalua-tion on the level of EXPRESSIVITY should by now be apparent. If we con-ceive of foregrounding in the basic Gestalt sense of a figure against a ground rather than in the sense of "sequential events on a time line," then foregrounding and evaluation can be seen as two sides of the same coin. Polanyi and Hopper (1981) define grounding from just this perspective:

background consists of (a) those elements of a discourse that are *predict-able* in a given context, hence less salient (corresponding to the cognitively based notions of "scripts" or "frames"), and (b) those that are *not evaluated* by various linguistic strategies; correspondingly, foreground is made up of (a) *unexpected* or "frame-breaking," hence more salient, items, and (b) those that *are evaluated* by one or more evaluation devices. It is therefore not unusual in languages to find the same linguistic markers serving these two pragmatic functions simultaneously, as I would claim is the case with the NP, shown in chapter 5 to operate in the EXPRESSIVE component as a device for internal evaluation (see also Fleischman 1986a). This is not to say that foregrounding and evaluation are fully congruent. As pointed out in §5.7.1, negative predications are evaluative in their contextualization of actually occurring events; nonetheless, they are usually regarded as background. We might say then that everything that is foregrounded is EXPRESSIVELY evaluated, but not everything that is evaluated is TEX-TUALLY foregrounded.

In a number of discourse studies that focus on narrative (Hopper and Thompson 1980; Wallace 1982; Chvany 1984; Reinhart 1984) it is suggested or at least implied that foreground and background should be viewed not as binary oppositions but as linguistic cluster concepts involving multiple constituent properties. One advantage of such an approach is that seeming exceptions to particular grammatical correlates (e.g., of clause type, aspect, or tense) do not undermine the foundation of the correlations themselves, but simply point up the fact that the linguistic marking of foreground and background involves an interplay of features that may or may not support one another. Though they often travel together, the various grammatical and semantic features associated with each of these two broad categories operate independently of one another. For example, both PR tense (vs. non-PR) and PFV aspect (vs. IPFV) generally correlate with foreground; however, the PR in many languages is either IPFV or neutral with regard to aspect, but in any case not PFV.

The cluster-concept approach also frees grounding from its traditional formulation as a binary opposition. The data of a number of recent studies, focusing on different linguistic correlates of grounding, suggest that the foreground-background contrast is better viewed as a spectrum or continuum in which saliency is a matter of degree, the different degrees being expressed through an interplay of the semantic and grammatical oppositions available in the language (Longacre 1981; Givón 1987). Considering just tense-aspect oppositions, we observe that English can modulate the degree of saliency within description through contrastive use of P, PROG P, and PROG PR (all with past time reference), while spoken standard Italian and certain genres of French have three possibilities for the event line: PC, PS, and PR, which similarly contrast not with regard to temporal reference but in terms of TEXTUAL and EXPRESSIVE meanings. Jones and Jones (1979) describe certain Mesoamerican languages that distinguish morphologically between pivotal and routine events, on the one hand, and between routine and downgraded events, on the other, this last category merging in turn with supportive information types (reported in Longacre 1981:338). Longacre suggests further that there may be resources to distinguish (again on the basis of morphological marking) crucial supportive material from routine supportive material.[146] This state of affairs may not be all that different from the discourse organization of early Old French, in which the PS reports descriptive material in orientation clauses as well as low-focus events in narrative clauses.

6.3. Grounding and parataxis

6.3.1. One of the most widely recognized features of *oral* narrative, artistic or conversational, is its paratactic organization. Formal grammatical apparatus for textual cohesion, in particular for coordination and subordination, is often at a minimum, with clauses merely juxtaposed asyndetically or linked by the minimal connectives "and" or "then." The asyndeton structure is illustrated in examples (6.18) and (6.19) below from twelfth-century French, while texts III, IV, and VI, from later stages in the development of Gallo-Romance (French and Occitan), illustrate linkage via semantically minimal clause-initial particles.

(6.18) Cil s'en repairent [PR] a Rome la citét,

The two men return [PR] to the city of Rome,

nuncent [PR] al pedre que nel pourent truver.

they announce [PR] to his [Alexis's] father that they could not [PS] find him;

Set il fut [PS] graim, ne l'estot [PS] demander.

As if you need [PR] ask whether he was [PS] sad!

La bone medre s'em prist a dementer [PS]

His worthy mother took to mourning [PS]

E sun ker filz suvent a regreter.

and often to lamenting for her dear son.   (XI:26–30)

(6.19) Dis blanches mules fist amener [PS] Marsilies

Marsile had ten white mules led out [PS],

Que li tramist [PS] li reis de Suatilie;

Li frein sunt [PR] d'or, les seles d'argent mises:

Cil sunt monté [PC] [147] ki le message firent [PS],

Einz en lur mains portent [PR] branches d'olive,

Vindrent [PS] a Charles ki France ad [PR] en baillie;

Ne·s poet guarder [PR] que alques ne l'engignent.

Li empereres se fait [PR] e balz e liez,

Cordres ad pris e les murs peciez [PC]

Od ses cadables les turs en abatied [PC],

Mult grant eschech en unt [PR] si chevaler

D'or e d'argent e de guarnemenz chers.

En la citét n'en ad remés [PC] paien,
Ne seit ocis u devient chrestïen.

that the King of Suatilie (had) sent [PS] him,

The bits are [PR] of gold, the saddles wrought in silver,

The men are mounted [PC], who were [PS] the messengers,

in their hands they carry [PR] olive branches.

They came [PR] to Charles, who has [PR] France in his keeping.

He cannot prevent [PR] them from deceptive dealing.

The Emperor is [PR] secure and jubilant,

He has taken Cordres, broken through [PC] its walls,

knocked down [PC] the towers with his catapults.

His knights now have [PR] much booty from this:

gold and silver, precious arms and equipment.

In the city there is not a pagan left [PC],
[who is] not killed or become a Christian.   (*Roland*, 89–102)

A structure of this type does not mean that logical and chronological relationships between events are lacking altogether, but simply that oral storytellers appeal to means other than syntax to convey them.

Consider the passage in (6.2.0a) from the *Cid*:

(6.20a)   A Minaya Albar Fañez   mataron [PS] le el cavallo . . .
Violo [PS] mio Çid   Ruy Diaz el Castelano:
acostos [PS] a un aguazil   que tenie [IMP] buen cavallo,
diol tal espadada [PS]   con el so diestro braço
cortol [PS] por la çintura   el medio echo [PS] en campo.

They killed [PS] his horse   [that of] Minaya Alvar Fañez . . .
Mio Cid, Ruy Diaz the Castilian   saw [PS] him [Alvar Fañez],
he went up to [PS] a bailiff   who had [IMP] a good horse,

thrust his sword far into him [PS]   with his right arm,
he cut him in two [PS] at the waist,   threw [PS] one half into the field.

(*Cid*, 748–751)

Compare this passage with a version of the same incident, taken from a thirteenth-century chronicle that incorporated epic material (connectives italicized):

(6.20b)   *Quando* el Cid vio [PS] a Aluar Hannez tornado a pie, dexosse [PS] yr a un algauzil de los moros que aduzie [IMP] muy bien cauallo, *et* diol [PS] tan grand colpe con la espada por la centura *que* todo le taio [PS] de parte en parte, *et* derribol [PS] a tierra . . .

When the Cid saw [PS] Alvar Fañez come back on foot, he betook himself [PS] to a Moorish bailiff who rode [IMP] a horse well, *and* dealt him such a blow [PS] through the waist with his sword *that* he cut [PS] him in two, *and* knocked [PS] him to the ground . . .   (*Primera crónica general*, p. 529)

Consider now the text in (6.21a), a fragment of a personal experience narration reported in Ochs (1979 : 67):

(6.21a)   So he decides that he he's gonna pass these cars
and, uh, he pulls out in the other lane
and starts passin' 'em,
and all of a sudden we see this big truck, you know . . .
This truck comin' for us,
and, uh, this guy was going pretty fast,
and we had passed one car,
and there's no way we can get in or out,
and uhm, this trucker's comin'
and he's just sort of bearing down on us
and honkin' his horn,
He wasn't slowing down . . .

When asked to describe the same scenario *in writing*, the speaker of this text produced the version given in (6.21b), in which the striking coordinative parataxis of the oral version is replaced by a hypotactic syntax, and tense switching is eliminated:

(6.21b)   After some five minutes of tailing these cars, my father decided it was time to pass the cars. He pulled into the other lane and accelerated. As we passed the first car we noticed a large Mack truck coming our way.

As these examples show, even in literate societies (the narrator of the texts in [6.21] appears literate by conventional standards) oral and written narrative styles rely on different strategies for organizing experiential data into stories. Clearly there is a trade-off: the deferred, mediated communication instituted by writing makes up for the absence of phonic and interactional diacritics precisely by appealing to a more elaborate syntax and to explicit grammatical structures of coordination and subordination, whereas oral discourse compensates for the limitations of parataxis in part by exploiting possibilities available through the verbal system in the form of tense-aspect contrasts.

Ong (1982b) describes the structures of thought and expression in primary oral cultures as "additive" rather than "subordinative"; "aggregative"—often filled with bulky formulas—rather than "analytic"; and "redundant" or "copious"—this last feature being particularly marked in oral delivery before a large audience. Chirographic cultures, on the other hand, look more to syntax. As he explains (1982b:38), "written discourse develops more elaborate and fixed grammar because it is more dependent simply upon linguistic structure, since it lacks the normal full existential contexts which surround oral discourse and help determine meaning somewhat independently of grammar." To this we might add that readers, moving at their own pace through a written text in which each sentence remains accessible as long as necessary, are able to process a more complex syntax than can listeners, whose decoding effort must keep pace with the flow of the narration. Accomplished oral story performers are sensitive to the pragmatic conditions of oral delivery and structure their performance texts accordingly (unlike many literate academics).

As stated above, the prevailing view in discourse studies is that main clauses carry the bulk of sequentially ordered new information and that various subordinate clauses carry discontinuous, nonsequential collateral information. Looking at the Complicating Action section of text III (*Aucassin and Nicolette*), we find this formula confirmed for narrative main clauses: each lettered clause introduces sequential new information packaged as a discrete "event" ("he *placed* his hand on his sword," "[he] STARTS TO ATTACK . . . ," "[he] STRIKES through the helmet, such that he BASHES him in the head," etc.). As for subordinate clauses, very few are in evidence. In this regard *Aucassin and Nicolette* is not unrepresentative of early Romance narrative, or of oral narrative in general, which tends to "juxtapose elements in two-dimensional space without subordinating them" (Zumthor 1984b:86). For the early vernaculars, however, the syntactic distinction between subordination and coordination is not entirely clear-cut.

6.3.2. Several investigators offer evidence for the tenu-ousness of the distinction between coordination and subordination in early Romance (Stempel 1964; Ageno 1971; Cerquiglini et al. 1976). The latter point out that the Old French particle *que*, traditionally viewed as a marker of subordination, might be better interpreted as simply a marker of clause-initial position, since in many instances it appears to be inter-changeable with the conventional coordination markers *et* and *si* (cf. *que* clauses m, o, and p of text III—which show both *et* and *que!*—and lines 27, 44, and 46 of text XII). The same claim can be made with regard to *si que* (so that—III: clause t; IV: 68, 72–73; XII: clause q), which weakly suggests a causal link but is essentially coordinative. However, it is also the case that following a temporal subordinate clause what would logically be the "main clause" at times begins with *et*, thus giving the impression of coordinated (temporal) subordinates, as in the example in (6.22) from Villehardouin:

(6.22) Et quant ce vint as lances baissier, *et* li Greu lor tornent le dos, si s'en vont fuiant et lor laissent le rivage.   "And when it came to lowering the lances, {*and*} the Greeks turn their backs on them, # [they] go take flight, and leave the shore to them."   (IV : 22–25)

As we shall see in §6.7 below, a rigid distinction between subordination and coordination has been called into question even for more "gram-matical" languages such as modern English.

With respect to clausal linkage patterns, there is a striking similarity be-tween early Romance narratives and their modern counterparts in infor-mal conversation. Compare texts III, IV, or VI in appendix 2 with the con-versational texts I and II or the fragment in (6.20a) above. The former are held together by the reiterated *et* and *si*, the latter by *and, so*, (*et*) *alors*, (*et*) *puis*. Halliday and Hasan (1976: 234f.) draw an important distinction be-tween "coordinate *and*," which establishes a purely *structural* relationship, and "conjunctive" or "additive *and*," which is restricted to a pair of sen-tences and functions to create textual *cohesion*. The clause-initial particles of early Romance narration represent in the majority of cases the purely structural variety, Old French *si* (vars. *se, s'*) being a case in point.

Si occurs predictably at the beginning of independent clauses where no subject is expressed (Old French is a *pro-drop* language), its referent having been given in preceding discourse; this particle comes immediately before the verb, thereby preventing it from occurring clause-initially (Old French is also a "verb-second" [V_2] language). Given that the texts generally contain few explicit grammatical linkages, *si* has been interpreted as a conjunction, translated variously as: "so," "so likewise" (in enumerations), "and yet," "yet," "and consequently," "and," "and then" (from the glossary to the Whitehead edition of *Roland*). What these glosses reveal is the modern reader's attempt to make explicit the logical connections that are conspicuously absent from medieval narrative, oral epic in particular. As modern text consumers in a culture of the written word, we have come to expect textual connective tissue to be explicit and grammaticalized; we demand syntax, and where it is lacking we supply it ourselves. Thus we interpret *si* as a conjunction, having come to expect a grammatical coordinator or subordinator in the environment in which this particle occurs. But in Old French, I submit, *si* is not a conjunction. I provisionally call it a discourse "structure signal" (Halliday and Hasan 1976), a pragmatic particle whose function seems to be to mark subject and/or topic continuity across clauses with no expressed subject (or, more accurately, across clauses with no preverbal subject; cf. XI:16), as in the example in (6.23) from Villehardouin (*si* is indicated in the translation by a "#"):

(6.23)   Et quant li Grieu les oïrent venir, *si* vuidierent la cité, *si* s'en alerent. Et il se hebergierent dedenz, *si* la garnirent et refermerent.   "And when the Greeks heard them come, # [they] evacuated the city, # [they] left. And they [the Crusaders] remained inside, # got it ready and fortified it."

(Villehardouin, §312)[148]

(Cf. also III: clauses b, d–f, j, s, w, ee; IV:f, p; VI:5,[149] 16, 50, 80, 84; X:40; XII:11, 17, 35, 47.) If we insist on assigning a "grammatical" function to *si*, we might call it a "same subject"/"topic continuity" marker, which is inserted in accord with the V_2 constraint.

Like many linguistic phenomena that remain fossilized in a language long after their *raison d'être* has disappeared, *si* is still found in the Middle French period alongside the subject pronouns that were coming more and more into use. Typically, however, *si* remains in sentences with subject inversion, with either lexical (6.24) or pronominal (6.25) subjects:

(6.24)   *Si* s'en ala li marchis Bonifaces de Montferrat [Subject] . . .   "The Marquis B. de M. left [lit., # went away the Marquis B. of M.]."

(Villehardouin, §123; cf. also text X:40)

(6.25)   *Si* leur bailla on [Subject] des deniers.   "Money was entrusted to them [lit., # to-them entrusted one some money]."   (Clari, §8:8–9)

Where *si* co-occurs with an expressed subject in a noninverted construction, it is generally in situations where the subject is at some remove from its verb, usually because of insertion of a relative clause:

(6.26) Et cil [Subject] qui empereres seroit par l'eslecion de cels, *si* aroit lo quart de tote la conqueste . . .   "And the one [Subject] who would be elected Emperor by them, # would receive one-fourth of the booty."

(Villehardouin, §234)

6.3.3. In his classic essay on the poetic technique of medieval French narrative, Erich Auerbach (1953:115) observes that in texts like *Alexis* or *Roland* "the urge to establish connections and pursue developments is feeble." He describes the structure of *Alexis* as "a string of autonomous, loosely related events . . . each [of which] contains one decisive gesture with only a loose temporal connection with those that follow or precede"; *Roland* similarly "strings independent pictures together like beads." This image is suggestive of how close the syntax of medieval verbal art was to that of medieval pictorial art, with its characteristic lack of perspective and tendency toward juxtaposition of independent pictures.[150]

Reporting on data from studies on children's acquisition of tenses in narration, Herring (1986a) observes that for the youngest children (three years), even for those who were able to produce some sort of discourse relevant to a set of pictures shown to them in a storybook, there was no evidence that they were aware of any overall, global connection among the pictures. What was elicited was on the whole "mere picture description, related in the deictically anchored present tense" (1986a:7). The similarity of this type of reporting to the technique of the *chansons de geste* is striking; this is not, however, to equate epic narration with primitivism, naïveté, or a childlike view of the world. Though historical grammars and manuals of the early vernaculars may give the impression that the paratactic style of early narrative texts reflects a more primitive state of linguistic development, a grammatically "simpler" language, the fallacy of this view has been adequately demonstrated (cf. Stempel 1964; Nordahl 1972; Peeters 1972). The move from parataxis to hypotaxis that accompanied the development of literacy and the need for a spoken vernacular to accommodate itself to writing should not be equated with linguistic "progress."[151] Beaman (1984) offers a convincing demonstration that subordination is not synonymous with syntactic complexity and that—just because written language is more highly subordinating—it is not therefore more complex syntactically than spoken language. The strategies used by oral storytellers for "narrative subordination" are as complex as those of written narrative; they are simply different.

Before leaving the matter of textual cohesion, a remark is in order concerning epic. Vinaver (1971:6) observes that the conventional definition of "parataxis" provides an umbrella for two distinct forms of expression:

> The absence of causal connectives may be merely apparent; they may be there even though they are not expressed; our mind then rushes into the artificially created verbal vacuum to supply by its own cogitations all that the poet has deliberately left unsaid. In such cases parataxis is a mere device . . . as in the great examples of biblical narrative. . . . The parataxis used in the French epic is of a different kind: it is genuine, not contrived; it invites simple acceptance, not elaboration; it does not conceal continuity and cohesion in silent intervals, but dispenses with such things, and any exegesis that attempts to supply them results in a distortion of the linguistic and poetic pattern of the work.

This statement refers to the fact, alluded to at several points in this discussion, that the two defining primes of narrative—causality and sequentiality—are only minimally in evidence in epic, an issue explored further in chapter 8. But it does not, as I read it, mean that connections between clauses or between events are not there. They are there, not permanently inscribed on parchment in the form of explicit formal connectives, but present *in posse* at a deeper semantic level, waiting to be reactualized by each listener in the context of another storytelling event. The connections reside not in the texts themselves but in the pragmatic context of oral narrative performances. Needless to say, these connections are often difficult to perceive for modern readers accustomed to texts in which the TEXTUAL operations of creating cohesion and signaling grounding are carried out largely by interclausal syntax. Much like contemporary conversational narratives, the early Romance texts make greater use of tense-aspect contrasts to create "texture" within text. While epics and ballads may not have pyramidal linear plots, they nonetheless have linguistic devices to foreground salient information (which need not be synonymous with a sharply profiled event line) and to create a certain level of textual cohesion (i.e., at the micro-syntactic level of clausal nexus, if not at the macro-syntactic level of larger narrative units). These functions are discussed in the next two sections.

6.4. Tense-aspect and grounding

As noted in chapter 3 (§3.6), a connection between parataxis and tense switching is hinted at in Antoine's 1959 monograph on coordination in

French. This connection is picked up by Blanc (1964), one of the few Romance philologists to link tense switching directly to techniques of oral composition and recitation. The decasyllabic meter of Old French epic, he argues, with its clearly marked 4 + 6 syllable hemistichs, precludes a complex syntactic structure; logical subordination is thus expressed in part by intonation and gesture, in part by shifts involving categories of the verb— all features identified by Wolfson as characteristic of performed stories. Blanc (1964:110) sees tense switching as "both a result of and a corrective to parataxis . . . a device which allows to make up for the lack of grammatical and chronological connections.[152] It can be seen to arise from the contradiction between the necessarily linear nature of recitation (in oral recitation events are necessarily placed one after another in time sequence)[153] and the discontinuous character of epic narrative. In *a world of disconnected events reported in the present,* relationships and continuity are rendered to a large extent by the change of . . . [categories] of the verb" (my emphasis). Recasting Blanc's argument in the terminology of the functional model used here, we might say that he sees tense alternation as a TEXTUAL strategy for creating cohesion and signaling grounding relationships, necessitated by epic parataxis.

Until the thirteenth century, grounding in French is handled largely through manipulation of categories of the verb within a predominantly paratactic main-clause structure. Gradually, from the fourteenth to seventeenth centuries, we see an increase in the use of explicit grammatical connectives, which in written narration eventually take over certain TEXTUAL functions earlier handled by tense-aspect variation. This move from parataxis to hypotaxis and the concomitant decline of tense switching go hand in hand with the shift from a predominantly oral textuality to one increasingly penetrated by writing.

The observations that follow apply to those genres of medieval narrative that conform to the narrative norm in having reasonably linear plots (which may include subplots), a formally expressed distinction between events and description, and P as the unmarked reporting tense.[154] By way of illustration I shall use texts III and VI, the Old French passage from *Aucassin and Nicolette* and the Old Occitan *razo* of Peire Vidal.

As discussed above, one of the normative correlates of grounding holds that in languages with a PFV/IPFV contrast for past time this aspectual contrast is used to distinguish events on the narrative line from collateral descriptive material. This is precisely what we see in the Old Occitan text, where the IMP and PLP are used in orientation clauses to report situations respectively simultaneous with and anterior to the main narrative events, which are reported either in the PS ("low-focus" events) or in the NP_a

("high-focus" events). In early Old French, however, this aspectual opposition could not be expressed unambiguously within the PAST system. Recall that the IMP was a low-frequency tense, "continuous action" being expressed largely by the PS in its durative reading. Thus in text III, the PS is alternately punctual, reporting events of the Complicating Action, and continuous, reporting collateral situations of Orientation.[155] The PA (lines 10, 23) marks situations for completion, specifically completion immediately prior to the event reported by the main verb that follows (cf. *n29*); these situations are not themselves on the time line (with time-line events, which are sequenced, the focus is generally on the inception of the situation, not on its completion viewed as an accomplished fact), but provide background for the events that are on the time line (e.g., "because/as soon as Aucassin's horse *had felt* [PA] the spurs, [he] carried him into the fray").

Looking at the sequence of lettered (temporally ordered) clauses in both texts, we see two tense-aspect categories: PS (consistently punctual) and NP_a. All the NPs could be replaced by PSs without altering the meaning. But if we substitute IMPs, the profile of the situations referred by these verbs changes from bounded narrative events on the time line to descriptive information of the type typically found in clauses of Orientation or in restricted clauses of Complicating Action. The point of this commutation exercise is simply to determine the profile of the NP in this type of discourse; like the PS, the NP reports temporally ordered, punctual events on the event line. But within the event category, these two temporally equivalent tenses differ with respect to saliency. Sequential events that the narrator opts to present in low focus (i.e., as background) are encoded in the PS, which in text III is likewise used for description and other nonsequential material, while events of high-focus (foregrounded events) are achievement situations reported in the NP. The contrast is especially noticeable at several points in the Complicating Action where the switch is from PS to PR.

In text III, the action of riding into the battle (clause a/PS) is clearly of lesser moment than the actions involved in the hero's actual clash with his enemies (b–f/NP); in clauses i–p, placing his hand on his sword (i/PS) is prefatory to the actions involved in the attack itself (j–p/NP), similarly for clauses r/PS and s/NP.[156] Text VI is interesting in that five of the six NPs (clauses b–f) appear as PSs in other manuscripts, and conversely six of the PSs (in narrative clauses) appear as NPs in other manuscripts (clauses n–p, v, aa), thus supporting Wolfson's (1979, 1982) statement that the diegetic PR does not occur in all instances in which it could (the predicates in question are all achievements!). Evidently, the various scribes who recopied the text had different feelings about use of the PR tense. In the manuscript

E version on which text VI is based, NPs co-occur with—and mark—narrative Peaks, as Peire enters Lady Adelaide's chamber and steals the kiss (b–f), and then again when she recognizes him (j).

A shift out of PR tense (i.e., from NP to P) seems to occur either (a) when there is an interruption in the narrative line for insertion of nonsequential material (e.g., in text III after clauses f and p, and again following the long passage of direct speech, deleted in the excerpt, in clause h), or (b) when the information reported in a narrative clause is not new information (e.g., in text VI, clauses g and k, which each repeat information provided in the preceding clause—f: "[he] *KISSES* her on the mouth" / g: "And she *felt* the kiss"; j: "[she] *LOOKS*" / k: "and *saw* that it was the prankster Peire Vidal"). In text III, where the switches PR → P occur following a break in the narrative line, the first clause to pick up the narrative line following the hiatus is predictably in the PS (clauses g, i, and q).

Conversational narratologists concur that a switch out of PR tense can mark a narrative boundary, a topic considered in more detail in part II of this chapter. This claim is supported by the examples in texts III and VI, in that an interruption in the event line (e.g., in text III between clauses f–g, h–i, and p–q) signals a transition: there may be a change of subject or topic, and this change is generally preceded by an insertion of nonsequential information.

As noted above, this particular juncture in a text—a break in the narrative line—favors insertion of time-line subordinate clauses. Clause g of text III is precisely this type of clause, and the only one in that text. Given that it introduces new information ("when Aucassin *heard* this"), it moves narrative time.[157] Following this "resumptive" P, the NP can appear once again on the event line as soon as the narrator wishes to report a high-focus, foregrounded event (in this instance, immediately in clause h). The NP alternates, on the one hand, with the PS, marking low-focus, backgrounded events, and, on the other, with the PS (Old French) or IMP (Old Occitan), marking nonsequential descriptive clauses, which in these texts do not use tense-aspect to discriminate foreground from background.

It should be clear from the discussion of the basic meanings of tense-aspect categories in chapter 1 why the PR should be selected in a significant number of languages to do the TEXTUAL work of foregrounding. By abandoning the distanced, dispassionate posture of the historian and re-presenting material in the fashion of an eyewitness observer, a narrator communicates to an audience that the information reported in the PR-tense clauses (events or description) is deserving of attention. The IMP can also serve as a foregrounding tense, either for description, if the unmarked descriptive tense is the PS (e.g., in Chrétien's romances), or more commonly on the event line (the NARR IMP found primarily in literary narration). The strong "pictorial" quality of the IMP underlies its use to foreground situations that a narrator views as more salient than those reported by the PRET, but less salient than those reported by the "dramatizing" PR.

6.5. Creating cohesion: The *chansons de geste*

Vinaver's statement quoted above about the structural disjunctiveness of Old French epic should not be interpreted to mean that at the level of micro-syntax there is no cohesion between sentences or that successive events have no relation to one another simply because they are not formally tied together by intersentential conjunctions. Consider the passage from *Roland* cited in (6.19) above. In the epic, more than in other genres of medieval Romance narrative, the cohesion normally provided by coordinating and subordinating conjunctions is in part established through tense-aspect.

The basic reporting tense of epic (universally) is the PR. However, a series of PRs in a narrative context does not convey the same sense of "sequence" as a series of PRETs (cf. §4.5.2), inasmuch as situations reported in the PR tense are not inherently punctual, bounded, and completed. Hatcher (1942:605) observes that when a succession of PRs is used, the effect is a rather monotonous staccato regularity: each act is represented as separate and independent, as having no particular relation with that which precedes or follows. But with a sequence PR–PC, in which the first situation is presented in its inception (since the NP_a focuses on the initial endpoints of situations) and the second as completed (in twelfth-century epics the PC is still primarily a PFV PR), it is as if the first precipitates the second to its conclusion, uniting the two into a global event, as in the example in (6.27):

(6.27) *VAIT* le *FERIR* [NP] en guise de baron, / *Trenchét* li AD [PC] li quens le destre poign. "Noble that he is, he *GOES TO STRIKE* [NP] him, / Count [Roland] *HAS* his [Marsile's] right hand *cut off* [PC]." (*Roland,* 1902f.)

Observe that the act of cutting off Marsile's right hand is not itself narrated—we see Roland approach his enemy; the next frame shows us the result: Marsile's right hand is missing. This technique is common in cinematographic narration, as are other features of the textuality of *Roland* (see §§6.8.2, 8.1.2). The same technique is used in the example in (6.29) where the PR → PC shift occurs between *laisses* (*laisse* boundaries are marked by a double slash).[158]

(6.28) Ço dist [PS] li reis: "*SUNEZ* [PR-IMPER] en vostre corn." // Gefreid
d'Anjou *AD* sun greisle *sunét* [PC]. "And the King said [PS]: '*SOUND* [PR-IMPER]
your horn.' // Geoffroy of Anjou *HAS sounded* [PC] his horn." (*Roland*, 2950–2951)

Tense switches of this type, which operate to split a macro-event into its
constituent phases, are a common device for establishing cohesion. The
distinct phases reported by verbs in individual clauses are bound together
into complex predicates, analogous to the serial verb constructions of certain African languages. A relationship is thus established between clauses
and, where the clauses in question cross *laisse* boundaries, between *laisses*
(cf. Blanc 1964). Hatcher (1942:605*n*) suggests that "we really have to
do with a certain type of hypotaxis: one which is dramatically suggested,
which seems to be created before us as the activity realizes itself."

The tense alternations that create cohesion between clauses (not necessarily in sequence) and between *laisses* also involve shifts other than PR →
PC. At times the order of these two tenses is reversed, as in example (6.29)
from Roland's death scene (the relevant predicates are boldfaced):

(6.29)   MUNTET [NP$_a$] sur un tertre desuz un arbre bel,
Quatre perruns i AD [NP$_v$] de marbre faiz,
Sur l'erbe verte si *EST caeit* [PC] envers,
La *S'EST pasmét* [PC], kar la mort li EST [NP$_v$] pres. //

Halt SUNT [NP$_v$] li pui e mult halt les arbres
Quatre perruns i AD [NP$_v$] luisant de marbre;
Sur l'erbe verte li quens Rollant *SE PASMET* [NP$_a$].

He CLIMBS [NP$_a$] a hill; there beneath a stately tree
ARE [NP$_v$] four blocks of stone, all made of marble,
[he] *HAS fallen* [PC] on the ground, on the green grass,
there [he] *HAS fainted* [PC], for death is [NP$_v$] at hand. //

The hills ARE [NP$_v$] high and high too the trees
there ARE [NP$_v$] four blocks of stone, of gleaming marble;
Count Roland *FAINTS* [NP$_a$] on the green grass.

(*Roland*, 2267–2273)

In the first *laisse* we are shown Roland on the ground, the result of his
having fainted (PC); in the second *laisse* the singer-composer returns to
"narrate" this event (in the NP). Though clause ordering in the epic is frequently not iconic to the stages of development of an action, as in this ex-

ample, cohesion is nonetheless established through a circular anaphoric nexus.

The example in (6.30) combines a tense shift with a change of situation type: the action in question is represented first as process by an accomplishment verb in the NP (boldfaced), then in its completion by a resultant state verb in the (durative) PS:

(6.30) *BAISSET* [NP$_a$] sun chef, si CUMENCET [NP$_a$] a penser. // Li empereres en *tint* sun chef *enclin* [PS]. "He *BOWS DOWN* [NP$_a$] his head, # BEGINS [NP$_a$] to meditate. // The Emperor *held* his head *bowed low* [PS]." (*Roland*, 137–138)

Note that when the diegetic PR$_a$ co-occurs with *accomplishments* ("bow down one's head"), the perception is of process, whereas with *achievements* ("begin to meditate") the perception is of beginnings. As with the preceding examples, the *fragmentation* of this situation into its constituent phases, accomplished through changes in tense, aspect, and/or situation type, operates paradoxically to create *cohesion* between the clauses or *laisses* that are thereby linked.

In *Aucassin and Nicolette* the alternating prose and verse *laisses* are linked to one another by a similar interstrophic anaphora, though in the prose, if not in the verse, the jarring tense switches characteristic of the epics have been eliminated in favor of temporal conjunctions (*entreusque* [while]):

(6.31) [Aucassins] . . . vers le palais *EST alés* [PC];
il en *monta* [PS] les degrés,
en une cambra *EST entrés* [PC],
si *comença* [PS] a plorer
et grant dol a demener
et s'amie a regreter . . .

Entreusque Aucassins *ESTOIT* [IMP] en la cambre et il *REGRETOIT* [IMP] Nicolette s'amie, li quens Bougars . . .

[Aucassin] *IS headed* [PC] for the palace;
he *climbed* [PS] the steps,
HAS gone into [PC] a chamber,
started [PS] to cry
and carry on with grief
and pine away for his friend . . .

While Aucassin *WAS* [IMP] in the chamber and he *WAS CARRYING ON* [IMP] over his friend Nicolette, Count Bougar . . .   (*AN*, 7:6–11, 8:1–2)

Repetition of events through an anaphoric *reprise* structure (with or without tense switching) is a common narrative strategy for creating textual cohesion. Compare the discourse structure of the example in (6.31) above with that of (6.14b), repeated here as (6.32):

(6.32)   Harry went down to the delicatessen and bought some bagels. After buying his bagels, he discovered his car had been stolen from the parking lot.

There are apparently languages in which *reprise* at the sentence level, as in (6.32), is mandatory in narration. Grimes (1975:96) reports on several languages in which events must be linked to preceding events through this type of repetition: "They went down the river. Having gone down the river, they entered the canoe. Having entered the canoe, they began to paddle. Having begun to paddle . . ." The anaphoric linkages of epic, however, differ from this type of narration in that events are not "chained" in iconic sequence using a conventional P tense of narration; rather they are "represented" in the PR from the perspective of a speaker-observer ostensibly reporting what he sees as he sees it. This report is not informed by the logical temporal ordering that is a product of retrospection, but is delivered in the nonlinear fashion of an on-the-scene observer (hence Blanc's [1964] comparison of the narrative technique of the *chansons de geste* with that of sportscasts).

Part II.   Boundary Marking: The "Space" of the Text

6.6.   Tense switching and the segmentation of narrative texts

In addition to choosing the material to be included in a story, a narrator must determine how this material, a nonlinear mass of experiential data, can be laid out in the linear space of narration. Even for minimally complex narratives, the linearization process is not a simple matter of packaging information into standardized units of action and lining them up seriatim along a time line like a string of beads. We have already seen that the beads of narrative are not all uniform; some are more salient than others, their prominence emerging through a contextual *mise en relief.*

Moreover, they are not spaced evenly along the string; typically they are grouped in clusters corresponding to the "episodes," "scenes," and "macroevents" into which narratives are subdivided, the boundaries between these units being marked by linguistic signals. It is to the use of tense-aspect categories for marking these internal boundaries (i.e., for demarcating the space of the text) that we shall now turn our attention.

6.6.1. Wolfson (1979, 1982) has advanced the claim that a switch between the P and the diegetic PR, in either direction, has a TEXTUAL function of marking event boundaries. As she states it (1982:115), "the switch from P to HP or HP to P has the effect of sequencing the otherwise indistinct series of narrative acts [= individual predicates], and each span or cluster that is thus created I call an event." [159] Though this hypothesis has been rejected by other investigators of tense switching in natural narration (Schiffrin 1981; Silva-Corvalán 1983; Ess-Dykema 1984; Herring 1986b), in part because of the difficulties with Wolfson's definition of an event (cf. §4.1.4), Schiffrin and Silva-Corvalán acknowledge that the shift *out of the* PR tense (i.e., from PR to P) can serve to partition a narrative into subunits (cf. also Wehr 1984:108f). This switch was shown above to occur at the point of a break in the narrative line; in the following paragraphs I shall pursue this line of argument further, showing that the breaks typically occur where there is a change of subject and/or of discourse topic (the two frequently coincide). The examples should be looked at in context in appendix 2.

In text I switches from NP to P occur following clauses f, i, and o. After each of these clauses nonsequential material is inserted (orientation or external evaluation), and the break marks a subject/topic shift. After clause g the narrator moves from talking about herself and her friends ("we") to talking about the guy in the car ("he"); after clause i she switches back to "we," and after o back again to "he." In text III, after clause f there is a switch from NP to P as the subject/topic shifts from Aucassin's enemies to Aucassin himself; a similar switch after clause p marks a change from talking about Aucassin to talking about Count Bougar. In text VI, the tense switch after clause f coincides with a topic shift from Peire Vidal to Lady Adelaide; and in text XI, the subject/topic shifts between clauses c and d from Alexis's mother to his bride, between clauses e and f from Euphemien to his two servants, and between clause o and the evaluative clause that follows back to Euphemien. Examples could be multiplied.

From these data it appears that where tense is used for "participant tracking," to demarcate spans of text focused on particular story participants, the switches are more often in the direction PR → P, though switches in the reverse direction necessarily also occur, particularly when the narration moves rapidly from one participant to another, as in text XI: b/c/d ("Thus said his father: . . . / Responds his mother: . . . / Thus said his bride: . . .") or in the short text given as example (3.12) in chapter 3. In the context of discussion of *focalization* in the next chapter I shall consider the empathetic dimension of tense switching as a tracking device for story participants.

In addition to demarcating participant-based spans, tense shifts—in particular shifts out of the PR tense—can also partition a text into spans centered around a setting or macro-event. Each span thus created typically begins in the P with an Orientation of one or more descriptive clauses or backgrounded events that "set the stage" for the ensuing narrative events in that span, which are reported in the PR and P tenses (for foregrounded and backgrounded events, respectively). The span may also include non-sequential material, reported either in the P or in speaker-based tenses (external evaluation). Typically a span concludes with a shift out of the PR tense and into the P, marking the onset of a new span. The passage from *Yvain* given as text XII constitutes one such span focused on the battle between Yvain and Esclados. Text IV is partitioned into three spans showing this overall structure, each centered around a macro- or project-event: the conquest of the harbor (lines 1–27), the journey to Galatha (28–41), and the battle for the tower (42–end). This pattern of an initial P followed by a series of PRs interspersed with PS has been widely observed in narratives (natural and artificial) in a range of older and modern languages.

6.6.2. Conversational narratologists have observed that tense switching occurs frequently where successive sentences (independent clauses) are separated by a temporal conjunction. Consider the examples in (6.33) and (6.34) from "Castia-gilos" (the conjunction *ab tan* [thereupon, with that] is boldfaced):

(6.33) Lo caval LAISSA [NP$_a$] al trotier e *dis* [PS]: "Amix, aten m'aisi." **Ab tan** VAY [NP$_a$] avan . . . "He LEAVES [NP$_a$] his horse with the groom and *said* [PS]: 'My friend, wait for me here.' **Thereupon** he GOES [NP$_a$] on ahead." (vv. 204–205)

(6.34) "[dialogue]" **Ab tan** *s'es fag* lo bras *liar* [PC] e·l cap *estrenher* fort ab benda, e dis [PS] que ia dieus ioy no·l renda, si ia la VA [PR], qui non lo·n FORSA [PR], c'amors . . . li TOL [PR] lo talen e·l TRASPORTA [PR]. **Ab tan** sonet [PS] a la porta lo senher n'Amfos autamen.

"[dialogue]" **Thereupon** he [Bascol] *has had* his arm *tied up* [PC] [in a sling] and his head *bound* tight with a bandage, and *said* [PS] {that} may God give him no joy, if ever he GOES AWAY [PR] without being FORCED to [PR], for love . . . TAKES AWAY [PR] his will and SENDS him OFF THE TRACK [PR]. **Just then** Lord Alfonso *knocked* [PS] loudly at the door.   (vv. 155–161)

There are sixteen occurrences of *ab tan* in this text (it is the highest frequency temporal conjunction). In fifteen of them *ab tan* occurs directly following a passage of direct speech, as in two of the three instances above, and thereby establishes *a discourse boundary between spans of mimetic and diegetic text*. Similarly, in novella 70 of Franco Sacchetti's *Three Hundred Tales*, three of the four instances of the temporal conjunction *alla (per) fine* (thereupon, with that) appear following passages of direct speech; in all four cases the adverb co-occurs with a resumption of the narrative line in the PS, as in the example in (6.35):

(6.35)   Quando Torello VEDE [PR] questo, DÀSSI [PR] delle mani su l'anche dicendo:
—Oimè, or siàn noi diserti;—e FASSI [PR] alle sponde guardando nel pozzo.
—Che faremo e che diremo?
Alla per fine *voltosi* [PS] al suo fante, il *pregò* [PS] per amor di Dio che si collasse nel pozzo.

When Torello SEES [PR] this, he SLAPS [PR] his thighs, saying:
—Oh no, now we're ruined;—and APPROACHES [PR] the edge of the well, looking in.
—What are we gonna do and what are we gonna say?
Thereupon he *turned* [PS] to his servant, he *begged* [PS] him for the love of God to lower himself into the well.   (novella 70, p. 230)

Givón (1987:179) ranks interclausal conjunctive particles along a continuum based on an iconic relationship between the size of the interruption between two clauses and the degree of discourse discontinuity between them. Virtually all the transitions marked by *ab tan* or *alla (per) fine* and a tense switch coincide with a perceptible interruption in the narrative line. Note that the second *ab tan* of (6.34) also coincides with a subject and topic switch from Bascol to Lord Alfonso. This is in line with Schiffrin's observation (1981:55) that sentences conjoined by a temporal conjunction commonly have non-coreferential subjects.

Ab tan and *alla per fine* are punctual or perfectivizing temporal adjuncts. In §6.1.4 I discussed other *punctual* time adverbs—notably conjunctive adverbs ("suddenly," "all of a sudden," "just then")—which signal new developments or unexpected turns in the story. Temporal conjunctions of this type occur predictably where there is a discontinuity, and the accompanying tense switches serve to mark the boundaries between one "span" and the next (what Wolfson would call "event" boundaries). The fact that the English adverbs listed above all have a basic temporal meaning leads to an interpretation of the clauses in which they occur as clauses of Orientation, analogous to the "when"-clauses discussed above, which are said to provide a temporal background for the narrative events that follow. But in this context *the REFERENTIAL meaning of these conjunctive adverbs is subordinate to their TEXTUAL function of marking a boundary on the narrative line;* this is perhaps clearer in the case of conjunctive adverbs that do not have a basic temporal meaning (e.g., *ab tan* above, or its near equivalent in modern French, *là-dessus*):

(6.36) Elle *a énuméré* [PC] tous ses défauts . . . puis elle *a raconté* [PC] le récit de ses malheurs avec lui et pourquoi il N'ÉTAIT [IMP] vraiment PAS SON GENRE, et **là-dessus** elle ANNONCE [NP] qu'elle VA L'ÉPOUSER, le type [GO-FUT]!

She *went through the list* [PC/PRET] of everything that's wrong with him . . . she *recounted* [PC/PRET] all her problems with him and why he really WASN'T HER TYPE [IMP] and **with that** she ANNOUNCES [NP] she's GOING TO MARRY THE GUY [GO-FUT]!

In part III of this chapter (§6.7.2) we will examine the use of the temporal conjunction *tant que* (until, as long as) as another TEXTUAL device to split certain situations into their constituent phases.

6.6.3. As stated above, the epic *laisses* do not correspond to definable units of narrative content; they are probably best viewed as performance units, subdivisions of "sittings." Auerbach, we recall, describes the epic *laisses* as "independent pictures"; just as pictures have borders, *laisses* have boundaries, which are often marked by shifts in tense. In Ruelle (1976:781) we read that the *Roland* poet returns to the P at the beginning of a *laisse*, notably where he wishes to signal a turning point in the action or recall earlier events. This accords with the observation above that new developments on the narrative line tend to be reported in the P. However, the concept of a narrative line is tenuous in the epic, in addition to which the most frequent *laisse*-initial PAST tense is not the PS but the PC, which is often simply a PFV aspect of the PR. The majority of epic *laisses* begin either *in medias res* with a PR (in description or direct speech),[160] or with an anaphoric PC/PERF,[161] which is also commonly used for closure of episodes.

The role of the PC in the textual articulation of *Roland* is analyzed by Hatcher (1942:606), who emphasizes both its "conclusive force . . . to bring a whole episode to a close [and] its introductory force to strike the opening chord for a new episode." Consider examples (6.37) and (6.38) below, in which the boundaries of macro-event spans (what Hatcher calls "episodes") are marked by the PC/PERF (boldfaced).[162] These boundaries (coded with a double asterisk) often coincide only approximately with those of *laisse* units.

(6.37) Cil le RECEIT [NP], s'i MET [NP] ·c· cumpaignons

He GETS HOLD OF [NP] him, # SETS [NP] upon him one hundred of his comrades

De la quisine des mielz e des pejurs.

from the kitchen, the best and the worst.

Icil li PEILENT [NP] la barbe e les gernuns,
Cascun le FIERT [NP] ·iiii· colps de sun puign,
Ben le batirent [PS] a fuz e a bastuns,

They TEAR OUT [NP] his beard and his moustache,
each one STRIKES [NP] him four blows with his fist,
they laid into [PS] him with cudgels and sticks,

E si li METENT [NP] el col un caeignun,
Si l'ENCAEINENT [NP] altresi cum un urs;
**Sur un sumer l'UNT mis [PC] a deshonor,
Tant le GUARDENT [NP] que·l RENDENT a Charlun.

and # PUT [NP] an iron collar around his neck,
they CHAIN [NP] him up as they would a bear;
**   On a packhorse, in dishonor, they HAVE **him put** [PC],
they GUARD [NP] him until they can TURN HIM OVER [NP] to Charles.
(vv. 1821–1829)

(6.38) **Li quens Rollant el champ EST **repairét** [PC]
TIENT [NP] Durendal, cume vassal i
FIERT [NP] . . .

**   Count Roland HAS **returned** [PC] to the battlefield,
He WIELDS [NP] Durendal, he STRIKES [NP] like a warrior . . .
(vv. 1870–1871)

The PC/PERF is a logical framing tense, not restricted to the *chansons de geste*. In chapter 5 we observed its overall frequency in Abstracts and Codas, which together frame the narrative diegesis. A number of prose *laisses* in *Aucassin and Nicolette* open with anaphoric repetition of an event narrated in the preceding *laisse* introduced by the PC formula *si con vos avés oï et entendu* (as you have now heard; cf. text III : 2). The closure provided by the PERF cannot be expressed using the PRET, whose "sequential" implicature leads us to expect continuation. For the twelfth-century *chansons de geste*, in which the PC is essentially still a PR with an aspectual feature of completion, this category is all the more appropriate to mark the closure of spans in which the unmarked tense for reporting information is the PR. The sequentiality of the PRET also renders it less appropriate than the PERF for signaling new developments, which often entail a break with what precedes.

Part III. Information Blocking: The "Tempo" of the Text

In addition to deciding on the content of a discourse and how it is to be organized, speakers also decide how much of it they think a listener can take in at one time. This decision is based in part on assumptions about what the listener already knows. Speakers package information into units or "blocks" (Grimes 1975), which may or may not correspond to some easily recognized substring of the content. In this final part of the chapter, I shall consider a number of ways in which tense switching is pressed into discourse-pragmatic service for the blocking of information in narrative, notably in texts that are recited and composed orally. The first section (§6.7) deals with several specifically oral strategies for distributing information in clauses and linking these clauses together. The second (§6.8) focuses on the use of tense-aspect categories to control the pacing of a text, i.e., the rate at which new information is introduced into the discourse, which in turn influences our perception of narrative tempo.

6.7. "Co-subordinate" nexus
6.7.1. It is generally assumed that conjoined clause structures in which the second (or all but the first) clause is subjectless fall under the heading of coordination. However, Foley and Van Valin (1984: chapter 6) propose a typology of clause-linkage patterns in which structures of this type are included in a syntactic halfway house they refer to as "*co-subordinate* nexus." According to this typology, three possible relations

may obtain between two clauses: coordination, co-subordination, and subordination, defined by the features [± dependent] and [± embedded]. Coordinated clauses carry a minus value for both features, subordinated clauses two plus values, while co-subordinate clauses are [+ dependent] but [− embedded] (1984 : 242f.). As an example of co-subordinate nexus, consider the first two clauses of (6.37), repeated here as (6.39):

(6.39)   Cil le *RECEIT* [NP], s'i *MET* [NP] ·c· cumpaignons / De la quisine des mielz e des pejurs. "He *GETS HOLD OF* [NP] him, # *SETS* [NP] upon him one hundred of his comrades / from the kitchen, the best and the worst."

These clauses could be rewritten in subordinate nexus without an appreciable change of meaning: "when/as soon as/once he gets hold of him, he sets one hundred of his comrades from the kitchen upon him."

This type of quasi-paratactic clausal linkage (analogous to the "conjunctive *and*" of Halliday and Hasan 1976) is extremely common in medieval Romance narrative, though not as common as full parataxis ("co-ordinative *and*"). Its function appears to be a pragmatic one of recipient-designing the packaging of information in texts to accommodate the conditions of story performance. Here once again the findings of natural narrative analysis may shed light on a particular strategy of information blocking common in medieval Romance.

In oral verse narration, information blocks are predetermined by the meter, with enjambment virtually absent in texts composed for performance. It is not accidental that these blocks rarely exceed eight syllables, and in texts composed *in* performance they often have fewer. The *chansons de geste* and the *Alexis* use a ten-syllable line divided into hemistichs of four and six syllables with a clearly marked caesura (see texts X, XI); the *romancero* uses a sixteen-syllable line divided into two eight-syllable hemistichs (texts VII, VIII). These metrical constraints function not only for artistic and compositional purposes, but also to ensure a reasonable blocking of information, consonant with what listeners are able to process in situations of aural text reception.

Looking at the discourse structure of the *orally composed* texts in this sample (VII–XI), we also observe that the density of new information is fairly low, its rate of introduction being controlled by anaphoric repetition of information and by the use of filler hemistichs, as in the second verse of each verse pair given in (6.40):

(6.40a)   Por la matanza va el viejo,   The old man goes in search of carnage
por la matanza adelante   of the carnage [that lies] ahead (VII : 15f.)

(6.40b) Recordó despavorida
y con un pavor muy grande

Terrified she recalled it [her dream],
filled with fear and dread   (VIII: 19f.)

(6.40c) "Ques esto, mesnadas,
o que queredes vos?"

"What is this, my men,
what do you wish?"   (IX: 33f.)

(6.40d) Le destre poign ad perdut,
n'en ad mie.

He has lost his right hand,
he has it no longer.   (X: 38f.)

(Other examples: VII: 75f.; VIII: 4, 14, 24, 42; IX: 12, 14; XI: 23f.) Though the presence of these filler clauses has generally been linked to considerations of rhyme or assonance, they also have an important TEXTUAL function: to slow down the rate of injection of new information to a reasonable level for this type of communicative situation.

6.7.2. Oral narratives of any length do not unfold in a single seamless continuum, but segment themselves naturally into chunks, which usually correspond to performance, prosodic, and information units. In the *chansons de geste*, for example, each "sitting" (a performance unit) is divided into *laisses* (a prosodic unit), which provide a meter or at times a countermeter for "spans" (an information unit) centering around a macro-event, participant, or setting.

A particularly interesting strategy for chunking information, tied clearly to the pragmatic and prosodic requirements of oral narration, is analyzed in Hatcher (1946) and involves the use of co-subordinate nexus for the representation of journeys. Consider the examples in (6.41)–(6.45):

(6.41) Tant *TRESPASSENT* [PR] de la meison que il *vindrent* [PS] en un vergier. "They *JOURNEY* [PR] so far/long from the house that they *came* [PS] to an orchard."   (*Yvain*, 5344f.)

(6.42a) Tant *chevalchat* [PS] qu'en Saraguce *fut* [PS]. "He *rode* [PS] so far/long that he *was* [PS] in Saragossa."   (*Roland*, 2818)

(6.42b) Tant *chevalcherent* [PS] que en Sarraguce *SUNT* [PR] . "They *rode* [PS] so far/long that they *ARE* [PR] in Saragossa."   (*Roland*, 2689 [X: 4–5])

(6.43) *Parrtios* [PS] de la puerta, por Burgos *AGUIJAVA* [IMP]. "He *left* [PS] through the gate [and] *SET OFF* [IMP] toward Burgos."   (*Cid*, 51)

(6.44) . . . si *S'EN VA* [PR] tant que ele *vint* [PS] au mur del castel. ". . . # [she] *GOES* [PR] so far/long that she *reached* [PS] the castle."   (*AN*, 16: 6–7)

Syntax of this type is designed to block information into relatively small clauses, each corresponding to a metrical unit and arranged with the appearance of a result clause structure (what Hatcher calls a "pseudo-result clause" structure). The alternative would be to package all of the information contained in the two clauses into a single clause ("they journey from the house to the orchard," "he/they rode as far as Saragossa," "he set off for Burgos") in which the goal of the motion verb is expressed only by a locative noun phrase. Many though not all sequences of this type involve tense switching, and the alternation patterns differ. The most common epic pattern is *tant* PS (movement verb) *que* PR (goal verb), as in (6.42b),[163] whereas in the romances the preferred pattern seems to be *tant* PR (movement) *que* PS (goal), as in (6.41) (Fotitch 1950:24ff; Wehr 1984:119). In *Aucassin and Nicolette* the co-subordinate structure occurs in both verse and prose, generally without tense switching—PS (movement) *tant que* PS (goal).[164]

The semantic structure of situations involving spatial motion consists of four elements: a source, a path, a goal, and the manner in which the motion is carried out. Languages differ regarding which of these elements must be expressed formally and how they are mapped onto grammar (see Talmy 1985). For example, English says "he ran across the street" or "he drove up to the house," conflating motion and manner in the verb root ("ran," "drove"), while path and goal are packaged together in what Talmy calls "satellites" of the verb complex, here adverbs and prepositional phrases ("across the street," "up to the house"). French, by contrast, configures these same motion events as *il a traversé la rue en courant, il s'est approché de la maison*, with motion and path expressed by the verb root (*traverser, s'approcher de*), goal by its complement (*la rue, la maison*), and manner—if expressed at all—by gerundive or other adverbial complements (*en courant*). In both cases the entire "journey" is contained in a single clause. In the medieval examples above, the linguistic expression of journeys is divided between two clauses, each with its own verb: motion and path (and optionally manner) are expressed by the verb of the first clause, while goal is expressed in a second clause by a verb (generally of little semantic weight) and a locative complement. (Source is not of concern here, because it does not involve the verb.)

The different tense patterns observed in the early Romance examples reflect a difference in *focus*, i.e., whether what is foregrounded—by a tense other than the PRET—is the path or the goal. In (6.42b) and (6.43) it is the arrival (goal), reported in the PR and IMP, respectively; in (6.41) and (6.44) it is the journey itself (path), reported in the PR. The nonfocal element is reported in the PS. But irrespective of whether tense switching occurs, these co-subordinate structures fulfill an important TEXTUAL function in *oral* narration; like filler clauses, they reduce the density of new information, thereby facilitating processing for the listener, while at the same time accommodating the demands of prosody.

6.7.3. An analogous blocking of information, reflecting the prosodic and pragmatic conditions of oral composition and delivery, occurs in the *romancero*. In chapter 3 (§3.5) I argued that tense in the *romancero* is not dictated by factors such as rhyme or meter, given the syntactic flexibility of the sixteen-syllable line. Clause structure, however, does seem to be influenced by rhyme. By way of example we shall consider texts with assonance in *-ía*, which favors the IMP. For convenience I transcribe the texts with one hemistich per line, following the tense-marking conventions used in the appendix and coding so-called main and subordinate clauses as M and S, respectively:

(6.45) *Despertó* muy congojado   [M] He *awoke* greatly distressed
con aquella voz que *OÍA* . . .   [S] by that voice he *WAS HEARING* . . .
Estando en esto *allegó*   [M] Thereupon there *arrived*
uno que nuevas *TRAÍA* . . .   [S] someone who *WAS BEARING* news . . .
        (Roderick cycle ballad, *Prim. #*5a; Menéndez y Pelayo 1944–1945:8:88f.)

(6.46) *Vino* allí un conde   [M] There *came* to that place a Norman
        normando   Count
que *PASABA* en romería;   [S] who was *PASSING THROUGH* on a
                pilgrimage;
supo que este hombre famoso   [M] he *learned* that this well-known man
en cárceles *PADECÍA*.   [S] *WAS SUFFERING* in jail.
Fuése para Castroviejo   [M] He *went* to Castroviejo
donde el conde *RESIDÍA* . . .   [S] where the Count *RESIDED* . . .
        (ballad of Fernán González, *Prim. #*15; Menéndez y Pelayo 1944–1945:8:103)

In all of these verses the first hemistich reports a narrative event in a main clause and in the unmarked event tense, the PS, while the second hemistich reports temporally simultaneous information in a subordinate clause, which logically calls for the IMP. This clause structure is clearly designed to accommodate the assonance in *-ía*. According to the narrative norm, focal or plot-advancing information (e.g., "the messenger came *with news*," "the famous man *was in jail*") is normally reported in main clauses; but in these examples the new information comes in subordinate clauses. Yet in an important sense none of this information is new: the *fabulas* of traditional ballads were well known, a circumstance that allowed their singers to block information in whatever form best suited the prosody. In many ballads, notably those assonating in -*ía* and -*a-a* (-*ía* and -*aba* are both IMP morphemes), the most appropriate blocking is via a structure of main clause followed by subordinate clause, PS followed by IMP. By contrast, in texts with assonance in -*ó* we frequently find second hemistichs with main clauses and, consequently, with PS verbs (-*ó* is the 3sg PS morpheme): for example, "Con cartas y mensajeros / el rey al Carpio *envió* . . ." (Through letters and messengers/the King *sent* [PS] to [Bernaldo del] Carpio . . .).

To sum up this argument, I shall insist once again that tense switching in the *romancero* is not governed by prosodic considerations, in the sense that it is not a grammatical anomaly explicable in terms of a need to provide rhymes or a proper number of syllables; however, the tenses associated with particular assonances are used to create a clause structure through which new information can be dispensed in carefully measured doses.

6.8. Pacing the discourse

Syntactic blocking patterns such as those described above are designed to reduce the rate at which new information is introduced, thereby slowing down the tempo of narration. Tense can also be used as a device to control the pacing of a narrative, accelerating or decelerating the tempo at appropriate points.

6.8.1. It has frequently been pointed out that an effect of the diegetic PR is to speed up the pace of narration, particularly when PR-tense verbs cluster, as in the examples in (6.47) and (6.48), from the texts in appendix 2, and (6.49), from Plautus's *Pot of Gold:*

(6.47) . . . l'en *porta par mi le presse,*	. . . [they] *carried him into the fray.*
se *SE LANCE TRES ENTRE MI SES ANEMIS;*	# He *THROWS HIMSELF AMIDST HIS ENEMIES,*
et il *GETENT LES MAINS* de toutes pars,	and they *GRAB AT HIM* from all sides,
si le *PRENDENT,*	# *TAKE HOLD OF HIM,*
si le *DESSAISISENT DE L'ESCU ET DE LE LANCE,*	# *DIVEST HIM OF HIS SHIELD AND HIS LANCE,*
si l'en *MANNENT* tot estrousement pris.	# *LEAD HIM AWAY,* securely captured.

(III : 24 – 29)

(6.48) *BALZO* dal letto mezzo addormentato, *DISCENDO LE SCALE, ENTRO NELLA VETTURA* e *PARTO*. . . . L'oste e la moglie . . . *CHIAMANO TUTTI I SERVI, CERCANO, ESAMINANO, MINACCIANO* . . .

I *LEAP OUT OF BED* half asleep, *GO DOWN THE STAIRS, GET INTO THE COACH,* and *LEAVE*. . . . The innkeeper and his wife . . . *SUMMON ALL THE SERVANTS,* SEARCH, INSPECT, THREATEN . . .   (V : 18–21, 33–36)

(6.49) Ubi illi *abiit,* ego *ME DEORSUM DUCO DE ARBORE: EXFODIO AULAM AURI PLENAM:* inde *EXEO* ilico. *VIDEO RECIPERE SE SENEM:* ille *NON ME VIDET.*

As soon as he *left,* I *SLIDE DOWN FROM MY TREE, DIG UP THE POT FULL OF GOLD,* and *TAKE OFF* right away. I *SEE THE OLD MAN COME HOME,* [but] he *DOESN'T SEE ME.*   (*Aulalaria,* 708–711; cited in Schlicher 1931)

Within accelerative passages of this type, the PR tense verbs occur in very short main clauses, at times consisting only of the verb itself and a subject pronoun if required; the clauses tend to be conjoined paratactically with no coordinating conjunctions (asyndeton); the verb occurs in clause-initial position (preceded only by particles if required); and subordinate clauses and background material are avoided, though they may occur elsewhere in the text. At issue here is obviously the PR_a, which focuses on the initial moment of situations and, irrespective of their inherent situation type, configures them into instantaneous achievements. It is the achievement profile in combination with the clausal properties described above that creates the impression of an acceleration in the tempo of narration.

The PR_a is also commonly used to "telescope" into semelfactive count situations what are really iterative mass situations ("slaying ten knights" and "wounding seven") or durative activity and accomplishment situations ("galloping back into battle"), as in the example in (6.50):

(6.50) et qu'il lor *ABAT DIS CEVALIERS*   And {that} he *SLAYS TEN OF THEIR KNIGHTS,*

et *NAVRE SET*   and *WOUNDS SEVEN,*

et qu'il *SE JETE* TOT ESTROSEEMENT *DE LE PRESE*   and {that} he *THROWS HIMSELF* HEADLONG *INTO THE FRAY*

et qu'il *S'EN REVIENT* LES *GALOPIAX* ARIERE.   and {that} he *COMES GALLOPING BACK.*

                (III : 45–49)

As a result of this linguistic condensation, iterated actions that occurred over a period of time are packaged as pseudo-narrative events that give the impression of having occurred at a single moment in time. In an appropriate syntactic context, such sequences similarly serve to speed up the tempo of narration at that particular point.

Though the phenomenon of PR-tense clusters can be found in highly literate written texts (e.g., in modern historiography; for examples, see Imbs [1960]:33; Herczeg 1958:373ff.), the syntax and tense usage of these passages are characteristic of—and as I see it ultimately derive from—oral narration.

6.8.2.   While the diegetic *action* PR can serve to accelerate the pace of a narrative in certain contexts, its counterpart the *visualizing* PR can have the opposite effect of slowing down the tempo, particularly when combined with stative predicates.

Consider first the example in (6.51) from a modern Italian short story by Grazia Deledda:

(6.51)   La rivoltella *È* lì, anche quella sera, sulla tavola da pranzo che *SERVE* da scrittoio, come la grande stanza, terrena, *E ADIBITA* a uso di salotto e, occorrendo, da sala e ufficio di consultazioni. Un lume a petrolio *RISCHIARA* la stanza; le finestre *SONO CHIUSE*, sebbene la notte, fuori, *SIA* già *UN PO' CALDA*, ricca di luna e di stelle.

That night too the revolver *IS* there, on the dining table that *IS USED* as a writing desk, in the same way as the large room on the ground floor *IS USED* as a sitting room and, when necessary, as an office and consultation room. A gas light *ILLUMINATES* the room; the windows *ARE CLOSED*, even though outside the evening *IS* a bit *WARM* perhaps, filled with light from the moon and the stars.
(“Forze Occulte,” p. 232)

Out of context it is not apparent that this is a passage of interior monologue. It reports the thoughts of a character as she contemplates the interior of a large room in an old house. The co-occurrence of the PR with stative predicates, a combination that typically occurs in *descriptive* rather than narrative passages, produces a perceptible slowing down of the narrative tempo, inviting readers to pause longer than they might otherwise over the descriptive details that are thereby foregrounded.

In similar fashion, the static, lyrical quality that critics commonly perceive in the “similar *laisses*” of the *chansons de geste, Roland* in particular, is produced in part through the decelerative power of the NP$_V$. In *Roland* the movement of narrative time is slowed to a halt at strategic points in the story—the narrative Peaks—by sequences of two or three *laisses* that repeat the same basic information with variations of detail. In Fleischman 1989a I discuss the use of this type of repetition-with-variation as a TEXTUAL device to regulate the pace of narration, once again by drastically reducing the rate at which new information is introduced. This "slowing down of the camera" is a foregrounding technique for marking Peaks, albeit Peaks that are lyrical rather than strictly narrative. Blanc (1964:105) calculates that the sets of similar *laisses* contain eighty percent PR tenses (included in this figure are many speaker-based PRs of direct speech). Though a number of these are of the action variety, it is the visualizing variety that slows narrative time to a halt at moments of high drama, such as *laisses* 133–135, when Roland finally consents to blow his olifant and in so doing bursts his temple and dies:

(6.52) Rollant *AD mis* [NP$_V$] [165] l'olifan a sa buche,   (133)
EMPEINT [NP$_a$] le ben, par grant vertut le *SUNET* [NP$_a$].
Halt *SUNT* [NP$_V$] li pui et la voiz *EST* [NP$_V$] mult lunge . . .

Li quens Rollant par peine e par ahans,   (134)
Par grant dulor *SUNET* [NP$_V$] sun olifan.
Parmi la buche en *SALT* [NP$_a$] fors li cler sancs,
De sun cervel le temple en *EST RUMPANT* [NP$_V$] . . .

Li quens Rollant *AD* la buche *SANGLENTE* [NP$_V$],   (135)
De sun cervel *RUMPUT* en *EST* [NP$_V$] li temples,
L'olifan *SUNET* [NP$_V$] a dulor e a peine . . .

Roland *HAS* the olifant *placed* [NP$_V$] at his lips,   (133)
He *SETS* [NP$_a$] it well, *SOUNDS* [NP$_a$] it with all his strength.
The hills *ARE* [NP$_V$] high and his voice *RANGES* [NP$_V$] far . . .

Count Roland with great pain and effort,   (134)
With great travail *IS SOUNDING* [NP$_V$] his olifant.
From his mouth the bright blood *COMES LEAPING OUT* [NP$_a$],
The temple in his forehead *IS BURSTING* [NP$_V$] . . .

Count Roland's mouth *IS FILLED WITH BLOOD* [NP$_V$],   (135)
The temple in his forehead *IS BURST* [NP$_V$],
He *IS SOUNDING* [NP$_V$] the olifant in great travail and pain . . .

                              (*Roland*, 1753–1755, 1761–1764, 1785–1787)

One effect of the repetition here is to blur the distinction between the NP$_a$ and the NP$_v$. The predicate *suner* (to sound a horn) is an activity. At its first appearance in *laisse* 133 it is perceived to be an action NP, referring to the moment at which Roland begins to blow his horn. As this verb is repeated in *laisses* 134 and 135 the tense becomes more of a visualizing NP, as we *watch* Roland blowing his horn through the slow-motion camera of the similar *laisses*.

Like the PR, the NARR IMP is also used to decelerate the tempo of narration. But whereas the decelerative PR occurs with atelic situations, primarily in descriptive passages, the NARR IMP enables a deceleration along the event line itself: "it makes us linger over the event's significance which the *qualité ponctuelle* of the Past Definite [PS] condenses too briskly" (Saunders 1969 : 154). See the examples in chapter 1 (§1.5.3).

6.8.3.   Each of the three phenomena considered in this section involves use of a tense other than the unmarked tense for that type of discourse (events or description) to do pragmatic work relating to the disposition of information in the text. The unmarked tense for the event line is the PRET; through the use of marked tenses to narrate events, the pace of a text can alternatively be speeded up, through the PR$_a$, or slowed down, through the NARR IMP. The unmarked tense for description is the IMP; through use of the PR$_v$ we are induced to linger over particular details, reported as states. In the case of activity and accomplishment predicates that have duration but also natural endpoints, on the one hand, the PR$_v$ can render them descriptive, moving them in the direction of states by obscuring their endpoints and privileging their duration; on the other, the PR$_a$ enables them to function as narrative events, moving them in the direction of achievements by shifting the focus onto their initial boundary.

The pragmatic functions of tense-aspect considered in this chapter— grounding, boundary marking, and monitoring information flow—all relate to the structure and organization of a narrative as TEXT. Certain of these functions relate in particular to textuality that is oral. The next chapter concentrates on pragmatic functions that operate in the EXPRESSIVE component, and certain of these manifest themselves most prominently in written texts, notably modern narrative fiction.

7 Expressive Functions

The decline of storytelling is only a concomitant that has quite gradually removed narrative from the realm of living speech. . . . The earliest symptom of a process whose end is the decline of storytelling is the rise of the novel at the beginning of modern times. What distinguishes the novel from a story (and from the epic in the narrower sense) is its essential dependence on the book. (BENJAMIN, "THE STORYTELLER")

J'avoue que certain emploi de l'imparfait de l'indicatif—de ce temps cruel qui nous présente la vie comme quelque chose d'éphémère à la fois et de passif, qui, au moment même où il retrace nos actions, les frappe d'illusion, les anéantit dans le passé sans nous laisser comme le parfait, la consolation de l'activité—est resté pour moi une source inépuisable de mystérieuses tristesses. (PROUST, *PASTICHES ET MÉLANGES*)

In a recent monograph on point of view in fiction we read: "It is virtually impossible for a narrator to tell a story without communicating, either explicitly or, as is more common, implicitly through a variety of means, some degree of distance or affinity, detachment from or involvement with the various subjects (events, objects, places, and especially personae) which constitute the story world. These affective relationships, which may be related to but are not identical with the ideological relationship of the narrator to the story, are a vital component of the 'message' the text communicates, crucial to its encoding, reception, and interpretation" (Lanser 1981:202). It is first of all on the level of ideology (i.e., of evaluations) that narrative "point of view" takes shape, insofar as an ideology governs the conceptual vision of the world in all or part of a text. In chapter 5 we looked at the role of tense as an EXPRESSIVE device for carrying out evaluation, in particular the prominent cross-language use of the PR for internal evaluations. But, as Lanser suggests, the "point" or "message" of a narrative is also communicated by the subjective colorations that events, objects, participants, and settings take on by virtue of being projected through the mediating filter of an individual subjectivity. These "affective relationships," which complete the notion of point of view, also receive linguistic expression through tense-aspect categories.

Lanser (1981) uses the term "stance" to refer to a speaker's relation to the message of an utterance. Every sentence in a text necessarily implies some stance, for "language is a powerfully committing medium to work in" (Fowler 1977:76). This fact tends to be obscured in studies on the language of fiction, since in the last century opinion about the novel has moved decisively against the intervention of the author in the text. Nonetheless, Fowler (1977:43f.) insists that "modal participation in what he writes is just as inevitable for the writer of fiction as it is for any other person who utters any sentence. . . . Syntactically 'unmarked' modality is still modality." With regard to narrative, the "syntactically unmarked" stance is that of the historian—whether this persona is identified with the author or the fictional Speaker—who reports events objectively in the PS/PRET.

In chapter 1 I set up a typology of narrating personae, each of which is associated with a tense-aspect category found in narration: the historian with the unmarked PRET, the memorialist with the PERF/PC, the painter with the IMP, and the performer with the PR. The Speaker's relationship to the content of the utterance is different for each of these personae. Although the Speaker normally remains the same throughout a text, his or her perspective on and relationship to people, places, objects, and events in the story world may change. The metaphor of narrating personae is intended to capture these different relationships, or points of view, which, like everything in a text, must be conveyed through language. What I propose to demonstrate in this chapter is how point of view is expressed through tense-aspect morphology operating in the EXPRESSIVE component.

7.1. Point of view and focalization

Discussion of point of view has been carried out largely in the camp of literary criticism; the theoretical underpinning for the concept comes similarly from the work of literary narratologists.[166] This is not to imply that either the concept of point of view or the linguistic means through which it is actualized in discourse is exclusive to literature. Literary narratologists recognize that although point of view is itself nonverbal, it must be conveyed through linguistic means; it is therefore surprising how few attempts have been made to identify in a linguistically informed way what these means are and how they operate. In particular, there has been minimal acknowledgment of the significant role played by categories of the verb, notably tense-aspect, in the linguistic encoding of point of view (exceptions are Bronzwaer 1970; Cohn 1978), or what I refer to, following Genette, as *focalization*.

Most theoretical works on point of view, Genette has observed, suffer from a confusion between what he calls "narrative mood" and "narrative voice," between the question "Who is the person whose point of view orients the narrative perspective?" and the very different question "Who is the narrator?" or "Who sees?" vs. "Who speaks?" (Genette 1980:186). It is often the case that narrators undertake to tell what another individual sees or has seen. Thus "speaking" and "seeing," "narration" and what Genette refers to as "focalization," may, but need not, be associated with the same agent. When focalization changes, what changes is not the narrative voice; the angle of vision through which events in a text are filtered will always be *verbalized* by the narrator. What changes is *the perception that orients the report*. This perception may be associated with a character in the story, or may simply be an unpersonified textual stance that we tend to endow with the qualities of a character.[167]

Example (7.1) from "L'Expiation," Victor Hugo's quasi-epic verse narrative about Napoleon, should serve to illustrate the distinction between Speaker/narrator and focalizer (also referred to as the "reflector"). Under orders from Napoleon, the French general Grouchy was to pursue the Prussian army, led by Blücher, then continue the march on to Waterloo. Instead, Grouchy was tricked and it was Blücher who arrived at Waterloo to reinforce the English. At a certain point in the battle, with things still looking up for the French, Bonaparte gazes across the plain of Waterloo and suddenly discerns in the distance an approaching figure he believes to be Grouchy. At this moment the narrator utters the sentences given in (7.1):

(7.1) Soudain, joyeux, il *dit* [PS]: Grouchy!—*C'ÉTAIT* [IMP] Blücher.
"Suddenly, joyful, he *said* [PS]: Grouchy!—It *WAS* [IMP] Blücher."
$[t_1 \text{ in } W_S]$ $[t_1 \text{ in } W_N]$

Commenting on this example, Ducrot (1979:13) observes that by using the IMP in the second sentence Hugo's narrator adopts the omniscient perspective of God or the historian who, at the moment in the story-world (W_S) when the approaching figure comes into view (t_1), already knows his identity. Had Hugo used the PS in place of the IMP, as in (7.1'):

(7.1') Il *dit* [PS]: Grouchy!—Ce *fut* [PS] Blücher.
$[t_1 \text{ in } W_S]$ $[t_2 \text{ in } W_S]$

this same narrator would instead be projecting the perspective of Napoleon, who would only identify the approaching figure as Blücher at a later moment (t_2) in story-time. In terms of chronology, the two situations referred to respectively by the two sentences in (7.1) are *simultaneous:* however, they refer to different worlds, the first sentence to the diegetic world (W_S), the second to the extradiegetic world of the narrator (W_N). By contrast, the situations referred to by the two sentences in (7.1') are *sequential,* both referring to the diegetic world W_S. In the actual passage from Hugo the narrator can, through a simple shift in tenses, both *narrate*—via the PS—the appearance of the person assumed by Napoleon at t_1 to be Grouchy and *comment*—via the IMP and from his own panchronic angle of vision—on the actual identity of this participant. The difference between the two versions of this example involves point of view or, more precisely, focalization, and this difference is expressed linguistically through a tense-aspect contrast.

Genette initially proposed a three-way typology of focalizations, distinguishing among sentences that are "externally focalized," "internally focalized," and "nonfocalized."[168] The nonfocalized perspective (also called "zero-focalization") corresponds to omniscient narration, where the narrator says more than any of the characters knows at a given moment, as in the IMP sentence of (7.1) above. With external focalization, the narrator says less than the focalized character knows, reporting only what can be perceived by an external observer. With internal focalization, the narrator is also a character and says only what that character knows or can perceive.

Focalization has both a subject and an object. The subject (the focalizer) is the agent (personified or not) whose perception orients the report; the object (the focalized) is what the focalizer perceives (Bal 1983). Just as the *focalizer* may be internal or external to the represented world, so too *focalized* objects may be perceived "from within" or "from without." Focalization from without limits all observation to outward manifestations, leaving the emotions to be inferred from them. This is the prototypical narrative stance of much biblical narrative and of epic, in which we are told only about the characters' actions, gestures, and directly quoted utterances. Consider the description of Charlemagne that closes the Oxford *Roland,* repeated here as (7.2)

(7.2) *PLURET* des oilz, sa barbe blanche *TIRET.*   "His eyes *WEEP,* he *STROKES* his white beard."   (v. 4002)

We are told nothing of Charlemagne's internal conflict at having to go off to war again; all we see are two gestures, which in the context of the story and of the feudal-warrior society that provides its cultural matrix say much more than what is conveyed by the referential meanings of the two clauses. By contrast, focalization from within reveals the inner life of focalized characters, either by making the characters their own focalizers, or by granting an external focalizer the privilege of penetrating the consciousness of focalized characters, an epistemic privilege available only in fiction. Among medieval Romance genres, it is courtly-chivalric romance that best develops external focalization from within (see text XII).

Inconsistencies have been pointed out in Genette's three-way typology, such that most theorists now operate with just a binary contrast—internal vs. external focalization—depending essentially on whether the focalizer is a character or the narrator.[169] The locus of an external focalization is outside W_S proper while that of an internal focalization is inside W_S.

Barthes (1966:18/1975:262) has proposed that the criterion for an internal focalization is the possibility of rewriting a narrative sequence in the first person (in terms of verisimilitude rather than strictly grammar) if it is not in that person already. If this is feasible, the segment is internally focalized; if not, the focalization is external. However, even in first-person narration focalization can be external when the temporal and psychological distance between the narrating-I and the experiencing-I is minimal (e.g., in the Crusade chronicles of Villehardouin or Robert of Clari, or in Camus's *The Stranger;* §7.7.1) or, alternatively, when the perception through which the story is rendered is that of the narrating-I rather than the experiencing-I (the unmarked focalization of Proust's *Remembrance of Things Past;* §7.4.1). We begin to see how the categories of "voice" and "point of view" become entangled. While the first-person substitution test is a necessary condition for internal focalization, it is not sufficient. For in first-person narration the grammatical "I" is a linguistic mark of two subjectivities: that of the narrating-I and that of the experiencing-I.

Whereas the thrust of the aforementioned discussions has been toward a conceptual *separation* between narrative voice and point of view, for Ricoeur (1985:99) the two are ultimately inseparable—a single function considered from the perspective of two questions: "Point of view answers the question 'From where do we perceive what is shown to us by the fact of being narrated?' Hence, from where is one speaking? Voice answers the question 'Who is speaking here?' If we do not want to be misled by the metaphor of *vision* when we consider a narrative in which everything is *recounted,* then vision must be taken to be concretization of understanding [cf. *n*168] hence, paradoxically, an appendix to hearing." As we shall see below, and as Genette also recognizes, in practice voice and focalization cannot be analyzed entirely independently of one another, even if we choose not to follow Ricoeur, who conflates them at the theoretical level.

For the remainder of our discussion I shall adhere to the revised binary formulation of focalization, with the following qualification: in most discussions of focalization there is an implication that the perception of a focalizer (narrator or character) remains constant. However, the narrating personae I have referred to as the historian, memorialist, painter, and performer are essentially *alternate focalizations of the narrator,* distinguished not so much along a scale of epistemic access to the mental states of story participants or to situations that cannot normally be observed as along a scale of subjective involvement with these situations and participants, yielding the different modes of reporting I have referred to respectively as diegetic, memorial, pictorial, and mimetic. It was Bakhtin (1973) who first suggested that a narrator speaks for a "polyphony" of voices, becoming a plurality of centers of consciousness irreducible to a common denominator. What he had in mind was a conversation *between narrators and their characters.* But is it not the "dialogization" *of the narrator's own voice* that offers the most compelling demonstration of the fundamental polyphony of narrative discourse?

Rimmon-Kenan (1983:77ff.) points out that the distinction between internal and external focalization has correlates—she refers to these as transformations (not in the TG sense)—in domains other than simply perception—in space, time, cognition, and expressivity. We shall consider the temporal transformation in §7.5 below. In its expressive, or what she calls "emotive," transformation, the external-internal opposition yields objective (neutral, uninvolved) vs. subjective (colored, involved) focalization (1983:80). While the perception of character-focalizers is unquestionably subjective, being limited to what they know or can observe, I would argue that the perception of narrator-focalizers can be equally subjective, a state of affairs that may reveal itself more strikingly in natural narratives than in fiction. Only the "degree-zero" focalization associated with the persona of the historian is relatively objective (absolute objectivity in narration is impossible), while the focalizations of the other personae that narrator-focalizers can adopt all involve a greater degree of subjectivity, the most subjective being that of the performer. By narrating in the PR tense, this persona strives to make narration resemble a current report, which is *a priori* internally focalized.

Focalization may remain stable throughout a narrative, but it can also alternate between different focalizers. Changes in focalization are generally taken to refer to changes in the *focalizer,* though they can also involve changes in how the focalized object is perceived (i.e., from "within" or "without"; examples in §§7.7.2–3). A change in focalizers can be entirely internal, from one character-focalizer to another, though more commonly it involves a shift from the narrator's external perspective to the internal perspective of a character. In such situations one voice narrates while another consciousness is responsible for the perceptions, thoughts, feelings, even to a degree the words that the narrator reports. The narrator retains phraseological control of the discourse, while yielding to a foreign point of view.

Most discussions of focalization concentrate on shifts between the subjectivity of the narrator and that of a character in instances where these two roles are not assigned to the same participant, the situation in third-person fiction. Consider the example in (7.3):

(7.3) Nessuno però la *VOLEVA* neppure la maestrina, perchè le stanze *ERANO GRANDI* e, d'inverno, gelate, e piene di topi e di scarafaggi. La serva non *CHIUDEVA OCCHIO* quando la signorina *DOVEVA USCIRE* di notte per il suo mestiere; e Giovanna, a sua volta, sebbene coraggiosa e senza pregiudizi, *POSSEDEVA* una rivoltella col relativo porto d'armi.

La rivoltella *E* lì, anche quella sera, sulla tavola da pranzo che *SERVE* da scrittoio, come la grande stanza, terrena, *E ADIBITA* a uso di salotto e, occorrendo, da sala e ufficio di consultazioni. Un lume a petrolio *RISCHIARA* la stanza; le finestre *SONO CHIUSE*, sebbene la notte, fuori, *SIA* già *UN PO' CALDA*, ricca di luna e di stelle.

Ma Giovanna *AVEVA PAURA* più delle stelle e del profumo del tasso e del lamento dell'assiolo sul ciglione, che dei malviventi notturni.

No one *WANTED* it [the house], not even the schoolteacher because the rooms *WERE LARGE* and freezing in the winter and full of mice and cockroaches. The servant *WOULDN'T CLOSE HER EYES* when her young mistress *HAD TO LEAVE* at night for her job; and similarly Giovanna, though normally free from fears or prejudices, *OWNED* a revolver and [*HAD*] a permit to use it.

That night too the revolver *IS* there, on the dining table that *IS USED* as a writing desk, in the same way as the large room on the ground floor *IS USED* as a sitting room and when necessary as an office and consultation room. A gas light *ILLUMINATES* the room; the windows *ARE CLOSED*, even though outside the evening *IS* a bit *WARM* perhaps, filled with light from the moon and the stars.

But Giovanna *WAS* more *AFRAID* of the stars and the perfume of the yew-tree and the cry of the owl on the embankment than of nocturnal criminals.

(Grazia Deledda, "Forze Occulte," p. 232)

The first paragraph of this passage, a description by the (unpersonified) narrator of the sinister atmosphere of an old house, is entirely in the IMP. At the second paragraph (boldfaced) the tense shifts abruptly to the PR, though the narrative *voice* remains that of the narrator. The IMP resumes in the third paragraph as the narrator proceeds with the description, now of the character Giovanna.

What are signaled by the alternation of paragraphs in the IMP and the PR are changes in focalization—from the *external* perspective of the narrator to the *internal* perspective of Giovanna, then back again to the narrator. The switch into PR provides a demarcative "traffic signal" marking a shift out of the unmarked diegetic mode and into the marked discourse form of *interior monologue* (further discussion and examples in §7.4). The boldfaced paragraph seeks a mimetic representation of Giovanna's thoughts *as they passed through her mind* at the past "now" in which she contemplates the room.

Once we enter the domain of first-person or purportedly experiential narration, where the grammatical "I" is shared by a narrator and his or her character-self, we are confronted with focalization shifts that involve the same "person" (human and grammatical). Whereas in third-person narration the contrast between the narrating discourse and the narrated discourse is formally supported by grammatical distinctions of person and tense (I-now vs. s/he-then), in first-person narration this contrast is more concealed, being no longer marked by distinctive pronouns. The task of identifying the referent of the grammatical "I," which is split into two (or more) subjectivities, devolves on other linguistic signals, in particular tense-aspect categories. In the following sections I shall consider a number of examples in which the grammatical "I" em-personates both the narrator's focalization as Speaker and the focalization of this same individual as a character in the story—what Banfield (1982) calls a "self in the past."[170]

7.2. The Speaker and the experiencer

Banfield (1982) identifies two sentence types of narrative fiction that differ according to whether or not they contain an experiencing-self at a moment corresponding to an act of consciousness. Consider the sentences in (7.4), which she cites to illustrate the distinction (1982:157):

(7.4a)   Elle *vit* [PS] la lune. "She *saw* [PS] the moon."

(7.4b)   Elle *VOYAIT* [IMP] la lune maintenant. "She *SAW* [IMP] the moon now."

The (a) version in the PS reports the activity of seeing the moon as a completed past event, and does so objectively, in the "historical" mode, whereas
the (b) version in the IMP implies that this event has been *experienced* at
some moment, and reports it by representing that experience. Sentences in
which a PAST-tense verb collocates acceptably with "now" (or some other
nonpast adverb), Banfield (1982 : 158) argues, represent past events "from
within a consciousness" and endowed with the "quality of the experiential." It should be noted that sentences of this type, which exemplify free
indirect discourse (§7.3), are only possible in, and constitute a distinctive
feature of, the marked context of narrative. In most languages only IPFV
tenses can co-occur with "now"; the sentence in (7.4c) with the (PFV) PS is
ungrammatical:

(7.4c)   *Elle *vit* [PS] la lune maintenant.[171]

As argued in chapter 1, the narrative stance of the PRET (the PS in written French) is distinct from those of all other tenses that occur in narrative texts by virtue of being the only stance that does not implicate an
experiencing-self in the report of events; the PRET is a nonexperiential
grammatical form, entirely detached from a speaking or experiencing subject. By obliterating all self-reference, the historian-narrator cuts deictics
loose from their normal connection to a Speaker, leaving them free to
gravitate to the here-and-now of the story characters, as in the boldfaced
sentences of free indirect discourse in (7.5) and (7.6):

(7.5)   When he had rung off Kate pondered a bit about the fancy Clemance had
taken to Reed, who appeared oddly skittish in the presence of the famous pro-
fessor. **Certainly the remark about the horrors of daughters having babies
had been [PLP] the absolutely uncharacteristic remark she had ever heard
[PLP] Reed make. Well, it was [P] probably one of the happier effects of the
turmoil that people no longer sorted themselves out [P] so neatly. Reed,
indeed, had become [PLP] a more righteous attender of the University than
she. He was [P] there now, hanging from pipes no doubt and contemplating
elevators.**   (Amanda Cross, *Poetic Justice*, p. 148)

(7.6)   Au coin de la rue Montmartre, il [Frédéric] *se retourna* [PS]; il *regarda*
[PS] les fenêtres du premier étage; et il *rit* [PS] intérieurement de pitié sur lui-
même, en se rappelant avec quel amour il les *avait* souvent *contemplées* [PLP]! **Où
donc VIVAIT-elle [IMP]? Comment la rencontrer maintenant?** La solitude SE
ROUVRAIT [IMP] sur son désir plus immense que jamais!
                    (Flaubert, *L'Education sentimentale*, pt. 1, chap. 4, p. 41)

On the corner of the Rue Montmartre he [Frédéric] *turned round* [PS]; he *looked at* [PS] the first-floor windows; and he *laughed* [PS] inwardly, pitying himself, recalling how lovingly he *had* often *gazed at* [PLP] them. **Where DID she LIVE [IMP] then? How to find her now?** Solitude OPENED UP [IMP] once more about his desire, which was vaster than ever!

(Flaubert, *Sentimental Education,* p. 52; trans. adapted)

The boldfaced sentences in (7.5) are the thoughts of the character Kate Fansler. The "now" of the last sentence is her now as she actualizes in her mind the (vicarious!) experience of her fiancé Reed "investigating" in the basement of the Political Science building.[172] In the boldfaced sentences of (7.6) the "now" of the second question is similarly a character-now, *not,* however, at the point in the current narrative plane at which the narrator recounts Frédéric's actions (in the PS) but at a now in Frédéric's past when he would routinely gaze at those same windows wondering about the enigmatic Mme Arnoux. It is Frédéric's thoughts at that past moment, re-experienced in his mind, that the IPFV P, the P of recollections (cf. *n*185), is able to recapture.

Among sentences that contain an experiencing-self, Banfield (1982) distinguishes further between those in which experiencer and Speaker coincide temporally (in which the now of the experiencing-self is also the now of the narrator) and those in which the now of the experiencing-self is in the past. To illustrate the contrast she cites the sentences given in (7.7) and (7.8) (whose original versions come from *Dubliners* and *Jane Eyre,* respectively) which differ according to whether the time adverb (the surface linguistic mark of the now) is past, as in the (a) versions, or present, as in the (b) versions:

(7.7a)   How my heart *beat*/WAS BEATING **then** as he came toward me!

(7.7b)   How my heart * *beat*/WAS BEATING **now** as he came toward me!

(7.8a)   How fast I *walked*/WAS WALKING **then**!

(7.8b)   How fast I * *walked*/WAS WALKING **now**!

As these sentences show, the *imperfective* PROG P can co-occur with either "now" or "then," while the *perfective* NON-PROG P is excluded from sentences with "now." Banfield comments that although the EXPRESSIVE force of all the sentences derives from their first-person self, that self is not located in the same moment in the two instances. Consciousness is always now, but it is not always the Speaker's present. The "now" of the (b) versions of these sentences is a past now. The cotemporality of P with now means that the experiencing-self in sentences like (7.4b), the boldfaced sentences of (7.5) and (7.6), or the PROG P versions of (7.7b) and (7.8b) is represented as a self-in-the-past. The exclamatory force represents a reaction *in the past* to a simultaneously past event. What is captured by the IPFV aspect of the PROG P (or the French IMP) is precisely this simultaneity of the event *qua* event and the character's experience of it *as it was occurring*. The expressivity of (7.7a) and (7.8a), on the other hand, represents a *present* reaction to a past event on the part of the narrating-self.

This focalization split between the narrating-self (Speaker) and the experiencing-self (experiencer) emerges with greater clarity if we expand the PROG P versions of (7.7a) by the addition of tags anchored to the Speaker's present, as in (7.9):

(7.9a)   How my heart WAS BEATING then . . . I remember now.
(experiencer = present / SPEAKER = present)

(7.9b)   How my heart WAS BEATING now . . . I realized then.
(experiencer = past / SPEAKER = present)

(7.9c)   How my heart WAS BEATING now . . . *I realize now.
(experiencer = past / SPEAKER = present)

As these examples show, the first-person voice (the grammatical "I") can be split between a Speaker and an experiencer. The temporality of the Speaker is always obligatorily present, hence the "now" of all the tags is a present now. The temporality of the experiencer may *also* be present, in which case Speaker and experiencer coincide, as in (7.9a); but the temporality of the experiencer may also be past, as in (7.9b) and (7.9c), in which case Speaker and experiencer do not coincide. (The ungrammaticality of [7.9c] results from the co-occurrence of two "nows" with different time reference in the same sentence.) This contrast within the first-person voice between Speaker and experiencer, between the focalization of the narrating-I and that of the experiencing-I, finds linguistic expression in English, French, and other languages, through a contrast between PFV and IPFV PAST tenses, a contrast that reveals itself most transparently when these tenses are combined with temporal-deictic adverbs.

Many languages distinguish two varieties of time adverbs: those that are anchorable only to S (Fr. *maintenant/en ce moment* [now], *aujourd'hui* [today], *demain* [tomorrow], *tout à l'heure* [in a bit/just now], *il y a huit jours* [a week ago]) vs. those whose temporal anchor can or must be a moment other than S (*dans trois jours* [in three days], *à ce moment-là* [then], *deux heures plus tard* [two hours later]). These two categories are often referred to respectively as absolute or deictic and relative or dependent adverbs (cf. C. Smith 1981 : 218–221). The example in (7.10) reports a sequence of past events in the expected tenses of the storytelling mode in written French (PS, IMP, and FUT-OF-P), which are combined, alternately, with absolute (boldfaced) and relative (italicized) time adverbs:

(7.10)   Le capomafia *alla* tranquilement *au lit* [PS] à minuit. Il *NE SE DOUTAIT PAS* [IMP] qu'il *SE COUCHAIT* [IMP] sur une bombe qui exploserait [FUT-OF-P] *six heures plus tard/dans six heures/* **demain.** "The Mafia boss *went* peacefully *to bed* [PS] at midnight. He *DIDN'T SUSPECT* [IMP] he *WAS SLEEPING* [IMP] on a bomb that would explode [FUT-OF-P] *six hours later/in six hours/* **tomorrow.**"

(cited in Kamp and Rohrer 1983)

Kamp and Rohrer hypothesize correctly that the difficulty of "tomorrow" in this context derives from the fact that the Mafia boss could not at midnight (R) have possessed the information contained in the relative clause, which, however, is reported in a way that would approximate the words he would have used at the time. If the PAST is cotemporal with an absolute nonpast adverb, then the sentence must be one of *free indirect discourse;* yet it makes no sense pragmatically to represent the propositional content of the relative clause in this way, since the Mafia boss could not have thought or said those words at that time. Nor is it his perception that governs the report; the entire sequence is focalized externally through the narrator.

Consider now examples (7.11)–(7.13) from Flaubert's *Sentimental Education:*

(7.11)   Ensuite, Arnoux *parla* [PS] d'une cuisson importante **que l'on** *DEVAIT* [IMP] *FINIR* **aujourd'hui, à sa fabrique.** Il *VOULAIT* [IMP] *la voir.* **Le train** *PARTAIT* [IMP] **dans une heure.**   (*L'Education sentimentale,* pt. 2, chap. 1, p. 127)

After that Arnoux *talked* [PS] about an important firing at his factory **that** *WAS DUE* [IMP] *TO BE FINISHED* **today.** He *WANTED* [IMP] *TO WATCH IT.* **The train** *WAS LEAVING* [IMP] **in an hour's time.**

(*Sentimental Education,* p. 133; trans. adapted)

(7.12)   Jamais Frédéric *n'avait été* [PLP] *plus loin* du mariage. D'ailleurs, Mlle Roques lui SEMBLAIT [IMP] une petite personne assez ridicule. Quelle différence avec une femme comme Mme Dambreuse! Un bien autre avenir lui ÉTAIT RÉSERVÉ [IMP]! Il en AVAIT [IMP] *LA CERTITUDE* aujourd'hui.

(pt. 3, chap. 2, p. 350)

Frédéric's thoughts *had never been* [PLP] *further* from marriage. Besides, Mademoiselle Roques STRUCK [IMP] him as a somewhat ridiculous little thing. What a difference with a woman like Madame Dambreuse! A very different future WAS AWAITING [IMP] him! He WAS [IMP] CERTAIN of that now.   (p. 347)

(7.13)   Il *se demanda* [PS] sérieusement, s'il serait [FUT-OF-P] un grand peintre ou un grand poète; et il *se décida* [PS] pour la peinture, car les exigences de ce métier le rapprocherait [FUT-OF-P] de Mme Arnoux. Il *avait* donc *trouvé* [PLP] sa vocation! Le but de son existence ÉTAIT [IMP] CLAIR maintenant, et l'avenir infaillible.

Quant il *eut refermé* [PA] *la porte,* il *entendit* [PS] . . .   (pt. 1, chap. 4, p. 50)

He *wondered* in all seriousness whether he would be [FUT-OF-P] a great painter or a great poet; and he *decided* [PS] in favor of painting, for the demands of this profession would bring [FUT-OF-P] him closer to Mme Arnoux. So he *had found* [PLP] his vocation! The object of his existence WAS [IMP] CLEAR now, and his future assured.

As soon as he *had shut* [PA] *the door,* he *heard* [PS] . . .   (p. 61)

In contrast to the pragmatic infelicity of (7.10), these examples from Flaubert are pragmatically acceptable inasmuch as the focalization shifts at the boldfaced sentences from the narrator to the characters, whose words and thoughts the narrator verbalizes. Flaubert's narrators typically glide in and out of characters' minds. Here the P—more precisely the IMP in its continuous reading as a "PAST cotemporal with now" (Banfield's term)—*is* acceptable with absolute deictic adverbs ("today," "now").

7.3.   Free indirect discourse

The boldfaced sentences in the examples from Flaubert above illustrate the discourse form known variously as *style indirect libre, erlebte Rede,* "represented speech and thought," "narrated monologue," or as it is referred to here, "free indirect discourse." Briefly, what demarcates sentences of free indirect discourse is the presence of features of direct speech (direct ques-

tions, exclamations, fragments, repetitions, deictics, emotive and conative words, overstatements, colloquialisms) reported in the fashion of indirect speech, i.e., with third-person pronouns and shifted tenses, but
normally without the characteristic inquit formulas such as "*X* said/thought
that . . . , wondered why . . ."

Free indirect discourse offers one linguistic means of identifying a
character-focalization; the words or thoughts of the character are translated into the discourse of the narrator, who imposes on them his or her
diegetic PAST tenses and third-person pronouns (but cf. *n*175). As Banfield
(1982:108) notes, free indirect discourse is neither an interpretation of the
character's speech or thought, which implies an evaluating Speaker, nor a
direct imitation of the quoted individual's voice; rather, the words or
thoughts of the self represented retain all their expressivity without suggesting that their grammatical form was that originally uttered, aloud or
silently.

From the standpoint of tense usage, it is not crucial to distinguish between free indirect *speech* and free indirect *thought;* however, the relationship of the discourse to what it represents is not the same. Short (1982)
situates the various strategies for representing a character's speech (S) and
thought (T) along the continuum of discourse "control" given in figure 10
(cf. also Leech and Short 1981:337ff.).

As indicated in figure 10, the norm for representing speech is the direct
mode, the norm for representing thought the indirect mode, since the
thoughts of others cannot be directly observed. Vis-à-vis the respective
norms, the free indirect mode constitutes a move in the direction of greater
character control of the discourse in the case of thought, while in the case
of speech the situation is the reverse. Another way of looking at this difference is to observe that free indirect thought speech involves a move toward
language, while free indirect speech involves a move away from the actual
language uttered by the character.

7.3.1.   By virtue of its special tense system as well as
other linguistic features, free indirect discourse reveals itself to be a marked
subcontext within narrative, in which certain of the expected grammatical features of diegetic discourse are not found (cf. Banfield 1982: chapter
2; Rimmon-Kenan 1983:111ff.; Bal 1985:138f.). Bronzwaer (1970) compares
the time-tense relationships of free indirect discourse (based on the usage
of Iris Murdoch's novels) with those that obtain in straight narration. A
distillation of his findings is given in figure 11.

With reference to figure 11, "time of speaking" refers to the Speaker's

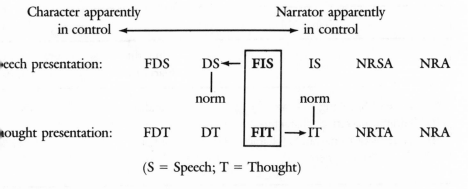

Character apparently in control ←				Narrator apparently → in control			

eech presentation: FDS DS← ⟮FIS⟯ IS NRSA NRA

thought presentation: FDT DT ⟮FIT⟯ →IT NRTA NRA

(S = Speech; T = Thought)

Examples:

DS/T (direct S/T): She said/thought, "I really like it here in Berkeley."
IS/T (indirect S/T): She said/thought that she really liked it there in Berkeley.
FDS/T (free direct S/T): I really like it here in Berkeley![a]
FIS/T (free indirect speech): She really liked it here in Berkeley.
NRS/TA (narrator's report of an S/T act): She expressed/pondered her
  pleasure at being in Berkeley.
NRA (narrator's report of an act): She liked Berkeley a lot.

[a] In FDS the reported utterance retains its original grammatical form, but either
or both of the features that signal the presence of a narrator—an inquit formula
and quote marks—are deleted.

Figure 10. The representation of speech and thought. After Short 1982:184.

---

present, "time of narrative" to the current narrative plane of the story. The
time-tense relationships for these two time spheres are the same in narration and free indirect discourse, except that the PERF does not appear in
the latter. On the other hand, Bronzwaer's table suggests that the formal
tense contrast between situations of the current narrative plane (II) and
situations that occurred before the current narrative plane (III) is obliterated, while the PR is replaced by the P in the "neutral time sphere" (IV)
used for generic or timeless statements (for examples, see Bronzwaer
1970:55ff.). My only question regarding his schema concerns time sphere
III, prenarrative events, for which my own data for free indirect discourse
in both English (cf. [7.5]) and French (cf. [7.13]) show the PLP (Bronzwaer
acknowledges, however, that the rarity of the PLP in his data may be an
idiosyncrasy of Murdoch's style; cf. *n*189).

Time Sphere	Tense	
	Straight Narration	Free Indire Discours
I. Time of Speaking (narrator-I)	PR and PERF	PR
II. Time of narrative (character-I)	P	P
III. Time prior to narrative (character-I)	PLP	P [?]
IV. Neutral time sphere	PR	P

Figure 11. Tense in narration and in free indirect discourse. After Bronzwaer 1970:51, 60.

7.3.2.   The prevailing view among literary narratologists is that free indirect discourse is a distinctive feature of *fiction* whose appearance in literature coincided with the emergence of the modern novel in the nineteenth century.[173] Although it has been demonstrated that this phenomenon is not exclusively literary,[174] it is felt to be characteristic enough of literature, more precisely of fiction, to impart a fictional flavor to other types of discourse in which it occurs (Bronzwaer 1970:49; Banfield 1982:260).

Cerquiglini (1984) cites two studies on naturally occurring speech in French that ostensibly document sentences that "come very close" to free indirect discourse. I have not been able to consult these studies, though the example given below as (7.14a) appears to be from one of them:

(7.14a)   Paul vient de téléphoner. **Il est très déprimé.**   "Paul just called. **He's very depressed.**"   (cited in Cerquiglini 1984:13)

Cerquiglini observes that the judgment expressed in the boldfaced sentence is not that of the speaker but of Paul—hence the sentence qualifies as a kind of free indirect discourse. Granted, this sentence may be read as focalized through Paul; but it may alternatively be read as either indirect speech from which the inquit formula ("he tells me/he says") has simply been deleted, as often happens in conversational narration, or alternatively as an inference on the part of the speaker (from what Paul has told me I infer that he's very depressed)—hence a sentence of the type referred to in figure 10 as a "narrator's report of an act," which falls under the heading of regular narration. The inferential reading of this sentence contains an "external focalization from within." Regular narration focalized in this way provides *the most indirect* method of reporting the contents of another mind (cf. figure 10), for which Dorrit Cohn (1978) has coined the useful term "psycho-narration." This term is intended to reflect both the subject matter of the discourse (the inner speech/thoughts of a character) and the fact that it is not only verbalized by but also focalized through the narrator.

Even if we read the boldfaced statement in (7.14a) as internally focalized through Paul, it still does not exemplify free indirect discourse, which is most reliably identified by its shifted tenses.[175] Cerquiglini's reading of it, however, raises the question of the relationship between internal focalization and free indirect discourse. Free indirect discourse, I submit, offers one way, but not the only way, in which an internal character-focalization can be expressed; what Cerquiglini has in mind seems to be internal focalization, though he does not use the term. He acknowledges, moreover, that paradigm sentences of free indirect discourse in French (i.e., those with IMP verbs) do not occur in conversation. Thus he characterizes the transposition of (7.14a), given in (7.14b):

(7.14b) Paul m'a téléphoné hier. Il *ÉTAIT* très déprimé, et *DEMANDAIT* mon secours. *POUVAIS*-je le rencontrer? "Paul called me yesterday. He *WAS* [IMP] very depressed and *ASKED* for my help. *COULD* I meet him?"

as "at the very least affected, in speech, or extremely literary" (1984:14).

7.3.3. Banfield (1982:228f., 240) considers and rejects the evidence of several earlier investigators who have sought to trace free indirect discourse back to the Middle Ages and even beyond. The case for a medieval avatar of the phenomenon is reopened, independently, in Stempel (1972) and Cerquiglini (1984) on the basis of more extensive documentation and sounder linguistic insights into the textual language of the French Middle Ages—a language that is written, in the elementary sense of being transcribed on parchment, yet in its linguistic structure still fundamentally oral.

Cerquiglini offers the examples given in (7.15) and (7.16), to which I add a parallel example, (7.17), all from the *Lais* of Marie de France (twelfth century). Sentences ostensibly in free indirect discourse are again boldfaced:

(7.15) Femme voleient qu'il preisist, / Mes il del tut les escundist: / **Ja ne prendra femme** [FUT] **a nul jur, / Ne pur aveir ne pur amur.** "They wanted him to take a wife, but he refused altogether, **never will he get married** [FUT], **neither for money nor for love.**"   ("Guigemar," 645–648)

(7.16)   Guigemar a la vile assise, / N'en turnerat [FUT] si sera prise. "Guige-mar has laid siege to the city, **he will not return** [FUT] **[until/unless] # [it] is captured.**"   ("Guigemar," 875–876)

(7.17) Quant la meschine oï parler	1	When the young lady heard [PS] the words
Celui que tant le peot amer,		of the one who can [PR] love her so much,
s'amur e sun cors li otreie.		she grants [PR] him her love and her being.
Ore est Lanval en dreite veie!		Now Lanval is [PR] on the right path!
Un dun li ad duné après:	5	Then she has a gift given [PC] to him:
Je cele rien ne vudra [FUT] mes		**Henceforth he will never want [FUT] anything**
Qu'il n'en ait a sun talent;		**that he will not have [PR SUBJ] aplenty;**
Doinst e despende largement,		**Let him give and spend [PR SUBJ] generously,**
Ele li troverat [FUT] asez.		**she will find [FUT] him the means.**
Mult est Lanval bien assenez:	10	Lanval is [PR] well provided for:
Cum plus despendra [FUT] richement,		**The more lavishly he will spend [FUT],**
E plus avra [FUT] or e argent!		**more gold and silver will he have [FUT]!**

                    ("Lanval," 131–143)

Cerquiglini argues that the boldfaced sentences in (7.15) and (7.16) repre-sent not the words of the narrator as Speaker (*locuteur*) but of the character Guigemar as *énonciateur*.[176] He buttresses his argument by appeal to the presence in these sentences of particles such as *si* (cf. §6.3.2) and *ja* (now), which he sees, following Marchello-Nizia (1985), as indexing a speaking subject. Given that the texts in which *si* and *ja* appear were all recited aloud by a speaker, or at least drew on a discursive tradition of oral perfor-mance, it is no surprise to find in them explicit marks of a spoken lan-guage. These marks, however, refer to the narrator (*locuteur*) not the focalizing character (*énonciateur*), even in situations where the character has maximal control over the discourse, in direct or free direct speech (cf. figure 10 and Sternberg 1982).

The examples in (7.15)–(7.17) all involve the FUT tense referring to situations as yet unrealized in the current narrative plane. The boldfaced sentences can be read either as a representation of the respective characters' thoughts about the future or as psycho-narration, based in the NP, about those thoughts. The passage in (7.17) begins with a clause in the PS (*oï parler*). According to the psycho-narration reading, it is the narrator who then switches to the NP in line 3. The sentence in line 4 may be read as external evaluation (by the narrator) with a PR anchored to discourse now (i.e., *at this point in the story* Lanval is finally on the right path); the same for the PR in line 10. The PC in line 5 is a PFV aspect of the NP, after which the tense switches to the FUT. The FUT clauses (lines 6–9, 11–12) can be read as straight narration, albeit externally focalized from within—the narrator has access to the mind of the fairy maiden and verbalizes what she knows.

I agree with Stempel and Cerquiglini that what is communicated in sentences of this type with FUT (or PR) tenses is knowledge that belongs to a character. But a distinctive feature of *fictional* narration that sets it apart from nonfiction is precisely the cognitive access that the narrator has to the mental states of other individuals and/or situations that cannot normally be observed; only in constructed narratives (i.e., fiction) that are true in constructed worlds can one individual penetrate—and represent through language—the subjectivity of another.[177] Cohn (1978:64) remarks on the attempts of certain modern novelists (e.g., Sartre, Joyce) to obliterate or at least blur the transitions in and out of a character's mind, making it difficult to distinguish the vocalized speech of the narrator (narration) from the inner speech of the character. As we shall see in the next chapter, such blurring occurs characteristically when narration is itself cast in the PR tense—which is often why writers base a Speaker's discourse in the PR. In examples (7.15)–(7.17) we confront a similar ambiguity, and it occurs precisely where (according to the "internal focalization" reading) the inner speech of a character is embedded into a passage where PR tense is used for narration as well as commentary. In the medieval examples, however, recitation *viva voce* by a real speaker presumably resolved the ambiguity through contrastive intonation and/or gesture, which often obviate the need for inquit formulas to assign utterances to their sources. Insofar as the Old French examples above do not exhibit one of the prime linguistic marks of free indirect discourse—shifted tenses—but employ instead the range of speaker-based tenses (PR, FUT, PC), I prefer to read them as psycho-narration, externally focalized from within, or alternatively as the inner speech of interior monologue.

The examples cited to this point in the chapter illustrate an important EXPRESSIVE function of tense-aspect oppositions: the signaling of focalization shifts. These have been either from an external narrator-focalizer to an internal character-focalizer or, in the case of the Old French examples (according to one reading), from an external focalization from without to a similar focalization from within. With the exception of (7.7)–(7.9), these examples have all involved vicarious, third-person narration. Yet focalization shifts also occur in first-person narration, where transitions between the subjectivity of the narrator, speaking from a present now, and that of his or her self-in-the-past are likewise signaled by oppositions involving tense. Here, however, I would argue we are no longer dealing with free indirect discourse but with its functional analogue: interior monologue.[178]

7.4. Interior monologue

Third-person fiction involves what Cohn (1978) has referred to as the "mimesis of other minds"; first-person fiction involves a different kind of mimesis, simulating speech acts such as autobiography or confession. In both instances we are dealing with "inner speech"; unlike quoted speech, which imitates a readily observable aspect of human behavior, inner speech purports to imitate a concealed linguistic activity whose existence cannot be objectively observed (Cohn 1978:77). The following passage from *Sentimental Education*, in which Frédéric puzzles over the semiotics of Mme Arnoux's gestures, illustrates the contrast (sentences of free indirect discourse italicized; quoted speech in single quotation marks):

(7.18) Il quitta ses amis; il avait besoin d'être seul. Son coeur débordait. *Pourquoi cette main offerte? Était-ce un geste irréfléchi ou un encouragement?* 'Allons donc! Je suis fou!' "He left his friends; he wanted to be alone. His heart was overflowing. *Why the offer of her hand? Was it an inadvertent gesture or an encouragement?* 'Come now, I must be mad!'" (*L'Education sentimentale*, p. 81)

In the two sentences of free indirect discourse Frédéric's consciousness remains suspended, as it were, on the threshold of verbalization (cf. figure 10) in a manner that cannot be achieved by direct quotation (the last sentence of the passage). However, removal of the quotation marks from this sentence—something Flaubert would never have done, preferring the

more subtle, less direct intrusion into the consciousness of his characters—
transforms it not into a sentence of free indirect discourse (tenses remain unshifted, first-person deictics are retained) but into one of interior
monologue.

7.4.1.   The examples in (7.19)–(7.21) are taken from
Proust's *Remembrance of Things Past*, in which the narrator Marcel—a figure identified with Proust himself who must nonetheless be considered
above all as a fictional Speaker within the text—recounts the experiences
of his life. In the passage given in (7.19) from the opening paragraphs of
book I (*Swann's Way*) Marcel describes his nightly childhood ordeal of
going to bed. He begins by recalling in the IMP certain habitual actions
associated with this ritual. To facilitate analysis I have segmented the text
into numbered clauses, marking focalizations at the right. Clauses of internal focalization (interior monologue) are boldfaced.

(7.19)

1	*J'APPUYAIS* tendrement mes joues contre les belles joues de l'oreiller	Marcel-narrator (external foc.
2	qui, pleines et fraîches, S O N T comme les joues de notre enfance.	from without)
3	Je *FROTTAIS UNE ALLUMETTE* pour regarder ma montre.	(habitual IMP)
4	**Bientôt minuit.**	Marcel-character (internal foc.)
5	C'EST L'INSTANT où le malade	Marcel-narrator
6	qui *a été obligé de partir* en voyage	COMMENTARY
7	et *a dû coucher* dans un hôtel inconnu,	(generic time
8	réveillé par une crise,	reference)
9	SE REJOUIT	
10	en apercevant sous sa porte une raie de jour.	
11	**Quel bonheur, C'EST déjà le matin!**	The Invalid
12	**Dans un moment les domestiques**	(internal foc.)
	SERONT LEVÉS,	
13	il POURRA SONNER,	
14	on VIENDRA lui **porter secours.**	

15 L'espérance d'être soulagé lui D O N N E du   Marcel-narrator
    courage pour souffrir.   (external foc.
16 Justement il A *cru entendre* des pas;   from within)
                                               COMMENTARY

17 les pas SE RAPPROCHENT,   The Invalid
18 puis S'ELOIGNENT.   (internal foc.)
19 Et la raie de jour qui *ÉTAIT* sous sa porte
20 A *disparu*.

21 C'EST MINUIT;   Marcel-character
22 on VIENT D'ÉTEINDRE le gaz;   (internal foc.)
23 le dernier domestique EST *parti*
24 et il FAUDRA RESTER toute la nuit à
    souffrir sans rémède.

25 Je *ME RENDORMAIS*,   Marcel-narrator
26 et parfois je *N'AVAIS* plus que de courts   (external foc.
    réveils . . .   from without)

1 *I WOULD LAY* [IMP] my cheeks gently   Marcel-narrator
    against the comfortable cheeks of my   (external foc.
    pillow,   from without)
2 which, plump and blooming, A R E [PR] like
    the cheeks of babyhood.
3 Or *I WOULD STRIKE* [IMP] *A MATCH* to look   (habitual IMP)
    at my watch.

4 **Nearly midnight.**   **Marcel-character**
                                   (internal foc.)
5 It I S [PR] T H E H O U R when an invalid,   Marcel-narrator
6 who HAS *been obliged to embark* [PC] *on a*   COMMENTARY
    journey
7 and who HAS *had to spend the night* [PC] in a   (generic time
    strange hotel,   reference)
8 awakened in a moment of illness,
9 REJOICES [PR]
10 at the sight of a streak of daylight showing
    under his bedroom door.

11 **Oh joy of joys! it is [PR] morning.**   **The Invalid**

12　The servants WILL BE ABOUT [FUT] in a	(internal foc.)
minute;	
13　he CAN RING [FUT],	
14　and someone WILL COME [FUT] to look	
after him.	
15　The thought of being made comfortable	Marcel-narrator
GIVES [PR] him the strength to endure	(external foc.
his pain.	from within)
16　Indeed, HE THINKS HE HAS *heard* [PC]	COMMENTARY
footsteps;	
17　they COME NEARER [PR],	The Invalid
18　and then DIE AWAY [PR].	(internal foc.)
19　And the ray of light that *GLIMMERED*	
[IMP] underneath his door	
20　HAS *disappeared* [PC].	
21　It IS MIDNIGHT [PR];	Marcel-character
22　the gas HAS [PR] JUST BEEN TURNED OFF;	(internal foc.)
23　the last servant HAS/IS *gone* [PC] [to bed],	
24　and [the invalid] WILL BE OBLIGED [FUT]	
TO LIE AWAKE in agony with no respite.	
25　I *WOULD FALL ASLEEP* [IMP],	Marcel-narrator
26　and often I *WOULD BE AWAKE* [IMP] again	(external foc.
for short snatches only . . .	from without)

(*Remembrance*, I : 3f.; trans. adapted)

Noteworthy in this passage are the subtle focalization shifts: from the external focalizations of the first-person narrator, recounting habitual activities in the IMP "from without" (clauses 1–3, 25–26) or offering a flash of omniscient insight into the thoughts of the invalid "from within" (15–16), to the internal focalizations: first, of Marcel as a child—*bientôt minuit* (4) and its sequel in 21–24 are the thoughts that would habitually be articulated in the child's mind each time this nightly drama would replay itself—then of the displaced invalid whose "inner transparency" (Cohn's term) is appropriately verbalized by a third-person pronoun (*il*) and three tenses of the communication mode—PR, FUT, and PC, all deictically anchored to the midnight now of this hypothetical experiencer (11–14, 17–21).

Note that time reference in the two sections of commentary (5–10, 15–16) is neutralized. The invalid is not a real story participant but a metaphorical exemplar whose actions stand in no temporal relation either to the events of the story-world or to the context of narration. The PR is thus involved here in its timeless meaning (5, 9, 15), with the PC its corresponding PERF, encoding situations completed prior to, and still relevant to, the reference point provisionally instituted by the now of this timeless PR (6, 7, 16).

If Proust's narrator represents the thoughts of the "other" in the third person and in tenses of direct speech, how does he render the thoughts of his own self-in-the-past? The *Remembrance* gives us entrée to two subjectivities, that of the hero and that of the narrator, their separation problematized by the shared first person. How are these two perspectives kept apart? Once again tense oppositions come into play to demarcate the interior monologues that "enclose the character in the subjectivity of a 'real experience' without transcendence or communication" (Genette 1980:179f.).

Several critics who have considered the question of inner speech reject the idea that interior monologue figures in Proust's arsenal of stylistic devices (Dujardin 1931; Raimond 1966; Genette 1980). "Nothing," writes Genette (1980:180), "is more foreign to Proustian psychology than the utopia of an authentic interior monologue whose inchoateness supposedly guarantees transparency and faithfulness to the deepest eddies of the 'stream of consciousness'—or of unconsciousness." It is Dujardin (1931:68) who insists on distinguishing between the "infralinguistic hodgepodge" of inchoate thoughts found in stream-of-consciousness novels and the more orderly sequences of ideas found in quotations of the mind from more traditional novels, reserving the term "interior monologue" for the modern "flowing" variety. It is in line with this distinction that he rejects the possibility of interior monologue occurring in Proust, who, he observes (1931:275), has an undeniable penchant for *explanation:* "the simple word 'because' transports us to the opposite pole from that of interior monologue." Though adherents to Dujardin's distinction have adopted such labels as "traditional monologue" or "silent soliloquy" for thought quotations cast in more ordinary discursive patterns, the term "interior monologue" is retained here. Cohn (1978:12f.) presents compelling arguments for not drawing a hard-and-fast distinction between these two types of thought quotation.

Genette acknowledges but a single instance of interior monologue in all of Proust's *Remembrance.* I give this example, in context, in (7.20) below. I again divide the passage into clauses, with extra space between functionally distinct sections of the narrative. The clauses I assign to interior monologue (8–9) appear in the double rectangle; those Genette assigns to interior monologue (8–10) are boldfaced.

(7.20)

1 Ces concerts matinaux de Balbec *N'ÉTAIENT PAS*   NARRATION
   ANCIENS.
2 Et pourtant, à ce moment relativement rapproché,   ORIENTATION
   je *ME SOUCIAIS* peu d'Albertine.   (narrator-I)
3 Même, les tout premiers jours de l'arrivée,
   je *n'avais pas connu* sa présence à Balbec.

4 Par qui donc l'*avais*-je *apprise?*   COMMENTARY
5 Ah! oui, par Aimé.   (narrator-I)
6 Il *FAISAIT UN BEAU SOLEIL* comme celui-ci.   [ORIENTATION]
7 Brave Aimé! Il *ÉTAIT CONTENT* de me revoir.

8 **Mais il N'AIME PAS Albertine.**	INTERIOR MONOLOGUE
9 **Tout le monde NE PEUT PAS L'AIMER.**	(character-I)

10 **Oui, C'EST lui qui m'A *annoncé* qu'elle *ÉTAIT* à**   COMMENTARY
    Balbec.   (narrator-I)
11 Comment le *SAVAIT*-il donc?

12 Ah! Il l'*avait rencontrée,*
13 il lui *avait trouvé mauvais genre.*

14 A ce moment, abordant le récit d'Aimé par une   NARRATION
    face autre . . .   (narrator-I)
    (*Recherche,* III : 84)

1 Those morning concerts at Balbec *WERE* [IMP] *NOT*   NARRATION
   REMOTE IN TIME.
2 And yet at that comparatively recent moment,   ORIENTATION
   I *WAS GIVING* [IMP] little thought to Albertine.   (narrator-I)
3 Indeed, on the very first mornings after my arrival,
   I *had not known* [PLP] of her presence at Balbec.
4 From whom *had* I *learned* [PLP] of it?   COMMENTARY
5 Oh, yes, from Aimé.   (narrator-I)
6 It *WAS* [IMP] *A FINE SUNNY DAY* like this.   [ORIENTATION]
7 A fine fellow, Aimé. He *WAS* [IMP] *GLAD* to see me
   again.

8	But he DOES NOT LIKE [PR] Albertine.	INTERIOR MONOLOGUE (character-I)
9	Not everybody CAN BE [PR] IN LOVE WITH HER.	

10 Yes, he's [PR] the one who told me that she *WAS*   COMMENTARY
    [IMP] at Balbec.   (narrator-I)

11 But how *DID HE KNOW* [IMP]?

12 Ah! he *had met* [PLP] her,
13 *had found* [PLP] *her undesirable.*

14 At that moment, looking back on Aimé's story   NARRATION
    from a different perspective . . .   (narrator-I)
                                     (*Remembrance*, II : 436)

A salient characteristic of Proust's narrative technique that appears in this passage (also in [7.19] and [7.21]) is his tendency to insert metanarrative commentary (external evaluation) by the narrator Marcel into his narration of the events of his life (cf. *n*180). In these sentences (4–7, 10–13) Marcel-narrator ponders aloud, at his now as Speaker, the source of information that he, as Marcel-character, had received in the past concerning Albertine's presence at Balbec. In the midst of this commentative musing, externally focalized through the narrating-I, the text slips briefly into an interior monologue in which the subjectivity we are confronted with is suddenly that of the experiencing-I in the past, no longer filtered through the voice of narrator but now internally focalized.

The line of demarcation between sentences that are externally and internally focalized is not at all sharply drawn, whence Genette's inclusion of the (boldfaced) sentence in line 10 within the monologue. Yet in terms of its focalization this sentence is no different from those in 4–5 or 11–13; these clauses all belong to the internal dialogue of Marcel-*narrator* with himself in the "commentative" mode and in the time frame of his own Speaker's present. *What demarcates the internally focalized sentences of interior monologue is the diacritical use of PR tense.* Only in clauses 8–9 are we given unmediated access to the thoughts of Marcel-character at a past now, albeit represented here in its erstwhile presentness. It is precisely at line 10 that the text shifts back to P tenses and back once again to the external focalization of the momentarily eclipsed narrator. Had Genette taken his cue from tense usage, he would have recognized that clause 10 lies outside the monologue. At clause 14 Marcel-narrator exits the commentative mode altogether and resumes narration.

Another striking example of Proust's pragmatic manipulation of tenses with respect to interior monologue/internal focalization occurs in the pivotal episode of the madeleine, which provides the catalyst for Marcel's discovery of the "involuntary memory" that sets him on his quest, across more than two thousand pages, for lost time and for his vocation as a writer.[179]

Some forty-five pages into his odyssey, Marcel recounts the occasion, some years after his sojourn at Combray, when his mother offered him a cup of tea and a madeleine; the aftertaste produced in him a most exquisite sensation, conjuring up childhood memories from Combray that he had assumed were lost. His reflections on this sensation are given in (7.21) below (sentences and relevant clauses are numbered):

(7.21)

D'où *avait pu* me *venir* cette puissante joie? (1)	Interior Mon. (character-I)
Je SENTAIS qu'elle ÉTAIT LIÉE au goût du thé et du gâteau, mais qu'elle le DÉPASSAIT infiniment, NE DEVAIT PAS ÊTRE de la même nature. (2)	NARRATION ORIENTATION (narrator-I)
D'où VENAIT-elle? (3) Que SIGNIFIAIT-elle? (4) Où l'appréhender? (5)	Interior Mon. (character-I)
Je BOIS une seconde gorgée où je NE TROUVE rien de plus que dans la première, une troisième qui m'APPORTE un peu moins que la seconde. (6)	HP NARRATION
IL EST TEMPS que je M'ARRÊTE, la vertu du breuvage SEMBLE DIMINUER.(7) IL EST CLAIR que la vérité que je CHERCHE N'EST PAS en lui, mais en moi.(8) Il l'y A *éveillée,* mais NE la CONNAÎT PAS, et NE PEUT QUE RÉPÉTER indéfiniment, avec de moins en moins de force, ce même témoignage que je NE SAIS PAS IN-TERPRÉTER et que je VEUX au moins POUVOIR LUI REDEMANDER ET RETROUVER INTACT, à ma disposition, tout à l'heure, pour un éclaircissement définitif. (9)	Interior Mon. (character-I)

Je *POSE* la tasse et *ME TOURNE* vers mon esprit. (10)   HP NARRATION

C'EST à lui de trouver la vérité. (11) Mais comment?   Interior Mon.
(12) **Grave incertitude, toutes les fois que l'esprit SE**   (character-I)
SENT DÉPASSÉ par lui-même; quand lui, le chercheur,
EST tout ensemble le pays obscur où il DOIT CHER-
CHER et où tout son bagage ne luis SERA de rien. (13)
Chercher? pas seulement: créer. (14) **IL EST EN FACE**
de quelque chose qui N'EST PAS encore et que seul il
PEUT RÉALISER, puis FAIRE ENTRER dans sa lumière.
(15)

Et je *RECOMMENCE* à me demander (16) quel POUVAIT   HP NARRATION
ÊTRE cet état inconnu, qui n'APPORTAIT aucune preuve
logique, mais l'évidence, de sa félicité, de sa réalité devant laquelle les autres S'ÉVANOUISSAIENT. (17) Je *VEUX*
ESSAYER de le faire réapparaître. (18) Je *RÉTROGRADE* par
la pensée (19) au moment où je *pris* la première cuillerée
de thé. (20) Je *RETROUVE* le même état, sans une clarté
nouvelle. (21)

(*Recherche,* I : 45f.)

Whence *could it have come* [PLP] to me, this all   Interior Mon.
powerful joy? (1)   (character-I)

I *SENSED* [IMP] that it *WAS CONNECTED* [IMP] to the   NARRATION
taste of tea and cake, but that it infinitely *TRANSCENDED*   ORIENTATION
[IMP] those savors, *COULD NOT* [IMP], indeed, BE of the   (narrator-I)
same nature as theirs. (2)

Whence *DID* it *COME* [IMP]? (3) **What *DID* it *SIGNIFY***   Interior Mon.
[IMP]? (4) **How to seize upon and define it?** (5)   (character-I)

I *DRINK* [HP] a second mouthful, in which I *FIND* [HP]   HP NARRATION
nothing more than in the first, a third, which *GIVES*
[HP] me rather less than the second. (6)

It IS TIME [PR] that I STOP [PR]; the potion APPEARS   Interior Mon.
TO BE LOSING ITS MAGIC [PR]. (7) **It IS PLAIN [PR]**   (character-I)
that the truth that I SEEK LIES NOT [PR] in the cup

but in myself. (8) The tea HAS *called up* [PC] in me,
but DOES NOT itself UNDERSTAND [PR], and CAN
only REPEAT [PR] indefinitely with a gradual loss of
strength, the same testimony; which I too CANNOT
INTERPRET [PR], though I HOPE at least TO BE ABLE
[PR] TO CALL UPON THE TEA FOR IT AGAIN and TO
FIND IT there presently, INTACT and at my disposal,
for my final enlightenment. (9)

I *PUT DOWN* [HP] my cup and *EXAMINE* [HP] my own mind. (10)	HP NARRATION
It IS [PR] for it to discover the truth. (11) But how? (12) What an abyss of uncertainty whenever the mind FEELS [PR] SOME PART OF IT TO HAVE STRAYED beyond its own borders; when it, the seeker, IS [PR] at once the dark region through which it MUST GO SEEKING [PR], where all its equipment WILL AVAIL [FUT] it nothing. (13) Seek? More than that; create. (14) It IS [PR] FACE TO FACE with something which DOES NOT so far EXIST [PR], to which it alone CAN GIVE REALITY AND SUBSTANCE [PR], [which it alone CAN] BRING [PR] into the light of day. (15)	Interior Mon. (character-I)
And I *BEGIN* [HP] to ask myself (16) what it *COULD* [IMP] *HAVE BEEN,* this unremembered state which *BROUGHT* [IMP] with it no logical proof of its existence, but only the sense [that it was] happy, [that it was] a real state in whose presence other states of consciousness *MELTED AND VANISHED* [IMP]. (17) I *WANT TO TRY* [HP] to make it reappear. (18) I *RETRACE* [HP] my thoughts (19) to the moment at which I *drank* [PS] the first spoonful of tea. (20) I *FIND* [HP] again the same state, illumined by no fresh light. (21)	HP NARRATION

(*Remembrance* I : 34f.)

The identification of focalizers and time levels in this passage is more complicated than in the previous passages, given the use of a single tense—the PR—for both HP narration and interior monologue. In the sentences of HP narration (6, 10, 16, 18–19, 21) the narrator is both Speaker and focalizer, and the time reference of the PR tense is the moment in Marcel's past of his first experience of involuntary memory, a moment referred to below as t_2. In the sentences of interior monologue (1, 3–5, 7–9, 11–15) the PR is not an HP but a PR cotemporal with now—a past now of the focalizing character Marcel. This now is not, however, the moment when Marcel *first* tasted the tea and madeleine, which we will call t_1 (this point in storytime is referred to by the single PS verb *pris* "drank" in clause 20), but rather some years later (t_2), when the same experience of tea and a madeleine would engender the exhilarating sensation he subsequently seeks to conjure up at will and which he describes *qua* narrator at t_3 (the present of the narration) in the passages marked NARRATION. The boldfaced sentences of interior monologue purport to offer a direct representation of the thoughts of Marcel-character at t_2; the remainder of the passage (save for the PS in clause 20 which refers to t_1) is spoken at t_3 by Marcel-narrator. As narrator, he uses the HP_a to report narrative events and the IMP for sentences of orientation (2) and restricted (subordinate) clauses within the Complicating Action (17). Within the monologue, the IMP (4) and PLP (1) function respectively as IPFV and PFV PASTs in relation to the character's now (= t_2).

Linguistic signs of the communicative mode, notably PR-tense verbs and absolute deictic adverbs (*tout à l'heure* "presently," sentence 9), are among the devices used by Proust to represent the unmediated thoughts of the character Marcel as he ponders—at t_2, evoked here in its presentness —the *recherche* he is about to undertake. It should be noted, however, that in the boldfaced section in 11–15, all PR verbs but the first are generic. They refer to habitual activities of the human mind (= the seeker) "toutes les fois que . . ."[180] And although grammatical person switches also in this section from first to third, what we are given is not the thoughts of an *il*, as in (7.19), but still those of a *je* (Marcel-character) reflecting on his own interiority personified as the "other" (= *il/le chercheur*).

7.4.2. I shall conclude this discussion of interior monologue, and of internal focalization, with an example drawn from text VII, the ballad of Beltrán. Like most traditional texts, this ballad presumably circulated orally for some time prior to its first printing in the sixteenth century. It belongs to the "Carolingian cycle," which recounts events from the Roland legend. This version relates a father's search for his son, the warrior Beltrán, who disappeared as Charlemagne's army was crossing the Pyrenees. The text is entirely in the third person except for passages of direct speech; however, it alternates narration with quasi-lyrical meditations by the narrator on the events of the story (a poetic form of "commentary"). In the section given in (7.22) below, Beltrán's father rides across the countryside searching for his son, whom he fears he will find dead. As the narrator tells us:

(7.22)   NARRATION

1 *vido* [PS] todos los franceses   he *saw* [PS] all the Frenchmen
2 y *no vido* [PS] a don Beltrán.   but *did not see* [PS] Sir Beltrán.

                    LYRIC MEDITATION

3 *MALDICIENDO IBA* [PROG P] el vino,   He *RODE ALONG CURSING* [PROG P]
                                               the wine,

4 *MALDICIENDO IBA* [PROG P] el pan,   he *RODE ALONG CURSING* [PROG P]
                                               the bread

5 el que *COMÍAN* [IMP] los moros,   —the bread the Moors *ATE* [IMP]
6 que no el de la cristiandad: {that} not that of the Christians—;
7 *MALDICIENDO IBA* [PROG P] el árbol   He *RODE ALONG CURSING* [PROG P]
                                               the tree

8 que solo en el campo *NASCE* [PR],   that *GROWS* [PR] only in the country;
9 que todas las aves del cielo   {that} all the birds in the sky
10 allí *SE VIENEN* [PR] *A ASENTAR,*   *COME* [PR] *THERE TO ALIGHT;*
11 que de rama ni de hoja   {that} from no branch, no leaf
12 no la *DEJABAN GOZAR* [IMP]:   *WOULD* they *TAKE PLEASURE* [IMP].
13 *MALDICIENDO IBA* [PROG P] el   He *RODE ALONG CURSING* [PROG P],
      caballero,   this knight

14 que *CABALGABA* sin paje;   who *RODE* [IMP] without a squire.

                    INTERIOR MONOLOGUE

15 si SE le CAE [PR] la lanza	If he DROPS [PR] his lance,
16 NO TIENE [PR] quien se la ALCE,	THERE IS NO ONE [PR] to RETRIEVE it;
17 y si SE le CAE [PR] la espuela	If he DROPS [PR] his spur,
18 NO TIENE [PR] quien se la CALCE:	THERE IS NO ONE [PR] to REPLACE it.

19 *MALDICIENDO IBA* [PROG P] la mujer   He *RODE ALONG CURSING* [PROG P]
                                               the woman

20 que tan solo un hijo *PARE* [PR];   who *BEARS* [PR] but a single son:

INTERIOR MONOLOGUE

21	si enemigos SE lo MATAN [PR]	If his enemies KILL [PR] him
22	NO TIENE [PR] quien lo	THERE IS NO ONE [PR] to
	vengar.	avenge him.

NARRATION

23	A la entrada de un puerto,	At the entrance to a pass
24	saliendo de un arenal,	coming out of a sand-pit,
25	*vido* [PS] en esto *estar* un moro	he *spied* [PS] a Moor there, who WAS
26	que VELABA en un adarve:	STANDING WATCH [IMP] on a
		sentry-walk.
27	*hablóle* [PS] en algarabía,	He *spoke* [PS] to him in Arabic
28	como aquel que bien la SABE	like one who KNOWS [PR] it
	[PR]: . . .	well: . . .

(VII : 21−48)

The narrator's lyric meditation begins at line 3 with a description of the old man's solitary wandering, represented *as process* by the IPFV PAST tenses (IMP and PROG P). The PRS in 8, 10, 20, and 28 are all general: *nasce* (8) and *se vienen* (10) hold true for all time moments within the locally defined context, whereas *sabe* (28) and *pare* (20) have global scope. The reference in 20 is atemporal or gnomic: anyone, anywhere, at any time, who speaks Arabic so well must *know* it; similarly, in 28 the old man curses all women who *bear* only one child, though in context this generic reference must also be read as the specific lament of this father who has lost his only son (cf. 21−22). At line 15, with no formal transition save the switch into the PR, we are suddenly admitted directly into the private thoughts of the old man as he considers his plight, wandering alone through enemy territory with no squire to attend him.

The passages of interior monologue in this text show a certain resemblance, *mutatis mutandis,* to the reflections of Marcel in (7.21). But this text is also an exemplar of traditional, orally composed poetry. The formal symmetry it exhibits, in particular the striking parallelism of clause structure, should not be seen as contrary to the spirit of interior monologue, which, as argued above, need not manifest itself in linguistically chaotic form. The syntactic symmetries of this text are a *formal* hallmark of a traditional poetic genre; what the PR-tense passages seek to communicate is still the unmediated thoughts of a focalizing character.[181] The rhythmic repetition of key formulaic phrases serves to foreground the poignancy of this mono-logic character-lament (the sentences beginning with *si* [if]) as well as the narrator's meditation into which it is embedded.

7.5. Tense, temporality, and focalization

It was suggested above (§7.1) that the external-internal focalization con-trast has correlates in other domains. With respect to the *time* correlate, Rimmon-Kenan (1983) points out that external focalization is either pan-chronic, in the case of an unpersonified focalizer, or retrospective, in the case of a narrating-I focalizing his or her own past, while internal focal-ization—which I take to include both free indirect discourse and inte-rior monologue—is synchronous with the information perceived by a character-focalizer. That is to say, external focalizers have at their disposal the full range of temporalities of a story (past, present, and future), whereas the temporal perspective of internal focalizers is generally confined to the now of the current narrative plane. The *synchronous* nature of character-focalizations suggests why it is that IPFV tenses are chosen as the gram-matical vehicles for the two discourse forms through which this internal perspective is conveyed: the "continuous" IMP or PLP for free indirect dis-course, the Speaker's PR for interior monologue. Each of these tenses, with the meanings actualized in internally focalized sentences, is cotem-poral with a now: the IMP with a now in the past, the PLP with an even more remote now, and the PR with a now that is also past (being the now of a particular moment in the story-world rather than the narrator's now) but is "presentified" insofar as an interior monologue re-presents the articulation of a thought process in consciousness.

The sentence of interior monologue corresponds to what Genette (1980:174) calls "immediate speech," which he contrasts with free indirect speech. In the latter mode the narrator's discourse "takes in hand" the character's speech or thoughts by lending them its voice, while it conforms to the tone of what the character said or thought (Ricoeur 1985:90f.). The narrator retains control of the discourse and there is no attempt at mimesis of the actual utterances of the quoted speaker. By contrast, in the immedi-ate speech of interior monologue the narrator is seemingly obliterated, and the character substitutes. This difference should suggest why the tenses of interior monologue are those of direct speech, whereas the less immediate, less vivid (because temporally more distant) PASTS (IMP/PLP) are used for the mediated language of free indirect discourse, which casts "a penumbral light" on the character's consciousness (Cohn 1978:103), just as they are for the mediated language of dream narrations (see below), which casts a penumbral light on the unconscious. Unlike the PR, which seeks to efface the narrator and offer a direct, quasi-mimetic rendering of the speech and thought of the character-focalizer, the IMP is the tense of a narrator, albeit a tense capable of retrieving an event from deep memory and recreating the experience of it, not in a feigned present, but at a past now.

7.5.1. The linguistic structure of dream narrations is a complex issue, only one facet of which is touched on here: tense usage. In their verbalizations of the contents of dreams, hallucinations, and other nonconscious states, speakers in a number of languages (Spanish, French, Italian, Rumanian, Dutch, and no doubt others) rely on the IMP as the unmarked reporting tense, as in the example in (7.23) from Galdos's novel *Doña Perfecta:* [182]

(7.23) *OÍA* [IMP] el reloj de la catedral dando las nueve; *VEÍA* [IMP] con júbilo a la criada anciana durmiendo con beatífico sueño, *SALÍA* [IMP] del cuarto muy despacito para no hacer ruido; *BAJABA* [IMP] *LA ESCALERA* tan suavemente que *NO MOVÍA UN PIE* [IMP] hasta no estar segura de poder evitar el más ligero ruido. *SALÍA* [IMP] a la huerta, deteniéndose un momento para mirar al cielo, que *ES-TABA TACHONADO* [IMP] de estrellas.

She *HEARD* [IMP] the cathedral clock striking nine; jubilant, she *SAW* [IMP] the old housemaid deep in a beatific sleep. She *WALKED OUT* [IMP] of the room ever so slowly so as not to make a noise; she *WENT DOWN* [IMP] *THE STAIRS* so quietly that she *DIDN'T LIFT HER FOOT* [IMP] until she was sure not to make the slightest sound; she *WALKED OUT* [IMP] to the garden, stopping for a moment to observe the sky, which *WAS STUDDED* [IMP] with stars.

(Benito Pérez Galdós, *Doña Perfecta,* p. 478)

In reports of this type, as in those of free indirect discourse or interior monologue, the event-description distinction is neutralized under the single IMP tense (the first six IMPs in the example are events, the last is descriptive). Use of the IMP for narrations of this type is motivated from the standpoint of both tense (P) and aspect (IPFV).

The IPFV aspect of the IMP is an appropriate category of grammar to represent the "out of focus" perspective of a speaker who is either too close to or too far from an experience to have it clearly in focus. The dream-narrator is obviously too close (Lunn 1985), while the narrator retrieving information from "deep memory" (cf. §§1.6.3, 2.2.2) is too far. The "in focus" perspective is that of the PRET, used to carve bounded events out of an experiential continuum. In verbalizations of dreamwork the boundaries of events are often blurred, and temporal sequence is confused. The pastness of the IMP correlates with the *mediated* nature of the language of dream narrations, given that distance in time (from S) is a frequent metaphorical vehicle for other more subjective kinds of distance languages find it appropriate to express (see Fleischman 1989b). Just as in free indirect discourse the language of the narrator provides a mediation and the linguistic form for the language (spoken or silent) of characters, so in dream narrations the ordered language of consciousness provides a mediation and the linguistic form through which the chaotic and unarticulated contents of the unconscious can be mapped onto narrative.[183] Were it not for the mediation provided by the language of consciousness, we might expect dreams to be reported in the PR, similar in this regard to interior monologues.

7.5.2. The perceived vividness of interior monologues derives from the effect of *presentness* produced by the PR in its minus-interpretation (present cotemporal with now). The fact that the PR is selected systematically across languages as the unmarked tense of interior monologues provides yet another example of a reversal of markedness values in a marked context (interior monologue being a marked subcontext within narrative). As we have seen, the PR occurs in both first- and third-person monologues, representing the subjectivities of both ego and other. The two oppositions need not coincide, whence my insistence, *pace* Ricoeur, on a separation at least at the theoretical level between voice and focalization. First-person narration (voice) may embed the unmediated discourse of either ego (examples [7.20], [7.21]) or other (7.19), while third-person narration, being an unpersonified narrative stance, is limited to representing other "third-person" subjectivities (7.22).

7.6. Time, tense, and memory in Proust

The EXPRESSIVE use of tenses in Proust could easily provide material for a monograph (several have been written on their REFERENTIAL use). The examples cited above give some indication of the linguistic complexities of Proust's narrative style and of ways in which tense-aspect comes into play in signaling point of view. Before leaving the subject of Proust's tenses, it is only appropriate to relate them to his theory of *time*.

In Mendilow (1965 [1952] : 135) we read:

Proust was fascinated at one and the same time by the power of time to subject modes of thinking to its control and by the power of the intuition to rescue events from its domination. In his voluminous novel, he held that the past in its purity cannot generally be recaptured because it has been modified by the experience intervening between the event and the time of recollection, and has undergone a change in the act of passing through the crucible of the mind. However, there were incidents that were never noted by the mind at the moment of their occurrence, and these slipped into the unconscious, unaffected by the chemistry of thought. *When on rare occasions a chance association recalls them from oblivion, they come up to the surface in their pristine form and become thereby free of time.* To develop the intuition that can apply this technique of recapturing the past free from time and its effects, to make events timeless, is his purpose, and provides the *point de repère* for the whole of his work. (my emphasis)

These observations shed particular light on the passage in (7.21), the episode of the madeleine, which is one of the incidents—the crucial one for Proust—serendipitously retrieved from oblivion by the "involuntary memory" that alone can render experiences timeless. It is the ultimate irrelevance of time to such experiences that motivates Proust's use of the PR tense (zero-interpretation) to translate these experiences into language, and of interior monologue as the discourse form capable of recapturing them in their "pristine," unmediated form.

7.6.1.   In a suggestive essay Banfield (1985) relates the tense-aspect oppositions available in the storytelling mode of modern written French to Proust's theory of time and memory as developed in the *Remembrance.* She identifies three varieties of past that French novels express via the two tenses PS and IMP. The "narrative past" (the domain of the PS) is used for past events that, whether experienced or not, for the narrator now belong to history; they constitute "an objective knowledge" (cf. *n*185). In contrast to this *historical* view of past events, the other two varieties, both encoded by the IMP, divide up the *experiential* past, "the personal realm of memory." These two experiential domains, the "habitual past" and the "past cotemporal with now," correspond to the two principal meanings of the IMP: habitual and continuous action.[184] Banfield associates these two meanings of the IMP, respectively, with Proust's concepts of voluntary and involuntary memory.

For Proust the essence of voluntary memory is "the recalling of a countless plurality of events which, as remembered, are converted into duplicates, repetitions, one of the other; no one of them has a date or numbered place in the series" (Banfield 1985:394)—hence the habitual reading of the IMP, which functions rather like a mass tense, as in (7.24)–(7.25):

(7.24) Souvent, quand M. de Cambremer m'*INTERPELLAIT* de la gare, je *VENAIS* avec Albertine . . . "Often, when M. de Cambremer WOULD CALL OUT to me from the station, I WOULD HAVE Albertine with me." (*Recherche*, II:1097)

(7.25) . . . la Place où on m'*ENVOYAIT* avant déjeuner, les rues où j'*ALLAIS* *FAIRE DES COURSES*, les chemins qu'on *PRENAIT* si le temps *ÉTAIT* beau. ". . . the Square where I WOULD BE SENT before lunch, the streets where I WOULD GO DO ERRANDS, the paths we WOULD TAKE if the weather WAS fine." (*Recherche*, I:47)

By contrast, both the narrative PAST, in (7.26) and (7.27), and the PAST cotemporal with now, in (7.28) and (7.29), are singular count tenses, which differ according to whether the individual past occurrence is objectively presented as history via the PS:

(7.26) Un jour d'hiver, comme je rentrais [IMP] à la maison, ma mère, voyant que j'avais froid [IMP], me *proposa* [PS] de me faire prendre . . . un peu de thé. "One winter's day, as I was returning [IMP] home, my mother, seeing that I was cold [IMP], *suggested* [PS] to me to have . . . some tea." (*Recherche*, I:45)

(7.27) Je *revis* [PS], du reste, sa femme cinq fois. "Moreover, I *saw* [PS] his wife five more times." (*Recherche*, II:1025)

or re-presented as happening at a now in the past by the IMP:

(7.28) Il *FAISAIT* déjà *NUIT* [IMP] maintenant quand j'*ÉCHANGEAIS* [IMP] la chaleur de l'hôtel—de l'hôtel devenu mon foyer—pour le wagon où nous *MON-TIONS* [IMP] avec Albertine. "It WAS GETTING DARK [IMP] now when I TRADED [IMP] the warmth of the hotel—the hotel [which had] become my home—for the train car that I BOARDED [IMP] with Albertine." (*Recherche*, II:1036)

(7.29) . . . alors combien tous les riens de la vie de Swann qui lui *SEMBLAIENT* [IMP] si tristes, au contraire parce qu'ils auraient en même temps *fait partie* [COND PERF] de la vie d'Odette auraient *pris* [COND PERF] . . . une sorte de douceur surabondante et de densité mystérieuse! ". . . then how completely all the trivial details of Swann's life, which *SEEMED* [IMP] to him now so gloomy, simply be-

cause they would, at the same time, *have formed part* [COND PERF] of the life of
Odette, . . . would *have taken on* [COND PERF] a sort of superabundant
sweetness and a mysterious solidity!"   (*Recherche*, I:299)

It is the P cotemporal with now, the IPFV P of free indirect discourse,
that makes a past moment become here-and-now again, and it is in this
sense that it "recaptures the past"—the essence of Proust's involuntary
memory. As Proust himself observes, this IMP of recollection "serves not
only to report people's words but their whole lives" (1920:78).[185] However, involuntary memory is only a precondition for recapturing the past
through narrative and through writing. Proust insists that the narrative
process is an emphatically conscious, deliberate, and intellectual one. He
employs various images to define this process as involving a retrospective
cognition of an inner life that cannot know itself at the moment of experience. As he observes in *Time Recaptured*: "One goes through an experience, but what one has experienced is like these negatives which show
nothing but black until they have been held up before a light, and they,
too, must be looked at from the reverse side; one has no idea what they
contain until they have been held up before the intelligence, and only
when it has thrown light upon them and intellectualized them do we distinguish—and with what effort!—the outline of what we have felt" (*Recherche*, III:896/*Remembrance*, II:1014, trans. adapted). One cannot, in
other words, produce narrative through the IMP of experiential memory,
just as one cannot produce it through the perceptual PR of current report;
narrative requires the retrospective intellection of the PS to bound recalled
experiences and order them into a coherent verbal configuration.

        7.6.2.   The pieces are now all sufficiently in place to sit-
uate Proust's theory of time and memory within the larger framework of
tense, perception, and memory outlined in chapters 1 and 2.
        The PR of Proust's interior monologues is the PR whose source is direct
perception, inasmuch as this discourse form seeks to re-present directly,
without the aid of a filtering narrator, what the mind's eye sees. At the
opposite pole is the objectified past event that has constituted itself as
knowledge; its locus is shallow memory, whence it can be recalled, through
a deliberate effort of retrospection, by the historicizing PS. Between these
two domains lies the experiential past of the IMP, the tense of recollection
(*le souvenir*), whose source is deep memory.[186] Of Proust's two paradigms
of memory, it is the involuntary variety that comes closer to Chafe's (1973)
characterization of deep memory. As indicated in table 3, incidents stored

in deep memory typically return to consciousness (to now) not through a voluntary effort of recall but by chance, and with a vitality lacking in experiences retrieved from shallow memory. As these incidents are recaptured they are relived by an experiencing subject, who is the focalizing agent, though not necessarily the Speaker who ultimately reports them.

The voluntary memory that Banfield associates with the habitual reading of the IMP is less easily fitted into this typology; if it can be associated with deep memory, the association is seemingly motivated by the loss or blurring of the distinctive features of individual events—what separates them from others of their kind. Just as painters often *abstract* a pictorial representation of an object from countless individual exemplars they have observed, conflating the details of one with those of another or dispensing with detail altogether, so the habitual IMP of Proust's voluntary memory summons the events of Marcel's life that have lost their uniqueness (they are no longer [+ specific]) but paradoxically are still subject to the domination of time—paradoxically, in that the distinctive features of events themselves recaptured by the involuntary memory have become permanently engraved though the events are no longer subject to time.

7.7. Point of view and the PERFECT

The one tense-aspect category that has so far not figured in this discussion of point of view is the PC/PERF. As pointed out in earlier chapters, the PERF is infrequent in narrative, all the more so in written fiction. In languages like standard French and standard Italian where the PC does double duty as a PERF and a PRET, the situation is more complicated. In such languages the PC/PRET is the unmarked tense of narration in speech as well as in less formal styles of writing. But in more formal varieties of written narration, fiction in particular, in which the unmarked tense is the PS, the PC's indelible link to a speaker (and to spoken language) stands in contradiction to the discourse itself. The PC can, however, be used for artistic purpose; the striking effect produced by the opening sentence of Proust's *Remembrance*: "longtemps je *me suis couché* [PC] de bonne heure" (for a long time I went to bed [PC] early) is impossible to convey in an English translation.

A narration in the PC is a discourse of personal recollections, of memoirs. The tense operates to reduce the distance between speaker-now and story-now, not to the extent possible via the PR—which seeks to obliterate retrospection and transform narration into a current report where seeing and speaking ostensibly take place simultaneously, but enough to neutralize considerably the objectivity of the report.

7.7.1.   In 1947 Albert Camus broke with French novel-istic protocol by casting the narration of *The Stranger* (*L'Etranger*) almost entirely in the PC. This radical move prompted a spate of commentary on the part of grammarians and literary critics.[187] Part of the oddity stems from the fact, noted above, that the PC focuses attention as much on the present world of the Speaker/narrator as on the past world of the story, the assumption being that the two are distinct. Yet for Camus's first-person narrator Meursault, they are not distinct: Meursault's past is of no conse-quence except as it bears on his present (his trial and imprisonment). Moreover, the only past that exists for him is a recent past, minimally dis-tanced from his present, which is in turn simply a "result," the outcome of recent past events. We are told nothing of Meursault's past prior to the moment of his mother's death, the point at which the novel begins with the sentences:

(7.30)   Aujourd'hui maman *est morte*. Ou peut-être hier, je ne sais pas. *J'ai reçu* un télégramme de l'asile . . .   "Mama *died* [PC] today. Or maybe yesterday, I don't know. I *received* [PC] a telegram from the old people's home."

(L'Etranger, p. 9)

It was pointed out above that the PS is normally incompatible with ab-solute deictic adverbs of time such as *aujourd'hui* (today) or *hier* (yester-day); thus if we replace the PC in the example above with PS the result is ungrammatical. If instead we substitute the IMP, as in (7.30′):

(7.30′)   Aujourd'hui maman *MOURAIT* [IMP]. *Ou peut-être hier, je ne sais pas. *Je *RECEVAIS* [IMP] un télégramme de l'asile.   "Today mama *WAS DYING* [IMP]. *Or maybe yesterday, I don't know. *I *WAS RECEIVING* [IMP] a telegram from the old people's home."

the result is hardly free indirect discourse. The first sentence by itself is grammatical, if slightly odd, but no longer a narrative event. With the first sentence in the IMP, the second becomes pragmatically very odd (a prob-lem of implicature), and the third ungrammatical as an independent sen-tence, if we assume that Meursault's narration is not simply the stream-of-consciousness monologue of a less than coherent mind. The PC alone is acceptable in these sentences, and it is, moreover, the only tense appro-priate to Camus's narrator-protagonist. The PC, accompanied by what Sartre (1947:118) refers to as the "inert PR," ideally captures the reality of Meursault, whose life is a succession of *faits accomplis*—not events that happened, but simply events that are "over now." Because there is no PS, there is no sequence, no logical chronology to the events Meursault reports, seemingly for his own benefit. Barrera-Vidal (1968:314) characterizes Meursault's discourse as "a transposition into the recent past of [his] internal dialogue with himself"—which amounts to a (failed) attempt to narrativize an interior monologue. The reader has difficulty discerning a narrative line, since these events seem to be synchronized in a time zone that can only be described as pre-present.

The French PS is the tense of a writer, the PC the tense of a speaker. Use of the PC in a novel thus has a METALINGUISTIC function of removing the text from the realm of literary fiction and bringing it to the level of banal, utilitarian speech (Wilmet 1976:63). Reading this text we feel as if we are listening to a natural narrative; yet we know we are reading a novel, a discourse context with which the inherent subjectivity of the PC is in contradiction. The rare instances of the PS in *The Stranger* (there are, I believe, seven) stand out like foreign bodies, momentarily instituting the language of a writer that Camus sought to camouflage under the purely functional discourse of a rather mundane Speaker.[188]

The PC, as Benveniste reminds us, is inseparable from a first-person report of witnessed events. *The Stranger* purports to be just that: a first-person Speaker's account of events in which he was a participant and, most importantly, from which he cannot distance himself sufficiently to report with any objectivity. Focalization becomes problematic inasmuch as Meursault-narrator can only on rare occasions be separated from Meursault-character. His relationship to events is that of the memorialist. As he tells us: "*J'ai appris* à me souvenir" (I have learned [PC] to remember, p. 112); and as he relives his past in memory, he imagines for himself another life, "*une vie où je pourrais me souvenir de celle-ci*" (a life in which I could remember this one, p. 168).

It is worth pointing out that Camus's tense innovation did not take hold, nor did it inaugurate a new narrative form; it remains in literary history as a grammatical "hapax," a mutation in the evolution of French novelistic language that failed to perpetuate itself. Other writers, however, have experimented with alternating the PC with other tenses, the alternation signaling changes in the narrator's relationship to focalized objects.

7.7.2. This discussion of focalization has thus far emphasized the use of tense alternations to signal shifts involving the *focalizer;* however, tense shifts also come into play to signal differences in the narrator's "empathetic involvement" (Bronzwaer 1970) with focalized objects, notably story participants.

Boyer (1985a, 1985b) discusses the use of PS/PC contrast in several "life narrations" in French. These are planned written texts (albeit in quasi-oral style) in which individuals recount the trajectory of their lives. In one of the *récits de vie* Boyer comments on, past situations associated with ego are reported logically in PC, while situations associated with third-person subjects (animate, inanimate, or propositional) are reported in the PS. More interesting is a second *récit de vie* in which situations associated with the narrator and her mother—who is dead, but for whom the narrator reveals considerable empathy—are reported in the PC, while those of all other story participants, including the narrator's husband, who is still alive, are in PS. This presumably unconscious alternation of tenses provides a sensitive linguistic barometer of the subjective proximity of the narrating ego to the various story participants.

In a similarly slanted discussion of tense usage, Osselton (1982) analyzes the use of the PC/PERF in a contemporary American novel, David Storey's *A Temporary Life*. The basic reporting tense is the PR. Osselton focuses on a passage involving a conversation among three story participants, Mrs. Newman, her daughter, and the narrator, Mr. Freestone, on the occasion of Freestone's first meeting with Mrs. Newman, with whom he will later have an affair. The "narrative events" in this passage are mostly sentences of direct speech together with their inquit formulas. While the *verba dicendi* associated with Mrs. Newman are all in the PR, those associated with her daughter are in the PC, as in the excerpt in (7.31):

(7.31) "I'm Elizabeth Newman," *the woman* SAYS.
A hand APPEARS.
"I wanted to thank you for all the trouble you took with Bec."
I SHAKE the hand.
"It was very kind of you," *she* SAYS.
"It was no trouble. None at all," I SAY.
"Can we give you a lift?" *the girl has said.*   (*A Temporary Life*, p. 73)

The effect of reporting the daughter's actions in the PC while those of the mother are reported in the PR is to focus our attention where Mr. Freestone's is—almost entirely on the mother (Osselton 1982:64). This alternation of tenses provides yet another way of signaling an internal focalization: the foregrounding and backgrounding of participants reflects the subjectivity of Mr. Freestone—as a character in the story, not as the narrator.

Where the PS is the unmarked narrative tense in a text, or is at least understood to constitute the norm for the type of discourse in question, the PC normally functions to *reduce the distance* between the narrator and entities in the story world; in Storey's text, where the unmarked tense is the PR, the PC serves just the opposite to *institute distance* between the narrator and story participants (Osselton notes that when the narrator has "mentally switched off" from both interlocutors, the *verba dicendi* introducing the speech of the mother as well as the daughter are in the PC).

This example provides an excellent illustration of the relativity of meanings that emanate from the pragmatic (TEXTUAL and EXPRESSIVE) components. In the unmarked context of the narrative norm, the marked PC has a minus value for the feature "distance." But in a different, marked context (i.e., as a figure against a different ground) the value for this feature is reversed: in Storey's novel the PC is [+ distant].[189] Once again we see confirmation of the *contextual* basis of concepts like markedness, foregrounding, and evaluation as expressed in texts through tense-aspect categories.

7.7.3. In both medieval epics and medieval romances *combat scenes* are a stock building block of narrative. They proceed according to norms known to the text composers and to their audiences and are constructed on the basis of conventional units of content (motifs): the taking and recovering of position, the attack with the lance, sword, and club, and the physical result of the attack. Combat scenes are typically narrated in the fashion of an eyewitness report (the analogy to a sportscast proposed in Blanc [1964] is entirely appropriate). The tempo is fast; the narrator reports the action in the PR tense as if without the mediation of intellectual processes. Fotitch (1950:72) has observed that in Chrétien's romances combat scenes are frequently narrated partly from the point of view of the spectator and partly from the point of view of the participants in the action; they are also interspersed with comments by the narrator. Consider the passages in (7.32) from *Roland* and (7.33) from Chrétien's *Yvain* (verses containing a PC are preceded by an asterisk):

(7.32) Li quens Gerins *SET* [NP$_v$]	I	Count Gerin *SITS* [NP$_v$] on his bay
el ceval Sorel		Sorél
E sis cumpainz Gerers en Passecerf;		and Gerer his companion on Passe-Cerf;
LASCHENT [NP$_a$] lor reisnes,		They *LOOSE* [NP$_a$] the reins, they
BROCHENT [NP$_a$]		both *RIDE OFF*
amdui a ait		[NP$_a$], spurring hard,
E *VUNT FERIR* [NP$_a$] un Paien	5	and *GO STRIKE* [NP$_a$] pagan Timozel,
Timozel,		

L'un en l'escut e li altre en l'osberc;

one on his shield, the other on his hauberk.

*Lur dous espiez enz el cors li UNT *frait* [PC],

*Their two lances HAVE *broken* [PC] in his body;

Mort le TRESTURNENT [NP$_a$] tres enmi un guarét.

They TURN [NP$_a$] him over dead, in a fallow field.

Ne l'*oï dire* [PS], ne jo mie ne·l SAI [PR]

I DO NOT KNOW [PR] and never *heard tell* [PS]

Li quels d'els dous *fut* [PS] li plus isnels. 10

10 which of the two *was* [PS] swifter.

(*Roland*, 1379–1387)

(7.33) Li uns l'autre a l'espee AS- SAUT [NP$_a$] 10

10 They ATTACK [NP$_a$] one another with swords;

si ONT au chaple des espees

they HAVE in this clash of swords

*les guiges des escuz *colpees* [PC]

cut through [PC] the shield straps

*et les escuz *dehaciez* [PC] toz

*and completely *split* [PC] the shields,

et par desus et par desoz

both on top and on the bottom,

si que les pieces an DEPENDENT [NP$_v$], 15

15 so that the pieces ARE LEFT HANGING [NP$_v$]:

n'il ne *s*'an CUEVRENT ne DESFAN- DENT [NP$_v$];

they can no longer COVER nor DE- FEND [NP$_v$] them;

*car si les ONT *harigotez* [PC]

*for # [they] HAVE *put* so many *holes* [PC] in them

qu'a delivre, sor les costez,

that directly on their sides,

et sor les piz, et sor les hanches,

and on their breasts, and on their flanks

ESSAIENT [NP$_a$] les espees blanches. 20

20 the shining swords LAND [NP$_a$ (mass verb)].

(XII : 10–20)

The distribution of tenses in these passages is as follows: the *actions* of each encounter, count or mass (Υ 20), are reported in the PR tense (NP$_a$); they are achievement predicates in narrative clauses. *Results* of these actions are reported in the PC (R 7; Υ 11–13, 17). Nonsequential descriptive material, packaged in the form of stative predicates (R 1; Υ 15), is reported by the NP$_v$. Narrator commentary (external evaluation), which is rare in *Roland* but happens to occur in this passage (9–10), is reported in the PR (PR cotemporal with now) and the PS.

The example from *Yvain* contains no commentary, though the passage from which it is excerpted (text XII) is heavily evaluated, albeit in a fashion quite different from that found in the *Roland* passage. The unmarked focalization of *Roland* is external *from without;* never does the narrator disclose knowledge of the internal states of his characters. What little evaluative commentary is offered is reported from the extradiegetic vantage of the narrator's own now and, appropriately, in tenses of the communicative mode (recall that in twelfth-century French the PS could be related to S— it was [± present relevance]). Chrétien's narrators, on the other hand, focalize *from within;* when the *Yvain* narrator tells us:

(7.34) . . . einz dui chevalier plus angrés ne *furent* [PS] de lor mort haster. *N'ONT CURE* [NP] de los cos gaster, que mialz qu'il *PUEENT* [NP] les *ANPLOIENT* [NP]. ". . . never *were* [PS] two knights more eager to hasten each other's death. They *HAVE NO DESIRE* [NP] to waste their blows, and *DELIVER* [NP] them as best they *CAN* [NP]." (XII : 24–27)

he is conveying information extracted from the minds of his characters at their now—hence the diegetic PR used to report this information.

To return to our point of departure, a switch to the PC marks a shift in the perspective from which events are reported. The NP$_a$ reports actions, the PC their results. Fotitch notes (1950 : 73) that at times the action proceeds so rapidly that certain acts can be grasped by listener-spectators only once they are completed—hence the PC as a PFV aspect of the NP$_a$, reporting the results of actions from the listener-spectators' point of view (the highly visual reporting technique of current reports makes the listener virtually a spectator). In (7.33) we see the two knights begin to attack one another (line 10); next we see that the shield straps have been "cut through" (12) and the shields themselves "split" (13)—hence they have "many holes" (17). As Fotitch observes, the relative freedom of Old French word order makes it possible to locate the participle virtually anywhere in the line, thus rendering the PC a more flexible vehicle for reporting fast-paced action than the PS. Where I depart from her analysis is with respect to the point of view expressed by the NP.

If I read Fotitch (1950 : 72) correctly, she seems to be claiming that the basic narrative tense of these combat scenes (the PR) reports events "from the viewpoint of the combat participants," as internally focalized through the knights themselves in the midst of combat. I find this view as implausible as having a football sportscast reported by the quarterback from the fifty-yard line. Where the PR/PC contrast signals a focalization shift, it is where the point of view of the omniscient narrator (PR) occasionally cedes to that of the listener-spectator (PC).

7.8. Tense-aspect and point of view in natural narration

In the preceding sections I have sought to illustrate one of the major EX-PRESSIVE functions of tense-aspect in the linguistic structuration of fictional narration: the use of tense-aspect contrasts to discriminate the different focalizations or perspectival filters through which elements of a story are projected in every narrative transaction between an author and a reader. The emphasis on modern fiction is not meant to imply that the use of tense-aspect to signal point of view is an exclusive prerogative of literary narrators. This pragmatic use of tense-aspect morphology is also well documented in natural narration. To cite but one example, Longacre (1976) reports on a type of storytelling in Oksapmin (a language of New Guinea) in which a particular person or group of persons is singled out as the "vantage point" (= focalizer); verbs that reflect the perception of this focalizing agent will have one type of morphology, while verbs that reflect the vantage point of other agents will have a different type of morphology. As the story unfolds, listeners are continually informed by the morphology whose perspective they are privy to.

Another pragmatic contrast that might fit under the heading point of view is expressed by languages with *evidentials* or analogous verb-based devices through which a speaker can adjust the epistemic modalization of a sentence or discourse.[190] Bulgarian, for example, uses verb morphology to distinguish different narrative stances according to the narrator's subjective distance from or involvement in events of the story-world. Bulgarian narrators are obliged to choose between reporting events in one of three ways: as *directly experienced*—what Chvany (1979) labels the "visualizing" mode; as perceived at some remove—the "direct reminiscing" mode; or merely *inferred*—the "indirect reminiscing" mode. These modes are signaled linguistically by combinations of tense, aspect, and mood. In a work of nonfiction, Chvany (1979:299) observes, the writer chooses one of these narrative stances and sticks with it. In fiction the narrator is free to shift from one perspective to another and usually does so. Givón (1982) describes a similar situation in Ute storytelling, whereby narrators can express differing degrees of deictic immediacy or involvement in a story through a choice of aspect markers.

7.9. Conclusion

This chapter concludes the discussion begun in chapter 5 of the major EX-PRESSIVE functions of tense-aspect: evaluation and point of view. As stated at the outset of this chapter, the two functions are connected, insofar as evaluative language provides a window onto focalization. In analyzing the use of tense-aspect to carry out evaluation (chapter 5), my emphasis was on natural narration, where I believe this function to have originated, and on narrative performance from the Middle Ages, which has certain pragmatic commonalities with story performance in natural language. By contrast, my analysis of point of view and focalization has emphasized modern literary fiction, which more than any other variety of narrative has exploited the possibilities available through tense-aspect contrasts. This is not to say that natural narration limits itself to the unmarked point of view of the narrator, nor that the narratorial point of view is limited to the unmarked perspective of the historian; it merely reflects the fact that certain strategies for conveying other points of view, such as free indirect discourse and interior monologue, seem to be excluded from natural narration—nor are they common in medieval story performance.

The possibilities for representing other subjectivities are distinctly greater in a text that does not advertise a speaker (i.e., in third-person fiction) than in a text where the linguistic presence of a real speaker is built into every utterance and can never be entirely concealed. This is precisely the point I sought to make concerning the traces of a speaker identified in the examples from Marie de France (§7.3.3): these "enunciative" particles reference not the voice of a fictional character but that of a real performer who verbalizes aloud all information reported in the text. Considered in terms of the discourse control cline represented in figure 10, except for sentences of direct (or, less commonly, free direct) speech, narrative utterances produced by a physically present speaker will necessarily gravitate toward the "narrator control" end of the continuum. Insofar as performed stories rely on tense-aspect to manipulate point of view, this manipulation occurs largely within the "voice" of the narrator through the various stances, or personae, that the narrator can adopt.

The concept of point of view raises crucial questions about representation and subjectivity. In the texts considered in this chapter point of view is consistently associated with a "psycho-realist" subject—an actual story participant to whom the author delegates the work of representation, and behind whom he or she hides (Britton 1987). From its position of "origin," this subject encloses the text within its point of view: everything appearing in the text is read, even when this is not explicitly stated, as filtered through the perceiving consciousness of the subject (1987:33f.). As we proceed into the next chapter, certain changes will be observed in the status of subjectivity—hence also of point of view. On the one hand, we shall see a promotion of subjectivity to the center of the fictional enterprise, with a concomitant displacement of the diegetic situation; rather than function as an "instrument" or transparency for the story, subjectivity now *is* the story. On the other hand, we shall see what certain critics have interpreted as an attempt to drain storytelling of subjectivity altogether—to replace the psycho-realist subject by pure acts of seeing (a literal reading of point of *view*). Significantly, in both cases the revision is accomplished by a privileging of seeing, of *visual perception,* as the source of representation, which carries with it a privileging of the PRESENT tense.

8 Metalinguistic Functions: Storytelling in the PRESENT

> *When the Narrative is rejected in favor of other literary genres, or when, within the narration, the preterite is replaced by less ornamental forms, fresher, more full-blooded and nearer to speech (the present tense or the present perfect), Literature becomes the receptacle of existence in all its density and no longer of its meaning alone.*
>
> (BARTHES, *WRITING DEGREE ZERO*)

> *On peut penser qu'il existe une logique visuelle, différente de la logique verbale. Car montrer n'est pas dire, et représenter n'est pas raconter.*
>
> (BLOCH-MICHEL, *LE PRÉSENT DE L'INDICATIF*)

One of the founding propositions of this book, spelled out in chapter 4, is that adult linguistic competence includes as one of its components a narrative norm—a set of shared conventions and assumptions about what constitutes a well-formed story. In the Western narrative tradition (broadly construed), the major tenets of this norm are (a) that narratives refer to specific experiences that occurred in some past world (real or imagined) and are accordingly reported in a tense of the PAST; (b) that while narratives contain both sequentially ordered events and non-sequential collateral material, it is the events that define narration; (c) that the default order of the *sjuzhet* in narratives is iconic to the chronology of events in the *fabula* they model; and (d) that narratives are informed by a point of view that assigns meaning to their contents in conformity with a governing ideology, normally that of the narrator. Though these tenets of normative narration are commonly infringed, the rhetorical or stylistic effects produced by infringements are possible only because the norm is in place.

In this chapter I examine a group of anomalies that illuminate the norm—poetic genres that violate some or all of the basic tenets of normative narration listed above. Section 8.1 deals with epic; though discussion focuses on the two most celebrated exemplars of vernacular epic in Romance, *Roland* and the *Cid,* many of the observations made about these texts are relevant to epic generally; 8.2 considers another genre of orally composed song-poetry, the ballad tradition of the *romancero,* with particular reference to the *romances viejos;* 8.3 returns to the subject of the HP, concentrating this time on its use in modern fiction; while 8.4 is devoted to the postmodern *nouveau roman*.

Readers may wonder about the motivation for bringing together these genres which from the standpoint of literary history or criticism make decidedly odd cohorts. What the genres share is a reliance on the PR tense as the grammatical vehicle for storytelling—or, more appropriately, for storytelling "against the grain." For in different ways and for different reasons, these genres all work in opposition to the narrative prototype, and the PR tense operates METALINGUISTICALLY to make this very statement.

The texts referred to in this chapter all belong to a body of discourses we now read as literature. Yet the two oral genres antedate the institution of belles-lettres by several centuries, while the *nouveaux romans* seek actively to challenge the foundation on which it rests—hence Sartre's characterization of them (1948:7) as "antinovels." Certain of the *nouveaux romans* do not purport to "tell a story" at all; thus attempts to disengage the rational line of action that they deliberately distort or to recuperate them using procedures appropriate to conventional realist fiction constitute exercises in misreading. But precisely because these novels call into question the defining primes of narration, they provide appropriate subject matter for this book, which has set as its task an inquiry into the linguistic structure of narrative. For just as certain linguistic protocols and categories of grammar have been shown to be instrumental to the process of narrativization, others are instrumental in denarrativization—in producing storytelling "against the grain."

8.1. Epic storytelling: Narration without time

Primary epic poetry confronts us with a special kind of storytelling in which narrativity, in the sense of a linear presentation of events informed by temporal and causal logic, is subordinated to other dimensions of a genre that is at once story, song, performance, and ritual.[191] Participants in an epic storytelling event, we recall, are generally familiar with the story—hence the possibility of fragmenting, reversing, even negating text chronology. Only when storytelling has been thus released from the basic REFERENTIAL function of conveying new information can NONREFERENTIAL functions—lyric (song), dramatic (performance), commemorative (ritual)—assume priority. And only when chronology and causality are subordinated to other considerations does the pragmatic logic of jarring tense alternations reveal itself.

Reflecting on similarities between the poetic techniques of French and Ukrainian epic, Burbelo (1986) proposes tense switching as a typological universal of the epic genre; he also acknowledges a connection between tense switching and oral performance. The retrospective vision characteristic of narration, he observes, is not characteristic of epic, which instead reports information more in the fashion of what I have here referred to as current report: "I sing what I see" (1986:46). The epic poet sings of past events but endeavors to report them as if observing them now, by means of a "retrospective dynamic PR tense" that represents action visually, via description rather than narration. It is the dual position of the epic singer—at once outside events looking back on them and inside them recreating the effects of being there—that produces, according to Burbelo (1986:47), the conspicuous P-PR alternation that is likewise characteristic of naturally occurring narration.[192]

8.1.1. *Tense and temporality in epic.* Epic is a genre in which the events of story-worlds detach themselves from their historical origins and become, as it were, timeless. For participants in epic storytelling events, there is little sense of the past being differentiated from the present. The *chanson de geste,* Hatcher (1946:10) remarks, "was conceived not as an historical account of things past, but as a re-enactment of events in the present"; the symbolic aspect of these events is underscored by the PR tense, which "divests them of their temporal contingencies" (Grunmann-Gaudet 1980:90). Goldin (1978:42) describes the *laisse* unit of *Roland* as: "immobiliz[ing] time, transform[ing] it into an edifice . . . in which all the heirs of Charlemagne were assembled. Through the singing of the song, their forebears became their companions, the empire of their descendants was restored. Charlemagne was *nostre emperere.*" Though Hispanists insist on the "historicity" of their local epic tradition (vis-à-vis the French *chansons de geste*), Gilman (1961:9) nonetheless concedes that the *Cid* poet "does not, like the historian, establish himself in his own present to narrate the past. The narration constitutes its own present, and in so doing converts familiar tenses into something new."

A discourse that is timeless, in the sense of collapsing the traditional divisions of the time continuum (past, present, and future), is appropriately vehiculated by a tense that can avoid a commitment to explicit temporality and to completion. This tense is the PR. Its IPFV aspect allows situations to be presented as not yet completed; yet unlike the IMP, which also presents situations as noncompleted, the PR makes no explicit reference to pastness. Though what is privileged in epic is the "timeless" or zero-interpretation of the PR, it is the meaning of "presentness"—available "under erasure" through the minus-interpretation—that creates the impression that events are happening now. Moreover, as Herring (1986b) has observed in regard to the capacity of the PR to transform particularized, time-bound narration into timeless storytelling, texts that rely on the PR tense typically have an interest or entertainment value that is independent of and often takes priority over their referential value as reports of information. This is certainly true of epic, whose nonreferential (social, cultural, political) functions have been extensively commented upon by literary critics and anthropologists.

8.1.2. Storytelling as descriptive visualization.

It is often pointed out that epic poets speak as if they were on the scene of events, giving an account of a spectacle taking place before their eyes. Although the relationship of epic singers to their material is in principle one of retrospection (memory) rather than simultaneity (perception), their reporting technique is closer to the current report formula. Blanc (1964) has noted the striking parallelism in tense usage between the *chansons de geste* and the current report genre of sportscasts. Like sportscasts, *Roland* and the *Cid* rely on the visualizing as well as the action NP (both expressed by the SIMPLE PR form); like individuals with eidetic imagery (cf. §1.6.3), they move back and forth between PR and P, as the singer shifts between a performative mode of visualization and a documentary mode of chronistic reporting.

For epic, the unmarked mode of reporting is what Burbelo calls "dynamic description" (the idea goes back to Lessing), a linguistic compromise between the dynamic movement of narration and the stasis of description. Action reported in the PR tense is action that is visualized, as in pictorial or cinematic narration (cf. *n*231). Gilman (1961:75) has suggested that the epic poet's strategy is to "convert his description into successive fragments of action." But as I see it, the process is the reverse: actions are arrested in their movement and observed via the descriptive PR.

In her suggestive reading of *Roland,* Hatcher (1942) likens the narrator's movements within the Old French tense system to the movements of a camera filming a movie. When the camera is held still in the foreground, the PS is used for "movement toward the camera" (i.e., from the background to the foreground), as in the example in (8.1), while the PR is used to capture "movement under camera," as in (8.2). Both examples involve the verbs *surdre* (rise up) and *venir* (come), boldfaced in the examples:

(8.1) PLURENT [PR] des oilz de   Their eyes FILL WITH TEARS [PR] in
doel et de tendrur   grief and pity

Por lor parenz par coer e par amor.

Li reis Marsilie od sa grant ost lor
SURT [PR].

Marsilie VIENT [PR] par mi une
vallee

Od sa grant ost que il out asemblee
[PA],

·xx· escheles ad li reis anumbrees
[PC];

LUISENT [PR] cil elme as perres d'or
gemmees

E cil escuz e cez bronies saffrees.

·vii· milie graisles i SUNENT [PR] le
menee;

Grant EST [PR] la noise par tute la
contree.

1447 for their kindred, with love, with all
their hearts.

King Marsile, with a vast army,
RISES UP before them.

Marsile COMES [PR] along a valley

1450 With the vast army that he had assembled [PA]:

the King has twenty divisions
formed and numbered [PC];

their helmets GLEAM [PR] with
gems beset in gold,

1453 and those bright shields, those
hauberks sewn with brass.

Seven thousand clarions SOUND
[PR] the pursuit,

Great IS [PR] the noise [that re-
sounds] across the land.

(*Roland*, 1446–1455; trans. adapted from Goldin)

(8.2) VENIR S'EN VOLT [PR] li
emperere Carles

Quant de paiens li SURDENT [PR]
les enguardes.

De cels devant i *vindrent* [PS] dui
messages,

Del amirail li NUNCENT [PR] la
bataille:

"Reis orguillos, nen est fins que t'an
alges . . ."

Carles li reis en ad prise [PC] sa
barbe,

Si li REMEMBRET [PR] del doel e
[del] damage,

Mult fierement tute sa gent
REGUARDET [PR],

Puis si s'ESCRIET [PR] . . .

2974 Charles the Emperor IS ABOUT TO
RIDE OFF [PR]

when before him the pagan
vanguards RISE UP [PR].

2976 From their front ranks two messengers *came* [PS];

they DECLARE [PR] battle in the Ad-
miral's name:

"Arrogant king, no point in running
off now . . ."

2982 With that King Charles has taken
[PC] his white beard in hand,

[he] REMEMBERS [PR] the pain,
the loss;

with fierce pride he LOOKS [PR] on
all his fighting men;

2985 Then # CRIES OUT [PR] . . .

(2974–2985)

As Hatcher observes (1942:620), in both passages the enemy's appearance is reported in the PR (*surt/surdent*) as the pagan army looms up suddenly over the crest of the hill. In (8.1) we then follow the camera, which moves to focus on Marsile and his men, from which vantage we observe them gleaming in their armor, sounding their trumpets, as they ride. Their action is described (not narrated) by the visualizing PR. But in (8.2) no description of the "comers" is given, for the camera is not shifted onto them; it remains focused on Charles. The two messengers make their way to the foreground (via the PS verb *vindrent*, v. 2976), where they stop before Charles, after which the PR tense resumes its work of describing his movements "under camera."[193]

The action-description opposition has also been invoked, if less convincingly, to explain the alternation of PS and PR in the *Cid*. Thus Gilman (1961) claims that this tense alternation—which he reads as primarily aspectual: PS = PFV, PR = IPFV—operates at once to distinguish action from description as well as to track story participants (cf. §3.9): the PS "celebrates" the *actions* of the hero and to a lesser degree those of other named (individuated) participants, while the PR is used for *description* of unnamed (nonindividuated) collectivities. Gilman adds nuance to this claim by insisting that it is not the identity or number of the grammatical subject per se that motivates tense choice, but the poet's "stylistic attitude" toward story participants—whether a participant is regarded as more heroic (PS) or less heroic (PR).

Testing Gilman's homology (PS : individual/heroic subject : : PR : collective/nonheroic subject) against the data of text IX, I find overall confirmation of the tendency for the PR to encode situations associated with unnamed collectivities (lines 13–16, 49–50, 55). However, the PR is also used with reference to the Counts of Carrión (56, 65)—a usage presumably explicable in Gilman's schema by their lack of heroism. Less explicable is the use of PR tense to report situations associated with the hero: the PR is used both to *describe* the Cid's appearance ("he *wears* his cape around his neck," 39), and to show him in action ("[he] *leads* [the lion] *around* like a trainer," 47). As for the "heroic" PS, it serves equally to report the cowardly activities of the Counts of Carrión (11–12, 17–28, 58, 63–64) and the heroic (40, 46, 48) as well as neutral (29–32, 37–38, 61) actions of the Cid, not to mention the movements of the lion (9–10, 41–44). On the basis of this passage, the most we can say concerning Gilman's homology is that with regard to *actions* there appears to be an overall correlation between individuated participants and the PS, and between collectivities and the PR_a; *description*, however, is uniformly in the PR_v.[194]

Gilman also argues (1961:83ff.) that the evaluative potential of IPFV tenses (he equates evaluation with description, which favors IPFV tenses and often involves value-marked qualifiers) stands in contradiction to the poet's "celebratory" attitude toward the hero, an attitude that ostensibly the PS alone can convey. To follow this argument one must understand that by "celebration" Gilman means that the poet simply states what the hero does, neutrally and objectively, allowing the actions to speak for themselves, rather than deliver them already evaluated (i.e., through qualifiers or *external* evaluation devices) as he does for other story participants. However, the so-called celebratory technique has been shown by Labov to be a device for *internal* evaluation (cf. §5.5.3 on evaluative action). Gilman is not alone among Romance medievalists in failing to recognize the evaluative potential that resides in the spare, objective discourse of epic.[195] Epic, as Schlegel (1884) observed, is unconcerned with the underlying causality of events, which are simply given (logical necessity in the representation of experience is a product of narrative thinking, and as such *a priori* subjective); the emotive rhetoric of a subjective perceiver is absent, as though the reflective and affective components of the mind had been bracketed, leaving only its capacity for sensory perception. What Gilman and others have failed to recognize is that evaluation need not be limited to external strategies—nor is it always located in the text itself. The unmodalized actions and gestures of epic figures await an investiture of meaning, which occurs in the pragmatic context of each performance. As we shall see in §8.4, the *nouveaux romans* similarly offer up images that are not empty but unfilled, awaiting the collaboration of the reader in the meaning-making process.

8.1.3. *Point of view: The spectator and the chronicler.* The surface objectivity of medieval epic and the absence of an evaluating narrator such as one finds in medieval romances (cf. Fleischman 1983b:295–298) lead Gilman (1961:81) to claim that epic fiction lacks point of view. If we interpret point of view narrowly to mean the positive manifestation of a psycho-realist subject through whom the story-world is projected, then Gilman's claim has some foundation. Yet I believe there is point of view in epic, and it is expressed linguistically through the interplay of tenses that articulate the discourse—PR, PS, PC, and IMP, each corresponding to a persona (whence a point of view) of the Speaker. Among these points of view, the most prominent are those associated with the PR and PS.

The PS/PR opposition in the *chansons de geste* has been shown to correlate with distinct modes of reporting information here called "chronicling" and "visualized representation" (Hatcher 1942, 1946; Goldin 1981). Each entails a distinct point of view. The PS is used when the Speaker wishes to present information as a statement of fact, adopting the objective point of view of a documentary historian. More commonly, though, epic Speakers adopt the point of view of an eyewitness observer who invokes the PR tense to describe events visualized in the mind's eye. To illustrate this contrast Hatcher (1946) cites the examples given in (8.3) and (8.4) involving the (boldfaced) verb *chevalcher* (to ride [off]). When used in the PR, she observes (1946 : 14), this verb always offers a picture of men on horseback, such that we *see* them riding along:

(8.3) Paien s'ADUBENT [PR] des os-
bercs sarazineis . . .

The pagans ARM THEMSELVES [PR] in
Saracen hauberks . . .

LAISSENT [PR] les muls e tuz les
palefreiz,

They LEAVE [PR] the mules and riding
horses,

Es destrers MUNTENT [PR], si CHE-
VALCHENT [PR] estreiz.

they MOUNT [PR] their war horses, #
RIDE [PR] close together.

Clers *fut* [PS] li jurz e bels *fut* [PS] li
soleilz,

The day *was* [PS] clear, the sun *was*
[PS] shining bright,

N'UNT [PR] guarnement que tut NE
REFLAMBEIT [PR SUBJ].

they HAVE [PR] NO armor that IS NOT
GLEAMING [PR SUBJ].

SUNENT MIL GRAILLES [PR] por ço
que plus bel SEIT [SUBJ].

They SOUND A THOUSAND TRUMPETS
[PR] to MAKE [SUBJ] it even finer.

(*Roland,* 994–1004; trans. adapted from Goldin)

But when *chevalcher* is used in the PS, as in (8.4), the sentence is intended merely as information:

(8.4) Paien d'Arabe des nefs SE SUNT
eissut [PC],

Pagans of Araby HAVE *come out* [PC] of
the ships,

Puis SUNT *muntez* [PC] es chevals e
es muls,

then they ARE *mounted* [PC] on their
horses, their mules,

Si *chevalcherent* [PS], que fereient
[COND] il plus?

[they] *rode off* [PS]; What else
would they do [COND]?

Li amiralz . . .

The Amiral . . .

Si ·n APELET [PR] Gemalfin, un sun
drut . . .

CALLS ON [PR] Gemalfin, one of his
dearest men . . .

(*Roland,* 2810–2814)

Hatcher comments on the "intellectualization" of the passage in (8.4):

once the statement is made that the pagans did the expected thing after mounting their horses (i.e., rode off), the camera shifts immediately from them to the Amiral, and they are left to ride off in a vacuum.

As noted in chapter 5, epic chronology is often disrupted by proleptic references to events that are still unrealized in the *fabula* at the point of first mention in the *sjuzhet*. Relevant to the claim that the PS is the tense of documentary reporting is the fact that these prolepses are systematically chronicled in the PS—what Grunmann (1976) refers to as the "anticipatory epic preterit." Consider the passage in (8.5) from *Roland*, which refers proleptically to Ganelon's trial and punishment for treason:

(8.5)	Karles li magnes en pluret [PR] si se demente [PR].		Charlemagne weeps [PR] for them, # [he] laments [PR].
	De ço qui calt [PR]? Nen avrunt sucurance [FUT].		What does it matter [PR]? They'll have [FUT] no aid from him.
	Malvais servis[e] le jur li *rendit* [PS] Guenes,	1406	Ganelon *served him badly* [PS] that day in Saragossa that
	Qu'en Sarraguce sa maisnee *alat vendre* [PS].		he *went and sold out* [PS] the barons of his household.
	Puis en *perdit* [PS] e sa vie e ses membres:		Then for what he did he *lost* [PS] his life and his limbs:
	El plait ad Ais en *fut jugét* [PS] a pendre,		At his trial at Aix he *was sentenced* [PS] to hang,
	De ses parenz ensembl'od lui tels trente	1410	and with him thirty of his kin,
	Ki de murir *nen ourent esperance* [PS].		who *did not expect* [PS] to die that death.

(*Roland*, 1404–1411; trans. adapted from Goldin)

This passage offers a paradigmatic illustration of the epic fusion of past, present, and future into a discourse that obliterates chronology. At the time of the current narrative plane, marked by the descriptive PR$_v$ of v. 1404 (where we *see* Charlemagne weeping and lamenting the losses to his army), the acts have already occurred (vv. 1406–1407) that will later be evaluatively referred to as "Ganelon's treason." The Speaker's statement in vv. 1406–1407 that Ganelon did Charles a "disservice" (*malvais service*) that day, "selling out" the barons of his household is a classic "narrative statement" (cf. §5.5.3) informed by the retrospective intelligibility of the historian's point of view. It is appropriately in the PS. This tense and point of view are continued through the end of the passage; however, at v. 1408 the temporal reference of the PS switches from the past to the future, with the cataphoric reference to Ganelon's trial at Aix where, some 2,400 verses later, he will be judged guilty of treason and hanged along with thirty of his relatives. In normative narration, future events of this type could not be reported by a P tense. If they were reported at all (which is unlikely since they compromise the structure of narrative tension), it would be by a FUT tense, as in the second sentence of v. 1405, which confirms the Speaker's omniscience yet maintains the temporal logic. But in a genre where omniscience is shared by Speaker and listeners, even events unrealized at the time of the current narrative plane can be referred to as historical fact, as knowledge, by the documentary PS.

In her reading of the PS/PR contrast in the *chansons de geste*, Hatcher also suggests that the PS is used to refer to details that are in some way subordinate to the main interest of a passage. This follows from her general view that the relation of PS to PR is one of "subordinate" to "dominant" (cf. also Blanc 1965:569). As Hatcher (1946:14f.) puts it:

The preterite (whether used factually—or descriptively in reference to an accessory detail) is the tense of subordination: it serves . . . as a foil for the present. The alternation of the two tenses offers a bas relief: the figures could not stand out in full relief were it not for the "depressions" of the preterite. To choose the present as the tense of narration for the epic was the first, the obvious step; but if this tense had to be used for every factual comment, for reference to every minor descriptive detail, its dramatic and pictorial force could not have been sustained, its emphasis on re-enactment in the present would have dwindled. (cf. also Wehr 1984:120)

What Hatcher is suggesting is a context-sensitive grounding relationship in which the PS provides background for the more crucial information reported by the foregrounding PR. This grounding relationship, I would add, holds for descriptive as well as eventive material.

If we put together the two readings of the PS/PR contrast that Hatcher proposes, but curiously does not connect—fact vs. description and subordinate vs. dominant—a picture of the *chanson de geste* emerges in which historical fact is backgrounded while visual spectacle is foregrounded. Not only is this picture accurate in terms of the esthetic of the genre, but it also dovetails with the way in which epic time moves.

As discussed in chapter 6, the "main line" of a narration consists of those units of information that advance narrative time. In the *chanson de geste*, as we have observed, the movement from one *laisse* to another often does not correspond to a progression in story time. Even in *laisses* that contain a substantial amount of "action" in rigorous sequence, like the one in (8.6) below, narrative time is halted rather than advanced; the movement is akin to marching in place.

(8.6) Li quens le FIERT [PR] tant vertuusement,	The Count STRIKES [PR] him so powerfully,
Tresqu'al nasel tut le elme li FENT [PR];	he SPLITS [PR] his helmet in two through the nosepiece,
TRENCHET [PR] le nes e la buche e les denz,	CUTS THROUGH [PR] the nose, the mouth, the teeth,
Trestut le cors e l'osberc jazerenc,	down through the trunk and the hauberk of eastern mail,
De l'oree sele les dous alves d'argent	[through] the two silver bows of that golden saddle
E al ceval le dos parfundement;	and deep into the horse's back.
Ambure *ocist* [PS] seinz nul recoevrement . . .	He *killed* [PS] them both, for them no recovery . . .

(Roland, 1644–1650)

In this rendering of the "epic blow" we observe the path of Roland's sword as it cuts through the pagan's helmet, nose, mouth, teeth, body, silver saddle, and ultimately his horse. Only after this sequence of actions is *described* in the PR is the macro-event that subsumes them *chronicled* in the PS: "he killed them both." Yet the chronicle line is the only one that moves narrative time. Otherwise the action is visualized, as if under a slow-motion camera, broken down into its component elements, and at the end set unobtrusively into the documentary record of the past. Passages describing the epic blow, like those describing many of the conventionalized gestures of epic action, are not intended to advance story time but to reveal the *qualities* of an agent—hence the choice of an IPFV tense rather than the narrating, historicizing PS.

8.1.4.   The discourse of epic cannot properly be characterized as narrative; it is more accurately a circumspection. The time of the telling moves in circles, not in a straight line. The primary building block of narrative—the event—is typically fragmented into its constituent acts, which are not narrated but described, as if seen through the lens of a video camera. The epic poet sings what he sees, bringing the past to life in dramatic performance, where it becomes imbricated with the present. All other points of view—those of the historian (PS), the memorialist (PC),

the painter (IMP)[196]—are backgrounded to that of the spectator/per-
former whose marked brand of storytelling—pared down, minimally
evaluated, disjunctive—is played out predominantly through the marked
PR tense.

8.2. *Romancero:* The fragmenting of narrative

Colin Smith (1964:3, 31) offers the following typological characterization
of the ballad as a form of verbal art:[197]

> The ballad is largely narrative in structure and tone, though it may have long
> passages in direct speech (particularly dialogue) and intensely dramatic moments.
> The narrator almost never intrudes himself upon the scene, but acts in an objec-
> tive, impersonal way, like the eye of the camera; but like the camera he often
> selects and highlights a significant detail. Facts are stated and left to work by
> themselves upon the hearer's imagination. There is often considerable emotional
> content, but the emotion is implied, not described and insisted on at length. . . .
> The ballad is concise and compact, fast-moving . . . [it] states circumstances and
> facts, never motives, and it cannot pause to analyze the emotions of the partici-
> pants. . . . Static descriptions are kept to a minimum, and everything is concen-
> trated upon the action and the words spoken. . . . Adjectives are few, never of the
> kind called "idle" (e.g., *green* grass). . . . If there is a need for static description, a
> few features are given and must serve to conjure up the rest in the imagination.

We observe from the preceding section that a number of these characteristics are shared with epic. This is not coincidental. The oldest ballads in the
Hispanic tradition—the Carolingian and indigenous historical *romances*—
are known to derive from medieval epics.

As the practice of chanting full-length epics declined in Spain during
the late fourteenth and early fifteenth centuries, these songs were not
simply forgotten or relegated to archives, as were for the most part their
French counterparts, the *chansons de geste*. Much of the epic material had
already been incorporated into chronicles in the thirteenth century. In addition, the most exciting and dramatic moments of the *cantares de gesta*
were excerpted and recast as ballads, which adapted both the metrical form
and much of the poetic technique of the earlier epics.[198]

The transformation of epic fragments into ballads during the fourteenth and fifteenth centuries was the work of professional poet-singers
who composed and performed the ballads, adapting them continuously to
suit public taste. The ability of particular stories to endure was due largely
to the storytelling skill of the poet-singers who appropriated them and to
their ability to attract and hold the attention of audiences in face-to-face

performance (Mirrer-Singer 1986). Many of their compositions were written down in the fifteenth and sixteenth centuries. At the same time, the most popular ballads continued to circulate, in variant versions, in the oral tradition.

8.2.1. Text structure. Most *romances* are relatively short, typically focusing on a single scene or episode, or a closely connected set of events. The *romance* given as text VII concerns itself with a single episode of the Charlemagne legend: Beltrán's father's search for his son, discovered to be missing after Charlemagne's troops have crossed the Pyrenees back into France.[199] The ballad contains only three events: the drawing of lots to determine who will go back to look for Beltrán (lines 5–10); the father's journey (11–48); and his dialogue with an Arab (49–80), the last event accounting for nearly half the text. Text VIII focuses similarly on a single episode of the Roland story. The version presented here reports the content of Alda's dream (15–40), its interpretation by her chambermaid (41–52), and the arrival the next morning of a letter announcing Roland's death (53–58). The first two of these events are speech events.

The "fragmentary" character of the *romances*—the fact that they typically focus on a single incident or episode extracted from a larger narrative—is not a universal characteristic of ballads. It is a distinctive feature of the Hispanic ballad tradition that relates to its ontogenesis as selected fragments of epic songs (Smith 1964:28). If a passage is excised from its context, much of it will remain unexplained, and its beginning may seem especially abrupt. In many *romances* nothing is told about the events that lead up to the ballad-situation, even though this may result in some obscurity. They simply begin *in medias res,* and often in the PR tense, as in the opening lines cited in (8.7):

(8.7a)   En Paris ESTA doña Alda . . .   "Lady Alda IS in Paris."
(*Prim.* #184; 1550 [text VII])[200]

(8.7b)   A Calatrava la Vieja la COMBATEN castellanos . . .   "Castilians ARE BE-
SIEGING Old Calatrava"   (*Prim.* #19; 1550)

(8.7c)   PÁRTESE el moro Alicante víspera de sant Cebrián . . .   "The Moor
Alicante IS HEADING OFF on the eve of St. Ciprian."   (*Prim.* #24; 1550)

(8.7d)   CABALGA Diego Lainez al buen rey besar la mano . . .   "Diego Laínez
RIDES OFF to kiss the noble King's hand . . ."   (*Prim.* #29; 1550)

The background orientation which opens text VII ("In the fields of Alventosa Sir Beltrán *was killed;* his presence *wasn't missed* until they crossed the pass") is atypical in explaining at the outset the events that led up to the situation on which the ballad focuses. Had some poet decided to excise these first four lines, the ballad would take on an entirely different structure. For without the information that Beltrán is already dead, we would be inclined to perceive in the slow parallel movement of the old man's wandering and in the statements of his exchange with the Arab a gradual and effective build-up of narrative tension (suspense) toward the Peak/Resolution in line 68 when the Arab ultimately reveals the location of Beltrán's body. *Mutatis mutandis,* this structure would be similar to that of text VIII, where the death of Roland is reported only at the end. Yet as we shall see below, the poet who composed the Beltrán ballad had another purpose in mind than to create a suspenseful narrative. Note that the events of lines 1–4, which occurred prior to the now of the ballad-situation, are reported in the PS; as we move into the ballad-situation itself in line 5, the singer shifts to the PR, which is the basic tense of the now of the ballad.

In the process of reworking by successive poet-singers, *romances* were frequently shortened and condensed. Through comparison of earlier and later versions it was observed that *romances* deriving from epic fragments tended over time to become shorter, more concise, and more schematic, as details and background material were progressively eliminated. This tendency reached its peak in the sixteenth century with the fashion for beginnings *ex abrupto* and truncated endings that stop short of a Resolution, producing a sense of suspense or mystery. While listeners and readers in the sixteenth century were still reasonably familiar with the epic legends, and knew, for example, that in a ballad that begins:

(8.8) ¡Afuera, afuera, Rodrigo, el soberbio castellano . . .   "Away with you, away, Rodrigo, most arrogant Castilian!"   (*Prim.* #37; 1550)

the unidentified Speaker is Princess Urraca and the addressee is the Cid (Rodrigo de Bivar), by the end of that century versions appear that are less fragmentary, with introductory and explanatory material added to aid the failing epic memories of listeners.

Smith (1964:31) observes that the "accident of fragmentism" that produced the historical ballads was, "by a collective stroke of genius, turned into a positive virtue" when ballads of nonepic origin were similarly cropped to give equally abrupt beginnings and/or endings. The example of this process most often cited is the ballad of Count Arnaldos, of which the most popular version (*Prim* #153)—the result of a strategic truncation in the sixteenth century—is an intensely lyrical piece of poetry about the sea and its mysteries, but it is not a narrative. The full "narrative" version was only discovered relatively recently among Sephardic Jews. The cropping of the Arnaldos ballad produced the opposite result from the hypothetical cropping of text VII suggested above. Without its initial four lines, the Beltrán ballad can be construed as a narrative; with those lines, the central section devoted to the old man's journey can no longer be construed as a dynamic progression in space and time (Complicating Action); rather, it reveals itself to be a static, lyrical meditation focused on thoughts and feelings expressed by IPFV tenses. Auerbach's observation (1953:538) that "exterior events have . . . lost their hegemony, they serve to release and interpret inner events" is as appropriate to this section of the Beltrán ballad as it is to the fiction of Virginia Woolf to which the statement in fact refers.

Chevalier (1971:64) characterizes the structure of *romances* as an overall dynamic movement into which units of stasis (*stases*) are inserted, each containing a degree of internal movement. I give a graphic representation of this structure in figure 12. The arrow moving from left to right indicates the dynamic movement, which accounts for whatever narrativity there happens to be. However, much of the information reported in *romances* is concentrated in the static units, represented by the rectangular blocks, whose internal movement is indicated by the spirals. To illustrate this schema, consider the structure of texts VII and VIII.

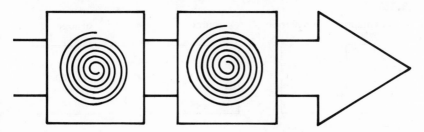

Figure 12. The structure of a *romance*.

Text VIII begins with a static block of parallelistic orientation (lines 1–16) describing Alda and her retinue. There follows a dynamic sequence of eleven lines in which the unpersonified Speaker reports the fact of Alda's dream, her awakening in terror, and a brief dialogic exchange with her ladies concerning the dream (17–28). The dream narration that follows (29–40) exemplifies one type of internal movement that can occur within a static unit. An inquit formula (41–42) provides the dynamic transition to the next *stase*, a dialogic block consisting of the chambermaid's interpretation of the dream and Alda's response (43–52). This is followed by a narrative statement announcing the arrival of letters (53–56) whose content— the news of Roland's death—is reported via the stative predicate *era muerto* (57–58).[201] A graphic representation of this structure is given in (8.9):

(8.9)

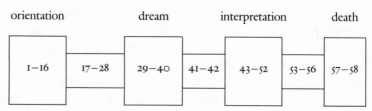

In text VII the dynamic segments include lines 5–8 (the soldiers draw lots to determine who will search for the missing warrior), 11–14 (the old man sets out on his journey), and 43–48 (he encounters and speaks with the Arab). Save for a few lines of orientation (1–4, 9–10), the remainder of this ballad consists of two large static blocks: the journey itself (15–42) and the dialogue with the Arab (49–80). This structure is represented graphically in (8.10).

(8.10)

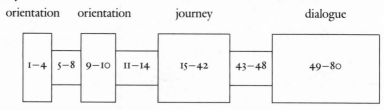

Within the *stase* corresponding to the journey (15–42), internal movement is expressed by the reiterated *maldiciendo iba*. The repetition of this phrase together with the marked imperfectivity of the PROG IMP contributes to a sense of movement—the rhythmic movement of horse and rider, albeit movement that leads nowhere in space or time. In narrative terms, the twenty-seven lines devoted to this peregrination constitute but a single "event." But the poetic technique of this ballad works precisely to de-emphasize narrativity in favor of a meditation on "internal events"—the old man's feelings, thoughts, and fears—to which temporal sequence is irrelevant.

By contrast, the internal movement of the direct speech block (49–80) does involve a measure of sequentiality, if only a dialogic sequentiality, leading to the information about the location of Beltrán's body (68–70). However, from that point on the story is dechronologized, in the sense that the Arab goes on to report events that occurred before the now of the ballad-situation (the seven lance wounds Beltrán received before he died). Given that *romances* frequently begin abruptly in the midst of the ballad-now, whose tense is either the PR or the IMP,[202] this flashback technique is an effective means of supplying explanatory background information about how the ballad-situation came about.

8.2.2. Temporal structure. With regard to story chronology, Smith (1964:31) claims that ballad narration tends to unfold "in proper logical order," though it may take great leaps. This claim is difficult to substantiate even for the more "narrative" *romances*. Text VIII (Alda) is exceptional in maintaining a rigorously iconic sequence. Text VII (Beltrán), as noted above, proceeds chronologically (at least in passages where chronology is relevant) until the Peak/Resolution (line 68), after which the Arab reports events that occurred before the ballad now. This technique of embedding a nonsequential account of prior events into direct speech is analyzed in Di Stefano (1976) to buttress his claim—which I support—that iconic sequence is not the norm for the *romancero*.

Di Stefano compares the ordering of *fabula* and *sjuzhet* in *romances* that deal with the same subject matter. Among examples he discusses are two *romances* about Bernardo el Carpio.[203] The very short ballad that begins "En los reinos de León," given in (8.11), is entirely narrative and atypically iconic in its presentation of material:

(8.11) En los reinos de León	In the kingdom of León
el casto Alfonso *REINABA* [IMP];	Alfonso the pure *REIGNED* [IMP];
hermosa hermana *TENÍA* [IMP]	he *HAD* [IMP] a beautiful sister,
doña Jimena *SE LLAMA* [PR].	her name *IS* [PR] Lady Jimena.
5 *Enamorárase* [PLP = PS] de ella	The Count of Saldaña
ese conde de Saldaña,	*fell in love* [PLP = PS] with her,
mas *NO VIVÍA ENGAÑADO* [IMP]	but *WAS NOT LIVING WITH ILLUSIONS* [IMP],
porque la infanta lo *AMABA* [IMP].	for the infanta *LOVED* [IMP] him also.

Muchas veces *fueron* [PS] *juntos*	Many times they *were together* [PS],
10 que nadie lo SOSPECHABA [IMP];	which no one ever SUSPECTED [IMP];
de las veces que *se vieron* [PS]	from the times they *saw each other* [PS]
la infanta *quedó preñada* [PS].	the infanta *became pregnant* [PS].
La infanta *parió* [PS] a Bernaldo	The infanta *gave birth* [PS] to Bernardo
y luego MONJA SE ENTRABA [IMP];	and then ENTERED A CONVENT [IMP].
15 *mandó* [PS] el rey *prender* al conde	The King *ordered* [PS] the Count *arrested*
y *poner*le muy gran guarda.	and *placed* under heavy guard.

(*Prim,* #8; 1550)

By contrast, in the ballad that begins "Por las riberas de Arlanza," in (8.12) below, these same events are reported by Bernardo, retrospectively and out of sequence, in a confrontational address to King Alfonso in which Bernardo demands acknowledgment of his legitimacy and redress for the wrongs to his parents. This verbal challenge constitutes the ballad-situation. The event or episode on which a ballad focuses, which establishes its now, is frequently the Peak or Resolution of a larger story. In many ballads this event is configured as a monologue or dialogue, in which a character relates, among other things, the events that led up to the ballad-situation. Typically, these events are not reported in chronological order. For ballads that begin *in medias res,* this technique offers an effective means of providing necessary background information.

(8.12)

Por las riberas de Arlanza	On the banks of the Arlanza
Bernardo del Carpio CABALGA [PR]	Bernardo el Carpio IS RIDING [PR],
con un caballo morcillo	with a reddish black horse
enjaezado de grama,	in scarlet harness,
5 gruesa lanza en la su mano,	a sturdy lance in his hand,
armado de todas armas.	armed in full armor.
Toda la gente de Burgos	All the people of Burgos
le MIRA [PR] como espantada.	GAZE AT [PR] him in amazement.
porque no SE S U E L E ARMAR [GEN PR]	for he DOES NOT W E A R HIS ARMOR [GEN PR]
10 sino a cosa señalada.	except when there is cause.
También lo MIRABA [IMP] el rey,	The King WAS WATCHING [IMP] him also,

que fuera *VUELA* [PR] una garza;
DIZIENDO ESTABA [P PROG] a los
   suyos:
"Esta ES [PR] una buena lanza;

15 si no ES [PR] Bernardo del Carpio
este es Muza el de Granada."

   Ellos estando en aquesto
Bernardo que allí *LLEGABA* [IMP],

ya sosegado el caballo
20 *no quiso dejar* [PS] la lanza;
mas puesta encima del hombro
al rey de esta suerte *HABLABA* [IMP]:
"Bastardo me LLAMAN [PR], rey,

siendo hijo de tu hermana
25 y del noble Sancho Dias,
ese conde de Saldaña;
DICEN [PR] que HA *sido* [PC] traidor,

y mala mujer tu hermana.
Tú y los tuyos lo HABÉIS *dicho* [PC],

30 que otro ninguno no *osara* [IMP
   SUBJ];
mas quien quiera que lo HA *dicho*
   [PC],
MIENTE [PR] por medio la barba;
mi padre *no fué* [PS] traidor,
ni mi madre mala mujer,
35 porque cuando *fuí engendrado* [PS]
ya mi madre ERA CASADA [IMP].

Pusiste mi padre *en hierros* [PS]
y a mi madre en orden santa,
y por que NO HEREDE [PR SUBJ] yo
40 QUIERES DAR [PR] tu reino a
   Francia.

who IS outside *FLYING* [PR] a heron;
He WAS SAYING [P PROG] to his
   retinue:
"This IS [PR] indeed a formidable
   lance;
if it IS [PR] not Bernardo del Carpio
[then] this IS [PR] Muza of
   Granada."
   Meanwhile,
here WAS Bernardo APPROACHING
   [IMP];
his horse [having] quieted down,
he *refused to put down* [PS] the lance;
but placing it on his shoulder,
SPOKE [IMP] thus to the King:
"They CALL [PR] me a bastard, oh
   King,
being the son of your sister
and the noble Sancho Díaz,
the Count of Saldaña.
They SAY [PR] he HAS *been* [PC] a
   traitor,
and your sister a wanton woman.
You and your people HAVE *said* [PC]
   this,
for no one else **would have dared;**

but whoever HAS *said* [PC] it

LIES [PR] by his beard.
My father *was no* [PS] *traitor,*
nor my mother a wanton woman;
for when I *was engendered* [PS],
my mother WAS already MARRIED
   [IMP].
You *put* my father *in chains* [PS],
and my mother in a holy order;
and so that I NOT INHERIT [PR SUBJ]
you WILL GIVE [PR] France your
   kingdom.

Morirán [FUT] los castellanos   Castilians will give their lives [FUT]
antes de ver tal jornada . . .   before seeing the day [that
                                             happens] . . .
y este rey de Zaragoza   and the King of Saragossa
me prestará su compaña . . .   will lend [FUT] me his support . . .
45 Mi padre MANDO [PR] que SUELTES   I ORDER [PR] you FREE [SUBJ] my
    [SUBJ],   father,
pues me *diste la palabra* [PS];   for you *gave* me *your word* [PS];
si no, en campo, como quiera   if not, on the [battle]field, or
                                             however,
será bien demandada [FUT]."   it will be exacted from you [FUT]."

                                                          (*Prim.* #12; 1550)

Of these two styles of reporting information, the more common is the one illustrated in (8.12), which Di Stefano labels "retrospective." The problem with his use of this term is that both styles of presentation involve a backward look; the difference is that in the iconic style of (8.11) the *sjuzhet* begins where the *fabula* begins and follows it chronologically, whereas in the noniconic style of (8.12) the temporal-deictic zero (the ballad now) is generally located somewhere toward the middle or end of the *fabula,* and events preceding it (bracketed above) are reported with no particular regard for chronology. In (8.12) the now—whose unmarked tense is the PR—is the moment of confrontation between Bernardo and the King. In many cropped ballads, however, even the backward look is eliminated, the only time depth being the duration of the ballad-situation itself.

In the discursive economy of the *romancero* considerable information is reported via direct speech. This is a characteristic that the *romancero* shares with and conceivably inherited from the epic, though it appears to be a typological feature of all performance storytelling and one that contributes to dramatization. The prominence of speech in the *romancero* also sheds light on its particular temporality and tense patterns.

Two distinct discursive systems operate in the *romancero:* the diegetic and the dialogic (including monologues), each with its own system of tenses. The unmarked tense of the dialogic mode is the PR, supported by other communicative tenses—PS (= PRET), PC (= PERF), and FUT—invoked for their basic temporal meanings. Given the prominence of direct speech in this genre, the PR has a high overall text frequency. Investigators have noted that "idiosyncratic" tense usage is virtually absent from dialogic passages; this can be verified with any of the *romancero* data cited here.[204]

For the diegetic mode, the event-line—such as it is—is rendered by the

PS, PR$_a$, or IMP; the unmarked event tense is the PS, while the PR$_a$ and IMP (a NARR IMP)[205] are used for evaluation and/or foregrounding. For the noneventive material that constitutes orientation, the unmarked tense is the IMP, with the PR$_v$ used for foregrounding. Where sentences of narration are embedded into dialogue, the distribution of tenses is that of the diegetic mode; thus when Bernardo del Carpio says in (8.12) "cuando *fui engendrado* [PS] ya mi madre *ERA CASADA* [IMP]" (when I *was engendered* [PS] my mother *WAS* already *MARRIED* [IMP]), the PS/IMP opposition distinguishes the event from the ongoing state.

   In line with his thesis that tenses in the *romancero* operate to position addressees inside or outside the story-world, Chevalier (1971) suggests that *within passages of stasis* this function is carried out by the PR/IMP alternation: through the PR the singer projects listeners directly into the world of the ballad; through the IMP he pulls them out again, or better, forces an awareness of the temporal *décalage* (1971:63f.). Suggestive as this interpretation is, it is not confirmed by my data. In the orientation passage that opens text VIII (lines 1–14), for example, a passage that relies entirely on the PR and IMP, it is difficult to see in the switches from PR to IMP (lines 7–8) and from IMP to PR (11–12) transitions in and out of the ballad-world; nor are such transitions visible in the parallel sections of text VII (lines 15–20, 23–42) which alternate similarly between the IMP (SIMPLE or PROG) and the PR. In the latter passages the IMP encodes the voice of the Speaker, describing for us with the rhythmic lyricism of repeated formulas a journey that has movement but no perceptible progression. When the poet switches into the PR he moves directly into the character's consciousness, bringing to language via the tense of "inner speech" the subvocal thoughts of this solitary wanderer through enemy territory. The transitions in and out of the character's mind are virtually seamless, marked only by shifts from one IPFV tense to another (cf. §7.4.2).

   If I read Chevalier correctly, certain of the functions he attributes to tenses in the *romancero* (e.g., use of the PS to translate the ballad into "real" time, and of the IMP to create an awareness of the temporal disjunction between the ballad-world and the world of the performance) run counter to the prevailing view of this genre as *timeless* storytelling. The events of a *romance*, like those of epic, have been stripped of temporality (Spitzer 1945:22) and have become independent of real (physical or historical) time. Even in the *romances históricos* the story-world is detached from its historical moorings and from any connection to an identifiable past. Even more striking than the *romances históricos* in this regard are the *romances noticieros*, whose original function was to spread the news of local events.

Albeit composed for particular historical occasions, the *romances noticieros* that have survived have done so largely through the ability of the poet-singers who appropriated them to transform local and contingent facts into stories of enduring human interest (cf. Mirrer-Singer 1986).

In a genre of this type it is not surprising to see the PRET, which ties events to an historical world, yield to the PR, which detemporalizes events and underscores a story's function as timeless entertainment. Each time the ballad of Beltrán is sung the soldiers DRAW LOTS—in the PR—to see who will go back to look for him; with each singing of the ballad of Alda, Roland's fiancée IS once again in Paris awaiting news of her beloved.

8.2.3. Romancero *as a* PR-*tense genre.* As in the case of the Romance epic, there are several reasons for considering the *romancero* to be a PR-tense genre rather than a genre of P-tense narration. First, there is the prominence of direct speech, whose unmarked tense is the PR. Direct speech is a typological feature of performed stories universally and one which ballad singers rely heavily; some *romances* are cast entirely or almost entirely in direct speech ("Abenámar," *Prim.* #78; "Morir os queredes, padre," *Prim.* #15). As pointed out above, information communicated directly through a character voice tends to be dechronologized; though character-Speakers often refer to situations in their past, they generally do not narrate.

A second reason for including the *romancero* among PR-tense genres is its prominent use of the PR as the basic tense of the ballad-now (the analogue of the current narrative plane in narrative genres). Bernardo el Carpio IS RIDING along the shores of the Arlanza, Alda IS in Paris, and Beltrán's father GOES OUT in search of his son's body. As suggested by figure 12, the bulk of the "action" of a *romance* is reported in static rather than dynamic fashion, through IPFV tenses that do not move story time forward.

Concerning my general claim that the "idiosyncrasies" of narrative tense usage have their origin in the pragmatics of oral story performance, it is relevant to point out that tense switching in the *romancero* occurs only in the traditional *romances,* those that have come down through oral tradition. The alternation phenomenon disappears once the genre comes to be cultivated by literate poets in what Chevalier (1971:102) refers to as *pièces d'auteur,* in the later *romances savants,* or in those of Lope, Góngora, or Quevedo inserted as set pieces into Golden Age drama—all instances of poetic *écriture.* Significantly, though, tense switching has persisted in *romances* still circulating in the modern Hispano-Portuguese oral traditions.

8.3. The HISTORICAL PRESENT and beyond

At various points in this discussion (§§1.7.4, 3.7–8) reference has been made to the HISTORICAL PRESENT, which I have sought to distinguish from the NARRATIVE PRESENT on the basis of distributional as well as discourse-typological criteria: while both varieties of diegetic PR privilege the plus-interpretation of the PR tense (their time reference is past), the NP is a spontaneous use of the PR that occurs consistently in *alternation* with tenses of the P and is linked to a performative mode of *oral* storytelling; by contrast, the HP is a stylistic feature of narrative *writing* that, while it can occur in alternation with the P,[206] also occurs in *sustained sequences* across descriptive and eventive clauses. It is this latter use of the HP—where it functions as the dominant grammatical vehicle of an entire text or of extended passages of a text—that concerns us here.

8.3.1.   Natural narratives are never recounted entirely in the diegetic PR. Ess-Dykema (1984 : 285) postulates a maximum text frequency of thirty percent for the PR to preserve an evaluative function. In a similar vein Weinrich (1973 : 106*n*) quotes Robert Petsch as saying that a narrative written entirely in the PR would be like a letter written with all the words underlined. The problem with these statements is their disregard of the fact that the TEXTUAL and EXPRESSIVE phenomena in question operate through contrast with contextual norms. Where the PR is the unmarked or statistically most frequent tense of a narrative, it will not also function as a device for evaluation and/or foregrounding. The question then arises; if, when used as the base tense of narration, the HP is not a device for foregrounding or evaluation, how does it function?

In chapter 3 I summarized the traditional view of the HP as a device to dramatize narration and render it more vivid. This view has validity insofar as it is founded on the visualizing property of the PR, which in ordinary language is primarily a descriptive tense, and on the ability of the PR to offer a mimetic representation of speech. These two properties together motivate use of the PR as a grammatical vehicle for performance, for *representation*. Less compelling is the second component of the traditional HP argument—that the effect of vividness produced by the HP derives from its ability to draw events out of the past and bring them into the present, since, other things being equal, what is present is more salient than what is not present. Yet representation need not entail "presentification." Section 3.7 points out the fallacy of linking the HP (or NP) to the minus-interpretation (presentness) rather than the zero-interpretation (timelessness) of the PR tense. It is the temporal neutrality of the PR that allows it to substitute for the P, or for any tense that makes explicit reference to time.

Like much of the consecrated terminology of grammar, the term HP has encountered resistance. Herring (1986b) finds it misleading, since "there is nothing necessarily 'historical' (in that it has nothing to do with time) nor 'present' (in that it derives from a tense form that is temporally unspecified) about it. As an exclusively narrative device, the basic function of which is to escape from the confines of 'pastness,' it might be better referred to as the 'narrative un-past'—certainly a less poetic title, but one that is descriptively accurate." While I agree that the HP operates to neutralize the temporal feature of "pastness" inherent in narration, I am not convinced that the qualifier "historical" is entirely infelicitous, at least not for a language like French. In narrative *écriture*,[207] which is the only type of discourse in which we find the HP, this tense substitutes for the PS in situations where the PC would be inadmissible, as an explicitly "historical" PAST. Buffin (1925:54) notes that the introduction of PR tense into past narration may compromise the homogeneity of the discourse by making it appear to be representation rather than narration. Yet it is precisely the desire to "represent" rather than merely "chronicle" the contents of a particular world that motivates a writer to choose the HP in place of the PS.

8.3.2.   Chapter 3 (§3.8) traces the origin of the HP in French back to the colloquial NP usage of the medieval period, at which time the language was essentially only a spoken language.[208] The use of PR tense has continued to this day in natural narration (cf. text II), though it declined significantly in written texts during the Middle French period (mid-fourteenth–sixteenth centuries). Surveying briefly its subsequent history (inevitably oversimplified), we observe that by the seventeenth century the diegetic PR was beginning to be cultivated in French as a rhetorical strategy in popular literature and in a brand of historiography that endeavored to preserve the old epic style. Buffin (1925:102) emphasizes that in these *avortements épiques du XVIIe siècle* we are already dealing with a sustained use of PR tense rather than the P-PR alternation characteristic of medieval usage. Normative grammarians of the classical period (seventeenth century) are highly vocal in their criticism of this usage, in particular where tenses alternate within a rhythmic phrase. Only in the eighteenth century with Voltaire, Diderot, and Rousseau does the HP finally establish itself in the arsenal of stylistic devices of respected writers, where it has remained ever since, albeit subordinated to the "historic tenses" (PS, IMP), which imposed their hegemony during the century of psychological realism—roughly 1850–1950, providing the grammatical foundation for the realist novel and narrative historiography. In the mid-decades of the twentieth century the PR once again reaffirms itself in fiction writing. Saunders (1969:161) goes so far as to claim this tense as "the new narrative centre of the language of fiction." But the PR of contemporary French fiction to which Saunders refers, which we shall examine in §8.4, is no longer a diegetic PR (plus-interpretation) that points temporally to a world in the past; it is interpretable alternately as a timeless PR (zero-interpretation) which, like that of the *chansons de geste,* refers to a world cut loose from any historical grounding and thus, appropriately, from historical tenses, or as a PR whose only reference is to the discourse itself, to the text as an adventure in writing (minus-interpretation). But before proceeding to the PR of postmodern fiction, let us consider the issues raised by fiction written in the HP.[209]

8.3.3. When used as the basic tense of a narration, the PR offers a number of inconveniences. Hamburger (1973:120f.), who regards the HP as superfluous in fiction,[210] points to the ambiguity likely to result from using a single grammatical form for distinct sentence types: in passages *narrated* in the HP there are nearly always sentences that for other reasons must be in the PR tense (narrator commentary, generic statements, inner speech and thought). How are these different types of sentences to be distinguished? For languages that rely on a PRET/IMP contrast to distinguish events from description, the risk of ambiguity is even greater, since the aspectual opposition is generally neutralized in the PR system (even where a PROG form is available, as in English, fiction tends to avoid it). Yet despite these difficulties, modern writers often base narrations in the HP, relying on context and on other elements of the discourse—temporal adverbs and conjunctions, clause type (main vs. subordinate), and especially situation type, which remains unaffected by tense-aspect changes—to disambiguate sentences of narration from sentences of Orientation, commentary, or interior monologue, if clarity is the objective. However, the motivation for choosing the HP is often, at least in part, a desire to blur these discursive distinctions.

Consider the passage in (8.13), the opening paragraphs of a short story by Elizabeth Tallent entitled "The Fence Party." The basic reporting tense is the HP (PRs of whatever sort are in uppercase; sentences are numbered):

(8.13) With the sound of the river forcing him to lift his voice and pitch it for her ears, Hart IS HOLDING FORTH to a woman with doctored auburn hair on the eccentricities of his father-in-law, a Nicaraguan refugee (1). She INCLINES HER HEAD (2)—an angle that MIMICS, and in a shady way PRETENDS TO PREDICT, intimacy (3). She HAS such a small, guarded face, crowned with the absurd hair (4), that he WANTS her to come closer (5). As a subject, fathers-in-law ARE a little poignant (6): Hart KNOWS (7) that this woman HAS *had* at least two (8). Acknowledging his own father-in-law PROVES that Hart IS a family man (9). He LIKES TO ESTABLISH that at once, and LET his amused account, falling into the gentlest irritation, SUGGEST that he MIGHT BE a slightly disappointed family man (10). That IS the second thing Hart LIKES TO MAKE KNOWN (11). He LIKES TO PRESENT the fact and the subtle hint of its contradiction together, a knot (12).

All afternoon, from a distance, Hart *followed* the auburn head among his guests (13) who *had been invited* to mend the old fence (14). . . . He *watched* her swinging a hammer, riding forward on its strokes with a carpenter's grace (15) . . . and *fell in love* (16). The party IS a reward for the fence's menders, and a housewarming as well (17), because Hart and his second wife, Caro, *bought* the house last winter (18). . . . He IS lucky in the weather (19), as he *knew* he would be (20). Only last week, the evenings *would have been too cold* for people to stand around drinking on the lawn (21). But not tonight, not when everyone FEELS FLUSHED and HIGH with work (22). Tonight COULD almost BE summer (23).

Hart PUTS his hand on the woman's arm (24), then KNOWS (25) that *was* a mistake (26), and PRETENDS, working thumb and forefinger, to rub out a mosquito (27) . . .

In this text the HP is used to report situations of the current narrative plane, which corresponds to the evening of the party. The PAST reports situations that occurred prior to this now, either "this afternoon" (13, 15, 16), "last winter" (18), an unspecified moment in the past (20), or the immediate past R of sentence (26), established by sentence (24). The single PLP (14) reports a situation that occurred in a before-past plane (before "this afternoon"), while the single PR PERF (8) refers to a period extending from the past through story now. Temporality, then, is clearly delineated. The twenty-one verbs in the PR, however, do not all refer to events of the current narrative plane. The question, as Hamburger suggests, becomes one of distinguishing the different types of sentence that the PR tense encodes, and the different focalizations.

The voice of the text is third-person. The first sentence is one of orientation, marked as such unambiguously by the PR PROG "is holding forth." Sentence (2) is a narrative event. Events in this passage—in sentences (2), (24), (25), and (27)—can be identified by their telic situation type (achievements or accomplishments; the normally stative "know" in [25] is converted to an achievement via the sequencer "then") together with the fact that they occur in main clauses. The coordinated clauses in (3) and (4) are clauses of orientation, again determined on the basis of their situation type (activities) and clause status (subordinate). The stative predicates of (4)–(8) suggest that these sentences are likewise orientation, though we cannot be sure that they are not the thoughts of Hart (they make sense rewritten in the first person) reported in the "inner speech" of interior monologue. As Cohn (1978:75) observes, narrating in the PR eliminates one of the clearest clues for distinguishing between narrator and character voices, especially when a text shifts to a generic or descriptive PR in the immediate vicinity of an interior monologue. This is precisely what we find in (6): the PR is generic ("fathers-in-law ARE a little poignant"), though we cannot be sure whether to assign the sentence to Hart (inner speech) or to the narrator (external commentary).[211] The remaining sentences of the first paragraph, all with stative predicates, suggest that the ambiguous sentences are spoken by the narrator, not by Hart (it is unlikely Hart would have this degree of distance on his own motives and behavior).

The second paragraph moves to a temporal plane before story-now (if this were conventional P-tense narration, the P verbs in [13], [15], [16], and [18] would presumably be PLPs). Sentences (13)–(16) appear to be Orientation, though, particularly where verbs of perception are involved that "link psyche and scene" (e.g., "watch" in [15]), the boundary between scenic description and psycho-narration becomes blurred (Cohn 1978). At sentence (17) the text returns to story-now with another PR-tense sentence of background Orientation by the narrator. Sentences (19)–(23) are again ambiguous: the voice of the narrator (Orientation) or the thoughts of Hart? We assign them to Hart this time because of the direct-speech syntax and absolute deictic adverbs ("last week," "tonight"). The narrative line resumes in the third paragraph with three ordered events reported in the PR.

As this text shows, it is possible to base narration in the HP, though not to the exclusion of the P, if different temporal planes are to be delineated, and not without ambiguity as to the status of certain sentences. In light of this ambiguity and of the linguistic complications involved in profiling "events" and discriminating narrative voices, we might wonder what motivates writers to base narration in the HP. As noted above, certain writers make a virtue of a linguistic dilemma, exploiting the PR precisely because of its ability to blur the distinction between events and description, or that between narration and inner language. But there appear to be other motivations as well for a sustained HP.

When used in narration, the PR takes on the temporal feature "past" but retains its IPFV aspect. This aspectual feature may be invoked to cancel the unmarked perfectivity of a retrospective report. Georges Bernanos's novella *Mouchette Revisited* (*Nouvelle histoire de Mouchette,* 1936) is the story of a tormented girl ultimately driven to suicide. For the majority of the text the operative tense system is that of the PR, i.e., PR, PC, and FUT, referring respectively to story-now, pre-now, and post-now events (the PC is also frequently a PERF or a PFV aspect of the PR). The basic narrative tense is the PR. Three pages from the end, however, the text shifts at a paragraph break to the P system:

(8.14)   Un des pans de l'étoffe légère usée par le temps RESTE PRIS [PR] sous la galoche de Mouchette, et la brusque secousse la DÉCHIRE [PR] de haut en bas. C'EST [PR] que la trame en EST *devenue* [PC] aussi fragile qu'une toile d'araignée. Un instant, la pauvre fille ESSAIE DE DÉGAGER [PR] ses mains,[212] mais la mousseline soyeuse, presque impalpable, S'ACCROCHE [PR] à la robe grossière, ACHÈVE DE S'EN ALLER [PR] par lambeaux.

Fut-ce [PS] à ce moment que Mouchette *subit* [PS] le deuxième assaut de la force obscure qui VENAIT DE S'ÉVEILLER [IMP] au plus profond, au plus secret de sa chair? Il *fut si violent* [PS] qu'elle *se mit à piétiner* [PS] sur l'étroite plate-forme en gémissant, ainsi qu'une bête prise au piège. La pensée de la mort N'ACHEVAIT pourtant PAS DE SE FORMER [IMP] . . .   (p. 1342)

One of the ends of the delicate material, worn thin over time, REMAINS CAUGHT [PR] under one of Mouchette's galoshes, and her abrupt movement TEARS [PR] it from top to bottom. For the thread HAS *become* [PC] as fragile as a spider's web. For an instant, the poor girl TRIES TO FREE [PR] her hands,[212] but the silky muslin, elusive to the touch, STICKS [PR] to the heavy fabric of the dress, [and] COMES OFF [PR] in shreds.

Was [PS] it at that moment that Mouchette *experienced* [PS] the second attack of that dark force that HAD JUST AWAKENED [IMP] in the most secret depths of her flesh? It *was so violent* [PS] that she *began to stamp* [PS] on the narrow platform, moaning like an animal caught in a trap. However, the thought of death HAD NOT yet COMPLETELY TAKEN SHAPE [IMP] . . .

Tense-aspect in this text provides a subtle grammatical window onto the psyche of Mouchette. As long as narration is in the PR, her fate remains open; death is not yet a certainty. But once the thought of suicide becomes irrevocable, the text moves first partially, then entirely into the P. The shift from HP to P that occurs in the passage above marks a transition from a future that is still open and undecided, expressed through the imperfectivity of the PR, to one that has become determined and whose closure is signaled by the perfectivity of the PS.

A similar privileging of the IPFV aspect of the PR occurs in Malraux's novel of the Spanish Civil War, *Man's Hope* (*L'Espoir,* 1937/1938), which chronicles the doomed struggle of the International Brigade to defend the north of Spain against the Nationalists. The text relies primarily on the P system, though there are nearly a dozen passages in which it reverts to the PR system, some fairly short, others extending for pages or even an entire chapter in which the P scarcely appears. In a suggestive reading of this text, Seylaz (1983) proposes that in the passages of HP narration Malraux seeks to introduce into the omniscient, retrospective point of view of the narrator, who knows already the outcome of the story, the contingent prospectivity of the point of view of the characters, for whom the outcome of the struggle is still in question and there is still hope. The shifts from PS to PR, in other words, mark shifts from an external to an internal focalization that once again privilege the aspectual component of the respective tenses. The PFV PS offers a retrospective view of events that for the narrator are completed and now constitute history; the IPFV PR enables a temporary release from the closure of this retrospectivity by reinstating the erstwhile contingency of a present in which the future is still undecided.

All the texts discussed heretofore in this section contain stretches of narration based in the HP, which replaces the P as the grammatical marker of story-now. But in order to maintain temporal perspective—the notion of a story-world with a past, present, and future—there must be recourse to other tenses, notably to the P. The way temporal perspective is produced in HP narration is by shifting forward the time-tense correlations of conventional narration such that the past, present, and future of the story-world are reported respectively by the P (PC in French), HP, and FUT tenses. *What* HP *narration does not do is relocate the story-world to speaker-now,* as many discussions of the HP would have it, *nor does it shift the focus of the discourse onto what is happening in the speaker's world.* For either of these moves—canceling retrospectivity or defocusing the experiencing-self in favor of the narrating-self—will produce a discourse that is no longer strictly narrative.

8.3.4.   Among modern fiction writers who have experimented with the PR-tense, Virginia Woolf has been one of the most successful in exploiting this tense to test the limits of the narrative form. I will illustrate this claim with a piece of her early short fiction entitled

"The Mark on the Wall."[213] In a suggestive reading of this text, which I take as my point of departure, Traugott (forthcoming) demonstrates how the use of tense figures prominently among the linguistic devices used by Woolf to subvert conventional narrative structure based on chronicles of events and to develop instead one of the major themes of her writing: a meditation on action and knowledge vs. perception and thought. Note that the categories of this opposition—action and knowledge, on the one hand, perception and thought, on the other—correlate in a motivated way with the P and PR tenses, respectively.

"The Mark on the Wall" leads us to expect a narrative. It begins conventionally in the P with a temporal clause of orientation (albeit epistemically modalized) followed by two coordinated narrative clauses:

(8.15)   Perhaps it *was* the middle of January in the present year (1) that I first *looked up* (2) and *saw* the mark on the wall (3). In order to fix a date IT IS NEC-ESSARY TO REMEMBER what one saw (4). So now I THINK OF THE FIRE; the steady film of yellow light upon the page of my book (5). . . . Yes, it *must have been* the winter time (6), and we *had* just *finished* our tea (7), for I REMEM-BER (8) that I *WAS SMOKING A CIGARETTE* (9) when I *looked up* (10) and *saw the mark on the wall* for the first time (11) . . .   (p. 77)

But already in clause (4) the text has moved out of the P and the would-be narrative mode into the speech mode as the Speaker reflects in the generic PR on the mental process one goes through in order to date a past event. This meditation continues for the duration of the passage given above, whose now is the Speaker's present, marked explicitly in sentences (5) and (8) by the PR cotemporal with now. Observe that the verbs in this passage are predominantly verbs of mental action ("think," "remember") or visual perception ("see," "look"). Reading this text as a conventional narration, we interpret sentences (6)–(9) as orientation and sentences (10) and (11) as coordinated narrative clauses, although the events referred to in (10) and (11) are the same as those referred to in (2) and (3). To the extent that narrative time has moved, it has moved in a circle.[214] The text continues more or less in this fashion—dearth of action, concentration of thought and perception verbs, predominance of the PR tense—virtually to the end. As Traugott (forthcoming) observes, it invites us to expect one world, a narrative world, but ultimately forces us to reconstrue it differently; for what appears to be a narrative turns out to be a meditative monologue that attacks narrative, "not only by commenting on the destructiveness of the genre, but in the use of language itself." Yet only in the last line of the text, given in (8.17) below, do we realize what has happened, and we are obliged to begin anew and reread with different expectations about the type of discourse that confronts us.

As long as our expectations are those appropriate to narrative, we search for a plot, a chronology, and a sequence of event-type units that can be construed as steps in the Speaker's coming to identify the mark on the wall. Yet in various ways that Traugott details, our initial reading strategy is undermined by the linguistic structure of the text (its use of deictics, manipulation of presuppositions, syntactic strategies for marking sentence focus, heavy use of stative predicates and of epistemic modality). On first reading we reach the end of the "story" poised between a nonnarrative text structure that relies on the PR and the apparent narrative imposed on it. Since the Speaker seems to be retracing the steps in the development of her thinking (by now we recognize that this is a story about thought), we expect to arrive ultimately at a Resolution, and we expect this Resolution to be cast in the same PR tense that temporally anchors the statements marking out the stages of the Speaker's apparent attempt to identify the mark on the wall. These statements are listed in (8.16):

(8.16) (a) If that mark *was* made by a nail . . . (p. 77)

(b) But as for that mark, I'M NOT SURE about it; I DON'T BELIEVE it was made by a nail after all; it's too big, too round, for that . . . (p. 77)

(c) And yet that mark on the wall IS NOT a hole at all. It MAY even BE CAUSED by some round black substance . . . (p. 78)

(d) In certain lights that mark on the wall SEEMS actually TO PROJECT from the wall. Nor IS it entirely circular. I CANNOT BE SURE, but it SEEMS TO CAST A perceptible SHADOW . . . (p. 80)

(e) And if I WERE TO GET UP at this very moment and ASCERTAIN that the mark on the wall IS really—what shall I say?—the head of a gigantic old nail . . . (p. 81)

(f) I MUST JUMP UP and SEE for myself what that mark on the wall really IS—a nail, a rose leaf, a crack in the wood? (p. 82)

(g) Indeed, now that I HAVE MY EYES FIXED ON IT, I FEEL that I HAVE *grasped* a plank in the sea . . . (p. 82)

Having followed this sequence, pieced together as the narrative line—notwithstanding the absence of any real "events";[215] there are only verbs of thought and perception—we are set up to expect as a Resolution the sentence given in the (a) version of (8.17). Instead we get the version in (b):

(8.17)   Someone IS STANDING OVER ME and SAYING—
". . . Curse this war; God damn this war! . . . All the same, I don't
see why we should have a snail on our wall."
(a) *Ah, that mark on the wall. It IS a snail.
(b) Ah, the mark on the wall. It *was* a snail.   (p. 83)

In a stroke this sentence dashes our operating hypothesis of a first-person
narration, for the identity of the mark was known all along to the Speaker,
who has not been recounting the itinerary of a discovery. As Traugott
(forthcoming) observes, we now find ourselves obliged to begin the text
all over again with revised expectations. For, contrary to what we were led
to believe, this was not a narrative but a moment of vision, a discourse to
be contemplated, and remembered, focusing this time on the thought processes, just as the Speaker does in contemplating—in the PR—the memory
of the mark.

Starting over, we recognize this text with its Speaker-based PR as a first-
person interior monologue in which the focus of attention is not on
the past actions of an experiencing-self,[216] but on the present thoughts
and perceptions of an analytic self. Cohn (1978:71) has observed that in
first-person fiction the time of most intense reflection is more often the
present than the past; the most memorable minds the genre has produced
(Sterne's Tristram Shandy, Proust's Marcel, Beckett's Molloy, Mann's Felix
Krull) thus belong to narrating-selves rather than experiencing-selves. The
next step in the process is to collapse the two psyches; not in the sense of
having the Speaker/narrator move toward the point of view of his or her
experiencing-self, but rather as Woolf does, by shifting the focus onto the
Speaker's activities in the present, which are cognitive activities rather than
events that happened.[217] The natural outcome of this move is a disabling of
retrospection—at least as anything more than just a backward look from
the vantage point of the focal present. Woolf's focus on the speaking-self
and on speaker-now renders the label "narrator" inappropriate for the
Speaker of this text. In genuine interior monologues, Cohn (1978:182) observes, "the temporal sequence of past events yields to the temporal sequence of present remembrance, and the past is thereby radically
dechronologized."

In her analysis of "The Mark on the Wall" Traugott effectively demonstrates how the movement between P and PR, in particular the unexpected
P of the last line, leads us to reject a reading of this text structured by the
conventional question of narrative: "What happened?" in favor of a reading which, like Woolf's own view of writing, is structured by the question:

"How did this make me think?"—a question that underlies the post-modernist view of reading as a process of rewriting.

"The Mark on the Wall" offers a striking demonstration of the META-LINGUISTIC use of PR tense for storytelling against the grain. An autonomous monologue on the superiority of thought and perception (concepts associated with the PR) over knowledge and action (concepts associated with the P), Woolf's text combines the two tenses in a discourse that undermines the narrative form itself. For what we assumed was *a narrative about thought,* undertaken in the HP, turns out to be *thoughts about narrative,* about the failure of narrative, spoken silently in the PR cotemporal with now. How different in spirit is this structural circularity from that of Proust in *Remembrance,* where the juncture between *the narration of past thoughts* and the *thoughts that give rise to narration*—thoughts incubated in Marcel's mind in the Guermantes library—ultimately gives birth to the narrator's vocation as a writer and to the 2,000-page narration that tells the tale. Yet, paradoxically, Woolf's attack on narrative can succeed only *because* the conventions of narration are so solidly in place as to permit their own deconstruction.

8.4. Transformations of narration in the *nouveau roman*

Literary history has conferred the label *nouveau roman* on the novels of a group of French writers—the best known being Samuel Beckett, Nathalie Sarraute, Alain Robbe-Grillet, Michel Butor, and Claude Simon—who, though not a coherent group or school, discovered at approximately the same time—the middle decades of the twentieth century—and at the outset independently that they could no longer write according to the literary and linguistic protocols consecrated by a long tradition of realist fiction. As one avatar of postmodernism, the *nouveau roman* represents not only a radical departure in creative writing, but also a critical project directed at challenging the assumptions and conventions of representational, realist fiction (typified by the novels of Balzac) and, through that, the habitual forms in which we define and "write" our lives. It is founded on a rejection of the principle that "to tell a good story is . . . to make what one writes resemble the prefabricated schemata people are used to, . . . their ready-made idea of reality" (Robbe-Grillet 1963: 30/1965: 31),[218] and, consequently, on a rejection of certain elements traditionally considered essential to the structure of narrative fiction: story, plot, characters, events. A novel, Robbe-Grillet (1963/1965) argues, should not "tell a story" in the sense referred to above; it is no longer the account of an adventure experienced by one or more characters, but the adventure of the novel's own coming into being: for the author, the novel being written; for the reader, the novel being read. A studied dramatization of the creative process, the *nouveau roman* "ceases to be the writing of a story to become the story of writing" (Ricardou 1967:166), a story that, as a result, is often unreadable as narrative.

A discussion of the goals, praxis, and ideology of postmodern fiction in France would take us beyond the scope of inquiry of this book.[219] Nor is it possible to attend adequately to the diversity of textual practice found among the *nouveaux romanciers,* even among the writers who represent the genre here: Robbe-Grillet, Simon, and Butor. Simon, for example, remained longer within the tradition of psycho-realist fiction than either Robbe-Grillet or Butor (Britton 1987). However, the three representative novels are contemporaneous (1957–1960), and all maintain a commitment to representation and to the convention of a psycho-realist subject whose point of view informs the text.

In Butor's *Second Thoughts* (*La Modification,* 1957/1958), the "action" takes place entirely in the mind of the Speaker, Léon Delmont, who carries on a silent dialogue with himself in the second person (*vous*) during the course of a night's train journey from Paris to Rome, in anticipation of leaving his wife and family in Paris (associated with the here-and-now of his life) and settling down with his mistress in Rome (his past). But in the course of the journey—which is essentially a journey through (his own psychic) time and through the self—Delmont has a change of heart (whence the novel's title) and returns the next morning to Paris. After the journey is over, he is able to live more comfortably in the present, having reconciled this present with his troubling past.

The French title of Robbe-Grillet's *Jealousy* (1957/1965) is purposefully ambiguous: *La Jalousie* refers both to the blinds (jalousies) through which the Speaker-focalizer, an unnamed husband, observes the world of the banana plantation outside his window and to the obsessional jealousy that progressively overcomes him as he constructs an involvement between his wife A... and the neighbor Franck. The novel consists entirely of what the jealous husband sees and has been interpreted alternately as an extreme example of objective, dehumanized narration—the purely visual perceptions of a focalizing eye behind which we have little sense of a focalizing "I"—and as an example of total subjectivity—the obsessive interior monologue of a tormented psyche. Both interpretations support the use of PR tense. Though there are some events in the novel (e.g., the events of A... and Franck's journey into town), they tend to be overshadowed by the seemingly interminable and minute description through which the husband's perceptions and reflections are primarily expressed.

Simon's *The Flanders Road* (*La Route des Flandres*, 1960/1985) likewise takes place entirely in the mind of an obsessional Speaker, Georges, embarked on the impossible task of reflecting on experience as it happens (cf. *n*21). As Georges lies in bed with Corinne, the widow of his commanding officer, the events of the novel—the wartime experiences of a small band of French cavalrymen who survived the destruction of their regiment in 1940—pass visually and chaotically through his mind and onto the pages of the text in the PR-tense mode of current report. As in the case of *Jealousy*, the text of the novel is entirely the product of an obsessional imagination, though Simon at times complicates point of view by introducing more than one focalization on the events Georges is concerned with; these are, however, embedded focalizations (of Iglesia the jockey and of Georges's fellow prisoner Wack), presented as part of the substance of Georges's memory, hence doubly focalized.

Narration presupposes that the activities of "experiencing" or "perceiving," "remembering," and "reporting" occur in the order listed here. But in a novel these activities can be made homologous, provided the writer suppresses all indications as to which is which, as Simon endeavors to do. *The Flanders Road* yields an ever-changing picture of the story-world as it is alternately experienced (or perceived) and remembered by Georges, albeit *without* the natural ordering of these activities that operates to produce narrative.[220] When Sturrock (1969:163) writes, "the distortion of the outside world, which may begin with our *perception* of it and be aggravated by the process of *memory*, is given further impetus still when we start to *verbalize* the contents of that memory" (my emphasis), his concern is with the resulting destabilization of the story-world. My concern is that the synchronization of these three activities, which the PR tense makes possible in fiction, produces a text that is no longer narrative.

To varying degrees, the *nouveaux romans* seek to break with certain of the basic conventions of narration since the Middle Ages: temporal sequence (a linear chronology of events); singulative events; a contrast between events and description, with the understanding that the former constitute the essential component of the discourse; and the assumption of a *fabula* outside the text that the text supposedly models. I shall examine these (interrelated) departures from the narrative norm in the two sections that follow. Critics who read the *nouveaux romans* (notably those of Robbe-Grillet) as experiments in extreme objectivity would claim, moreover, that they lack point of view. In several of these respects the *nouveaux romans* seem to return to a textual practice observed in vernacular epics, notwithstanding profound differences between the two genres in ideology, compositional technique, and cultural and pragmatic context.

8.4.1. *Dechronologizing story-time.*   In texts like *Jealousy, Second Thoughts,* or *The Flanders Road* there is essentially no time line, no linear sequence of events. Attempts to discern a narrative line are doomed to failure, for "narrative time" in these texts does not advance. As Robbe-Grillet observes (1963:130, 133/1965:152, 155, trans. adapted and corrected), insofar as the modern novel "is concerned most often with mental structures, which are devoid of time, . . . time in the modern novel seems to be cut off from temporality. It no longer passes." Tenses are used to obliterate the perception of passing time that they normally evoke in narrative discourse. The conceptualization of time as a continuum stretching backward (and conceivably forward) from the Speaker's present is no longer appropriate; there is only the here-and-now of the text: "an *elsewhere* is no more possible than a *formerly*" (Robbe-Grillet 1963:131/1965:153). The PR tense that serves as the grammatical vehicle of such texts is thus not the HP but a Speaker's PR, a PR cotemporal with now (minus-interpretation).[221] Banishing temporality from his novels, Robbe-Grillet constructs them on the foundation of a "perpetual present," his objective being not to create a dynamic linear pattern of events but to represent a totality, a static whole resembling a picture, as in the passage from *Jealousy* given in (8.18) below. Like the zoom lens of a camera in slow motion, the focalizing eye of the jealous husband scrutinizes the movements of the wife—or, more accurately, her body parts and hairbrush as the brush moves through her hair, as if independent of a controlling agent (PRs in uppercase):

(8.18)   The brush DESCENDS the length of the loose hair with a faint noise that HAS something of the sound of a breath and a crackle. No sooner [has it] reached the bottom than it quickly RISES AGAIN toward the head, where the whole surface of its bristles SINKS IN before gliding down over the black mass again. [The brush is] a bone-colored oval whose short handle DISAPPEARS almost entirely in the hand that firmly GRIPS it.

Half of the hair HANGS DOWN the back, the other hand PULLS the other half over one shoulder. The head LEANS to the right, offering the hair more readily to the brush. Each time the latter LANDS at the top of its cycle behind the nape of the neck, the head LEANS farther to the right and then RISES again with an effort, while the right hand, holding the brush, MOVES AWAY in the opposite direction. The left hand, which loosely CONFINES the hair between the wrist, the palm, and the fingers, RELEASES it for a second and then CLOSES ON it again, gathering the strands together with a firm, mechanical gesture, while the brush CONTINUES its course to the extreme tips of the hair. The sound, which gradually VARIES from one end to the other, IS at this point nothing more than a dry, faint crackling, whose last sputters OCCUR once the brush, leaving the longest hair, IS ALREADY MOVING UP the ascending part of the cycle, describing a swift curve in the air which BRINGS it above the neck, where the hair LIES FLAT on the back of the head and REVEALS the white streak of a part. (*Jealousy*, p. 66; trans. adapted)[222]

In a conventional narrative this entire passage might be reduced to a single narrative or restrictive clause: "She brushed/was brushing her hair."

The novel proceeds unrelentingly in this fashion, with all sense of narrativity stifled by the overwhelming minutiae of descriptions that seem to go nowhere, or at least nowhere they have not been before. For just as events and descriptions are frequently repeated in the *chansons de geste*, so the *nouveaux romans* return to scenes, gestures, and objects we have already seen. In the three passages from *Jealousy* given in (8.19) we observe the repetitive ritual of cocktails, punctuated by banal conversations reiterating the contents of earlier conversations:

(8.19a) A... HAS JUST BROUGHT OUT the glasses, the two bottles, and the ice bucket. She BEGINS SERVING: the cognac in the three glasses, then the soda, and finally three transparent ice cubes, each of which IMPRISONS a bundle of silver needles in its heart. . . .

They SIP their drinks.

"If all goes well," Franck SAYS, "we'll be in town and have an hour or two before lunch."

"Yes, of course. I'd prefer that too," A... SAYS.

They SIP their drinks.

Then they CHANGE the SUBJECT. Now both of them HAVE *finished* the book they HAVE BEEN READING for some time; their remarks CAN therefore REFER to the book as a whole: that is both to the outcome and to the earlier episodes (subjects of past conversations). . . .

They SIP their drinks.   (pp. 74–75)

(8.19b) A..., who HAS *gone to get* the drinks herself, SETS DOWN the loaded tray on the low table. She UNCORKS the cognac and POURS it into the three glasses lined up on the tray. Then she FILLS them with soda. Having distributed the first two, she SITS DOWN in her turn in the empty chair, holding the third glass in one hand.

This is when she ASKS if the usual ice cubes will be necessary, declaring that these bottles COME OUT of the refrigerator . . .   (pp. 85–86)

(8.19c)   IT IS ALMOST TIME for cocktails, and A... HAS not *waited* any longer to call the boy, who APPEARS at the corner of the house, carrying the tray with the two bottles, three large glasses and the ice bucket. . . . he carefully PUTS DOWN the tray, near the novel with the shiny paper jacket.

It is the latter that PROVIDES the subject for the conversation. . . . A... and Franck DISCUSS it animatedly while sipping the mixture of cognac and soda served by the mistress of the house in the three glasses.   (p. 137)[223]

In *The Flanders Road* too the Speaker returns to information that has already been reported, events that reiterate themselves in his memory with variations not unlike those found in the *chansons de geste* (e.g., the death of the horse and that of Captain de Reixach, the latter ultimately becoming fused with the death of an ancestor who fought in the Revolution). As in the *chansons de geste,* repetition serves as a foregrounding device (cf. Fleischman 1989a). In *The Flanders Road,* however, it is irrelevant how many times or in what order the variants are reported, for there is no external order to provide a template for iconic sequence in the text.

Cohn (1978) coins the term "memory monologues" to refer to *The Flanders Road* and similar novels that read like interior monologues verbalizing the activity of remembering. In memory monologues the logic of the *sjuzhet* bears no relation to a temporally ordered *fabula;* events are dechronologized and the only continuity is that of the spontaneously remembering mind, the only logic that of "the private associations that determine mnemonic thought sequences" (Cohn 1978:183). It is therefore not surprising that *The Flanders Road,* again like the *chansons de geste,* contains cataphoric references. These mark the discourse as that of a Speaker who knows everything from the outset and—unlike omniscient narrators of conventional fiction—is under no constraint to withhold information until the appropriate point in the *sjuzhet.* In the case of epic singers such violations of chronology are licensed by the fact that the *fabula* is shared knowledge; the dechronologized *sjuzhet* therefore poses no problem for listeners attempting to follow the story. In *The Flanders Road* dechronologization is problematic only to the extent that the reader insists on finding a chronology in the text. For in effect, the purpose of Simon's blurring of temporality, like Robbe-Grillet's attempt to abolish time altogether, is to eliminate all notion of an external *fabula* that the text is assumed to model.[224] The reader is supposed to feel that the configurational operation that transforms unordered reality into ordered narration has been disabled.

A conspicuous linguistic feature of Simon's novels is his use of the PR PTC, a form of the verb that, through its explicit tenselessness, can abort any sense of chronology that might creep in simply through the linearity of discourse. Simon is reported as having said in an interview, "the use of the present participle enables me to locate myself outside conventional time" (Sturrock 1969 : 101), by which we are to understand the time of public reference; he relies on the PR PTC to relocate the action of his novels in the mind's time, the here-and-now of the remembering subject, where, through language, the inputs to consciousness drawn from perception (the present) and from memory (the past) can be conflated. The temporal relativity of the PR PTC—it expresses pure, nondeictic simultaneity—denies the situation it reports any recognizable beginning or end, thereby preserving the essential discontinuities of memory, and prevents deictic anchoring. By stringing together clauses with PR PTCs, anchored minimally, if at all, to a finite verb, as in the example in (8.20) below, Simon conveys a sense of movements that merely replace one another, suspended in time; they have no positive temporal reference (past or present) and no logical relation to one another (causality):

(8.20)   . . . Georges DECLARING that he had decided to work on the land, and supported (although he pretended not to hear her although PRETENDING to speak to them both together, and yet TURNING noticeably towards her [his mother] alone and TURNING noticeably AWAY from his father, and yet SPEAKING to him, and noticeably PAYING NO ATTENTION to her or anything she might say), supported then by Sabine's noisy, obscene, and uterine approval . . .
(The Flanders Road, p. 173)[225]

In monologic fiction that seeks to represent no external world but only the contents of a Speaker's mind, tense switching is a recurrent feature, though the PR tense predominates. But unlike conventional PAST-tense narration in which the functions of tense switching are in large part not temporal (REFERENTIAL) but pragmatic (TEXTUAL/EXPRESSIVE), the marked genre of monologic fiction generally convokes the tenses for their basic REFERENTIAL meanings, as Speakers reflect on their present or formulate general ideas (PR), recall their past (P), and speculate about the future (FUT). The prominence of the P varies considerably in these texts, in proportion to the role played by memory. In *The Flanders Road* it is considerable; less so but still significant in *Second Thoughts,* and infinitesimal in *Jealousy,* where temporality is entirely reduced to the now of the telling, the "perpetual present" beneath which no time depth lurks. But no matter how much of the text is concerned with the content of memories, the past—which is a remembered past, not a past-become-knowledge—is inevitably tied to the Speaker's present, and thus commented on and exclaimed upon, but not narrated.

8.4.2. *The discourse of visual perception.* The PR is the privileged tense of description. By radically foregrounding description at the expense of events, in particular, minutely detailed description of the most seemingly mundane reality, the *nouveau roman* effects another departure from the narrative prototype that contributes significantly to the feeling that time does not move, that there is no "story" in the traditional sense of the term. To invoke Robbe-Grillet once again (1963:133/1965:155): "Description makes no headway, contradicts itself, turns in circles. Moment denies continuity."

The *nouveaux romanciers* have often been referred to as *l'école du regard*, a label that derives from a particular way of looking at the world that excludes anything beyond what the eye can see and what can be apprehended purely by visual perception. Commentators on the *nouveau roman* point consistently to the prominence of visual images in the textual practice of these writers.[226] The reader of a *nouveau roman* becomes of necessity a spectator, an observer of visual reality in its microscopic detail. Sartre's *Nausea* (1938/1949) opens with the passage given in (8.21) below, which purports to be the first page, undated, of the notebooks of Antoine Roquentin, "here published without alteration":

(8.21)   The best thing would be to write down events from day to day. Keep a diary to see clearly—let none of the nuances or small happenings escape even though they might seem to mean nothing. And above all, classify them. I must tell how I see this table, this street, the people, my packet of tobacco, since *those* are the things which have changed. I must determine the exact extent and nature of this change. . . . I must always be ready, otherwise it will slip through my fingers. I must never[227]   but carefully note and detail all that happens.

Naturally, I can write nothing definite about this Saturday and the day-before-yesterday business. I am already too far from it . . .   (*Nausea*, 1949:7)

Among the striking features of this mode of writing, we observe: the shrinking of the event as the crucial component of storytelling; the need to work in fine detail; the equal attention given to objects and to people; the insistence on "how" rather than "when"; and above all, a desire to record what one sees, what is happening, at the moment—the antithesis of the historian's "narrative statements" (§5.5.3), which retrospectively invest acts and actors with meanings. Narrative in the traditional sense of a causally related sequence of past events has undergone a radical transformation; the thrust of the postmodern novel is the evocation of a milieu in the present, which reaches us filtered through a strongly visual focalizer—several critics have suggested a camera eye—that circles around objects and agents, registering its perceptions in a discourse dominated by the descriptive PR tense.

In their handling of description, as in their handling of temporality, the *nouveaux romanciers* do not offer homogeneity. The function of description in Robbe-Grillet, Britton (1987:44f.) argues, is, paradoxically, to limit observation, to make the focalized object disappear; he often produces descriptions in which the visual properties of objects, while being noted with apparent scrupulousness, are deliberately emptied of all sensuous significance (cf. the hair-brushing passage in [8.18]). Simon does just the opposite; his descriptions are vivid and sensuous, in a way which seems to belong to an earlier tradition of realist writing. But, notwithstanding their differences, the *nouveaux romanciers* seem to be united in foregrounding the descriptive mode and the activity of visual perception.

Robbe-Grillet privileges visual perception notably in his early novels, *The Voyeur* and *Jealousy*. What the phenomenal world offers to the eye is opacity: objects that have no accompanying meanings but are simply there,[228] characters that lack any psychological penetration, a world of surfaces beneath which there is no depth of meaning, just as there is no time depth, no past, underlying the insistent present. In an essay entitled "On Several Obsolete Notions" (first published 1957), Robbe-Grillet insists (1963:28/1965:28) that "the novel of characters belongs entirely to the past"; though we still refer to them as characters, the human objects focalized in many *nouveaux romans* differ minimally from their inanimate counterparts. There is no depth to them; their emotions must be inferred from what can be externally perceived (they are externally focalized from without). Consider the following description of A...—who lacks even a full name—observed through the horizontal slats of the jalousies that striate and distort the perceptions of the focalizing subject in *Jealousy*:[229]

(8.22) It IS only at a distance of less than a yard that the elements of a discontinuous landscape APPEAR in the successive intervals, parallel chinks separated by the wider slats of grey wood: the turned wood balusters, the empty chair, the low table where a full glass IS STANDING beside the tray holding the two bottles, and then the top part of the head of black hair, which at this moment TURNS toward the right, where above the table SHOWS a bare forearm, dark brown in color, and its paler hand holding the ice bucket. A...'s voice THANKS the boy. The brown hand DISAPPEARS. The shiny metal bucket, [which IS] immediately FROSTED OVER, REMAINS where it has been set on the tray beside the two bottles.

The knot of A...'s hair, seen at such close range from behind, SEEMS to be extremely complicated. IT IS DIFFICULT TO FOLLOW the convolutions of different strands: several solutions SEEM POSSIBLE at some places, and in others none.

(pp. 59–60)[230]

Scrutinized at such close range, the figure of A... can only appear fragmented: a hand, a forearm, a knot of hair, its individual strands; a voice, not a character, thanks the boy. Verbalizing his perceptions as he observes, in the PR-tense mode of a current report, the focalizer is unable to gain perspective on focalized objects, his vision (cognitive as well as sensory) distorted by the lack of distance and the slats of the jalousies, a reification of his own profoundly distorting jealousy.

A goal of the *école du regard* was to arrive at an objective description in which objects (animate and inanimate) could be observed in their pristine form, stripped of the meanings they accumulate through contact with individual subjectivities. Two people looking at an object will not see the same object, since its significance is different for each one. Their respective imaginations have worked with the public fact, integrated it into private systems of relationships, and stored it in memory. It is only by virtue of having passed through the crucible of memory that the data of perception acquire meanings. By obliterating the past through the vehicle of "that perpetual present which makes all recourse to memory impossible" (Robbe-Grillet 1963:131/1965:152), the novelist seeks to project a world with no predetermined meanings, a world of *unevaluated* public facts. As Robbe-Grillet states in a 1956 essay entitled "A Future for the Novel" (1963:19/1965:20, trans. adapted):

In the earlier novel, the objects and gestures that served as background for the plot disappeared completely, leaving behind only their *meanings:* the empty chair became only absence or expectation, the hand placed on a shoulder became a sign of friendliness, the bars on the window became only the impossibility of leaving. . . . But in the cinema, one *sees* the chair, the movement of the hand, the shape of the bars.[231] Their meaning remains obvious, but instead of monopolizing our attention, it becomes something added, even something in excess, because what affects us, what persists in our memory, what appears as essential and irreducible to vague mental notions are the gestures themselves, the objects, the movements, and the outlines, to which the image has suddenly (and unintentionally) restored their *reality*.

A world of objects with no preestablished meanings—things and people that exist solely because of their presence to an observer—is a world in the present that can only be represented in language by the PR tense—hence the title of Bloch-Michel's essay on the *nouveau roman: Le Présent de l'indicatif*. As Bloch-Michel observes (1963:55ff.), the world of things past is the memory of their meanings; for it is memory that transforms indifferent objects, neutral public facts, into things we cherish or abhor, things we miss when they are gone or are glad to be rid of. When things install themselves in our memory it is not as they are objectively but *as they are for us,* invested with the meanings and associations we have attached to them, which develop only through familiarity with them *over time.* Meaning thus presupposes a past. Memories cannot be introduced into a world where things exist only in the present. By casting the novel in the PR tense—the PR cotemporal with now—the *nouveaux romanciers* have chosen a grammatical form that "contains only presence, but is devoid of meanings" (Bloch-Michel 1963:56), meanings in the sense of prior evaluations reflecting a particular subjectivity.

Subjectivity in fiction is normally linked to the Speaker, whom—unless we are told otherwise or led to believe is unreliable—we assume to be the purveyor (real or proxy) of evaluations and the reference point for the ideology of the text. In Robbe-Grillet's novels it is precisely because the Speaker refuses to evaluate the contents of the story-world or to guide readers along paths of meaning that his novels have been interpreted as excessively *chosistes* and lacking a human element.[232] But for Robbe-Grillet subjectivity in the postmodern novel is located not in the Speaker, but in the reader/spectator, who must assume responsibility for the production of meaning.[233] Thus he insists that the images the *nouveau roman* proposes to the reader are not gratuitous or meaningless, as critics have often thought, but meaningful—in the sense of *inviting* not imposing interpretation.

Insofar as this controversy of interpretation surrounding the *nouveau roman* has focused on characterization, it presents an interesting paradox. The "objective" approach to characterization (cultivated by Robbe-Grillet and in its most extreme form in certain novels of Nathalie Sarraute) seemingly stands in opposition to the purport of techniques such as free indirect discourse, interior monologue, or psycho-narration (external focalization from within), all of which open windows, more or less transparent, into characters' minds and psyches. Yet, as we have seen, certain of the *nouveaux romans* can themselves be construed as interior monologues, insofar as everything "takes place" within the consciousness of the speaking subject. Thus the "death of the novel of characters" that Robbe-Grillet proclaims in the *nouveau roman* is at once, paradoxically, an affirmation of the novel of characters; for while *focalized characters* may be reduced to sets of externally *un*evaluated descriptions of what is perceivable on the surface, this opens the way for an excursion into *focalizing characters* (Speakers), whose subjectivity is communicated, however, through more subtle techniques of internal evaluation, in particular, by allowing their *percep-*

tions to "speak for themselves." It is this paradox, here construed as a function of different kinds of evaluation, that appears to be the source of the alternate interpretations of Robbe-Grillet's novels as aiming at total objectivity or total subjectivity.

The point at issue here is that both interpretations—which are not incompatible with one another—motivate the choice of PR tense. On the one hand, the PR is the logical grammatical vehicle of a discourse that claims to be an objective (unevaluated) *description* of focalized objects (things and people) as they offer themselves directly, in the *present*, to the *perception* of a speaking subject. This is the present of current report. On the other hand, the PR is also the tense of interior monologue, the discourse that purports to offer an unmediated representation of subjectivity. In both cases, we have to do with verbal representations that are unconcerned with time movement and sequences of events—the essence of narrativity—and are unmediated by retrospective reflection or a configurational act. Thus in both cases what is at issue is the minus-interpretation— the PR cotemporal with now, which METALINGUISTICALLY establishes the discourse as something other than narration.

8.4.3. A literature of speech.   The *nouveau roman* has been referred to as a "literature of speech" insofar as it challenges the traditional view of literary language as something more than a graphic transcription of utilitarian spoken language whose unmarked tense is the PR. Like Camus's *The Stranger* (§7.7.1), the *nouveau roman* seeks to move the language of fiction in the direction of ordinary conversation with its disjunctions, false starts, repair mechanisms, and apparent incoherencies. Consider the example in (8.23) from a diegetic passage of Butor's *Second Thoughts* (all marks of speech are italicized, including speaker-based tenses):

(8.23)   *There you go again* [PR], playing *that* game *you get into* [PR] so often, giving names to *your* fellow passengers; but *this one's* [PR] not really right for *that* little boy *wriggling* [PR] in his seat, *who's* [PR] so much younger than *your* son *now;* better call him, *let's say, André;* [and] the woman *who's holding* [PR] his hand and *taking him out* [PR] *will be* [FUT] Madame Polliat; *as for* the young couple, *forget* the literary allusions, just Pierre, and, *let's see* [IMPER], Cécile *is out of the question* [PR], but Agnès would do just fine . . .

(*Second Thoughts,* p. 118, trans. adapted)[234]

Clearly this is not a narrative in the HP, whose time reference is that of the PS/IMP (the commutation test produces a number of anomalous sentences). At issue here is the PR cotemporal with now, the tense of a speaker observing his own actions in the present and commenting on them to himself (cf. *n*214). The "action" of this novel is played out entirely in speech and thought, silently, through an autonomous monologue.

Yet despite Butor's attempt to collapse the distinction between the storytelling and speech modes, it cannot be entirely obliterated. Consider the passage in (8.24), in which quoted speech reverts to normative time-tense correlations:

(8.24) Next Tuesday, when you go [FUT] into her bedroom, you'll surely tell her [FUT] all about your journey and you'll say [FUT] to her: "I had gone [PLP] to Rome to prove to Cécile that I was choosing [IMP] her rather than you, I had gone [PLP] intending to ask her to come and live with me for good in Paris . . ."
Then your own voice cries out [PR] within you in a wail of terror . . .
(*Second Thoughts*, p. 150)[235]

In this novel the so-called storytelling mode is simply a marked variety of speech in which events, reported in the PR, cannot be pinned down in time. They are located, in Saunders's words (1969:144), "in a space or vacant lot between the past and the future," setting up tensions that involve the reader almost as a participant in the story (the referential ambiguity of *vous*).

In *The Flanders Road* the text between quotation marks often extends for pages, at times embedding speech into speech, to the point where the distinction between mimetic and diegetic discourse becomes irrelevant. The passage given in (8.25) below is diegetic, insofar as it is not enclosed between quotation marks and begins with the most common of narrative sequencers, "then," conventionally used to introduce events; yet both its syntax (the main line of the sentence is repeatedly interrupted with explanatory parentheticals) and the insistent qualifiers (*c'est-à-dire* [that is], *cette espèce de* [that kind of], *plutôt* [rather], *pour ainsi dire* [somehow]) mark the discourse as that of a speaker, not a literary narrator. This is what this text purports to be: the experiences of the war "speaking themselves" through the consciousness of Georges:

(8.25) Puis ils (tous les trois: l'homme décharné, Iglésia et Georges—eux maintenant vêtus comme des valets de ferme, *c'est-à-dire* vaguement gênés, vaguement mal à l'aise, comme si—au sortir de leur lourde carapace de drap, de cuir, de courroies—ils se sentaient à peu près nus, sans poids dans l'air léger) furent de nouveau dehors, flottant dans *cette espèce de* vastitude, de vacuité, de vide cotonneux, entourés de tous côtés par le bruit où *plutôt* la rumeur pour ainsi dire tranquille de la bataille . . .
(*La Route des Flandres*, p. 115)

Then they (all three: the fleshless cadaver, Iglésia, and Georges—they now dressed like farm-hands, *that is,* vaguely uncomfortable, vaguely embarrassed, as if— abandoning their heavy carapace of cloth and leather—they felt almost naked, weightless in the weightless air) were outside again, floating in *that kind of* enormous emptiness, that cottony void surrounded on all sides by the sound or *rather* the somehow calm murmur of battle . . .   (*The Flanders Road,* p. 88)

While postmodern fiction may have gone far in eliminating the "story" from the novel, its trace (in Derrida's sense) remains in the structure of difference through which speech between quotation marks distinguishes itself from speech without quotation marks, and through which the latter constitutes itself as antinarrative.[236]

8.4.4. *Preliterate and postmodern fiction: Points of contact.*   In a number of respects, as we have seen, the textual practice of the *nouveaux romans* resembles that of orally performed epics: a preference for descriptive circularity over linear plot; paratactic organization of content units;[237] parallelism and repetition of words, events, and scenes;[238] emphasis on perceptions and visual representation; refusal to penetrate the surface of focalized characters and objects; and prominence of speech. In drawing this comparison I do not mean to imply that the artistic objectives of epic singers and *nouveaux romanciers* are at all the same, nor are their reasons for incorporating these features into their respective textual practice. I invoke the commonalities principally with a view toward demonstrating, in the context of the theory of tense and narrativity being proposed here, the motivations underlying the choice in both genres of the marked PR tense, whose METALINGUISTIC function is to identify the discourse as something other than narrative.

The *nouveau roman* also resembles the epic in its endeavor to avoid explicit evaluations and to eliminate the modalizing filter of a positively expressed point of view. This is not to say that these texts lack an ideology, nor that the worlds they propose to us are devoid of "meanings," as certain commentators have suggested. However, in neither genre is the source of meanings and values to be found where we normally expect to find it in conventional storytelling—in the textual persona of the Speaker-narrator. Where, then, are meanings produced? For vernacular epic they emerge in a pragmatic space of shared cultural, political, and moral values that unite a community of listeners gathered to participate in a "storytelling event" whose significance for that community clearly transcends the entertainment value of the story being performed. For the *nouveau roman,* if we accept Robbe-Grillet's views on the matter, meaning resides in the reader-become-spectator, who observes and participates in the novel's coming into being; only through this active collaboration between author and reader do the familiar objects of reality become invested with meanings, meanings that are therefore always new.

8.5. PRESENT-tense fiction: Where is it moving?

As Genette (1980 : 218f.) points out, PR-tense fiction is inherently unstable, tending to veer either in the direction of a highly objective "behaviorist" report that seeks to suppress all traces of a speaking subject or, conversely, toward the complete interiority of the monologic novel, which uses the action merely as a pretext for exploring the consciousness of a perceiving or remembering subject. Of the texts and genres considered in this chapter, epic and *romancero* seem to come under the first rubric; "The Mark on the Wall," *Second Thoughts,* and *The Flanders Road* under the second. Robbe-Grillet's *Jealousy,* as we have seen, has been read in both ways: as an extreme example of objective, dehumanized reporting and as the obsessive monologue of a tormented psyche.

It is also significant that both paths to which Genette refers lead away from narrative toward the two nonnarrative macro-genres: lyric and drama. The examples of PR-tense storytelling surveyed in this chapter all involve a measure of dechronologization and a shrinking of specifically narrative elements. This opens the way, on the one hand, for performed stories to approach actual dramatic performance, and, on the other, for the discourse of reflections and perceptions to approach lyricism. A pure monodrama written for stage performance, Cohn (1978 : 157f.) observes, would differ from an interior monologue to be read only in its author's intentions; likewise, a dramatic monologue in which a lone speaker articulates a contemporary experience is the lyric analogue of the prose monologue in the novel. Parallel observations have been made concerning the traditional oral genres that rely on PR tense: The *laisse* unit of the *chansons de geste* has been described as a "lyrical arrest" (Goldin 1978) in the commemorative dramatization of the founding events of a national past, a drama in which historical agents and events shed their ephemeral pastness and enter the timeless realm of legend. The oldest of the *romances* preserve the most dramatic moments of earlier epic legends; infused with direct speech and passages of sustained lyricism, they also convert erstwhile historical events into timeless song.

In sum, the choice of a tense in fiction clearly is more than just a grammatical agenda. Let us recall once again Sartre's observation that *tense* holds the key to a text's "special strangeness." Texts that rely on the PR tense are texts that in different but not dissimilar ways have moved away from the narrative prototype toward the monologic (lyric) or dialogic (drama) genres, whose unmarked tense is likewise the PR. In so doing these texts privilege a METALINGUISTIC function of the PR, which, according to my theory of tense and narrativity, is to announce a language that cannot be narrative according to the rules of narrative's own game.

Conclusion

He who tells the story has the power to do away with the
opacity . . . of the existences that make it up.

(BARTHES, *WRITING DEGREE ZERO*)

We have no idea of what a culture would be like where no
one knew any longer what it meant to narrate things.

(RICOEUR, *TIME AND NARRATIVE*)

Since the advent of structuralism we have become accus-
tomed to thinking of grammar as a relatively stable structure or system that
all adult members of a speech community possess in reasonably similar
form, and in which *forms*—the recognized categories of the grammar—
have *meanings* or *functions* that hold constant independently of context
(the so-called basic meanings). Recently, however, Hopper (1987) has proposed that we abandon such *a priori* notions of grammar in favor of a view
of grammar as "emergent"—not as a synchronically stable bedrock of
form-meaning or form-function correlations, but as a set of linguistic
transactions that are continually negotiated in individual contexts of actual
communication. "Structure," in this postmodernist view of grammar, is
thus always provisional and always deferred. The relationship Hopper
(1987:142) posits between "regularity" ("grammar" in the traditional sense)
and "discourse" (speakers' use of the forms in specific contexts, or what is
here called "pragmatics") is a dialectical one: "structure, or regularity,
comes out of discourse and is shaped by discourse as much as it shapes
discourse in an on-going process."

This dialectic between "regularity" and "discourse" (i.e., between grammar and pragmatics) underlies the approach to tense and narrativity that I
have taken in this book. For if we equate the REFERENTIAL functions of
tense-aspect categories with "regularity" and their TEXTUAL, EXPRESSIVE,
and METALINGUISTIC functions with "discourse," it is evident that the
functions that have been of primary concern here are those that "emerge"
in specific contexts: contexts of *narration*, understood as a distinct variety

of linguistic activity. Granted, the contexts in which these functions operate no longer necessarily involve face-to-face interaction of the type Hopper has in mind. Yet one of the principal claims I have sought to establish is that it was initially in situations of *interactive oral storytelling* that the narrative functions of tense-aspect categories were developed, functions that have continued and still continue to be renegotiated in contexts of natural narrative performance. Certain of these functions have by now been extended beyond the original performance contexts (e.g., the HP, the NARR IMP, and the discourse contrast commonly associated with the aspectual opposition PFV-IPFV) and have also undergone a measure of *grammaticalization* (integration into the grammar), redefining in the process the categories in question. These developments illustrate the dialectical nature of emergent grammar: for, on the one hand, we have observed how the basic REFERENTIAL meanings of these categories motivate particular TEXTUAL, EXPRESSIVE, and METALINGUISTIC uses—the most salient example perhaps being that of the PR tense—and, on the other, how the latter uses in turn reshape the grammar, both synchronically and ultimately diachronically.

Whereas approaches to grammar based on mentally represented rule systems would presumably exclude from the domain of "grammar" meanings produced in the pragmatic and metalinguistic components, an emergent view of grammar not only allocates a place for these meanings within the province of grammar, but also acknowledges their prominent role in its continual restructuring. Even among functional models of language, those that view synchronic grammars as relatively fixed systems of form-function correlations have difficulty incorporating the specifically narrative functions of tense-aspect categories, which constitute a system of their own in certain respects, one in which form-function correlations are not always the same as those that obtain in ordinary speech. Even within the broad context of narrative, specific varieties (oral vs. written, spontaneous vs. planned, performed vs. unperformed, fictional vs. nonfictional) or specific genres (epic, chronicle, novel, personal anecdote) may set up pragmatically determined subcontexts with their own potentially distinctive uses of the forms of grammar. Bronzwaer (1970) takes this line of argument to its logical terminus, claiming that *an individual text* can set up a discourse micro-context, negotiating its own unique system of tense-aspect functions, provided these remain relatively constant throughout the text and do not clash with the prevailing grammar of the language. Yet certain of these "clashes," construed as renegotiations of the grammar, may eventually take hold and thereby reconfigure the system itself. While Camus's experiment with the PASSÉ COMPOSÉ failed to reshape the grammar of novelistic fiction in French, Flaubert's renegotiation of the IMP and the postmodern renegotiation of the PR were ultimately more successful.

The differential functioning of tense-aspect categories within successively narrower discourse contexts is what motivated my analysis of tense-aspect functions in terms of markedness, and more specifically in accord with the principle that markedness values commonly reverse in contexts that are themselves marked. We have seen this principle worked out most strikingly with regard to the PR and PRET; the PR is in the first instance the unmarked tense of ordinary language (the unmarked context), in relation to which narrative constitutes a marked context whose unmarked tense is accordingly the PRET (a marked category in ordinary language). Yet within the context of narrative, where the PRET is now unmarked, we find genres such as the epic, *romancero, nouveau roman,* and other monologic fiction, which represent marked micro-contexts that define themselves in opposition to the narrative norm and accordingly select the PR, which is marked in a narrative context, as their unmarked tense. At each level of the hierarchy a slightly different grammar emerges through the interaction of REFERENTIAL meanings and context. Within each grammar thus constituted, tense-aspect morphology can function REFERENTIALLY (providing temporal reference and aspectual information) as well as TEXTUALLY (to signal grounding relationships, mark discourse boundaries, control the tempo of the discourse), EXPRESSIVELY (to communicate evaluations and mark point of view), and METALINGUISTICALLY (to broadcast the nature of the discourse).

One of the claims that founds this book, though not an original claim, is that narrative constitutes a special category of linguistic performance whose grammar differs in certain significant respects from the grammar of nonnarrative language. Under the narrative umbrella I have chosen to analyze in conjunction with one another a variety of discourse types that contrast along such (intersecting) lines as spoken vs. written, spontaneous vs. planned, literary vs. nonliterary, fictional vs. nonfictional—discourses that are not generally brought together in the context of a single inquiry. The data base for this book accordingly includes texts representing a number of different languages at different stages in their histories, as well as a diversity of storytelling genres: vernacular epics and medieval romances, hagiography and historiography, traditional ballads, pseudo-biography, avant-garde fiction, and personal-experience anecdotes. My decision to bring these texts together was motivated by their parallel use of tense-aspect morphology for purposes that are PRAGMATIC or METALINGUISTIC as well as REFERENTIAL. Though the particulars often differ, as might be expected given differences among tense-aspect systems, the basic strategies are very much the same, across languages and across genres.

The more original claim this book makes, which is in line with Hopper's notion of emergent grammar, is that the NONREFERENTIAL uses of tense-aspect morphology, certain of which have now become grammaticalized, developed as motivated pragmatic responses to the conditions of narrative performance in spontaneous interactive contexts. Regrettably, we have little reliable documentation on "natural" narrative performance in the early stages of the languages in question. However, a comparison of modern natural narratives with artificial performance texts that have come down from the early periods—at which time textual language was much closer to spoken language than is the case today—reveals some striking similarities in discourse organization, notably with regard to the NONREFERENTIAL use of tenses. Hence my decision to adopt an analytical framework developed for conversational narration as a methodological starting point for analyzing the linguistic structure of more complex narrations of poetic or historiographic purport. I cite in this context a view shared by many narratologists, that "oral storytelling in conversational contexts [constitutes] the primary site for understanding narrative structure. Once we understand what every competent speaker is doing when s(he) recounts the experiences in his/her life or the lives of other people, we will be in a somewhat better position to understand the transformation of the 'story' into written, fictional, and literary artifacts" (Polanyi 1981:316). It is my hope that this book has succeeded in furthering the goal articulated in Polanyi's statement and, in a broader context, that it will further the dialogue that has already begun to take place among linguists, literary theorists, anthropologists, historiographers, and others concerned with understanding the workings of one of our most basic and most powerful hermeneutic constructs for making sense of the data of experience: narrative.

Appendix 1. Coding Conventions

The following typographic conventions are used to code tense-aspect categories; correlations with language-specific *forms* are noted where appropriate. As a rule the entire predicate is coded, not just the verb.

DIEGETIC PRESENT (NP or *HP)*   *ITALIC BOLD UPPERCASE*
   (includes PRESENT SUBJUNCTIVE, marked [SUBJ])
   Time reference: story-now
PRESENT COTEMPORAL WITH NOW   ROMAN UPPERCASE
   Time reference: speaker-now
G E N E R I C   P R E S E N T   S P A C E D   U P P E R C A S E
   Time reference: all relevant time-moments, with global or local inter-
   pretation determined by context
preterit (PERFECTIVE PAST)*   *italic lowercase*
   (includes IMPERFECT SUBJUNCTIVE, marked [IMP SUBJ])
   *Certain languages have two exponents of PFV PAST, simple and
   complex (Fr. PASSÉ SIMPLE/PASSÉ COMPOSÉ), often in complemen-
   tary distribution according to discourse type. Both are given in *italic
   lowercase* where their function is PRETERIT.
IMPERFECT (IMPERFECTIVE PAST)**   *ITALIC UPPERCASE*
   **For languages like English, which do not mark the PFV/IPFV con-
   trast morphologically, the single PAST form is given in *lowercase italic*
   irrespective of its contextually determined aspect. Only the PROG
   PAST is given *IMPERFECT* marking.

PRESENT *perfect****   UPPERCASE AUX. + *italic ptc.*

(where linked to a diegetic PR [HP or NP] the form is in *bold/italic* [I HAVE ***spoken***]; where linked to a PR cotemporal with now it is in Roman type [I HAVE *spoken*])

> ***For languages like modern French and Italian, in which the complex PAST may function as either PRETERIT or PRESENT PERFECT, the appropriate *functional* marking is used.

anterior past/pluperfect   *lowercase italic* + **bold**

(including those with simple past time reference)

FUTURE   UPPERCASE BROKEN UNDER-

(includes GO-FUTURE)   SCORING

future-of-the-past/conditional   lowercase broken underscoring

(includes GO-FUTURE-OF-THE-PAST)

Transcription Conventions

Verse texts are transcribed with one line of verse per line of transcript, prose texts with one clause per line of transcript; where verses or clauses exceed a single line, the second line is indented. Direct speech is included with its *verbum dicendi* as part of a single clause.

Clause coding: Narrative clauses are preceded by a letter in the left margin. Restricted, free, coordinated, and summative result clauses are marked, where appropriate, in the right margin (centered for passages with side-by-side translations).

Major structural components of the narrative are indicated at the right of each text: COMPLICATING ACTION is only marked at its onset; it is understood to include clauses of ORIENTATION or EVALUATION whether these are marked explicitly as EMBEDDED or not.

Omissions and additions: where words or lines of the original text are omitted (e.g., passages of direct speech), this is indicated by ellipses. In the early Romance texts (original versions) letters or words not appearing in the manuscript but supplied by an editor are enclosed in square brackets.

In the translations words in square brackets are words that I have added for a smoother reading; words in curly brackets translate words in the original text that would normally be omitted in an idiomatic translation, but which I have included because of their relevance to points of analysis. The number sign (#) indicates the place of anaphoric *si* (no translation equivalent) in Old Gallo-Romance texts.

Appendix 2. Texts

(repr. in Menéndez y Pelayo 1944–1945, 8:414f., first printed in the *Cancionero de romances* of 1550).

IX. *Poema de mio Cid,* stanza 112 (episode of the lion)—epic song, Old Spanish. Date controversial, probably beginning of the thirteenth century. Text from edition by Colin Smith.

X. *La Chanson de Roland,* Oxford manuscript, vv. 2686–2723 (episode of the pagans' lament)—epic song, Old French. Composed ca. 1100. Text from edition by Frederick Whitehead; translation adapted from that of Frederick Goldin, with line numbers adjusted to match those of Whitehead's edition.

XI. *La Vie de St. Alexis,* Hildesheim version (manuscript *L*), early twelfth century, stanzas 21–32 (episode of the failure of his father's men to recognize Alexis dressed as a beggar)—hagiography, Old French (Anglo-Norman dialect). Probably composed late eleventh century. Text from edition by C. Storey.

XII. Chrétien de Troyes, *Le Chevalier au lion (Yvain),* vv. 815–875 (episode of Yvain's combat with Esclados)—chivalric romance, Old French (Champagne dialect), late twelfth century. Text from edition by Mario Roques (based on Guiot manuscript); translation adapted from edition by William Kibler.

XIII. *Récit de vie* of Xavier-Edouard Lejeune—synoptic narrative biography, French. Text from Lejeune 1985:5.

(Full bibliographic data on editions provided in section I of the references.)

Text I.   "The Car Breakdown"

Synopsis: Some girls, counselors at a summer camp, borrow a car to go out for lunch; the car breaks down in an out-of-the-way place; they enlist the help of a man passing by, whose undesirable appearance leads them to fear being kidnapped.

Oh it *was so crazy*	1	(EVALUATIVE)
I REMEMBER THIS.		ABSTRACT
Maybe I SHOULDN'T SAY IT now.		
It *was really a weird thing.*		
We *were* at camp	5	ORIENTATION
and we *did this crazy thing.*		
We *were* all *going out for lunch*		

    it *was our birthdays*
    and we *were C.I.T.'s*
    so we *were allowed to.*   10

a. We *borrowed someone's car*   COMPLICATION
b. And we *got blown out.*
c. And w—so, the car *stalled*
    but we *didn't ca—couldn't call*   ORIENTATION
    because we *were supposed t' be* out t' lunch   15
    and why *were* we here?
    Cause we **had moved . . . off the road** t' party.
    So we *were* in this car
    in this—an' we *were* in Allentown
    it's real dinky   20
    an' it's like real hick town off o' Allentown.
    right around there in this factory.
d. We just *pulled into this lot*
    it *was* just in this lot   ORIENTATION
e. and all of a sudden the buzzer *SOUNDS*   25
f. and all these guys hh *COME* hh *OUT*
    and we *didn't know what t' do*   ORIENTATION
    cause we *were stuck.*
g. So we *asked some guy t' come over an' help us.*
h. So he *OPENS THE CAR*   30
i. and everyone *GETS OUT* except me and my
      girlfriend.
    We *were* in the front   ORIENTATION
    we just *didn't feel like getting out*
j. And all of a sudden all these sparks
    START T' FLY
k. So the girl *SAYS,*   35
    "Look, do you know what you're doing?   EVALUATION
    Because y' know um . . . this is not my car
    an' if you don't know what you're doing,
    just don't do anything."
l. And he *SAYS,*   40
    "Yeh, I have t' do it from inside."
m. And all of a sudden he *GETS IN THE CAR,*
n. *SITS DOWN,*
o. and *STARTS T' TURN ON THE MOTOR.*   PEAK
    We *thought* he was taking off with us   45 EVALUATION

We really *thought*—h—he *was*—
he *was* like real—with all tattoos and
   smelled—   ORIENTATION
an' we *thought* that was it! hhh

p. But he *got out* hhh after awhile.   RESOLUTION
I really *thought* I was gonna die   50 EVALUATION
or be taken someplace far away.
It *was so crazy,*
because we *couldn't call* anybody.
It *was really funny.*

Text II.   "The Hitchhiking Adventure"

Synopsis: Two girls vacationing at a camp go off on an excursion; they miss
the bus back and are obliged to hitchhike.

Alors, C'ÉTAIT UN SOIR DE CONGÉ.   1 ORIENTATION
Deux cheftaines ÉTAIENT DE CONGÉ,
alors on *avait décidé* d'aller aux Sables-
   d'Olonne
et alors on *était parti* en car.
Et même déjà dans le car on *s'était amusé*   5
parce qu'on PRÉPARAIT une . . .
on PRÉPARAIT UNE ESPÈCE DE VEILLÉE,
la fête du directeur ÉTAIT le lendemain, je
   CROIS.
On *avait fait une chanson* avec des paroles
   adaptées,
on *s'était bien amusé.*   10
Alors donc on *était allé passer la journée là-*
   bas,
puis le soir on *avait* . . . on *avait manqué le*
   car, oui.
Le car DEVAIT PARTIR vers cinq heures,
on *s'était pas arrangé* pour y être à temps,
on *avait manqué le car.*   15

a. Alors on SE DIT: COMPLICATION
    "Il faut absolument rentrer ce soir à la
    colonie."

Evidemment on aurait *pu* . . .   ORIENTATION
on aurait *pu rester à la colonie de garçons*
qui *ÉTAIT* aux Sables-d'Olonne,   20
mais enfin il *FALLAIT RENTRER* à la colonie,
    quoi.

b. Alors on *a décidé de faire du stop.*

c. On *PART* sur la route qui . . .
    qui *ALLAIT VERS LA FAUTE,* quoi,   ORIENTATION

d. et puis on *ESSAIE D'ARRÊTER DES VOITURES.*   25
    Mais C'EST PAS ÇA: EVALUATION
    Tantôt elles *ÉTAIENT PLEINES,*   ORIENTATION
    tantôt *C'ÉTAIENT RIEN QUE DES MESSIEURS,*
    alors on *N'OSAIT PAS* trop.   (restricted
    Ou bien alors . . . ou bien C'ÉTAIT alors . . .   30   clauses)
    ils *S'ARRÊTAIENT* tout de suite,
    mais ils *N'ALLAIENT PAS À LA FAUTE.*

e. On *a fait un grand bout à pied,*
    on *N'ARRIVAIT PAS À TROUVER QUELQU'UN.*
    Et puis on *ÉTAIT EN TRAIN DE SE DEMANDER*   35   ORIENTATION
        si on continuerait ou non,
    parce qu'on *avait déjà fait un bon bout.*

f. "Mais si on trouve rien,
    il vaut autant rester aux Sables-d'Olonne."

g. Enfin, on *s'est obstiné* quand même.   40   (summative
                                                                 result clause)

    Et puis on *avait arrêté une petite*   ORIENTATION
    fourgonnette.

h. Elle *S'ARRÊTE,*

i. Un monsieur *DESCEND* et nous *DIT:*
    "Bien! montez derrière."
    Y AVAIT sa femme et puis un tout petit bébé.   45   ORIENTATION

j. Alors il nous *a fait monter* derrière;

k. il nous *a emmenées* jusqu'à . . .
    C'ÉTAIT à peine la moitié du chemin.

l. Mais on *s'est dit:*
    "C'est que . . . c'est pas tout!   50   PEAK₁
    Mais il faut trouver quelque chose pour
    continuer,"
    parce que *C'ÉTAIT EN PLEINE NATURE.*   EVALUATIVE
    Y AVAIT ABSOLUMENT RIEN.   ORIENTATION
    Alors à la (?),

m. on *SE MET À NOUVEAU AU CROISEMENT DES*   55
   CHEMINS,
   parce que là *Y AVAIT* deux . . .   ORIENTATION
   deux routes possibles,
   une qui *ALLAIT SUR LA FAUTE*
   et puis une qui *ALLAIT* . . .   60
   JE NE SAIS PLUS, SUR UNE AUTRE DIRECTION.
n. Alors on *s'est mis* sur la route de la Faute,
   et puis on *ATTENDAIT.*   (restr. clause)
   Puis C'E S T que là, alors,   ORIENTATION
   C'ÉTAIT un petit chemin,
   C'ÉTAIT vraiment un petit chemin.   65
   La route E S T à peine . . .
   elle E S T . . .
   mais elle E S T pas très fréquentée.
   Alors on *COMMENÇAIT A DÉSESPÉRER,*   (restr. clause)
o. on *ARRÊTE.* . . , on *a arrêté plusieurs voitures*   70   (mass verbs)
   qui *S'ARRÊTAIENT* toutes . . .   ORIENTATION
   presque toutes tout de suite,   (restricted
   ou qui *TOURNAIENT,* ou alors . . .   clauses)
p. Enfin y E N A une qui *S'ARRÊTE.*
   Elle *ÉTAIT PLEINE,* mais pleine.   75   ORIENTATION
q. Et puis on . . . Elle *S'ARRÊTE.*
r. Puis ils nous *ont fait monter* derrière.
   On *AVAIT JUSTE UNE TOUTE PETITE PLACE,*   ORIENTATION
   et on *ÉTAIT* deux, oui.
   Les deux dames *AVAIENT* déjà trois ou quatre   80
   gosses.
   Y AVAIT . . .
   ils *ÉTAIENT ÉTENDUS* dans des espèces de lits.
   C'ÉTAIT une fourgonnette aussi.
   Et puis . . . *Y AVAIT* trois dames,
   et puis un . . . un jeune homme;   85
   et puis devant *Y AVAIT* deux messieurs:
   C'ÉTAIENT les maris des dames, je PENSE.
s. Alors on *s'est mis dans un coin*
   pour ne pas tenir trop de place,   ORIENTATION
   parce qu'elles nous *FAISAIENT UN PEU DES*   90
   SALES YEUX!
   Et puis au bout d'un moment alors . . .

et elles *AVAIENT PAS L'AIR CONTENTES* du
   tout . . .

t. on *a commencé à lier conversation un peu,*
   parce que *C'ÉTAIT PAS DRÔLE*   ORIENTATION
   de se regarder comme ça.

u. Alors on leur *a parlé un peu.*

v. Alors *IL Y EN A* une qui me *DIT:*
   "Je ne vois vraiment pas pourquoi   PEAK₂
   mon mari s'est arrêté.
   Eh bien oui. D'habitude, vous savez . . .   100
   Vous avez eu beaucoup de chance qu'il
   vous prenne."
   C'ÉTAIT UNE CHANCE parce
      qu'autrement! . . .   EVALUATION
   Et ils *HABITAIENT* juste à côté de la colonie,   ORIENTATION
   ils *ÉTAIENT EN VACANCES* à la Faute.

w. Alors on *est arrivé* en même temps que le car,   105   RESOLUTION
   C'E S T bien simple,
   puisque *Y AVAIT* plusieurs équipes   ORIENTATION
   qui *étaient venues* nous attendre au car,

x. on *les a retrouvées* là-bas   RESOLUTION
   en même temps que le car.   110   (repeated)
   C'ÉTAIT UNE CHANCE parce que vraiment,   EVALUATION
   Y AVAIT PAS beaucoup d'autos qui *PASSAIENT*   ORIENTATION
      pour aller à la Faute.
   Y AVAIT bien dans l'autre direction
   parce qu' *I L Y A* des villes plus importantes   115
   dans l'autre côté.
   Tandis que vers la Faute, *Y AVAIT* pas grand-
      chose.

Text II.   "The Hitchhiking Adventure"
(translation)

So, *IT WAS A FREE NIGHT.*   1   ORIENTATION
Two counselors *WERE OFF,*
so we **had decided** to go to Sables d'Olonne,
and so we **had taken off** on the bus.
And even on the bus we **had had a good time**   5

because we *WERE PLANNING* a . . .
we *WERE PLANNING A KIND OF GET-*
  TOGETHER,
the camp director's party *WAS* the next day, I
  THINK.
We **had made up a song** and changed the
  words,
we **had really had a good time.**   10
So we **had gone to spend the day** there,
then in the evening we **had** . . . we **had**
  missed the bus.
The bus *WAS SUPPOSED TO LEAVE* around five
  o'clock,
we **hadn't made arrangements** to get there
  on time,
[and] we **had missed the bus.**   15

a. So we *SAY TO EACH OTHER:*   COMPLICATION
  "We absolutely have to get back to camp
    tonight."
  Obviously, we could have . . .   ORIENTATION
  we could have *stayed at the boys' camp*
  that *WAS* at Sables d'Olonne   20
  but we really *HAD TO GET BACK* to [our]
    camp, you know.
b. So we *decided to hitchhike.*
c. We *GET OUT* on the road that . . .
  that *WENT TO LA FAUTE,* you know,   ORIENTATION
d. and then we *TRY TO STOP SOME CARS.*   25
  But THAT'S NOT THE THING: EVALUATION
  Either they *WERE FULL,*   ORIENTATION
  or else there *WERE ONLY MEN,*
  so we *WEREN'T TRYING* all that hard.   (restricted
  Or else . . . uh . . . or else . . . they   30   clauses)
    WOULD . . .
  they *WOULD STOP* right away,
  but they *WEREN'T GOING TO LA FAUTE.*
e. [So] we *walked a good bit,*
  we *WEREN'T HAVING MUCH LUCK FINDING*
    SOMEONE.
  And so we *WERE BEGINNING TO WONDER*   35   ORIENTATION
  whether we should go on or not,

'cause we *had already walked quite a bit.*

f. "But if we don't find anything,
we might as well stay at Sables d'Olonne."

g. Anyway, we *kept on going.*   40   (summative
                                                           result clause)

And then, we *had stopped this little van.*   ORIENTATION

h. It *STOPS,*

i. This man *GETS OUT* and *SAYS* to us:
"Alright, get in the back."
THERE WAS his wife and a little tiny baby.   45   ORIENTATION

j. So he *had us get in* the back seat;

k. he *took* us as far as . . .
It *WAS* barely half way.

l. But we *said to each other:*
"But . . . but, we're not there yet!   50   PEAK₁
We've got to find something for the rest of
the way,"
'cause it *WAS OUT IN THE MIDDLE OF*
NOWHERE.   EVALUATIVE
THERE WAS ABSOLUTELY NOTHING THERE.   ORIENTATION
So then at (?)

m. we *GO STAND AT THE CROSSROAD* again   55
'cause there, *THERE WERE* two . . .   ORIENTATION
two possible roads,
one that *WENT TO LA FAUTE*
and one that *WENT TO . . .*
I DON'T KNOW, *SOMEWHERE ELSE.*   60

n. So we *started off* on the road to La Faute,
and we *WERE WAITING.*   (restr. clause)
So, I T ' s, you know, uh,   ORIENTATION
IT *WAS* a pretty small road,
[I mean,] IT *WAS* really a small road.   65
The road I s hardly . . .
it's . . .
but hardly anybody U S E S it.
So we *WERE STARTING TO GIVE UP,*   (restr. clause)

o. we *STOP.* . . , we *stopped a few cars*   70   (mass verbs)
which *WOULD* all *STOP* . . .   ORIENTATION
almost all of them right away,   (restricted
or *WOULD TURN,* or else . . .   clauses)

p. Finally, T H E R E ' s this one that *STOPS.*

It *WAS FULL*, [I mean] really full.   75   ORIENTATION
q. And so we . . . it *STOPS*.
r. So they *had* us *get in* in back.
There *WAS HARDLY ANY ROOM*,   ORIENTATION
and there *WERE* two of us, yeah.
The two women *HAD* three or four kids.   80
THERE WAS . . .
they *WERE STRETCHED OUT* on these . . .
like . . . beds.
It *WAS* a van too.
And then . . . *THERE WERE* these three women,
and then a . . . a young guy;   85
and then in front *THERE WERE* two men:
they *WERE* the husbands of the women, I
THINK.
s. So we *squeezed into a corner*
so as not to take up too much room,   ORIENTATION
'cause the women *WERE* already *GIVING US*   90
KINDA DIRTY LOOKS!
And so after that . . .
and they *DIDN'T LOOK VERY HAPPY* [about it]
at all . . .
t. we *started to make some conversation*,
'cause it *WASN'T* very much *FUN* to sit there   ORIENTATION
just looking at each other like that.   95
u. So we *talked to them a little*.
v. Then *THERE'S* this one *SAYS* to me:
"I really don't see why   PEAK₂
my husband stopped [for you].
I mean, really. Usually, you know . . .   100
You were really pretty lucky that he picked
you up."
IT WAS really *LUCK* because otherwise . . .   EVALUATION
And they *LIVED* right near the camp,   ORIENTATION
they *WERE ON VACATION* at La Faute.
w. So we *got there* the same time as the bus, 105   RESOLUTION
I T ' s just like that,
'cause *THERE WERE* several groups   ORIENTATION
that *had come* to meet us at the bus,

x. we *met up with them* there   RESOLUTION
    at the same time as the bus.   110   (repeated)
IT *WAS* really *LUCK*, 'cause   EVALUATION
THERE WEREN'T very many cars {that *WERE*}   ORIENTATION
    GOING BY
    headed toward La Faute.
THERE WERE lots of them (going) the other
    way
'cause T H E R E A R E bigger towns   115
    on the other side.
Whereas over by La Faute, THERE WASN'T
    really very much.

Text III. *Aucassin et Nicolette,* prose laisse #10

Synopsis: While supposedly engaged in combat on his father's behalf against Count Bougar of Valence, young Aucassin rides distractedly among his enemies thinking only of his beloved Nicolette; suddenly he springs into action, wreaks havoc among Bougar's knights, defeats the Count himself, and delivers him to his father for surrender.

X. Or DIENT et CONTENT

Aucassins *fu armés* sor son ceval,   1   ORIENTATION
si con vos AVÉS *oï* et *entendu.*
Dix! con li *sist* li escus au col
    et li hiaumes u cief et li renge
    de s'espee sor le senestre hance!   5
Et li vallés *fu grans et fors*   (free clause)
    et biax et gens et bien fornis,
et li cevaus sor quoi il *sist*   (free clause)
    rades et corans,
et li vallés l'*ot* bien *adrecié*   10
    par mi la porte
Or NE QUIDIÉS vous   EXTERNAL
qu'il *pensast [IMP SUBJ]* n'a bués   EVALUATION
    n'a vaces n'a civres prendre,

ne qu'il *ferist [IMP SUBJ] cevalier.*   15
   ne autres lui.
Nenil nient!
onques *ne l'en sovint;*
ains *pensa tant a Nicolette*
   sa douce amie   20
qu'il *oublia ses resnes*
et quanques il *dut faire;*
et li cevax qui *ot senti les esperons*   COMPLICATION
a. *l'en porta par mi le presse,*
b. se *SE LANCE TRES ENTRE MI SES ANEMIS;*   25
c. et il *GETENT LES MAINS* de toutes pars,
d. si le *PRENDENT,*
e. si le *DESSAISISENT DE L'ESCU ET DE LE*
   LANCE,
f. si l'en *MANNENT* tot estrousement pris,
et *ALOIENT* ja *PORPARLANT*   30 (restr. clause)
   de quel mort il feroient morir.
g. Et quant Aucassins *l'entendi:*
h. "Ha! Dix," *FAIT* il, "douce creature!
   sont çou mi anemi mortel . . . ?"
Li vallés *fu grans et fors,*   35 ORIENTATION
et li cevax so quoi il *sist fu remuans;*   (free clauses)
i. et il *mist le main a l'espee,*
j. si *COMENCE A FERIR*   (mass verbs)
   a destre et a senestre
k. et *CAUPE HIAUMES ET NASEUS*   40 (coordinated
   ET PUINS ET BRAS   clauses)
l. et *FAIT UN CAPLE* entor lui,   (project verb)
   autresi con li senglers   EVALUATION
   quant li cien *l'A S A L E N T* en le forest,
m. et qu'il lor *ABAT DIS CEVALIERS*   45 (coord. clauses)
n. et *NAVRE SET*   (mass verbs)
o. et qu'il *SE JETE*
   tot estroseement *DE LE PRESE*
p. et qu'il *S'EN REVIENT LES GALOPIAX ARIERE,*
   s'espee en sa main.   50
Li quens Bougars de Valence *oï dire*   ORIENTATION
   c'on penderoit Aucassin son anemi,

si *VENOIT* cele part;

q. et Aucassins *ne le mescoisi mie:*

r. il *tint l'espee en la main,*   55

s. se le *FIERT* par mi le hiaume   ⎫

t. si qu'i li *ENBARE EL CIEF.*   ⎬   PEAK
                                                          ⎭
   Il *fu si estonés*

u. qu'il *caï a terre;*

v. et Aucassins *TENT LE MAIN,*   60

w. si le *PRENT*

x. et l'en *MAINNE PRIS*
      par le nasel del hiame

y. et le *RENT A SON PERE.*

z. "Pere," *FAIT* Aucassins,   65
   "ves ci vostre anemi
   qui tant vous a gerroié
   et mal fait:
   vint ans ja dure ceste guerre;
   onques ne pot iestre acievee par home."   70
   [. . .]

[In the remainder of the *laisse* the action is presented largely through direct
discourse, introduced consistently by *FAIT* (he goes)]

aa. "Enondu!" *FAIT* il
      "je vous afie quanque il vous plaist."

bb. Il li *AFIE;*   RESOLUTION

cc. et Aucassins le *FAIT MONTER* sor un ceval,

dd. et il *MONTE* sor un autre,   75

ee. si le *conduist*

ff. tant qu'il *fu* a sauveté.

Text III.   *Aucassin and Nicolette* (translation)

X. Now they TELL and RECOUNT

Aucassin *was* on his horse, fully *armed,*   1 ORIENTATION
as you HAVE now *heard.*
God! How [*well*] his shield *sat* on his neck
   and his helmet on his head

and his sword-belt on his left hip.   5
And the lad *was big and strong,*   (free clause)
and handsome and comely, with fine features,
and the horse he *was sitting on*   (free clause)
[*was*] swift and spirited.
And the boy *had led him right up*   10
through the gate.
Now DON'T GO IMAGINING   EXTERNAL
he *was thinking [IMP SUBJ] about cattle*   EVALUATION
or cows, or about catching goats,
nor that he *was attacking [IMP SUBJ]* any   15
knights
or others [*were attacking*] him.
Perish the thought!
It never occurred to him.
Rather he *was thinking so much*
about his sweet friend, *Nicolette,*   20
that he *forgot all about the reins*
and everything he *had to do.*
And the horse, [once he] *had felt the spurs,*   COMPLICATION
a. *carried him into the fray.*
b. # He THROWS HIMSELF AMIDST HIS ENEMIES, 25
c. and they GRAB AT HIM from all sides,
d. # TAKE HOLD OF HIM,
e. # DIVEST HIM OF HIS SHIELD AND HIS
      LANCE,
f. # LEAD HIM AWAY, securely captured.
   And ALONG THEY WENT TALKING of   30   (restr. clause)
   how they would have him killed.
g. And when Aucassin *heard* this:
h. "Oh God!," he GOES, "my sweet one,
      are these my mortal enemies . . . ?"
   The lad *was big and strong,*   35   ORIENTATION
   and the horse he *sat on was spirited;*   (free clauses)
i. And he *placed his hand on his sword,*
j. # STARTS TO ATTACK   (mass verbs)
      left and right,
k. and SLASHES HELMETS AND NOSE GUARDS,   40   (coordinated
      AND WRISTS AND ARMS,   clauses)

l. and *WREAKS SLAUGHTER* all around him,   (project verb)

   just like a wild boar   EVALUATION

   when hounds ATTACK it in the forest.

m. And {that} he *SLAYS TEN OF THEIR KNIGHTS,*   45   (coord. clauses)

n. and *WOUNDS SEVEN,*   (mass verbs)

o. and {that} he *THROWS HIMSELF*

     HEADLONG INTO THE FRAY

p. and {that} he *COMES GALLOPING BACK,*

     sword in hand.   50

   Count Bougar of Valence *heard tell*   ORIENTATION

   that they would hang his enemy Aucassin

   if he *CAME* that way.

q. And Aucassin *did not fail to spot him:*

r. He *took his sword in hand,*   55

s. # *STRIKES* through the helmet,   ⎫

t. such that he *BASHES HIM IN THE HEAD.*   ⎬ PEAK

   He [Bougar] *was so stunned*   ⎭

u. that he *fell to the ground.*

v. And Aucassin *OFFERS [HIM] HIS HAND,*   60

w. # *TAKES HIM,*

x. and *LEADS HIM OFF*

     by the nose-piece of his helmet,

y. and *SURRENDERS HIM TO HIS [A'S] FATHER.*

z. "Father," *GOES* Aucassin,   65

   "here is your enemy

   who has waged war against you for so long

   and done so much evil:

   this war has been going on for twenty years;

   never could it be ended by any man."   70

   [. . .]

[In the remainder of the *laisse* the action is presented largely through direct speech, introduced consistently by *FAIT* (he goes)]

aa. "In God's name," he *GOES,*

     "I promise you anything you like."

bb. He *GIVES HIM HIS WORD.*   RESOLUTION

cc. and Aucassin *PUTS HIM ON A HORSE,*

dd. and *MOUNTS* another himself,   75

ee. # *led him away*

ff. until he *reached* safety.

Text IV.   Geoffroy de Villehardouin, *La Conquête de Constantinople*, §§155–161

(Note: Starred PRS [*] are NPS that appear as PSS in one or more of the later MSS.)

Synopsis: As part of the military effort of the Fourth Crusade, the Latin army engages in battle with the Christian Greeks at Constantinople; the part of this battle transcribed below, in which Villehardouin was a participant, involves the capture of the tower of Galatha.

(155)	Li termes *vint* si con *devisez fu;*		I ORIENTATION
	et li chevalier *furent* es uissiers tuit,		
	avec lor destriers,		
	et *furent* tuit *armé,*		
	les helmes *laciez* et li cheval *covert*		
	et y *ensellé;*		
	et les autres genz qui N'AVOIENT MIE	5	
	SI GRANT MESTIER en bataille		
	furent es granz nés tuit;		
	et les galees *furent armees* et *atornees*		
	totes.		
(156)	Et li matins *fu biels,* aprés le solei un		
	poi levant.		
	Et l'emperieres Alexis les ATTENDOIT		
	a granz batailles		
	et a granz corroiz de l'autre part.	10	
a.	Et on SONE* les bozines,		COMPLICATION
	et chascune galie *fu* a un uissier *liee*		(restr. clause)
	por passer oltre plus delivreement.		
	Il NE DEMANDENT* MIE chascuns qui		
	DOIT ALER devant;		EVALUATION
b.	mais qui ançois PUET ançois ARIVE*	15	
c.	Et li chevalier *issirent* des uissiers,		
d.	et SAILLENT* EN LA MER trosque a la		PEAK₁
	çainture,		
	tuit armé, les hielmes laciez et les		ORIENTATION
	glaives es mains;		
	et li bon archier, et li bon serjant,		

et li bon arbalestrier,

chascune conpagnie ou endroit ele 20
arriva.

(157) Et li Greu *firent mult grant semblant*   (summative result)
del retenir.   project verb

Et quant ce *vint* as lances baissier,

e. et li Greu lor TORNENT LE DOS,

f. si S'EN VONT* FUIANT

g. et lor LAISSENT* LE RIVAGE   25

Et SACHIEZ que onques plus   EXTERNAL
orgueilleusement

nuls pors *ne fu pris.*   EVALUATION

h. Adonc CONMENCENT* li marinier A
OUVRIR LES PORTES des uissiers
et A GITER LES PONS FORS;

i. et on COMENCE* LES CHEVAX A
TRAIRE;   30

j. et li chevalier CONMENCENT A
MONTER SOR LOR CHEVAUS,

k. et les batailles SE CONMENCENT A
RENGIER

si com il DEVOIENT.   EVALUATION

(158) l. Li cuens Baudoins de Flandres et de
Hennaut CHEVAUCHE*,

qui *L'AVAN GARDE FAISOIT,*   35   ORIENTATION

et les autres batailles aprés chascune

si cum eles CHEVAUCHIER DEVOIENT.   EVALUATION

m. Et *alerent* trosque la ou l'emperere
Alexis *avoit esté logiez.*

Et il *s'en fu tornez* vers   ORIENTATION
Costantinople,

et *laissa tenduz trés et paveillons.*   40

Et la *gaignerent assez* nostre gent.   (summative result)
project verb

(159) De nostres barons *fu* tels *li conseils*
que il *se hebergeroient* sor le port devant la tor de Galathas,

ou la caiene FERMOIT qui MOVOIT de
Costantinoble;   ORIENTATION

Et SACHIEZ de voir que par cele   45

chaiene *CONVENOIT ENTRER*
qui al port de Costantinople *VOLOIT
ENTRER;*
et bien *virent* nostre baron,
se il *NE PRENOIENT CELE TOR* et *ROM-
POIENT CELE CHAIENE,*
que il *ESTOIENT MORT ET
MALBAILLI.*

n. Eisi *se herbergierent la nuit*   50
   devant la tor et en la juerie,   ORIENTATION
   que l'en A P E L L E l'Estanor,
   ou *IL AVOIT* mult bone ville et mult
   riche.

(160) o. Bien *se fissent* la nuit *eschaugaitier;*
   et l'endemain, quant *fu hore de tierce,*   55   ORIENTATION
  p. si *firent une assaillie* cil de la tor de
   Galathas
   et cil qui de Costantinople lor *VE-
   NOIENT AÏDIER* en barges;   (restr. clause)
  q. Et nostre gent *CORENT* * *AS ARMES.*   PEAK$_2$
  r. La *assembla* Jaches d'Avesnes,
   et la soe maisnie, *a pié;*   60
   et SACHIEZ que il *fu mult chargiez*   EVALUATIVE
   et *fu feruz par mi le vis* d'un glaive   ORIENTATION
   et *en aventure de mort.*
   Et un sien chevaliers *fu montez* a
   cheval,   ORIENTATION
   qui *AVOIT NOM* Nicholes de Janlain,   65
  s. et *secorut mult bien son seignor,*
   et le *fist mult bien,*   EVALUATION
   si que il en *ot grant pris.*   (summative result)

(161) t. Et li criz *fu levez* en l'ost;
  u. et nostre gent *VIENENT* * de totes   70   PEAK$_3$
   pars,
  v. et les *mistrent enz* mult laidement,   RESOLUTION
   si que assez *en i ot* de mors et de pris.   (summative result)
   Si que de tels *i ot* qui *ne guenchirent
   mie a la tor,*
  w. ainz *alerent as barges* dunt il *erent
   venu;*

et la *en rot assez de noiez,*   75   (summative
et alquant en *eschaperent.*   result clauses)
Et cels qui *guenchirent a la tor,*
x. cil de l'ost les *tindrent si prés*
   que il *ne porent la porte fermer.*
Enqui *refu granz* li estors a la porte,   80
y. et la lor *tolirent par force,*   ⎫
z. *et les pristrent laienz:*   ⎬   RESOLUTION
   la *en i ot* assez de morz et de pris.   (summative result)

(162)   Einsi *fu* li chastiaus de Galathas *pris*   ABSTRACT
       et li porz *gaigniez* de Costantinoble   85
       par force [. . .]

Text IV. Geoffroy de Villehardouin, *The Conquest of Constantinople* (translation)

(155)   The time [for departure] *arrived* as   ORIENTATION
       had been determined,   I
       and the knights *were* [assembled] in
          the transport ships with their
          steeds
       and *were* all *armed,*
          their helmets *fastened* and their
          horses *saddled* and *equipped;*
       and the others, who HAD LESS CRU-
          CIAL FUNCTIONS in battle,   5
       were all in the large vessels.
       and the galleys *were* fully *armed* and
          decked out.

(156)   And the morning *was beautiful,* just
       after sunrise.
       And the Emperor Alexis WAS AWAIT-
          ING them on the other side
          with many battalions and much   10
          equipment.

a. And the trumpets SOUND*   COMPLICATION
   and each galley *was tied* to a transport   (rest. clause)
       ship in order to
       facilitate the crossing.

	And *NO ONE ASKS* * who *SHOULD GO* first:		EVALUATION
b.	[but] whoever *CAN, GETS THERE* * first.	15	
c.	And the knights *disembarked* from the transport ships,		
d.	and *JUMP* * *INTO THE SEA* up to their waists		PEAK₁

and *JUMP* * *INTO THE SEA* up to their waists — PEAK₁

fully armed, helmets fastened, swords in hand; — ORIENTATION

and the good archers, and the good officers, and the good crossbowmen,

each company [disembarked]   20
where it *arrived*.

(157)   And the Greeks *put up a great show of resistance*.   (summative result) project verb

And when it *came* to lowering the lances,

e. {and} the Greeks *TURN THEIR BACKS ON THEM,*

f. # *GO* * *TAKE FLIGHT,*

g. and *LEAVE* * *THE SHORE TO THEM.*   25

And KNOW that *never was* a harbor *conquered* with greater pride.   EXTERNAL EVALUATION

h. Then the sailors *BEGIN* * *TO OPEN THE DOORS* of the transport ships and *TO THROW DOWN THE RAMPS.*

i. and they *BEGIN* * *TO BRING OUT THE*   30 *HORSES;*

j. and the knights *BEGIN TO MOUNT THEIR HORSES,*

k. and the battalions *BEGIN TO FORM* as they *WERE INSTRUCTED.*   EVALUATION

(158)   l. Count Baldwin of Flanders and Hainaut *RIDES FORTH* *,

[the one] who *WAS LEADING THE*   35 ORIENTATION *VANGUARD,*

and the other battalions each in turn as they *WERE INSTRUCTED TO RIDE.*   EVALUATION

m. And they *proceeded* to where the Emperor Alexis *had been camped,*
   And he *had gone back* to   ORIENTATION
   Constantinople,
   and *left his tents and pavilions in place.*   40
   And there our men *collected a great*   (summative result)
   deal of booty.*   project verb

(159)   The *decision* of our nobles *was*
        that they would set up camp at the
        harbor in front of the tower of
        Galatha,
        where the channel ENDED, which BE-   ORIENTATION
        GAN at Constantinople;
        And KNOW in truth that whoever   45
        WISHED TO ENTER the harbor of
        Constantinople
        HAD TO DO SO via this channel;
        And our nobles *saw* clearly
        that if they DID NOT TAKE THE
        TOWER and BLOCK THE CHANNEL,
        then they WERE AS GOOD AS DEAD.

n. Thus they *set up camp for the night*   50
   in front of the tower and in the Jew-   ORIENTATION
   ish quarter,
   which IS CALLED Estanor,
   where THERE WAS an important and
   wealthy town.

(160) o. They *kept careful watch* that night;
        and the next morning, when *the hour* 55 ORIENTATION
        of tierce was at hand,

p. those from Galatha tower *made an*
   attack
   and those from Constantinople CAME   (restr. clause)
   TO HELP THEM in barges,

q. And our men RUN * TO TAKE ARMS.   PEAK₂

r. There Jacques d'Avesnes
   and his men *fought on foot;*   60
   And KNOW that he *was sorely pressed*   EVALUATIVE
   and *was struck in the face* with a lance   ORIENTATION
   and *in danger of dying.*

And one of his knights *was mounted*   ORIENTATION
on his horse,

[one] who WAS NAMED Nicolas de   65
Jainlain,

s. and *came swiftly to the aid of his lord,*

and he *performed so well*   EVALUATION

that he *received great praise* for his   (summative result)
service.

(161)   t. And the cry *went up* among the
troops;

u. and our men COME * RUNNING from   70   PEAK₃
all sides,

v. and they *did them in* so thoroughly   RESOLUTION

that *there were* a great number cap-   (summative result)
tured and killed.

And *there were* those who *did not go
for the tower,*

w. but rather *went for the barges* whence
they *had come,*

and *there were a considerable number*   75   (summative
drowned,   result clauses)

and some *escaped.*

And those who *went for the tower,*

x. our men *held them so tenaciously*

that they *could not close the gate.*

There at the gate the battle still *raged,*   80

y. and they *took it [the gate] from them
by force,*   RESOLUTION

z. and *locked them up inside;*

there were many prisoners and   (summative result)
casualties.

(162)   Thus *was* the tower of Galatha *taken*   ABSTRACT
and the harbor of Constantinople
conquered by force [. . .]   85

Text V.   "Theft Narrative" from the memoirs of Lorenzo Da Ponte

Synopsis: Da Ponte recounts the tale of a journey he was obliged to make from Prague to Vienna. En route his money disappears; he returns to the inn where he spent the night, and the money is finally located hidden in a servant girl's dress.

> *Fui obbligato a partire* per Praga,   I ORIENTATION
> dove si doveva rappresentare per la prima
>   volta il Don Giovanni di Mozart
> per l'arrivo della principessa di Toscana in
>   quella città.
> *Mi fermai otto giorni* per dirigere gli attori
> che dovevano rappresentarlo;   5
> ma, prima che *andasse [IMP SUBJ] in scena,*
> *fui obbligato di tornar* a Vienna
> per una lettera di fuoco che *ricevei* dal Salieri   (EVALUATION)
> in cui, fosse vero o no, M'INFORMAVA
> che l'Assur doveva rappresentarsi imme-   10
>   diatamente per le nozze di Francesco
> e che l'imperatore gli *aveva ordinato di*
>   *richiamarmi.*
> a. *Tornai* dunque a Vienna, viaggiando di e   COMPLICATION
>   notte;
>   ma a mezza strada, sembrandomi d'essere
>   stanco,
> b. *domandai d'andar a letto* per un paio di ore.
> c. *Mi coricai,*   15
>   e quando i cavalli ERANO PRONTI,
> d. *si venne* a chiamarmi.
> e. *BALZO DAL LETTO* mezzo addormentato,
> f. *DISCENDO LE SCALE,*
> g. *ENTRO NELLA VETTURA*   20
> h. e *PARTO.*
> i. A qualche distanza *giungemmo a una barriera,*
> j. ove mi *DOMANDANO UNA PICCOLA SOMMA* pel
>   mio passaggio.
> k. *METTO LA MANO IN TASCA*
>   e qual *fu la mia sorpresa*   25 EVALUATION
> l. quando *non trovai un soldo* nel borsellino   PEAK₁
>   dov'io *posi* la mattina *cinquanta zecchini*   ORIENTATION
>   che l'impresario di Praga m'*aveva pagato* per
>   quell'opera:
>   *pensai* d'averli perduti nel letto
>   dove m'*ero coricato* vestito.   30

m. *RITORNO* subito a quell'osteria,

n. non *V'ERA* un soldo.

o. L'oste e la moglie, persone veramente di garbo,
   CHIAMANO TUTTI I SERVI,

p. *CERCANO,*   (four

q. *ESAMINANO,*   35 coordinated

r. *MINACCIANO;*   clauses)

s. ma *NESSUNO CONFESSA* di aver guardato in
   quel letto.

   Una fanciulletta di cinque anni al più,   ORIENTATION
   ch'*aveva veduto una delle serve rifar il letto*
   per un altro forestiero: 40

t. Mamma, mamma!—*esclamò*—la Caterina ha   PEAK$_2$
   rifatto il letto quando il signore partì.

u. L'ostessa *fece spogliare la Caterina*

v. e le *trovò* nel seno *i cinquanta zecchini.*   RESOLUTION
   Perdei due ore di tempo in questa faccenda;   45 EVALUATION
   ma, lieto d'aver trovato quel danaro,

w. *pregai* quella buona gente *di perdonare a quella
   lor serva*
   e, senza fermarmi che a cambiar cavalli,

x. *arrivai* il giorno dopo a Vienna.

Text V.   "Theft Narrative" from the memoirs of Lorenzo Da Ponte (translation)

I was obliged to leave for Prague,   1 ORIENTATION
where Mozart's "Don Giovanni" <u>was to be
   performed</u> for the first time
for the arrival in that city of the Princess of
   Tuscany.
I stayed there a week to direct the actors
who <u>were to perform it;</u>   5
but, before it *could be [IMP SUBJ] staged,*
I was obliged to return to Vienna
because of an urgent letter I *received* from   EVALUATION
   Salieri,
in which I WAS INFORMED, whether it was
   true or not,

that "Assur" was to be performed immedi-   10
ately for the marriage of Francis,
and that the Emperor *had ordered him to re-*
call me.

a. So I *returned* to Vienna, traveling day and   COMPLICATION
night;
but halfway there, finding myself tired,
b. *I asked if I might go to sleep* for a few hours.
c. *I lay down,*   15
and when the horses *WERE READY,*
d. *they came* to call me.
e. *I LEAP OUT OF BED* half asleep,
f. *GO DOWN THE STAIRS,*
g. *GET IN THE COACH,*   20
h. and *LEAVE.*
i. And a ways from there *we reached a roadblock,*
j. where they *ASK ME FOR A SMALL SUM* for my
passage.
k. *I REACH MY HAND IN MY POCKET*
and what *was my surprise*   25   EVALUATION
l. when *I didn't find a cent* in the bag   PEAK₁
where that morning *I [had] put fifty zecchini*   ORIENTATION
that the Prague empresario *had paid* me for
that opera:
I thought I had lost them in the bed
where I *had lain down* in my clothes.   30
m. I quickly *RETURN* to that inn,
n. *THERE WASN'T* a cent.
o. The innkeeper and his wife, very upstanding
people, *SUMMON ALL THE SERVANTS,*
p. *THEY SEARCH,*   (four
q. *INSPECT,*   35   coordinated
r. *THREATEN;*   clauses)
s. but *NO ONE CONFESSES* to having looked in
that bed.
A little girl of five (years) at most,   ORIENTATION
who *had seen one of the servants remake the*
bed for another guest: 40
t. *exclaimed:* "Mama, mama, Caterina remade the   PEAK₂
bed when the gentleman left."
u. The innkeeper's wife *ordered Caterina to undress*

v. and *found* in her bosom *the fifty zecchini.*   RESOLUTION
    I lost two hours' time in that business;   45 EVALUATION
    but, happy to have found the money,

w. *I asked* the good people *to pardon their servant,*
    and, without stopping except to change
        horses,

x. *arrived* in Vienna the next day.

Text VI.   *Razo* of the troubadour Peire Vidal

(Note: This legend appears in two versions, one in manuscript *H,* the
other common to manuscripts *E, N₂, P,* and *Re.* The text reproduced here
is that of *E.* Where one of the other manuscripts, notably *N₂,* shows a PR
for a PS (PRET) in *E,* this PS is marked with a plus sign [+]; for the reverse
situation where *E* shows a PR the PR verb is starred [*].)

Synopsis: The troubadour Peire Vidal is a reputed lady's man; for some
time he has been trying to make headway with Lady Adelaide, the wife of
his patron, Sir Barral. While Barral is away on a journey, Peire sneaks into
Adelaide's bedroom and steals a kiss. When Adelaide discovers that it is
not her husband but the wily Peire Vidal, she makes a scene that results in
Peire's exile overseas. He remains there for a long time, composing many
songs. Ultimately he returns to Provence and is pardoned.

Peire Vidal   I ABSTRACT
—si com ieu vos AI *dig*—
S'ENTENDIA EN TOTAS LAS BONAS DONAS
e *CREZIA* que totas li volguesson be per amor.
E si S'ENTENDIA EN ma dona n'Alazais,   5 ORIENTATION
qu'ERA moiller d'En Barral, lo senhor di
        Marceilla,
lo quals VOLIA MEILS a Peire Vidal c'az ome
        del mon,
per lo ric trobar e per las ricas folias
        que Peire Vidal DIZIA e FAZIA;
e CLAMAVON SE abdui "Rainier."   10
E Peire Vidal si ERA PRIVATZ de cort e de

cambra d'En Barral, plus c'ome del mon.

En Barrals si *SABIA* be

que Peire Vidals *SE ENTENDIA* en la moiller,

e *TENIA LO·I A SOLATZ* e tuit aquill c'o   15
SABION.

E si *S'ALEGRAVA* de las folias qu'el *FAZIA* ni
DIZIA

e la dona ho *PRENDIA EN SOLATZ*,

si com *FAZION* totas las autras donas en que
Peire Vidal *S'ENTENDIA;*

e cascuna li *DIZIA PLAZER*

e·ill *PROMETIA* tot so que·ill *plagues* [IMP   20
SUBJ] e qu'el *DEMANDAVA;*

et el *ERA SI SAVIS*

que tot ho *CREZIA.*

E quan Peire Vidal *SE CORROSAVA AB ELA,*

En Barrals *FAZIA ADES LA PATZ*

e·ill *FAZIA PROMETRE* tot so qu'el   25
DEMANDAVA.

E quan *venc* un dia,   COMPLICATION

a. Peire Vidal si *saup*

qu'En Barrals *s'era levatz*

e que la dona *ERA TOTA SOLA* en la cambra.

b. Peire Vidal *INTRA* * *EN LA CAMBRA*   30

c. e *venc s'en* + *al leit* de ma dona N'Alazais   (coordinated

d. e *TROBA* * *LA DORMEN.*   clauses)

e. Et *AGENOILLA SE* * davan ella

f. e *BAIZA* * *LI LA BOCA.*   PEAK (CO-

g. Et ella *sentit lo baizar*   35 ordinated

h. e *crezet* qu'el *fos* [IMP SUBJ] En Barrals, sos clauses)
maritz,

i. e rizen ela *se levet.*

j. E *GARDA*   PEAK
(coordinated

k. e *vit* qu'el *ERA·l* fol de Peire Vidal;   clauses)

l. e *comenset a cridar* e *a far gran rumor.*   40

m. E *vengron* + las donzelas de lains,
quant ho *auziron,*

n. e *demandaron*†: "Quez es aiso?"

o. E Peire Vidal *s'en issit*[†] fugen.

p. E la dona *mandet*[†] *per En Barral*   45

q. e *fes li gran reclam* de Peire Vidal,
    que l'*avia baizada.*   ORIENTATION

r. E ploran l'en *prequet* qu'el en *degues* [IMP
    SUBJ] ades *penre venjansa.*

    Et En Barrals, si com valens hom et adregz,   (restricted
    si *pres lo fait a solatz*   50   clause)

s. e *comenset a rire* et *a repenre* la moiller,
    quar ela *avia faita rumor*   ORIENTATION
    d'aiso que·l fols *avia fait.*
    Mas el non la·n *poc castiar*

t. qu'ela non *mezes [IMP SUBJ] en gran rumor lo
    fait,*   55
    e sercan et enqueren lo mal de Peire Vidal;
    e gran MENASAS FAZIA de lui.   (restricted

u. Peire Vidal, per paor d'aquest fait, *montet*[†] *en*   clause)
    una nau

v. et *anet s'en*[†] *en Genoa;*

w. e *lai estet*   60
    tro que pueis *passet outra mer* ab lo rei   ORIENTATION
    Richart.
    Que·ill *fo mes en paor*
    que ma dona N'Alazais li VOLIA FAR TOLRE
    LA PERSONA.

w.' *Lai estet longua sazo*
    e lai *fes maintas bonas chansos,*   65   (restricted
    recordan del baizar qu'el *avia emblat.*   clause)
    E *dis*—en una chanso que *dis* "Ajostar e
    lasar"—
    que de leis *non avi' agut negun guizardo,*
    "Mas una petit cordo . . ."
    [song fragment]   70
    Et en autre luec el *dis:*
    [. . . song fragment]
    Et en autra chanso el *dis:*
    [. . . song fragment]

w." Ainsi *estet longua sazo outra mar,*   75
    que non AUSAVA VENIR ni TORNAR en

Proensa.

En Barrals,

que li *VOLIA AITAN DE BE*   ORIENTATION

com vos *AVES auzit*,

x. si *preguet* tan sa moiller   80

y. qu'ela li *perdonet lo furt del baizar*

z. e *lo·i autreget* en do.   RESOLUTION

aa. En Barrel si *mandet*[†] *per Peire Vidal*,   (coordinated

bb. e si·ll *fes mandar grassia e bona volontat* a sa   clauses)
    moiller.

cc. Et el *venc* ab gran alegreza a Marceilla,   85

dd. et ab gran alegreza *fo reseubutz* per En Barral
    e per ma dona N'Alazais.

z.' Et *autreget li lo baizar* en do   RESOLUTION'

    qu'el li *avia emblat*.   ORIENTATION

    Don Peire Vidal *fes aquesta chanso* que D I T Z;   CODA

    "Pos *tornatz* SUI en Proensa,"   90

    la qual vos AUZIRETZ.

Text VI.   *Razo* of the troubadour Peire Vidal (translation)

Peire Vidal   I ABSTRACT

—as I HAVE *told* you—

COURTED ALL THE NOBLE LADIES

and *BELIEVED* they were all quite taken with
    him.

And he *COURTED* Lady Adelaide,   5 ORIENTATION

who *WAS* the wife of Sir Barral, the lord of
    Marseille,

who *WAS FONDER* of Peire Vidal than of any-
    one in the world,

because of his skill as a poet and for the
    amusing things

that Peire Vidal *WOULD SAY* and *DO*;

and the two of them *CALLED* each other
    "Rainier."   10

And Peire Vidal *WAS A PRIVILEGED MEMBER*

of Sir Barral's court and of his house, more
so than anyone else.
Sir Barral KNEW very well
that Peire Vidal WAS COURTING HIS WIFE,
but TOOK IT AS A JOKE like everyone else who 15
KNEW about it.
And # he DELIGHTED IN the spirited things
that Peire Vidal WOULD SAY and DO,
and his wife ENJOYED them [also],
as DID all the other ladies whom Peire Vidal
COURTED;
and each one WOULD SAY SWEET THINGS to
him
and he WOULD PROMISE whatever they
wanted [IMP SUBJ]
and WOULD ASK FOR.   20
And he WAS SO CLEVER
that he BELIEVED it all.
And whenever Peire Vidal WOULD GET UPSET
WITH HER [Lady Adelaide],
Sir Barral WOULD MAKE PEACE straightaway
and WOULD MAKE his wife PROMISE whatever 25
Peire ASKED.

	And it *came about* one day		COMPLICATION
a.	[that] Peire Vidal *learned*		
	that Sir Barral **had gone away**		
	and that the lady WAS ALL ALONE in their chamber.		
b.	Peire Vidal GOES INTO* THE ROOM	30	
c.	and *came*† *up to* Lady Adelaide's bed		(coordinated
d.	and FINDS* HER SLEEPING.		clauses)
e.	And he KNEELS DOWN* beside her		
f.	and KISSES* HER ON THE MOUTH.		PEAK (co-
g.	And she *felt the kiss*	35	ordinated
h.	and *thought* it *was* [IMP SUBJ] Sir Barral her husband.		clauses)
i.	And smiling, she *got up*.		
j.	And LOOKS,		PEAK (co-
k.	and *saw* that it WAS the prankster Peire Vidal;		ordinated

l.   and *began to scream* and *make a ruckus.*   40 clauses)

m. And her ladies *came*[†] from inside,
     when they *heard this,*

n.   and *asked*[†]: "What is this?"

o.   And Peire Vidal *ran*[†] *fleeing out* the door.

p.   And the lady *sent for*[†] Sir Barral   45

q.   and *complained vigorously* about Peire Vidal,
     who **had kissed her.**   ORIENTATION

r.   And, in tears, she *asked* that he *should [*IMP
     SUBJ*] take vengeance* immediately.
     And Sir Barral, a savvy and kind person,   (restricted
     # *took the matter lightly*   50 clause)

s.   and *started to laugh* and *reproach* his wife,
     because she **had made such a fuss**   ORIENTATION
     about what the prankster **had done.**

t.   But he *couldn't keep her* from *making [*IMP
     SUBJ*] a fuss* about the matter,   55
     seeking out Peire Vidal and demanding
     punishment;
     And she MADE vociferous THREATS.   (restricted

u.   Peire Vidal, frightened by this business,   clause)
     boarded[†] a ship

v.   and *set off*[†] *for Genoa;*

w. and he *remained there*   60
     until he later *crossed the sea* with King   ORIENTATION
     Richard.
     For he *was frightened* lest Lady Adelaide SEEK
     TO HAVE HIM PUT TO DEATH.

w.' He *remained there for a long time*
     and there *composed many beautiful songs,*   65 (restricted
     recalling the kiss that he **had stolen.**   clause)
     And he *said*—in a song that *said* "Ajostar e
     lasar"—that he **had received from her no
     reward,** "other than a little cord . . ."
     [song fragment]   70
     and in another place he *said:*
     [. . . song fragment]
     and in yet another song he *said:*
     [. . . song fragment]

w.'' And so he *stayed overseas a long time,*   75
for he DIDN'T DARE RETURN to Provence.
Sir Barral,
who WAS SO FOND of him,   ORIENTATION
as you HAVE *heard,*

x.   # *pleaded* so with his wife   80
y.   that she *forgave the stolen kiss*
z.   and *bestowed it upon him* as a gift.   RESOLUTION
aa. Sir Barral # *sent*[†] *for Peire Vidal*   ⎫ (coordinated
bb. and # *conveyed to him the forgiveness and* ⎬ clauses)
     goodwill of his wife.   ⎭
cc. And he [Peire] *came* to Marseille with   85
     great joy,
dd. and with great joy *was received* by Sir Barral
     and Lady Adelaide.

z.' And she *granted him* as a gift *the kiss*   RESOLUTION'
     that he *had stolen.*   ORIENTATION
     Sir Peire Vidal *composed this song,* which CODA
     G O E S :
     "I HAVE *come back* to Provence,"   90
     that you WILL HEAR.

Text VII.   "En los campos de Alventosa . . ."

(Note: The 16-syllable *romancero* verse lines are transcribed here with each 8-syllable hemistich as a separately numbered line.)

Synopsis: This ballad recounts a fragment of the legend of the Battle of Rencesvals dealing with the death of Beltrán, supposedly a noble who accompanied Charlemagne on his campaign in Spain but did not return to France with the rest of the army. The ballad focuses on the poignant journey of Beltrán's father to search for the body of his son.

1   En los campos de   ORIENTATION   In the fields of
     Alventosa   Alventosa
     mataron a don Beltran,   *Sir Beltrán was killed,*
     nunca lo echaron ménos   *his presence wasn't missed*

hasta los puertos pasar.

until they crossed the pass.

5 a. Siete veces ECHAN SUERTES
quién lo VOLVERÁ a buscar;

COMPLICATION

Seven times they DRAW LOTS:
Who WILL GO BACK to look for him [?]

b. todas siete le *cupieron*
al buen viejo de su padre;

all seven *fell*
to the worthy old man, his father;

las tres *fueron* por malicia,

ORIENTATION

three *were* through cunning,

10 y las cuatro con maldad.

and four through malice.

c. VUELVE RIENDAS al caballo,

He GIVES REIN to his horse

d. y VUÉLVESELO A BUSCAR
de noche por el camino,
de dia por el jaral.

and GOES OUT IN SEARCH OF HIM,
by night on the pathways,
by day through the brush.

15 Por la matanza VA el viejo,

LYRIC

The old man GOES OUT in search of carnage,

por la matanza adelante;

MEDITATION

of the carnage [that lies] ahead;

los brazos LLEVA CANSADOS
de los muertos rodear;

his arms ARE WEARY
from turning over corpses;

no HALLABA al que BUSCA,

he COULDN'T FIND the one he SEEKS,

20 ni ménos la su señal;

nor even any trace of him;

e. *vido todos los franceses*
f. y *no vido a don Beltrán.*

he saw all the Frenchmen
but *didn't see Sir Beltrán.*

MALDICIENDO IBA el vino,	LYRIC	He *RODE ALONG CURSING* the wine,
MALDICIENDO IBA el pan,	MEDITATION	he *RODE ALONG CURSING* the bread
25 el que *COMIAN* los moros,		—the bread the Moors *ATE*,
que no el de la cristiandad:		(that) not that of the Christians—
MALDICIENDO IBA el árbol		he *RODE ALONG CURSING* the tree
que solo en el campo N A S C E,		that G R O W S only in the country;
que todas las aves del cielo		(that) all the birds in the sky
30 allí S E V I E N E N A A S E N T A R		C O M E there T O A L I G H T.
que de rama ni de hoja		(that) from no branch, no leaf
no la *DEJABAN GOZAR:*		*WOULD* they *TAKE PLEASURE.*
MALDICIENDO IBA el caballero,		He *RODE ALONG CURSING,* this knight
que *CABALGABA* sin paje;		who *RODE* without a squire.
35 si SE LE CAE LA LANZA NO TIENE QUIEN SE LA ALCE [SUBJ],	EVALUATION (INTERIOR	If he DROPS HIS LANCE, THERE IS NO ONE TO RETRIEVE [SUBJ] IT.
y si SE LE CAE LA ESPUELA	MONOLOGUE)	If he DROPS HIS SPUR,
NO TIENE QUIEN SE LA CALCE:		THERE IS NO ONE TO REPLACE IT.
MALDICIENDO IBA la mujer		He *RODE ALONG CURSING* the woman
40 que tan solo un hijo P A R E;		who B E A R S but a single son;
si enemigos SE LO MATAN	EVALUATION	If his enemies KILL HIM
NO TIENE QUIEN LO VENGAR.	(INTER. MONOLOGUE)	THERE IS NO ONE TO AVENGE HIM.

(NARRATION RESUMES)

A la entrada de un puerto,	ORIENTATION	At the entrance to a pass
saliendo de un arenal,		coming out of a sand-pit,
45 g. *vido* en esto *estar* un moro		he *spied* a Moor there,
que VELABA en un adarve:	(restricted clause)	who WAS STANDING WATCH on a sentry-walk.
h. *hablóle* en algarabía,		He *spoke* to him in Arabic
como aquel que bien la SABE:		like one who KNOWS it well:
—Por Dios te RUEGO, el moro,	DIALOGUE	"In God's name I PRAY, Moor,
50 me DIGAS una verdad:		TELL me in truth:
caballero de armas blancas		a man in white armor,
si lo *viste* acá pasar,		did you *see* him pass by here?
y si tú lo TIENES preso,		and if you HAVE him prisoner
a oro te lo PESARAN,		you WILL BE GIVEN his weight in gold,
55 y si tú lo TIENES muerto		and if you HAVE him dead
DÉSMELO para enterrar,		GIVE ME his body to bury,
pues que el cuerpo sin el alma		for a body without a soul
solo un dinero no VALE.		IS WORTH not a penny."
—Ese caballero, amigo,		"This man, my friend,
60 DIME tú qué señas TRAE.		TELL me what he LOOKS like."
—Blancas armas SON las suyas		"His armor IS white
y el caballo es alazan,		and his horse sorrel,
y en el carrillo derecho		and on his right cheek

65	él TENIA una señal, que siendo niño pequeño se la *hizo* un gavilan.		he HAD a mark that in his childhood a sparrow-hawk *gave* him."
	—Este caballero, amigo, MUERTO ESTA en aquel pradal; las perinas TIENE en el agua.	PEAK/ RESOLUTION	"This man, my friend, LIES DEAD in yonder meadow; his feet ARE in the water,
70	y el cuerpo en el arenal: siete lanzadas TENIA desde el hombro al carcañal, y otras tantas su caballo desde la cincha al pretal.		his body in the sand-pit; seven lance wounds he BORE from his shoulder to his heel, and his horse just as many from the cinch to the breast-strap.
75	No le DÉS CULPA al caballo, que no se las PUEDES DAR; que siete veces lo *sacó* sin herida y sin señal, y otras tantas lo *volvió*		DO NOT BLAME the horse, for him you CANNOT BLAME; seven times he *dragged* him out without a mark or a wound, seven more times he *brought* him *back*,
80	con gana de pelear.		eager for the fight."

Text VIII.   "En París está doña Alda . . ."

(Note: The 16-syllable *romancero* verse lines are transcribed here with each 8-syllable hemistich as a separately numbered line.)

Synopsis: This ballad recounts an episode from the Roland legend in which Roland's fiancée Alda relates a disturbing dream to her serving ladies. One of her ladies interprets it for her as prefiguring Roland's death, which is confirmed the next day with the arrival of a letter.

1	En Paris ESTÁ doña Alda,	ORIENTATION	Lady Alda *IS* in Paris,
	la esposa de don Roldan,		the fiancée of Lord Roland,
	trescientas damas con ella		three hundred ladies with her
	para la acompañar;		to provide her company.
5	todas VISTEN un vestido,		They *ARE* all *WEARING* the same gown,
	todas CALZAN un calzar,		they *ARE* all *WEARING* the same slippers,
	todas COMEN a una mesa,		they *ARE* all *EATING* at the same table,
	todas COMIAN de un pan,		they all *WOULD EAT* the same bread,
	sino ERA doña Alda,		*WERE IT NOT* for Lady Alda,
10	que ERA la mayoral.		who *WAS* the eldest.
	Las ciento HILABAN oro,		One hundred of them *WERE EMBROIDERING* in gold,
	las ciento TEJEN cendal,		one hundred of them *ARE WEAVING* fine silk,
	las ciento TAÑEN instrumentos		one hundred of them *ARE PLAYING* instruments
	para doña Alda holgar.		to bring pleasure to Lady Alda.
15	Al son de los instrumentos	COMPLICATION	With the sound of the instruments
	doña Alda *adormido SE HA:*		Lady Alda *HAS fallen asleep.*
	ensoñado había un sueño,		*a dream she had dreamed,*
	un sueño de gran pesar.		a very disquieting dream.
	a. *Recordó* despavorida		Terrified, she *recalled* it,

20	y con un pavor muy grande,		filled with fear and dread;
b.	los GRITOS DABA tan grandes	(coordinated	her cries RANG OUT so loudly
c.	que SE OIAN en la ciudad.	clauses)	they WERE HEARD in the city.
d.	Allí *hablaron* sus doncellas,		Then her ladies in waiting *spoke up,*
	bien OIRÉIS lo que DIRAN:	(formula)	LISTEN well now to what they WILL SAY:
25	—Qué ES aquesto, mi señora?		—What IS this, my lady?
	Quién ES el que os *hizo mal?*		Who IS it that *made* you *upset?*
e.	—Un sueño *soñé,* doncellas,		—A dream I *dreamed,* my girls,
	que me HA *dado* gran pesar:	EVALUATION	which HAS *given* me great fright:

	(EMBEDDED DREAM NARRATION)		
	que ME VEIA en un monte	ORIENTATION	I SAW MYSELF on a mountain,
30	en un desierto lugar:		in a place totally deserted.
	de so los montes muy altos		Above the high mountains
a'.	*un azor vide volar,*	COMPLICATION	I *saw a hawk fly;*
b'.	tras dél VIENE una aguililla		behind him COMES an eagle
	que lo AHINCA muy mal.	(restricted clause)	who IS rapidly GAINING on him.
35	El azor con grande cuita		The hawk in great distress
c'.	*metióse so mi brial;*		*hid himself beneath my tunic;*
	el aguililla con grande ira		the eagle full of rage
	de allí LO IBA A SACAR;		WAS GOING TO PULL HIM OUT;

d'. con las uñas LO DES- PLUMA,	(coordinated	with his claws he PULLS OUT HIS FEATHERS,
40 e'. con el pico LO DES- HACE.	clauses)	with his beak he DOES HIM IN.

f. Alli *habló* su camarera,

  bien OIRÉIS lo que   (formula)
    DIRA:
  —Áquese sueño,   DIALOGUE
    señora,
  bien os lo ENTIENDO
    SOLTAR:
45 el azor ES vuestro
    esposo
  que VIENE de allen
    la mar;
  el águila SEDES vos
  con la cual HA DE CASAR,
  y aquel monte ES la
    iglesia
50 donde os HAN DE VELAR.

g. —Si así ES, mi
    camarera,
  bien te lo ENTIENDO
    PAGAR.
  Otro día de mañana
h. CARTAS de fuera le   PEAK
    TRAEN:
55 TINTAS VENIAN de   EVALUATION
    dentro,
  de fuera ESCRITAS CON
    SANGRE,
  que su Roldan *era*   RESOLUTION
    muerto
  en la caza de
    Roncesvalles.

Then her chamber-
  maid *spoke up,*
now you WILL HEAR:
  what she WILL SAY:
"That dream, my lady,

I KNOW HOW TO UN-
  RAVEL it for you:
the hawk IS your
  husband
who IS COMING from
  across the sea;
the eagle IS you,
whom he IS TO WED;
and the mountain IS the
  church
where the veiling cere-
  mony IS TO BE HELD."
"If it IS as you say, my
  chambermaid,
I KNOW HOW TO RE-
  WARD you properly."
The next morning
they BRING her LETTERS
  from afar
—they CAME STAINED
  on the inside,
on the outside WRITTEN
  IN BLOOD—
that her Roland *had*
  been killed
in the massacre at
  Rencesvals.

Text IX.   *Poema de mio Cid,* stanza 112

(Note: The anisosyllabic verse lines are here transcribed with each hemistich as a separately numbered line.)

Synopsis: This episode serves to reveal the cowardliness of the Cid's sons-in-law, Diego and Ferrán González, nobles of Carrión. The Cid is holding court in Valencia. While he is dozing, a lion escapes from its cage; the sons-in-law recoil in fear. The Cid awakens and gently leads the lion back into its cage. The sons-in-law are shamed.

1	En Valençia *SEYE* mio Çid	ORIENTATION	The Cid *WAS* in Valencia
	con todos sus vassallos,		along with all of his vassals,
	con el amos sus yernos		with him also his two sons-in-law,
	los ifantes de Carrion.		the infantes of Carrión.
5	*YAZIES EN UN ESCAÑO,*		HE *WAS LYING ON A BENCH,*
	DURMIE el Campeador;		the Cid *WAS ASLEEP;*
	mala sobrevienta		a frightening escapade
	SABED que les *cuntio*	ABSTRACT COMPLICATION	*befell* them, KNOW this!
	a. *salios* de la red	(coordinated	The lion *escaped* from the cage
10	b. e *desatos* el leon.	clauses)	and *untied himself.*
	c. *En grant miedo se vieron*		[The nobles] *showed their great fear*
	por medio de la cort;		for all the court to see.
	d. *EMBRAÇAN LOS MANTOS*		They *WRAP THEMSELVES IN THEIR CAPES*
	los del Campeador		the Cid's men,
15	e. e *ÇERCAN EL ESCAÑO*	(coordinated	and *SURROUND HIS BENCH,*
	f. e *FINCAN SOBRE SO SEÑOR.*	clauses)	and *HUDDLE ABOUT THEIR LORD.*
	Ferran Gonçalez non *vio* alli do*s alçasse* [IMP SUBJ],	EVALUATION	Ferrán González *couldn't see* where to *hide* [IMP SUBJ],

nin camara abierta nin torre,		no open room, no tower.
g. *metios so'l escaño*		He *hid underneath the bench,*
20 tanto *ovo el pavor;*	(restricted	*so terrified was* he.
Diego Gonçalez	clause)	Diego González
h. *por la puerta salio*		*fled out the door,*
diziendo de la boca:		saying (from his mouth):
"Non VERE Carrion!"	EVALUATION	"Never again WILL I SEE Carrión!"
25 Tras una viga lagar		Behind the beam of the wine-press
i. *metios* con grant pavor,		he *hid,* terrified,
el manto y el brial		his cape and tunic
j. todo suzio lo *saco.*		—now soiled!—he *removed.*
k. en esto *desperto*		With this, [the Cid] *awakened*
30 el que en buen ora *naçio*	(formula)	the one *born* at a propitious moment.
l. *vio çercado el escaño*		he *saw his bench surrounded*
de sus buenos varones:		by his noble vassals:
m. "Ques esto, mesnadas,		"What IS this, my men,
o que QUEREDES vos?"		what do you WISH?"
35 n. —"Hya, señor ondrado,		"Oh, honored Lord,
rebata nos dio el leon!"	PEAK (?)	what *a fright* the lion *gave* us!"
o. Mio Çid *finco el cobdo,*		The Cid *propped up on his elbow,*
p. *en pie se levanto*		he *rose to his feet*
EL MANTO TRAE al cuello	ORIENTATION	—he WEARS HIS CAPE around his neck—
40 q. e *adeliño pora[l] leon;*		and *advanced toward the lion.*
r. el leon quando *lo vio*		The lion, when he *saw him,*
s. assi *envergonço*		*humbled himself* just like this:

s′. ante mio Çid *la cabeça premio*		he *bowed his head* before the Cid
s″. y *el rostro finco;*		and *lowered his face.*
45 mio Çid don Rodrigo		The Cid, don Rodrigo,
t. *al cuello lo tomo*		*took him by the neck*
e *LIEVA LO ADESTRANDO,*	(restricted clause)	and *LEADS HIM AROUND* like a trainer,
u. *en la red le metio.*	RESOLUTION	[then] *put him back in the cage.*
A maravilla lo *HAN*	EXTERNAL	—They *THINK* it a miracle,
50 quantos que i *SON*	EVALUATION	those who *ARE* gathered there—
v. e *tornaron se* al (a)palaçio		and *returned* to the palace
pora la cort.		via the court.
w. Mio Çid *por sos yernos demando* [1]		The Cid *asked for his sons-in-law*
x. e *no los fallo,*		and *did not find them;*
55 mager *LOS ESTAN LAMANDO*	(restricted	though [they] *ARE CALLING FOR THEM,*
NINGUNO *NON RESPONDE.*	clauses)	*NEITHER ONE ANSWERS.*
y. Quando los *fallaron*		When they *found* them,
z. assi *vinieron* sin color;		they *came* like this, their color lost.
non *viestes tal guego*	EXTERNAL	—Never *did you see such a comedy*
60 commo *IVA POR LA CORT!*	EVALUATION	as *PASSED THROUGH THAT COURT!*—
aa. *Mandolo vedar* mio Çid el Campeador.		The Cid *ordered it stopped.*
Muchos *tovieron por enbaidos*	EVALUATIVE	Many *took for cowards*
los ifantes de Carrion;	CODA	the nobles of Carrión;
65 fiera cosa *LES PESA*		heavily it *WEIGHS ON THEM*
desto que les *cuntio.*		this incident that *occurred.*

[1] The verb *demando* (asked for) is metrically part of line 54, but to facilitate clause analysis has been moved to the line above where its subject is found.

Text X.   *La Chanson de Roland,*
vv. 2686–2723

(Note: Segmentation into clauses does not consistently match segmentation according to lines of verse. Verse numbers for the Old French text are indicated in square brackets.)

Synopsis: Baligant, the leader of all pagandom, returns with his men to Saragossa to find his people distressed over the damage that has been inflicted on them in their war with Charlemagne and the Franks; in particular, Roland has cut off the right hand of their chieftain Marsile. The information in these two *laisses* is presented largely through direct speech: first by the pagans collectively, then by Marsile's wife Bramimonde, who expresses the collective fear for their fate at the hands of Charlemagne.

194.

1 a. *Dist* Baligant: "Car
      chevalchez, barun!   [2686]
      L'un PORT [SUBJ] le
      guant, li alt[r]e le
      bastun!"

   b. E cil RESPUNDENT:
      "Cher sire, si FERUM."

   c. Tant *chevalcherent*

5 d. que en Sarraguce SUNT,

   e. PASSENT .X. PORTES,   (mass verb)
      [2690]

   f. TRAVERSENT .IIII.   (mass verb)
      PUNZ, tutes les rues

      u li burgeis ESTUNT

      Cum il APROISMENT en
      la citét amunt,

10 g. Vers le paleis *oïrent*
       grant fremur;

194.

Said Baligant: "Lords,
   time for you to ride!
One BEAR [SUBJ] the
   glove, the other the
   staff!"

And they REPLY:
   "Dear Lord, we
   SHALL DO that."

They *rode and rode*

until they ARE in
   Saragossa,

they PASS THROUGH
   TEN GATES,

RIDE ACROSS FOUR
   BRIDGES and through
   the streets

where the townspeople
   LIVE.

As they APPROACH, on
   the heights of the city,
round the palace they
   heard a great
   murmur:

Asez *I AD* de cele gent paienur,	(restr. clause)	swarms of that pagan race *ARE GATHERED* there,
h. *PLURENT*	(4 coordinated	they *WEEP*
i. e *CRIENT,*	clauses)	and *SHOUT,*
j. *DEMEINENT GRANT DOLOR,*	[2695]	*DISPLAY THEIR HEAVY GRIEF,*
15 k. *PLEIGNENT LUR DEUS* Tervagan e Mahum e Apollin		*LAMENT THEIR GODS* Tervagant and Mohammed and Apollin,
dunt il *MIE NEN UNT*	(restricted clause)	whom they *NO LONGER HAVE.*
l. *DIT* cascun a l'altre: "Caitifs, que *DEVENDRUM?*	PEAK	each *SAYS* to the other: "What *WILL BECOME* of us?
Sur nus *EST venue* male confusiun,	(?)	Destruction and dis-honor *HAVE befallen* us,
Perdut AVUM le rei Marsiliun;	[2700]	we *HAVE lost* our King Marsilion;
20 Li quens Rollant li *tren-chat* ier le destre poign.		yesterday Count Roland *cut off* his hand;
Nus n'*AVUM* mie de Jurfaleu le blunt,		We no longer *HAVE* Jurafleu the blond
Trestute Espaigne *IERT* hoi *EN LUR BANDUN."*		All of Spain *WILL BE* *UNDER THEIR FLAG* today!"
m. Li dui message *DESCENDENT* al perrun.		The two messengers *DISMOUNT* at the stone block.
195.		195.
n. *LUR CHEVALS LAISENT* dedesuz un' olive,	[2705]	They *LEAVE THEIR HORSES* under an olive tree;
25 o. Dui Sarrazin *par les resnes les pristrent,*		two Saracens *took their reins.*

E li message par les
  mantels *se tindrent*;

And the messengers *held*
  each other by their
  cloaks;

p. Puis SUNT *muntez* sus el
  paleis altisme.

then they ARE *up* in that
  towering palace.

q. Cum il *entrerent en la*
  cambre voltice,

As they *entered [the*
  King's] high-vaulted
  chamber,

r. Par bel amur malvais *sa-* [2710]
  luz li firent:

in perfect love they *gave*
  him dire greetings:

30   "Cil Mahumet ki nus AD
  en baillie

"MAY Mohammed who
  HAS us in his hands,

E Tervagan e Apollin,
  nostre sire,

and Tervagant, and
  Apollin our Lord

SALVENT [SUBJ] le rei e
  GUARDENT [SUBJ] la
  reine."

SAVE the King and
  WATCH OVER [SUBJ]
  the Queen."

s. *Dist* Bramimunde: "Or PEAK (?)
  OI mult grant folie.

Said Bramimonde:
  "What madness DO I
  HEAR!

Cist nostre deu SUNT [2715]
  EN RECREANTISE,

These gods of ours ARE
  FAILURES,
  DESERTERS!

35   En Rencesval *malvaises*
  vertuz firent,

miserable wonders they
  performed at
  Rencesvals:

Nos chevalers i UNT
  lessét ocire.

they HAVE *allowed* our
  men to be killed,

Cest mien seignur en
  bataille *faillirent:*

they *abandoned* my lord
  in battle:

Le destre poign AD
  perdut,

he HAS *lost* his right
  hand,

N'EN AD MIE;

he HAS IT NO LONGER.

40   Si li *trenchat* li quens [2720]
  Rollant li riches.

The powerful Count
  Roland *cut it off.*

Trestute Espaigne
  AVRAT Carles EN
  BAILLIE.

Charles WILL HAVE all
  of Spain IN HIS
  POWER.

Que DEVENDRAI, du-
luruse caitive?

What WILL BECOME
of me, a wretched
captive!

E! lasse, que NEN AI un
hume ki m'OCIET
[SUBJ]!"

Alas, me, HAVE I NO
ONE TO KILL [SUBJ]
me too!"

Text XI.   *La Vie de St. Alexis,* stanzas 21–32 (vv. 101–157)

Synopsis: Count Euphemien of Rome sends two vassals out in search of his son Alexis, who has been missing for many years; when they find him, the two men fail to recognize Alexis, who is dressed as a mendicant friar; when they return, having failed in their mission, Alexis's mother grieves.

I   Or REVENDRAI al pedra ed a la medra   DISCOURSE   (21)
    Ed a la spuse qued il *out espusethe.*   TRAFFIC SIGNAL
    Quant il ço *sourent* qued il *fud* si *alét,* COMPLICATION
a. Ço *fut granz dols* quet il UNT *demenét*
5   E granz deplainz par tuta la citiét. [105]
b. Ço *dist* li pedres: "Cher filz, cum t'AI
    perdut!"
c. RESPONT la medre: "Lasse! qu'EST   (22)
    devenut?"
d. Ço *dist* la spuse: "Pechét le m'AT *tolut!*
    E! chers amis, si pou vus AI *oüt!*
10 Or SUI si GRAIME que NE PUIS
    ESTRA plus." [110]
e. Dunc PRENT li pedre DE SE[S] *meilurs ser-*   (23)
    ganz,
f. Par multes terres FAIT QUERRE SUN AM-
    FANT;
g. Jusque an Alsis en *vindrent* dui *errant:*
h. Iloc *truverent danz Alexis* sedant, [114]
15 i₁. Mais *n'a[n]conurent* sum vis ne   PEAK   (24)
    sum semblant. *
    Si AT *li emfes sa tendra carn mudede,*   *orientation*
i₂. *Nel reconurent* li dui sergent sum pedre;   PEAK'
j. A lui medisme UNT *l'almosne dunethe;*
k. Il *la receut* cume li altre frere.

20 i₃/l. *Nel reconurent,* sempres *s'en returnerent.*   PEAK″
        [120]
     i₄. *Nel reconurent* ne *ne* l'*UNT anterciét.*   PEAK‴   (25)
     m. Danz Alexis an *LOTHET DEU* del ciel
        D'icez sons sers qui il *EST*   EVALUATIVE
        provenders;   ORIENTATION
        Il *fut* lur sire, or *EST* lur almosners; [124]
25   NE VUS SAI DIRE cum il *s'en firet liez.*   EXTERNAL
     n. Cil *S'EN REPAIRENT* a Rome la citét,   EVALUATION   (26)
     o. *NUNCENT* al pedre que *nel pourent truver.*   EXTERNAL
        Set il *fut graim,* NE L'ESTOT DEMANDER.   EVALUATION
     p. La bone medre *s'em prist a dementer*
30   E sun ker filz suvent *a regreter.* [130]
        "Filz Ale[x]is, pur quei*[t] portat* ta medre?   (27)
        Tu m'IES *füit,* DOLENTE en SUI *remese.*
        NE SAI le leu ne N'EN SAI la contrede
        U t'ALGE [SUBJ] QUERRE; tute en SUI
        ESGUARETHE. [134]
35   Ja mais N'IERC LEDE, kers filz, ne
          N'ERT tun pedre . . ."
[The mother's lament continues in direct speech for ca. 20 verses, here
omitted: the episode concludes at v. 157 with the poet's commentary:]
36   Ne POET ESTRE ALTRA, *TURNENT EL*   EVALUATION/   (32)
        CONSIRRER;   RESOLUTION
        Mais la dolur *NE POTHENT UBLÏER.* [157]
*Clause i, which marks the Peak of the episode, is repeated 4 times within
a space of 7 verses (15, 17, 20, 21).

Text XI.   *The Life of St. Alexis*
(translation)

I   Now I WILL COME BACK TO his father   DISCOURSE   (21)
       and mother   TRAFFIC SIGNAL
     and to the bride whom he *had married.*
     When they *learned* that he [Alexis] *had*   COMPLICATION
       gone,
     a. it *was their great sorrow* that they *(HAVE)*
        displayed
5   and a great lamentation throughout the
       city.

b. Thus *said* his father: "My dear son, how I
   HAVE *lost* you!"
c. *RESPONDS* his mother: "Wretched me!   (22)
   What HAS *come about?*"
d. Thus *said* his bride: "Sin HAS *taken him*
   from me!
   Ah, my dear friend, so little [time] HAVE I
   had you!
10   Now I AM SO SAD, sadder I CANNOT BE."
e. Then his father *TAKES HIS TWO BEST*   (23)
   HENCHMEN,
f. [and] *SENDS* them over many lands *TO*
   SEARCH FOR HIS SON;
g. The two *came wandering* as far as Alsis:
h. There they *found Lord Alexis* sitting down,
15   i₁. But they *didn't recognize* his face or his   PEAK
   appearance. *
   So much HAS *the child changed his*   ORIENTATION   (24)
   appearance,
   i₂. his father's two men *didn't recognize* him.   PEAK'
   j. *To him—to him!—they HAVE given alms.*
   k. He *received* them like his fellow
   mendicants.
20   i₃/l. They *didn't recognize* him, immediately   PEAK"
   they *returned.*
   i₄. They *didn't recognize* him, nor HAVE *they*   PEAK'''   (25)
   picked him out.
m. Thereupon Lord Alexis *PRAISES GOD* in
   heaven
   for those men, his servants, whose alms-   EVALUATIVE
   man he now *IS*;
   He once *was* their lord; now he *IS* their   ORIENTATION
   alms-seeker.
25   I CANNOT TELL YOU how *jubilant he was*   EXTERNAL
   over it.   EVALUATION
n. The two men *RETURN* to the city of Rome,   (26)

---

*Clause i, which marks the Peak of the episode, is repeated 4 times within a space
of 7 verses (15, 17, 20, 21).

o. they ANNOUNCE to his father that they
    could not find him.

    AS IF YOU NEED ASK whether he *was*   EXTERNAL
    sad!   EVALUATION

p. His worthy mother *took to mourning*
30   and often *to lamenting* for her dear son.
    "Alexis, my son, why did your mother
    carry you [in her womb]?   (27)
    You HAVE *fled* from me, grieving HAVE I
    remained.
    I KNOW NOT the place, I KNOW NOT the
    land
    where to GO [SUBJ] IN SEARCH of you; I
    AM completely UNDONE.
35   NEVER again WILL I BE HAPPY, DEAR
    son, NOR WILL your father BE . . ."
[The mother's lament continues in direct speech for ca. 20 verses; the
episode concludes at v. 157 with the poet's commentary:]
36   IT CANNOT BE OTHERWISE; they *RESIGN*   EVALUATION/   (32)
    THEMSELVES;   RESOLUTION
    But they *CANNOT FORGET* their sorrow.

Text XII. Chrétien de Troyes, *Le Chevalier au lion (Yvain)*, vv. 815–875
(Episode of Yvain's combat with Esclados)

(Note: Text is transcribed with one line of verse per numbered line of transcript. Starred [*] NPs appear as PSS in other manuscripts, per Foerster ed.,
which combines readings from different manuscripts.)

Synopsis: The knight Yvain engages in combat with Esclados the Red.
After much bitter fighting, with serious blows dealt on both sides, Yvain
deals the culminating blow to Esclados, slashing through his helmet and
splitting his head open. Realizing the fight is over for him, Esclados departs the field of combat.

1   a. et maintenant qu'il   COMPLICATING   and as soon as they
      s'antrevirent,   ACTION   *saw one another,*

b. *s'antrevindrent* et
sanblant firent

they *came at each other*
and *looked as if*

qu'il *s'antrehais-*   (EVALUATION)
sent [IMP SUBJ] de
mort.

they *bore* each other a
mortal *hatred* [IMP
SUBJ].

Chascuns *ot* lance   (ORIENTATION)
roide et fort;

Each *had* a sturdy and
strong lance.

5   c. si *S'ANTREDONENT SI*   (mass verb)
GRANZ COS

They *DEAL EACH
OTHER SUCH
MIGHTY BLOWS*

d. qu'andeus les escuz de
lor cos

that they *PIERCE
THROUGH* both the
shields

(series of
coordinated
clauses)

e. *PERCENT*, et
li hauberc
DESLICENT;

at their sides and
SMASH each other's
hauberks,

f/g. les lances *FANDENT ET
ESCLICENT,*

they *SHATTER* and
SPLINTER the
lances,

h. et li tronçon *VOLENT
AN HAUT.*

and the pieces *FLY
INTO THE AIR.*

10   i. Li uns l'autre a l'espee   (mass verb)
ASSAUT

They *ATTACK* one
another with
swords;

si *ONT* au chaple des
espes

they *HAVE* in this
clash of swords

les guiges des escuz
colpees

cut through the shield
straps

et les escuz *dehachiez*
toz

and completely *split*
the shields,

et par desus et par
desoz

both on top and on
the bottom,

15   si que les pieces an   EVALUATIVE
DEPANDENT,   ORIENTATION

so that the pieces *ARE
LEFT HANGING;*

n'il ne *S'AN CUEVRENT*
ne *DESFANDENT;*

they can no longer
COVER nor *DEFEND*
them;

car si *les ONT
harigotez*

for # they *HAVE put
so many holes in them*

qu'a delivre, sor les costez,		that directly on their sides,
et sor les piz, et sor les hanches,		and on their breasts, and on their flanks
20 *ESSAIENT* les espees blanches.	(mass verb)	the shining swords *LAND.*
Felenessemant *S'ANTR'ES-PRUEVENT*,	EVALUATIVE ORIENTATION	They *TEST EACH OTHER* cruelly;
n'onques d'un estal *NE SE MUEVENT*		*NEVER DO* THEY *MOVE* further from their positions
ne plus que *feïssent* [IMP SUBJ] dui gres;		than *would* [IMP SUBJ] two blocks of stone;
einz dui chevalier plus *angrés*	(restricted	never *were* two knights more *eager*
25 ne *furent* de lor mort haster.	clauses)	to hasten each other's death.
N'*ONT CURE* de lor cos gaster		They *HAVE NO DE-SIRE* to waste their blows,
que mialz qu'il *PUEENT* les *ANPLOIENT*;	(mass verb)	and *DELIVER THEM AS BEST THEY CAN.*
j/k. les hiaumes *AN-BUINGNENT* et *PLOIENT*	(coordinated clauses)	They *DENT* and *BEND* each other's helmets,
l. et des haubers les mailles *VOLENT*,		and the links of mail *FLY* from their hauberks,
30 m. si que del sanc assez *SE TOLENT*;		such that much blood *FLOWS.*
car d'ax meïsmes *SONT* si *CHAUT*	EVALUATIVE ORIENTATION	For their hauberks *ARE* now so *HOT*
lor hauberc, que li suens *NE VAUT*		from the fighting, that *NEITHER IS WORTH*
a chascuns gueres plus d'un froc.		much more than a frock.

n.	Anz *EL VIS SE FIERENT* d'estoc,	(mass verb)	Then they *STRIKE ONE ANOTHER'S FACES* with their blades;
35	*S'EST MERVOILLE* comant *TANT DURE* bataille si fiere et si dure	EVALUATION	# It's *A WONDER* such a fierce and bitter battle *COULD LAST SO LONG;*
	Mes andui *SONT DE SI FIER CUER*		but they *ARE* both OF SUCH STALWART COURAGE
	que li uns por l'autre a nul fuer		that <u>neither would on any account</u>
	<u>de terre un pié</u> <u>ne guerpiroit</u>		<u>yield a foot of ground</u> to the other
40	se *JUSQU'A MORT NE L'ENPIROIT;*		if he *WERE NOT VIR-TUALLY AT THE POINT OF DEATH.*
	et de ce *firent molt que preu*	EVALUATIVE ORIENTATION	And in this they *proceeded most honorably:*
	c'onques lor cheval an nul leu		*never* in a single spot *did* they *strike*
	ne ferirent ne *maheignierent*	(generic actions)	or *wound* the horses,
	qu'il *ne vostrent* ne *ne deignierent,*		*nor did* they *desire to* nor *deign to;*
45	mes toz jorz *A CHEVAL SE TIENENT* *	(restricted	but they *REMAIN* * *ALWAYS ON HORSE-BACK,*
	que *NULE FOIZ A PIÉ NE VIENENT* *:	clauses)	*NEVER RESORT TO* * *COMBAT ON THE GROUND;*
	s'an fu la bataille *plus bele.*		# thus the battle *was more splendid.*
o.	En la fin, son hiaume *ESCARTELE* au chevalier mes sire Yvains;	PEAK	Finally, he *SMASHES* the knight's helmet my Lord Yvain [does];
50	p. del cop *fu estonez* et *vains*	(result)	the knight *was stunned* and *weakened*

q. li chevaliers; molt s'esmaia		by the blow; he *was confounded,*
qu'ainz si felon *cop* n'essaia,		for never *did* he *experience* such *a blow,*
qu'il li *ot* desoz le chapel	EVALUATIVE ORIENTATION	for he *had,* beneath his hood,
le chief fandu jusqu'au cervel,		*his head split apart* down to the brain,
55 tant que del cervel et del sanc		such that the chain-mail of his shining hauberk
TAINT la maille del hauberc blanc,		*IS STAINED* with brains and with blood,
don si tres grant *dolor santi*		from which he *felt* such terrible *pain*
qu'a po li cuers ne li *manti.*		that his heart *nearly failed* him.
r. S'il *s'an foï,* N'A* MIE TORT,	RESOLUTION/ EVALUATION	If he *fled,* HE IS* NOT TO BE BLAMED,
60 qu'il *se santi navrez* a mort;		since he *felt himself* mortally *wounded;*
car riens *ne* li *valut* desfansse.		for defending himself *was to no avail* now.

Text XIII.   *Récit de vie* of Xavier-Edouard Lejeune (plot summary)

Synopsis: Summary of the events in the life of that narrator's grandfather.

Il *DESCEND D'*une longue lignée de "manouvriers" de Laon. Son grand-père *ÉTAIT* chiffonnier, ses oncles artisans (potier, cordonnier, ébéniste). Sa mère, jeune couturière, *MONTE À PARIS.* En 1845, elle *MET AU MONDE UN ENFANT,*—lui. Pour pouvoir continuer à travailler, elle le *PLACE EN NOURRICE,* puis *LE CONFIE À SES GRANDS-PARENTS,* à Laon. De 1848 à 1855, il y *PASSE UNE ENFANCE* heureuse et libre dont il GARDERA toujours LA NOSTALGIE. Quand il *A DIX ANS,* sa mère *LE REPREND* avec elle à Paris, où il *TERMINE RAPIDEMENT SON ÉDUCATION:* en 1858, à treize ans, il *COMMENCE À TRAVAILLER,* comme calicot, dans les grands magasins de nouveautés alors en pleine expansion. De 1858 à 1872, changeant très souvent de magasin, il *PARCOURT* le commerce de la nouveauté et il *OBSERVE*, en direct, ce monde que plus tard Zola PEINDRA dans "Au bonheur des dames." En 1868, il *SE MET EN MÉNAGE* avec une ouvrière en couture aussi pauvre que lui, originaire d'une famille de juifs hollandais fraîchement installée en France. De 1869 à 1875, ils *ONT CINQ ENFANTS*. Finie l'instabilité. Xavier-Edouard *COMMENCE UNE NOUVELLE CARRIÈRE* comme représentant dans le commerce de la fourrure: pendant quarante ans, de 1872 à 1912, il FERA CE MÉTIER, et, les trente dernières années, dans la même maison, chez Félix Jungmann. Une vie de travail acharné et d'économie, pour pouvoir élever les enfants et aboutir à une modeste aisance. Jungmann, le patron, parti de rien, *a fait fortune* en moins de trente ans; il *REÇOIT LA LÉGION D'HONNEUR:* il *HABITE* avenue du Bois. Quand Xavier-Edouard *PREND SA RETRAITE* en 1912, on lui *DONNE UNE "MÉDAILLE D'HONNEUR"* pour les vieux serviteurs ayant trente ans de maison; il *SE RETIRE À MONTMORENCY* dans un pavillon de meulière. Sa femme *MEURT* en 1915, lui en 1918.

Text XIII.   *Narrative of the Life* of Xavier-Edouard Lejeune (translation)

He *DESCENDS FROM* a long line of "manual laborers" from Laon. His grandfather *WAS* a ragman, his uncles artisans (a potter, a cobbler, a cabinet-maker). His mother, a young seamstress, *GOES UP TO PARIS.* In 1845, she *GIVES BIRTH TO A CHILD*—him. In order to continue working, she *SENDS HIM TO A NURSE,* then *ENTRUSTS HIM TO HIS GRANDPARENTS* in Laon. From 1848 to 1855, he *SPENDS A* happy, carefree *CHILDHOOD,* which he WILL always REMEMBER NOSTALGICALLY. When he *IS SIX,* his mother *TAKES HIM BACK WITH HER* in Paris, where he *QUICKLY FINISHES HIS EDUCATION:* in 1858, at thirteen, he *BEGINS WORKING* as a draper's assistant in the big dry goods stores, on the rise at the time. From 1858 to 1872, moving from store to store, he *COVERS THE TERRITORY* of the dry goods business and *OBSERVES,* through firsthand experience, the world that Zola WILL later DEPICT in "Au bonheur des dames." En 1868, he *ENTERS INTO MARRIAGE* with a young seamstress, as poor as he, from a family of Dutch Jews recently settled in France. Between 1869 and 1875, they *HAVE FIVE CHILDREN.* End of financial instability. Xavier-Edouard *EMBARKS ON A NEW CAREER* as a representative in the fur business: for forty years, from 1872 to 1912, he WILL CARRY OUT THIS OCCUPATION, the last thirty of these with the same firm: Felix Jungmann's. A life of hard work and sacrifice in order to raise his children and achieve a modest level of comfort. Jungmann, the boss, [who had] started off with nothing, *made a fortune* in less than thirty years; he RECEIVES THE MEDAL OF THE LE-GION OF HONOR; he LIVES on the Avenue du Bois. When Xavier-Edouard RETIRES in 1912, he IS GIVEN A "MEDAL OF HONOR" for thirty years of service; he RETIRES TO MONTMORENCY to an old stone farmhouse. His wife DIES in 1915, he in 1918.

Notes

Introduction

1. The terms "tense" and "tense-aspect" are often used interchangeably, since many of the paradigms that traditional grammars label "tenses" combine temporal and aspectual information. This is typical of languages whose verb morphology is organized principally around tense distinctions (English, Romance), with aspect bundled into the tense morphemes.

2. Typographic conventions used in the coding of texts are explained in appendix 1.

3. For languages that distinguish IMPERFECTIVE (IPFV) and PERFECTIVE (PFV) aspect within the PAST system, it is the PFV PAST, often referred to as the PRETERIT or AORIST, that is the unmarked tense of narrative. Unless the IMP is specified, PAST refers to the PFV PAST.

4. Halliday and Hasan (1976) refer to the first three components as IDEATIONAL, TEXTUAL, and INTERPERSONAL, Traugott (1982) as PROPOSITIONAL, TEXTUAL, and EXPRESSIVE. While the first two categories are virtually equivalent conceptually, EXPRESSIVE has the advantage over INTERPERSONAL of not being limited to interactive phenomena. For what is communicated at this level is not only the *interpersonal* (i.e., information about the relationship *between* speech-act participants) but also, and equally important, the *personal* (i.e., the speaker's perspective on, or evaluations of, elements of the text).

The assignment of tense-aspect functions to the components of this model is not always a clear-cut issue. For example, I have chosen to include point of view within the EXPRESSIVE component for the reason that it presents the contents of a story world as subjectively filtered through the consciousness of a particular participant. However, point of view might alternatively be considered TEXTUAL in the sense that it assigns "stretches of text" to different story participants. Nor is it assumed that the model adopted here is the only one appropriate to the classification of tense-aspect functions; an advantage it has over other functional models is relative simplicity—only four categories, which are, moreover, sufficiently broad to account for a considerable number of tense-aspect functions.

5. Van Dijk (1975) coins the term "artificial" as an umbrella for the varieties of narrative found in stories, novels, and other types of literature, as well as myths, folktales, and epics—in contrast to the "natural" narratives that occur in ordinary conversation.

6. To save space yet at the same time provide adequate discourse context for examples, I have included in appendix 2 a selection of thirteen texts representative of the genres here under consideration. Twelve of the texts are narrative, some containing a story in its entirety, others excerpts, but all are structurally complete; the last text of the group is a type of plot summary.

7. "Storytelling" is not always congruent with "performance." In some cultures storytelling is regarded as a kind of "straight talk," distinct from other varieties of speech to which the label "performance" appropriately applies (cf. Bauman 1977).

8. It is argued in chapter 1 that the "basic meaning" of the PRESENT tense in many languages is "timelessness," in the sense of absence of any positive temporal reference.

Chapter 1. Working Definitions and Operational Preliminaries

9. "Situation" is used as a cover term for the predicate classes traditionally referred to as events, processes, and states, or, according to the typology proposed by Vendler (1967), as states, activities, achievements, and accomplishments. Working definitions of these *situation types* are given in §1.3.

10. A system that relates entities to a (shifting) reference point is termed a deictic system. The most straightforward instance of a deictic system is one in which the speaker's here-and-now is taken as the center, or zero-point. Tense is deictic in that it establishes the temporal location of situations in relation to the speaker's now. For a general discussion of deixis, see Fillmore (1975), Lyons (1977: chapter 15), and, with particular reference to tense, Comrie (1985: §1.5).

11. A major advance in semantic theory has been the recognition of a distinction between the "meaning" of a linguistic item, in terms of its conventionalized semantic representation, and the "implicatures" that can be drawn from the use of the item in a particular context. An example would be use of the sentence "it's getting late" to prompt a visitor to leave. The literal meaning of this sentence is an observation about the time of day. But in most contexts the literal meaning of this sentence is not particularly relevant to the conversation; the hearer thus deduces that this sentence is not intended literally, but rather that the speaker has an ulterior motive, which by a chain of reasoning can be deduced to be that the speaker wants the hearer to leave. For a general discussion of conversational implicature, see Grice (1975), Lyons (1977:592–596), and, with respect to tense, Comrie (1985: §1.7).

12. On the interaction of aspects and situation types, see Comrie (1976), Dry (1983), and Smith (1983); the latter two refer to situation types as "temporal schemata."

13. Reference to examples drawn from these texts is by text number (in Roman numerals) and line number (e.g., III : 45–58). Prose texts are transcribed with one clause per line of transcript; each line of transcript is numbered. For clauses exceeding a single line of transcript, the second line is indented. Directly quoted speech is included with its discourse-introducing verb as a single clause. Verse narratives (texts VII–XII) are transcribed with one line of verse per line of transcript. Clauses preceded by a letter are those containing the sequential events of the story.

14. Per Grice's maxim of quantity: "make your contribution as informative as is required" (Grice 1975). Had the speaker moved more than once and wanted to convey this information, a numeral quantifier (twice, six times) would presumably have been added.

15. In the French grammatical tradition this usage is often referred to as the IMPARFAIT PITTORESQUE. Cf. Buffin (1925 : 109ff.), Imbs ([1960] : 92f.), Muller (1966), Saunders (1969 : 154ff.), Martin (1971 : 98, 170f.), Ducrot (1979); for Italian, Ronconi (1943) and Bertinetto (1986 : §6.4). Though most investigators acknowledge the NARR IMP as a phenomenon of modern literature, Lerch (1922) argues for popular origins in Old French, subsequent eclipse during the classical period, then resurgence in the nineteenth century as a cultivated stylistic device—a history much like that of the HP (see §§3.8, 8.3.2).

16. Variants of this formula introduce the prose *laisses* 1, 6, 10, 12, 18, 28, and 36.

17. I have coined this term as an umbrella for the several varieties of PR that have past time reference. See also *n*22.

18. The disappearance of the PASSÉ SIMPLE from standard spoken French (it is retained in certain regional dialects) has been amply discussed and need not concern us here. Among many treatments of the subject, see Foulet (1920), Buffin (1925), Schogt (1964), and Saunders (1969). Martin (1971 : 399–402) surveys previous discussion. This development postdates the period of classical French (seventeenth century).

Most Italian grammars repeat the claim that the contrast between the PASSATO PROSSIMO (in its PRET meaning) and the PASSATO REMOTO is one of spoken vs. written language. For a more nuanced picture, see Centineo (forthcoming).

19. The literature on French tenses contains numerous comparisons of these two tenses; among more recent pronouncements, cf. Martin (1971), Boyer (1979, 1985a, 1985b), Boulle (1981), Kamp and Rohrer (1983), and Vet and Molendijk (1985).

20. These are not the only varieties of narration in French. In less formal written varieties (e.g., journalistic or informal autobiographical narration), as well as more formal spoken varieties (e.g., in radio interviews), both PS and PC occur, the contrast expressing TEXTUAL and EXPRESSIVE meanings. Cf. Boyer (1979, 1985a, 1985b), Monville Burston and Waugh (1985), and Waugh and Monville Burston (1986).

21. If one accepts Derrida's view of *différance* (1968/1973), no narration can ever be simultaneous with the action it reports. What is conventionally understood as a simultaneous narration is one in which the distance between seeing and speaking is minimal.

22. The term "diegesis," which goes back to Plato's *Republic,* is used here to refer to sentences of *narration proper.* As used in this sense, diegesis contrasts, on the one hand, with *directly quoted speech,* which is "mimetic" (an imitation of real speech), and, on the other, with *commentary* by the narrator, which is neither mimetic—in that it is not a representation of speech but speech itself—nor diegetic—in that it refers not to the story-world but to the world of the narrator at the time of the narrating. On the evolution of the term "diegesis" in the critical metalanguages of literary and film theory, see Lanser (1981:19f.), Sternberg (1982), Rimmon-Kenan (1983:106ff.), and Ricoeur (1985:180).

This meaning of diegesis underlies my use of the term "diegetic PR" as a cover term for two distinct varieties of PR tense, both referring to the (past) time-frame of a story-world: the so-called HISTORICAL PRESENT (HP) and what I call the NARRATIVE PRESENT (NP). These contrast according to the type of narrative text in which they occur and according to their distribution in the text. The NP is exclusively a phenomenon of orally performed narratives, where it occurs in alternation with the PAST, while the HP is a cultivated feature of planned written narratives that generally occurs in sustained sequences. The relationship between these two varieties of diegetic PR is taken up in chapter 3.

23. For French, this claim has been advanced in Hatcher (1942), Brunot and Bruneau (1949), Imbs (1956), and Antoine (1959); for Spanish, in Gilman (1961) and Szertics (1967); for Italian, in Folena (1952), Ambrosini (1961), and Aigotti (1974).

24. Cf. Schächtelein (1911), Foulet (1919:§§325–326), Martin (1971:175ff.), and Ménard (1973:§146) for French; Stussi (1960–1961), Ambrosini (1961), Aigotti (1974), and Bertinetto (1987) for Italian.

25. Cf. text IV:65, where the same predicate *avoir (a) nom* occurs in the IMP.

26. For statistics on the textual frequency of tenses at various periods in French, see Martin (1971); also Blanc (1964) for the older language and Wilmet (1970) for Middle French. De Felice's (1957) statistics for the earliest French texts are invalidated by his failure to distinguish tense usage in dialogue from that in narrative diegesis (see §3.2 below), while Picken's figures for Old French (1979) are invalidated by an assumption of isomorphism between tense-aspect forms and meanings.

27. Among many commentators on Old French, cf. Brunot and Bruneau (1949:500), Fotitch (1950), Blanc (1964), Worthington (1966), and Schøsler (1973, 1985); on Old Spanish, Company (1983:254ff.); on Old Italian, Ageno (1964:200ff.).

28. A new *laisse* frequently begins with an anaphoric repetition of the last situation reported in the preceding *laisse.* The new *laisse* presents the situation from a different perspective, usually by a change of tense or aspect. In the last verse of *laisse* 212 (in the Whitehead edition) the command is given for Geoffroy of Anjou to sound his horn; in the first verse of *laisse* 213 this action is represented as completed, a meaning I have sought to capture in the translation through use of the passive.

29. In all three of the major early Romance vernaculars the temporal value of the PLP or PA is often not "before-past" but simply "past." The reading suggested here—PLP as an explicitly PFV "contextual variant" of the PS—has been proposed by Aigotti (1974) for the Old Italian TRAPASSATO REMOTO; for other investigators this form expresses "immediate completion" (Ambrosini 1961; Ageno 1964:299; cf. also Bertinetto 1986:479ff.), a reading that would also fit this example: "as soon as they were finished eating, his horse . . ." "Immediate completion" is also an appropriate meaning for the two PA verbs of text III (lines 10, 23).

Use of before-past tenses with simple past time reference is discussed in cross-linguistic perspective in Fleischman (1989b), where it is argued that this substitution often involves a metaphorical use of "distance in time" to express distance along other axes that receive linguistic coding in particular languages. Cf. also Dahl (1985:120).

30. Martin (1971:351) provides statistics based on six texts spanning the fourteenth and fifteenth centuries. During this period the diegetic PR declines from 30.5 percent to 0.84 percent overall text frequency.

Chapter 2. A Theory of Tense-Aspect in Narrative Based on Markedness

31. Among many treatments of markedness, cf. Jakobson (1957), Greenberg (1966), and Waugh (1982). In what follows I draw largely on Waugh's discussion and on Comrie (1976: chapter 6).

32. The difference between the minus- and zero-interpretations corresponds to the distinction made in logic and semiotics between relationships of contradictories (black vs. not-black, PAST vs. NONPAST) and relationships of contraries (black vs. white, PAST vs. PRESENT). The tense opposition in question is generally one of contradictories.

33. Admittedly, most narratives depart in some way from this normative profile, which probably reveals itself as much in the breach as in strict observance.

34. The association of PAST in narration with realis events offers another instance of a reversal in a marked context of a correlation normally operative in the unmarked context: the association of PRESENT with realis and PAST with irrealis. This correlation is founded on the metaphor of distance from a deictic center: a situation that is happening here-and-now (i.e., at the deictic center) can normally be vouched for by a speaker, who experiences it as actual and real. A situation that took place in the past (i.e., at some distance from the deictic center) has a different epistemic status; at the moment it is reported (S) it is no longer actual and real. In other words, temporal distance from now correlates with an epistemic distance from "reality" (cf. Steele 1975; James 1982; Fleischman 1989b). In narrative the temporal-deictic center is no longer the speaker's here-and-now (S) but an R in the past established by the discourse.

35. Sequentiality is not in principle part of the meaning of any tense but an implicature of PFV aspect in a narrative context. This point is developed in chapter 4.

36. Cluster concept or spectrum approaches have been fruitfully invoked with respect to other linguistic phenomena traditionally viewed as either/or propositions, such as subjecthood (Keenan 1976), transitivity (Hopper and Thompson 1980), discourse saliency (Longacre 1981; Chvany 1984, 1985; Fleischman 1985), and topicality. Andersen (1987) links this "post-binary bliss" that the field of linguistics is experiencing to a shift of interest from language structures to discourse (cf. also Hopper 1987).

37. The temporality of the PERF must be represented as [+ past] and [+ present], the past-present opposition being one of contraries not contradictories (cf. *n*32).

38. The "habitual" reading of the IMP is [− semelfactive], the "continuous" reading [+ semelfactive]. For its PR counterpart, the diegetic PR_v, only the continuous ([+ semelfactive]) reading occurs.

39. Following the conventional view in discourse studies, situations reported by an IPFV verb are normally backgrounded. While the correlation between IPFV aspect and background, PFV aspect and foreground, holds for the "narrative norm," it is argued in chapter 6 that *any* tense-aspect category can be used for foregrounding, provided it functions as the contextual "figure" against the "ground" established by some other category.

40. The IPFV P is commonly used for reporting events in dreams, visions, hallucinations, make-believe, and other states removed from reality; cf. Fleischman (1989b).

41. As Ducrot (1979 : 11) writes, "a statement in the IMP cannot be perceived as a narrative because its temporal topic [cf. §1.5.3] is not presented as a sequence of moments in time but as an unanalyzable bloc. . . . The listener does not have the impression of an unfolding of events outside of himself. What he is given is *depiction*, not narration" (my emphasis).

Chapter 3. "Ungrammatical" Tenses: Background of the Question

42. Kiparsky (1968) cites examples of tense switching, strikingly parallel to those documented in older Romance, from Vedic Sanskrit, Ancient Greek, Old Irish, Old Norse, and Latin, and from modern Icelandic and Albanian. For Ancient Greek, see also Rodemeyer (1889), von Fritz (1949), and Ruipérez (1982), the last offering a summary of previous discussion. On biblical Greek, see Enos (1981) and references provided there. For Old Norse, see Lehmann (1939), Sprenger (1951), Wood (1965), and Thomas (1974); for early Irish, Thomas (1974), Tristram (1983), and Fulk (1987). For Latin, see Emery (1897)—dated, but still of value, Schlicher (1931), Serbat (1975–1976), and, with particular reference to the historians, Chausserie-Laprée (1969) and Mellet (1980).

Among older languages within the Indo-European family, the phenomenon has been commented on in Middle Welsh (Evans 1964 : 119d), Old and Middle High German (for references, see Frey 1946 : 43*n*1), and notably English at various stages of its development. The narrative use of tenses, in particular the HP, in Middle and Early Modern English receives attention from Graef (1889) and Visser (1964, 1966 : §§760–779); cf. also Benson (1961) on Chaucer; Zimmerman (1973) on

Gawain; Steadman (1917) and Roloff (1921) on Middle English generally. Frey (1946) concentrates on the HP in Modern German fiction, but also surveys the Indo-European tradition. Chvany (1980) offers an insightful treatment of narrative tense-aspect usage in Old Russian (*Song of Igor's Campaign*).

Among modern languages of greater genetic remove, Gensler (1976) looks into the HP in a dialect of colloquial Arabic, Herring (1985a, 1986b) in Tamil and Japanese; on Japanese, see also Brannen (1979), Soga (1983), and Szatrowski (1985).

43. Cf. Sandmann (1957), Blanc (1964), Stefenelli-Fürst (1966), Paden (1977), and Pickens (1979). For Old French, discussion has concentrated on the *Song of Roland:* Bockhoff (1880), Hatcher (1942, 1946), Blanc (1965), Ruelle (1976), Grunmann-Gaudet (1980), and Goldin (1981); tense usage in the *Song of William* is examined in Grunmann (1976), and in the *Charroi de Nîmes* in Schøsler (1985, 1986). Tense switching in the unique exemplar of Old Spanish epic extant in its entirety, the *Poem of the Cid,* is discussed in Sandmann (1953), Gilman (1961), Myers (1966), Szertics (1967), and Montgomery (1968).

44. Tense usage in the Old French *Life of St. Alexis* (Hildesheim version) receives monographic treatment in Garey (1955); cf. also Yvon (1960) and Uitti (1973:50f., 1979); Paden (1977) cites examples from the *Alexis* as well as from other, late Latin and early Gallo-Romance hagiographic texts; statistics on tense usage from several saints' lives are included in the survey in Pickens (1979). Tense switching has also been observed in late medieval passions; albeit dramatized, these were often as much straight narration as theater. On the *Minstrels' Passion (Passion des jongleurs)*, see Perry (1981:54ff.). Tense alternations in the Old Spanish verse *Life of St. Mary the Egyptian (Vida de Santa María Egipciaca)* are noted briefly in the edition by Alvar (1972).

45. See Dembowski (1963:48–56) on Robert of Clari, Beer (1968:41*n*) on Villehardouin. Several chroniclers (Robert of Clari, Joinville, Froissart) are included in Blanc's cross-genre survey (1964) of temporal patterns in Old French narrative.

46. On tense switching in the *lais* of Marie de France, see Worthington (1966), Pickens (1979), and Beck (1988).

47. On romance in general, see Foulet (1919:§220), Sutherland (1939), Blanc (1961, 1964), Worthington (1966), Ollier (1978), and Pickens (1979). More narrowly, Schøsler (1985) focuses on the *Prose Tristan,* Wehr (1984) on the *Quest for the Holy Grail (Queste del Saint Graal)* and the Old Occitan romance of *Flamenca* (all thirteenth century), while Fotitch (1950) and Wigger (1978) devote monographs to the most celebrated of Old French *romanciers,* Chrétien de Troyes (late twelfth century), whose *Yvain* is also discussed in Uitti (1979).

48. Tense usage in this unique exemplar of the *chantefable* genre has been discussed by Foulet (1919, 1920), Blanc (1964), Schøsler (1973), and Stewart (1977). Schøsler finds the tense usage of dialogue (verse and prose) and prose narration to differ from that of verse narration; the latter conceivably reflects an earlier stage of linguistic development, while the former offers a closer approximation to the verbal system of spoken French in the thirteenth century.

49. The first to call attention to the tenses of the *romancero* was Spitzer (1911);

the matter has subsequently been taken up by Gilman (1961, 1967, 1972), Szertics (1967, 1974), Chevalier (1971), Sandmann (1974), Di Stefano (1976), and Mirrer-Singer (1986).

50. Examples in Paden (1977) and in the preferred edition of the *vidas* and *razos* (Boutière and Schutz 1964 : xxxix–xliv). The *vidas* purport to be mini-biographies of the poets whose songs they accompany, while the *razos* are intended as background information, explicating the historical contexts in which the songs were purportedly composed. It is now generally recognized that these ancillary narrative genres are as often as fictional as the primary lyric texts that they accompany—and from which their information is frequently drawn.

51. Brief references in Sandmann (1953).

52. The question arises whether tense switching can occur in lengthy narrative monologues, that is, where what is essentially "narration" is packaged as the direct speech of a character. The answer seems to be no, except in the narrative style known as *skaz* (see §4.6.3) and in the *romancero* (§8.2). Isolated instances of tense switching in direct speech in Old French have been noted by Blanc (1964 : 99*n*), Stefenelli-Fürst (1966 : 15, 52ff.), and Ollier (1978 : 101).

53. Cf. Burton (1980), Banfield (1982), Sternberg (1982), and Tannen (1982b, 1986).

54. Though story performance clearly moves narration in the direction of a dramatic representation, the theoretical distinction between diegesis and mimesis can never be collapsed. As Genette (1980 : 164) puts it, "in contrast to dramatic representation, no narrative can 'show' or 'imitate' the story it tells. All it can do is tell it in a manner which is detailed, precise, 'alive,' and in that way give it more or less the *illusion of mimesis*—which is the only narrative mimesis, for this single and sufficient reason: that narration, oral or written, is a fact of language, and language signifies without imitating."

55. Foulet was conceivably the first to posit a double stylistic tradition for medieval French: a "poetic style" for verse narrative in contrast to a "literary style" for prose and drama (the fragility of this opposition is demonstrated in Schøsler 1973 : 98f.). The idea of two grammars is then taken up by Gilman (1972 : 153), who refers to the language of the *romancero* as an "autonomous language, poetically derived from the mother tongue and grammatically different from the language of the *cantares de gesta*," and again by Schøsler (1973, 1985, 1986), who distinguishes, for French texts from ca. 1050–1300, a grammar of narrative from a grammar of direct speech. Where the two differ, Schøsler hypothesizes that narrative usage probably reflects an earlier stage of linguistic development.

56. This same argument is put forth with respect to tense switching in the *Cid* (Menéndez-Pidal 1908) and the *romancero* (Szertics 1967), and to certain uses of the HP in the writings of Latin historians (Chausserie-Laprée 1969).

57. She calculates 1,600 verbs in the PR as against 375 in the PS and 325 in the PC. However, PRs are not distinguished as to type or function; thus the figure of 1,600 includes, in addition to PRs whose temporal reference is "past," also generic PRs and PRs referring to the now of the performance.

58. My own examination of *Roland* does not bear out Hatcher's reading on this point. Goldin (1981:176) also has observed that the principles of tense usage in *Roland* often have nothing to do with temporal relations between events.

59. In line with this view, Visser (1966:§774) seeks to explain the absence of tense switching in *Old* English by appealing to the fact that the OE (alliterative) verse texts do not have a fixed meter and that neither rhyme nor meter is relevant to the prose texts. As we shall see, the evidence of other poetic traditions poses a serious challenge to the prosodic hypothesis. Furthermore, the rigid distinction Visser makes between verse and prose usage in Middle English has been called into question (Casparis 1975:21).

60. Similarly Benson (1961) and Casparis (1975) with respect to the diegetic PR in Chaucer, and McKay (1974) for the PR in ancient Greek. Ruipérez (1982:§259), however, points out that the diegetic PR in Greek is neither punctual nor durative, but neutral with respect to aspect; the frequent punctual readings (i.e., the fact that the PR more often replaces the AORIST than the IMPERFECT) are determined contextually and/or lexically (*Aktionsart*). For Latin, the IPFV interpretation of the diegetic PR, which goes back to Hoffmann (1884), is most persuasively argued in Schlicher (1931).

61. There appear to be languages (e.g., Tamil, Japanese) in which the diegetic PR substitutes for the IPFV rather than the PFV P (see Herring 1985a, 1986b). In such cases we would not want to claim that the PR is functioning aspectually—nor in "HP narration" (§8.3), where the PR tense appears in sustained sequences, encoding PFV (eventive) and IPFV (descriptive, characterizing) situations alike, and thereby blurring the distinction.

62. The idea that "present" is the default time reference underlies the claim that the PR is the unmarked tense of ordinary language.

63. Notwithstanding the validity of Kiparsky's claim that the PR in early Greek is a neutral or timeless form (the argument appears earlier in von Fritz 1949:196, and ultimately goes back to Wackernagel 1920:162ff.), his interpretations of the data he cites—for the most part decontextualized sentences—have been called into question not only for Greek (Levin 1969), but also for Vedic, Old Norse, and early Irish (Thomas 1974; Tristram 1983).

64. The vividness hypothesis has similarly been rejected by Frey (1946) for German; Visser (1966) for English; and Gilman (1961), Chaurand (1966), Reid (1970), and Paden (1977) for early Romance. Among conversational narratologists this position has been argued most forcefully by Wolfson (1979, 1982).

65. A theoretical question here arises: whether the "same story" can be told more than once. Most ethnomethodologists insist on the uniqueness of every "storytelling event" (understood as an individual story performance together with the context of its telling). Not only are the precise words used in each telling never the same, but, more importantly, each telling is tuned to the circumstances in which it occurs, subtly reflecting the concerns of the participants and their relations to each other and to the content of the story, as well as the fact that the story is being inserted at a particular juncture in a conversation, presumably to make a point relevant to the topic of discussion (cf. Georges 1969; Polanyi 1981). Such tailoring of stories to their situation contexts is known as *recipient design*. For other views on this question, cf. Wilensky (1982), Bauman (1986: chapter 5), and Shuman (1986: chapter 4). *Mutatis mutandis,* the above observations apply as well to vernacular narrative genres of the Middle Ages for which we assume a degree of improvisational composition-in-performance.

66. In Fleischman (1986b, 1989a) the repetitive sequences of *Roland*'s "similar *laisses*" are shown to function as one kind of "rhetorical underlining" (Longacre's term) through which narrative peaks are marked in surface syntax.

67. This difference forms the basis of the distinction posited in Bertinetto (1986:334f.) between the "dramatic PR" and the "narrative PR" (= my NP and HP, respectively). He notes that for Italian these two varieties of diegetic PR can also differ aspectually: only the "narrative PR" (HP) has habitual readings, but only the "dramatic PR" (NP) occurs in the PROG. These constraints hold for other languages with PROG aspect as well.

68. "Spontaneous" and "rhetorical" are not mutually exclusive. As argued above, rhetorical/stylistic devices are employed in virtually every utterance. Even where they are used consciously, the language user (writer or speaker) is often unaware of how or why they function to produce a desired effect.

69. Along similar lines, Herring (1986b) observes that tense switching in Tamil is particularly characteristic of the Puranic stories (tales about the lives of the gods), a variety of orally performed folk narrative that is likewise sung to musical accompaniment.

70. This position has also been argued by Serbat (1975–1976, 1980) and Mellet (1980) for the diegetic PR in Latin, and among conversational narratologists by Wolfson (1979, 1982). It is discussed further in chapter 6 (§6.6.1).

71. It is unclear whether Gilman intends "subject" in the traditional grammatical sense of the nominal argument governing verb agreement or in the sense of a sentence topic or even focus.

72. In addition to those cited, cf. Fotitch (1950) on Chrétien's romances and Zimmermann (1973) on the Middle English *Gawain.*

73. The correlation PFV (PS/PC) : singular/individuated :: IPFV (PR) : collective/unindividuated is fairly stable in the *chansons de geste* for the verbs *dire* (say) and *parler* (speak); however, the verb *respondre* (reply) appears regularly in the PR, irrespective of its grammatical subject.

74. This coherence between direct speech and its reporting sentence underlies my decision, in transcribing the texts in appendix 2, to code direct speech as part of the same "narrative clause" as its introducing verb.

75. As a *verbum dicendi* the English verb "go," like its French counterpart *faire,* is consistently in the PR.

76. Grimes (1975:91ff.) introduces the term "spans" to refer to stretches of text within which there is some kind of uniformity, be it of setting (all the actions that take place in a single spatial location), of *participant orientation* (stretches during which a single participant maintains a relatively high level of activity relative to other participants), or even of temporal setting (actions that take place without mention being made of discontinuities in the temporal line or without the intervention of a temporal adverb).

77. Cf. among others, Crosby (1936), Ong (1982b), Zumthor (1984a,b), and Roy (1988). The primary texts themselves also occasionally document the practice of reading aloud (e.g., Wace's *Romance of Rou,* the Occitan romance of *Flamenca,* the chronicles of Joinville and Froissart, and the most celebrated example, Dante's tale of Paolo and Francesca, *Inferno* V : 127–138).

78. Blanc (1964 : 116) links tense switching in the *Prose Lancelot* to the constructivist technique of "interlace." Romances of this type consist of an interlocking series of episodes; one is interrupted and another begins, only to be superseded in turn and followed by yet another until the first is picked up again, etc. In four out of five instances suspension of an episode is in the PR, resumption in the P, typically via a PASSÉ SIMPLE or PASSÉ ANTÉRIEUR (the PA is a PFV "before-past") in an anaphoric time clause. Chapter 6 examines the TEXTUAL considerations underlying this tendency for beginnings (of texts, episodes) and resumptions (of disjunctive episodes or of the "event line" following a break) to be reported in a PFV tense of the PAST. On the poetics of interlace, see Vinaver (1970, 1971), Ryding (1971), and Lacy (1974).

79. On the complex issue of defining literacy for the Middle Ages, the reader is referred to Bäuml (1980) and to Stock's monograph (1980) examining the role of "the text" in the twelfth century in creating a new type of interdependence between orality and writing. Stock explores how the functions of oral discourse changed under the influence of the written word, a change not so much from oral *to* written as from an earlier state, predominantly oral, to various combinations of oral *and* written.

80. On differences between an orally composed (and performed) text and a recitation/reading of a prepared written text, see Bäuml (1977, esp. pp. 90ff.).

81. Objections to the concept of transitional texts are raised by Scholes and Kellogg (1966) and by Bäuml (1984).

82. For an alternative, more concrete typology of oral text situations, based on compositional technique, mode of performance, and mode of reception, see Walker (1971).

83. "Literature" is here understood to refer to that body of discourses or texts that, within a society, are considered worthy of dissemination, transmission, and preservation in essentially constant form and are not perceived as simply everyday communication, a purely utilitarian use of language (Fabre and Lacroix 1974 : 70; Bright 1981 : 171). Resonating with this definition, which ultimately goes back to Hockett (1958), is John Ellis's pragmatic statement (1974 : 50) that "literature is not distinguished by defining characteristics but by the characteristic *use* to which those texts are put by the community."

84. The mini-narrative divisions I have proposed do not coincide strictly with the paragraph numbers given in parentheses at the left margin of text IV. This paragraph numbering *does not,* however, reflect the manuscripts, which differ among themselves in this regard. It was introduced by a nineteenth-century editor and has been generally adhered to since. From a comparison of the actual paragraph divisions of manuscripts *A* and *B,* representative of the two major manuscript families, Poirion (1978) concludes that modern editors have segmented Villehardouin's material according to a principle of chronology that was *not* the author's own organizational principle and that effectively camouflages his thinking and artistry. Poirion argues for a spatial rather than chronological organization: composition according to *scenes* built up around a nucleus of direct speech (cf. Labov 1982; Bauman 1986: chapter 4, for examples from very different genres in which stories are constructed around quoted speech). Poirion sees this spatial ground plan as the logical form for what he perceives to be Villehardouin's compositional enterprise: the forging of a narrative on the basis of memory—Villehardouin's own subjective memory of events in which he was often a participant—complemented by a variety of documentary sources. The passage cited in the appendix is paragraphs 85–87 of manuscript *A*, 109–110 of manuscript *B*. For *A*, 85 = 155mid–157, 86 = 158–161, 87 begins with 162; for *B*, 109 = 155, 110 = 159–162mid.

85. On the theatricality of medieval performed stories, see in particular Frappier's observations (1969:169–176) on the dialogues and monologues of Chrétien's *Yvain* and Alonso's vividly imaginative account (1944) of the *Cid* as "semirepresentation"—something between recital and full-fledged theater. On gesture and other paratextual features in the early epics, see Chasca (1967:118f.), Smith and Morris (1967), and Brault (1978:111–115).

Chapter 4.   Narrative Discourse: Typological Considerations

86. On the various formalist and structuralist avatars of this distinction, see Culler (1980) and Ricoeur (1985:180n40).

87. The unmarked point of view in a narrative is that of the narrator. But it is also the case that narrators undertake to tell what others have seen or experienced. Thus "speaking" and "seeing," narration and point of view, or what Genette (1980) has labeled *focalization,* may but need not be associated with the same agent. This question is taken up in chapter 7.

88. "Story schemata" should not be confused with "story grammars." The former are mental objects; the latter are rule sets, theoretical formalizations that relate the ordering of surface-text categories to the underlying schemata (Beaugrande 1982:410; Wilensky 1982:426).

For a critical overview of the literature on story grammars, see Beaugrande (1982) and Rimmon-Kenan (1983: chapter 2). Just as TG sentence grammars claim to be able to discriminate between grammatical and ungrammatical sentences of a language, a major goal of story grammars is to distinguish stories from nonstories. Yet in the considerable literature on what constitutes a well-formed story—whether from the perspective of cognitive psychology, artificial intelligence, or literary theory—little attention has been paid to *cultural* differences in story structure. Virtually all story grammars (and story schemata!) that have been proposed have a decidedly Western bias, especially as regards the need for closure or resolution: Western narrative consumers require that "the sense of an ending" (Kermode 1967) be superimposed upon mere succession. Jarrett (1984) reports that American Indian coyote tales are often frustrating to Anglo-American readers because the adventures are relentlessly episodic, building to no final climax or conclusion. Medieval romances often elicit the same response from modern students for the same reason. With respect to narrative fiction, Virginia Woolf credited Chekhov with helping us see that "inconclusive stories are legitimate" (reported in Dick's introduction to *The Complete Shorter Fiction of Virginia Woolf*, p. 1).

89. "Punctual" would be preferable to "instantaneous"; of the two telic situation types, only achievements are instantaneous, whereas both achievements and accomplishments are punctual.

90. Cf. the section of *Time and Narrative, I* entitled "Historical Time and the Fate of the Event" (Ricoeur 1984:206–225). Other philosophers of history (William H. Walsh, William Dray) have referred to these experiential umbrella structures as "colligations": verbal constructs that allow us to apprehend a set of historical situations under a common denominator.

91. Bronzwaer (1970) discusses Michael Frayn's novel *A Very Private Life*, which casts storytelling at least in part in the FUT.

92. These observations emerged from discussion with Susan Herring.

93. Thus Banfield (1982:3) writes, "Narrative, understood as that modern genre known as 'narrative fiction' . . . has come to incarnate literature itself."

94. Interested readers are referred to Searle (1974, 1979), Schmidt (1976), and Adams (1985), among linguistically oriented discussions, while Toliver (1974) and Ricoeur (1984, 1985, 1988) tackle the question in the context of broad-ranging explorations of temporality and narrative representation; see in particular Ricoeur (1988: chapter 5).

95. When reference is specifically to the participants in the embedded communicative context, initial uppercase is used. Just as the Speaker in this model (which is not restricted to *narrative* fiction) corresponds to a narrator, the Hearer corresponds to what literary theoreticians label the "implied reader" or "narratee" (for references to critical discussion on this participant, see Lanser 1981:53n60). Adams finds the "implied" participants superfluous in that they are not part of the context in any pragmatic sense, though he acknowledges the usefulness of the "implied author" concept, introduced by Booth (1961), as a convenient reference point for the ideology of the text, a hook on which to hang its norms and values.

96. Cf. Lanser (1981:110): "the act of communication is visible in novelistic fiction as in few forms of written discourse. Indeed, the semantics of novelistic discourse, with its terms like 'teller' and 'audience,' emphasizes oral conventions, perhaps revealing discomfort with the fact of mass communication, a wish to restore the ancient, less complicated relationship between teller, story, and listener that seems to characterize the oral traditions and the folktale."

97. This distinction is admittedly an oversimplification of a complex issue that is not pursued further here. Suffice it to note that among experience narratives some are more "self-oriented," others more "other-oriented" (Stahl 1983; Genette 1980 draws an analogous distinction).

98. A major methodological flaw of several studies on tense usage in Old French (Wigger 1978; Pickens 1979) is their mechanical application of Weinrich's categories to the verbal system of Old French.

99. Benveniste refers to this category as the "*-rait* form" (*il ferait*) to avoid privileging either its temporal (FUT-OF-P) or modal (COND) meaning.

100. Comrie (1985:26ff.) insists that sequentiality is not part of the *meaning* of the PS (or of any PFV P) but simply an implicature that emerges from general conversational principles (specifically, Grice's maxim of manner: be orderly) in the particular context of narrative. The most "orderly" presentation (Grice 1975) in narration is for the chronological order of events to be reflected directly in the order of presentation (iconic sequence), if the speaker is capable of doing so (i.e., if he or she knows the order of events). It is the interaction among the meaning of PFV aspect, the narrative context, and this conversational principle that gives rise, in neutral contexts, to a sequential interpretation for a succession of PFV events (Comrie 1985:28).

Relevant to Weinrich's claim that sequentiality is an exclusive property of the PS, which has developed into the NARR tense par excellence in French, is an observation made by Dahl (1985) apropos of languages with specialized NARR tenses (certain Niger-Congo languages). He speculates (1985:114) that the original function of such tenses was as the second member of constructions of the type "*x* and (then) *y*," which would explain the synchronic tendency for verbs in NARR tenses to be "in some way subordinated to or otherwise syntactically connected to the preceding verb."

101. Of eleven instances of the formula *m(i)en escïent(re)* in *Roland* this is the only one not occurring in direct speech. Metanarrative interventions of this type by the composer-reciter are rare in the *chansons de geste*.

102. Elsewhere Butor (1969:81) comments that "whenever one wants to describe a real progression of consciousness . . . the second person is the most effective." With this in mind I have adapted Stewart's translation using the PR PROG as the equivalent of the French PR. In chapter 8 we shall look again at this text (§8.4) as an example of monologic fiction that takes place entirely in the silent language of its Speaker. Butor's use of *vous* is more than just an injunction to the reader. It has been suggested that the second person of *Second Thoughts* originates in psychic repression, marking a gap in the self-awareness of the narrator, who in the first instance is addressing himself and only secondarily the readership (Sturrock 1969:169f.). Monologic language makes the "I" and the "you" coincide, each pronoun containing the other within itself; nor do we need psychologists to tell us that the self often takes itself for an audience. "You" is appropriately the pronominal form of individuals who perform acts of self-reflection, who scrutinize their own consciousness. In line with Sturrock's observation above, it is significant to note that the second-person form chosen for this dialogue with the self is not the pronoun of familiarity (*tu*) but that of estrangement (*vous*). For references to other texts that "compulsively buttonhole a second person who seems to be simultaneously inside and outside the fictional scene, inside and outside the speaking self," see Cohn (1978:178ff., 304*n*15).

103. The issue of empathetic presuppositions in medieval narrative confronts the sociohistorical philologist with a particularly thorny problem that cuts across the question of genre: implicated in the texts of different genres are different story-world conventions and different sets of beliefs on the part of text producers and recipients. Any attempt to reconstruct these presuppositions, largely through intertextual hermeneutic procedures, would clearly fall outside the perimeter of this investigation. Fortunately, medievalists working within the reader-response framework have begun to take steps in this direction (see in particular Jauss 1970; Gumbrecht 1981).

104. Östmann (1981) argues that "you know" functions as a pragmatic formula used when the speaker wants the addressee to *accept as mutual knowledge* (or at least be cooperative with respect to) the propositional content of the utterance. Formulaic language in general is acknowledged by oral theorists to be a convenient way of signaling shared knowledge, of which involvement formulas such as "you know" are perhaps the most explicit articulation. *Sabet* (var. *sabed*) occurs twenty-seven times in the *Cid*.

105. It has been argued that these formulas of direct address to an audience cannot be taken as incontrovertible evidence of oral performance, given that expressions such as Sp. *commo oyredes* (as you will hear), *commo oyestes* (as you heard) are often "purely conventional phrases that persist into the 16th century" (Walker 1971: 41). The question of "oral residue" in literate texts is addressed in chapter 3 (§3.10), where it is pointed out that the writers' imitations of or references to the oral style are themselves significant.

106. I assume that in this text Speaker$_1$ = COMPOSER and Hearer$_1$ = LISTENERS. A more detailed analysis of the *skaz* structure of "Castia-gilos" must be deferred to a separate study.

107. In expository writing we use the PR to speak of authors long dead as "saying" *x* or *y* that is found in their *extant* works, whereas we would not use this tense to report on the content of works known indirectly, the actual text having been lost. Accessible (hence timeless) information is referred to in the PR, ephemeral information in the P.

108. This recalls Benedetto Croce's distinction between "chronicle" and "history": a chronicle is history cut off from the living present and, in this sense, applied to a dead past. History, properly speaking, is viscerally linked to the present and to action (cited in Ricoeur 1984: 255*n*).

Chapter 5. The Linguistic Structure of Narrative

109. These terms are used in place of what I have elsewhere (Fleischman 1985, 1986a) referred to as speech-event time and narrated-event time. This distinction between speaker-now and story-now should not be confused with that between the *time of the telling* and *time of the tale* (*temps du signifiant* vs. *temps du signifié*, *Erzählzeit* vs. *erzählte Zeit*). The time of the tale refers to duration and chronology in the story-world (*fabula*), the time of the telling to the ordering of material in the text that models that world (*sjuzhet*). Into this schema Ricoeur (1985: 77ff.) introduces a third kind of time, a fictive experience of time projected by the conjunction/disjunction between the time of the telling and the time of the tale.

110. I translate the Sp. FUT *oiréis* with an IMPER; the second FUT verb refers to the discourse itself: *lo que diran* is "what they will say" in the verses that follow.

111. The discussion in this section draws on Kamp and Rohrer (1983).

112. The IPFV tense options given in (5.11) are also acceptable with "four hours later."

113. But as Ricoeur (1984:152) points out, in many narratives *propter hoc* is not always easily extracted from *post hoc* inasmuch as the "logic" of a story (the causal relationships linking successive events) often reveals itself only at the end; only by "reading backward" from the conclusion do we understand why things had to "turn out" as they did.

114. Cf. Toliver (1974:3): "a liking for continuous plots is unquenchable and leads us to invent them even where we do not find them—which is nearly everywhere." The gaps that inevitably occur in every literary text have been a particular focus of concern in reader-oriented approaches to narrative, which have sought to formalize the processes through which the reader/listener/spectator fills in these gaps (see Iser 1971).

115. Cf. Sternberg (1978), Genette (1980), Bal (1985). A case against iconic sequence and for "anachrony" (as the norm for presenting material in narrative fiction) is argued in Mendilow (1952), Barbara Herrnstein Smith (1981), and Rimmon-Kenan (1983); also in Shuman (1986) for adolescent natural narratives.

116. Among many commentaries on *Roland*'s lack of causal and temporal verisimilitude, see Vinaver (1971), Grunmann-Gaudet (1980), Goldin (1981), Lock (1981, 1985).

117. Beginning *in medias res* was not only a characteristic of the orally composed genres of the Middle Ages, but also of romances composed in writing. The rhetorical manuals that set forth the guidelines for poetic composition recommended artificial order as being more elegant than natural order (Faral 1924:60).

118. This claim requires qualification. For languages with PROG aspect, the PROG PR can appear in Orientation and still refer to the story-world (*"I'm walking into the house* when all of a sudden . . ."); likewise stative verbs ("Lady Alda *is* in Paris"; "swarms of that pagan race *are gathered* there"). In *Roland* nonstative verbs can appear in Orientation clauses in the SIMPLE PR, as they do in HP narration. But in all instances what is at issue is the visualizing, not the action PR.

119. Direct speech is acknowledged to be the most common linguistic strategy for marking narrative Peaks (Longacre 1981; Li 1986). In Fleischman (1986b, 1989a) I discuss the use of direct speech to mark narrative Peaks in *Roland*.

120. The Peak at clause o (line 44) is in the PS in the manuscript on which our text is based (manuscript E), but in the PR in another manuscript (N_2).

121. Given the limited use of subordination in the *romancero* and the fact that *que* is a loose, catch-all conjunct often inserted for metrical reasons, I would not insist in calling the sentence in lines 57—58 subordinate. It may conceivably represent a sentence of *free indirect discourse* reporting Alda's interior verbalization of the news of Roland's death. The IMP verb *era muerto* (was dead/had been killed) supports this reading.

122. The composer-singers of the *chansons de geste* are here an exception. The minstrel formulas *De ço qui chalt?* (To whom does it matter?—vv. 1405, 1840, 1913) and *Que fereient il plus/el?* (What more/else could they do?—vv. 1185, 2691, 2812) are among the rare instances of external evaluation in *Roland*.

123. Villehardouin's undisguised bias on the events he narrates typically takes the form of external evaluation of this sort; cf. §§220, 271, 379, 409 of the Faral edition.

124. Observe the parallelism between the temporal structure of "narrative statements" and that of relative tenses, in particular the PLP. Three temporal positions are implied in a narrative statement: the focal event (= E), a subsequent event in reference to which the first event takes on historical significance (= R), and the configurational moment of historical consciousness (= S). The ordering of these three moments—E < R < S—matches the temporal structure of a before-past tense.

125. Narration of this type is pragmatically acceptable only in artistic story performance, where the entertainment value of the text and/or the pleasure of "putting it all together" offset logical and chronological discontinuities. The most successful medium for this kind of multiple-story narration is film, for obvious reasons.

126. The opening paragraph of this thirteenth-century prose romance informs us that Walter Map was commissioned by his lord King Henry to complete the vast romance project known as the *Prose Lancelot* or *Vulgate Cycle* by telling of *The Death of King Arthur*. The "story" referred to in these passages is that told by Map, which underlies the anonymous Old French text cited here. In line with the argument put forth in chapter 4 concerning the timelessness of fiction—the story remains ever accessible—the PR-tense verbs referring to this story (boldfaced) are appropriately generic/timeless.

127. As seen in chapter 6, the main-subordinate clause distinction is not always a reliable indicator of whether a clause is "on the time line." In particular, temporal subordinates introduced by "when" or other perfectivizing adverbs can refer to sequentially ordered events (see §6.1.2).

128. Texts I–VI are limited to the diegetic PR_a; texts VII–XII also make use of the diegetic PR_v, which does not occur in narrative clauses. Though both types occur in *Alexis*, only the action variety appears in the passage excerpted as text XI.

129. I distinguish *project* situations ("wage war," "raise cattle," "have a dinner party"), which subsume a variety of *diverse actions* under a single project label, from what I call *mass* situations ("slay seven knights," "eat up all the chocolates," "give a series of lectures"), which package together multiple iterations of the *same action*. Mass situations are often produced by quantifying singulative count situations (cf. II:70–73; X:6, 7).

130. For an opposing view, see Labelle (1987); regrettably, her supporting data (1987:16) consist of decontextualized sentences whose discourse status cannot be verified by the reader.

131. Note that clauses k, m, and n contain mass verbs, clause l a project verb (cf. *n*129), all converted to achievements by the NP. This telescoping technique, combined with a syntax of simple short clauses, creates an impression of staccato, quasi-robotic movement on the part of Aucassin.

132. The number sign (#) marks the place of the Old French clause-initial particle *si*, whose pragmatic function is discussed in chapter 6 (§6.3.2).

133. For Wolfson (1982: 43ff.), the two verbs form part of the same event—in this case a speech act—and therefore maintain the same tense, though she admits exceptions. Silva-Corvalán (1983: 772) argues that in an action-speech sequence the two verbs are treated by speakers as a single complex verb, analogous to serial verb constructions and that this "holistic" view motivates use of the same tense for both verbs.

134. In this text the PS *dis* is used consistently to introduce direct speech, while the PR *ditz* introduces indirect speech. This distribution of tenses provides a piece of counterevidence to Fotitch's suggestion (1950) that introduction-to-discourse verbs tend to select the PR because of their affinity to the communication mode (cf. §3.9.1).

Chapter 6.   Textual Functions

135. In Fleischman (1985) I refer to this TEXTUAL function as "narrative subordination," a metaphor based on the analogy between the syntax of a sentence and that of a text, both involving the hierarchical arrangement of elements according to the relative importance the speaker/narrator attaches to them.

136. On this analogy, see Wallace (1982), Chvany (1984), and Reinhart (1984). For an overview of the foreground-background distinction with respect to discourse, see Weber (1983), van Peer (1986: chapter 1), and Givón (1987).

137. Similarly, Matthiessen and Thompson (1988) speak of "nuclei" and "satellites" of a discourse, Reid (1976) of "high" and "low" focus (on events).

138. Among experimental studies to demonstrate the psycholinguistic validity of foreground-background in discourse, see Erbaugh (1987). Alternatively, it has been suggested that only the concept of foreground has real psycholinguistic validity, background being everything that is not foreground (Dan Slobin, personal communication). This view also finds support in the recent literature: with respect to aspect, Chvany (1984) observes that in Russian the correlation between PFV aspect and foreground appears to be stronger than that between IPFV and background, while with respect to clause-type Thompson (1987) finds a stronger link in English between main clauses and foreground than between subordinate clauses and background. The correlations are taken up below.

139. Hopper and Thompson (1980) define transitivity as a cluster concept involving ten oppositional variables. These are listed below in SMALL CAPS, with the opposing values (or for scalar variables the end values of the continuum) given in parentheses. The boldfaced feature correlates with high transitivity, the nonboldfaced with low transitivity. The variables include: (1) PARTICIPANTS (**2 or more participants—A[gent] and O[bject]**/single participant), (2) KINESIS (**action**/nonaction), (3) ASPECT (**telic**/atelic), (4) PUNCTUALITY (**punctual**/non-punctual), (5) VOLITIONALITY (**volitional**/nonvolitional), (6) AFFIRMATION (**affir-mative**/negative), (7) MODE (**realis**/irrealis), (8) AGENCY (**A high in potency**/A low in potency), (9) AFFECTEDNESS OF OBJECT (**O totally affected**/O not affected), and (10) INDIVIDUATION OF OBJECT (**O highly individuated**/O nonindividu-ated). Every clause in a text is assigned an overall transitivity rating based on its combined scores for the above variables, each of which represents a different facet of "the effectiveness or intensity with which the action is transferred from one par-ticipant to another" (Hopper and Thompson 1980:252).

140. According to Hopper (1979a, 1982a), "completion," now considered the basic meaning of PFV aspect, arose as a secondary meaning derived from the need to bound events in discourse in order to recount them as a sequence.

141. Chung and Timberlake (1985:217) point out that, as applied to states, closure (= boundedness) implies a complete change of state, specifically *inception* rather than termination.

142. Here as elsewhere for twelfth-century French, I translate the PC (*sont asis*) as a PFV PR ("are seated") rather than as a PERF.

143. Chvany (1984) offers Slavic data that challenge the conventional associa-tion between PFV aspect and foreground, IPFV aspect and background. These data suggest that, in Russian, aspect does not grammaticalize grounding, as Weinrich, Hopper, and others have claimed for other languages including French.

144. Only 40 occurrences in 4,000 lines, or 1 per 100 lines.

145. Cf. Weinrich (1973:115): "It is . . . impossible to decide *a priori* what in a narrative is to be assigned to . . . the foreground. . . . The foreground is what an author wishes to make foreground."

146. Longacre (1981) reports the findings of studies on discourse organization in a variety of unrelated languages, certain of which (Biblical Hebrew, Halbi [an Indo-European language of India], Northern Totonac [Mexico]) show just such a "spectrum" correlation between levels of grounding, or information relevance, and tense-aspect categories and situation types. While the particulars of each linguistic system are different, the basic strategies are parallel.

147. The auxiliary construction *sunt monté* is one of many PCs in *Roland* that are ambiguous between a present state reading ("they *are mounted*") and a past with present relevance ("they *have mounted*"). Cf. also *ad remés* (is not left/has not remained; v. 101).

148. Note that where a subject pronoun is inserted (*et il se herbergierent de-denz*, "and *they* remained inside") it seems to function as a marker of switch ref-erence (i.e., it signals a change of subject), while *si* marks subject continuity. This discourse-pragmatic analysis of *si* will be pursued in more detail in a separate study. Most grammars of Old French at least make reference to this particle. It is dis-cussed most extensively by Rychner (1970: chapter 6) and Marchello-Nizia (1985).

149. The occurrence of *e* together with *si* in this clause (*e si entendia en ma dona Adelaide*), also in lines 16 and 84, buttresses my claim that *si* should not be viewed as merely a coordinating conjunction meaning "and."

150. The juxtapositional "narrative syntax" of the *chansons de geste* has been likened to that of the Bayeux tapestry (Lock 1981:292) and the tympanum of the Madeleine at Vézelay (Hatzfeld 1952:8); cf. also Vinaver (1964b:480f.).

151. Interestingly, several hundred years later a move in the opposite direction seems to have taken place: Leech and Short (1981:249ff.) note a progressive tendency in English fiction writing over the past three centuries to dispense with formal sentence connectives and to rely instead on inferred connections or simple juxtaposition.

The pejorative connotations that attach to parataxis in certain quarters may be historical in origin. In the classical tradition paratactic constructions belonged to the "low style," being decidedly oral rather than written (Vinaver 1964b:481).

152. The absence of explicit subordinators ("before," "after," "because") has also been identified as a distinctive feature of performed stories (Wolfson 1982:41).

153. This is even truer of written narrative, which shares with its oral counterpart the condition of unfolding through (reading) time. The constraints of linearity can be relaxed to a degree only in cinematic or certain other forms of *visual* narrative in which stories unfold in both space and time, thus facilitating violations or fragmentation of the conventionally linear representation of time. Much has been written on this subject: for synoptic overviews, see Segre (1979) and Sternberg (1978).

154. Neither the epics nor the *romances* meet these criteria, being as much descriptive and lyrical as they are narrative, and their grounding patterns differ accordingly from those of normative narration. Discussion of these genres is deferred to chapter 8.

155. The frequency of the IMP in the verse stanzas of *Aucassin and Nicolette* is lower than average for the thirteenth century. In the excerpt from Villehardouin (text IV), composed earlier in the same century, the IMP is better represented. In the latter text all verbs of continuous action (i.e., verbs in "restricted" clauses) occur in the IMP except the verb *être* (to be).

156. The situations reported in the NP also score consistently higher on the transitivity and saliency hierarchies (see §6.1.3) than those reported in the PS.

157. The only other "when"-clause in text III (line 44) contains a general PR. In text VI:42, the clause *quant ho auziron* (when they heard this) is also a time-line subordinate; it is not coded as a narrative clause because it is reported out of sequence (in the chronology of the *fabula* her ladies "heard this," line 42, before they "came from inside," line 41).

158. The *laisse* is the strophic unit of the *chansons de geste* and of certain other Old French texts. It consists of a variable number of verses (from five to thirty-five in *Roland*) united by a common assonance (the later epics use rhyme). The *laisse* does not correspond to a recognizable unit of narrative content (event, scene, episode), nor does it have a definable narrative structure, though there is often a perceptible decline in tension at the end. The intricate patterns through which epic *laisses* are linked to one another are analyzed in Rychner (1955).

159. Wolfson (1978, 1979, 1982) adopts the term "(Conversational) Historical Present" to refer to the PR tense that alternates with the P in naturally occurring performed stories (= my NP).

160. The paragraph divisions (*pericopae*) of the Gospel according to St. Mark, which shares a number of "orality" features with vernacular epic (asyndeton, parataxis, heavy use of direct speech and of the diegetic PR), also are marked by a shift to the PR tense (see Enos 1981).

161. Similarly in early Biblical Hebrew, the PERF aspect (anteriority) tends to be used at the opening of new thematic paragraphs where not only participants but also themes change (Givón 1977).

162. Cf. Zimmermann (1973) on the use of the PERF to bound macro-events in the Middle English *Gawain*.

163. Cf. *Roland*, vv. 402–403, 405–406, 2842, 3697. The example in (6.42a) is the sole instance of *tant* PS *que* PS.

164. Cf. *AN* 18:2, 19:3–7, 20:27, 28:24, 30:16, 34:10. The example in (6.44), in which tense switching does occur, is somewhat atypical.

165. I read this PC as a resultant-state PR: "Roland has the olifant placed at his lips" (i.e., as an NP, rather than as a PERF). Cf also *nn*140 and 147.

Chapter 7.   Expressive Functions

166. The extensive literature on this topic cannot be surveyed here; for a range of viewpoints, cf. Friedemann (1910), Doležel (1967, 1980), Stanzel (1971), Uspensky (1973), Cohn (1978), Genette (1980), and Lanser (1981), the last providing a history of critical discussion for the Western literary tradition. In Doležel (1980) point of view is linked to the problem of "authentication": the credibility of various sources of information in a fictional text; here we see yet another instance where narrative theory has coopted a grammatical category associated with the verb, in this instance evidentiality (defined in *n*190).

167. This distinction between the speaking subject and the source of subjectivity was first suggested by Brooks and Warren (1943), whose term "focus of narration" inspired Genette's term "focalization." Genette coined his term to avoid the explicitly visual connotations associated with the roughly equivalent terms "point of view," "vision" (Pouillon 1946), or "field." Once Genette made focalization a topic of critical interest, his typology of focalizations was refined by other theorists, notably Bal (1983) and Vitoux (1982); these refinements are considered below.

168. His typology was inspired by that of Pouillon (1946), who speaks of "seeing from the outside" (external focalization), "seeing with" (internal focalization), and "seeing from behind" (zero-focalization). Pouillon derived this classification from the striking analogy he perceived between narrative fiction and "real psychological understanding" (1946:69).

169. As Bal (1983) has convincingly demonstrated, Genette's original typology is based on two different criteria: while his distinction between nonfocalized and internally focalized utterances refers to the perceiving subject (the focalizer), that between internally and externally focalized utterances refers to the perceived object (the focalized).

170. As Banfield (1982:195) writes: "in first-person narration the *I* is divided by time into a SELF caught always in the NOW of consciousness and a SPEAKER narrating in a moment for which the NOW of consciousness is always past." The distinction between what Banfield calls SPEAKER and SELF appears in the critical literature under variant nomenclatures: *erzählendes Ich* vs. *erlebendes Ich* (Spitzer 1928), *sujet d'énonciation* vs. *sujet d'énoncé* (Todorov 1970), narrator-I vs. character-I (Bellos 1978). Cf. also Butor (1969), Bronzwaer (1970), and Hamburger (1973).

171. An exception to the constraint against co-occurrence of "now" with PFV PAST tenses is provided by inchoatives, which mark the beginning of a process. Nef (1980:148) cites the example: *maintenant les couvertures commencèrent [PS] à le gêner* (now the blankets began [PS] to bother him). But this "now" is as much, if not more, a discourse-referential adverb than a temporal adverb; it marks a new narrative development, reported appropriately by a converted achievement. Without the inchoative auxiliary *gêner* remains an activity and the sentence is ungrammatical (**maintenant les couvertures le gênèrent*).

172. Note that in (7.5) the so-called experiencing-self of the last sentence is Kate, although the activities she "reexperiences" in her mind are not her own, but Reed's.

173. For those who hold this view, the appearance of free indirect discourse is linked to the moment when third-person fiction enters the domain previously reserved for first-person (epistolary or confessional) fiction (Cohn 1978:133ff.). Cerquiglini (1984:14) adds that the "modern" phenomenon of free indirect discourse in French, whose most distinctive linguistic mark is the IMP, not only begins but ends with the nineteenth-century novel, its text frequency already on the decline by the mid-twentieth century. Leech and Short (1981:332) cite several studies claiming evidence of free indirect discourse in pre-nineteenth-century fiction in England.

174. Bronzwaer (1970) offers examples from nonfictional, albeit written texts— a linguistics article, a letter to a magazine, a popular history book; Leech and Short (1981:332) cite a study documenting the phenomenon in a seventeenth-century account of Lancaster witch trials. Haberland (1986) claims that, in Danish, sentences of free indirect discourse also occur in conversational narration. Likewise Polanyi (1981:159) for English; however, the two examples she cites in support of her claim do not hold up to scrutiny.

175. A qualification: my emphasis on shifted tenses (and third-person pronouns) as the defining mark of free indirect discourse is based on a norm of past-tense, third-person narration. Yet the free indirect mode can occur in first- as well as third-person narration, PR- as well as P-based. The crucial issue, as Leech and Short (1981:329ff.) point out, is that the choice of tense and person in the reported utterance must be consistent with the primary discourse situation (i.e., with the tense and person of the reporting utterance). Leech and Short's definition of free indirect discourse is accordingly fairly broad, based on "family resemblance" rather than on the obligatory presence of specific linguistic features.

176. The terms *locuteur* and *éconciateur* (= speaker/narrator and focalizer, respectively) belong to the metalanguage of the French *théories de l'énonciation,* elaborated in slightly differing formulations by Oswald Ducrot (see esp. Ducrot 1984: chapter 8) and Antoine Culioli (see Simonin 1984). I find these terms problematic insofar as both seem to imply a *speaking* subject; yet only the *locuteur* speaks, *sensu stricto,* even when quoting directly.

177. When conversational narrators appear to do this, as in (7.14a), the statement must technically be viewed as an inference, not an assertion.

178. According to Leech and Short's criteria for free indirect discourse stated in *n*175 above (i.e., consistency in tense and person between the reporting and the reported discourse), interior monologue could be included under the heading of free indirect discourse. According to the stricter grammatical criteria adopted here, however, the two differ.

179. This episode (*Recherche,* I : 44ff./*Remembrance,* I : 34f.) has conceivably received more critical attention—not surveyed here—than any other in the novel. For a perceptive reading of the passage (and of the *Remembrance* as a whole) with particular regard to Proust's handling of time, see Ricoeur (1985 : 130−152) and references provided there, also Genette (1980), esp. chapter 1. Proust's own thoughts on the role of tense in narrative fiction are set forth in his essay "About Flaubert's Style" (Proust 1920/1948).

180. These digressions in the generic PR are a distinctive feature of Proust's narrative style, which "displays all the disillusioned wisdom the narrator has culled from his iterative past" (Cohn 1978 : 148).

181. Alternatively, this passage may be read as extradiegetic narrator commentary embedded into the lyric meditation, in which case the PR verbs would have past time reference. As shown in chapter 8, it cannot always be determined unambiguously whether the source of certain utterances—particularly utterances in the PR tense—is a character or the narrator.

182. Though this passage is taken from a constructed (fictional) dream narration, the claim that the IMP is in many languages the unmarked reporting tense for dreams is based on naturally occurring dream narrations.

183. This statement radically oversimplifies the process through which the contents of the dreamer's unconscious come to be articulated in language. In *The Interpretation of Dreams* Freud distinguishes two stages in this process, both of which are prior to language. The first maps the "latent content" of the dream (repressed wishes) onto a "manifest content," mainly in the form of disconnected and symbolically disguised images. At a second stage this manifest content, when recalled in waking consciousness, is again reordered ("secondary revision") as a precondition for remapping the dream content (now already twice transformed) onto linguistic structures capable of being reported. It is not coincidental that data retrieved from the unconscious come to be reported via the same grammatical category as data retrieved from deep memory.

184. Banfield does not draw the analogy between the "past cotemporal with now" and the continuous action meaning of the IMP, though it fits with her argument, completing the four-term homology, the other equation being the more transparent association of the "habitual past" with the habitual action meaning of the IMP.

185. Cf. Groethuysen (1935−1936 : 189, 180f.): "Recollection" [*le souvenir*] and memory [*la mémoire*] are not the same thing. In my recollections . . . I *relive* what has taken place, I relive my life. Recollection is the evocation of a past which is experienced, just as recall [*rappel*] is the evocation of a past become knowledge."

186. Of interest in this context is Genette's analysis (1966:74) of time, tense, and memory in the opening section of Robbe-Grillet's *Voyeur*. The first forty pages of the novel contain four temporal planes: the main character's present, recent past, distant past (recollections of childhood), and hypothetical future. Of these, Genette observes, it is the distant past that stands out linguistically; while the other three rely essentially on the PS, the traditional tense of the novel and of real *actions,* the events that constitute the distant past are reported subjectively as *recollections,* and no one expects to see them enlivened into real action. They are accordingly reported in IPFV tenses, notably the IMP.

187. For an overview of the controversy surrounding the PC as a tense of written narration in French, see Wilmet (1976). On Camus's use of this tense, see Barrera-Vidal (1968), on whose reading of the text I draw.

188. On the introduction of spoken language into French novelist discourse, see Bloch-Michel (1963:114ff.), also Barthes's essay "Writing and Speech" (in Barthes 1967).

189. A parallel example involving the PLP is discussed in Bronzwaer (1970). Looking at the use of this tense with simple past time reference in the novels of George Moore and Iris Murdoch, he observes that both writers use the PLP to adjust the degree of empathetic involvement projected by the narrator. But whereas Moore invokes the PLP to signal a lesser degree of empathy, Murdoch uses it to express greater empathy. Bronzwaer explains the difference as a function of contrast with shifting contextual norms: for Moore, PLP is the norm, and P the marked form used to signal moments of heightened empathy; for Murdoch, the markedness relationship is the reverse.

190. Jakobson (1957) introduced the term "evidential" as a tentative label for a verbal category that indicates *the source of the information on which a speaker's statement is based.* As currently understood, evidentiality covers a range of distinctions involved in the identification of "data source," not all of which are verb-based in all languages. I discuss the use of tenses to express evidential meanings (and vice versa) in Fleischman (1989b).

Chapter 8.   Metalinguistic Functions: Storytelling in the PRESENT

191. The term "primary" (= vernacular) is used to distinguish traditional, orally composed epics from later art epics in which literate writers consciously sought to imitate the poetic technique of vernacular epic forms.

192. Save for the analogy to natural narrative, Burbelo's observations on epic are not new; the critical literature contains similar statements about other epics that exhibit tense switching and rely heavily on the PR: the *chansons de geste* (Hatcher 1942, 1946; Blanc 1964, 1965), the *Cid* (Gilman 1961), Vergil's *Aeneid* (von Albrecht 1970), and the *Song of Igor's Campaign* (Chvany 1980), to cite but a few of the better-known Western epics. I cite Burbelo (among many commentators on the poetic technique of epic) because his observations are supported by data from a less-familiar tradition and thereby shed new light on the extent to which certain features of primary epic, including its tenses and temporality, are documented across languages.

193. With reference to the thirteenth-century romances of *Flamenca* (Old Occitan) and the *Quest for the Holy Grail* (Old French), Wehr (1984:108ff.) describes movements in and out of the narrative foreground in terms of a similar "zoom" technique. She interprets foreground spatially as a zone of "high focus of attention" for the participant whose point of view orients the report at the moment in question (narrator or focalizing character). Actions occurring within this zone are reported in the PR. When a new participant is introduced into the foreground, his entry will be reported in the PS if a verb of "coming" is used (focus on the source of the movement); conversely, if the entry is reported from the perspective of the focalizer who sees the new participant approach (focus on the goal), the tense of this verb of perception will be the PR. By means of the PR an action is drawn into the zone of high focus of attention (PS → PR); as participants move out of this zone their actions are reported once again in the PS (PR → PS).

194. The PS is more prominent in the *Cid* than in most French epics, where the PR predominates (Hatcher 1946:10). This difference conceivably reflects a more historical and less mythical attitude toward the events of the story-world, which, as Hispanists are quick to point out, are closer in time to the poem than the historical events of *Roland* are to the Oxford text. In other words, the statistical prominence of the "chronicling" tense in the *Cid* would seem to correlate with the poet-singer's more historical attitude toward his material.

195. For example, in claiming that "there is little room for mature evaluation or for reflection" in the solidly oral genres, Pickens (1979:169) appears to equate evaluation with narrator commentary (= external evaluation) of the type found more commonly in the romances.

196. The pictorial point of view associated with the IMP is statistically insignificant in *Roland,* though in the *Cid* the IMP accounts for sixteen percent of all verbs (Gilman 1961:23). The higher frequency of the IMP in the *Cid* may well explain the lower frequency of the PR in that text, since the two IPFV tenses compete to a degree for territory that in the Old French poems, *Roland* in particular, belongs entirely to the PR$_v$.

197. For literary-historical background on the *romancero,* I draw primarily on the introduction to Smith's *Spanish Ballads* (1964), which surveys the major critical questions and provides references to the primary sources of scholarship.

198. Much of the original epic material has been lost, at least in poetic form. From what is hypothesized to have been an extensive epic production in medieval Spain, the sole text to survive in its entirety is the *Cid*. The legends of "the *infantes* of Lara/Salas," the "siege of Zamora," and the "campaign of Huesca" have been reconstructed from historical chronicles, largely through the text-archeological efforts of Ramón Menéndez Pidal (see especially Menéndez Pidal 1951). In Alvar (1972) each poetic legend is given in reconstructed verse form, in its documented chronistic versions, and finally as it evolved into ballads.

199. This episode appears to be a distinctively Spanish embroidery on the Charlemagne legend. No figure with the name Beltrán appears in any known versions of the *Song of Roland.*

200. The ballads cited here appear in Wolf and Hoffmann's *Primavera y flor de romances* (1856), of which the 2d ed. has been reprinted (with additions and corrections) as vols. 8–9 of Menéndez y Pelayo 1944–1945. For convenience, ballads are referred to by the number assigned to them in the *Primavera,* followed by the date of the collection in which they were first printed.

201. This verb may be read either as an adjectival state—"was dead" (for which modern Spanish would use *estar* rather than *ser*)—or as a stative passive of the verb *morir* in a transitive use no longer possible in modern Spanish—"was [= had been] killed."

202. In ballads that begin *in medias res,* the PR or IMP is often preceded by the adverb *ya* (now, already): *Ya comienzan [PR] los franceses con los moros pelear . . .* (Now the French are beginning to do battle with the Moors); *Ya cabalga [PR] Diego Ordóñez . . .* (Diego Ordóñez is now riding off); *Ya se salía [IMP] el rey moro . . .* (The Moorish King was leaving). Investigators have commented on the predilection of this adverb for IPFV tenses (cf. Szertics 1967:106–114); like adverbs that anchor NARR IMPs (cf. §1.5.3), *ya* provides a temporal reference point for situations presented as ongoing. When this occurs at the outset of a text, it has the effect of plunging the listener *already* into the midst of the action.

203. The Bernardo ballads derive from a lost epic and from legends incorporated into chronicles, all of dubious historicity. In adapting a legend about Charlemagne, the Leonese invented Bernardo to defeat Roland and the Twelve Peers at Rencesvals. Of greater human interest and dramatic potential, however, was that part of the legend that dealt with Bernardo's birth and the fate of his parents. Neither ballad here under consideration directly reflects an epic fragment; both were composed in the sixteenth century on the basis of chronistic accounts (Smith 1964:59).

204. The only consistent tense idiosyncrasy of the dialogic mode is use of the IMP where a PR would be expected. For a summary of interpretations of this dialogic IMP, see Mirrer-Singer (1986: chapter 2).

205. Cf. (8.11), line 14: *y luego MONJA SE ENTRABA* (and then [she] ENTERED A CONVENT); (8.12), line 22: *al rey de esta suerte HABLABA* ([he] SPOKE thus to the King).

206. Reporting on the HP in English, Casparis (1975:21) observes that where this tense alternates with the P, the switching creates the effect of a spontaneous, uninhibited narrator whose discourse sounds more genuinely colloquial. This statement seems to suggest that the alternating HP is a stylistic calque on NP usage—whence it originated (§3.8)—whose effect is different from that of a sustained PR tense.

207. The French term *écriture* is difficult to translate; it occupies a lexical space that encompasses not only the English notion of "writing," but also such notions as "writerliness," "style," "construction," and "inscription."

208. This diachronic argument also applies to English and presumably to other languages as well.

209. Among many discussions of the HP as a stylistic phenomenon of literary and historiographic narration, see Seylaz 1983 (French), Casparis 1975 (English),

Herczeg 1958 (Italian), Mellet 1980 (Latin), and Sorella 1983 (general survey, focus on Italian). For a more detailed history of the PR tense in literary French, see Buffin (1925: part II, chapter 4) and Saunders (1969). Germane also, though its focus is on the PASSÉ SIMPLE, is Barthes's essay "Writing and the Novel" (in Barthes 1967).

210. Since the PRET, in Hamburger's view, signals "fictionality" not "pastness," there is no need for an explicit "unpast" that neither disrupts nor underscores the fictional effect (1973: 119); all the PR can do is compromise the distinction between narrative and nonnarrative sentences in the text.

211. A PR-tense statement that leaves the reader uncertain as to its origin, Cohn (1978: 75) observes, is a clear sign of a successful merger of narrator and character voices. The same is true for statements in the IMP in free indirect discourse; cf. the example from Flaubert given in (7.6).

212. Note that because this discourse is in the PR, a punctualizing adverb ("for a second") is required to mark the predicate "try to free her hands" unambiguously as a narrative event.

213. This piece was written in 1917 and first published in a volume of stories and sketches entitled *Monday and Tuesday* (1921). The version to which I refer appears in Dick's (1985) edition of *The Complete Shorter Fiction*.

214. Cohn (1978: 8) reports a statement by Woolf herself that modern fiction would eventually return to its "circular tendency," and adds (1978: 193f.) that the figure of the (vicious) circle recurs inevitably in texts cast predominantly in the PR cotemporal with now, the tense in which one takes stock of one's circumstances.

215. The only two action verbs in these sentences are modalized ("if I were to get up," "I must jump up"); they refer to actions that do not actually occur.

216. Cohn (1978) coins the term "autonomous monologue" to refer to texts of this type that constitute in their entirety someone's inner language.

217. Here is the full citation from Auerbach (1953: 538) alluded to above: "In Woolf's case exterior events . . . have lost their hegemony, they serve to release and interpret inner events, whereas before her time (and still today in many instances) inner movements function to prepare and motivate exterior happenings." This striking reversal of what normative narration regards as foreground and background suggests yet another reason why grounding should remain independent of the notion of ordered events.

218. Much of the theoretical as well as fictional writing (insofar as a distinction can be drawn) of the *nouveaux romanciers* is available in translation; shorter quotations are from the English editions, though both references are given; the first date refers to the French edition, the second to the English.

219. For perspectives on this enterprise, the reader is referred to Bloch-Michel (1963), Sturrock (1969), Ricardou (1971, 1973), and Heath (1972), among theoreticians and critics closer to the event, and, for more recent assessments reflecting the critical orientations of the 1980s, to Stoltzfus (1985), Sherzer (1986), and Britton (1987). The discussion that follows draws on all these sources.

220. In natural narration or other varieties of nonfictional narration, "reporting" must be seen as an activity distinct from "remembering" (we can recall an experience without reporting it, but we cannot communicate our memories to others without speaking or writing them); only in fiction writing can the "report" be eliminated as a separate activity, since fiction writing alone has linguistic conventions (discussed in chapter 7) for extracting thoughts (perceptions, memories) directly from the consciousnesses that articulate them.

221. For obvious reasons, I avoid the term "narrator" in reference to the Speaker of a *nouveau roman,* even though it is used in much of the critical literature, including statements by the novelists themselves.

222. Le long de la chevelure défaite, la brosse DESCEND avec un bruit léger, qui TIENT du souffle et du crépitement. A peine arrivée en bas, très vite, elle REMONTE vers la tête, où elle FRAPPE de tout la surface des poils, avant de glisser derechef sur la masse noire, ovale couleur d'os dont le manche, assez court, DISPARAIT presque entièrement dans la main qui l'ENSERRE avec fermeté.

Une moitié de la chevelure PEND dans le dos, l'autre main RAMÈNE en avant de l'épaule l'autre moitié. Sur ce côté (le côté droit) la tête S'INCLINE, de manière à mieux offrir les cheveux à la brosse. Chaque fois que celle-ci S'ABAT, tout en haut, derrière la nuque, la tête PENCHE davantage et REMONTE ensuite avec effort, pendant que la main droite—qui TIENT la brosse—S'ÉLOIGNE en sens inverse. La main gauche—qui ENTOURE les cheveux sans les serrer, entre le poignet, la paume et les doigts—lui LAISSE un instant libre passage et SE REFERME en rassemblant les mèches à nouveau, d'un geste sûr, arrondi, mécanique, tandis que la brosse CONTINUE sa course jusqu'à l'extrême pointe. Le bruit, qui VARIE progressivement d'un bout à l'autre, N'EST plus alors qu'un pétillement sec et peu nourri, dont les derniers éclats SE PRODUISENT une fois que la brosse, quittant les plus longs cheveux, EST EN TRAIN déjà DE REMONTER la branche ascendante du cycle, décrivant dans l'air une courbe rapide qui la REPORTE au-dessus du cou, là où les cheveux SONT APLATIS sur l'arrière de la tête et DÉGAGENT la blancheur d'une raie médiane (*La Jalousie,* pp. 64–65).

223. (a) A... VIENT D'APPORTER les verres, les deux bouteilles et le seau à glace. Elle COMMENCE À SERVIR: le cognac dans les trois verres, puis l'eau minérale, enfin trois cubes de glace transparente qui EMPRISONNENT en leur coeur un faisceau d'aiguilles argentées. . . .

Ils BOIVENT à petites gorgées.

"Si tout va bien, DIT Franck, nous pouvons être en ville vers dix heures et avoir déjà pas mal de temps avant le déjeuner.

—Bien sûr, je préfère aussi," DIT A...

Ils BOIVENT à petites gorgées.

Ensuite ils PARLENT d'autre chose. Ils ONT *achevé* maintenant l'un comme l'autre la lecture de ce livre qui les OCCUPE depuis quelque temps; leurs commentaires PEUVENT donc PORTER sur l'ensemble: c'est-à-dire à la fois sur le dénouement et sur d'anciens épisodes (sujets de conversations passées). . . .

Ils BOIVENT à petites gorgées. (pp. 81–83)

(b) A... qui EST *allée chercher* elle-même les boissons, DÉPOSE le plateau chargé sur la table basse. Elle DÉBOUCHE le cognac et en VERSE dans les trois verres alignés. Elle les EMPLIT ensuite avec l'eau gazeuse. Ayant distribué les deux premiers, elle VA S'ASSEOIR à son tour dans le fauteuil vide, tenant le troisième en main.

C'est alors qu'elle DEMANDE si les habituels cubes de glace seront nécessaires, prétextant que ces bouteilles SORTENT du réfrigérateur. (pp. 105–106)

(c) IL EST PRESQUE L'HEURE de l'apéritif et A... n'A pas *attendu* davantage pour appeler le boy, qui APPARAIT à l'angle de la maison, portant le plateau avec deux bouteilles, trois grands verres et le seau à glace. . . . il PLACE le plateau avec précaution près du roman à couverture vernie.

C'est ce dernier qui FOURNIT le sujet de la conversation. . . . A... et Franck en PARLENT avec animation, tout en buvant à petites gorgées le mélange de cognac et d'eau gazeuse servi par la maîtresse de maison dans trois verres (pp. 215–216).

224. Cf. Robbe-Grillet's statement: "It was absurd to suppose that in the novel *Jealousy* . . . there existed a clear and unambiguous order of events, one that was not that of the sentences of the book, as if I had amused myself by mixing up a pre-established calendar the way one shuffles a deck of cards. The narrative was on the contrary made in such a way that any attempt to reconstruct an external chronology would lead, sooner or later, to a series of contradictions, hence to an impasse. . . . There existed for me no possible order outside that of the book. The latter was not a narration imbricated with a simple tale external to itself, but the unfolding of a story that had no reality other than that of the *sjuzhet* [*récit*], that occurred nowhere except in the mind of the writer, and of the reader" (1963:132f./1965:154, trans. adapted).

225. . . . Georges DÉCLARANT qu'il avait décidé de s'occuper des terres, et soutenu (quoiqu'il fît semblant de ne pas l'entendre, quoique AFFECTANT de leur parler à tous deux également, et tourné cependant ostensiblement vers elle seule [sa mère] et SE DÉTOURNANT ostensiblement de son père, et cependant S'ADRESSANT à lui, et NE TENANT ostensiblement AUCUN COMPTE d'elle ou de ce qu'elle pouvait dire), soutenu, donc, par la bruyante, obscène et utérine approbation de Sabine . . . (*La Route des Flandres*, p. 233).

226. The title of Britton's (1987) study on Claude Simon—*Writing the Visible*—captures in a phrase the paradox inherent in the *nouveaux romanciers'* attempts to figure visual reality in writing, to offer textual descriptions of visual objects.

227. "Le mieux serait d'écrire les événements au jour le jour. Tenir un journal pour y voir clair. Ne pas laisser échapper les nuances, les petits faits, même s'ils n'ont l'air de rien, et surtout les classer. Il faut dire comment je vois cette table, la rue, les gens, mon paquet de tabac, puisque c'est *cela* qui a changé. Il faut déterminer exactement l'étendue et la nature de ce changement. . . . Je dois être toujours prêt, sinon elle me glisserait encore entre les doigts. Il ne faut rien   mais noter soigneusement et dans le plus grand detail tout ce qui se produit.

"Naturellement je ne peux plus rien décrire de net sur ces histoires de samedi et d'avant-hier, j'en suis déjà trop éloigné . . ." (*Nausée*, p. 11).

At the point of apparent ellipsis the novel inserts the following footnote: "Un mot est raturé (peut-être 'forcer' ou 'forger'), un autre, rajouté en surcharge, est illisible" ("Word crossed out (possibly 'force' or 'forge'), another word added above, is illegible") (*Nausea*, p. 7).

228. Recall Schlegel's characterization of epic referred to above (§8.1.2).

229. The truncation of the wife's name is not irrelevant to the thrust of discussion in this section, which is to establish the connection between the PR-tense and fiction that privileges description. The function of proper names, Searle (1958:171f.) argues, is to refer without describing. If there were a consensus among speakers about the set of descriptions that constitute the "identity" of an object or individual, then proper names would be superfluous, being essentially shorthand formulas for elaborate definite descriptions. But given that consensus of this sort is lacking, we avail ourselves of proper names, which enable us to refer without raising the question of what the object is. Proper names function not as descriptions, but as "pegs on which to hang descriptions." By eschewing the proper name, Robbe-Grillet must resort to "elaborate description" to construct an identity for the wife. The irony, of course, is that the detailed descriptions that substitute for the proper name are in no way a "consensus" view of this character, but the radically skewed perceptions of a single unbalanced focalizer. The fact that this focalizing character has no name at all (nor is he ever the object of descriptions) obviates in his case even the possibility of reference.

230. c'est à une distance de moins d'un mètre seulement qu'APPARAISSENT dans les intervalles successifs, en bandes parallèles que SÉPARENT les bandes plus larges de bois gris, les éléments d'un paysage discontinu: les balustres en bois tourné, le fauteuil vide, la table basse où un verre plein REPOSE à côté d'un plateau portant les deux bouteilles, enfin le haut de la chevelure noire, qui PIVOTE à cet instant vers la droite, où ENTRE EN SCÈNE au-dessus de la table un avant-bras nu, de couleur brun foncé, terminé par une main plus pâle tenant le seau à glace. La voix de A... REMERCIE le boy. La main brune DISPARAIT. Le seau de métal étincelant, qui SE COUVRE bientôt DE BUÉE, RESTE posé sur le plateau à côté des deux bouteilles.

Le chignon de A... vu de si près, par derrière, SEMBLE d'une grande complication. IL EST TRÈS DIFFICILE D'Y SUIVRE dans leurs emmêlements les différentes mèches: plusieurs solutions CONVIENNENT, par endroit, et ailleurs aucune (pp. 51–52).

231. Hence Robbe-Grillet insists that "the cinema knows only one grammatical form: the present tense of the indicative" (1963:130/1965:151).

232. The radical objectivity of epic that Schlegel so insisted on has met with similar charges of "ignoring the human factor" (Gilman 1961:78*n*). In *For a New Novel* Robbe-Grillet (1963:117f./1965:138f.) insists that, contrary to the common critical interpretation, "total subjectivity" is at the heart of the *nouveau roman*, the supposed "objectivity" of his novels being a critical misapprehension derived from their orientation toward objects. These statements call to mind Jakobson's comment, in his essay "On Realism in Art" (1971:41), that while the revolutionary artist deforms the existing canons for the sake of a closer imitation of reality, the conservative public misunderstands the deformation of the canon as a distortion of reality!

233. As he observes in the essay "Time and Description in Fiction Today" (1963:133f./1965:155f.), "These descriptions whose movement destroys all confidence in the things described, these heroes without naturalness as without identity, this present which constantly invents itself, as though in the course of the very writing, which repeats, doubles, modifies, denies itself without ever accumulating in order to constitute a past—hence a 'story' in the traditional sense of the word—all this can only invite the reader (or the spectator) to another mode of participation than the one to which he was accustomed. . . . For far from neglecting him, the author proclaims his absolute need of the reader's cooperation, an active, conscious, *creative* assistance. What he asks of him is no longer to receive a ready-made world, completed, full, closed upon itself, but on the contrary to participate in a creation, to invent in his turn the work—and thus to learn to invent his own life."

234. Ainsi *vous recommencez* [PR] à jouer à *ce* jeu qui *vous est* [PR] familier, donner un nom à chacun de *vos* compagnons de voyage, mais *celui-ci convient* [PR] plutôt mal à *ce* petit garçon qui *s'agite* [PR] sur sa place, puisqu'il *est* [PR] bien plus jeune que votre fils *maintenant;* il vaudrait mieux le baptiser André, *par exemple;* la femme qui le *prend* [PR] par la main et le *fait sortir* [PR] *sera* [FUT] Madame Polliat; *quant au* jeune couple, *non,* pas d'allusions littéraires, simplement Pierre et, *voyons* [IMPER], Cécile *est exclu* [PR], mais Agnès conviendrait très bien . . . (*La Modification,* p. 106).

235. Mardi prochain, lorsque vous entrerez [FUT] dans sa chambre, en effet vous lui raconterez [FUT] tout ce voyage et vous lui direz [FUT]: "J'étais allé [PLP] à Rome pour prouver à Cécile que je la choisissais [IMP] contre toi, j'y étais allé [PLP] dans l'intention de lui demander de venir vivre avec moi définitivement à Paris . . ."

Alors terrorisée s'élève [PR] en vous votre propre voix qui se plaint [PR]. . . . (*La Modification,* p. 135).

236. Cf. Joyce's comment apropos of Édouard Dujardin's novel *Les Lauriers sont coupés* (which Joyce believed to be the first interior-monologue novel): "In that book . . . the reader finds himself installed, from the very first lines, in the thought of the main character; and the uninterrupted flow of his thought, *completely replacing the usual form of narrative,* informs us of what that character *is doing* and what *is happening* to him" (cited in Larbaud's preface to Dujardin 1925: my emphasis).

237. Genette (1966:77) compares the articulation of actions in Robbe-Grillet's novels to the paratactic organization of the Bayeux tapestry (cf. *n*150 above); cf. also Sherzer (1986:3–4).

238. On functions of repetition in the *nouveau roman,* see Sherzer (1986: chapter 2); in the Old French epic, Fleischman (1986b, 1989a). Sherzer also sees repetition, parataxis, acausality, and achrony as features connecting postmodern French fiction with the oral performance of preliterate and nonliterate societies (1986:172).

References

I. Texts Cited

a. Latin and early Romance

Alexis   *La Vie de Saint Alexis.* Edited by C. Storey. Oxford: Blackwell, 1968.

AN   *Aucassin et Nicolette: Chantefable du XIIIe siècle.* Edited by Mario Roques. 2d rev. ed. Classiques Français du Moyen Age. Paris: Champion, 1973.

Book of Good Love   Juan Ruiz. *Libro de buen amor.* Edited with an introduction and English paraphrase by Raymond S. Willis. Princeton, N.J.: Princeton University Press, 1972.

Castia-gilos   Ramon Vidal de Besalù. "Castia-gilos." Text from Karl Appel, *Provenzalische Chrestomathie.* Leipzig: Reisland, 1907.

Chastelaine de Vergi   *La Chastelaine de Vergi.* Edited by Gaston Raynaud. 3d ed. rev. by Lucian Foulet. Paris: Champion, 1912.

Cid   *Poema de mio Cid.* Edited with introduction and notes by Colin Smith. Oxford: Clarendon, 1972.

Clari   Robert de Clari. *La Conquête de Constantinople.* Edited by Philippe Lauer. Classiques Français du Moyen Age. Paris: Champion, 1924.

Death of King Arthur   *La Mort le roi Artu: Roman du treizième siècle.* Edited by Jean Frappier. Textes Littéraires Français. Paris: Droz, 1964.

Erec   In *Les Romans de Chrétien de Troyes.* Edited by Mario Roques. Vol. 1, *Erec et Enide.* Classiques Français du Moyen Age. Paris: Champion, 1970.

First General Chronicle   Alfonso X, King of Castile and León. *Primera crónica general: Estoria que mando componer Alfonso el Sabio y se continuaba bajo Sancho IV en 1289.* Madrid: Bailly-Balliere e hijos, 1906.

Flamenca   *Flamenca.* In *Les Troubadours,* vol. 1. Translated by René Lavaud and René Nelli. Bruges: Desclée de Brouwer, 1960.

Froissart   Jean Froissart. *Chroniques: Début du premier livre, Edition du manuscrit de Rome Reg. lat. 869.* Edited by G. T. Diller. Geneva: Droz, 1972.

Guigemar   In *Les Lais de Marie de France.* Edited by Jean Rychner. Classiques Français du Moyen Age. Paris: Champion, 1973.

Jaufre   *Jaufre.* In *Les Troubadours,* vol. 1. Translated by René Lavaud and René Nelli. Bruges: Desclée de Brouwer, 1960.

Lancelot   In *Les Romans de Chrétien de Troyes.* Edited by Mario Roques. Vol. 3, *Le Chevalier de la charrette (Lancelot).* Classiques Français du Moyen Age. Paris: Champion, 1983.

Lanval   In *Les Lais de Marie de France.* Edited by Jean Rychner. Classiques Français du Moyen Age. Paris: Champion, 1973.

Minstrels'   *La Passion des jongleurs.* Edited by Anne A. Perry. Paris: Beau-
Passion   chesne, 1981.

Pathelin   *Maistre Pierre Pathelin: Farce du XVe siècle.* 2d rev. ed. by Richard T. Holbrook. Classiques Français du Moyen Age. Paris: Champion, 1970.

Pot of Gold   Plautus. *Aulularia.* With notes and an introduction by Wilhelm Wagner. New York: Arno Press, 1979.

Primavera   *Primavera y flor de romances* (of Wolf and Hoffmann, 1856). Repr. by Marcelino Menéndez y Pelayo as vols. 8 and 9, with additions, of *Antología de poetas líricos castellanos.* Santander: Oldus, 1944 (original ed. 1899).

Prose Tristan   *Le Roman de Tristan en prose: Les deux captivités de Tristan.* Edited with introduction, notes, and glossary by Joel Blanchard. Bibliothèque Française et Romane. Série B: Editions critiques de textes, 15. Paris: Klincksieck, 1976.

Razo of Peire   In J. Boutière and A.-H. Schutz, *Biographies des troubadours:*
Vidal   *Textes provençaux des XIIIe et XIVe siècles.* Edited by Jean Boutière and I.-M. Cluzel. Paris: Nizet, 1964.

Roland   *La Chanson de Roland.* Edited by F. Whitehead. Oxford: Blackwell, 1970. / *The Song of Roland.* Trans. Frederick Goldin. New York: Noonan, 1978.

Saint Mary the   *Vida de Santa María Egipciaca.* Ed. Manuel Alvar. 2 vols. Ma-
Egyptian   drid: CSIC, 1970–1972.

     La Vida de Santa María Egipciaca traducida por un juglar anónimo hacia 1215. Ed. María S. de Andrés Castellanos. Madrid: Anejos del Boletín de la Real Academia Española, 1964.

Song of William   Jeanne Wathelet-Willem. *Recherches sur la Chanson de Guillaume: Etude accompagnée d'une édition.* Paris: Les Belles Lettres, 1975.

Three Hundred   Franco Sacchetti. *Trecentonovelle.* In *Opere.* Edited by Aldo Bor-
Tales   lenghi. Milan: Rizzoli, 1957.

Villehardouin   Geoffroy de Villehardouin. *La Conquête de Constantinople.*
2d ed. 2 vols. Edited by Edmond Faral. Paris: Les Belles
Lettres, 1961.

Yvain   In *Les Romans de Chrétien de Troyes.* Edited by Mario Roques.
Vol. 4, *Le Chevalier au lion (Yvain).* Classiques Français du
Moyen Age. Paris: Champion, 1971. / *The Knight with the
Lion, or, Yvain.* Edited and translated by William W. Kibler.
Garland Library of Medieval Literature, 48. New York:
Garland, 1985.

b. Modern

Bernanos, Georges. 1936. *Nouvelle histoire de Mouchette.* In *Oeuvres romanesques.*
Bibliothèque de la Pléiade. Paris: Gallimard, 1961.

Bradbury, Malcolm. 1976 [c1975]. *The History Man.* Boston: Houghton Mifflin.

Butor, Michel. 1957. *La Modification.* Paris: Editions de Minuit. / *Second Thoughts.*
Translated by Jean Stewart. London: Faber and Faber, 1958.

Camus, Albert. 1949 [c1942]. *L'Etranger.* Paris: Gallimard. Repr. 1961. / *The
Stranger.* Translated by Stuart Gilbert. New York: Alfred A. Knopf, 1977
[c1946].

Chekhov, Anton P. 1946. "Spat' xočetsja" [Sleepy]. In *Izbrannye sočinenija.* Moscow:
Gos. izd-vo khudož. lit-ry.

Cross, Amanda. 1972 [c1970]. *Poetic Justice.* New York: Avon Books.

———. 1986. *No Word from Winifred.* New York: Dutton.

Deledda, Grazia. 1939. "Forze Occulte." In *Il cedro del Libano: Novelle.* Milan:
Garzanti.

Flaubert, Gustave. 1869. *L'Education sentimentale: Histoire d'un jeune homme.* With
introduction, notes, and summary of variants by Edouard Maynial. Paris:
Garnier, 1961. / *Sentimental Education.* Translated by Robert Baldick. Har-
mondsworth: Penguin, 1964.

Hugo, Victor. 1853. "L'Expiation." In *Les Châtiments.* Paris: Nelson Editeurs, 1957.

Lesage, Alain René. 1715–1735. *Gil Blas.* Introduction by Emile Faguet. Edition
Lutetia. Paris: Nelson Editeurs, n.d.

Malraux, André. 1937. *L'Espoir.* Paris: Gallimard. / *Man's Hope.* Translated by
Stuart Gilbert and Alistair Macdonald. New York: Modern Library, 1938.

Pérez Galdós, Benito. *Doña Perfecta.* In *Obras completas,* vol. 4. Introduction, biography, and notes by Federico Carlos Sainz de Robles. Madrid: Aguilar, 1954.

Proust, Marcel. 1913–1927. *A la recherche du temps perdu.* 3 vols. Edited by Pierre
Clarac and André Ferré. 3 vols. Bibliothèque de la Pléiade. Paris: Gallimard,
1954. / *Remembrance of Things Past.* 2 vols. Translated by C. K. Scott-Moncrieff.
New York: Random House, 1934.

———. 1919. *Pastiches et mélanges.* Paris: Gallimard.

Robbe-Grillet, Alain. 1957. *La Jalousie.* Paris: Editions de Minuit. / *Two Novels by
Robbe-Grillet: Jealousy and In the Labyrinth.* Translated by Richard Howard.
New York: Grove Press, 1965.

————. 1981. *Djinn—Un trou rouge dans les pavés disjoints*. Paris: Editions de Min-uit. / *Djinn*. Translated by Yvonne Leonard and Walter Wells. New York: Grove Press, 1982.

Sartre, Jean-Paul. 1938. *La Nausée*. Paris: Gallimard. / *Nausea*. Translated by Lloyd Alexander. Paulton and London: New Directions, 1949.

Simon, Claude. 1960. *La Route des Flandres*. Paris: Editions de Minuit. / *The Flan-ders Road*. Translated by Richard Howard. London: John Calder / New York: Riverrun Press, 1985.

Storey, David. 1973. *A Temporary Life*. New York: Dutton.

Tallent, Elizabeth. 1985. "The Fence Party." *New Yorker* (September 16, 1985).

Woolf, Virginia. 1921. "The Mark on the Wall." In *The Complete Shorter Fiction of Virginia Woolf*. Edited by Susan Dick. London: Hogarth Press, 1985.

————. 1927. *To the Lighthouse*. New York: Harcourt Brace and World.

II. Critical Works

Adams, Jon-K. 1985. *Pragmatics and Fiction*. Pragmatics and Beyond, 6.2. Amster-dam: Benjamins.

Ageno, Franca Brambilla. 1964. *Il verbo nell'italiano antico: Ricerche di sintassi*. Milan: Riccardi Editore.

————. 1971. "Osservazioni sull'aspetto e tempo del verbo nella 'Commedia.'" *Studi di grammatica italiana*, vol. 1, 61–100. Florence: Sansoni.

Aigotti, Daniela. 1974. "Tempo e aspetto nell'italiano antico." Diss., Università di Torino.

Albrecht, Michael von. 1970. "Zu Vergil's Erzähltechnik." *Glotta* 48 : 219–229.

Alonso, Dámaso. 1944. "Estilo y creación en el *Poema de Mio Cid*." *Ensayos sobre poesía española*, 69–111. Buenos Aires: Revista de Occidente Argentina. Repr. in D. A., *Obras completas*, 2 : 107–143. Madrid: Gredos, 1973.

Alvar, Manuel. 1972. *Cantares de gesta medievales*. México: Porrua.

Ambrosini, Riccardo. 1961. "L'uso dei tempi storici nell'italiano antico." *L'Italia Dialettale* 24 : 13–124.

Andersen, Henning. 1972. "Dipthongization." *Language* 48 : 11–50.

————. 1987. "From Auxiliary to Desinence." In *Historical Development of Auxili-aries*, edited by Martin Harris and Paolo Ramat, 21–51. Trends in Linguistics. Studies and Monographs 35. Berlin: Mouton De Gruyter.

Antoine, Gérald. 1959, 1962. *La Coordination en français*, 2 vols. Paris: D'Artrey.

Auerbach, Erich. 1953. *Mimesis*. Translated by Willard Trask. Princeton: Princeton University Press (first published in German, 1946).

Augustine of Hippo. *Confessions*. Translated by R. S. Pine-Coffin. Harmonds-worth: Penguin Books, 1961.

Bache, Carl. 1986. "Tense and Aspect in Fiction." *Journal of Literary Semantics* 15.2 : 82–97.

Bakhtin, Mikhail. 1971. "Discourse Typology in Prose." In Matejka and Pomorska, eds. 1971, 176–196.

————. 1973. *Problems of Dostoevsky's Poetics.* Translated by R. W. Rotsel. Ann Arbor: Ardis Publications (first published in Russian, 1929).

Bal, Mieke. 1977. *Narratologie: Essais sur la signification narrative dans quatre romans modernes.* Paris: Klincksieck.

————. 1983. "The Narrating and the Focalizing: A Theory of Agents in Narrative." *Style* 17.2:234–269. Originally published as "Narration et focalisation," chapter 1 of Bal 1977.

————. 1985. *Narratology: Introduction to the Theory of Narrative.* Translated by Christine van Boheemen. Toronto: University of Toronto Press. Original title *De theorie van vettellen en verhalen.* 2d revised ed. Muiderberg: Coutinho, 1980.

Banfield, Ann. 1982. *Unspeakable Sentences: Narration and Representation in the Language of Fiction.* Boston: Routledge and Kegan Paul.

————. 1985. "Grammar and Memory." *BLS* 11:387–397.

Barrera-Vidal, A. 1968. "La Perspective temporelle dans *L'Etranger* de Camus et dans *La Familia de Pascual Duarte* de José Camilo Cela." *Zeitschrift für romanische Philologie* 84:309–322.

Barthes, Roland. 1966. "Introduction à l'analyse structurale des récits." *Communications* 8:1–27. Translated 1975 as "An Introduction to the Structural Analysis of Narrative." *New Literary History* 6:237–272. Repr. in R. B., *Image-Music-Text.* London: Fontana, 1977.

————. 1967. *Writing Degree Zero.* Translated by Annette Lavers and Colin Smith. Preface by Susan Sontag. New York: Hill and Wang (first published in French 1953).

Bauman, Richard, ed. 1977. *Verbal Art as Performance.* Rowley, Mass.: Newbury House. Repr. 1984. Prospect Heights, Ill.: Waveland Press.

Bauman, Richard. 1986. *Story, Performance, Event: Contextual Studies of Oral Narrative.* Cambridge: Cambridge University Press.

Bäuml, Franz. 1977. "The Unmaking of the Hero: Some Critical Implications of the Transition from Oral to Written Epic." In *The Epic in Medieval Society, Aesthetic and Moral Values,* edited by Harald Scholler, 86–99. Tübingen: Niemeyer.

————. 1980. "Varieties and Consequences of Medieval Literacy and Illiteracy." *Speculum* 55:237–265.

————. 1984. "Medieval Texts and the Two Theories of Oral Formulaic Composition: A Proposal for a Third Theory." *New Literary History* 16.1:51–66.

Beaman, Karen. 1984. "Coordination and Subordination Revisited: Syntactic Complexity in Spoken and Written Narrative Discourse." In Tannen, ed., 1984a, 45–80.

Beaugrande, Robert de. 1982. "The Story of Grammars and the Grammars of Stories." *Journal of Pragmatics* 6:383–422.

Beck, Jonathan. 1988. "On Functional Multiplicity of Tense-Aspect Forms in Old French Narrative." *Romance Philology* 42:129–143.

Beer, Jeanette M. A. 1968. *Villehardouin, Epic Historian.* Geneva: Droz.

————. 1981. *Narrative Conventions of Truth in the Middle Ages.* Geneva: Droz.

Bellos, David M. 1978. "The Narrative Absolute Tense." *Language and Style* 11:231–237.

Benjamin, Walter. 1969. "The Storyteller." In *Illuminations,* translated by Harry Zohn. New York: Schocken Books (original German ed. 1955).

Benson, Larry D. 1961. "Chaucer's Historical Present, Its Meaning and Uses." *English Studies* 42:65–77.

Benveniste, Emile. 1959. "Les Relations de temps dans le verbe français." *Bulletin de la Société Linguistique de Paris* 54:237–250. Repr. in E. B., *Problèmes de linguistique générale,* I:69–82. Paris: Gallimard, 1966.

Bertinetto, Pier Marco. 1986. *Tempo, aspetto e azione nel verbo italiano: Il sistema dell'indicativo.* Florence: Accademia della Crusca.

———. 1987. "Structure and Origin of the 'Narrative' Imperfect." In *Papers from the Seventh International Conference on Historical Linguistics (Pavia, September 1985),* edited by A. G. Ramat et al., 71–85. Amsterdam: Benjamins.

Blanc, Michel H. A. 1961. "The Use of Narrative Tenses in Thirteenth-Century French Prose." Diss., University of London.

———. 1964. "Time and Tense in Old French Narrative." *Archivum Linguisticum* 16.2:96–124.

———. 1965. "Le Présent épique dans la *Chanson de Roland.*" *Actes du Xe Congrès International de Linguistique et Philologie Romanes (Strasbourg, 1962),* 565–578. Paris: Gallimard.

Bloch-Michel, Jean. 1963. *Le Présent de l'indicatif: Essai sur le nouveau roman.* Paris: Klincksieck.

Bockhoff, Heinrich. 1880. "Der syntaktische Gebrauch der Tempora im Oxforder Texte des Rolandsliedes." Diss., Universität Münster.

Bolinger, Dwight. 1947. "More on the Present Tense in English." *Language* 23:434–436.

Booth, Wayne. 1961. *The Rhetoric of Fiction.* Chicago: University of Chicago Press.

Boulle, Jacques. 1981. "L'Aoriste et le parfait dans une perspective énonciative: L'Example du bulgare et du français." In *Actants, voix et aspect verbaux.* Actes des Journées d'Etudes Linguistiques des 22 et 23 Mai 1979, 129–149. Angers: Presses de l'Université d'Angers.

Boutière, Jean, and A.-H. Schutz. 1964. *Biographies des troubadours: Textes provençaux des XIIIe et XIVe siècles.* Revised ed. by Jean Boutière, with Iréné Cluzel. Paris: Nizet.

Boyer, Henri. 1979. "L'Opposition passé simple/passé composé dans le système verbal de la langue française." *Le Francais Moderne* 47.2:121–129.

———. 1985a. "L'Economie des temps verbaux dans le discours narratif." *Le Français Moderne* 53.1/2:78–89.

———. 1985b. "Le Temps dans la mise en scène du récit de vie comme écriture." *Pratiques* 45:52–64.

Brannen, Noah S. 1979. "Time Deixis in Japanese and English Discourse." In *Explorations in Linguistics,* edited by G. Bedell et al., 37–57. Tokyo: Kenkyusha.

Brault, Gerard J. 1978. *The Song of Roland: An Analytical Edition.* University Park: Pennsylvania State University Press.

Bright, William. 1982. "Poetic Structures in Oral Narrative." In Tannen, ed., 1982d, 171–184.

Britton, Celia. 1987. *Claude Simon: Writing the Visible*. Cambridge: Cambridge University Press.

Bronzwaer, W. J. M. 1970. *Tense in the Novel*. Groningen: Wolters-Noordhoff.

Brooks, Cleanth, and Robert Penn Warren. 1943. *Understanding Fiction*. New York: Crofts.

Brunot, Ferdinand, and Charles Bruneau. 1949. *Précis de grammaire historique de la langue française*. Paris: Masson.

Buffin, J. M. 1925. *Remarques sur les moyens d'expression de la durée et du temps en français*. Paris: Presses Universitaires de France.

Bull, William E. 1960. *Time, Tense, and the Verb*. University of California Publications in Linguistics, 19. Berkeley and Los Angeles: University of California Press.

Burbelo, V. B. 1986. "Pro deyaki osoblivosti aktualizatsii kategorii chasu v epichonomu teksti" [On Certain Peculiarities of Tense Category Actualization in Epic Text]. *Movoznavstvo* 20.2:45−49.

Burton, Deirdre. 1980. *Dialogue and Discourse: A Sociolinguistic Approach to Modern Drama Dialogue and Naturally Occurring Conversation*. London: Routledge and Kegan Paul.

Butor, Michel. 1969. *Essais sur le roman*. Paris: Gallimard. Repr. 1975.

Carlson, Lauri. 1981. "Aspect and Quantification." In Tedeschi and Zaenen, eds., 1981, 31−64.

Casparis, Christian Paul. 1975. *Tense without Time: The Present Tense in Narration*. Schweizer Anglistische Arbeiten, 84. Berne: Francke.

Centineo, Giulia. Forthcoming. "Tense Switching in Italian: The Alternation between *Passato Prossimo* and *Passato Remoto* in Oral Narration." In Fleischman and Waugh, eds., forthcoming.

Cerquiglini, Bernard. 1981. *La Parole médiévale*. Paris: Editions de Minuit.

———. 1984. "Le Style indirect libre et la modernité." *Langages* 73:7−16.

Cerquiglini, Bernard, Jacqueline Cerquiglini, Christiane Marchello-Nizia, and Michèle Perret-Minard. 1976. "L'Objet 'ancien français' et les conditions propres à sa description linguistique." In *Méthodes en grammaire française*, edited by Jean Claude Chevalier and Maurice Gross, 185−200. Paris: Klincksieck.

Chafe, Wallace L. 1973. "Language and Memory." *Language* 49:266−281.

———. 1982. "Integration and Involvement in Speaking, Writing, and Oral Literature." In Tannen, ed., 1982d, 35−44.

———. 1987. "Cognitive Constraints on Information Flow." In Tomlin, ed., 1987, 21−51.

Chasca, Edmund de. 1967. *El Arte juglaresco en el "Cantar de Mio Cid"*. Madrid: Gredos (1st ed. 1955, *Estructura y forma en "El Poema de mio Cid"*).

Chatman, Seymour. 1978. *Story and Discourse: Narrative Structure in Fiction and Film*. Ithaca and London: Cornell University Press.

Chaurand, Jacques. 1966. "Le temps grammatical dans quelques 'mondes au présent': L'Enfance, la geste médiévale, et le nouveau roman." *Le Français Moderne* 34:210−224, 254−263.

Chausserie-Laprée, Jean-Pierre. 1969. *L'Expression narrative chez les historiens latins.* Paris: Boccard.

Chevalier, Jean-Claude. 1971. "Architecture temporelle du 'romancero tradicional.'" *Bulletin Hispanique* 73:50–103.

Chung, Sandra, and Alan Timberlake. 1985. "Tense, Aspect, and Mood." In Shopen, ed., 1985, 3:202–258.

Chvany, Catherine V. 1979. "Grammatical Categories in the Narrative of Elin Pelin's *Zemja.*" *Folia Slavica* 3.3:296–316.

———. 1980. "The Role of Verbal Tense and Aspect in the Narration of the *Tale of Igor's Campaign.*" In *The Structural Analysis of Narrative Texts,* edited by Andrej Kodjak et al., 2:7–23. New York University Slavic Papers. Columbus, Ohio: Slavica.

———. 1984 (author's copyright). "Backgrounded Perfectives and Plot Line Imperfectives: Towards a Theory of Grounding in Text." In *The Scope of Slavic Aspect,* edited by M. S. Flier and A. H. Timberlake, 247–273. UCLA Slavic Studies, 12. Columbus, Ohio: Slavica, 1985.

———. 1985. "Foregrounding, Saliency, Transitivity." *Essays in Poetics* 10.2:1–23.

Clanchy, M. T. 1979. *From Memory to Written Record: England 1066–1307.* London: Edward Arnold.

Cohn, Dorrit. 1978. *Transparent Minds: Narrative Modes for Presenting Consciousness in Fiction.* Princeton: Princeton University Press.

———. Forthcoming. "Fictional *versus* Historical Lives: Borderlines and Borderline Cases." *Journal for Narrative Technique.*

Company, Concepción. 1983. "Sintaxis y valores de los tiempos compuestos en el español medieval." *Nueva Revista de Filología Hispánica* 32:235–257.

Comrie, Bernard. 1976. *Aspect.* Cambridge: Cambridge University Press.

———. 1981. "On Reichenbach's Approach to Tense." In *Papers from the Seventeenth Regional Meeting, Chicago Linguistic Society,* edited by R. A. Hendrick, C. S. Masek, and M. F. Miller, 24–30. Chicago: Chicago Linguistic Society.

———. 1985. *Tense.* Cambridge: Cambridge University Press.

Costello, Edward T. 1979. "Modality and Textual Structuration." *Poetics and Theory of Literature* 4:299–314.

Coulmas, Florian, ed. 1986. *Direct and Indirect Speech.* Berlin: Mouton de Gruyter.

Crist, Larry S. 1981. "*Halt sunt li pui:* Remarques sur les structures lyriques de la *Chanson de Roland.*" In *[Actes del] VIII Congreso de la Société Rencesvals (Pamplona-Santiago de Compostela, 1978),* 93–100. Pamplona: Institución Príncipe de Viana.

Crosby, Ruth. 1936. "Oral Delivery in the Middle Ages." *Speculum* 11:88–100.

Culler, Jonathan. 1980. "*Fabula* and *Sjuzhet* in the Analysis of Narrative." *Poetics Today* 1:27–37.

Dahl, Osten. 1985. *Tense and Aspect Systems.* Oxford: Blackwell.

Danto, Arthur C. 1965. *Analytical Philosophy of History.* Cambridge: Cambridge University Press.

De Felice, Egidio. 1957. "Problemi di aspetto nei più antichi testi francesi." *Vox Romanica* 16:1–51.

Dembowski, Peter F. 1963. *La Chronique de Robert de Clari: Etude de la langue et du style*. University of Toronto Romance Series, 6. Toronto: University of Toronto Press.

Derrida, Jacques. 1968. "La Différance." In *Théorie d'ensemble*, 41–66. Paris: Seuil. Repr. in English as "Différance." In *Speech Phenomena and Other Essays on Husserl's Theory of Signs*, 129–160. Evanston: Northwestern University Press, 1973.

Di Stefano, Giuseppe. 1976. "Discorso retrospettivo e schemi narrativi nel romancero." In *Linguistica e letteratura*, I : 25–55. Pisa: Giardini.

Doležel, Lubomir. 1967. "The Typology of the Narrator: Point of View in Fiction." In *To Honor Roman Jakobson*, I : 541–552. The Hague: Mouton.

———. 1980. "Truth and Authenticity in Narrative." *Poetics Today* 1.3 : 7–25.

Dorfman, Eugene. 1969. *The Narreme in Medieval Romance Epics*. Toronto: University of Toronto Press.

Dowty, David. 1979. *Word Meaning and Montague Grammar*. Dordrecht: Reidel.

Dray, William H. 1971. "On the Nature and Role of Narrative in Historiography." *History and Theory* 10 : 153–171.

Dry, Helen Aristair. 1981. "Sentence Aspect and the Movement of Narrative Time." *Text* 1.3 : 233–240.

———. 1983. "The Movement of Narrative Time." *Journal of Literary Semantics* 12.2 : 19–53.

Du Bois, John W. 1987. "The Discourse Base of Ergativity." *Language* 63 : 805–855.

Ducrot, Oswald. 1979. "L'Imparfait en français." *Linguistische Berichte* 60 : 1–23.

———. 1984. *Le Dire et le dit*. Paris: Editions de Minuit.

Duggan, Joseph J. 1973. *The Song of Roland: Formulaic Style and Poetic Craft*. Berkeley and Los Angeles: University of California Press.

———. 1987. "Appropriation of Historical Knowledge by the Vernacular Epic." In *Grundriss des romanischen Literaturen des Mittelalters*, vol. II, *Historiographie*, edited by Hans Ulrich Gumbrecht et al., 285–311. Heidelberg: Carl Winter.

Dujardin, Edouard. 1925. *Les Lauriers sont coupés*. Preface by Valéry Larbaud. Introduction by Olivier de Magny. Paris: Messein. Repr. Paris: "10/18," 1968.

———. 1931. *Le Monologue intérieur*. Paris: Messein.

Eisner, Judith. 1975. "A Grammar of Oral Narrative." Diss., University of Michigan.

Ellis, John. 1974. *The Theory of Criticism*. Berkeley and Los Angeles: University of California Press.

Emery, Annie Crosby. 1897. *The Historical Present in Early Latin*. Ellsworth, Maine: Hancock.

Enkvist, Nils Erik. 1981. "Experiential Iconicism in Text Strategy." *Text* 1.1 : 77–111.

Enos, Ralph. 1981. "The Use of the Historical Present in the Gospel according to St. Mark." *Journal of the Linguistic Association of the Southwest* 3.4 : 281–298.

Erbaugh, Mary S. 1987. "A Uniform Pause and Error Strategy for Native and Non-Native Speakers." In Tomlin, ed., 1987, 109–130 (title listed in Contents as "Psycholinguistic Evidence for Foregrounding and Backgrounding").

Ess-Dykema, Carol J. van. 1984. "The Historical Present in Oral Spanish Narratives." Diss., Georgetown University.

Evans, D. Simon. 1964. *A Grammar of Middle Welsh.* Dublin: Dublin Institute for Advanced Studies.

Fabre, Daniel, and Jacques Lacroix. 1974. *La Tradition orale du conte occitan,* vol 1. Paris: Presses Universitaires de France.

Faral, Edmond. 1924. *Les Arts poétiques du XIIe et du XIIIe siècle: Recherches et documents sur la technique littérature du moyen âge.* Paris: Champion. Repr. Geneva: Slatkine, 1982.

——. 1934. *La Chanson de Roland: Etude et analyse.* Paris: Mellottée.

Faye, Paul-Louis. 1933. "L'Equivalence passé défini-imparfait en ancien français." *University of Colorado Studies* 20.4 : 267–308.

Fillmore, Charles W. 1975. *Santa Cruz Lectures on Deixis 1971.* Bloomington: Indiana University Linguistics Club.

Fleischman, Suzanne. 1982. *The Future in Thought and Language: Diachronic Evidence from Romance.* Cambridge Studies in Linguistics, 36. Cambridge: Cambridge University Press.

——. 1983a. "From Pragmatics to Grammar: Diachronic Reflexions on the Development of Complex Pasts and Futures in Romance." *Lingua* 60 : 183–214.

——. 1983b. "On the Representation of History and Fiction in the Middle Ages." *History and Theory* 22.3 : 278–310.

——. 1985. "Discourse Functions of Tense-Aspect Oppositions in Narrative: Toward a Theory of Grounding." *Linguistics* 23 : 851–882.

——. 1986a. "Evaluation in Narrative: The Present Tense in Medieval 'Performed Stories.'" *Yale French Studies* 70 : 199–251.

——. 1986b. "'Overlay' Structures in the *Song of Roland:* A Discourse-Pragmatic Strategy of Oral Narrative." *BLS* 12 : 108–123.

——. 1989a. "A Linguistic Perspective on the *Laisses Similaires:* Orality and the Pragmatics of Narrative Discourse." *Romance Philology* 43.1.

——. 1989b. "Temporal Distance: A Basic Linguistic Metaphor." *Studies in Language* 13 : 1–50.

——. Forthcoming. "Verb Tense and Point of View in Narrative." In Fleischman and Waugh, eds., forthcoming.

Fleischman, Suzanne, and Linda R. Waugh, eds. Forthcoming. *Discourse-Pragmatic Approaches to the Verb: The Evidence from Romance.* London: Routledge, Chapman and Hall.

Folena, G. 1952. *La crisi linguistica del Quattrocento e l'Arcadia di Sannazzaro.* Florence: Olschki.

Foley, William A., and Robert D. Van Valin. 1984. *Functional Syntax and Universal Grammar.* Cambridge Studies in Linguistics, 38. Cambridge: Cambridge University Press.

Fotitch, Tatiana. 1950. *The Narrative Tenses in Chrétien de Troyes: A Study in Syntax and Stylistics.* CUASRLL, 38. Washington, D.C.: Catholic University of America Press.

Foulet, Lucien. 1919. *Petite syntaxe de l'ancien français.* 3d ed. Paris: Champion. Repr. 1974.

——. 1920. "La Disparition du prétérit." *Romania* 46 : 271–313.

Fowler, Roger. 1977. *Linguistics and the Novel*. London: Methuen.

Frappier, Jean. 1969. *Etude sur "Yvain" ou "Le chevalier du lion" de Chrétien de Troyes*. Paris: Société d'Edition d'Enseignement Supérieur.

Frey, John R. 1946. "The Historical Present in Narrative Language, Particularly in Modern German Fiction." *Journal of English and Germanic Philology* 45 : 43–67.

Friedemann, Käte. 1910. *Die Rolle des Erzählers in der Epik*. Leipzig: H. Haessel. Repr. Darmstadt: Wissentschaftliche Buchgesellschaft, 1965.

Fritz, K. von. 1949. "The So-Called Historical Present in Early Greek." *Word* 5 : 186–201.

Frye, Northrup. 1957. *Anatomy of Criticism*. Princeton: Princeton University Press.

Fulk, Robert D. 1987. "The Historical Present in Medieval Irish Narrative." *Zeitschrift für Keltische Philologie* 42 : 330–343.

Gallais, Pierre. 1964. "Recherches sur la mentalité des romanciers français du moyen âge." *Cahiers de Civilisation Médiévale* 7 : 479–493.

Gallie, W. B. 1968. *Philosophy and the Historical Understanding*. New York: Schocken Books.

Garey, Howard B. 1955. *The Historical Development of Tenses from Latin to Old French*. Language Diss. no. 51, *Language* 31.1 : 2, Supplement.

Genette, Gérard. 1966. "Vertige fixé." In *Figures I*, 69–90. Paris: Seuil.

———. 1980. *Narrative Discourse: An Essay in Method*. Translation by Jane E. Lewin of "Discours du récit," a portion of *Figures III* (1972). Ithaca: Cornell University Press.

Gensler, Orin. 1976. "Tense in ʕaḡarma Arabic." Berkeley, Cal.: MS.

Georges, Robert A. 1969. "Toward an Understanding of the Storytelling Event." *Journal of American Folklore* 82 : 313–328.

Gilman, Stephen. 1961. *Tiempo y formas temporales en el "Poema del Cid"*. Madrid: Gredos.

———. 1967. Review of Szertics 1967. *Modern Language Notes* 83 : 339–343.

———. 1972. "On 'Romancero' as a Poetic Language." In *Homenaje a Casalduero*, 151–160. Madrid: Gredos.

Givón, Talmy. 1977. "The Drift from VSO to SVO in Biblical Hebrew: The Pragmatics of Tense-Aspect." In *Mechanisms of Syntactic Change*, edited by Charles N. Li, 181–254. Austin: University of Texas Press.

———, ed. 1979a. *Discourse and Syntax*. Syntax and Semantics, 12. New York: Academic Press.

———. 1979b. "From Discourse to Syntax: Grammar as a Processing Strategy." In Givón, ed., 1979a, 81–112.

———. 1982. "Evidentiality and Epistemic Space." *Studies in Language* 6 : 23–49.

———. 1983. *Topic Continuity in Discourse*. Amsterdam: Benjamins.

———. 1984. *Syntax: A Functional-Typological Introduction*, vol. 1. Amsterdam: Benjamins.

———. 1987. "Beyond Foreground and Background." In Tomlin, ed., 1987, 175–188.

Gleason, H. A. 1968. "Contrastive Analysis of Discourse Structure." *Georgetown University Monograph Series on Languages and Linguistics* 21 : 39–64.

Goffman, Erving. 1974. *Frame Analysis*. New York: Harper and Row.

Goldin, Frederick, trans. 1978. *The Song of Roland*. New York: Norton.

Goldin, Frederick. 1981. "Le Temps de chronique dans la *Chanson de Roland*." In *[Actas del] VIII Congreso de la Société Rencesvals (Pamplona-Santiago de Compostela, 1978)*, 173–183. Pamplona: Institución Príncipe de Viana.

Gonda, Jan. 1956. *The Character of the Indo-European Moods*. Wiesbaden: Harrassowitz.

Goody, Jack, and Ian Watt. 1968. "The Consequences of Literacy." In *Literacy in Traditional Societies*, edited by J. G., 27–68. Cambridge: Cambridge University Press.

Gougenheim, Georges. 1929. *Etudes sur les périphrases verbales de la langue française*. Paris: Les Belles Lettres. Repr. Paris: Nizet, n.d.

Graef, A. 1889. "Die präsentischen Tempora bei Chaucer." *Anglia* 12:532–577.

Grassi, C. 1966. "Sull'aspetto verbale, con particolare riferimento al latino." In *Problemi di sintassi latina*, 93–250. Florence: La Nuova Italia.

Greenberg, Joseph H. 1966. *Language Universals, with Special Reference to Feature Hierarchies*. The Hague: Mouton.

Grice, H. Paul. 1974. "Logic and Conversation." In *Speech Acts,* edited by Peter Cole and Jerrold Morgan, 41–58. Syntax and Semantics, 3. New York: Academic Press.

Grimes, Joseph E. 1975. *The Thread of Discourse*. The Hague: Mouton.

———. 1978. *Papers on Discourse*. Dallas: Summer Institute of Linguistics.

Groethuysen, B. 1935–1936. "De quelques aspects du temps: Notes pour une phénoménologie du récit." *Recherches Philosophiques* 5:139–195.

Grunmann, Minette. 1976. "Temporal Patterns in the *Chanson de Guillaume*." *Olifant* 4.1:49–62.

Grunmann-Gaudet, Minette. 1980. "The Representation of Time in the *Chanson de Roland*." In *The Nature of Medieval Narrative*, edited by M. G.-G. and Robin F. Jones, 77–98. Lexington, Ky.: French Forum.

Guillaume, Gustave. 1929. *Temps et verbe*. Paris: Champion.

Gumbrecht, Hans Ulrich. 1981. "Strangeness as a Requirement for Topicality: Medieval Literature and Reception Theory." *L'Esprit Créateur* 21:5–12.

Haberland, Hartmut. 1986. "Reported Speech in Danish." In Coulmas, ed., 1986, 219–253.

Halliday, M. A. K., and Ruqaiya Hasan. 1976. *Cohesion in Spoken and Written English*. London: Longman.

Hamburger, Käte. 1973. *The Logic of Literature*. 2d rev. ed. Translated by Marilyn Rose. Bloomington: Indiana University Press.

Harris, Martin B. 1982. "The 'Past Simple' and the 'Present Perfect' in Romance." In *Studies in the Romance Verb,* ed. M. B. H. and Nigel Vincent, 42–70. London: Croom Helm.

Hatcher, Anna Granville. 1942. "Tense-Usage in the *Roland*." *SP* 39:597–624.

———. 1946. "Epic Patterns in Old French." *Word* 2:8–24.

Hatzfeld, Helmut. 1952. *Literature through Art: A New Approach to French Literature*. New York: Oxford.

Heath, Stephen. 1972. *The Nouveau Roman: A Study in the Practice of Writing*. London: Elek.

Herczeg, Giulio. 1958. "Valore stilistico del presente storico in italiano." In *Omagiu lui Iorgu Iordan,* 371–379. Bucharest: Academia Republicii Populare Romîne. Repr. in *Saggi linguistici e stilistici.* Florence: L. Olschki, 1972.

Herring, Susan. 1985a. "Narration and the Present Tense: The Tamil Narrative Present." Berkeley, Cal.: MS.

———. 1985b. "Special Field Annotated Bibliography: Tense, Aspect, and Narrative Structure." Berkeley, Cal.: MS.

———. 1986a. "The Present Tense in Narration: Developmental Implications of a Unified Historical Present Account." Paper presented at the Workshop on the Acquisition of Temporal Structures, Chicago Linguistic Society, April 1986.

———. 1986b. "Marking and Unmarking via the Present Tense in Narration: The Historical Present Redefined." Berkeley, Cal.: MS.

Hockett, Charles F. 1958. *A Course in Modern Linguistics.* New York: Macmillan.

Hoffmann, Emanuel. 1884. *Die Zeitfolge nach dem Praesens Historicum im Latein.* Vienna: Konegen.

Hoffmann, J. B., and A. Szantyr. 1963. *Lateinische Syntax und Stilistik.* Munich: Beck'sche.

Hopper, Paul J. 1979a. "Aspect and Foregrounding in Discourse." In Givón, ed., 1979a, 213–241.

———. 1979b. "Some Observations on the Typology of Focus and Aspect in Narrative Language." *Studies in Language* 3.1:37–64.

———. 1982a. "Aspect between Discourse and Grammar: An Introductory Essay for the Volume." In Hopper, ed., 1982b, 3–18.

———, ed. 1982b. *Tense-Aspect: Between Semantics and Pragmatics.* Typological Studies in Language, 1. Amsterdam: Benjamins.

———. 1986. "Discourse Function and Typological Shift: A Typological Study of the VS/SV Alternation." In *Language Typology 1985: Papers from the Linguistic Typology Symposium, Moscow, 9–13 December 1985,* edited by Winfred P. Lehmann, 123–141. Current Issues in Linguistic Theory, 47. Amsterdam: Benjamins.

———. 1987. "Emergent Grammar." *BLS* 13:139–157.

Hopper, Paul J., and Sandra A. Thompson. 1980. "Transitivity in Grammar and Discourse." *Language* 56.2:251–299.

———, eds. 1982. *Studies in Transitivity.* Syntax and Semantics, 15. New York: Academic Press.

Hornstein, Norbert. 1977. "Towards a Theory of Tense." *Linguistic Inquiry* 8:521–527.

Hymes, Dell. 1974. "Breakthrough into Performance." In *Folklore, Performance, and Communication,* edited by D. Ben Amos and K. Goldstein, 11–74. The Hague: Mouton.

Imbs, Paul. 1956. *Les Propositions temporelles en ancien français.* 2 vols. Pubs. de la Faculté des Lettres de l'Université de Strasbourg, 120. Paris: Les Belles Lettres.

———. [1960.] *L'Emploi des temps verbaux en français moderne.* Bibl. Française et Romane, série A, 1. Paris: Klincksieck.

Iser, Wolfgang. 1971. "The Reading Process: A Phenomenological Approach." *New Literary History* 3:279–299.

Jakobson, Roman. 1938. Discussion following paper by J. Marouzeau, "Fait de langue et fait de style." In *Actes du Quatrième Congrès International de Linguistes (Copenhagen, 1936)*. Copenhagen: Munksgaard.

———. 1957. *Shifters, Verbal Categories and the Russian Verb*. Cambridge, Mass.: Harvard University Russian Language Project. Repr. in *Selected Writings*, vol. 2, *Word and Language*, 130–147. The Hague–Paris: Mouton, 1971.

———. 1960. "Closing Statement: Linguistics and Poetics." In *Style in Language*, edited by Thomas A. Sebeok, 350–377. Cambridge, Mass.: MIT Press.

———. 1971. "On Realism in Art." Translated by Karol Magassy. In Matejka and Pomorska, eds., 1971, 38–46 (first published in Czech, 1921).

James, Deborah. 1982. "Past Tense and the Hypothetical: A Cross-Linguistic Study." *Studies in Language* 6.3 : 375–403.

Jarrett, Dennis. 1984. "Pragmatic Coherence in an Oral Formulaic Tradition: I Can Read Your Letters/Sure Can't Read Your Mind." In Tannen, ed., 1984a, 155–171.

Jauss, Hans Robert. 1963. "Chanson de geste et roman courtois." In *Chanson de geste und höfischer Roman*, 61–77. Heidelberger Kolloquium, 30. Heidelberg: Carl Winter.

———. 1970. "Literary History as a Challenge to Literary Theory." *New Literary History*. 2 : 7–37. Repr. 1974 in *New Directions in Literary History*, edited by Ralph Cohen. Baltimore: Johns Hopkins University Press.

Jespersen, Otto. 1935. *The Philosophy of Grammar*. London and New York. Repr. 1965. New York: Norton Library.

Jones, Larry, and Linda K. Jones. 1979. "Multiple Levels of Information Relevance in Discourse." In *Discourse Studies in Mesoamerican Languages*, vol. 1, edited by L. K. J., 3–28. Summer Institute of Linguistics Publications, 58. Dallas: Summer Institute of Linguistics and University of Texas at Arlington.

Joos, Martin. 1964. *The English Verb*. Madison: University of Wisconsin Press.

Kalmár, Ivan. 1982. "Transitivity in a Czech Folk Tale." In Hopper and Thompson, eds., 1982, 241–259.

Kamp, Hans, and Christian Rohrer. 1983. "Tense in Texts." In *Meaning, Use and Interpretation in Language*, edited by Rainer Bäuerle, Christoph Schwarze, and Arnim von Stechow, 250–269. Berlin/New York: Springer.

Kayser, Wolfgang. 1970. "Qui raconte le roman?" *Poétique* 4 : 498–510.

Keenan, Edward L. 1976. "Towards a Universal Definition of Subject." In *Subject and Topic*, edited by Charles N. Li, 303–334. New York: Academic Press.

Kermode, Frank. 1967. *The Sense of an Ending: Studies in the Theory of Fiction*. New York: Oxford University Press.

Kiparsky, Paul. 1968. "Tense and Mood in Indo-European Syntax." *Foundations of Language* 4 : 30–57.

———. 1974. "Oral Poetry: Some Linguistic and Typological Considerations." In *Oral Literature and the Formula*, edited by Benjamin A. Stolz and Richard S. Shannon, 73–106. Ann Arbor: Center for the Co-ordination of Ancient and Modern Studies.

Kuen, Heinrich. 1934. Review of Wartburg, *Evolution et structure de la langue française*. *Zeitschrift für französische Sprache und Literatur* 58 : 489–507.

Kuroda, S.-Y. 1976. "Reflections on the Foundations of Narrative Theory from a Linguistic Point-of-View." In *Pragmatics of Language and Literature*, edited by Teun A. van Dijk, 108–140. Amsterdam and New York: North Holland.

Labelle, Marie. 1987. "L'Utilisation des temps du passé dans les narrations françaises: Le Passé Composé, L'Imparfait et Le Présent Historique." *Revue Romane* 22.1:3–29.

Labov, William. 1972. "The Transformation of Experience in Narrative Syntax." In *Language in the Inner City*, 354–396. Philadelphia: University of Pennsylvania Press.

———. 1982. "Speech Actions and Reactions in Personal Narrative." In Tannen, ed., 1982a, 219–247.

Labov, William, and Joshua Waletzky. 1967. "Narrative Analysis: Oral Versions of Personal Experience." In *Essays on the Verbal and Visual Arts*. Proceedings of the 1966 Annual Spring Meeting of the American Ethnological Society, edited by June Helm (McNeish), 12–44. Seattle: University of Washington Press.

Lacy, Norris J. 1974. "Spatial Form in Medieval Romance." *Yale French Studies* 51:160–169.

Lanser, Susan S. 1981. *The Narrative Act: Point of View in Prose Fiction*. Princeton: Princeton University Press.

Leech, Geoffrey N., and Michael H. Short. 1981. *Style in Fiction: A Linguistic Introduction to English Fictional Prose*. London: Longman.

Lehmann, Willibald. 1939. *Das Präsens Historicum in den Islendinga Sogur*. Würtzburg-Aumühle: K. Triltsch.

Lejeune, Philippe. 1985. "Autobiographie et histoires de famille." *Pratiques* 45:5–11.

Lerch, Eugen. 1922. "Das Imperfektum als Ausdruck der lebhaften Vorstellung." *Zeitschrift für romanische Philologie* 42:311–331, 384–425.

Levin, Saul. 1969. "Remarks on the 'Historical Present' and Comparable Phenomena of Syntax." *Foundations of Language* 5:386–390.

Li, Charles N. 1986. "Direct and Indirect Speech: A Functional Study." In Coulmas, ed., 1986, 29–45.

Lock, Richard. 1981. "Patterns of Narrative and Patterns of Time in the *Chanson de Roland*." In *[Actas del] VIII Congreso de la Société Rencesvals (Pamplona-Santiago de Compostela, 1978)*, 291–297. Pamplona: Institución Príncipe de Viana.

———. 1985. *Aspects of Time in Medieval Literature*. New York: Garland.

Longacre, Robert E. 1976. *Anatomy of Speech Notions*. Lisse: De Ridder.

———. 1981. "A Spectrum and Profile Approach to Discourse Analysis." *Text* 1:337–359.

———. 1983. *The Grammar of Discourse*. New York and London: Plenum.

Lunn, Patricia V. 1985. "The Aspectual Lens." *Hispanic Linguistics* 2:49–61.

Lyons, John. 1977. *Semantics*. 2 vols. Cambridge: Cambridge University Press.

Mandler, Jean M., and Marsha S. Goodman. 1982. "On the Psychological Validity of Story Structure." *Journal of Verbal Learning and Verbal Behavior* 21.5:507–523.

Mandler, Jean M., and Nancy S. Johnson. 1977. "Remembrance of Things Parsed: Story Structure and Recall." *Cognitive Psychology* 9:111–151.

Marchello-Nizia, Christiane. 1985. *Dire le vrai: L'adverbe "si" en français médiéval*. Publications Romanes et Françaises, 168. Geneva: Droz.

Martin, Robert. 1971. *Temps et aspect: Essai sur l'emploi des temps narratifs en moyen français*. Paris: Klincksieck.

Martin, Robert, and Marc Wilmet. 1980. *Manuel du français du moyen âge, 2, Syntaxe du moyen français*. Bordeaux: SOBODI.

Matejka, Ladislav, and Krystyna Pomorska, eds. 1971. *Readings in Russian Poetics: Formalist and Structuralist Views*. Cambridge, Mass.: MIT Press.

Matthiessen, Christian, and Sandra A. Thompson. 1988. "The Structure of Discourse and 'Subordination.'" In *Clause Combining in Grammar and Discourse*, edited by John Haiman and Sandra A. Thompson, 275–301. Typological Studies in Language, 18. Amsterdam: Benjamins.

McKay, K. L. 1974. "Further Remarks on the 'Historical Present' and Other Phenomena." *Foundations of Language* 11 : 247–251.

Mellet, Sylvie. 1980. "Le Présent 'historique' ou 'de narration.'" *L'Information Grammaticale* 4 : 6–11.

Ménard, Philippe. 1973. *Manuel du français du moyen âge, 1, Syntaxe de l'ancien français*. Revised ed. Bordeaux: SOBODI.

Mendilow, A. A. 1952. *Time and the Novel*. Introduction by J. Isaacs. New York: Humanities Press. Repr. 1965.

Menéndez Pidal, Ramón. 1908. *Cantar de mio Cid: Texto, gramática y vocabulario*. Madrid: Bailly-Balliere e Hijos. Repr. Madrid: Espasa-Calpe, 1944.

———. 1951. *Relíquias de la poesía épica española*. Madrid: Espasa-Calpe.

———. 1957–1964. *Romancero Tradicional*, vols. 1 and 2. Madrid: Gredos.

Menéndez y Pelayo, Marcelino. 1944–1945. *Tratado de los romances viejos*, vols. 2–4 (= vols. 7–9 of *Antología de poetas líricos castellanos*). Edición Nacional de las Obras Completas de Menéndez y Pelayo, vols. 22–24. Santander: Aldus (original ed. Madrid, 1899).

Mink, Louis O. 1968. "The Anatomy of Historical Understanding." *Review of Metaphysics* 20 : 667–698.

Mirrer-Singer, Louise. 1986. *The Language of Evaluation: A Sociolinguistic Approach to the Story of Pedro el Cruel in Ballad and Chronicle*. Purdue University Monographs in Romance Languages, 20. Amsterdam and Philadelphia: Benjamins.

Mitchell, W. T. J., ed. 1981. *On Narrative*. Chicago: University of Chicago Press.

Montgomery, Thomas. 1968. "Narrative Tense Preference in the *Cantar de Mio Cid*." *Romance Philology* 21 : 253–274.

Monville Burston, Monique, and Linda R. Waugh. 1985. "Le Passé simple dans le discours journalistique." *Lingua* 67 : 121–170.

Mourelatos, Alexander P. D. 1981. "Events, Processes, States." In Tedeschi and Zaenen, eds., 1981, 191–212.

Muller, C. 1966. "Pour une étude diachronique de l'imparfait narratif." In *Mélanges de grammaire française offerts à M. Maurice Grevisse*, 252–269. Gembloux: Duculot.

Müller, Günther. 1968. "Erzählzeit und Erzähltezeit." In *Morphologische Poetik, Gesammelte Aufsatze*, edited by Elena Müller, 269–286. Tübingen: Niemeyer (originally published 1948).

Munro, Pamela. 1982. "On the Transitivity of 'Say' Verbs." In Hopper and Thompson, eds., 1982, 301–318.

Myers, Oliver T. 1966. "Assonance and Tense in the *Poema del Cid.*" *PMLA* 81:493–498.

Nef, Frédéric. 1980. "Maintenant₁ et maintenant₂: Sémantique et pragmatique de 'maintenant' temporel et non-temporel." In *La Notion d'aspect*, edited by Jean David and Robert Martin, 145–165. Metz: Centre d'Analyse Syntaxique.

Nordahl, Helge. 1972. "Parataxe rhétorique dans la *Chanson de Roland.*" *Revue des Langues Romanes* 80:345–354.

Ochs, Elinor. 1979. "Planned and Unplanned Discourse." In Givón, ed., 1979a, 51–80.

Ollier, Marie Louise. 1978. "Le Présent du récit: Temporalité et roman en vers." *Langue Française* 40:99–112.

Olson, David R. 1977. "From Utterance to Text: The Bias of Language in Speech and Writing." *Harvard Educational Review* 47:257–281.

Ong, Walter J., S.J. 1965. "Oral Residue in Tudor Prose Style." *PMLA* 80:145–154. Repr. in W. J. O., *Rhetoric, Romance, and Technology*, 23–47. Ithaca: Cornell University Press, 1971.

———. 1982a. "Oral Remembering and Narrative Structures." In Tannen, ed., 1982a, 12–24.

———. 1982b. *Orality and Literacy: The Technologizing of the Word*. London and New York: Methuen.

Ortega y Gasset, José. 1961. *History as a System and Other Essays toward a Philosophy of History*. New York: Norton (first published in Spanish, 1941).

Osselton, N. E. 1982. "On the Use of the Perfect in Present-Tense Narrative." *English Studies* 63.1:63–69.

Östmann, Jan-Ola. 1981. *"You Know": A Discourse-Functional Study*. Amsterdam: Benjamins.

Paden, William D., Jr. 1977. "L'Emploi vicaire du présent verbal dans les plus anciens textes narratifs romans." In *XIV Congresso internazionale di linguistica e filologia romanze (Napoli, 15–20 aprile 1974)*, 4:545–557. Naples: Macchiaroli/Amsterdam: Benjamins.

Pascal, Roy. 1962. "Tense and the Novel." *Modern Language Review* 57.1:1–12.

Peabody, Berkeley. 1975. *The Winged Word: A Study in the Technique of Ancient Greek Oral Composition as Seen Principally through Hesiod's "Works and Days."* Albany: SUNY Press.

Peeters, Léopold. 1972. "Syntaxe et style dans la *Chanson de Roland.*" *Revue des Langues Romanes* 80:45–59.

Peirce, Charles Sanders. 1932. *Collected Writings*, vol. 2, *Elements of Logic*. Cambridge, Mass.: Harvard University Press.

Perry, Anne A., ed. 1981. *La Passion des jongleurs*. Paris: Beauchesne.

Pickens, Rupert T. 1979. "Historical Consciousness in Old French Narrative." *French Forum* 4.2:168–184.

Poirion, Daniel. 1978. "Les Paragraphes et le pré-texte de Villehardouin." *Langue Française* 40:45–59.

Polanyi, Livia. 1981. "Telling the Same Story Twice." *Text* 1.4 : 315–336.

————. 1982. "Linguistic and Social Constraints on Storytelling." *Journal of Pragmatics* 6 : 509–524.

————. 1985. *Telling the American Story: A Structural and Cultural Analysis of Conversational Storytelling.* Norwood, N.J.: Ablex.

————. 1986. "Narrative Organization and Disorganization." Paper presented at the Workshop on the Acquisition of Temporal Structures in Discourse. University of Chicago, April 1986.

Polanyi, Livia, and Paul J. Hopper. 1981. "A Revision of the Foreground-Background Distinction." Paper presented to the Winter Meeting, Linguistic Society of America, New York.

Pouillon, Jean. 1946. *Temps et roman.* Paris: Gallimard.

Pratt, Mary Louise. 1977. *Toward a Speech-Act Theory of Literary Discourse.* Bloomington: Indiana University Press.

Prince, Gerald A. 1982. *Narratology: The Form and Function of Narrative.* Janua Linguarum, Series Maior, 108. The Hague: Mouton.

Propp, Vladimir. 1958. *Morphology of the Folktale.* Bloomington: Indiana University Press. 2d ed. rev. by Louis A. Wagner. Austin: University of Texas Press, 1968 (orig. published in Russian, 1928).

Proust, Marcel. 1920. "A propos du style de Flaubert." *Nouvelle Revue Française* 14.1 : 72–90. / "About Flaubert's Style." In *Marcel Proust: A Selection from His Miscellaneous Writings.* Translated by Gerard Hopkins. London: Wingate, 1949.

Quine, Willard van Orman. 1960. *Word and Object.* Cambridge, Mass.: Technology Press of the Massachusetts Institute of Technology.

Raimond, Michel. 1966. *La Crise du roman, des lendemains du naturalisme aux années 20.* Paris: Corti.

Reichenbach, Hans. 1947. *Elements of Symbolic Logic.* London: Collier-Macmillan. Repr. New York: Free Press, 1966.

Reid, T. B. W. 1955. "On the Analysis of the Tense System of French." *Revue de Linguistique Romane* 19 : 23–38.

————. 1970. "Verbal Aspect in Modern French." In *The French Language: Studies Presented to Lewis Charles Harmer,* edited by T. G. S. Combe and Peter Rickard, 146–171. London: Harrap.

Reid, Wallis J. 1976. "The Quantitative Validation of a Grammatical Hypothesis: The Passé Simple and the Imparfait." *Papers of the Northeastern Linguistic Society (NELS),* 7. Repr. in *Columbia Working Papers in Linguistics* 4 (1977): 59–77.

Reinhart, Tanya. 1984. "Principles of Gestalt Perception in the Temporal Organization of Narrative Texts." *Linguistics* 22 : 779–809.

Ricardou, Jean. 1967. *Problèmes du nouveau roman.* Collection "Tel Quel." Paris: Seuil.

————. 1971. *Pour une théorie du Nouveau Roman.* Paris: Seuil.

————. 1973. *Le Nouveau Roman.* Paris: Seuil.

Ricoeur, Paul. 1984, 1985, 1988. *Time and Narrative,* 3 vols. Translated by Kathleen McLaughlin (vol. 3 by Kathleen Blamey) and David Pellauer (orig. published in French: Paris: Seuil, 1983, 1984, 1985). Chicago: University of Chicago Press.

Rimmon-Kenan, Shlomith. 1983. *Narrative Fiction.* London: Methuen.

Riquer, Martín de. 1959. "Epopée jongleuresque et épopée romanesque à lire." In *Actes du Colloque de Liège: La Technique littéraire des chansons de geste*, 75–82. Paris: Les Belles Lettres.

Robbe-Grillet, Alain. 1963. *Pour un nouveau roman*. Paris: Editions de Minuit. / *For a New Novel: Essays on Fiction*. Translated by Richard Howard. New York: Grove Press, 1965.

Rodemeyer, K. Th. 1889. *Das Präsens historicum bei Herodot und Thukydides*. Leipzig: G. Fock.

Roloff, H. 1921. "Das Präsens historicum im Mittelenglischen." Diss., Universität Giessen.

Ronconi, Alessandro. 1942. "Il presente storico italiano e il suo aspetto." *Lingua Nostra* 4:34–36.

———. 1943. "L'imperfetto narrativo." *Lingua Nostra* 5:90–93. Repr. in A. R., *Interpretazioni grammaticali*. Padua: Liviana, 1958.

Roy, Bruno. 1988. "La Cantillation des romans médiévaux: Une voie vers la théâtralisation." *Le Moyen Français* 19:148–162.

Ruelle, Pierre. 1976. "Temps grammatical et temps réel dans la *Chanson de Roland*." In *Mélanges de langue et de littérature romanes offerts à Carl Theodor Gossens*, edited by G. Colón and R. Kopp, 2:777–792. Berne: Francke/Liège: Marche Romane.

Ruipérez, Martín Sánchez. 1982. *Structure du système des aspects et des temps du verbe en grec ancien*. Translated by Marc Plénat and Pierre Serça. Paris: Les Belles Lettres (orig. published in Spanish, Salamanca: CSIC, 1954).

Rychner, Jean. 1955. *La Chanson de geste, essai sur l'art épique des jongleurs*. Geneva and Lille: Droz.

———. 1970. *Formes et structures de la prose française médiévale: L'Articulation des phrases narratives dans "la Mort Artu"*. Neuchâtel: Faculté des Lettres/ Geneva: Droz.

Ryding, William. 1971. *Structure in Medieval Narrative*. The Hague: Mouton.

Sandmann, Manfred G. 1953. "Narrative Tense of the Past in the *Cantar de Mio Cid*." *Studies . . . Presented to John Orr*, 258–281. Manchester: Manchester University Press. Repr. in French in Sandmann 1973, 123–144.

———. 1957. "Die Tempora der Erzählung im Altfranzösischen." *Vox Romanica* 16:287–296. Repr. in French in Sandmann 1973, 167–174.

———. 1960. "Syntaxe verbale et style épique." In *Atti del VIII Congresso Internazionale di Studi Romanzi (1956)* (Florence) 2:379–402. Repr. in Sandmann 1973, 145–165.

———. 1968. Review of Stefenelli-Fürst 1966 in *Romance Philology* 21:570–574.

———. 1973. *Expériences et critiques*. Bibliothèque Française et Romane, Série A, 25. Paris: Klincksieck.

———. 1974. "La 'mezcla de los tiempos narrativos' en el Romancero viejo." *Romanistisches Jahrbuch* 25:278–293.

Sartre, Jean-Paul. 1947. *Situations*, I. Paris: Gallimard.

———. 1948. Preface to Nathalie Sarraute, *Portrait d'un inconnu*. Paris: Gallimard (English trans. 1955).

Saunders, H. 1969. "The Evolution of French Narrative Tenses." *Forum for Modern Language Studies* 5:141–161.

Schächtelein, Paul. 1911. *Das Passé défini und Imparfait im Altfranzösischen. Zeitschrift für romanische Philologie* Beiheft 30. Halle: Niemeyer.

Scheub, Harold. 1977. "Body and Image in Oral Narrative Performance." *New Literary History* 8.3:345–367.

Schiffrin, Deborah. 1981. "Tense Variation in Narrative." *Language* 57:45–62.

Schlegel, August Wilhelm von. 1884. *Vorlesungen über schöne Literatur und Kunst,* vol. 1, *Die Kunstlehre* (= Berliner Vorlesungen, 1801–1802). Heilbrunn: Henninger.

Schlicher, John J. 1931. "Historical Tenses and Their Functions in Latin." *Classical Philology* 26:46–59.

Schmidt, Siegfried J. 1976. "Towards a Pragmatic Interpretation of 'Fictionality.'" In *Pragmatics of Language and Literature,* edited by Teun A. van Dijk, 161–178. Amsterdam: North Holland.

Schoch, Josef. 1912. *Perfectum Historicum und Perfectum Präsens im Französischen, von seinem Anfängen bis 1700.* Halle: Niemeyer.

Schogt, H. G. 1964. "L'Aspect verbal en français et l'élimination du passé simple." *Word* 20:1–17.

Scholes, Robert. 1981. "Language, Narrative, and Anti-Narrative." In Mitchell, ed., 1981, 200–208.

Scholes, Robert, and Robert Kellogg. 1966. *The Nature of Narrative.* Oxford: Oxford University Press.

Schøsler, Lene. 1973. *Les Temps du passé dans "Aucassin et Nicolette".* Etudes Romanes de l'Université d'Odense. Odense: Odense Universitetsforlag.

———. 1985. "L'Emploi des temps du passé en ancien français: Etude sur quelques textes manuscrits." *Razo* (Cahiers du Centre d'Etudes Médiévales de Nice) 5:107–119.

———. 1986. "L'Emploi des temps du passé en ancien français: Etude sur les variantes manuscrites du *Charroi de Nîmes.*" In *Mémoires de la Société Néophilologique de Helsinki* 44 (Actes du 9ᵉ Congrès des Romanistes Scandinaves. Helsinki 13–17 août 1984), edited by Elina Suomela-Härmä and Olli Välikangas, 341–352. Helsinki: Société Philologique.

Searle, John R. 1958. "Proper Names." *Mind* 67.266:166–173.

———. 1975. "On the Logical Status of Fictional Discourse." *New Literary History* 6:319–332.

———. 1979. *Expression and Meaning.* Cambridge: Cambridge University Press.

Segre, Cesare. 1979. "Analysis of Tale, Narrative Logic, and Time." In *Structures and Time,* translated by John Meddemmen, 1–64. Chicago: University of Chicago Press (orig. published in Italian, 1974).

Serbat, Guy. 1975–1976. "Les Temps du verbe en latin." *Revue des Etudes Latines* 53:367–405; 54:308–352.

———. 1980. "La Place du présent de l'Indicatif dans le système des temps." *L'Information Grammaticale* 7:32–39.

Seylaz, Jean-Luc. 1983. "Sur le présent narratif: A la recherche d'une définition formelle." *Rivista di Letterature Moderne e Comparate* 36 (n.s.): 207–219.

Sherzer, Dina. 1986. *Representation in Contemporary French Fiction.* Lincoln and London: University of Nebraska Press.

Shopen, Timothy, ed. 1985. *Language Typology and Syntactic Description,* vol. 3, *Grammatical Categories and the Lexicon.* Cambridge: Cambridge University Press.

Short, Michael. 1982. "Stylistics and the Teaching of Literature with an Example from James Joyce's *Portrait of the Artist as a Young Man.*" In *Language and Literature,* edited by Ronald Carter, 179–182. London: George Allen and Unwin.

Shuman, Amy. 1986. *Storytelling Rights: The Use of Oral and Written Texts by Urban Adolescents.* Cambridge: Cambridge University Press.

Silva-Corvalán, Carmen. 1983. "Tense and Aspect in Oral Spanish Narrative: Context and Meaning." *Language* 59.4:760–780.

Simonin, Jenny. 1984. "De la nécessité de distinguer énonciateur et locuteur dans une théorie énonciative." *Documentation et Recherche en Linguistique Allemande Contemporaine* (Vincennes) 30:55–62.

Smith, Barbara Herrnstein. 1981. "Narrative Versions, Narrative Theories." In Mitchell, ed., 1981, 209–232.

Smith, Carlota S. 1980. "Temporal Structures in Discourse." In *Time, Tense, and Quantifiers.* Proceedings of the Stuttgart Conference on Tense and Quantification, 355–374. Tübingen: Niemeyer.

———. 1981. "Semantic and Syntactic Constraints on Temporal Interpretation." In Tedeschi and Zaenen, eds., 1981, 213–237.

———. 1983. "A Theory of Aspectual Choice." *Language* 59.3:479–501.

Smith, C. Colin, ed. 1964. *Spanish Ballads.* Oxford: Pergamon Press.

Smith, C. Colin, and J. Morris. 1967. "On 'Physical Phrases' in Old Spanish Epic and Other Texts." In *Proceedings of the Leeds Philosophical and Literary Society, Literary and Historical Section* 12.5:129–190.

Soga, Matsuo. 1983. *Tense and Aspect in Modern Colloquial Japanese.* Vancouver: University of British Columbia Press.

Sorella, Antonio. 1983. "Per un consuntivo degli studi recenti sul presente storico." *Studi di Grammatica Italiana* 12:307–319.

Spitzer, Leo. 1911. "Stilistisch-Syntaktisches aus den Spanisch-portugiesischen Romanzen." *Zeitschrift für romanische Philologie* 35:257–308.

———. 1928. "Zum Stil Marcel Prousts." In L. S., *Stilstudien,* 2:365–497. Munich: Hueber.

———. 1945. "Los Romances españoles." *Asomante* 1:7–29.

Sprenger, Ulrike. 1951. *Praesens historicum und Praeteritum in der altisländischen Saga: Ein Beitrag zur Frage Freiprosa-Buchprosa.* Basel: Benno Schwabe.

Stahl, Sandra. 1983. "Personal Experience Stories." In *Handbook of American Folklore,* edited by Richard M. Dorson, 268–275. Bloomington: Indiana University Press.

Stanzel, Franz. 1971. *Narrative Situations in the Novel.* Translated by James Pusack. Bloomington: Indiana University Press.

Steadman, J. M. 1917. "The Origin of the Historical Present in English." *Studies in Philology* 14:1–46.

Steele, Susan. 1975. "Past and Irrealis: Just What Does It All Mean?" *International Journal of American Linguistics* 41 : 200–217.

Stefenelli-Fürst, Friederike. 1966. *Die Tempora der Vergangenheit in der Chanson de Geste.* Wiener Romanistische Arbeiten, 5. Vienna-Stuttgart: Wilhelm Braunmuller.

Stein, Nancy L. 1982. "The Definition of a Story." *Journal of Pragmatics* 6 : 487–507.

Stempel, Wolf-Dieter. 1964. *Untersuchungen zur Satzverknüpfung im Altfranzösischen.* Braunschweig: Westermann.

———. 1972. "Perspektivische Rede in der französischen Literatur des Mittelalters." In *Interpretation und Vergleich: Festschrift für Walter Pabst,* edited by Eberhard Leube and Ludwig Schrader, 310–329. Berlin: Erich Schmidt.

Sternberg, Meir. 1978. *Expositional Modes and Temporal Ordering in Fiction.* Baltimore: Johns Hopkins University Press.

———. 1982. "Proteus in Quotation-Land: Mimesis and the Forms of Reported Discourse." *Poetics Today* 3.2 : 107–156.

Stewart, Joan Hinde. 1977. "Some Aspects of Verb Usage in *Aucassin et Nicolette.*" *French Review* 50 : 429–436.

Stock, Brian. 1980. *The Implications of Literacy: Written Language and Models of Interpretation in the Eleventh and Twelfth Centuries.* Princeton: Princeton University Press.

Stoltzfus, Ben. 1985. *Alain Robbe-Grillet: The Body of the Text.* London and Toronto: Associated University Presses.

Sturrock, John. 1969. *The French New Novel.* London: Oxford University Press.

Stussi, Alfredo. 1960–1961. "Imperfetto e passato remoto nella prosa volgare del quattrocento." *L'Italia Dialettale* 24 : 125–133.

Sutherland, Danuta R. 1939. "On the Use of Tenses in Old and Middle French." In *Mélanges M. K. Pope,* 329–337. Manchester: Manchester University Press.

Szatrowski, Polly E. 1985. "The Function of Tense-Aspect Forms in Japanese Conversations: Empirical and Methodological Considerations." Diss., Cornell University.

Szertics, Joseph. 1967. *Tiempo y verbo en el Romancero Viejo.* 2d ed. Biblioteca Románica Hispánica, 97. Madrid: Gredos, 1974.

———. 1974. "Observaciones sobre algunas funciones estilísticas del pretérito indefinido en el romancero viejo." *Explicación de Textos Literarios* 2.3 : 189–197.

Talmy, Leonard. 1978. "Figure and Ground in Complex Sentences." In *Universals of Human Language,* edited by Joseph H. Greenberg, vol. 4, *Syntax,* 625–649. Stanford: Stanford University Press.

———. 1985. "Lexicalization Patterns: Semantic Structure in Lexical Forms." In Shopen, ed., 1985, 3 : 57–149.

Tamir, Nomi. 1976. "Personal Narrative and Its Linguistic Foundation." *Poetics and Theory of Literature* 1 : 403–429.

Tannen, Deborah. 1979. "What's in a Frame? Surface Expectations for Underlying Expectations." In *New Directions in Discourse Processing,* edited by Roy Freedle, 137–181. Norwood, N.J.: Ablex.

———, ed. 1982a. *Analyzing Discourse: Text and Talk.* GURT 1981. Washington, D.C.: Georgetown University Press.

———. 1982b. "Oral and Literate Strategies in Spoken and Written Narrative." *Language* 58.1 : 1–21.

———. 1982c. "The Oral/Literate Continuum in Discourse." In Tannen, ed., 1982d, 1–16.

———, ed. 1982d. *Spoken and Written Language: Exploring Orality and Literacy.* Norwood, N.J.: Ablex.

———, ed. 1984a. *Coherence in Spoken and Written Discourse.* Advances in Discourse Processes, 12. Norwood, N.J.: Ablex.

———. 1984b. "Spoken and Written Narrative in English and Greek." In Tannen, ed., 1984a, 21–41.

———. 1986. "Introducing Constructed Dialogue in Greek and American Conversational and Literary Narrative." In Coulmas, ed., 1986, 311–332.

———. Forthcoming. "Ordinary Conversation and Literary Discourse: Coherence and the Poetics of Repetition." In *Uses of Linguistics,* edited by Edward H. Bendix. *Annals of the New York Academy of Science.*

Tedeschi, Philip J., and Annie Zaenen, eds. 1981. *Tense and Aspect.* Syntax and Semantics, 14. New York: Academic Press.

Thomas, Werner. 1974. "Historische Präsens oder Konjunktionsreduktion? Zum Problem des Tempuswechsels in der Erzählung." *Sitzungsberichte der wiss. Ges. an der J. W. Goethe-Universität Frankfurt/Main* 12.2 : 31–62.

Thompson, Sandra A. 1987. "'Subordination' and Narrative Event Structure." In Tomlin, ed., 1987, 435–454.

Todorov, Tzvetan. 1966. "Les Catégories du récit littéraire." *Communications* 8 : 125–151.

———. 1969. *Grammaire du Décameron.* The Hague: Mouton.

———. 1970. *L'Enonciation.* Paris: Didier-Larousse.

Toliver, Harold. 1974. *Animate Illusions: Explorations of Narrative Structure.* Lincoln: University of Nebraska Press.

Tomlin, Russell S., ed. 1987. *Coherence and Grounding in Discourse.* Typological Studies in Language, 11. Amsterdam and Philadelphia: Benjamins.

Traugott, Elizabeth Closs. 1979. "Against the Discourse Origins of Tense and Aspect." MS.

———. 1982. "From Propositional to Textual and Expressive Meanings: Some Semantic-Pragmatic Aspects of Grammaticalization." In *Perspectives on Historical Linguistics,* edited by Winfred P. Lehmann and Yakov Malkiel, 245–271. Amsterdam: Benjamins.

———. Forthcoming. "Semantics, Pragmatics, and Textual Analysis." *Language and Style.*

Traugott, Elizabeth Closs, and Mary Louise Pratt. 1980. *Linguistics for Students of Literature.* New York: Harcourt Brace Jovanovich.

Traugott, Elizabeth Closs, and Suzanne Romaine. 1985. "Some Questions for the Definition of 'Style' in Socio-Historical Linguistics." *Folia Linguistica Historica* 6 : 7–39.

Tristram, Hildegard L. C. 1983. *Tense and Time in Early Irish Narration.* Innsbrucker Beiträge zur Sprachwissenschaft. Vorträge und Kleinere Schriften, 32. Innsbruck: Institut für Sprachwissenschaft der Universität Innsbruck.

Uitti, Karl D. 1973. *Story, Myth, and Celebration in Old French Narrative Poetry 1050–1200.* Princeton: Princeton University Press.

———. 1979. "Narrative and Commentary: Chrétien's Devious Narrator in *Yvain.*" *Romance Philology* 33 : 160–167.

Uspensky, Boris. 1973. *A Poetics of Composition: The Structure of the Artistic Text and a Typology of Compositional Form.* Translated by Valentina Zavanin and Susan Wittig. Berkeley and Los Angeles: University of California Press.

van Dijk, Teun A. 1975. "Action, Action Description, and Narrative." *New Literary History* 6 : 273–294.

van Peer, Willie. 1986. *Stylistics and Psychology: Investigations of Foregrounding.* London: Croom Helm.

Vaugelas, Claude Favre de. 1663. *Remarques sur la langue françoise utiles a ceux qui veulent bien parler et bien escrire.* Paris: L. Billaine.

Vendler, Zeno. 1967. *Linguistics in Philosophy.* Ithaca: Cornell University Press.

Verkuyl, Henk. 1972. *On the Compositional Nature of the Aspects.* Dordrecht: Reidel.

Vet, Co, and Arie Molendijk. 1985. "The Discourse Functions of the Past Tenses of French." In *Temporal Studies in Sentence and Discourse,* edited by Vincenzo Lo Cascio and Co Vet, 133–159. Groningen-Amsterdam Series in Semantics, 5. Dordrecht-Riverton: Foris.

Vinaver, Eugène. 1964a. "La Mort de Roland." *Cahiers de Civilisation Médiévale* 7 : 133–143. Repr. in Vinaver 1970, 49–74.

———. 1964b. "From Epic to Romance." *Bulletin of the John Rylands Library* 49 : 476–503.

———. 1970. *A la recherche d'une poétique médiévale.* Paris: Nizet.

———. 1971. "Roland at Roncevaux." In E. V., *The Rise of Romance,* 1–14. Oxford: Clarendon.

Vising, Johann. 1888–1889. "Die realen Tempora der Vergangenheit im Französischen und den übrigen romanischen Sprachen." *Französischen Studien* 6 : 1–228; 7 : 1–113.

Visser, F. Th. 1964. "The Historical Present in Middle English Verse Narratives." In *English Studies Presented to R. W. Zandvoort on the Occasion of His Seventieth Birthday.* Suppl. to *English Studies* 45 : 135–143.

———. 1966. *An Historical Syntax of the English Language,* vol. 2, *Syntactical Units with One Verb.* Leiden: Brill.

Vitoux, Pierre. 1982. "Le Jeu de la focalisation." *Poétique* 51 : 359–368.

Wackernagel, Jakob. 1920. *Vorlesungen über Syntax mit besonderer Berücksichtigung von Griechisch, Latein und Deutsch.* 2 vols. Basel: E. Birkhäuser.

Walker, Roger M. 1971. "Oral Delivery or Private Reading? A Contribution to the Debate on the Dissemination of Medieval Literature." *Forum for Modern Language Studies* 7 : 36–42.

Wallace, Stephen. 1982. "Figure and Ground: The Interrelationships of Linguistic Categories." In Hopper, ed., 1982b, 201–223.

Walsh, John K. Forthcoming. "Performance in the *Poema de mio Cid.*" *Romance Philology.*

Wartburg, Walther von. 1937. *Evolution et structure de la langue française*. 10th ed. Berne: Francke, 1971.

Watts, Richard J. 1984. "Narration as Role-Complementary Interaction: An Ethnomethodological Approach to the Study of Literary Narrative." *Studia Anglica Posnaniensia* 17 : 157–164.

Waugh, Linda R. 1982. "Marked and Unmarked: A Choice between Unequals in Semiotic Structure." *Semiotica* 38.3/4 : 299–318.

Waugh, Linda R., and Monique Monville Burston. 1986. "Aspect and Discourse Function: The French Simple Past in Newspaper Usage." *Language* 62: 846–877.

Weber, Jean-Jacques. 1983. "The Foreground-Background Distinction: A Survey of Its Definitions and Applications." *Language in Literature* 8.1 : 1–15.

Wehr, Barbara. 1984. *Diskurs-Strategien im Romanischen*. Romanica Monacensia, 22. Tübingen: Gunther Narr.

Weinrich, Harald. 1973. *Le Temps*. Translated by Michèle Lacoste. Paris: Seuil (orig. published in German, 1964).

White, Hayden. 1980. "The Value of Narrativity in the Representation of Reality." *Critical Inquiry* 7 : 5–27. Repr. in Mitchell, ed., 1981, 1–23.

Wierzbicka, Anna. 1974. "The Semantics of Direct and Indirect Discourse." *Papers in Linguistics* 7.3/4 : 267–307.

Wigger, Marianne. 1978. *Tempora in Chrétiens "Yvain," Eine textlinguistische Untersuchung*. Studia Romanica Linguistica, 6. Frankfurt am Main: Peter Lang.

Wilensky, Robert. 1982. "Story Grammars Revisited." *Journal of Pragmatics* 6 : 423–432.

Wilmet, Marc. 1970. *Le Système de l'indicatif en moyen français*. Geneva: Droz.

———. 1976. "Le Passé-composé narratif." In M. W., *Etudes de morphosyntaxe verbale*, 61–82. Paris: Klincksieck.

Woisetschlaeger, Erich F. 1976. *A Semantic Theory of the English Auxiliary System*. Bloomington: Indiana University Linguistics Club.

Wolfson, Nessa. 1978. "A Feature of Performed Narrative: The Conversational Historical Present." *Language in Society* 7 : 215–237.

———. 1979. "The Conversational Historical Present Alternation." *Language* 55.1 : 168–182.

———. 1982. *The Conversational Historical Present in American English Narrative*. Topics in Sociolinguistics, 1. Dordrecht: Reidel/Cinnamson, N.J.: Foris.

Wood, Cecil. 1965. "The So-Called Historical Present in Old Norse." In *Scandinavian Studies Honoring Henry Goddard Leach*, edited by C. F. Bayernschmidt and E. J. Friis, 105–110. Seattle: University of Washington Press.

Worthington, Martha Garrett. 1966. "The Compound Past Tense in Old French Narrative Poems." *Romance Philology* 19 : 397–417.

Yvon, Henri. 1960. "Emploi dans la *Vie de St. Alexis* (XIᵉ siècle) de l'imparfait, du passé simple et du passé composé de l'indicatif." *Romania* 31.2 : 244–250.

Zimmermann, Rüdiger. 1973. "Verbal Syntax and Style in *Sir Gawain and the Green Knight*." *English Studies* 54 : 533–543.

Zink, Michel. 1985. *La Subjectivité littéraire*. Paris: Presses Universitaires de France.
Zumthor, Paul. 1975. "Autobiographie au Moyen Age?" In P. Z., *Langue, texte, enigme*, 165–180. Paris: Seuil.
——. 1983. *Introduction à la poésie orale*. Paris: Seuil.
——. 1984a. *La Poésie et la voix dans la civilisation médiévale*. Essais et Conférences, Collège de France. Paris: Presses Universitaires de France.
——. 1984b. "The Text and the Voice." *New Literary History* 16.1 : 67–92.

Concept and Name Index

Index of Texts Cited